A Life-Span Approach to Nursing Care for Individuals with Developmental Disabilities

A Life-Span Approach to Nursing Care for Individuals with Developmental Disabilities

edited by

Shirley P. Roth, R.N., M.S.N.

*Clinical Services Coordinator
National Children's Center
Home Health Agency
Washington, D.C.
and
Clinical Instructor
George Mason University
College of Nursing and Health Science
Fairfax, Virginia*

and

Joyce S. Morse, R.N., M.A., P.N.P.

*Director of the Children's Services Division
The Matheny School and Hospital
Peapack, New Jersey
and
Adjunct Professor of Nursing
College of St. Elizabeth
Convent Station, New Jersey*

·P A U L·H·
BROOKES
PUBLISHING C°

Baltimore • London • Toronto • Sydney

Paul H. Brookes Publishing Co.
P.O. Box 10624
Baltimore, Maryland 21285-0624

Typeset by The Composing Room of Michigan, Inc.,
Grand Rapids, Michigan.
Manufactured in the United States of America by
The Maple Press Company, York, Pennsylvania.

Permission to reprint the following quotations is gratefully acknowledged:

Page 94: List of essential components of a sound quality assurance program. Source:
Edward P. Richards III and Katharine C. Rathbun, *Medical risk management: Preventive legal strategies for health care providers,* Aspen Publishers, Inc. © 1982.

Pages 94–95: A numbered list from Meisenheimer, C.G. (1985). *Quality assurance: A complete guide to effective programs*. Gaithersburg, MD: Aspen Publishers, Inc. Reprinted by permission of the author.

Library of Congress Cataloging-in-Publication Data

A life-span approach to nursing care for individuals with
developmental disabilities / edited by Shirley P. Roth and Joyce S. Morse.
  p.   cm.
Includes bibliographical references and index.
ISBN 1-55766-151-0
1. Developmental disabilities—Nursing. I. Roth, Shirley P.,
1947– . II. Morse, Joyce S., 1945– .
  [DNLM: 1.   Mental Retardation—nursing. 2.   Psychiatric Nursing.
3.   Delivery of Health Care. 4.   Mental Retardation—rehabilitation.
WY 160 L722 1944]
RJ506.D47L53 1994
610.73′68—dc20
DNLM/DLC
for Library of Congress   94-910
                                                                        CIP

British Library Cataloging-in-Publication data are available from the
British Library.

Contents

Contributors

Lee Barks, R.N., M.N., A.R.N.P.
President and Consulting Clinical
  Nurse Specialist
Developmental Health, Inc.
1 Village Green
Longwood, Florida 32779

Marisa Cenci Brown, M.S.N., R.N.
Project Coordinator
Community Service Division
Georgetown University
University Affiliated Program
Washington, D.C. 20007

Patricia W. Clausen, R.N., M.S.N.
Adult Health Coordinator
Fairfax County Health Department
10777 Main Street, Suite 203
Fairfax, Virginia 22030

Sally L. Colatarci, R.N., B.S.N.
Director of Nursing
The Matheny School and Hospital
Peapack, New Jersey 07977

Jeannie Frank, R.N., M.S.N.
Certified Pediatric Nurse Practitioner
CIGNA Health Care
Pediatric Urgent Care
1711 West Temple Street
Los Angeles, California 90026

Teresa A. Free, Ph.D., R.N.C.
Associate Professor
University of Kentucky
College of Nursing
760 Rose Street
Lexington, Kentucky 40536-0232

Jacki Miller, M.S., R.N.
Director of Nursing
Central Wisconsin Center for
  the Developmentally Disabled
317 Knutson Drive
Madison, Wisconsin 53704

Joyce S. Morse, R.N., M.A., P.N.P.
Director of the Children's Services Division
The Matheny School and Hospital
Peapack, New Jersey 07977
and
Adjunct Professor of Nursing
College of St. Elizabeth
Convent Station, New Jersey 07961

Deborah A. Natvig, R.N., Ph.D.
Administrator of Health Programs
Whitten Center
Clinton, South Carolina 29325

Wendy M. Nehring, R.N., Ph.D., FAAMR
Assistant Professor of Maternal–Child
  Nursing
University of Illinois College of Nursing
Chicago, Illinois 60612

Donna Rice O'Brien, R.N.C., M.S., A.N.P.
Private Consultant
Professional Health Care Consulting
and
President
Nurses of the Developmentally Disabled—
  New Jersey
P.O. Box 387
Convent Station, New Jersey 07961

Betty Runion Rice, M.S.N., R.N.
Instructor in Nursing
George Mason University
4400 University Drive
Fairfax, Virginia 22030

Shirley P. Roth, R.N., M.S.N.
Clinical Services Coordinator
National Children's Center
  Home Health Agency
2300 Good Hope Road SE
Washington, D.C. 20020
and
Clinical Instructor
George Mason University
College of Nursing and Health Science
Fairfax, Virginia 22030

Linda J. Ross, R.N., M.A., C.P.N.P.
Director of Nursing
Westchester Institute for Human Development
Cedarwood Hall
Valhalla, New York 10595

Fay F. Russell, R.N.C., M.N., B.S.N.
Chief of Nursing
The University of Tennessee, Memphis
Boling Center for Developmental Disabilities
711 Jefferson Avenue
Memphis, Tennessee 38105

Carolyn I. Steadham, R.N.C., M.S.N.
Pediatric Clinical Nurse Specialist
University of Southern California
   Medical Center
Pediatric Pavilion
1129 North State Street
Los Angeles, California 90033

Kathlyn J. Steele, R.N., M.S.
Director of Staff Training and Development
Central Wisconsin Center for the
   Developmentally Disabled
317 Knutson Drive
Madison, Wisconsin 53704

Brent C. Toleman, M.A.
Director of Training
Providence Center, Inc.
80 West Street, Suite 120
Annapolis, Maryland 21401

Foreword

The history of care given to individuals with developmental disabilities is a legacy of institutional atrocities and neglect. Individuals with developmental disabilities have been a stigmatized population whose lives were not valued, and those who cared for them have historically had low recognition and received few accolades. Individuals with congenital or acquired conditions that affected their mental or physical capacities have always needed assistance to carry on with their lives, and their quality of life has been questioned. For years, their care was custodial and caregivers traditionally have been nonprofessionals.

Today, individuals with developmental disabilities are leading productive lives and living with their families or in community living situations. No longer locked away and hidden in institutions, they are part of the community population that health care providers encounter. They may be patients at clinics, in hospitals, in community health centers, or in schools, with episodic problems or with chronic, lifelong conditions complicated by their developmental disabilities. Although all nurses may be involved with caring for persons with developmental disabilities in their respective settings, some nurses have pursued advanced knowledge and developed a better understanding of the practice of developmental disabilities nursing.

Developmental disabilities nursing as a specialty has traced its history concurrently with the legislative and social changes in caring for individuals with disabilities. From a variety of nursing areas of practice, including maternal–child nursing, psychiatric/mental health nursing, and community health nursing, developmental disabilities nursing has evolved with a theoretical and practice foundation from a hybrid of behavioral, biological, and social sciences. Several influential nurses, including Kathryn Barnard, Ada Axelrod, Una Haynes, and others with clinical skills, personal concerns, professional wisdom, and organized leadership brought the presence of nursing and systematic nursing skills into the field of developmental disabilities. They paved the way for professional nurses to become experts in this field. Developmental disabilities nursing has become a unique and recognized specialty of professional nursing, incorporating a range of interdisciplinary skills, knowledge, and research into a recognized system of care delivery.

Few books exist on caring for individuals with developmental disabilities across the life span, and none uses a comprehensive nursing approach. Now, through the work of Shirley P. Roth and Joyce S. Morse, *A Life-Span Approach to Nursing Care for Individuals with Developmental Disabilities* gives the reader a foundation of this specialty information, with contributions and references from many of those nurses who are leaders in the field of developmental disabilities nursing. Roth and Morse integrate a holistic and comprehensive approach to caring for individuals with developmental disabilities that can be used by all nurses. In addition, this book offers all health professionals a refreshing perspective to clinical practice in providing care for this population.

Caring for persons with developmental disabilities is a complex enterprise. Their health and well-being are often compromised in some way by their special needs. They are often treated in traditional systems that compartmentalize their problems into mental/educational, physical/medical, or psychosocial domains. Yet, their health, which interrelates their medical and nonmedical conditions, is haphazardly addressed by medical, school, and community health care professionals, whereby their medical conditions, cognitive limitations, or social problems supersede all other considerations. However, some aspects of health care and medical care are not significantly different for persons with developmental disabilities than for those without. Some aspects of health care for the infant, toddler, school-age child, and adolescent with a developmental disability must address their special needs. The health care provider in the school, community, or hospital setting should operate with an understanding of developmental disabilities that is discussed with authority and insight in this book.

Within the health care professional's collection of tools, skills, knowledge, and expertise should be an underlying philosophy or orientation of care. A holistic, life-span approach to care is essential for nurses to cross the professional–client threshold and embark on a therapeutic relationship with client and family. Patients and families deserve integrated services that are individually and culturally sensitive, developmentally appropriate, and family-centered. This approach should be based on a framework stemming from a professional perspective that is enriched with specific knowledge about developmental disabilities. Care given to individuals with developmental disabilities should not be a fragmented, single-discipline package, but rather a fully integrated health care service. Wherever community health, school, or acute care nurses are involved with some aspect of caring for individuals with developmental disabilities, they should draw from this nursing framework and incorporate relevant special developmental considerations into the care they give. This book provides a comprehensive reference of content from developmental disabilities nurse experts for all clinicians to use, and presents this information for the first time in one volume in the context of professional nursing.

The role of the nurse involved with caring for people with developmental disabilities is particularly important. Whether as a member of a collaborative team or a case manager in a particular setting, the nurse should ultimately perform in the full professional role as clinician, teacher, counselor, advisor, advocate, researcher, and leader of care. This requires the nurse to operate from a theoretical base according to the nursing code of ethics regardless of social or economic status, personal characteristics, or the nature of health problems. Roth and Morse use Orem's theoretical framework and incorporate into many chapters of the book a collection of standards of care, position statements, and practical guidelines that help nurses value the uniqueness of each person and look for assets, strengths, and potential rather than limitations, inabilities, or deficits.

The chapters in the book addressing nursing process and practice begin with a general foundation of information from which the specific considerations of caring for individuals with developmental disabilities can be applied. Roth and Morse draw from a self-care theoretical framework and North American Nursing Diagnosis Association (NANDA) nursing diagnostic procedures to specify an approach to assessing, planning, implementing, and evaluating nursing care for infants, children, adolescents, and adults with developmental disabilities. The goals of care for working with this population are consonant with a professional nursing's system of assessing, diagnosing, and treating human responses to real and potential problems for any individual. However, an additional understanding of physical, behavioral, cognitive, sensory, socioemotional, and neuromuscular problems related to an underlying developmental condition must be incorporated into the process. The chapters on theory and assessment elaborate on these aspects and incorporate case examples to clarify them, and the book uses a consistent strand of nursing analysis throughout. Additionally, the chapters on seizures, medications, and infections are of particular interest to many community health care providers working with individuals with developmental disabilities. Other topics of particular interest to the developmental disabilities nurse addressed in the book include sexuality, quality of life, and quality of care.

In the closing chapters of the book, Roth and Morse introduce several contemporary issues related to developmental disabilities nursing. These areas include the complex integration of technology, and medical, adaptive, and supportive assistance in living; and the emerging nursing role related to case management of persons with developmental disabilities. Both of these areas will continue to evolve during the 1990s and new debates will arise as these issues play out.

This book gives the general pediatric, maternal–child, community, and school nurse a fountain of information for building an effective practice. In all areas of practice, nurses function with a philosophy of care and a professional process that allow them to individualize and evaluate care of clients. Roth and Morse have compiled a book that can assist nurses in all settings where individuals with developmental disabilities seek care—a book that gives special recognition to the rich and substantive information in the field of developmental disabilities nursing.

Veronica D. Feeg, Ph.D., R.N., FAAN
Associate Professor of Nursing,
George Mason University,
and Editor, Pediatric Nursing

Preface

This book brings together a unique body of nursing knowledge specific to the care of individuals with developmental disabilities across the life span. It is intended as a reference guide for nurses who provide services to individuals with developmental disabilities and their families in a variety of practice settings. As a result of demographic changes, technological advances, and increased life expectancy, more persons with developmental disabilities are receiving nursing care and health services in community-based systems such as schools, workshops, supported employment settings, outpatient clinics, and acute and long-term care facilities. As the trend toward deinstitutionalization grows stronger and the development of community-based living options expands, for many individuals, the family unit may be composed of nonrelated persons residing in congregate living situations such as group homes and supported living environments. Promoting optimal health care for each person with developmental disabilities in such a variety of living and work settings is both demanding and rewarding. This book will enable nurses to better understand and meet the health care needs of individuals with developmental disabilities and their families.

Since the 1970s, developmental disabilities nursing has emerged as a subspecialty area of nursing practice. It is a specialty that draws on knowledge from the more traditional areas of maternal–child health, mental health, and community health nursing practice. This book emphasizes prevention, wellness, and the delivery of person-centered services within the context of the family and the community. This approach is consistent with social trends toward normalization and the full inclusion of persons with developmental disabilities in the mainstream of society and the health care delivery system.

Excellence in nursing practice for this special population demands a sound knowledge base, creativity, resourcefulness, and the ability to recognize the unique strengths and assets of each person with developmental disabilities. The contents of this book provide the reader with techniques designed to involve each person with developmental disabilities as an active participant and self-advocate in maintaining wellness and in preventing disease.

The contributors to this book bring years of experience in the delivery of nursing services to individuals with developmental disabilities. They are nurse–clinicians, educators, and administrators from diverse geographical and practice settings. In each chapter an attempt has been made to provide practical examples of best practice strategies that are sensitive to a variety of cultures and ethical concerns. It was not possible to emphasize the full implications of multicultural diversity and ethical considerations as they relate to developmental disabilities nursing practice in this volume. Each of these topics merits fuller nursing exploration and research.

As the book evolved, ongoing changes in legislation at the federal, state, and local level resulted in modifications for terminology and the use of language. This had the potential to obscure the authors' intent. In cases where there was conflict between the language of nursing and the field of developmental disabilities, the authors have chosen to utilize terminology familiar to nurses. For example, in Chapter 15, the term *case manager* and the federal nomenclature of Qualified Mental Retardation Professional (QMRP) are used rather than the current developmental disabilities term of *service coordinator*.

This book represents a compilation and synthesis of information based on a wellness approach to meet the health care needs of persons with developmental disabilities across the life span. It is the authors' hope that this volume will broaden the reader's perspective and stimulate ongoing dialogue.

Acknowledgments

It would never have been possible to complete this book without the help of many individuals. The editors gratefully acknowledge the cooperative spirit and commitment of the chapter contributors in defining the roles of the nurse in developmental disabilities. During the initial stages of transforming our ideas into a book, Veronica Feeg's belief in the importance of this project kept us motivated. Special thanks are extended to the staff at Paul H. Brookes Publishing Co., especially to Melissa Behm who was receptive to the initial proposal; Sarah Cheney, whose patience and insights were invaluable; and Theresa Donnelly, who provided inspiration and guidance when the "going got tough."

Typing support for this project was provided by Jay Roth and Eunice Bajkowsky. Without their commitment and support, as well as unfailing patience, tolerance, and positive attitude about "yet one more revision," we never would have been able to complete this work.

We would like to thank the administration and staff of the National Children's Center Home Health Agency, especially Adrena Mahu for her support and confidence in this project. The Board of Directors, administration, staff, and families of The Matheny School and Hospital were unselfish in their support and encouragement.

We are indebted to our many nursing colleagues, including those at George Mason University, the College of St. Elizabeth, the Nursing Division of the American Association on Mental Retardation, the members of Nurses of the Developmentally Disabled (NODD), and those students and staff nurses who challenged us to clearly articulate our thoughts and ideas.

We acknowledge the significant contribution that many individuals with developmental disabilities and their families have made over the years in shaping our philosophy and understanding of nursing roles. We would like to thank Dr. Robert Sapin, Dr. Robert Schonhorn, Ms. Virginia Williams, Dr. Lawrence Taft, and the many other health professionals for acting as role models and mentors.

To those family members and close friends who tolerated our preoccupation with writing, our difficult schedules, and absences from special events, we can only say "thank you."

This book is dedicated to
Jay and Mark, Michelle and Sharon

A Life-Span Approach to Nursing Care for Individuals with Developmental Disabilities

1

A History of Nursing in Developmental Disabilities in America

Wendy M. Nehring

OBJECTIVES

On completion of this chapter, the reader will be able to:

- Define the importance of the nursing profession to the field of developmental disabilities.
- Describe the nursing care of persons with developmental disabilities since the late 1800s.
- Discuss the education of nurses, over time, as it relates to developmental disabilities.
- Describe developmental disabilities nursing as a specialty in nursing.

OVERVIEW

Studying history allows one to examine the past, identify the present, and predict the future. Unfortunately, histories of the field of developmental disabilities often overlook the story of developmental disabilities nursing. However, it is hoped that an historical discussion of the role of the nurse in developmental disabilities will fill this void and guide us in creating a clearer vision of the future.

Throughout history, persons with developmental disabilities have been stigmatized by the general public, yet nurses have been present since the 1700s to care for these individuals and act as advocates for their concerns when needed (Twardzicki, 1970).

HISTORICAL PERSPECTIVES OF NURSING CARE

Early American Mental Hospitals

The first American mental hospitals, or asylums, were built in the early 1700s. Philadelphia General Hospital, or "Block-

1

ley Hospital," built in 1731, was one of the earliest American mental hospitals. A large institution, Blockley had an almshouse, an insane asylum, a residence for homeless children, a general and maternity hospital, and a venereal hospital housed in the attic. In an article on the history of nursing at Blockley, Dr. Joseph McFarland (1932) wrote:

> in the "good old days" so few nurses were employed that the patients were never adequately cared for. Of them a few were probably kindly and careful, doing their duty in so far as they understood it, but the greater number were ignorant and often vicious women, recruited from a very low class of society, and not infrequently were convalescent patients, who, having recovered their health and having nowhere to go, remained to "nurse" others. Not infrequently their inability to read the directions on the bottles of medicine led to disastrous and unexpected consequences and even to loss of life. (pp. 632–633)

Following an investigation of Blockley Hospital in 1883, and after consultation with Florence Nightingale, Alice Fisher was recruited to become the Chief Nurse in 1884 and head the training school for nurses at Blockley Hospital in 1885. Prior to this position, Fisher was the Chief Nurse of a hospital in England. During her tenure in Philadelphia, she initiated the movement for improved nursing care for individuals with developmental disabilities, among many other accomplishments (Dietz & Lehozky, 1967; McFarland, 1932).

Nurse Training and Staff Shortages

Because of the poor conditions in mental hospitals and asylums across the country, the Virginia Colony took the lead in passing a law to improve the nursing care of patients in these institutions. Prior to the passage of this law, "mental" nurses were not required to have special training. Now, nurses were strongly urged to obtain an education in order to

care adequately for their patients (Peppe & Sherman, 1978).

As nurses began to be formally trained during the 1800s in this country, the number of patients with mental retardation and developmental disabilities who resided in institutions remained high. The ratio of nurses to patients in 1850 was 1 to 50 (Santos & Stainbrook, 1949). In 1933, six states had a ratio of 1 nurse to 3,771 patients and the lowest ratio was found in 13 states that boasted of having 1 nurse to 83 patients (How, 1933). Twenty years later, the ratios between nurses and their patients were declining. In state hospitals this ratio was highest, averaging 1 nurse to 400.48 patients. Private hospitals were second, with an average of 1 nurse to 15.67 patients. Psychiatric departments of general hospitals had the best ratio, with an average of 1 nurse to 7.07 patients (Fitzsimmons, 1944).

As more persons were identified as having developmental disabilities, more registered nurses were needed to care for these individuals. By 1964, in public institutions alone, 9,659 registered nurses were required for the adequate care of the people living in these institutions. However, only 2,651 registered nurses were available (American Association on Mental Deficiency, 1964; National Institute of Mental Health, 1965). Because registered nurses were in such short supply, institutions began using licensed practical nurses (Central Wisconsin Center, 1961). The personnel shortage was so great that one institution's director remarked that, if an applicant for an aide's position could "read, write, and walk, they are hired [and] jail records are checked" (Gunderman, personal communication, October 3, 1966).

Early Nursing Care

At the beginning of the 19th century, individuals with developmental disabilities remained grossly neglected by society. Care at this time was custodial and segregated from society. The majority of those who provided care for these individuals were members of religious orders who, for the most part, lacked adequate training and had little or no medical knowledge. Out of fear, many of the often well-intentioned caregivers placed those for whom they cared in straitjackets, muffs, iron collars, belts and chains, enclosed cribs, and/or wristlets (Marshall, 1937).

During this time, persons with mental retardation and developmental disabilities and persons with mental illness were cared for and housed together. There was no distinction between diagnoses. All were placed together under the label of "insanity" or "mental enfeeblement." As late as 1930, a textbook on psychology and psychiatry by C. B. Burr described mental retardation under the heading of "paranoia and pellagrous insanity."

Dorothea Dix Dorothea Dix (1802–1877) did more than any other woman in history to alter the course of nursing care for individuals with developmental disabilities. A dynamic and devoted advocate, Dix changed America's view of individuals with mental illness and of those with developmental disabilities. She brought about monumental change in the care of patients, the conditions of hospitals and asylums, and the laws regarding individuals with mental illness and developmental disabilities (Deutsch, 1936; Dix, 1976).

However, sharing the prejudice of her time, Dix viewed mental retardation as a "consequence of depravity and intemperate parenting" (Scheerenberger, 1983). She advocated separate education and living facilities for individuals with mental retardation because she believed they would encounter "injurious influences" that would keep them from receiving proper care at home (Scheerenberger, 1983). In her 1847 Appeal to the Illinois General Assembly for better treatment for all residents of mental hospitals, Dix stated:

> For it is only those who would advance the idea that the insane can be taken care of in their own dwellings, I repeat, that recovery is as rare as it is nearly hopeless while the patient remains with his family, exposed to all the exciting causes which have developed the malady. (Dix, 1847, p. 3)

Therefore, although Dix did much to reform the care and treatment of persons with mental illness and mental retardation, she did help establish many institutions in this country.

The Colony Plan An initial attempt at humane care was the colony plan, instituted at the Templeton Colony on the grounds of the Massachusetts School for the Feeble-Minded in 1899. This plan was an attempt to separate persons by disorders and provide schooling and vocational training to those able to be trained (Mastin, 1916). The writers of the colony plan dictated that "the patient ought to be as little trouble as possible to the nursing staff, and putting him to bed was an expeditious method of keeping him out of the way as much as possible" (Santos & Stainbrook, 1949, p. 61). Persons often were placed in bed as early as 4:00 P.M. (Santos & Stainbrook, 1949).

Linda Richards Linda Richards (1840–1925), influenced by the work of Dix, has been referred to as America's first trained nurse. Prior to her appointment as a superintendent of nursing at Taunton Insane Hospital in Massachusetts in 1899, Richards stated, "Although I had always found grounds for refusal of these requests [to work with the insane], my judgment finally told me that such schools were a necessity, and at last I entered upon this branch of work" (Richards, 1911, p. 108). Serving at three insane hospitals from 1899 to 1911, Richards was able to motivate many nurses to care for the individuals who resided in these institutions.

Evolution of Treatment Approaches

Medical Model/Unidisciplinary Approach By the turn of the 20th century, medical knowledge regarding persons identified as having mental illness or developmental disabilities began to emerge. With these advances came the medical model, a unidisciplinary approach that described both mental illness and mental retardation as pathology or illness. Only the discipline of medicine was involved in the care of these individuals, and physicians alone provided service delivery. With an emphasis on nutrition and elimination, this structure mandated that the nurse's sole duty was to follow the physician's orders (Foley, 1990).

Multidisciplinary Approach After World War I, Freud's (1965) work on psychoanalysis led to the development of a new perspective on mental illness and, in turn, developmental disabilities, which were categorized under mental illness. This new perspective utilized a multidisciplinary approach. Central to this approach was that, as "team leader," the physician would consult members of the other disciplines regarding their opinions on a particular case. Each discipline completed an assessment and sent the findings back to the physician. Using the information contained in these reports, the physician developed a plan of intervention (Foley, 1990).

Interdisciplinary Approach After World War II, the interdisciplinary approach emerged as the prevailing technique. Within this model, professionals from each discipline completed their individual assessments, gathered together to discuss their findings, and *jointly* decided on a plan of care (Foley, 1990).

Transdisciplinary Approach In 1969, a group of interested nurses from the United Cerebral Palsy Association, Inc.,

the National Association for Retarded Citizens (now The Arc), and the Central Wisconsin Colony and Training School, the University of Wisconsin Extension, and a representative from the federal government, gathered together to discuss guidelines for nursing care in residential centers, with one outcome being a description of the transdisciplinary approach. In this approach, the boundaries between disciplines are blurred and the professionals, along with the individual concerned and his or her family, work equally together to identify needs, plan care, implement interventions, and evaluate progress (Hutchison, 1978). For the first time, the individual and his or her family were viewed as central to planning future care and programming.

Changes in Nursing Care and Treatment

The care and treatment of individuals with mental retardation and developmental disabilities also began to evolve and were altered dramatically from 1900 through the 1980s. Changes in nursing care from 1910 to 1963 are illustrated in Table 1. Through the 1930s, it is evident that nurses assisted the patients with their daily needs of hygiene, elimination, nutrition, and safety (Brett, 1929; Mabon, 1910; Purcell, 1911). Nursing reports and charting emerge with the advent of multidisciplinary care (Dick, 1941). After World War II, the expanded nursing role necessary for interdisciplinary care is apparent in the increased shift to nurses of autonomous responsibilities (i.e., case finding, nursing assessment, and writing and managing the nursing care plans) (Dunsdon, 1963; McClure, 1951).

Behavioral Therapy During the 1960s behavioral therapy became a central feature of the care of individuals with developmental disabilities. Wright, Erb, and Lawrence (1961), all nurses, described a remotivation technique that

Table 1. Changes in nursing care of persons with developmental disabilities from 1910 to 1963

1910	1929[c]	1941[d]	1951[e]	1963[f]
1. Assessment of patient's signs and symptoms[a]	1. Rounds to assess: (a) physical and mental condition of patient, (b) elimination, and (c) check for bruises and marks on patient	1. Daily nursing reports	1. Prevention of mental retardation/ developmental disability	1. Basic nursing needs: (a) physical care, (b) emotional understanding, and (c) mental stimulation
2. Hydrotherapy, including packs and hot air baths, massage[a]	2. Medications	2. Daily therapy reports	2. Finding and reporting cases	2. Supervise 24-hour care of patients
3. Feeding—including special feedings; spoon, tube and rectal feedings[a]	3. Personal hygiene of patient	3. Daily baths for patients	3. Assisting with the diagnostic exam of the child and the interview with the parents	3. Ordering supplies
4. Care of seizures[a]	4. Treatment—enemas, continuous baths, and packs as needed	4. Daily errands for nurses	4. Assisting with the obtaining of specimens for lab tests	4. Supervising housekeeping chores
5. Direction in entertainment, occupation, and diversion of patients[a]	5. Serve meals and feed those patients most sick and negativistic	5. Daily check of patient's clothing	5. Giving reassurance and guidance to the parents following the physician's interpretation of the disease	5. Keeping a time schedule for the aides
6. Care of bedridden patients[a]	6. Take patient's temperature, pulse, and respiration	6. Meals to patients, three times daily	6. Carrying out orders for medical treatment and sedation	6. Being a substitute parent –teacher
7. Reduced use of restraints to prevent suicide attempts and use after surgery[a]	7. Toilet the patient regularly	7. Daily linen count by nurses	7. Understanding and satisfying the fundamental needs of the child	7. Assessing progress in self-care skills, including feeding, toileting, dressing, and personal hygiene
8. Gain confidence of the patient[b]	8. Hydrotherapy and baths as needed	8. Daily charting on admission and treatment wards	8. Understanding the problems peculiar to the patient's mental status and social position and those created by basic drives	8. Total care for patients severely retarded and/or physically handicapped
9. Elimination—guard against the patient retaining his or her urine and/or feces[b]	9. Care for patient's fingernails	9. Patients to occupational therapy shop daily, admission and treatment wards only	9. Recognizing and reflecting the patient's feelings to relieve tension	9. Assisting patients to ambulate
10. Toilet training[b]	10. Occupational therapy	10. Assisting patients to dress	10. Outlining a balanced daily life based on defined objectives	10. Giving medications
11. Provide the patient with time out-of-doors[b]		11. Daily housekeeping by nurses		11. Serving as liaison between institution and community
12. Reduce masturbation (due to sexual relations of parents during pregnancy)[b]				

[a]Information from Purcell (1911).
[b]Information from Mabon (1910).
[c]Information from Brett (1929).
[d]Information from Dick (1941).
[e]Information from McClure (1951).
[f]Information from Dunsdon (1963).

was part of an overall regimen of behavioral therapy. This technique, carried out by attendants and supervised by nurses, focused on the development of staff–patient trust and included poetry readings, group discussions about life outside of the institution using audiovisual aids (i.e., maps, pictures), and field trips. Conceived as an alternative to strictly custodial care, this approach focused on group participation and group interaction skills but did not attempt to educate participants.

Care Groups In 1965, Pat McNelly, Director of Nursing at the Central Wisconsin Center in Madison, initiated "care groups" that advocated minimal staffing for groups of patients, a precursor to primary nursing. This approach brought up to three nurse's aides together to care consistently for a specified group of patients over a period of 7 months or more. The patients were categorized by either geographical location of their rooms or functional level. Nurses supervised the aides assigned to these groups. Long-term care planning could be achieved better this way. Relationships between the staff and patients also strengthened with increased, consistent care (Miller, 1979).

Two years later, Una Haynes directed a project supported by the United Cerebral Palsy Association and the National Association for Retarded Children that produced *Guidelines for Nursing Standards in Residential Centers for the Mentally Retarded* (1968). These guidelines originated from a 1964 evaluation study by the Division on Special Studies of the American Association on Mental Deficiency (AAMD) (now known as the American Association on Mental Retardation [AAMR]) of personnel and institutional facilities across the country. The members of the Nursing Subdivision of the AAMD thought that this also would be an opportunity to evaluate current nursing practice and needs. These guidelines, which were the outcome of this evaluation, served to standardize nursing care for persons with mental retardation living in institutions. Nurses were beginning to take an independent and active role in the care of persons with mental retardation and developmental disabilities.

Professional and Legislative Reforms In the 1960s, the Kennedy administration instituted reforms that greatly improved services for persons with developmental disabilities. These reforms extended and advanced nursing roles in the field of developmental disabilities as a result of increased federal monies that were made available to universities for training grants. Murray and Barnard (1966) described the evolution of nursing education, citing nurse specialists who eventually would go on to receive advanced nursing degrees. Advanced theoretical and practical knowledge in the fields of mental retardation and developmental disabilities, abnormal growth and development, genetics, and family dynamics, as well as research skills, were taught in these graduate nursing programs.

New Principles in Mental Retardation and Developmental Disabilities The wide range of services outlined by President Kennedy's Panel on Mental Retardation were significantly augmented by four connected principles: *normalization* (later, social role valorization), the *developmental model,* the *least restrictive environment,* and *mainstreaming.* The concept of normalization allowed for all individuals, including those with mental retardation and developmental disabilities, to lead their lives as they chose (e.g., what to eat, where to go to spend time, and when to sleep). Nurses were encouraged to consider normalization in their daily care, in their teaching of families, and in their interactions with other professionals and the lay public (Engelhardt, 1978).

New advances were being made in our understanding of normal and abnormal human development. Nurses, as well as all disciplines, were learning and teaching others about how persons with mental retardation and developmental disabilities develop their physical and cognitive skills over time.

Much reform was occurring in the area of education. Students of all cognitive and physical abilities were being placed in the optimal learning and physical environment. Least restrictive environments and mainstreaming became the terminology used for this type of education. School nurses working with students with mental retardation and developmental disabilities played a key role in these changes. The signing of PL 94-142 (the Education for All Handicapped Children Act of 1975) ensured equal education for all children, and nurses were instrumental in screening and identifying health needs of children at risk for possible mental retardation and developmental disabilities. Nurses also participated in the development of individualized education programs (IEPs), as well as their implementation and evaluation. In fact, nursing was listed as a "related service" under PL 94-142 (National Association of State School Nurse Consultants, 1982). School nurses today continue to function in this capacity.

Deinstitutionalization In general, the 1970s was an explosive decade for the expanding role of nursing in the field of mental retardation and developmental disabilities. Deinstitutionalization of the many residents with mental retardation and developmental disabilities was mandated, for example, after Geraldo Rivera uncovered the horrific conditions at the Willowbrook State School, New York, in 1972. Other factors leading up to this massive residential shift were the photographic essay by Burton Blatt and Fred Kaplan entitled *Christmas in Purgatory* (1966); landmark court cases regarding treatment of residents in these institutions (e.g., *Wyatt v. Stickney,* 1972) and

due process (e.g., *Lessard v. Schmidt,* 1972); support by national associations, such as The Arc and The Association for Persons with Severe Handicaps; the 1971 amendments to Title XIX (Medicaid); and a great public outcry. During this time, nurses employed in institutions and in the community worked together to help individuals with mental retardation and developmental disabilities and their families make decisions regarding health care needs, future housing, social interaction, and other key aspects of integration in the community (Curry, 1978).

Nursing Diagnoses for Individuals with Developmental Disabilities The documentation of nursing care was altered significantly with the introduction of nursing diagnoses in the late 1970s. The concept of nursing diagnoses to identify, categorize, and standardize nursing care garnered a national effort and became a part of future standards of care written for various nursing specialties, such as developmental disabilities nursing (Gordon, 1976). In 1987, Miller, Steele, and Boisen developed nursing diagnoses specific to persons with developmental disabilities in long-term care settings using the NANDA (North American Nursing Diagnosis Association) nomenclature. These diagnoses pertain to actual or potential conditions and include ineffective breathing patterns, alterations in bowel elimination (constipation), alterations in nutrition (less than body requirements), fluid volume deficit, and impairment of skin integrity (actual/potential). These medical problems, of course, had been nursing concerns for a number of years, but the development of nursing diagnoses specific to individuals with developmental disabilities paved the way for more effective nursing treatment.

The Nurse as Case Manager PL 99-457 (the Education of the Handicapped Act Amendments of 1986), passed in 1987 and amended in 1992, centers on the child with developmental disabilities between the ages of birth and 5 years. Nurses and nursing care are an integral part of this law because of its emphasis on health services. Within the context of this legislation, health professionals are viewed as case managers and service providers. In an early intervention setting, nurses assess the child's nutritional status, growth and development, feeding patterns, possible complications of the identified disease process, current dental care, immunization status, well-baby care, safety measures, and vision and hearing levels. The nurse also assumes the roles of consultant and teacher. As the case manager, the nurse further serves to refer, interpret for, and assist the individual and his or her family in any manner necessary (Godfrey, 1991).

Changing Image of Developmental Disabilities Nurses

The reputation and public image of the nurse involved in the care of individuals with mental illness and mental retardation has evolved over time. Developmental disabilities nurses historically have received little respect, even within their own profession. For example, in the first article on "mental nurses" that appeared in the new *American Journal of Nursing* ("Work of nurses," 1901), the author apologized for her work in this field and stated, "I hope that this short paper will at least entertain you, and perhaps instil [sic] a little more interest and a kindlier feeling towards our cousin nurses" (p. 515). This attitude betrays the little appreciation present at the time for the developmental disabilities nurse.

How (1933) specified the requirements for a good "mental" nurse. She believed these requirements should include:

- graduation from an accredited school of nursing;
- registration in the state in which she is practicing;

- at least a year of experience with psychiatric patients either as part of her three-year course or postgraduate work [nurses could take a postgraduate course, usually 3 months in length, in psychiatric nursing after they completed a general nursing course];
- membership in the district and state nurses' association and active interest in the progress of nursing;
- subscription to the nursing journals and *Mental Hygiene Quarterly*;
- interest and ability to participate in community affairs;
- she should be wholesome and without organic or functional disease;
- intellectually alert;
- and most important is her personality. She should be able to adapt harmoniously, get along with others cheerfully, and do her share for the upkeep of morale. (p. 797)

There are many nurses who have helped to shape the current image and practice of nurses in the field of developmental disabilities. These nurses joined together during the 1960s and 1970s to produce research projects, initiate new care techniques, introduce new and expanded nursing roles in the field, publish educational materials, and be active politically and in organizations specific to this group. Among these influential nurses were Kathryn Barnard (University of Washington, Seattle), Ada Axelrod (National Association for Retarded Children), Una Haynes (United Cerebral Palsy Association), Margaret Wright (Embreeville State Hospital), Natalie Twardzicki (Wrentham State School, New Jersey), Doris Haar (Nursing Consultant, Bureau of Health Services, Division of Mental Retardation, Washington, DC), and Patricia McNelly (Central Wisconsin Center, Madison).

Nurses Today in the Field of Developmental Disabilities

Currently, nurses working in the field of developmental disabilities are employed in a number of settings (primary, secondary, and tertiary). The level and type of care they deliver varies as much as the setting in which they work. The majority of nurses caring for persons with developmental disabilities worked in institutional settings up until the 1970s. Some of these settings served individuals with specific disabilities, such as blindness (Perkins Institute and Massachusetts School for the Blind), deafness (Gallaudet University), and physical disabilities and blindness (the Matheny School and Hospital). Nurses now interact with persons with mental retardation, developmental disabilities, and dual diagnoses in homes, ambulatory care settings, independent nursing practices, schools, University Affiliated Programs, occupational health settings, early intervention programs, home health programs, and hospice programs (Browne & Walsh, 1989; Cullinane & Shishmanian, 1989; Curtis, Begin, & Blinkhorn, 1989; Hodas, Blaber, & Keane, 1989). With the shift toward deinstitutionalization, intermediate care facilities, group homes, and community independent living arrangements (CILAs), new knowledge, methodologies, services, and practice arenas are being created for nurses for the present and future.

Nurses also are pursuing careers in the fields of mental retardation and developmental disabilities as independent practitioners/entrepreneurs working in communities throughout the United States. A holistic life-span approach is possible in this arena as the nurse combines his or her skills and knowledge of theory from nursing and other related disciplines. Using their skills in physical assessment and history taking, these nurses are able to provide a service to individuals, their families, and agencies at a lesser cost than physicians. In some states, nurse–practitioners are able to prescribe certain medications. Of course, much cooperation between physicians,

other health professionals, service agencies, and government funding agencies (i.e., Medicaid, Supplemental Security Income) must be achieved for successful practice. Much information on research and practice experiences will be written about this type of nursing care in the years to come.

STANDARDS OF NURSING PRACTICE AND A NURSING POSITION STATEMENT

Nurses have collaborated since the mid-1960s to produce four documents describing the nursing service, nursing organization, and educational programs and research expected of nurses employed in the fields of mental retardation and developmental disabilities. Nurses have used these standards in all areas of institutional and community practice and educational settings.

The first set of standards to be developed was directed by Una Haynes (1968) and was entitled *Guidelines for Nursing Standards in Residential Centers for the Mentally Retarded* (discussed earlier). This document provided information to guide nursing care. Such areas as the interdisciplinary team role, the safety of the environment, health supervision, daily skilled nursing care of the patient, and the use of nursing care plans were specified. An evaluation form delineating all points was included for institutional use.

The *Standards of Nursing Practice in Mental Retardation/Developmental Disabilities*, published in 1984, focuses on clinical nursing care. The nine standards listed include the topic areas of health and functional assessment, nursing diagnoses, nursing care plans, "normalized" nursing interventions, evaluation of care, interdisciplinary collaboration, peer evaluation, participation in continuing education, and contribution to nursing theory, nursing practice, and interdisciplinary research (Aggen & Moore, 1984).

The third set of standards was developed in 1987 (with a revision set for 1994) for Clinical Nurse Specialists. The *Standards for the Clinical Nurse Specialist in Developmental Disabilities/ Handicapping Conditions* was published by the American Association of University Affiliated Programs. Using these standards, the advanced practice nurse (having either a master's or doctoral degree) is evaluated on his or her use of interdisciplinary theory relevant to appropriate patient care, use of a systematic plan of care for the patient and his or her family, collaboration with other disciplines and family members regarding the plan of care, collaboration with community agencies and resources, provision of appropriate health education, provision of programs based on patient and community needs, provision of leadership and advocacy in areas of concern for persons with mental retardation and developmental disabilities, and contribution to interdisciplinary research involving this population (Austin, Challela, Huber, Sciarillo, & Stade, 1987).

Standards also have been proposed in the specific areas of early intervention and nursing. A task force from the American Nurses' Association has drafted the *National Standards of Practice for Early Intervention Services* (Task Force on Nursing Practice Standards, 1990). The California Nurses' Association also published their own document, *Nursing Standards for Early Intervention Services for Children and Families at Risk* (California Nurses' Association, 1990).

In 1989, the Nursing Division of the American Association on Mental Retardation (AAMR) approved a nursing position statement on the role and function of the professional nurse in the fields of mental retardation and developmental disabilities. Providing a comprehensive statement on the nursing care of the individual with mental retardation and developmental disabilities across the life span and incorporating all possible service settings, the proactive nature of nursing today is stressed (Steadham, 1993). This document is presented in Appendix F of Chapter 2, this volume.

NURSING EDUCATION IN DEVELOPMENTAL DISABILITIES

With the advent of mental hospitals or asylums and public laws proclaiming the need for appropriate nursing care for individuals with developmental disabilities, the first "mental" nursing training school was established at the McLean Hospital in Massachusetts in 1883. Three years later, Florence Nightingale interceded to appoint Alice Fisher as the first nursing director of the mental nursing school at "Blockley Hospital" in Philadelphia, Pennsylvania. Correspondence indicated that Fisher was paid $1,000 per year for her services both to the school and to the hospital. Classes began at 8:00 P.M. because the student nurses could not be taken off the wards during the day. The only textbook used in the Blockley School of Nursing was the one Fisher brought with her from England. Student nurses received $5.00 for their first year and $10.00 for their second year of training (McFarland, 1932).

By the turn of the century, the United States had 35 training schools located in mental hospitals and 10 independent educational facilities. Early training included instruction in making beds, keeping the wards clean, nutrition and feeding (including forced feeding), patient hygiene, observation and documentation of patients' symptoms, patient grooming, medications and remedies, use of cold and hot water in treatments, safety, restraints, and the transporting of the patient (Santos & Stainbrook, 1949).

Training in mental nursing continued to be an unaccepted career choice during the early 1900s. Societal disapproval was so great that many graduating from these training programs did not remain employed in nursing. This was evidenced by the McLean School 22 years after its founding. The report stated that, of the school's 568 graduates, 361 were women and 207 were men. Of those graduates, 29 had died and 112 (approximately one third) of the women had married and left the profession. Of those still employed, several had gone into medical professions other than nursing, a few were ministers, four were lawyers, and four were massage operators (Russell, 1907). In the face of such statistics, nurses and hospitals began advocating for the schools of general nursing and mental nursing to combine, or for a year of postgraduate training in mental nursing to be offered to nurses graduating from general nursing programs (Peppe & Sherman, 1978).

However, nursing education remained approximately the same for the first two decades of the 20th century. The mental nursing training programs were increased to 3 years in length, and work hours continued to be in excess of 12 a day, including classwork, with only about 6 hours off per week. Owing to their long work hours, nursing students usually stayed on the hospital grounds and ate in the same cafeteria as the patients (Tucker, 1916). It was no wonder that few nurses went into this field.

By the 1920s, courses were being offered on mental retardation and developmental disabilities to nurses in locations outside the institutional training schools. A special 3-month course of theoretical and clinical instruction on mental retardation was offered to graduate nurses by the Department of Public Welfare in New York City. The course content included the topics of:

> types and classification of mental deficiency; social manifestations and results of feeblemindedness and epilepsy; history and development of care for the mentally deficient; methods of testing, group testing, personality studies, etc; principles and methods of education, social service, aftercare and field work; hygiene and sanitation in institutions; institutional organization and management; causes, phenomena, and treatment of epilepsy; physiology and anatomy of the brain and nervous system; occupational therapy, and physical training. (How, 1923, p. 842)

Students also were required to learn hobbies and recreational activities as part of their coursework so that they could teach and participate in such activities with the patients (Ingram, 1935). However, of the 25,971 nursing graduates in the 1930–1931 school year, only 524 were specialized in mental nursing (How, 1933).

Reflecting a general move toward combining the training for general and mental nurses, over the next 20 years many nursing schools affiliated with mental hospitals began to close their doors (Fitzsimmons, 1944). Uniform training for all nurses soon became a reality. Short-term in-service programs pertaining to the health care needs of individuals with mental retardation also first appeared in the late 1930s (Peppe & Sherman, 1978).

The initiation of the University Affiliated Programs (UAPs) in Mental Retardation in the 1960s focused attention on the interdisciplinary training needs of professionals. Nurses were offered both preservice and in-service programs. Content in all areas of theory, practice, and research applying to persons with mental retardation and developmental disabilities was highlighted. Three important pamphlets were developed for nurses regarding the care of persons with mental retardation and developmental disabilities: *A Guide for Public Health Nurses Working with Mentally Retarded Children* (Holtgrewe, 1964), *Guidelines for Continuing Education in Developmental Disabilities* (Haynes et al., 1978), and

School Nurses Working with Handicapped Children (Igoe et al., 1980). The University Affiliated Programs also sponsored nursing workshops for nurses interested in mental retardation throughout the late 1960s and 1970s.

An unpublished paper by Hiltz (1970) found that schools of nursing had very few theory hours devoted to mental retardation. There were even fewer hours provided in clinical settings. Judkins and Harrison (1979) conducted a federally funded national survey of all baccalaureate nursing programs to determine what theoretical and clinical content on mental retardation was being taught in nursing and in other courses found in other departments. Ten schools were chosen for in-depth interviews during site visits. The authors found that there was a general lack of use of available facilities, the priority for such subject content was low, no program objectives were found, and most schools instead suggested regional programs for instruction. What subject content there was included assessments, communication, community living, family interaction, role of the nurse, and treatments. Usually the faculty in charge of the lectures were nursing specialists in the field. Clinical sites were varied and ranged from community based to institutional. The courses were required in some schools and elective in others. Usually the content was found in the course on pediatric nursing. Theory presentation lasted an average of 2–27 hours and clinical experience from 0–130 hours. Objective tests, supervised work, and family case studies were used. It appeared that nursing curricular content in mental retardation was emphasized only when a University Affiliated Program was located on campus or a nursing faculty member was a specialist or interested in this field (Judkins & Harrison, 1979).

Under the leadership of Kathryn Barnard, the University of Washington at Seattle School of Nursing led the nation in innovative curricular content in mental retardation. In 1964, the School of Nursing offered a postgraduate course and continuing education program in mental retardation, funded by the Children's Bureau. Assessment skills, growth and development, behavior analysis, forms of care (both medical and psychosocial) for both the patient and his or her family, communication techniques, and learning to compose a nursing framework of care were stressed in these curricula (Seidel, 1976). Later, in 1989, the University of Washington at Seattle School of Nursing was also one of the first to offer a postgraduate program in early intervention, representing a major move forward in training nurses in an extended role in providing health care for children in a new educational setting (Brandt & Magyary, 1989).

The opportunities for nurses in the fields of mental retardation and developmental disabilities expanded in the 1970s to include genetics. Graduate programs in nursing and genetics were begun at the University of Iowa, Iowa City; the University of Miami; the Eunice Kennedy Shriver Center, Waltham, Massachusetts; and the University of Cincinnati College of Nursing and Health (Kenner & Berling, 1990).

During the 1970s, grant monies were available for nursing research on mental retardation and developmental disabilities. Therefore, there was increased nursing curricular content in these areas. Beginning in the late 1970s, however, governmental grant priorities were in other health issues; thus, much less nursing curricular time was given to this area of study. Now, with increased genetic knowledge as a result of the Genome Project, very low birth weight babies surviving and living longer, pediatric acquired immunodeficiency syndrome, and increased screening, testing, and documentation of developmental disabilities in children, there has been an increased interest in nursing knowledge regarding developmental disabiliities.

NURSING IN DEVELOPMENTAL DISABILITIES AS REFLECTED IN THE LITERATURE

For many years, the primary writing by nurses on topics related to developmental disabilities appeared in the *American Journal of Nursing*. Other articles appeared mostly in journals related to this field, the *American Journal on Mental Retardation* (formerly *American Journal of Psycho-Aesthetics* and *American Journal of Mental Deficiency*), the *Journal of Mental Science*, and the *American Journal of Insanity*. Often the early articles, (prior to 1940) were written by physicians about nurses. With the advent of advanced nursing roles and specialty roles, publications began to appear in journals specific to the specialty.

The most prolific period of writing on developmental disabilities by nurses occurred during the 1960s and 1970s, beginning with the advent of reforms issued by the Kennedy administration. Three articles on developmental disabilities appeared in the September 1963 issue of the *American Journal of Nursing*. Margaret Wright (1963) wrote about elderly persons with mental retardation, the care in institutions, the amount of curricular content in mental retardation, and the dearth of prepared nurses in this field—all issues relevent to nursing today. Other significant articles written during this time focused on nursing in institutions (Dunsdon, 1963) and nursing in the community (Woodfall, 1963).

Mental Retardation, published by the AAMD, first appeared in 1963. A nurse wrote an article for that first issue on in-service training (Harrison, 1963). Other topics to appear during this year in journal articles authored by nurses included public health nursing services for children with mental retardation, primary health programs in culturally deprived areas, and the operant learning theory (Edwards & Tilly, 1963; Fackler, 1963; Hawley, 1963). These authors came from backgrounds in administration, education, and clinical practice.

Unfortunately, the nurse's role in the field of developmental disabilities has been neglected in more recent literature. Nursing articles written on topics related to developmental disabilities and mental retardation diminished after the Johnson presidency. To date, there are only a handful of books that have been written by nurses on caring for an individual with developmental disabilities. Although some of these works now are rather dated, they are all worth reviewing to gain a sense of recent history and changes in care and treatment (see Table 2).

DEVELOPMENTAL DISABILITIES NURSING IN PROFESSIONAL ORGANIZATIONS

In order to strengthen special nursing interests, nurses have joined together to form their own organizations or become a part of an established organization. An important development in the late 1800s was the founding of the Association of Medical Officers of American Institutions for Idiots and Feeble-Minded Persons, established in 1876 by six superintendents of institutions from across America. The purpose of the organization was:

> the discussion of all questions relating to the causes, conditions, and statistics of idiocy, and to the management, training, and education of idiots and feeble-minded persons; it will also lend its influence to the establishment and fostering of institutions for this purpose. (Meeting of Superintendents, 1877, pp. 4–5)

Table 2. Books on mental retardation and developmental disabilities written by nurses

Author(s)	Title	Year
Penny	*Practical Care of the Mentally Retarded and Mentally Ill*	1966
Penny	*Substitute Parents*	1967
Barnard and Powell	*Teaching the Mentally Retarded Child*	1972 (2nd Ed., 1976)
Powell	*Assessment and Management of Developmental Changes and Problems in Children*	1976 (2nd Ed. 1981)
Krajicek and Tearney-Tomlinson	*Detection of Developmental Problems in Children*	1977 (2nd Ed., 1983)
O'Neill, McLaughlin, and Knapp	*Behavioral Approaches to Children with Developmental Delays*	1977
Siantz	*The Nurse and the Developmentally Delayed Adolescent*	1977
Curry and Peppe	*Mental Retardation: Nursing Approaches to Care*	1978
Blackwell	*Care of the Mentally Retarded*	1979
Haynes	*A Developmental Approach to Casefinding among Infants and Young Children*	1980
Zelle and Coyner	*Developmentally Disabled Infants and Toddlers*	1983
Cohen	*Clinical Genetics in Nursing Practice*	1984
Graff, Ault, Guess, Taylor, and Thompson	*Health Care for Students with Disabilities: An Illustrated Medical Guide for the Classroom*	1990
Fraley	*Nursing and the Disabled across the Lifespan*	1992

This organization is now known as the American Association on Mental Retardation (AAMR, 1987). It was 54 years later, in 1930, before a nurse could hold full membership in this organization.

Beginning in 1896, nurses interested in mental retardation and developmental disabilities nursing, or other specialties, could join the American Nurses' Association (ANA). In a survey by the American Nurses' Association in 1941, only 2% of its membership were mental nurses (Anderson, 1941). Nurses interested in the fields of mental retardation and developmental disabilities were encouraged to join either the Council of Maternal-Child Nursing or the Council of Community Health Nursing. There were not enough nurses interested in mental retardation and developmental disabilities to begin their own council (Nehring, 1985).

In 1964, nurses joined the newly organized subdivision of nursing in the American Association on Mental Deficiency. In 1966, nursing placed its first lectures and discussions on the agenda for the annual conference. Recruitment of membership was the major issue. In 1969, nursing became the seventh division in the AAMD; Pat McNelly was the first vice-president of the division. The Nursing Division of the AAMD grew rapidly. By 1972, a record high enrollment of 418 was reached. Today the Nursing Division of AAMR has approximately 375 members. Una Haynes (in 1974) and Doris Haar (in 1981) both received national awards from the AAMD, the Special Award and the Leadership Award, respectively. Nurses have become active in all aspects of the organization but have yet to hold the national presidency.

Nurses involved in the care of persons with mental retardation or developmental disabilities also belong to other specialty interdisciplinary and nursing organizations. Many nurses involved with the UAPs are members of their organization, the American Association of University Affiliated Programs. Other nurses belong to and participate in the activities of the United Cerebral Palsy Association and/or The Arc. Moreover, very active state and regional nursing organizations for nurses working with persons with mental retardation and developmental disabilities include the New York State Mental Retardation/ Developmental Disabilities Nurses; the Nurses of the Developmentally Disabled (NODD, in New Jersey, which recently obtained a national charter); and similar groups in Louisiana, Washington, D.C., Massachusetts, Ohio, and Wisconsin. Other state and regional nursing groups continue to form. Specific educational materials for individuals with mental retardation and developmental disabilities (e.g., an infection control manual from a Boston, Massachusetts, group and a computer program used to address health and nursing care needs from the OMRDD Bureau of Training and Development in Albany, New York) also have been developed by individuals and groups for widespread use.

FUTURE DIRECTIONS

This chapter has focused on the history of the field of developmental disabilities nursing. Future nursing theories or elaborations on current theories, new interventions, increased quantities of and advances in technologies, genetic advances, and employment opportunities will enhance nursing practice in developmental disabilities. The future of the health care system in America will mandate quality services at reduced costs, and nurses, especially the advanced practitioners, are in a position to meet the public's health care needs. Nurses will be called on to collaborate in complicated health conditions such as human immunodeficiency virus infection, and

they will continue to provide assessment, intervention, and evaluation of the effects of conditions on the individual and his or her family according to a systematic approach.

Developmental disabilities content will increase in nursing curricula as more persons are diagnosed with developmental disability, whether etiologic or environmental in nature. The topics of aging, minorities, and lower social classes cannot be discussed thoroughly without mention of developmental disabilities. For example, much of the research being done on Alzheimer disease is focused on the neuropathological changes in persons with Down syndrome. More advanced practitioners will be trained for the care of persons of all ages, and this training will include content on developmental disabilities.

With deinstitutionalization and a greater public awareness of our "global community," more attention will need to be paid to the population of persons with developmental disabilities. Not since the 1960s and early 1970s has nursing been in such an influential position to alter the health care for persons with developmental disabilities and the public in general. With the future revision of the standards of practice for advanced nurse–practitioners in developmental disabilities, the new position statement for professional nurses, and future certification available at the baccalaureate and advanced degree levels, the position of nursing in this interdisciplinary field remains solid and stable. Much will be written about nurses in the coming years regarding developmental disabilities in each area of theory, practice, and research.

REFERENCES

Aggen, R.L., & Moore, N.J. (1984). *Standards of nursing practice in mental retardation/developmental disabilities*. Albany: New York Office of Mental Retardation and Developmental Disabilities.

American Association on Mental Deficiency. (1964). *Standards for state residential care*. Washington, DC: Author.

American Association on Mental Retardation. (1987, May 31). *Annual general membership* meeting minutes from the 111th Annual Meeting of the American Association on Mental Retardation. Denver, CO.

Anderson, E.C. (1941). Open road ahead in psychiatric nursing. *American Journal of Nursing, 41,* 1183–1188.

Austin, J., Challela, M., Huber, C., Sciarillo, W., & Stade, C. (1987). *Standards for the clinical nurse specialist in developmental disabilities/handicapping conditions.* Washington, DC: American Association of University Affiliated Programs.

Barnard, K.E., & Powell, M.P. (1972). *Teaching the mentally retarded child.* St. Louis: C.V. Mosby.

Blackwell, M. (1979). *Care of the mentally retarded.* Boston: Little, Brown.

Blatt, B., & Kaplan, F. (1966). *Christmas in purgatory.* Boston: Allyn & Bacon.

Brandt, P.A., & Magyary, D.L. (1989). Preparation of clinical nurse specialists for family-centered early intervention. *Infants and Young Children, 1*(3), 51–62.

Brett, E.A. (1929). A study of the nursing care given to mental patients in the Cook Co. Hospital. *American Journal of Nursing, 29,* 143–147.

Browne, C.M., & Walsh, C.A. (1989). Midlevel practitioners: Expanded roles. In I.L. Rubin & A.C. Crocker (Eds.), *Developmental disabilities: Delivery of medical care for children and adults* (pp. 425–435). Philadelphia: Lea & Febiger.

Burr, C.B. (1930). *Practical psychology and psychiatry* (6th ed.). Philadelphia: F.A. Davis.

California Nurses' Association. (1990). *Nursing standards for early intervention services for children and families at risk.* San Francisco: Author.

Central Wisconsin Center. (1961). *Report of the Board of Public Welfare.* Unpublished manuscript, Madison, Wisconsin.

Cohen, F.L. (1984). *Clinical genetics in nursing practice.* Philadelphia: J.B. Lippincott.

Cullinane, M., & Shishmanian, E. (1989). Community nursing services. In I.L. Rubin & A.C. Crocker (Eds.), *Developmental disabilities: Delivery of medical care for children and adults* (pp. 47–54). Philadelphia: Lea & Febiger.

Curry, J.B. (1978). The transition from institution to community living. In J.B. Curry & K.K. Peppe (Eds.), *Mental retardation: Nursing approaches to care* (pp. 239–246). St. Louis: C.V. Mosby.

Curry, J.B., & Peppe, K.K. (1978). *Mental retardation: Nursing approaches to care.* St. Louis: C.V. Mosby.

Curtis, S.J., Begin, B.A., & Blinkhorn, P.L. (1989). Delivery of nursing services in an intermediate care facility for the mentally retarded. In I.L. Rubin & A.C. Crocker (Eds.), *Developmental disabilities: Delivery of medical care for children and adults* (pp. 418–425). Philadelphia: Lea & Febiger.

Deutsch, A. (1936). Dorothea Lynde Dix: Apostle of the insane. *American Journal of Nursing, 43,* 1011–1017.

Dick, K.R. (1941). Nursing in a state hospital: A study of nursing hours in the Worchester (Massachusetts) State Hospital. *American Journal of Nursing, 41,* 401–407.

Dietz, L.D., & Lehozky, A.R. (1967). *History and modern nursing* (2nd ed., pp. 75–76, 92–93). Philadelphia: F.A. Davis.

Dix, D. (1847). *Appeal to Illinois General Assembly for better treatment of the insane.* Archives at the Midwest Nursing History Center, University of Illinois, Chicago.

Dix, D. (1976). Memorial to the legislature of Massachusetts, 1843. In M. Rosen, G.R. Clark, & M.S. Kivitz (Eds.), *The history of mental retardation: Collected papers* (Vol. 1, pp. 1–30). Baltimore: University Park Press.

Dunsdon, E. (1963). Nursing service in a large institution. *American Journal of Nursing, 63,* 75–77.

Edwards, M., & Tilly, R.T. (1963). Operant conditioning: An application to behavioral problems in groups. *Mental Retardation, 1,* 18–20.

Engelhardt, K.F. (1978). Principles of normalization. In J.B. Curry & K.K. Peppe (Eds.), *Mental retardation: Nursing approaches to care* (pp. 33–41). St. Louis: C.V. Mosby.

Fackler, E. (1963). Community organization in culturally deprived areas. *Mental Retardation, 1,* 12–14.

Fitzsimmons, L.W. (1944). Facts and trends in psychiatric nursing. *American Journal of Nursing, 44,* 732–735.

Foley, G.M. (1990). Portrait of the ARENA evaluation: Assessment in the transdisciplinary approach. In E.D. Gibbs & D.M. Teti (Eds.), *Interdisciplinary assessment of infants: A guide for early intervention professionals* (pp. 271–286). Baltimore: Paul H. Brookes Publishing Co.

Fraley, A.M. (1992). *Nursing and the disabled across the life span.* Boston: Jones and Bartlett Publ.

Freud, S. (1965). *New introductory lectures on psychoanalysis* (J. Strachey, Trans.). New York: Norton. (Original work published 1933).

Godfrey, A.B. (1991). Providing health services to facilitate benefit from early intervention: A model. *Infants and Young Children, 4*(2), 47–55.

Gordon, M. (1976). Nursing diagnosis and the diagnostic process. *American Journal of Nursing, 76,* 1298–1300.

Graff, J.C., Ault, M.M., Guess, D., Taylor, M., & Thompson, B. (1990). *Health care for students with disabilities: An illustrated medical guide for the classroom.* Baltimore: Paul H. Brookes Publishing Co.

Harrison, J.H. (1963). Discussion of the article on in-service training. *Mental Retardation, 1,* 16–17.

Hawley, E.F. (1963). The importance of extending public health nursing services to related children living at home. *Mental Retardation, 1,* 243–247.

Haynes, U. (1968). *Guidelines for nursing standards in residential centers for the mentally retarded* (V.R.A. Grant #714-T68). Washington, DC: United Cerebral Palsy Associations, Inc. and the National Association for Retarded Children.

Haynes, U. (1980). *A developmental approach to*

casefinding among infants and young children (DHEW Publ. No. (HSA) 79-5210). Washington, DC: U.S. Department of Health, Education, and Welfare.

Haynes, U., Bumbalo, J., Cook, C., Haar, D., Krajicek, M., Slamar, C.F., & Smith, L.L. (1978). *Guidelines for continuing education in developmental disabilities.* Kansas City, MO: American Nurses' Association.

Hiltz, A. (1970). *Mental retardation and delivery of health care services: Implications for professional nursing education.* Unpublished manuscript, Catholic University of America, Washington, DC.

Hodas, A.S., Blaber, K.A., & Keane, J.M. (1989). Nurses in community-based residential school programs. In I.L. Rubin & A.C. Crocker (Eds.), *Developmental disabilities: Delivery of medical care for children and adults* (pp. 54–61). Philadelphia: Lea & Febiger.

Holtgrewe, M.M. (1964). *A guide for public health nurses working with mentally retarded children* (Publication 3422-1964). Washington, DC: Superintendent of Documents.

How, A. (1923). Something new in nursing. *American Journal of Nursing, 23,* 842–843.

How, A. (1933). From the standpoint of the superintendent of nurses. *American Journal of Nursing, 33,* 794–798.

Hutchison, D.J. (1978). The transdisciplinary approach. In J.B. Curry & K.K. Peppe (Eds.), *Mental retardation: Nursing approaches to care* (pp. 65–74). St. Louis: C.V. Mosby.

Igoe, J.B., Green, P., Heim, H., Licata, M. Macdonough, G.P., McHugh, B.A., Smith, L.L., & Tjornhom, B.H. (1980). *School nurses working with handicapped children* (NP-60). Kansas City, MO: American Nurses Association.

Ingram, M.E. (1935). Teaching the social side of mental nursing. *American Journal of Nursing, 35,* 330–333.

Judkins, B.L., & Harrison, A. (1979). *Education of nurses in mental retardation: National survey of NLN accredited baccalaureate nursing programs in the United States* (HEW Special Training Grant 1D10 NU 02012-01). Unpublished manuscript, University of Utah, Salt Lake City.

Kenner, C., & Berling, B. (1990). Nursing in genetics: Current and emerging issues for practice and education. *Journal of Pediatric Nursing, 5,* 370–374.

Krajicek, M., & Tearney-Tomlinson, A.I. (1977). *Detection of developmental problems in children.* Baltimore: University Park Press.

Lessard v. Schmidt. (1972). No. 71-C-602, U.S. District Court, Eastern District of Wisconsin.

Mabon, W. (1910). The nursing care of the insane. *American Journal of Nursing, 10,* 887–896.

Marshall, H.E. (1937). *Dorothea Dix: Forgotten samaritan.* New York: Russell & Russell.

Mastin, J.T. (1916). The new colony plan for the feeble-minded. *Journal of Psycho-Aesthetics, 21,* 25–35.

McClure, C. (1951). Nursing therapy in mental deficiency. *American Journal of Mental Deficiency, 55,* 108–116.

McFarland, J. (1932). The history of nursing at the Blockley Hospital. *Medical Life, 146,* 631–644.

Meeting of superintendents. (1877). *Proceedings of the Association of Medical Officers of American Institutions for Idiotic and Feebleminded Persons,* pp. 4–6. Philadelphia: J.B. Lippincott & Co.

Miller, J.A. (1979). *A history of nursing at Central Wisconsin Center for the Developmentally Disabled.* Unpublished manuscript, University of Illinois, Chicago.

Miller, J., Steele, K., & Boisen, A. (1987). The impact of nursing diagnoses in a long-term care setting. *Nursing Clinics of North America, 22,* 905–911.

Murray, B.L., & Barnard, K.E. (1966). The nursing specialist in mental retardation. *Nursing Clinics of North America, 1,* 631–639.

National Association of State School Nurse Consultants. (1982). National association of school nurse consultants define role of school nurse in "P.L. 94-142—Education for All Handicapped Children Act of 1975." *The Journal of School Health, 52,* 475–478.

National Institute of Mental Health. (1965). *Patients in public institutions for the mentally retarded, 1965.* Washington, DC: Author.

Nehring, W.M. (1985, June 1). *A comparison of two A.N.A. surveys.* Paper presented at the 109th Annual Conference of the American Association on Mental Retardation, Los Angeles.

O'Neill, S.M., McLaughlin, B., & Knapp, M.B. (1977). *Behavioral approaches to children with developmental delays.* St. Louis: C.V. Mosby.

Penny, R. (1966). *Practical care of the mentally retarded and mentally ill.* Springfield, IL: Charles C Thomas.

Penny, R. (1967). *Substitute parents.* Springfield, IL: Charles C Thomas.

Peppe, K.K., & Sherman, R.G. (1978). Nursing in mental retardation: Historical perspective. In J.B. Curry & K.K. Peppe (Eds.), *Mental retardation: Nursing approaches to care* (pp. 3–18). St. Louis: C.V. Mosby.

Powell, M.L. (1976). *Assessment and management of developmental changes and problems in children.* St. Louis: C.V. Mosby.

Purcell, M. (1911). Nursing care of the insane. *American Journal of Nursing, 11,* 430–434.

Richards, L. (1911). *Reminiscences of America's first trained nurse.* Philadelphia: J.B. Lippincott.

Russell, W.L. (1907). Nursing the insane. *American Journal of Nursing, 7,* 926–933.

Santos, E.H., & Stainbrook, E. (1949). A history of psychiatric nursing in the nineteenth century, Parts I and II. *Journal of the History of Medicine, 4,* 48–74.

Scheerenberger, R.C. (1983). *A history of mental retardation.* Baltimore: Paul H. Brookes Publishing Co.

Seidel, M.A. (1976). *Career development in the*

health professions. Unpublished manuscript, University of Washington, Seattle.

Siantz, M.L. (1977). *The nurse and the developmentally disabled adolescent.* Baltimore: University Park Press.

Steadham, C.I. (1993). The role of the professional nurse in developmental disabilities. *Mental Retardation, 31,* 179–181.

Task Force on Nursing Practice Standards. (1990). *National standards of practice for early intervention services* (working draft). Kansas City, MO: American Nurses' Association.

Tucker, K. (1916). Nursing care of the insane in the United States. *American Journal of Nursing, 16,* 198–202.

Twardzicki, N. (1970). *The role of nursing in mental retardation.* Unpublished document, University of Washington, Seattle.

Woodfall, R.E. (1963). Care for the mentally retarded. *American Journal of Nursing, 63,* 80–82.

The work of nurses in asylums. (1901). *American Journal of Nursing, 1,* 515–518.

Wright, M.M. (1963). Care for the mentally retarded: Scope of the problem. *American Journal of Nursing, 63,* 70–74.

Wright, M.M., Erb, A., & Lawrence, P. (1961). *Remotivation technique in the nursing care of the mentally retarded.* Philadelphia: American Psychiatric Association.

Wyatt v. Stickney (1972). No. 3195-N, U.S. District Court, Middle District of Alabama, North Division.

Zelle, R.S., & Coyner, A.B. (1983). *Developmentally disabled infants and toddlers.* Philadelphia: F.A. Davis.

2

An Overview of Developmental Disabilities Nursing

Joyce S. Morse

OBJECTIVES

On completion of this chapter, the reader will be able to:

- Describe current issues in the field of developmental disabilities nursing.
- Identify strategies that promote self-advocacy for persons with developmental disabilities.
- Discuss the role of the family in caring for individuals with developmental disabilities across the life span.
- Describe the role of the nurse in facilitating optimal development of the individual with developmental disabilities.

OVERVIEW

Nurses interact with persons with developmental disabilities in a wide variety of settings, including homes, schools, hospitals, clinics, workshops, and competitive employment. Basic nursing education programs provide the practitioner with general skills that then must be enhanced to meet the needs of individuals with developmental disabilities. Like other existing and/or emerging subspecialty areas of nursing practice (e.g., organ transplantation, gerontology, and addictions/chemical dependency nursing), the specialty of developmental disabilities nursing (also known as developmental nursing) must describe and define its scope of practice. The purpose of this chapter is to present the basic concepts and trends applicable to the practice of developmental disabilities nursing.

DEFINITIONS OF TERMS

Developmental disability is a broad term that refers to a wide variety of conditions that interfere with the ability of an individual to function effectively in society. These conditions can be mental and/or physical, and may include environmental deprivation as well as biological limitations. PL 95-602 (the Rehabilitation, Comprehensive Services, and Developmental Disabilities Amendments of 1978) defines a developmental disability as:

A severe, chronic disability of a person which:
  Is attributable to a mental or physical impairment or a combination of mental and physical impairment
  Is manifested before the person attains 22 years of age
  Is likely to continue indefinitely
  Results in substantial limitations in three or more of the following areas of major life activity:
    Self-care
    Receptive and expressive language
    Learning
    Mobility
    Self-direction
    Capacity for independent living
    Economic sufficiency
  Reflects the person's need for a combination and sequence of special, interdisciplinary or generic care, treatment, or the services which are of lifelong or extended duration and are individually planned and coordinated. (U.S. House of Representatives, 1978, pp. 51–52)

The inclusion of the requirement for substantial functional limitations in three or more major life areas in the above definition was intended to assure provision of services to individuals with more severe impairments (Kiernan, Smith, & Ostrowsky, 1986). This requirement is most relevant to adolescents and adults because the life areas specified in the federal definition have little relevance for infants and limited relevance for young children. More recently, PL 99-457 (Education of the Handicapped Act Amendments of 1986) specifically recognized the need for comprehensive early intervention services and enhanced educational services for infants and young children with disabilities, including those with mental retardation (American Association on Mental Retardation, 1992).

Extensive information is available about many developmental disabilities, such as cerebral palsy, Down syndrome, seizure disorders, neural tube defects, learning disabilities and attention deficit hyperactivity disorder, and autism. Nurses who interact with persons with developmental disabilities need an understanding of the characteristics that define and describe various developmental disabilities in order to comprehend the nurse's role. It is beyond the scope of this chapter to address all of these disabilities; therefore, mental retardation has been selected as an example because it typifies a developmental disability.

Individuals who are classified as having a developmental disability also may have **mental retardation.** Mental retardation refers to substantial limitations in present functioning. It is characterized by significantly subaverage intellectual functioning, existing concurrently with related limitations in two or more of the following applicable adaptive skills areas: communication, self-care, home living, social skills, community use, self-direction, health and safety, functional academics, leisure, and work. Mental retardation manifests before age 18.

The following four concepts are essential to the application of the definition of mental retardation:

Valid assessment considers cultural and linguistic diversity as well as differences in communication and behavioral factors;

The existence of limitations in adaptive skills occurs within the context of community environments typical of the individual's age peers and is indexed to the persons' individualized needs for supports;

Specific adaptive limitations often coexist with strengths in other adaptive skills or other personal capabilities;

With appropriate supports over a sustained period, the life functioning of the person with mental retardation will generally improve. (American Association on Mental Retardation, 1992, p. 1)

Developmental delay is a general term that refers to an individual's failure to meet developmental milestones. Delays do not always indicate the presence of developmental disabilities; they may represent short-term problems that resolve over time as the individual "catches up" developmentally. In other cases, however, what appears first as a delay in development may later manifest as a developmental disability when developmental progression ceases. In some settings, the term *developmentally delayed* is utilized to describe individuals in need of or receiving services (Capute & Accardo, 1991). Infants and young children with developmental delays should be referred to an early intervention program for educational interventions to promote optimal development (see Russell & Free, chap. 3, this volume).

GROWTH AND DEVELOPMENT

Growth may be defined as "an increase in size" (*Webster's New World Dictionary*, 1991). Development refers to "advancement from lower to more advanced stages of complexity; the emerging and expanding of the individual's capacities through growth, maturation, and learning" (Whaley & Wong, 1991, p. 106). Human growth and development is an orderly, predictable process. It begins with the embryo and continues throughout the life span. The phases of growth and development are influenced by many hereditary and environmental influences, such as the parent–child relationship and the living environment. The growth process includes not only physical development but also emotional and social development. Table 1 summarizes theories of cognitive, moral, and personality development.

Development is linked closely to the maturation of the central nervous system, and follows a cephalocaudal pattern, progressing from head to foot. For example, an infant gains head control first, then sitting balance, and then achieves crawling, then standing, and finally walking. Development generally follows a fixed sequence of events; thus, babies sit before they crawl and stand before they walk. This gives us a frame of reference to utilize when assessing a child's developmental status and comparing it to the norms. Several aspects of development may be occurring simultaneously at any given time.

Developmental disabilities affect the typical processes involved in growth and development. Therefore, in order to advocate for and support the best possible program for the individual with developmental disabilities, the nurse should have a thorough understanding of that individual's developmental status. The nurse must be familiar with landmarks in the growth and development process. This information enables the nurse to utilize a developmental rather than a chronological approach to the individual with developmental disabilities. This approach focuses on the abilities and the assets of the individual.

Developmental Assessment in Nursing

Within the health care system, a normal component of the nursing process is developmental assessment. Appendices A,

Table 1.   Summary of personality, cognitive, and moral development theories

Stage/age	Psychosexual stages (Freud)	Psychosocial stages (Erickson, 1963)	Cognitive stages (Piaget, 1969)	Moral judgment stages (Kohlberg, 1968)
I—Infancy Birth to 1 year	Oral sensory	Trust vs. mistrust	Sensorimotor (birth to 18 months)	
II—Toddlerhood 1–3 years	Anal–urethral	Autonomy vs. shame and doubt	Preoperational thought, preconceptual phase (transductive reasoning) (e.g., specific to specific) (2–4 years)	Preconventional (premoral) level Punishment and obedience orientation
III—Early childhood 3–6 years	Phallic– locomotion	Initiative vs. guilt	Preoperational thought, intuitive phase (transductive reasoning) (4–7 years)	Preconventional (premoral) level Naive instrumental orientation
IV—Middle childhood 6–12 years	Latency	Industry vs. inferiority	Concrete operations (inductive reasoning and beginning logic)	Conventional level Good boy, nice girl orientation Law-and-order orientation
V—Adolescence 13–19 years	Genitality	Identity and repudiation vs. identity confusion	Formal operations (deductive and abstract reasoning)	Postconventional or principled level Social contract orientation Universal ethical principle orientation (no longer included in revised theory)
VI—Early adulthood		Intimacy and solidarity vs. isolation		
VII—Young and middle adulthood		Generativity vs. self-absorption		
VIII—Later adulthood		Ego integrity vs. despair		

Adapted from Erickson (1963), Kohlberg (1968), and Whaley and Wong (1991).

B, and C at the end of this chapter contain information that can be utilized by the nurse to assess the developmental status of the infant, toddler, and pre–school-age child. The developmental tasks and milestones of the school-age child and the adolescent are described in Appendices D and E. Formal developmental assessment tools, such as the Denver II (Sperhac & Salzer, 1991) also can be used by the nurse as part of the assessment process. Specific instructions for the use of such tools can be found in most pediatric nursing textbooks. The results of the developmental assessment can be utilized to give parents information about activities to promote optimal development. They also can be the basis for providing anticipatory guidance about the stages yet to come. These results also help to identify a child with developmental delays.

Developmental Assessment in Education

Within the educational setting, developmental status typically is assessed by studying the various domains or areas of skill development. The domains used to assess developmental status are cognition, communication, social/adaptation, and fine motor and gross motor functioning. In the communication domain, language is the best predictor of future intellectual functioning (Shapiro, 1992). In the cognitive domain, Jean Piaget's stages of cognitive growth provide a framework for understanding the sequence of cognitive development as well as the limitations that may be imposed by developmental disabilities.

According to Piaget, cognition is an active and interactive process in which learning results from the constant interaction between the child and his or her environment. These interactions help the child to construct an understanding of how the world operates (Piaget, 1969). The cognitive theory of learning describes the way in which learning occurs in concert with the cognitive developmental stages. Piaget believed that intellectual development progressed through four definitive stages between birth and 14 years of age:

Sensorimotor stage:	Birth to 2 years
Intuitive or preoperational stage:	2–7 years
Concrete operations stage:	7–11 years
Formal operations stage:	11–16 years

Each stage is a major transformation from the previous one, and children must move through these stages in sequential order. As the individual passes from one stage to the next, more complex and abstract abilities are acquired. An individual who is unable to progress through all of the stages is limited in his or her ability to adapt as an adult (Shapiro, 1992).

In the sensorimotor stage, the child responds to the environment primarily through the senses. Responses usually are related to the situation; for example, the infant will cry because of hunger. As the infant grows and develops, he or she experiments and finds ways to interact with the environment. Placing objects in the mouth in order to experience the taste, temperature, texture, and shape is an example of a baby's interaction with his or her environment. At this stage, most learning occurs as the result of trial and error. Many people with severe cognitive deficits do not progress beyond this stage in the learning process, despite advances in chronological age.

During the intuitive or preoperational stage, the child uses language in a meaningful way. The predominant mode of thinking is intuitive and highly imaginative. The child says what he or she thinks, and can use symbols to represent objects that are not present. For example, a 3-year-old child may enjoy pretending that a doll is a real baby and "feed" it make-believe food. At this stage, the child can classify and group some objects and distinguish certain quantities, such as "big" versus "little." Individuals with moderate cognitive limitations rarely progress beyond this stage of cognitive development, even as they age.

In the stage of concrete operations, children learn to test things for themselves and become almost too literal in their thinking. Skills such as counting, sorting, building, and manipulating fit this level of thinking. The child can arrange objects according to size or weight. The child also can generalize new learning, solve some mathematical problems, and read well. At this stage a limited understanding of time concepts such as "past" and "future" is beginning to emerge. Individuals with mild cognitive limitation usually remain at this level of intellectual development as they grow older (Shapiro, 1992).

During the stage of formal operations, children learn to test hypotheses, to use self-reflection, and to include the perspectives of others. It is during this stage that the individual develops the ability to isolate a problem, review it systematically, and figure out all possible solutions to that problem.

Standardized curricula are available to assist a child to overcome delays or disabilities identified in educational assessments (e.g., *The Carolina Curriculum for Infants and Toddlers with Special Needs* [Johnson-Martin, Jens, Attermeier, & Hacker, 1991]). It is also important to consider the effects of sociocultural factors when developing strategies that support learning (Bricker & Woods Cripe, 1992). Successes in early intervention programs demonstrate the effectiveness of an interactional approach that incorporates family involvement and promotes learning in persons with developmental disabilities.

DEVELOPMENTAL DISABILITIES

Incidence and Prevalence

The availability of epidemiological data specific to developmental disabilities reflects the difficulties in obtaining accurate data about specific disabilities. The terms *incidence* and *prevalence* are used as measures of frequency. **Incidence** measures the occurrence of new cases in a specific period of time, and **prevalence** identifies the number of cases existing at a specific time. Incidence is more accurate in the investigation of etiology and the assessment of the effectiveness of prenatal and perinatal programs, whereas prevalence has become the method utilized to plan for services needed by persons with developmental disabilities and their families (Lipkin, 1991).

Data collection depends on case identification. Case identification is easiest when the disability has a well-defined etiology. For example, the individual with Down syndrome is clearly identifiable based on chromosomal analysis. When the etiology is less well defined, case identification is based on a requirement for evidence of loss of function, lack of performance, or limitation of role fulfillment. The search for such evidence can delay case identification, as is also true when social or psychological criteria are used. Case identification also has presented problems in investigating the epidemiology of other, more recently identified, developmental disabilities. These include speech and language disorders, hearing and visual impairments, autistic disorders, and the minimal dysfunction syndromes such as learning and behavior disorders (including learning disabilities and attention deficit hyperactivity disorder) (Lipkin, 1991).

Case identification often is based on the concepts of impairment, disability, or handicap, as defined below:

Impairment: A disturbance in structure or function resulting from anatomical, physiological, or psychological abnormalities. For example, a person may have an impairment of vision that requires eyeglasses for reading.

Disability: The degree of observable and measurable physical or mental impairment. For example, a person may have uncorrected vision of 20/60.

Handicap: The total adjustment to disability necessitated by an impairment or disability that limits or prevents functioning at a usual level. For example, a person with 20/60 vision would be handicapped in reading or driving a car because of the vision problem. (Stanhope & Lancaster, 1992, p. 537)

The nurse must be able to interpret statistical information about developmental disabilities and integrate it into nursing practice. The National Health Interview Survey conducted by the U.S. Department of Health and Human Services in 1987 estimated health impairment and disability in persons under the age of 18 (National Center for Health Statistics, Schoenborn, & Marano, 1988). It did not consider cognitive or behavioral impairments. The results showed that 5.7 million children have some sort of impairment or disability. Additional survey data on the prevalence of various chronic conditions among 10- to 24-year-olds are presented in Table 2.

The most extensive statistical information available in the field of developmental disabilities is about mental retardation and cerebral palsy. This is probably because these two disorders were among the first to be identified historically, and are fairly easy to diagnose clinically (Lipkin, 1991).

Mental Retardation Munro (1986) estimated an overall prevalence of mental retardation of 1% of the general population. McLaren and Bryson (1987) estimated an overall prevalence of between 0.8% and 1.2%. Others (Baird & Sadovnick, 1985; Grossman, 1983; Hagberg, Hagberg, Lewerth, & Lindberg, 1981)

have estimated the prevalence of mental retardation at closer to 3%. In the United States, this means that there are approximately 6 million people with mental retardation. The differences in data may be the result of differences in ascertainment. For example, persons who speak English as a second language or those from financially impoverished environments may test poorly, and thus may have low IQ test results that imply mild mental retardation (Shapiro, 1992). Worldwide statistics reflect a prevalence rate of 3–4 cases per 1,000 persons (Baird & Sadovnick, 1985; Fryers, 1984; McQueen, Spence, Winsor, Garner, & Pereira, 1986).

Cerebral Palsy The overall incidence of cerebral palsy ranges from 0.6 to 2.4 per 1,000 persons, depending on the study. Spastic cerebral palsy is the most common subtype, accounting for 63%–94% of the identified cases (Pharoah, Cooke, Rosenbloom, & Cooke, 1987). There are slightly more males than females affected (Lagergren, 1981). Compared with other chronic conditions (deafness, blindness, musculoskeletal im-

Table 2. Prevalence and rate per 1,000 persons of selected chronic conditions for persons 10–24 years of age: United States, 1986–1988 (based on total U.S. population of 10- to 24-year olds: 53,654,000)

Chronic conditions	Prevalence, 10–24 years old	Rate per 1,000 persons
Arthritis	633,000	11.8
Asthma	2,696,000	502.0
Cerebral palsy	65,000[a]	1.2[a]
Cleft palate	46,000[a]	0.9[a]
Congenital heart disease	144,000	2.7
Diabetes	218,000	4.1
Epilepsy	273,000	5.1
Hearing impairments	1,425,000	26.6
Liver diseases (including cirrhosis)	33,000[a]	0.6[a]
Malignancies—all sites	21,000[a]	0.4[a]
Mental retardation	698,000	13.0
Multiple sclerosis	9,000[a]	0.2[a]
Paralysis of extremities, complete or partial	97,000	1.8
Speech impairments	561,000	10.5
Spina bifida	11,000[a]	0.2[a]
Visual impairments	1,003,000	18.7

Source: Unpublished data from the National Health Interview Survey, National Center for Health Statistics. Compiled with the assistance of John Gary Collins, Division of Health Interview Statistics.

[a] Does not meet standards of statistical reliability.

pairment, diabetes mellitus, asthma, epilepsy, etc.), cerebral palsy was found to be the most limiting on children's activities (Newacheck & Taylor, 1992). In Lagergren's study (1981), 82% of individuals with cerebral palsy had at least one associated disability and 42% had three or more associated disabilities. These included cognitive disorders (31%), communication disorders (41%), visual impairments (50%–92%), hearing impairments (10%), seizure disorders (40%), and orthopedic deformities, as well as behavioral and emotional disorders.

Etiology

Developmental disabilities are either congenital or acquired. They may be visible or invisible. They may be stable or progressive, depending on the etiology of the specific disorder or syndrome (Batshaw & Perret, 1992).

The etiologies of developmental disabilities and mental retardation are multitudinous. They are most easily divided into prenatal, perinatal, postnatal, and unknown categories. Prenatal etiologies include chromosomal, (e.g., trisomy 21), single gene (e.g., Lesch-Nyhan syndrome), multifactorial (e.g., myelomeningocele), and environmental (e.g., congenital infections, maternal drug use). The perinatal etiologies include prematurity/low birth weight and hypoxia. Postnatally, trauma, infections, and neglect can result in mental retardation and/or developmental disabilities (American Association on Mental Retardation, 1992; Haggerty, 1984).

Prevention

Nurses play an important role in the prevention of developmental disabilities. *Primary prevention* includes family planning services, genetic counseling, comprehensive prenatal care, immunizations, and decreasing the use of tobacco, drugs, and alcohol. *Secondary prevention* consists of early intervention to promote optimal development. Nursing

services in early intervention include case finding, case management, health assessment, assisting families to cope with actual or potential health problems, administration of medications or treatments, and collaboration with other members of the interdisciplinary team. *Tertiary prevention* focuses on the prevention of secondary disabilities. Physical stimulation, nutritional counseling, cognitive stimulation, attention to developmentally appropriate safety issues, and family assessment and support are examples of tertiary prevention (Stanhope & Lancaster, 1992). See Russell and Free (chap. 3, this volume) for an expanded discussion of secondary and tertiary prevention concepts.

DEVELOPMENTAL DISABILITIES NURSING

Developmental disabilities nursing (sometimes referred to as *developmental nursing*) describes the subspecialty of nursing practice that deals with assisting the individual with developmental disabilities to attain/maintain an optimal level of wellness across the life span. Individuals served by the developmental nurse have disorders that reflect a variety of health, cognitive, communication, social adaptation, sensory, perceptual, gross motor, and fine motor strengths and limitations. These are manifested over time and impact on the family as well as the individual.

Developmental nursing has its roots in the practice of maternal–child nursing, psychiatric/mental health nursing, and community health nursing. Developmental nurses integrate, adapt, and modify information from many disciplines into their practice. A generalized knowledge base permits the nurse to synthesize information from the behavioral, biological, and social sciences. The result is a unique, holistic approach to the care of the individual and his or her family. Table 3 identifies the assumptions and beliefs that form the concep-

Table 3. Assumptions and beliefs about developmental disabilities nursing

Assumptions	Beliefs
1. The service delivery system for individuals with developmental disabilities is complex and does not always include provisions for health care. 2. Access to primary, secondary, and tertiary health care makes a difference in the quality of life for persons with developmental disabilities. 3. Nursing, as a profession, is the product of education and practice based on research. 4. Nursing care of individuals with developmental disabilities occurs primarily in community-based settings.	1. Health care and the services of a registered professional nurse should be available to all individuals with developmental disabilities. 2. In formulating health policy, individuals with developmental disabilities and their families should be included. 3. The nurse as a provider, the individual with developmental disabilities, and the family can form an effective partnership to advocate for and effect changes in health services and policies. 4. The environment affects the health of persons with developmental disabilities, as well as others. 5. For individuals with developmental disabilities, the prevention of the illness and secondary complications of their disabilities is essential for health. 6. Health practices that promote wellness must be carried out throughout the life span of individuals with developmental disabilities. 7. The individual with developmental disabilities is the only constant member of the interdisciplinary treatment team. 8. Individuals with developmental disabilities must be encouraged and taught to be active participants in their own health care.

Adapted from the American Nurses' Association (1980) and the American Association on Mental Retardation (1990).

tual basis for the contemporary practice of developmental nursing.

The Nursing Division of the American Association on Mental Retardation (AAMR) has developed a position paper, shown in Appendix F, that describes the role of the nurse who provides services to individuals with developmental disabilities (AAMR, 1992). The AAMR position paper emphasizes the promotion of wellness and normalization in the delivery of nursing services to individuals with developmental disabilities. It also stresses education, prevention, and a holistic approach to the integration of health care services in habilitation. The nurse's role in contributing to and improving the quality of life for persons with developmental disabilities and their families is emphasized (AAMR, 1992).

Special Issues in Developmental Disabilities Nursing

Complex Medical Needs/Medical Fragility Many individuals with developmental disabilities have concurrent medical conditions. Often, the medical needs of an individual are complex and interrelated but, the individual is medically stable (i.e., is not in need of continual health intervention merely to maintain a state of wellness).

Felicia is a vivacious 18-year-old woman with a medical diagnosis of static encephalopathy that manifests as cerebral palsy and spastic quadriplegia accompanied by mild dysphagia and slight dysarthria. She has a seizure disorder that is well controlled with oral medication. She has a nonprogressive scoliosis. Felicia sees a nurse–practitioner for her primary health care. On an annual basis she has routine

(continued)

audiology, optometry, dental, and gynecological evaluations. She is monitored by a neurologist and orthopedist as necessary. Felicia has had no serious illnesses, accidents, or hospitalizations during the past 5 years. Last year, she was treated for one episode of otitis media and one episode of strep throat. Both illnesses responded well to oral antibiotic therapy. Despite her medical diagnosis, Felicia is generally well. The focus of her health interventions is on prevention of illness, early detection and prompt treatment of episodic illness, and health teaching to promote Felicia's ability to manage her own health care needs.

Thus, Felicia's concurrent medical conditions are stable and do not present an ongoing threat to her general health. Medical care for such individuals is not significantly different than that for an individual without developmental disabilities.

In contrast, the term *medical fragility* (a condition also referred to as having complex medical needs) is sometimes utilized to indicate how vulnerable some individuals are to seemingly slight changes that can seriously compromise their health status. The intensity of health services required by Ron to maintain an optimal level of wellness reflects the complexity of his health problems. Managing these problems requires a variety of highly individualized and specialized supports and services that must be integrated in order to assure a coordinated service plan.

Service Availability All of the developmental disabilities place demands on the health care system. Many individuals with developmental disabilities and their families require extensive social,

psychological, and educational services in order to optimize positive life outcomes. Nurses must be cognizant of demographic trends in order to plan for and deliver appropriate interventions to this population.

In order to meet the demand for services to individuals with developmental disabilities, government expenditures at the federal, state, and local levels have increased approximately 150% between 1962 and 1984 (Castellani, 1987). In 1985, the largest portion of these federal dollars was spent for reimbursement for institutional care. Federal efforts then were redirected to focus on assistance to community and local programs. In 1989, legislation was enacted to focus on the costs and benefits of respite care programs (Overview of Respite Care Programs, 1990). Presently there are wide variations in the abilities of individual states to implement these programs. This can leave huge gaps in the delivery of services provided to individuals with developmental disabilities. Early intervention programs, respite care services,

Ron is a quiet, serious 28-year-old who has cerebral palsy with spastic quadriplegia. He is nonambulatory and spends most of his time in his wheelchair. Ron is unable to swallow food by mouth, so he is fed via a gastrostomy tube. He also has chronic reactive airway disease (secondary to prematurity, chronic aspiration, and progressive scoliosis). Ron is vulnerable to malnutrition, metabolic disturbances, and infection as a result of the complex pathophysiology of his interrelated medical problems.

multidisciplinary supports in the school system, vocational training, and supported employment programs are only a few of the services that are needed in a community. The nurse must be knowledgeable about the availability of resources and services in each community. The nurse can function as an advocate for program development and funding as state and local policies are being developed.

Normalization and Mainstreaming in Health Care Services The principle of *normalization* forms the philosophical basis of service delivery to persons with mental retardation and/or developmental disabilities in this country (Wolfensberger & Kurtz, 1969). In the 1950s in Scandinavia, Nirje and Bank-Mikkelsen promulgated the concept of normalization as "letting the mentally retarded obtain an existence as close to normal as possible" (Wolfensberger, 1980, p. 7). In the United States, the focus of the normalization movement has been to promote a high quality of life for each person with developmental disabilities within the least restrictive environment (Wolfensberger, 1991). This has meant the development of community-based programs for persons with developmental disabilities that promote freedom of choice for the individual, and meet age-appropriate as well as special developmental needs.

In the education setting, *mainstreaming* is the process whereby children with developmental disabilities receive their education in regular classroom settings. It is the result of PL 94-142 (the Education for All Handicapped Children Act of 1975), which mandated a free, appropriate public education in the least restrictive environment. As of 1991, school districts are mandated to implement a policy of *inclusion*. This means that all students, regardless of special needs, are to be educated in the regular classroom. Programs that are challenging and geared to the individual student's

capabilities must be provided, along with any needed supports and assistance. An inclusive school system must be sensitive, flexible, and responsive to unique needs. It must support teachers as well as students. In an inclusive school, each individual has his or her needs met and has a sense of belonging, acceptance and support from peers and other members of the school community (Stainback & Stainback, 1990).

In the health care system, changes have become necessary in order to respond to the needs of persons with developmental disabilities. Mainstreaming medical care is a result of the normalization movement. As persons with developmental disabilities left the institutional placements common in the 1950s, 1960s, and 1970s, it was necessary to identify a systems approach that would ensure the effective delivery of high-quality health care services. Rubin and Crocker (1989) emphasize the importance of stable primary health care with an identified "medical home." This means that a health care provider, such as an internist, pediatrician, or nurse practitioner, is responsible for the coordination of all routine and specialty health care to individuals with developmental disabilities in order to maintain wellness and minimize the secondary complications of any physical disability. Primary care nurses are uniquely qualified to provide care to these individuals (Morse & Ayers, 1982). Community health nurses also have a role in coordinating health care, participating in team meetings, and acting as contacts to provide communication and education about relevant health issues to the individual, his or her family, and the program staff (Crocker, Yankauer, & Conference Steering Committee, 1987).

Social Role Valorization and Vulnerability As a successor to the concept of normalization (Wolfensberger, 1972), *social role valorization* is a term proposed by Wolfensberger in 1983. It implies the use of cultural values to enable, establish, or maintain (valued) social roles for people. Individuals who have developmental disabilities may be perceived as "different" from others. Although there are many differences between individuals, being different does not always have a negative connotation or automatically devalue a person. It is society's cultural norms that give negative value to some differences. For example, in some cultures, an individual with a seizure disorder may be considered to be "touched by the gods," which has a strong positive social value. In another culture, the same individual might be labeled as "neurologically impaired" and suffer from a strong negative social valuation (Wolfensberger, 1983).

The way in which a person is perceived has a direct impact on how the person will be treated by others. Individuals who are socially devalued may be treated in ways that diminish their dignity, adjustment, growth, competence, health, wealth, and life span (Wolfensberger, 1989). Individuals who are socially devalued are also vulnerable. *Vulnerability* is a condition in which individuals or groups are highly susceptible to harm. For persons with developmental disabilities, vulnerability is characterized by personal, social, and environmental variables (Dever, Sciegaj, & Wade, 1988). Health risks, limited control, disenfranchisement, victimization, powerlessness, and disadvantaged status are some of the major concepts that contribute to an understanding of vulnerability.

The concept of *health risk* is based on a model of the natural history of a disease, in which certain aspects of physiology, personal habits, and the social or physical environment make it likely that an individual will develop a particular health problem. For example, like others with the same medical diagnosis, an individual with spina bifida is prone to skin breakdown secondary to immobility, impaired sensation, and poor circulation. As a result of concern for risk factors and high-risk groups, there has been increasing attention to the needs of such people, who constitute a *special population group*. The U.S. Public Health Service defines a special population group as an age group, minority group, or low-income group with a greater likelihood of developing particular diseases or conditions than the population as a whole. These groups include persons with developmental disabilities, medically indigent persons, homeless persons, and frail elderly persons, to name just a few (Nichols, Wright, & Murphy, 1986).

In our culture, individuals share control and responsibility for their health status with society as a whole (Dever et al., 1988). Tim's biological condition (Down syndrome) determines the kind of health issues he will face. Society determines the type of health services and reimbursement that are available to Tim. In this regard, Tim has *limited control* of his health options.

Disenfranchisement refers to a feeling of separation from mainstream society. Disenfranchised groups often are per-

Tim is an active 38-year-old man who has Down syndrome. For most of his life, Tim lived at home. His mother assumed primary responsibility for coordinating Tim's health care and seeing that he followed his physician's recommendations. Last year Tim moved into a supervised apartment. Now he must schedule his own appointments and follow up on recommendations for continued care. Even with some assistance from his apartment manager, Tim has had an increase in the number and frequency of health problems experienced over the past year.

ceived to be nonproductive members of society. People who are homeless, frail, elderly, or pregnant adolescents, and persons with developmental disabilities are often invisible to and isolated from society as a whole. These groups are poorly represented and may be forgotten in terms of health and social planning (Sebastian, 1985).

In the United States, there is a focus on the individual's responsibility for maintaining health through lifestyle choices; for example, smoking and overeating are seen as irresponsible/negative behaviors. Persons who "fail" to manage their health may be blamed for becoming ill. Blaming the victim of illness for that illness (*victimization*) is one way in which society relieves itself of responsibility for social and environmental issues as well as issues surrounding the delivery of health care services (Grau, 1987).

During difficult economic times, the emphasis on cost containment restricts access to government-sponsored health care. Limits to access can be both economic and social. Economically, individuals may have to pay more for services as fewer and fewer services are covered by third-party payers. There may be only partial reimbursement for previously covered services, and there may be higher deductibles. Socially, many services have strict eligibility criteria that may exclude some people from receiving

needed services. These trends combine to place many persons with disabilities in a state of *powerlessness*.

Typically, health planning focuses on meeting the needs of the majority of the population. Persons with developmental disabilities and other vulnerable groups have limited input in the health planning to meet their needs. They have a more *disadvantaged status* than mainstream groups. Because of their minority status, persons with developmental disabilities are often thought of as unable to credibly advocate for their own interests. Advocacy for access to adequate and appropriate health services for individuals with developmental disabilities is an important role of the nurse.

Advocacy The concept of advocacy can be described as "a set of beliefs that results in action aimed at defending, maintaining, or promoting a cause" (Neufield, 1979, p. 45). In our society, it is usually the family that functions as an advocate for its dependent members. Because most individuals with developmental disabilities live with their families in the community, the essential role of families as advocates is well established (Kornblatt & Heinrich, 1985).

Historically, in small or rural communities, the church or the community itself also assisted a family to support a person with a developmental disability.

Hannah is a 46-year-old woman who utilizes a power wheelchair for mobility. She is employed part time as a clerk in her community library. Hannah would like to work full time but, if her income were to increase, she might jeopardize her eligibility for Medicaid and Social Security/disability benefits. Hannah currently receives her health care in the outpatient clinic of the local municipal hospital. Because of recent cutbacks in funding, the subsidized wheelchair-accessible van that provided her transportation to the clinic no longer operates a route near her home. Although Hannah needs health services, she is in a quandary. The cost of private transportation to the clinic will deplete her financial resources. For this month, Hannah might have to choose between transportation to health care and groceries. Such a decision fails to promote her independence.

As society has become more complex and urban, this informal network has been unable to advocate successfully for the needs of its members. At the same time, human service organizations have become so large, complex, and impersonal that even competent individuals may feel intimidated by "the system" (Kornblatt & Heinrich, 1985). Advocacy serves to bridge the gap between what an individual with developmental disabilities needs and what the service system can provide.

The advocacy role in contemporary nursing practice is well defined. The American Nurses' Association (ANA) Code for Nurses (1985) states that *"the goal of nursing action is to support and encourage the client's responsibility and self-determination"* (p. 1). In the role of advocate, the nurse must consider the person's physical, psychological, social, and environmental capabilities.

Sometimes conflict can arise as the nurse carries out the advocacy role. The nurse must be aware of his or her own value systems. It often is easier for the nurse to inform, support, and affirm another person's decision when it is congruent with the nurse's own values. In order for the nurse to provide information to any individual, the nurse should:

Assess the individual's understanding of the situation.

Provide correct information.

Communicate with the individual's cognitive level and literacy skills in mind.

Use visual and tactile aids to reinforce comprehension.

Discuss relevant factors that will affect the individual's decision (e.g., financial and ethical issues).

Discuss the possible consequences of the individual's decision.

Conflict also can arise within families, and the nurse must balance his or her role as advocate for an individual with consideration of the desires and values of the individual's family members.

Kohnke (1982) stated that nurse advocates must assure individuals that they have the right to obtain information and the responsibility to make their own decisions. The person with developmental disabilities can build his or her decision-making skills by recognizing the progression of activities experienced as part of the decision-making process. Nurses can assist persons with developmental disabilities in the development of decision-making skills through use of the following strategies: information exchange, written contracts, setting priorities, and

---

Keisha is a 24-year-old woman with a great sense of humor. She has mild cognitive deficits and a seizure disorder. She resides in a supervised apartment with two other young women. Keisha is employed as a clerk in a bookstore. She has a boyfriend, and they are planning to be married. Keisha arrives at her adult nurse–practitioner's office for her annual physical exam, accompanied by her mother. Keisha starts to ask the nurse about sexual activity. Her mother cuts off the discussion, stating "Keisha won't ever need that sort of stuff." Keisha interjects, "I'm getting married and I want to know more about sex." The nurse must respond to Keisha's request for information while being sensitive to the mother's point of view. The nurse suggests that Keisha schedule a follow-up appointment with her for a private session to discuss sexuality issues. The nurse can also support Keisha's mother to accept Keisha's responsible attitude toward seeking appropriate intervention.

role playing to determine the consequences of different options.

It can be difficult for the nurse to attain balance between "doing for" and "promoting autonomy." The nurse should remember that the goal of advocacy is to promote the individual's ultimate degree of self-determination, given the individual's current and potential status. For most individuals, this goal can be realized (Cary, 1992).

Nurse advocates, as proponents for social change, must become familiar with the legislative issues that affect the lives of persons with developmental disabilities. Legal remedies are the tools through which change becomes legitimized. The Americans with Disabilities Act of 1990 (ADA) is an example of the use of the judicial system to advocate for the rights and needs of special interest groups. The ADA prohibits discrimination based on disability and has expanded greatly the basic civil rights of individuals with developmental disabilities. This law creates opportunities for full participation in all aspects of society.

ROLE OF THE FAMILY IN DEVELOPMENTAL DISABILITIES NURSING

Across the life span, every individual with developmental disabilities must be viewed within the context of his or her family. The needs and wants as well as the abilities of each family member must be considered as programs are developed and implemented.

Cultural and Ethical Considerations

Every individual is born into a family. The term *family* can be interpreted and defined in a wide variety of ways. There are biological relationships, economic perspectives, and social as well as moral and functional descriptors that can be applied. Friedman (1986) defined family as "composed of [two or more] people who are emotionally involved with one another and live in close geographic proximity" (p. 6). Emotional involvement is a "perception of reciprocal obligations, a sense of commonness, and a sharing of certain obligations, coupled with a caring commitment to one another" (Friedman, 1986, p. 6). Within each culture the structure and goals of the family vary; however, the basic functions of the family are to provide for the future of society and the stabilization of its culture (R. Johnson, 1984).

According to Lynch and Hanson (1992), culture is "a framework that guides and bounds life practices" (p. 3). A culture is composed of individuals who share a set of values, beliefs, practices, and information that is learned and integrated into one's life. Material manifestations of culture include dress, food, and art; whereas nonmaterial manifestations of culture include ideas, beliefs, and feelings (Elkin & Handel, 1989). The culture in which an individual is reared determines factors as varied as the type of food he or she will eat, the language spoken, the ideals of behavior, and the understanding of social roles. The nurse must recognize his or her own cultural biases and be sensitive to how these will interact with the culture of a family with a member who has developmental disabilities, or "culture shock" may occur. Typically, culture shock refers to "a normal and universal response to the unfamiliar" (Hanson, 1992, p. 23). It is the result of encounters between two culturally dissimilar groups, and can lead to misunderstanding, frustration, and anger, or it can be used in a positive way to increase tolerance and open one's consciousness to new ways of behaving and interacting.

Increasingly, the United States is characterized by multicultural diversity. As we approach the year 2000, it is estimated that 38% of all children under the age of 18 will be nonwhite and non-Anglo (Bureau of the Census, 1988). It is important for the nurse to appreciate and respect differences among cultures in order to be effective as an interventionist. Nurses traditionally have provided services to individuals within the context of the family unit. It is the role of the nurse to foster the integrity of the family and its culture throughout the life span of the individual with developmental disabilities.

The emergence of a multicultural perspective for nursing interventions exists concurrently with bioethical considerations. Bioethical issues can emerge even prenatally. Wolfensberger (1991) stated that it is unethical to test for the presence of congenital and/or genetic deficiencies during pregnancy. He argued that, if the results of the testing reveal a deformed or defective fetus and an abortion ensues, the medical profession and the parents have devalued the intrinsic worth of human life. It is more common, however, for bioethical controversy to begin with the birth of an infant who has serious genetic or health impairments with accompanying (or presumed) mental retardation (Orelove & Sobsey, 1991). The focus of the controversy can be the right of the individual to medical treatment.

The present-day practice of selective nontreatment of newborns with severe disabilities is a continuation of the historical practice of infanticide. The practice transcends cultures and always has existed. It is based on social and economic considerations and may take the form of withdrawing or withholding treatment that is necessary to support life, or the withholding of sustenance (Weir, 1984).

In 1984, PL 98-457 (the Child Abuse Prevention and Treatment Act) went into effect. This legislation defines "medical neglect" as "the withholding of medi-

cally indicated treatment from a disabled infant with a life threatening condition." The specific definition of "withholding of treatment" is: "The failure to respond to the infant's life threatening condition by providing treatment (including appropriate nutrition, hydration, and medication) which, in the treating physician's . . . reasonable medical judgment will most likely be effective in ameliorating or correcting all such conditions . . ." (Child Abuse Prevention and Treatment Act, Child Abuse Amendments, 1984).

Withholding of medical treatment is not considered to be "medical neglect" when:

1. The infant is chronically and irreversibly comatose; or
2. The provision of such treatment would merely prolong dying, not be effective in ameliorating or correcting all of the infant's life threatening conditions, or otherwise be futile in terms of the survival of the infant; or
3. The provision of such treatment would be virtually futile in terms of the survival of the infant and the treatment itself under such circumstances would be inhumane. (Child Abuse Prevention and Treatment Act, Child Abuse Amendments, 1984)

The federal legislation provides guidelines for practice, and each state's Child Protective Service Agency has the authority to enforce the federal regulations. However, a host of moral and ethical dilemmas remain unresolved. Among these are the role of parents versus the role of medical professionals in the decision-making process, the meaning of terms such as *quality of life* and *meaningful life,* and what impact the projected cognitive ability of the newborn should have in the decision-making process.

Once an infant with significant disabilities has reached early childhood, ethical issues focus on the "right to education." In 1975, the federal government passed PL 94-142 (the Education for All Handicapped Children Act). This legislation mandated that an appropriate education be made available to every child, regardless of his or her disability. Subsequent federal legislation expanded the right to education position by supporting the development of early intervention programs for infants birth through 3 years (see Russell & Free, chap. 3, this volume, for a detailed discussion).

As with the "right-to-treatment" issue, the educational issue is fraught with legal, ethical, and philosophical landmines. Arguments have been made against the universal educability of all children, the limited gains that can be made by some individuals versus the high cost of providing services, defining appropriate services, and even defining what constitutes education for persons with severe multiple disabilities. There has been particular concern focused on those individuals with profoundly impaired cognition in addition to multiple physical handicaps. Some, such as Orelove and Sobsey (1991), believe that, for education to be effective for persons with multiple disabilities, teachers and technology must be utilized differently than they are in contemporary school settings (Morse & Colatarci, chap. 14, this volume).

For adults with developmental disabilities, ethical issues focus on guardianship and consent as well as the freedom to live, work, and marry with access to support services on an "as necessary" basis. At the present time, most service system funds are tied into programs rather than disbursed to individuals. A person-centered approach to service delivery for adults with developmental disabilities should evolve from the needs of the individual and would:

1. Recognize the importance of involving persons with developmental disabilities and their families in planning and making choices about their lives.
2. Recognize that choices should be made based on their knowledge of options and adequate information.
3. Sensitize family and staff to understand and facilitate choices and preferences of persons with developmental disabilities.
4. Encourage program options beyond the traditional developmental disabilities service systems (Anderson & Moran, 1993).

For the aging adult with developmental disabilities, ethical concerns are emerging about retirement, integrated leisure options, health services (including the use of psychoactive medication), and death with dignity (Jacobson, Sutton, and Janicki, 1985; Janicki, 1988). Wolfensberger (1991) has expressed concern that older persons with developmental disabilities might be at risk of medical neglect or undertreatment because of perceived devaluation of their social role within the context of society as a whole.

Because the nurse works with families and individuals with developmental disabilities at all stages of the life cycle, it is important for the nurse to be cognizant of and sensitive to cultural and ethical considerations. The nurse must appreciate that each culture and every family will take a unique approach to the issues that confront them in daily life. A nonjudgmental approach combined with insight into the nurse's own value system will be an asset in resolving cross-cultural or divergent philosophical approaches to care.

Developmental Stages of Families

In order to develop interventions that are most supportive to families, the nurse should be aware that every family experiences developmental stages that are analogous to the developmental stages of an individual. According to family development theory, these developmental stages reflect general features of family life through a longitudinal view of the family life cycle. This implies that there are successive phases and patterns that occur within the family over the years and that there is a high degree of interdependence between family members. Therefore, families change each time members are added to or subtracted from the family (Duvall & Miller, 1985; Friedman, 1986). These changes, known as critical transition points, cause changes in the status and roles of family members. The healthy family is able to perform all roles appropriately according to the family member's ages, competencies, and needs during the life cycle. Table 4 provides an overview of family developmental tasks and stages.

Response to a Child with a Developmental Disability

For every family, the adjustments and realignments each member must make during times of change are stressful. When a family has a child with a disability, the stress is amplified. Each family will respond uniquely to the needs of such a child, altering its style of functioning to incorporate those needs. Over time, a new pattern of family response develops as the family achieves a measure of acceptance of or adjustment to the child's condition (Figure 1).

The most common response to being told that a child has a disability is some combination of shock, disbelief, guilt, and an overwhelming feeling of loss. Kubler-Ross (1969) described the stages of grieving over such situations, including denial, depression, anger, guilt, bargaining, and acceptance. Fortier and Wanlass (1984) have labeled the stages in their model as impact, denial, grief, focusing attention, and closure:

Impact usually occurs at the time of medical diagnosis. It is characterized by anxiety and family disorganization.

Denial appears to be a defense mechanism. It is illustrated by the parents' searching for a second opinion in the hope that the original diagnosis was incorrect.

Grief is manifested as feelings of anger, guilt, and sadness. It may result in blaming others for the child's diagnosis.

Focusing attention is the stage during which parents can begin to accept help from others and begin to adapt to their life situation realistically.

Closure is the final stage. At this point the parents accept the fact that their

---

Table 4.   Stages of family development according to Wright and Leahy (1984) and Duvall (1977)

Stage I—Marriage and an Independent Home: Establish identity as a married couple, realign relationships with birth family and spouse's family, make decisions about childbearing.

Stage II—Families with Infants: Maintain the marital relationship, incorporate infant into the family; include grandparenting roles.

Stage III—Families with Preschoolers: Socialize children; children and parents adapt to separations.

Stage IV—Families with School-Age Children: Children develop peer relationships, parents adjust to the influences of peers and school.

Stage V—Families with Teenagers: Adolescents develop more independence, parents refocus on marriage and career issues, parents have increasing concerns and responsibilities related to their own parents.

Stage VI—Families as Launching Centers: Parents and young adults establish independent identities. Marriage relationship and expectations renegotiated.

Stage VII—Middle-Age Families: Couple reinvests in marital relationship, concurrent development of independent interests; realignment of relationships to include in-laws and grandchildren; deal with disabilities and death of older generation.

Stage VIII—Aging Families: Roles shift from leisure to semiretirement or full retirement; focus on maintaining functioning as an individual and a couple while adapting to age; prepare for own death while dealing with the possible/actual loss of siblings, peers, spouse.

Adapted from Wright and Leahy (1984) and Duvall (1977).

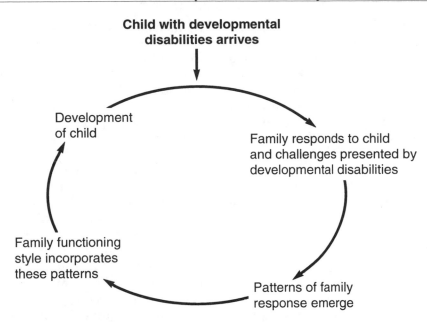

Figure 1.   Impact of a child with developmental disabilities on family function. (Modified from Center for Children with Chronic Illness and Disability [1992].)

child's diagnosis has disrupted and will continue to disrupt normal family life. The family develops mechanisms to incorporate the child into family life.

This model suggests progression through a sequence of stages that are time bound and culminate in parental acceptance of or adjustment to the child's condition. According to the model developed by Fortier and Wanlass, this family has reached the stage of closure. They have accepted the fact that Arlene's diagnosis

requires ongoing adjustments in their family life and schedules in order to accommodate her needs.

Chronic sorrow is a model in which parental reaction is one of functional adaptation to, but not acceptance of, the child's condition. Olshansky (1962) defined chronic sorrow as a natural, nonneurotic, and understandable response to a tragic act that remains constant throughout a child's life, whether the child is at home or institutionalized. The intensity of sorrow is said to vary between parents and families (Clements,

---

Arlene is an adorable 4-year-old with wispy blond hair and an engaging smile. She has cerebral palsy. She is very aware socially but is totally dependent physically. She is enrolled in a preschool program sponsored by the local Easter Seals society. In a parent support group, her mother talks about how supportive her husband's employer has been, allowing him to work his 40-hour week in 4 days. This permits her to schedule her full-time job around his schedule, so they do not need baby sitters for Arlene. They still must juggle at least 1 day per week, but they are not constantly taking time off from work to take Arlene to school, therapy, and doctor appointments.

Copeland, & Loftus, 1990; Clubb, 1991; Copley, 1991; Damrosch & Perry, 1989), among situations, from time to time, and within the same person (Wikler, Wasow, & Hatfield, 1983). The emotion of chronic sorrow is affected by factors such as a person's personality, ethnic group, religion, and social class (Fraley, 1990). Phillips (1991) suggested that, for chronic sorrow to be present, there must be hopelessness regarding progress, cure, or normalcy. Time seems to be a crucial factor in the development of chronic sorrow. The certainty and permanence of the condition need to evolve (Frey, Greenberg, & Fewell, 1989). Denial seems to preclude the development of this phenomenon (Phillips, 1991).

A sense of sadness and a lack of hope preface Keith's father's touching statement. It typifies the presence of chronic sorrow as described by Olshansky.

Family Coping Strategies

Thomas, Barnard, and Sumner (1991) defined family coping as "the collective behaviors and/or thought processes of family members for the purpose of dealing with an identified threat or challenge to the family or a member" (p. 2). Examples of family coping include changing work schedules in order to place a child with a disability on a special, adapted van (behavior) or their belief (thought process) that the child with a developmental disability will recover and become "normal."

Practiced coping refers to the use of coping skills that have proven to be helpful to the family in the past. *Novel coping* describes behaviors that are developed by the family when they recognize that their practiced coping skills are not being effective in a given situation. Families are most likely to be receptive to novel ways of coping after they have tried the ways that are most familiar to them.

Assessment of family coping is important in order to identify the unique ways each family manages stress. This assessment serves as a guide to the nurse in selecting interventions and supports that promote that family's way of coping. The timing of the assessment of family

---

Keith is an alert and socially responsive 9-year-old boy. Lesch-Nyhan syndrome was diagnosed by genetic testing when he was 10 months old. An apparently normal baby at birth, his parents noted developmental delays and dystonia at about 5 months of age. Shortly thereafter, Keith began to cause injuries to himself. These were described as scratching, rubbing, and/or biting behaviors that he seemed unable to control. At home, his parents have developed a variety of mittens, splints, and straps in an effort to protect Keith from self-injury. Presently, Keith attends his local elementary school. He is popular with other students and staff. A specially designed wheelchair provides maximum protection from the possibility of self-injury.

During a parent support group meeting, Keith's father spoke eloquently about Keith's life. "It hurts me to know that I can't hug my son without worrying that one of us will get hurt. I understand his disease, but I look at other families with [handicapped] kids and wish that the only thing wrong with Keith was cerebral palsy. This is not getting better. Keith is getting bigger and more difficult to handle physically. My wife used to be able to manage him by herself; now it takes the two of us just to give him a bath. We're getting older and worry about what will happen to Keith. What if his kidneys get worse? He already has been in the hospital for stones. He could never have dialysis. I can't bear to think about the future for all of us."

coping is important, because families experience a period of adjustment when dealing with any stressor, and cope differently at the beginning of the adjustment process than they do later in the process. The nurse, therefore, can get a different impression of the family's coping skills depending on the timing of the assessment. Sometimes professionals do not recognize a family's coping mechanisms as they move through the early stages of adjusting to a new situation. It takes time for families to adjust to crises and organize their coping strategies (Thomas, 1992).

A number of useful tools are available for the nurse to utilize in assessing family coping. One of these is the Coping Health Inventory for Parents (CHIP) (McCubbin, McCubbin, Nevin, & Cauble, 1987). This measure is designed to assess coping styles of parents dealing with a chronic condition in their child. It assesses coping in the following areas:

Family integration, cooperation and definition of the situation

Maintaining social support, self-esteem and psychological stability

Understanding the health care situation through communication with other parents and consultation with the health care team. (Thomas, 1992, p. 2)

Using the CHIP gives the nurse and the family a way to develop and strengthen optimal coping strategies. Future research directed toward resilience and effective coping strategies will enable nurses and other professionals to better assist families with children who have developmental disabilities (Center for Children with Chronic Illness and Disability, 1991).

Resilience is the "tendency for a child, adult or family to rebound from stressful circumstances or events and resume usual activity, accord, and success" (Center for Children with Chronic Illness and Disability, 1992, p. 100). Some family strengths that support resilience are listed in Table 5. Resilient families learn to balance the special needs of the child with a disability with the other

Table 5. Family strengths that support resilience

FAMILY SIZE	More, rather than fewer, siblings enhance family life.
ATTITUDES	Families must be able to see their situation as an opportunity for enrichment and satisfaction.
RESOURCES	When financial, medical, emotional, and social needs of the family are met, they can focus on the other aspects of family life. All family members are negatively affected when the family's needs exceed their resources.
MARRIAGE	A strong, harmonious relationship enables parents to share the challenges and satisfactions of raising a child with a chronic condition.
COMMUNICATION	Successful family life is enhanced by honest, frequent communication.
SHARING INFORMATION	Family members need to share information and fears.
TWO-WAY COMMUNICATION	The individual with developmental disabilities needs to share feelings with parents and siblings.
COPING	Each family must develop strategies that support effective coping. Family meetings, prayer, and humor all can be helpful.
BELIEFS	Parents must agree on what is important to them about child rearing, and how these beliefs can be applied to the person with developmental disabilities.
ADDITIONAL PROBLEMS	Family life becomes more complicated in the presence of additional stressors such as parental illness, unemployment, or a death in the family.

Adapted from Center for Children with Chronic Illness and Disability (1991)

needs of the family on several levels. Decisions about health-related services, special education needs, and home treatment and therapies must be integrated into other family decisions. Time, energy, and money also must be shared. The family must establish priorities based on shared values of family members. They protect their sense of identity by maintaining normal family routines, and by protecting themselves from too much outside intrusion (Turnbull & Turnbull, 1986). Nurses can support families and encourage healthy resilience by providing information about the disability, helping the family access needed services, and encouraging family members to express their feelings and communicate with one another.

Supporting Families as Primary Care Providers

In the past, individuals with developmental disabilities, especially mental retardation, were cared for outside of the home. Institutions and agencies became the primary care providers. It generally was acknowledged that only professionals knew how to manage the needs of these individuals. Therefore, children and adults with mental retardation, mental illness, sensory disabilities, and other disabilities were placed in residential institutions. However, isolation from home and community experiences was found to inhibit personal and social development. The advocacy movement of the 1970s resulted in the closing or reduction in size of large public residential facilities. The residential facilities that have remained open as part of state and county mental retardation service systems are smaller and more highly regulated, and primarily serve people with significant and multiple disabilities, many of whom have complex medical and psychiatric disorders (Kurtz & Berman, 1991).

Since the 1970s there has been a shift in social policy. According to this trend,

families would be supported and strengthened as the primary care providers for the family member with a developmental disability. Family support systems may be described as programs, benefits, or arrangements that facilitate, enhance, or optimize members and the functioning of the family as a unit by supporting individual family members (Whaley & Wong, 1991).

Nurses are familiar with a *family-centered care model* of service delivery. In this system the family is recognized as the constant in the child's life. Every effort is made to support, respect, encourage, and enhance the competence of the family unit (B. Johnson, McGonigel, & Kaufman, 1989). Within this philosophy, the role of professionals is to support families in their natural caregiving skills as well as encouraging decision making that is based on their unique skills as individuals and families. The needs of all family members are considered (Shelton, Jeppson, & Johnson, 1987).

Enabling and *empowerment* are the basic concepts in family centered care. Enabling is the process whereby professionals create the opportunities and means for family members to demonstrate their present understanding and competencies as well as acquiring the new ones necessary to meet the needs of the child and the family. Empowerment is the result of interactions between families and professionals that maintain the locus of control within the family unit and foster their own strengths, abilities, and actions (Whaley & Wong, 1991).

The parent–professional partnership is a powerful mechanism for enabling and empowering families of persons with developmental disabilities. In a parent–professional partnership, parents have the rightful role of deciding what is important for themselves and their family; the professional's role is to support and strengthen the family's ability to nurture and promote its members' development in a way that is both enabling and empowering (Whaley & Wong, 1991).

An optimal parent–professional relationship should include trust, competence, and an equal relationship between the parent and the professional. When one of these attributes is missing, expectations of that attribute persist, which can distort and confuse the existing relationship (Pimentel, 1991). As a member of the interdisciplinary treating team that provides care to the individual with developmental disabilities, the nurse has an obligation to advocate for and facilitate the strongest parent–professional partnership possible.

SUMMARY

Health and wellness are fundamental aspects of life. For individuals with developmental disabilities and their families, health status will impact on personal and family functioning. It will affect the outcome of assessments, and determine the need for environmental supports and services that facilitate optimal functioning. The developmental nurse utilizes a holistic approach to assist these individuals and their families to maintain autonomy in making decisions that promote wellness across the life span. The nurse has a responsibility to ensure that habilitation goals that re-

late to the promotion of healthy behavior, prevention of illness, treatment of disease, and amelioration of health-related disability are included in the development and implementation of the individual's program plan at every stage of the life cycle (AAMR, 1992). Morse and Colatarci (1992) have listed those goals pertaining to the maintenance of emotional and physical health for individuals with developmental disabilities:

Identify and/or communicate a change in health status.

Understand the impact of medical diagnoses.

Attain/maintain:

the ability to manage his or her own health care.

the ability to consume adequate nutrients to support growth and/or good health.

adequate respiratory function to permit activity without (respiratory) distress.

regular elimination of body waste.

adequate activity level to maintain/promote good health.

a rest pattern sufficient to meet biological and emotional needs.

positive relationships with family, peers, and others.

the ability to adapt to changes in sexual function.

the ability to cope with environmental stressors.

REFERENCES

Aggen, R.L., & Moore, J.J. (1984). *Standards of nursing practice in mental retardation and developmental disabilities.* Albany, NY: Office of Mental Retardation and Developmental Disabilities.

American Association on Mental Retardation. (1990). *Nursing division position paper.* Washington, DC: Author.

American Association on Mental Retardation. (1992). *Mental retardation: Definition, classification, and systems of support* (9th ed.). Washington, DC: Author.

American Nurses' Association. (1980). *A concep-*

tual model of community nursing practice. Kansas City, MO: Author.

American Nurses' Association. (1985). *Code for nurses.* Kansas City, MO: Author.

Anderson, D.J., & Moran, P. (1993). Health services for older people with mental retardation/developmental disabilities. *Impact, 6*(1), 18.

Austin, J., Challela, M., Huber, C., Sciarillo, W., & Stade, C. (1987). *Standards for the clinical nurse specialist in developmental disabilities/handicapping conditions.* Washington, DC: National Maternal Child Health Clearinghouse.

Baird, P.A., & Sadovnick, A.D. (1985). Mental retardation in over half-a-million consecutive live births: An epidemiological study. *American Journal of Mental Deficiency, 89,* 323–330.

Batshaw, M.L., & Perret, Y.M. (1992). *Children with disabilities: A medical primer* (3rd ed.). Baltimore: Paul H. Brookes Publishing Co.

Bricker, D., & Woods Cripe, J.J. (1992). *An activity-based approach to early intervention.* Baltimore: Paul H. Brookes Publishing Co.

Brown, F., & Lehr, D.H. (Eds.). (1989). *Persons with profound disabilities: Issues and practices.* Baltimore: Paul H. Brookes Publishing Co.

Capute, A.J., & Accardo, P.J. (Eds.). (1991). *Developmental disabilities in infancy and childhood.* Baltimore: Paul H. Brookes Publishing Co.

Cary, A.H. (1992). Promoting continuity of care: Advocacy, discharge planning, and case management. In *Community health nursing: Process and practice for promoting health* (3rd ed., pp. 265–267). St. Louis: Mosby-Year Book.

Castellani, P. (1987). *The political economy of developmental disabilities.* Baltimore: Paul H. Brookes Publishing Co.

Center for Children with Chronic Illness and Disability. (1991). *Children adapt (Children's Health Issues,* Vol. 1, No. 1). Minneapolis, MN: Author.

Center for Children with Chronic Illness and Disability. (1992). *Longitudinal research: Measuring what helps kids and families thrive (Springboard,* Vol. 2, No. 1). Minneapolis, MN: Author.

Clements, D.B., Copeland, L.G., & Loftus, M. (1990). Critical times for families with a chronically ill child. *Pediatric Nursing, 16,* 157–161.

Clubb, R. (1991). Chronic sorrow: Adaptation patterns of parents with chronically ill children. *Pediatric Nursing, 17,* 461–466.

Copley, M.F., & Bodensteiner, J.B. (1987). Chronic sorrow in families of disabled children. *Journal of Child Neurology, 2,* 67–70.

Crocker, A.C., Yankauer, A., & Conference Steering Committee. (1987). Basic issues. *Mental Retardation, 25,* 227–232.

Damrosch, S.P., & Perry, L.A. (1989). Self-reported adjustment, chronic sorrow and coping of parents of children with Down syndrome. *Nursing Research, 38*(1), 25–30.

Dever, G.E.A., Sciegaj, M., & Wade, T.E. (1988). Creation of a social vulnerability index for justice in health planning. *Family and Community Health, 10*(4), 23.

Duvall, E. (1977). *Family development.* Philadelphia: J.B. Lippincott.

Duvall, E., & Miller, B. (1985). *Marriage and family development* (6th ed.). New York: Harper & Row.

Elkin, F., & Handel, G. (1989). *The child and society: The process of socialization.* New York: Random House.

Erickson, E. (1963). *Childhood and society.* New York: Jeffrey Norton Publisher.

Evans, P., Elliot, M., Alberman, E., & Evans, S. (1985). Prevalence and disabilities in 4-to-8-year olds with cerebral palsy. *Archives of Disease in Childhood, 60,* 940–945.

Fortier, L.M., & Wanlass, R.L. (1984). Family crisis following the diagnosis of a handicapped child. *Family Relations, 33,* 13–24.

Fraley, A.M. (1990). Chronic sorrow: A parental response. *Journal of Pediatric Nursing, 5,* 268–273.

Frey, K.S., Greenberg, M.T., & Fewell, R.R. (1989). Stress and coping among parents of handicapped children: A multidimensional approach. *American Journal on Mental Retardation, 94,* 240–249.

Friedman, M. (1986). *Family nursing: theory and assessment* (2nd ed.). Norwalk: Appleton-Century-Crofts.

Fryers, T. (1984). *The epidemiology of severe intellectual impairment: The dynamics of prevalence.* Orlando, FL: Academic Press.

Grau, L. (1987). Illness engendered poverty among the elderly. *Women's Health, 12*(3/4), 103–118.

Grossman, H.J. (Ed.). (1983). *Classification in mental retardation.* Washington, DC: American Association on Mental Deficiency.

Hagberg, B., Hagberg, G., Lewerth, A., & Lindberg, U. (1981). Mild mental retardation in Swedish school children: I. Prevalence. *Acta Pediatrica Scandinavica, 70,* 441–444.

Haggerty, R.J. (1984). Symposium on chronic disease in children: Foreword. *Pediatric Clinics of North America, 31,* 1–2.

Hanson, M.J. (1992). Ethnic, cultural, and language diversity in intervention settings. In E.W. Lynch & M.J. Hanson (Eds.), *Developing cross cultural competence: A guide for working with young children and their families* (pp. 3–18). Baltimore: Paul H. Brookes Publishing Co.

Jacobson, J.W., Sutton, M.S., & Janicki, M.P. (1985). Demography and characteristics of aging and aged mentally retarded persons. In J. R. Patton, M. Beirne-Smith, & J.S. Payne (Eds.), *Mental retardation* (pp. 115–150. Englewood Cliffs, NJ: Prentice Hall.

Janicki, M.J. (Ed.). (1988). Symposium on aging and mental retardation. *Mental Retardation, 26,* 177–217.

Johnson, B., McGonigel, M., & Kaufman, R. (Eds.). (1989). *Guidelines and recommended practices for the individualized family service plan.* Washington, DC: Association for the Care of Children's Health.

Johnson, R. (1984). Promoting the health of families in the community. In M. Stanhope & J. Lancaster (Eds.), *Community health nursing* (pp. 470–483). St. Louis: Mosby-Year Book.

Kiernan, W.E., Smith, B.C., & Ostrowsky, M.B. (1986). Developmental disabilities: Definitional issues. In W.E. Kieran & J.A. Stark (Eds.), *Pathways to employment for adults with developmental disabilities* (pp. 11–20). Baltimore: Paul H. Brookes Publishing Co.

Kohlberg, L. (1968). Moral development. In D.L. Sills (Ed.), *International encyclopedia of the social sciences.* New York: MacMillan.

Kohnke, M.F. (1982). *Advocacy risk and reality*. St. Louis: C.V. Mosby.

Kornblatt, E.S., & Heinrich, J. (1985). Needs and coping abilities of families of children with developmental disabilities. *Mental Retardation, 23,* 13–19.

Kubler-Ross, E. (1973). *On death and dying.* New York: Macmillan.

Kurtz, M.B., & Berman, W. (1991). Medical issues in residential placement. In A.J. Capute & P.J. Accardo (Eds.), *Developmental disabilities in infancy and childhood* (pp. 235–250). Baltimore: Paul H. Brookes Publishing Co.

Lagergren, J. (1981). Children with motor handicaps: Epidemiological, medical and socio-pediatric aspects of motor handicap in children in a Swedish county. *Acta Paediatrica Scandinavica, 70* (Suppl. 289), 1–69.

Lipkin, P.H. (1991). Epidemiology of the developmental disabilities. In A.J. Capute & P.J. Accardo (Eds.), *Developmental disabilities in infancy and childhood* (pp. 43–67). Baltimore: Paul H. Brookes Publishing Co.

Lynch, E.W., & Hanson, M.J. (Eds.). (1992). *Developing cross cultural competence: A guide for working with young children and their families.* Baltimore: Paul H. Brookes Publishing Co.

McCubbin, H., McCubbin, M., Nevin, R., & Cauble, A.E. (1987). C.H.I.P.: Coping Health Inventory for Parents. In H.I. McCubbin & A.I. Thompson (Eds.), *Family assessment inventories for research and practice* (pp. 1–20). Madison: University of Wisconsin.

McLaren, J., & Bryson, S.E. (1987). Review of recent epidemiological studies of mental retardation: Prevalence, associated disorders, and etiology. *American Journal on Mental Retardation, 92,* 243–254.

McQueen, P.C., Spence, M.W., Winsor, E.J.T., Garner, J.B., & Pereira, L.H. (1986). Causal origins of major mental handicaps in the Canadian Maritime Provinces. *Developmental Medicine and Child Neurology, 28,* 697–707.

Morse, J.S., & Ayers, B.G. (1982, August). *Establishing community-based health services for the deinstitutionalized.* Paper presented at the meeting of the International Association for the Scientific Study of Mental Deficiency, Toronto, Ontario, Canada.

Morse, J.S., & Colatarci, S. (1992). *Goals pertaining to emotional and physical health for individuals with developmental disabilities.* Unpublished manuscript.

Munro, J.D. (1986). Epidemiology and the extent of mental retardation. *Psychiatric Clinics of North America, 9,* 591–624.

National Center for Health Statistics, Schoenborn, C.A., & Marano, M. (1988). *Current estimates for the National Health Interview Survey: United States, 1987* (Vital and Health Statistics Series 10, No. 166; DHHS Publication No. PHS 88-1594). Washington, DC: U.S. Department of Health and Human Services.

Neufield, G.R. (1979). The advocacy role and func-

tions of developmental disabilities councils. In R. Wiegerink & J.W. Pelosi (Eds.), *Developmental disabilities: The DD movement* (pp. 45–60). Baltimore: Paul H. Brookes Publishing Co.

Newachek, P.W., & Taylor, W.R. (1992). Childhood chronic illness: Prevalence, severity, and impact. *American Journal of Public Health, 82,* 364–371.

Nichols, J., Wright, L.K., & Murphy, J.F. (1986). A proposal for tracking health care for the homeless. *Journal of Community Health, 11:* 204.

Olshansky, S. (1962). Chronic sorrow: A response to having a mentally defective child. *Social Casework, 43,* 190–193.

Orelove, F.P., & Sobsey, D. (1991). *Educating children with multiple disabilities: A transdisciplinary approach* (2nd ed.). Baltimore: Paul H. Brookes Publishing Co.

Orem, D. (1991). *Nursing: Concepts of practice.* New York: McGraw-Hill.

Overview of respite care programs, GAO/R-HRD-90-125 (1990). Washington, DC: U.S. Government Printing Office.

Pharoah, P.O.D., Cooke, T., Rosenbloom, L., & Cooke, R.W.I. (1987). Trends in birth prevalence of cerebral palsy. *Archives of Disease in Childhood, 62,* 379–384.

Phillips, M. (1991). Chronic sorrow in mothers of chronically ill and disabled children. *Issues in Comprehensive Pediatric Nursing, 14,* 111–120.

Piaget, J. (1969). *The theory of stages in cognitive development.* New York: McGraw-Hill.

Pimentel, A.E. (1991). The family system in developmental disabilities. In A.J. Capute & P.J. Accardo (Eds.), *Developmental disabilities in infancy and childhood* (pp. 189–196). Baltimore: Paul H. Brookes Publishing Co.

Rubin, I.L., & Crocker, A.C. (Eds.). (1989). *Developmental disabilities: Delivery of medical care for children and adults.* Philadelphia: Lea & Febiger.

Sebastian, J.G. (1985). Homelessness: A state of vulnerability. *Community Health, 8* (3), 11.

Shapiro, B.K. (1992). Normal and abnormal development: Mental retardation. In M.L. Batshaw & Y.M. Perret, *Children with disabilities: A medical primer* (3rd ed.) (pp. 259–289). Baltimore: Paul H. Brookes Publishing Co.

Shelton, T.L., Jeppson, E.S., & Johnson, B. (1987). *Family centered care for children with special health care needs.* Washington, DC: Association for the Care of Children's Health.

Sperhac, A.M., & Salzer, J.L. (1991). A new developmental screening test: The Denver II. *Journal of the American Academy of Nurse Practitioners, 3*(4), 152–157.

Stainback, W., & Stainback, S. (Eds.). (1990). *Support network for inclusive schooling: Interdependent integrated education.* Baltimore: Paul H. Brookes Publishing Co.

Stanhope, M., & Lancaster, J. (1992). *Community health nursing: Process and practice for promoting health* (3rd ed.). St. Louis: Mosby-Year Book.

Teel, C.S. (1991). Chronic sorrow: Analysis of the

concept. *Journal of Advanced Nursing, 11,* 1311–1319.

Thomas, R. (1992, April). Family coping. *NCAST National News* (University of Washington, Seattle: Nursing Child Assessment Satellite Training Program).

Thomas, R., Barnard, K.E., & Sumner, G.A. (1991). *Family nursing and diagnosis as a framework for family assessment.* Paper presented at the second International Family Nursing Conference, Portland, Oregon.

Turnbull, A.P., & Turnbull, H.R. (1986). *Families, professionals, and exceptionality: A special partnership.* Columbus: OH: Charles E. Merrill.

U.S. Department of Commerce, Bureau of the Census. (1988). *Current population reports* (Series P-60, No. 161). Washington, DC: Author.

U.S. House of Representatives. (1978). Conference report: Comprehensive rehabilitation services amendments of 1978 (Report No. 95–1780, pp. 51–52). Washington, DC: U.S. Government Printing Office.

Vgotsky, L. (1978). *Mind in society.* Cambridge, MA: Harvard University Press.

Webster's New World Dictionary (3rd College Ed.). (1991). New York: Simon and Schuster.

Weir, R. (1984). *Selective nontreatment of handicapped newborns.* New York: Oxford University Press.

Whaley, L.F., & Wong, D.L. (1991). *Nursing care of infants and children* (4th ed.). St. Louis: Mosby-Year Book.

Wikler, L., Wasow, M., & Hatfield, E. (1983). Seeking strengths in families of developmentally disabled children. *Social Work, 28,* 313–315.

Wolfensberger, W. (1972). *The principle of normalization in human services.* Toronto, Ontario, Canada: National Institute on Mental Retardation.

Wolfensberger, W. (1980). The definition of normalization: Update, problems, disagreements, and misunderstandings. In R.J. Flynn & K.E. Nitsch (Eds.), *Normalization, social integration, and community service.* Baltimore: University Park Press.

Wolfensberger, W. (1983). Social role valorization: Proposed new term for the principle of normalization. *Mental Retardation, 21,* 234–239.

Wolfensberger, W. (1989). An overview of social role valorization and some reflections on elderly mentally retarded persons. In M.J. Janicki (Ed.), *Symposium on Aging and Mental Retardation, 26,* 177–217.

Wolfensberger, W. (1991). Reflections on a lifetime in human services and mental retardation. *Mental Retardation, 29,* 1–15.

Wolfensberger, W., & Kurtz, R. (Eds.). (1969). *Management of the family of the mentally retarded: A book of readings.* Chicago: Follet Educational Corp.

Wong, D., & Whaley, L.F. (1990). *Clinical manual of pediatric nursing* (3rd ed.). St. Louis: Mosby-Year Book.

World Health Organization. (1980). *International classification of impairment, disabilities, and handicaps: A manual of classification to the consequences of disease.* Geneva: Author.

Appendix A.   Milestones
in Growth and Development: Infancy

Age (months)	Gross motor	Fine motor	Sensory	Communication	Socialization/ cognition
1	Assumes flexed position with pelvis high, but knees not under abdomen when prone (at birth, knees flexed under adomen)	Hands predominantly closed	Visual acuity approaches 20/100	Cries to express displeasure	Is in sensorimotor phase— stage I, use of reflexes (birth–1 month) and
	Can turn head from side to side when prone, lifts head momentarily from bed	Grasp reflex strong	Able to fixate on moving object in range of 45 degrees when held at a distance of 20–25 cm (8–10 inches)	Makes small throaty sounds	stage II, primary circular reactions (1–4 months)
	Has marked head lag, especially when pulled from lying to sitting position	Hand clenches on contact with rattle	Follows light to midline	Makes comfort sounds during feeding	Watches parent's face as she or he talks to infant
	Holds head momentarily parallel and in midline when suspended in prone position		Quiets when hears a voice		
	Assumes asymmetric tonic neck reflex position when supine				
	Makes crawling movements when prone				
	When held in standing position, body limp at knees and hips				
	In sitting position back is uniformly rounded, absence of head control				
3	Able to hold head more erect when sitting, but still bobs forward	Actively holds rattle but will not reach for it	Follows object to periphery (180 degrees)	Squeals to show pleasure	Displays considerable interest in surroundings
				Coos, babbles, chuckles	

(*continued*)

(continued)

Age (months)	Gross motor	Fine motor	Sensory	Communication	Socialization/ cognition
3 (continued)	Has only slight head lag when pulled to sitting Assumes symmetric body position Able to raise head and shoulders from prone position to a 45- to 90-degree angle from table; bears weight on forearms When held in standing position, able to bear slight fraction of weight on legs Regards own hand	Grasp reflex absent Hands kept loosely open Clutches own hand, pulls at blankets and clothes	Locates sound by turning head to side and looking in same direction Begins to have ability to coordinate stimuli from various sense organs	Vocalizes when smiling "Talks" a great deal when spoken to Cries less during periods of wakefulness	Ceases crying when parent enters room Can recognize familiar faces and objects, such as feeding bottle Shows awareness of strange situations
6	When prone, can lift chest and upper abdomen off table, bearing weight on hands When about to be pulled to a sitting position, lifts head Sits in high chair with back straight Rolls from back to abdomen When held in standing position, bears almost all of weight Hand regard is absent	Resecures a dropped object Drops one cube when another is given Grasps and manipulates small objects Holds bottle Grasps feet and pulls to mouth	Visual acuity 20/60 to 20/40 Adjusts posture to see an object Prefers more complex visual stimuli Can localize sounds made above the ear Will turn head to side, then look up or down	Begins to imitate sounds Babbling resembles one-syllable utterances such as *ma, mu, da, di, hi* Vocalizes to toys, mirror image Laughs aloud Takes pleasure in hearing own sound (self-reinforcement)	Recognizes parents; begins to fear strangers Holds arms out to be picked up Has definite likes and dislikes Begins to imitate (coughs, protrudes tongue) Excites on hearing footsteps Laughs when head is hidden in a towel Has frequent mood swings, from crying to laughing, with little or no provocation Briefly searches for a dropped object (object permanence beginning)

(*continued*)

Age (months)	Gross motor	Fine motor	Sensory	Communication	Socialization/ cognition
9	Crawls, may progress backward at first Sits steadily on floor for prolonged time (10 minutes) Recovers balance when leans forward but cannot do so when leaning sideways Pulls self to standing position and stands holding onto furniture	Uses thumb and index finger in crude pincer grasp Preference for use of dominant hand now evident Grasps third cube Compares two cubes by bringing them together	Localizes sounds by turning head diagonally and directly toward sound Depth perception is increasing	Responds to simple verbal commands Comprehends "no-no"	Is in stage IV, coordination of secondary schemata Parent (mother) is increasingly important for own sake Shows increasing interest in pleasing parent Begins to show fears of going to bed and being left alone Puts arms in front of face to avoid having it washed Searches for an object if sees it hidden
12	Walks with one hand held Cruises well May attempt to stand alone momentarily Can sit down from standing position without help	Has neat pincer grasp Releases cube in cup Attempts to build two-block tower but fails Tries to insert a pellet into a narrow-neck bottle but fails Can turn pages in a book, many at a time	Discriminates simple geometric forms (e.g., circle) Amblyopia may develop with lack of binocularity Can follow rapidly moving object Controls and adjusts response to sound; listens for sound to recur	Says two or more words besides *dada, mama* Comprehends meaning of several words (comprehension always precedes verbalization) Recognizes objects by name Imitates animal sounds Understands simple verbal commands (e.g., "Give it to me," "Show me your eyes")	Shows emotions such as jealousy, affection (may give hug or kiss on request), anger, fear Enjoys familiar surroundings and explores away from parent Is fearful in strange situation, clings to parent May develop habit of "security blanket" or favorite toy Has unceasing determination to practice locomotor skills

(*continued*)

(*continued*)

Age (months)	Gross motor	Fine motor	Sensory	Communication	Socialization/ cognition
12 (*continued*)					Searches for an object even if has not seen it hidden, but searches only where object was last seen

Adapted from Whaley and Wong (1991).

Appendix B.   Milestones in Growth and Development: Toddlerhood

Age (months)	Gross motor	Fine motor	Sensory	Communication	Socialization/ cognition
15	Walks without help (usually since age 13 months) Creeps up stairs Kneels without support Cannot walk around corners or stop suddenly without losing balance Assumes standing position without support Cannot throw ball without falling	Constantly casting objects to floor Builds tower of two cubes Holds two cubes in one hand Releases a pellet into a narrow-necked bottle Scribbles spontaneously Uses cup well but rotates spoon	Able to identify geometric forms; places round object into appropriate hole Binocular vision well developed Displays an intense and prolonged interest in pictures	Uses expressive jargon Says four to six words, including names "Asks" for objects by pointing Understands simple commands May use head-shaking gestures to denote "no" Uses "no" even while agreeing to the request	Tolerates some separation from parent Less likely to fear strangers Beginning to imitate parents, such as cleaning house (sweeping, dusting), folding clothes, mowing lawn Feeds self using cup with little spilling May discard bottle Manages spoon but rotates it near mouth Kisses and hugs parents, may kiss pictures in a book Expressive of emotions, has temper tantrums
18	Runs clumsily, falls often Walks up stairs with one hand held	Builds tower of three to four cubes Release, prehension,		Says 10 or more words Points to a common object, such	Great imitator ("domestic mimicry") Manages spoon well

(continued)

(continued)

Age (months)	Gross motor	Fine motor	Sensory	Communication	Socialization/ cognition
18 *(continued)*	Pulls and pushes toys Jumps in place with both feet Seats self on chair Throws ball overhand without falling	and reach well developed Turns pages in a book, two or three at a time In a drawing, makes stroke imitatively Manages spoon without rotation		as shoe or ball, and to two or three body parts	Takes off gloves, socks, and shoes and unzips Temper tantrums may be more evident Beginning awareness of ownership ("my toys") May develop dependency on transitional objects, such as "security blanket"
30	Jumps with both feet Jumps from chair or step Stands on one foot momentarily Takes a few steps on tiptoe	Builds tower of eight cubes Adds chimney to train of cubes Good hand-finger coordination; holds crayon with fingers rather than fist Moves fingers independently In drawing, imitates vertical and horizontal strokes, makes two or more strokes for cross		Gives first and last name Refers to self by appropriate pronoun Uses plurals, names one color	Separates more easily from mother In play, helps put things away, can carry breakable objects, pushes with good steering Begins to notice sex differences; knows own sex May attend to toilet needs without help except for wiping

Adapted from Whaley and Wong (1991).

Appendix C.   Growth and Development: Preschool

Age (years)	Gross motor	Fine motor	Communication	Socialization/ cognition
3	Rides tricycle Jumps off bottom step Stands on one foot for a few seconds Goes up stairs using alternate feet (may still come down using both feet on the step) Broad jumps May try to dance, but balance may not be adequate	Builds tower of 9 or 10 cubes Builds bridge with three cubes Adeptly places small pellets in narrow-necked bottle In drawing, copies a circle, imitates a cross, names what he or she has drawn, cannot draw stickman but may make circle with facial features	Has vocabulary of about 900 words Uses primarily "telegraphic" speech Uses complete sentences of three to four words Talks incessantly, regardless of whether anyone is paying attention Repeats sentence of six syllables Constantly asks questions	Is in preconceptual phase Is egocentric in thought and behavior Has beginning understanding of time; uses many time-oriented expressions, talks about past and future as much as about present, pretends to tell time Has improved concept of space as demonstrated in understanding of prepositions and ability to follow directional command Has beginning ability to view concepts from another perspective
4	Skips and hops on one foot Catches ball reliably Throws ball overhand Walks down stairs using alternate footing	Imitates a gate with cubes Uses scissors successfully to cut out picture following outline Can lace shoes, but may not be able to tie bow In drawing, copies a square, traces a cross and diamond, adds three parts to stick figure	Has vocabulary of 1,500 words or more Uses sentences of four to five words Questioning is at peak Tells exaggerated stories Knows simple songs May be mildly profane if associates with older children Obeys four prepositional phrases, such as "under," "on top of," or "in front of"	Is in phase of intuitive thought Causality is still related to proximity of events Understands time better, especially in terms of sequence of daily events Is unable to conserve matter Judges everything according to one dimension, such as height, width, or first Immediate perceptual clues dominate judgment Can choose longer of two lines or heavier of two objects

(continued)

(continued)

Age (years)	Gross motor	Fine motor	Communication	Socialization/ cognition
4 *(continued)*			Comprehends analogies, such as, "If ice is cold, fire is _____" Repeats four digits Uses words liberally but frequently does not comprehend meaning	Is beginning to develop less egocentrism and more social awareness May count correctly but has poor mathematic concept of numbers Still believes that thoughts cause events Obeys because parents have set limits, not because of understanding of reason behind right or wrong
5	Skips and hops on alternate feet Throws and catches ball well Jumps rope Skates with good balance Walks backward with heel to toe Jumps from height of 12 inches, lands on toes Balances on alternate feet with eyes closed	Ties shoelaces Uses scissors, simple tools, or pencil very well In drawing, copies a diamond and triangle; adds seven to nine parts to stickman; prints a few letters, numbers, or words, such as first name	Has vocabulary of about 2,100 words Uses sentences of six to eight words, with all parts of speech Names coins (nickel, dime, and so on) Names four or more colors Describes drawing or pictures with much comment and enumeration Asks meaning of words Asks inquisitive questions	Begins to question what parents think by comparing them to age-mates and other adults May notice prejudice and bias in outside world Is more able to view other's perspective, but tolerates differences rather than understands them Tends to be matter-of-fact about differences in others May begin to show understanding of conservation of numbers through counting objects regardless of arrangement

Adapted from Whaley and Wong (1991).

Appendix D.   Growth and Development: School Age

Age (years)	Motor	Cognition	Adaptive	Socialization
6	Gradual increase in dexterity Active age; constant activity Often returns to finger feeding More aware of hand as a tool Likes to draw, print, and color	Knows whether it is morning or afternoon Defines common objects such as fork and chair in terms of their use Obeys triple commands in succession Shows personal right hand and left ear Says which is pretty and which is ugly of a series of drawings of faces Describes the objects in a picture rather than simply enumerating them Reads from memory; enjoys oral spelling game Is in period of more tension, but is intellectually more stimulating	At table, uses knife to spread butter or jam on bread At play, cuts, folds, pastes paper toys, sews crudely if needle is threaded Cannot tie knot Enjoys making simple figures in clay Takes bath without supervision; performs bedtime activities alone Likes table games, checkers, simple card games Has own way of doing things Tries out own abilities	Can share and co-operate better Has great need for children of own age Often engages in rough play Does what child sees adults doing Often has temper tantrums Had difficulty owning up to misdeeds Giggles a lot Has increased socialization, such as tattling
7	Gross motor actions are cautious but not fearful More cautious in approaches to new performances Repeats performances to master them Posture more tense and unstable; maintains one position longer	Notices that certain parts are missing from pictures Can copy a diamond Repeats three numbers backward Reads ordinary clock or watch correctly to nearest quarter hour; uses clock for practical purposes More mechanical in reading; often does	Uses table knife for cutting meat; may need help with tough or difficult pieces Brushes and combs hair acceptably without help or "going over"	Is becoming a real member of the family group Likes to help and have a choice Is less resistant and stubborn Spends a lot of time alone; does not require a lot of companionship Boys take part in group play with boys; girls prefer playing with girls

(continued)

(continued)

Age (years)	Motor	Cognition	Adaptive	Socialization
7 *(continued)*		not stop at the end of a sentence, skips words such as *it, the, he,* and so on		
8–9	Movement fluid; often graceful and poised Always on the go; jumps, chases, skips Increased smoothness and speed in the motor control Dresses self completely Eyes and hands are well coordinated	Gives similarities and differences between two things from memory Repeats days of week and months in order; knows the date Describes common objects in detail, not merely their use Makes change out of a quarter Reads classic books but also enjoys comics	Makes use of common tools such as hammer, saw, or screwdriver Uses household and sewing utensils Helps with routine household tasks such as dusting, sweeping Assumes responsibility for share of household chores Looks after all of own needs at table Buys useful articles; exercises some choice in making purchases Goes about home and community freely, alone or with friends	Easy to get along with at home; better behaved Likes the reward system Dramatizes Is more sociable Is better behaved Is interested in boy–girl relationships but will not admit it Likes to compete and play games More critical of self
10–12	Posture is more similar to an adult's; will overcome lordosis Pubescent changes may begin to appear, especially in females Body lines soften and round out in females	Writes occasional short letters to friends or relatives on own initiative Uses telephone for practical purposes Responds to magazines, TV, or other advertising by mailing coupons Reads for practical information or own enjoyment stories or library books of adventure or romance, or animal stories	Does occasional or brief work on own initiative around home and neighborhood Is sometimes left alone at home for short period Is successful in looking after own needs or those of other children left in own care Makes useful articles or does easy repair work Writes brief stories Produces simple paintings or drawings Washes and dries own hair	Likes family; family really has meaning Likes mother and wants to please her in many ways Demonstrates affection Likes dad too; he is adored and idolized Respects parents Loves friends; talks about them constantly Chooses friends more selectively Loves conversation Has beginning interest in opposite sex Is more diplomatic

Adapted from Whaley and Wong (1991).

Appendix E. Growth and Development: Adolescence

Dimension	Early adolescence (11–14 years)	Middle adolescence (14–17 years)	Late adolescence (17–20 years)
Growth	Rapidly accelerating growth; reaches peak velocity Secondary sex characteristics appear	Growth decelerating Stature reaches 95% of adult height Secondary sex characteristics well advanced	Physically mature Structure and reproductive growth almost complete
Cognition	Limited ability for abstract thinking Clumsy groping for new values and energies Comparison of "normality" with peers of same sex	Developing capacity for abstract thinking Enjoys intellectual powers, often in idealistic, altruistic terms Concern with philosophic, political, and social problems	Established abstract thought Able to view problems comprehensively Intellectual and functional identity established
Identity	Preoccupied with rapid body changes Trying out various roles Measurement of attractiveness by acceptance or rejection of peers Conformity to group norms	Reestablishes body image as growth decelerates Very self-centered; increased narcissism Tendency toward inner experience and self-discovery Has a rich fantasy life Idealistic Able to perceive future implications of current behavior and decisions	Body image and gender role definition nearly secured Irreversible sexual identity Phase of consolidation of identity Comfortable with physical growth Social roles defined and articulated
Sexuality	Self-exploration and evaluation Limited dating Limited intimacy	Multiple plural relationships Decisive turn toward heterosexuality (if homosexual, knows by this time) Exploration of "sex appeal" Feeling of "being in love," tentative establishment of relationships	Forms stable relationships and attachment to another Growing capacity for mutuality and reciprocity Preeminence of individual as dating partner Intimacy involves commitment rather than exploration and romanticism

(continued)

55

(*continued*)

Dimension	Early adolescence (11–14 years)	Middle adolescence (14–17 years)	Late adolescence (17–20 years)
Emotionality	Most ambivalence Wide mood swings Intense daydreaming Anger outwardly expressed with moodiness, temper outbursts, and verbal insults and name calling	Tendency toward inner experiences; more introspective Tendency to withdraw when upset or feelings are hurt Vacillation of emotions in time and range Feelings of inadequacy common; difficulty in asking for help	More constancy of emotion Anger more apt to be concealed

Adapted from Whaley and Wong (1991).

Appendix F. AAMR Nursing Position Statement—1993

Nurses who provide services to persons with developmental disabilities play an important role as health and wellness coordinators, communicating and interpreting health related information to clients who have a disability, families who have a member with a disability, and to other professionals.

This is further delineated in the American Nurses' Association Social Policy Statement which states that specialization in nursing practice permits new applications of knowledge and refined nursing practices to flow from the specialist to the generalist in nursing practice, thus ensuring progress in the general practice of nursing.

The Nursing Division of the American Association on Mental Retardation (AAMR) endorses specific practice standards for the beginning practitioner as well as for the experienced clinical specialist in the field of developmental disabilities nursing. These standards provide specific criteria and outcome measures which can be used as effective tools in evaluating the quality of services provided by the professional nurse on the interdisciplinary team. Settings in which standards can be applied include large public agencies, small private residential facilities located in the community, and agencies providing services to families caring for a family member with an actual or potential developmental disability.

The position of the AAMR Nursing Division is that every person with a developmental disability, regardless of that individual's health status, is entitled to the services of a registered professional nurse. The nurse has the skills to assess, diagnose, plan, implement interventions, and reevaluate those plans and interventions as well as educate recipients of service and staff. An understanding of the interaction between physical, affective, and cognitive systems enables the nurse to enhance the contributions of all other professionals on the interdisciplinary team and improves the quality of life for persons with developmental disabilities and their families.

Nurses endorse the promotion of wellness and normalization in providing services to individuals with developmental disabilities. The nursing profession, committed to the concepts of prevention of health problems and promotion of wellness, focuses primarily on interventions which maximize the psychosocial, physical, affective, cognitive, and developmental strengths of persons with developmental disabilities and their families and minimize deficits in these areas.

From American Association on Mental Retardation. (1993). *Nursing division position paper*. Washington, DC: Author; reprinted by permission.

It is the responsibility of the professional nurse to conduct nursing assessments of individuals and families, identify health needs and potential problems, provide primary intervention for those problems, initiate and coordinate referrals to other professionals where appropriate, monitor the findings and interventions of those professionals, keep records of changes that may result from health problems, and function as an advocate for the client. Additionally, the Registered Nurse is expected to provide health-related education to persons with developmental disabilities, families, staff, community. In advanced practice roles, the nurse also conducts research with the goal of improving health practices, promoting safety and accident prevention, and assisting families in adapting to existing health problems. The professional nurse interprets health care interventions for other team members, and provides leadership in the holistic integration of health interventions into the total habilitation program.

3

The Nurse's Role in Habilitation

Fay F. Russell and Teresa A. Free

OBJECTIVES

Upon completion of this chapter, the reader will be able to:

- Identify and apply the major principles of habilitation for people with developmental disabilities.
- Recognize the evolving habilitation needs of individuals with developmental disabilities across the life span.
- Identify approaches to habilitation appropriate to different age groups and analyze advantages and disadvantages of various approaches.
- Identify conditions that place families at risk for having children with developmental disabilities and delineate problems encountered in case finding.

OVERVIEW

This chapter reviews major principles and concepts related to habilitation of individuals with developmental disabilities across the life span. Team models for providing health, developmental, and educational services to individuals with disabilities and their families are described and nursing approaches to habilitation and models for implementing

family-centered care programs of habilitation are presented. The role of the nurse in prevention and early identification of children having, or being at risk for, developmental disabilities is profiled.

DEFINING HABILITATION

Habilitation describes the process by which individuals develop new skills and abilities. (In contrast, **rehabilitation** is the process by which an individual relearns a lost skill or behavior.) The habilitation of persons with developmental disabilities is complex because they often have many unique needs. Not only do they require special assistance in learning, but often they have physical or health conditions that require the collaboration of skilled professionals in providing ongoing assessments, planning, interventions, and evaluations for many areas of functioning.

Individuals with developmental disabilities often need help to acquire skills of daily living, social and communication skills, a healthy lifestyle, and a personal means of self-actualization. Habilitation needs include attention to self-care, receptive and expressive language, learning, mobility, self-actualization, activities of daily living, and economic sufficiency, with the goals of achieving as much independence, productivity, and community participation as possible across the life span. Habilitation that is planned with the family in consultation with professionals will enable the individual with a disability or at risk for disability to best reach his or her potential.

Concepts Related to Habilitation

Community-based service delivery offers services to individuals with developmental disabilities or special health care needs in community settings that also are frequented by persons without disabilities. This includes relying on primary care agencies to serve as "medical homes" for persons with or without disabilities, with a relative reduction in centralization of tertiary or specialized services (Crocker, Yankauer, & Conference Steering Committee, 1987).

Medical homes provide primary health care and care coordination to each client. *Care coordination,* described below, involves collaboration of a health professional with the individual and the family in setting goals, planning assessments, and choosing appropriate interventions and resources.

Family-centered care provides care to the individual in need of special services within the context of his or her family, individualized by consideration of health care and developmental needs of all family members, family structure, and cultural, social, economic, and religious factors. Health care professionals always must remember that the family is the constant in the life of the individual, that the family's role is to be supported, and that professionals must collaborate with the family in making decisions and giving care.

Care coordination, or *case management,* plans for the provision of interventions for individuals with special needs by identifying and helping families gain access to the programs or services that will provide the interventions. Care coordination involves advocating for families and interfacing with larger community systems for planning, facilitating, monitoring, and follow-up. The coordination of assessments, plans, and implementation of support services by professionals and agencies avoids duplication or conflicts between the services provided. The care coordinator for each client serves as the single point of contact for the individual and his or her family in acquiring the services and help needed.

Major Principles of Habilitation for Persons with Developmental Disabilities

1. Habilitation of persons with developmental disabilities will require ongoing assessment and intervention in many areas, including physical, behavioral, cognitive, sensory, socioemotional, and neuromuscular functioning.

2. Each person with developmental disabilities should have a "medical home" for primary health care, as well as access to specialty care for a continuum of services.

3. Coordination of comprehensive health services with an emphasis on prevention should be available across the life span to persons with developmental disabilities.

4. An array of habilitative services for persons with developmental disabilities should be available to serve age-related needs and special needs across the life span.

5. Habilitative goals should include increased independence, productivity, and community participation across the life span.

PLANNING FOR HABILITATION

Because the needs of individuals with developmental disabilities are often complex and involve many areas, teams of professionals are needed to best assess and assist the individual and the individual's family in comprehensive habilitation. A team is a group of people, representing many disciplines, each of whom possesses particular clinical expertise. Each must make individual decisions and contribute information needed for group decisions. Team members are responsible for communicating their knowledge of the person's needs from the perspective of their discipline and for collaborating in setting goals, identifying and implementing appropriate interventions, and evaluating the person's progress. The team has a common purpose: to offer the best plan for promoting the development of each individual at risk for or having developmental disabilities.

Teams include primarily health, social service, behavioral, and educational professionals and may be health oriented or education oriented. Table 1 lists the pro-

fessionals who are likely to be members of such teams. Because the developmental delay of any individual impacts every member of the family, it is important for teams to be family focused. The individual and his or her family will require an array of services that change over time according to the individual's age, specific risk or disability, health status, and family environment (Challela, 1986). Therefore, the individual and his or her parents should be included on the team; a court-appointed guardian may be called upon to represent the interests of the individual who does not have a family. Joining forces to solve problems with the individual and his or her family in developing a common plan of care increases that plan's effectiveness.

Table 1. Composition of health-oriented teams and education-oriented teams

Health-oriented teams may be composed of:
Audiologists
Dentists
Nurses (especially maternal–child or pediatric nurses)
Nutritionists
Occupational therapists
Ophthalmologists
Physical therapists
Physician specialists in developmental disabilities
Podiatrists
Primary physicians and/or developmental pediatricians
Psychologists
Social workers
Special education teachers
Speech-language pathologists

Education-oriented teams may be composed of:
Leisure/recreation therapists
Music therapists
Occupational therapists
Physical therapists
Prevocational/vocational specialists
Reading specialists
Resource teachers
School nurses
School psychologists
Social workers
Special education teachers
Speech therapists
Vision specialists

The nurse is an essential member of the team for the family with an individual who has developmental disabilities. The nurse lends the team expertise in health assessment and supervision, parent–child and family interactions, promoting growth and development, supporting family functioning and competencies, and anticipatory guidance (Challela, 1986). The nurse participates on the health-oriented team along with physician specialists, nutritionists, physical and occupational therapists, social workers, and communication specialists. The roles of the nurse include providing nursing assessments and interventions related to health promotion and illness prevention, and acting to facilitate the learning of new skills by an individual with disabilities so that he or she may attain the highest possible quality of life.

Models of Team Organization

There are three predominant team models: multidisciplinary, interdisciplinary, and transdisciplinary. The *multidisciplinary team* consists of professionals from the disciplines required to meet the needs of the individual with a special disability or at special risk and the needs of his or her family. The professionals independently evaluate the person and make recommendations to the team leader, who communicates the findings and plan of care to the family and the individual, who are not part of the team. The multidisciplinary team model is based on the traditional medical model (Urey & Bloom, 1988). One member, usually the physician, is the team leader and takes primary decision-making responsibility. This model introduces multiple perspectives and approaches to assessment and intervention, but reinforces that professionals should maintain the boundaries of their discipline. Thus, one team member's perspective dominates, and any conflict felt by others usually is not expressed. The multi-

disciplinary team model permits limited integration of assessments and interventions, with likely redundancy of client evaluations and recommendations.

The *interdisciplinary team* consists of professionals from a variety of disciplines who independently or together evaluate the individual at risk for or having a developmental disability from the perspective of their own disciplines. Each shares his or her findings with the other team members, and all team members collectively formulate the plan of care. The plan will include recommendations reflecting the domains of the disciplines involved, which are communicated by the case manager (care coordinator) to the individual and his or her family, who may have limited participation on the team. In this model, each discipline is valued for the contribution it uniquely brings to assessment and treatment; each professional is considered an equal partner in the team. The model permits the leadership of the team to develop in response to the priority of needs for individuals being served and allows case management assignments to be rotated among team members. However, it reinforces the idea that the professionals of each discipline should offer services only in the practice domains defined by their discipline, with little boundary crossing; thus, conflicts may arise between the perspectives of the various disciplines. The interdisciplinary team model assumes equal participation of disciplines, lending them autonomy but requiring much attention to communication of findings and recommendations to the case manager, as well as among team members (Urey & Bloom, 1988).

Both the multidisciplinary and interdisciplinary team models have been used successfully over the years to provide comprehensive services to individuals with developmental disabilities and their families. However, neither model includes them on the team as full participants in assessment and intervention planning. The recognition of the valuable contribution that can be made by the individual and his or her family has led to the development of the *transdisciplinary team* model. This model assumes there is a body of knowledge, including assessments and interventions, common to many disciplines that is needed for the care of individuals with special risks or disabilities. It includes parents, guardians, and other service agencies on the team with roles equal to team professionals in identifying and prioritizing the needs of the individual and in implementing plans of care. The emphasis is on collaboration between parents (or families) and professionals to deliver family-centered care. The transdisciplinary team model is based on a developmental model, blending the medical model and an educational model. Team members are encouraged to teach other members the knowledge and skills of their discipline required by persons with developmental disabilities and to learn from all members of the team. Thus, the model places the commitment of the team on teaching, learning, and working collaboratively with other team members to meet the needs of these individuals. In addition, professionals and agencies within and outside the team are consulted regarding specialized expertise unique to their disciplines, which exists at a level above the knowledge and skills common across disciplines. This requires achievement and maintenance of advanced knowledge and refined skills in his or her discipline on the part of each professional. The transdisciplinary team model fosters integration of assessments, plans, interventions, and recommendations, thus preventing redundancy. However, it may be less cost-effective if there is no pre-screening or triaging of individuals at risk for a developmental delay (Hutchison, 1978; Urey & Bloom, 1988).

A *transagency team* is a team composed of representatives of many disciplines who also represent more than one agency. This team uses an interdisciplinary or transdisciplinary team process as described above (Garland, Woodruff, & Buck, 1988).

Interdisciplinary Training

Because there is a need for communication among and service provision by professionals from many disciplines in the habilitation of individuals at risk for or having developmental disabilities, interdisciplinary training programs are offered to undergraduate and graduate professional students by University Affiliated Programs (UAPs) at universities that offer degrees in the helping professions. The students engage in didactic and clinical experiences that enhance their ability to provide best-practice, individualized family-centered, community-integrated, and coordinated support and services to individuals with developmental disabilities and their families. Although some learning experiences are tailored for the clinical preparation specific to each profession, other content is offered across professions and usually includes information on the nature of health care delivery systems; family-centered and community-based service delivery; infant and child development and assessment; case management (care coordination); regulatory requirements, including eligibility and case finding; development of individualized family service plans; care delivery and interagency coordination; how to help families with transitions to services; and research to improve care for individuals with disabilities.

Developing an Individualized Family Service Plan

Because of the language of PL 99-457 (the Education of the Handicapped Act Amendments of 1986), Part H, habilitation plans are referred to as individualized family service plans (IFSPs). Nurses recognize IFSPs as being much like nursing care plans; educators see them as similar to individualized education programs (IEPs) for children over age 3. IFSPs include information on the child's present developmental status, including physical, cognitive, receptive and expressive language, psychosocial, and self-help levels of function that are established by objective assessments. Also, the IFSP includes identification of the individual's and the family's strengths and needs, goals, priorities and time frames, and best available resources for meeting the goals. The total environment of the individual at risk for, or having, a developmental disability is considered in the habilitation plan, including family, cultural (as discussed by Morse, chap. 2, this volume), and economic factors. Development of the IFSP is an ongoing interactive process between the family and the care coordinator (case manager) in which a written document of individual and family assessments, established goals, and specific strategies for goal achievement is produced and modified when needed. Projected dates for initiation of services, goal achievement, and transition to future services are recorded.

The IFSP process is more important than the written plan because the collaboration between parents and professionals in identifying goals, expectations of the child, and realistic interventions is the embodiment of family-centered care. The involvement of the family in setting goals, making plans for goal achievement, implementing strategies, and evaluating the child's progress is a unique departure from nursing care plans or IEPs of the past, when professionals planned for the child and bestowed the plan on the family without considering their needs, opinions, or decision-making ability. The purpose of IFSPs is to enable families to make informed choices about

what they want for their child and what services they will use to reach their goals and meet their needs. It is the family who sets priorities and determines the course of the child's care. Families should be encouraged to participate in developing and evaluating the habilitation plan.

APPROACHES TO HABILITATION ACROSS THE LIFE SPAN

Table 2 provides health, developmental, and emotional health considerations for planning habilitation across the life span. Throughout the life span of an individual with developmental disabilities, nursing care should be family centered.

Infants and Toddlers

Early intervention services are coordinated, comprehensive programs that promote development for infants and preschool children with disabilities or for those at risk for developmental delays. The benefits of early intervention for preventing and reducing developmental disabilities have been recognized through national priorities and legislation. In 1986, PL 99-457, Part H, created legislation to help state and local governments establish statewide, comprehensive, coordinated systems of early intervention services for young children and their families. This legislation authorizes services for infants and toddlers through age 2 who are experiencing developmental delays or who have a physical or mental condition that places them at risk for developmental delays (U.S. Department of Education, 1989). In 1991, PL 99-457 was reauthorized in the Individuals with Disabilities Education Act (IDEA) (PL 102-119, Part H). Changes in terminology and additions to the act are noted in Table 3.

What made this law unique are the targeted age group and its mandate for the involvement of families in the plan-

Table 2. Planning for habilitation across the life span

Age group	Goals for physical health	Goals for development	Goals for mental health
Infants and toddlers (birth to 3 years)	Prevention or early management of common childhood illnesses Immunizations Health promotion Adequate nutrition for growth needs Treatment to limit impact of disability	Progress in motor, affective, communication, adaptive, and cognitive development with the least possible deviation from normal and with the parent as the primary intervener	Development of basic trust Development of autonomy and independence Nuturing parent–child interactions Family needs met
Preschoolers (3–5 years)	Health promotion Safety issues Illness prevention Dental care	Transition to preschool setting Success in social, self-help, and play skills	Good self-esteem Discipline that teaches the natural positive and negative consequences of behavior
School-age children (6–12 years)	Health promotion Safety issues Prevention of infectious disease Vision and hearing adequate or adequately corrected for learning	Adaptation to school setting Progress in learning academic skills Appropriate behavior for classroom setting Ability to attend to the learning environment	Enjoyment of school and friends Early intervention for aggressive, self-injurious, or destructive behavior
Adolescents (13–21 years)	Health promotion, prevention of unhealthy habits such as smoking Accident prevention Sexual development, STD prevention, appropriate contraception	Goals made for future Progress in prevocational skills Respects self and others Deals with issues of sexuality	Good self-concept Prevention of delinquent behavior Friendships
Adults (21–55 years)	Promotion of a healthy lifestyle, especially diet and exercise Accident prevention	Living as independently as possible Adequate job training Successful employment	Productivity Friendships Healthy leisure and social activities Integration into the larger community
Older adults (over 55 years)	Early detection and management of chronic illness Maintaining a healthy lifestyle	Adapting to body changes Retirement when ready Maintaining stimulating activities	Early detection of depression, anxiety, and loneliness Healthy leisure and social activities

ning, implementation, and evaluation of services. The law also acknowledges the complexity of the needs of a young child with disabilities through recognition that no single discipline or agency will likely have the knowledge, resources, or skills required to best serve the child and family. The mandate for case management (care coordination) is an attempt to reduce duplication, fragmenta-tion, and inaccessibility of services across disciplines and agencies.

PL 102-119, Part H, defines early intervention services as developmental services provided, under public supervision, at no cost to families. These services are designed to meet the child's needs in one or more of the following areas of development: physical, cognitive, communication, social–emotional,

Table 3.   Changes in legislation authorizing early intervention services for infants and toddlers

Education of the Handicapped Act Amendments of 1986 (PL 99-457, Part H)	Individuals with Disabilities Education Act of 1991 (PL 102-119, Part H)

Previous language
  Case management
  Language and speech development
  Psychosocial development
  Self-help skills
  Family strengths and needs
	New language
	  Service coordination
	  Communication development
	  Social–emotional development
	  Adaptive development
	  Family resouces, priorities, and concerns

Previous authorized services
  Family training and counseling
  Home visits
  Special instruction
  Speech pathology and audiology
  Occupational therapy
  Physical therapy
  Psychological services
  Case management services
  Medical services only for diagnosis or evaluation
  Early identification, screening, and assessment
  Health services needed to benefit from other
    early intervention services
	Additional authorized services
	  Vision
	  Assistive devices and technology
	  Transportation

Previous personnel qualified to provide early intervention services
  Nurses
  Audiologists
  Nutritionists
  Occupational therapists
  Physical therapists
  Psychologists
  Social workers
  Special educators
  Speech-language pathologists
	Additional qualified personnel
	  Family therapists
	  Orientation and mobility specialists
	  Pediatricians and other physicians

and adaptive development. Qualified personnel, including nurses, provide services that may include health care, family training, counseling, and home visits, and must include case management. Service providers and the family together develop and review an IFSP to best meet the needs of the child.

Individual early intervention programs usually are targeted to specific groups:

1. Infants and children with genetic or biological conditions known to cause developmental deviations or disabilities (e.g., Down syndrome, sensory impairments such as blindness or deafness)
2. Infants and children at biological risk (e.g., premature or very low birth weight infants)
3. Infants and children at environmen-

tal risk (e.g., born to adolescent mothers or to families living below the poverty level)
4. Infants and children at compounded biological and environmental risk (e.g., mother chemically dependent during pregnancy and postnatally, or technology-dependent children of parents at low socioeconomic and/or low education levels)

Early intervention programs are coordinated by multidisciplinary, interdisciplinary, or transdisciplinary teams who provide services that may include assessments, planning, interventions for health needs, growth, nutrition and feeding, sensorimotor performance, speech-language and auditory ability, psychosocial needs, parent–child interactions, cognitive ability, and family needs. Nurses, as members of the team, often coordinate and provide direct services for the child and family. The integrated perspective the nurse brings to the team blends health promotion, habilitation, and family-centered care. The nurse also assesses the child's health status and its potential impact on growth and developmental outcomes. Using the health promotion perspective, the nurse recommends and educates the family and other team members about interventions that will maintain and improve the child's health and development (Savage & Culbert, 1989).

Nurse generalists, prepared at the diploma, associate, and baccalaureate levels, and nurse specialists, prepared at master's and doctoral levels, participate at a variety of levels in early intervention programs (Brandt & Magyary, 1989). Standards of nursing practice for early intervention services have been developed by a task force of maternal–child nurses through the University of Kentucky grant, Leadership Development for Nurses in Early Intervention (Consensus Conference Committee, 1993). Standards of care and standards of professional performance, along with rationale and process criteria, are delineated and address levels of participation (see Table 4).

Approaches to Early Intervention

Child-Centered Early Intervention In this approach, professionals consider only the child in their assessments, plans, interventions, and evaluations. This approach is limited in its value to the child, because the family is the key to health, growth, and the developmental potential of the child. The love, trust, affection, and attachment of the child to the family are the springboard to all interventions that encourage physical, emotional, social, and developmental growth.

Family-Centered Early Intervention In this approach, all assessments, plans, interventions, and evaluations of the child are considered in the context of the family.

The family collaborates with professionals in identifying the child's strengths and needs; in setting priorities, goals and expectations; and in implementing interventions.

Models of Early Intervention

Center-Based Early Intervention In this model, all assessments, plans, and interventions are carried out in a developmental center. The family brings the child to participate in services provided by the team. The format of the intervention may be presented as a "program," wherein specific assessments or instruction, training, or counseling are planned and implemented in a series of sessions. The advantages of this approach include efficiency of the child and family being seen by many team members. Individual team members may be able to evaluate and work with more than one child in the course of a session. Families enrolled in a program often become a source of support for each other, and ongoing relationships are established between families as well as between the family and professional team members. Center-based sessions permit multiple assessments of the child, which always give a broader, more reliable picture of the child's abilities. The disadvantages may be that long distance, lack of transportation, or care of other children make it difficult for the family to participate.

Home-Based Early Intervention In this model, one or two professionals see the child and family, usually on a weekly basis, for assessments and interventions that are carried out in the child's own home environment. Planning may include other members of the professional team and likely would take place at a developmental center or clinic setting, not in the home. Advantages include the individualization of the time spent with the child and family. The planning for a child's care is more realistic when made with the child's daily environment in perspective. Eliminating the need for

Table 4.   National standards of nursing practice for early intervention services (1993 revision)

Standard of Care

Standard 1.   Assessment

The nurse systematically collects, records and analyzes comprehensive and accurate data.

Standard 2.   Diagnosis

The nurse analyzes assessment data, utilizes scientific principles and professional judgment, and collaborates with the family in determining appropriate nursing diagnoses.

Standard 3.   Outcome Identification

The nurse, in collaboration with the family, identifies expected outcomes which support the health and development of infants/children and the values and priorities of their families.

Standard 4.   Planning

The nurse in collaboration with the family and the interdisciplinary team participates in the development of the individualized family service plan (IFSP).

Standard 5.   Implementation

The nurse, in partnership with the family, implements actions identified on the individualized family service plan (IFSP) that promote, maintain, or restore health and development.

Standard 6.   Evaluation

The nurse, in collaboration with the family and interdisciplinary team, evaluates the progress of infants/children and their families toward attainment of outcomes.

Standards of Professional Performance

Standard 1.   Quality of Care

The nurse is accountable for promoting quality of care in early intervention services/systems.

Standard 2.   Performance Appraisal

The nurse who provides early intervention services participates in self evaluation.

Standard 3.   Education

The nurse maintains appropriate knowledge and skills in order to effectively implement the standards of practice and specialty guidelines for early intervention services.

Standard 4.   Collegiality

The nurse in early intervention services contributes to the professional development of peers, colleagues, and others.

Standard 5.   Ethics

The nurse's decisions and actions on behalf of infants/children and their families are determined in an ethical manner.

Standard 6.   Collaboration

The nurse collaborates with the family and other members of the interdisciplinary interagency team in providing care to infants/children and their families.

Standard 7.   Research

The nurse applies appropriate, scientifically-sound empirical research and theory as a basis for nursing practice decisions.

Standard 8.   Resource Utilization

The nurse, in collaboration with the family and the interdisciplinary team, pursues strategies to enhance access to and utilization of adequate health care and educational services.

Adapted from the Consensus Conference Committee. (1993). *National Standards of Nursing Practice for Early Intervention Services.* Maternal and Child Health HRSA Project MCJ-215052. Contact: Dr. Gwen Lee, Project Director, College of Nursing, University of Kentucky, Lexington, KY 40536-0232; reprinted with permission.

transportation or care of other children is a tremendous help for some families, especially those with limited incomes. A disadvantage is that some team members may not actually see the child, al-though they are called on to help through planning and evaluating assessments done by others.

Combination of Center and Home Intervention Services   In this model, assessments, planning, and some components of care, such as speech therapy or audiology assessment, are conducted in a developmental center, but many interventions are carried out in the home by the primary caregiver in the family and one or two professionals who visit on a regular basis. Advantages are that all team members have opportunities to assess the child and family. Transportation and child care demands are limited. Disadvantages are that the family probably will not establish ongoing relationships with all the team members or with other families because of the limited time they are in the center.

Preschool Children

The 3- to 5-year-old child who has developmental disabilities or is at risk will benefit from preschool programs that encourage socialization, play, self-help, self-determination, and school readiness skills. Learning to follow directions, to share, to make friends, to enjoy books and songs and table activities, to take turns and be considerate of others, and to attend to the teacher are important for success in later school and life experiences. Nurses will need to help families and children make the transition to programs in which parents are not as fully involved as they have been in early intervention, such as day care, Head Start, or other preschool programs.

Nurses in early intervention programs must recognize that the child's transition to a new program may be particularly stressful for families. Common concerns are: 1) having to transfer feelings of trust, support, and friendship from one set of professionals to another; 2) shifting to a new service delivery system in which care may be more child focused and less family focused and families are not included as fully in planning and intervention activities; 3) changing to a new system of service coordination in which there may no longer be one des-

ignated case manager; and 4) changing to a new model of care delivery in which the child may leave a home-based program to enter a center-based program and the new team may be more education oriented than health oriented or more interdisciplinary than transdisciplinary in nature (Hains, Rosenkoetter, & Fowler, 1991).

Children and parents must be prepared for the changes they will experience (Rosenkoetter, 1992). Parents' contacts and participation with the new program teachers and professionals will be important determining factors for the child to receive optimal benefit from the program. Parents' satisfaction with the program will be reflected in the child's adaptation.

Approaches to Nursing Care

Primary Care Interventions This approach emphasizes the prevention of acute illnesses to which children may be vulnerable. The nurse educates parents on the transmission of communicable diseases and how to prevent illnesses through immunizations, good hand washing and skin care, and avoiding infectious contacts.

Secondary Care Interventions This involves the early recognition, management, and/or referral of physical, developmental, or emotional conditions that may result in disability.

Tertiary Care Interventions This approach focuses on managing and monitoring the progress of known disabilities. Examples of nursing care at this level would be serial assessments and evaluations of developmental progress for children with developmental problems, monitoring and administering medications, or managing tracheostomy care (Savage & Culbert, 1989).

Models of Care

Primary Care Clinics In this model, nurses and nurse–practitioners provide direct care and teaching to children and their families. Children with disabilities can be cared for in the same clinics that serve children without disabilities, especially for the delivery of "well child care" and management of common childhood illnesses. Consultation and periodic referral for specialty care is appropriate when the medical management needed is beyond the scope of primary care.

Developmental Centers In this model, nurses, as part of evaluation and health care teams, assess children and their families, participate with families and the health care team in identifying the child's strengths and needs, and plan for health care and educational interventions that will foster positive health and developmental outcomes. Some developmental centers may provide preschool programs that handle a large number of children with disabilities, particularly those with complex or multiple disabilities. The nurse may serve as a consultant to the teachers and staffs of these programs for the management of acute and chronic health problems that arise.

Special Care Needs A special care need that may be identified in the preschool period is *management of a behavior disorder*. Many young children with developmental disabilities also have behavior disorders that disrupt their cognitive, social, and emotional development and may even threaten their physical health and safety (Drotar & Sturm, 1991; Toleman, Brown, & Roth, chap. 11, this volume). A wide variety of behavior problems can occur, including feeding problems such as rumination or pica, stereotypic motor movements such as head banging or finger biting, hyperactivity, aggression, and impairment of social and communication development (Drotar & Sturm, 1991). Parents are often the first to be concerned about a child's unusual behaviors because the behaviors cause difficulty in daily family activities. Drotar and Sturm (1991) suggested that mental health intervention by professional specialists usually is

warranted when the behavior is interfering with developmental progress or when parents are especially stressed and concerned that the behavior is psychologically or interpersonally abnormal.

School-Age Children

School-age children with developmental disabilities receive educational programming within school systems, as first legislated by PL 94-142 (the Education for All Handicapped Children Act) in 1975. Teams including educators assess school-age children for learning needs and for health, sensory, motor, or psychosocial problems that will interfere with learning. Nurses may be part of evaluation teams that are school based or developmental center based. Nurses also will see school-age children in primary care settings and in hospitals. In all settings, nurses must assess school-age children with developmental risks or disabilities to determine if learning needs are being met. Special attention is given to vision screening, hearing screening, auditory and visual processing, speech and language ability, social and self-help skills, and peer relations because deviations interfere with learning. Health care issues and safety concerns also are addressed.

Every child's educational program should provide the opportunities that maximize his or her potentials and abilities. Educational goals for children with special needs include participation in general classrooms as much as possible. They also should have opportunities to utilize all school resources on a regular basis, including computer, library, music, and physical education programs, along with opportunities for interaction throughout the day with peers without disabilities. Inclusive education—the concept of including children with special needs in the same learning environment as all other children to the greatest extent possible—aims at meeting these goals. At the same time, a specially equipped lunchroom or bathroom or communication assistance should be provided as needed. Assistive technology advances in adaptive and communication equipment are helping children with special needs to learn in the regular classroom (see Morse & Colatarci, chap. 14, this volume). Students with special needs, such as behavioral disorders or autism, may require the services of specially trained mental health professionals, based either inside or outside the school system.

Approaches to Nursing Care

Primary Care   Physicals and health maintenance visits are recommended for the purposes of screening, diagnosis, management and/or referral, prevention, and health teaching. Nurses and nurse–practitioners are in an excellent position to provide the comprehensive care and teaching needed by children who have disabilities and their families.

Assisted Care   The nurse acts as a resource and advocate for children who require special care or devices such as wheelchairs, nasogastric or gastrostomy tube feedings, tracheostomies, or physical assistance with activities of daily living while at school. Delivery of health supportive services is a challenge for teachers who have limited knowledge or training regarding the health care needs of the individual.

Models of Care   Models of care would include primary care clinics that provide prevention and health promotion care and clinics that provide health care in the school setting. School nurses or public health nurses who serve schools may provide direct care or, more likely, teaching that helps teachers and school staff understand and confidently manage children with complex health conditions.

Nursing Assessment   Whether the nurse is clinic based or school based, components of the nursing assessment that are emphasized for the school-age child who has a developmental disability are health, social, and education needs. The health care of the school-age child may be especially fragmented if the child sees several specialists, as well as a primary care provider, and is dependent on an array of educational professionals and paraprofessionals for meeting his or her needs. The nurse is especially important in helping families obtain and coordinate the health services needed.

Assessment of social relationships and friendship circles is very important. Nurses may need to help and encourage parents to find neighborhood and school activities where children have good opportunities to make friends. Children with disabilities can be included in all the activities in which their peers without disabilities engage. Children who have disabilities also have the special talents needed in any group activity—a winning smile, a quick joke, an encouraging word, a helping hand. Special attention in finding the least restrictive school and social environment will aid any child in becoming more fulfilled and stimulated.

Adolescents

As children who have a developmental disability reach adolescence, health and education considerations usually become more focused on preparing for the future. Caregivers will need to work with families to ensure that the adolescent becomes as independent and productive as possible. In the past, parents and community agencies sometimes mistakenly assumed that the schools were preparing adolescents with developmental disabilities for a vocation and community living, only to discover, after the students' graduation, that the school assumed the parent would make all decisions about the child's future and that a community agency would be "out there" to provide a job and help with life skills. With the vision of an adolescent with developmental disabilities becoming an active participant in his or her community, parents and schools together must plan and provide functional, as well as academic, educational programming.

Functional Programming Functional programs for students in middle school and high school teach the skills needed to live in the real world, and are geared to giving those individuals with unique and challenging educational needs a meaningful and appropriate educational preparation. Functional programs (sometimes referred to as community-based education or instruction) provide learning opportunities in both the classroom and the community. The skills students learn will help them function successfully in daily life. Usually functional programs address four life areas (Kleinert, Guitinan, & Farmer, 1991):

Community: This area uses community resources to support independent daily life. Students learn such processes as shopping, street crossing, driving a car or use of public transportation, banking, getting to the doctor or dentist for scheduled appointments, and exchange of money in restaurants or other businesses.

Domestic: This area focuses on daily life skills that take place in one's house. Students may learn personal grooming, meal preparation, housekeeping, clothing care and laundering, and use of the telephone.

Recreation/Leisure: In this area, the individual participates in activities that are fun as well as provide for learning and a healthy lifestyle. Students can be helped to develop an interest in crafts, sports, visiting the library, or joining a club or recreational group, and can be encouraged to visit friends, to attend dances or sporting events or theater or art exhibits, to eat out, or to develop a hobby.

Vocational: The emphasis in this area is in learning the skills necessary for having a job. Students must learn to get to work on time, to ask for help when needed, and to organize their work day, as well as learn how to perform satisfactorily on the job.

Functional programs are more effective when the student goes to the actual environment for learning and becomes progressively independent in the learning activity (i.e., goes to a grocery store for shopping, exchanges money in a business, rides public transportation to and from school, holds a job on a regular or part-time basis). Functional programs also are more effective when they are planned and implemented by the adolescent, his or her parents, the health team, and the school team together, and when they are begun early (Shutz, 1988; Smull & Bellamy, 1991). The planning for transition to living in the community as an adult should begin at least by age 14, paralleling the academic planning that occurs when a teen enters high school.

Approaches to Nursing Care Approaches for nursing care of the adolescent include the primary care and assisted care approaches described for school-age children.

Models of Care Models of care include general primary care clinics or special clinics provided for adolescents with developmental disabilities. Pediatric, adolescent, or family nurse–practitioners may direct and provide care in the special clinics, which usually are run part-time and operate on certain hours or days of the week within a larger primary care facility. These nurses often develop and coordinate the clinic's interdisciplinary services and provide direct nursing services, including anticipatory guidance to adolescents and parents regarding health, developmental, and sexual concerns.

Special Care Needs The teen with disabilities may desire having boyfriend–girlfriend relationships. Nurses help families adjust to managing menstruation, contraceptive, and intimacy needs of the adolescent. Special planning, teaching, and reassurance often are required for assisting the female teen during a gynecological exam.

Helping parents cope with having a teenager in the home includes discussing the management of acting-out behavior, nutritional needs of the growing adolescent, and good skin care, as well as assessing the educational and vocational needs that are individualized to the abilities and interests of the adolescent (see Steadham, chap. 7, this volume).

Adults

Adults with developmental disabilities reside in a variety of settings. They live alone, with their families or relatives, in group homes or boarding homes, or in larger institutional settings. Group home living is in a residence in which one or more persons with mental retardation live with staff who provide care, supervision, and training (Hauber, Bruininks, Hill, Lakin, & White, 1984). In institutional living, a large number of persons with mental retardation live in a facility where they are cared for by staff employed by the institution. Placement of an adult with multiple, complex health needs in an appropriate, safe environment may require many nursing procedures and interventions, such as skin care treatments and dressings, injections, intravenous fluid or medications, ostomy care, oxygen, and other specialized respiratory care (Uehara, Silverstein, Davis, & Geron, 1991). The trend is movement away from institutional living toward group homes and other community living options where medical needs can be met. Interventions that promote independence and maximize skills and abilities are included in

planning habilitation of the adult with developmental disabilities.

Adults with disabilities have the same basic needs as any adult but require additional supports to live successfuly and happily in the community. *Supported living* refers to flexible, coordinated, individualized services that enable persons to live in a home of their choice, to be included in community activities, and to have their rights respected and autonomy promoted. The supports should be individualized to the needs, desires, and hopes of each person and will vary in what is required for each of the following areas:

- Continuing education, for ongoing learning of skills, interests, or vocational training
- Financial and legal planning for management of income, personal finances, and guardianship
- Recreation and leisure, for learning and to experience the fun of being with friends
- Residential, for access and management of the home and individual choices
- Self-determination, for expression of choices, preferences, control of one's life, independence, and dignity
- Sexual expression and affection, for expression of responsible and appropriate sex roles and behaviors
- Transportation, for mobility within the community
- Vocational, for holding a job and earning a fair wage to foster independence, self-esteem, and empowerment

Approaches to Health Maintenance Approaches to health maintenance during the long adult phase of life are preventive and health promoting in nature. The primary goal for health is that the adult follows a healthy lifestyle. This will include adaptive living skills of which daily skin care, dental hygiene, exercise and dietary habits that maintain appropriate weight, and avoidance of use of tobacco and other addictive substances are components. Adults require early diagnosis and treatment of illness and sexuality counseling. Health care providers must assess the emotional and mental health of clients, because a dual diagnosis of mental retardation and mental illness may be overlooked. Utilization of community services appropriate to the needs identified and active follow-up are necessary to help each adult with developmental disabilities reach his or her individual potential.

Models of programs for adults include health services, employment services, and activity-related programs. Health programs provide prevention and health promotion services. Necessary care and services are discussed and planned with the adult individual and, depending on the person's level of functioning and decision-making ability, with the person's advocate. Supported employment focuses on wages, support, and integration of persons with severe disabilities (Rusch, Hughes, Johnson, & Minch, 1991), and, as part of habilitation, meets self-actualization, self-sufficiency, and social interaction needs. Activity-related programs assist in meeting training, leisure, and social needs.

Older Adults

Older adults with developmental disabilities reside alone or in group homes, intermediate care facilities, developmental centers, board and care homes, or the homes of family members who act as caregivers (Martinson & Stone, 1993). Nursing home care also may become necessary when more complex skilled care needs arise. Health and habilitation issues in older adults are usually complex because physical, mental, and emotional changes occur that require alterations in the habilitation plan. Hearing, vision, musculoskeletal, cardiovascular, and central nervous system changes will require evaluation and replanning of

goals and interventions. Primary health care and coordination of services will be crucial to optimal functioning of the older adult with developmental disabilities.

Approaches to Health Maintenance
Approaches to health maintenance during the older adult phase of the life span are largely the same as those for persons without disabilities. As persons with developmental disabilities grow older, they become more like those their own age who do not have developmental disabilities, yet become increasingly different from each other in interests, needs, preferences, and functional competence (Lottmann, 1993). Concerns of less stamina and lowered energy level have been reported by caregivers of older persons with disabilities. Other changes include general health decline, problems in walking (usually related to arthritis), and skill changes, as well as cognitive changes (Anderson & Moran, 1993). A slight increase in health conditions requiring medication can be expected as persons with developmental disabilities grow older (Anderson & Moran, 1993).

Many older adults with disabilities (approximately 40% of older adults with Down syndrome) experience symptoms associated with Alzheimer's disease. As with other older adults, early changes noted are memory loss, getting lost in a familiar environment, and more limited verbal skills. Other health issues related to older persons with disabilities include hearing and visual loss, thyroid disease, heart disease, and mobility impairment, which may be due to decreased muscle tone, lax ligaments, spinal curvature, and hip problems. The mobility problems intensify as arthritis and bunions (which have a 90% incidence in persons with Down syndrome) develop (Adlin, 1993).

Many older persons with developmental disabilities have a dual diagnosis of psychosis, anxiety, or depression; psychotropic drug use among older persons with dual diagnosis is an area of concern that currently needs monitoring and research. Studies in this country indicate that half of the drug regimens prescribed to older persons with developmental disabilities are inappropriate for the diagnosis (Anderson & Polister, 1993). Polypharmacy prevails as an issue for all older adults. Careful monitoring of the effects and interactions of psychotropic and other drugs for aging adults is essential.

Program Models Person-centered care coordination provides the individualized planning and implementation required to meet the personal and health care preferences of older persons who have disabilities. Barriers to this model include the sparsity of health services designed to meet the needs of older adults, lack of planning and capability for handling emergencies or crises in agencies that serve older persons, and low numbers of adequately trained professionals (Anderson & Factor, 1993). More geriatric nurse–clinicians and nurse–practitioners are being prepared to manage the health care of the older population. These specially trained nurses will be able to function as care coordinators and can help meet the challenge of complex health care needs.

SPECIAL ISSUES IN HABILITATION

Prevocational and Vocational Services

Historically, persons with developmental disabilities were expected to do menial chores in institutional settings and at home, without compensation and with little or no advancement. When special education services began in the late 1960s, they included prevocational and vocational training. Jobs were difficult to secure then and have remained so. It has been estimated that one third of the population with developmental disabilities are employable, but less than half of that portion are employed

(Frank, Sitlington, Cooper, & Cool, 1990).

Kiernan, McGaughey, and Schalock (1988) categorized employment for individuals with developmental disabilities as:

1. *Sheltered employment,* located separately from the mainstream work site, where there is close care and supervision with compensations that are less than minimum wage
2. *Transitional training for employment,* which provides time-limited support leading to competitive employment, with wages typically below the minimum
3. *Supported employment,* which provides ongoing support to workers in mainstream sites where persons with developmental disabilities are employed, with pay less than minimum wage
4. *Competitive employment,* which is a regular job that is not subsidized, with pay at or above minimum wage

In the late 1980s and early 1990s, the jobless rate among adults with mental disabilities ranged between 50% and 80% (Frank et al., 1990). This jobless rate is reported to be for causes other than inability to perform a regular, full-time job. If employed, adults with mental retardation tend to work part-time, earn less, and, in depressed economic conditions, are the last to be hired and first to be fired (Frank et al., 1990). One follow-up study of special education students (Roessler, Brolin, & Johnson, 1990) reported that less than 50% of young adults with mild mental retardation, but 70% of those with learning disabilities, became employed. Most of these held low-paying clerical, sales, or service jobs. More men are employed than women, and men are employed for more hours per week than women. This study also indicated that the quality of life for young people with developmental disabilities is positively related to their employment status and level of daily living, personal–social, and occupational skills (Roessler et al., 1990). It is important for special education programs to prepare students for successful employment in better paying jobs that exist in the community, through such options as local industries that offer on-the-job training.

Concerns beyond the mere employment of persons with developmental disabilities have been expressed in recent studies. Rusch et al. (1991) described interactions between co-workers and supported employees and found that supported employees frequently were involved in associating (87%), evaluating (66%), advocating (56%), and training (55%) relationships with co-workers without disabilities, but experienced befriending only 23% of the time. Chadsey-Rusch, De-Stefano, O'Reilly, Gonzales, and Collet-Klingenberg (1992) found that some workers with mental retardation experienced loneliness in the workplace, but it was not a pervasive feeling. Now that integrated employment is a reality for many persons with mental retardation, more studies of feelings and adjustment to work situations are needed.

Much remains to be done in refining prevocational and vocational services that secure the appropriate employment needed by persons with developmental disabilities. This responsibility falls to schools, supportive citizens groups, businesses, and vocational counselors trained to assist people with special needs. All activities that facilitate appropriate, successful employment are integral to the habilitation of persons with developmental disabilities.

Living Options

Litigation over such issues as the right to education and treatment provided the impetus that forced changes in living arrangements (Walker, 1988). The individual's need should be the criterion for choosing a living arrangement option, rather than the efficacy of any single system of service. The issue of quality of life must be considered as individual choices become available for persons with mental retardation and developmental disabilities (Walker, 1988). When living options are being considered, the health care needs of the individual also must be considered. Persons with disabilities and complex health issues need specialized, appropriate care. For these individuals, living and transportation arrangements must allow adequate monitoring by a nurse, nurse–practitioner, or primary care physician, with specialty consultation as needed.

Group homes, intermediate care facilities, independent and supervised living arrangements, adult foster care, and a variety of other alternative housing arrangements are options available to persons with developmental disabilities. In general:

Supported living in small group homes and in intermediate care facilities within a community provides clients with structure for their day and on-site supervision on a 24-hour basis.

Semi-independent living, often in apartments, affords an alternative for clients who need some supervision, the amount of which varies and is determined individually. The goal is to provide opportunity for independence and self-sufficiency appropriate to an individual's abilities.

Independent living arrangements offer limited support services and require more independent decision making by the individual. Usually much planning, training, and practice is invested in preparation as a person moves toward independent living. When a crisis or unusual circumstances arise, support and supervision will be needed from an interdisciplinary or transdisciplinary team.

When communities work to plan and provide living arrangements for persons who have developmental disabilities, citizen opposition sometimes occurs (Dudley, 1988). Usually such opposition diminishes as the programs become operational over time. Social integration, one goal of community living, should occur within the larger community. This may involve such activities as shopping at stores, attending religious services, eating at restaurants, and attending sports events. Too often, however, few close associations with neighbors are reported by persons with developmental disabilities (Dudley, 1988).

IDENTIFICATION OF FAMILIES AT RISK FOR HAVING A CHILD WITH A DEVELOPMENTAL DISABILITY

Human development from infancy through adulthood progresses through stages and growth phases that are predictable and amenable to description by theoretical models. Great individual variation occurs within the normal parameters of developmental events. Development is the product of genetic, biological, and environmental factors that may either limit or promote the individual's potential. Those persons whose development fails to evolve as expected by the family and by health and developmental care professionals are recognized as having developmental disabilities.

For the nurse who provides care to families with children, the goal of habilitation is achieved by identification of families at risk coupled with a threefold effort at prevention. *Primary prevention* involves interventions designed to prevent developmental disabilities whenever possible. Early and adequate preconceptual and prenatal health care for a woman of childbearing age will contribute to the growth and development status of the fetus and increase the likelihood of delivering a healthy newborn.

For example, one condition characterized by mental retardation, fetal alcohol syndrome (FAS), can be prevented if a woman abstains from alcohol during pregnancy.

Secondary prevention involves early identification and intervention when a developmental disability is suspected, to facilitate recovery and prevent further disability. For example, children who cannot see or hear well will have difficulty learning. Early correction of impaired sensory abilities will prevent communication and cognitive development from being affected.

Tertiary prevention involves making appropriate interventions when developmental delays are present to achieve the greatest possible recovery from or reduction in the extent of developmental disability (Drash, Raver, & Murrin, 1987). For example, children with chronic conditions such as bronchopulmonary dysplasia, failure to thrive, or Down syndrome will have some degree of disability, but early best-practice treatment, good preventive measures, and early developmental stimulation will limit the disability as much as possible.

Nurses can use standardized screening tools (e.g., the Denver II [Frankenburg et al., 1990a] and the Battelle Developmental Inventory Screening Test [Newborg, Stock, Wynek, Guidubaldi, & Svinicki, 1984]) or standardized assessment tools (e.g., the Bayley Scales of Infant Development [Bayley, 1969]) to help document developmental delays in infants and children. In addition, a thorough knowledge of the factors known to be associated with impaired development helps in identifying families at risk for having a child with a developmental disability.

Factors Associated with Developmental Disabilities

At all levels of prevention, it is helpful for the nurse to recognize the genetic, biological, and environmental factors associated with developmental disabilities.

Genetic Factors Genetic factors include chromosomal abnormalities, single-gene defects, and multifactorial disorders.

Chromosomal Abnormalities Chromosomes are microscopic bodies in cell nuclei that contain genes, the basic units of heredity. The term that denotes possession of the correct complete chromosome set in a human cell nucleus is *euploidy*. The euploidic number of chromosomes in most body (somatic) cells is 46. Somatic cells have 22 pairs of autosomes (chromosomes common to both sexes) and two sex chromosomes, the 23rd pair. Deviations from euploidy result in chromosome abnormalities such as deletion or duplication. For example, trisomy refers to the presence of 47 chromosomes, with one pair of autosomes having an extra member. One manifestation is trisomy 21, also known as Down syndrome, in which there are three chromosomes instead of two for the 21st pair. Individuals with Down syndrome will have some degree of developmental disability.

Single-Gene Defects These defects occur when there is disruption of the normal alignment of genes on a chromosome in the cell nucleus. Proteins are aligned to form genes and genes are aligned to form the deoxyribonucleic acid (DNA) chains of each chromosome. The arrangement order of genes represents a code for the body's production of proteins that perform many functions, such as giving the body structure and performing metabolic activities.

Single-gene defects involve a mistake in the genetic code and may result in either a dominant or a recessive disorder. Autosomal dominant disorders tend to be structural defects that are physically evident and occur in many of an affected individual's relatives, all to varying degrees. Most dominant disorders do not cause mental retardation, although some do, such as myotonic dystrophy (Cohen, 1984). Autosomal recessive disorders tend to cause biochemical abnormalities that inhibit normal metabolic processes. Usually the result is an inactivated enzyme that either prevents the breakdown of toxic substances or produces a chemical deficiency. For a recessive disorder to occur, both the mother and father must carry the abnormal gene, although neither exhibits the disorder (this is called the carrier state). The affected child must inherit both of the abnormal genes in the chromosome set he or she receives. Recessive disorders usually result in mental retardation as well as other disabilities and include such disorders as phenylketonuria, Tay-Sachs disease, cystinosis, galactosemia, and maple syrup urine disease (Cohen, 1984).

Multifactorial Disorders These disorders have a polygenic plus environmental causation that cannot be as easily described or predicted as the chromosomal or gene defects. Examples are cleft lip or palate, heart defects, and neural tube defects. These do not necessarily, but often do, cause developmental disabilities.

Biological Factors Biological factors that may cause mental retardation or developmental disabilities include:

- Premature birth or perinatal asphyxia
- Exposure to teratogens or toxins either prenatally, as in fetal alcohol syndrome (FAS), or postnatally, as with toxic lead exposure
- Trauma such as severe head injury, especially when accompanied by coma for greater than 24 hours (Reilly, Lutz, Spiegler, & Lynn, 1987)
- Intrauterine infections, such as cytomegalovirus
- Maternal diseases, such as diabetes, that place the fetus at risk for many malformations and neonatal instability
- Central nervous sytem malformations, including brain anomalies

Environmental Factors Environmental factors include home situations in which animate (caregiver) and/or inanimate (food, shelter, learning materials [including toys]) resources are inadequate to nurture the child's social–emotional and cognitive growth. In the home, the primary caregiver (usually the mother) not only stimulates and interacts with the infant or child but mediates the child's experiences with the environment. The caregiver stimulates thought, language, and communication by drawing the child's attention to elements in the environment, labeling them, and demonstrating their functions. Through daily behavioral dialogues that capture the child's affection and trust, the caregiver becomes the child's most important teacher.

The primary caregiver begins teaching the child from the day of birth through interactions with the infant. In some homes, the infant does not receive nurturing, growth-fostering opportunities to learn from his or her mother or primary caregiver for a variety of reasons. These may include personal illness or functional disabilities of the mother (or caregiver), deprived environment and lack of resources basic to daily living, chaotic or stress-laden social situations, and lack of knowledge by the caregiver regarding the infant's needs for developmental stimulation. The infant or child who misses positive learning opportunities on a daily basis, which include interactive, reciprocal communication with the caregiver and play with toys, will not be able to develop normally.

Parental factors contributing to high-risk home environments include lack of preparation for parenthood, lack of social support, and family dysfunction or economic difficulties.

Adolescent Parents   Studies show that adolescents interact with their infants differently from adult mothers (Parks & Arndt, 1990; Roosa, Fitzgerald, & Carson, 1982; Ruff, 1987). Adolescents provide fewer audiovisually stimulating toys, talk less to their infants, spend less time in mutual gaze, and respond less to their infants' distress vocalizations (Roosa et al., 1982; Ruff, 1987). Compared to adult mothers, they are less nurturing of social–emotional growth by virtue of more negative comments, less praise, fewer smiles, and less reinforcement of the infant's attempts to interact (Ruff, 1987). It may be that adolescents are unaware of how early infants see, hear, and respond to their environment, or benefit from mothers' talk (Becker, 1987). Furthermore, when compared to adult mothers, adolescents perceive caregiving behaviors to have less influence on the infant's health, behaviors, and intelligence (Parks & Arndt, 1990).

Poverty   Children raised in impoverished homes are at greater risk for poor health (Wise & Meyers, 1988). Not only do poor children suffer more illness and trauma, but they also have greater severity of illness and trauma. Poor children are more often the victims of unintentional trauma, especially house fires and motor vehicle accidents, than are nonpoor children, and they incur more injuries caused by violence (Wise & Meyers, 1988). With special significance for long-term neurodevelopmental consequences, poor children have a higher prevalence of low birth weight (less than 2,500 g) and very low birth weight (less than 1,500 g). Hearing loss also is more prevalent in poor children, affecting speech, language, and learning.

Children with disabilities require consistent, enriching developmental activities that low-income parents are the least able to provide (Parker, Greer, & Zuckerman, 1988). Poverty reduces access to the interventions that will prevent or limit the disabilities resulting from chronicity and severity of illness and trauma. Unemployed and underemployed families cannot pay for medical care, do not have insurance benefits, lack transportation to medical care facilities, and often lack information on and understanding of health care phenomena as a result of low education levels. In their daily lives, stressed by unmet basic needs and social situation difficulties, these families usually do not see preventive health care as a priority. Lack of prenatal care and pediatric health assessment/promotion visits contribute to child morbidity.

Dysfunctional or Chaotic Homes These situations are present especially when caregivers are chemically dependent on alcohol or other drugs. Children born to mothers who have abused alcohol or other drugs during pregnancy are at risk for both the physical effects of this prenatal exposure and for growing up in a nonnurturing environment (Free, Russell, Mills, & Hathaway, 1990). Mothers who drink heavily may have a child with FAS or fetal alcohol effects (FAE). FAS is characterized by poor prenatal and postnatal growth, midface dysmorphia, and mild to moderate mental retardation. Children with FAS have special difficulty with object relations, understanding of cause and effect, and anticipation of consequences. Children who are less severely affected or who have mothers who drank less heavily may exhibit FAE. Children with FAE show less severe FAS physical characteristics and learning difficulties.

Children exposed to cocaine and other central nervous system stimulants demonstrate the effects of maternal, placental, and fetal vasoconstriction. Consequences for the infants are irritability, tremulousness, and jitteriness that last up to 6 months. Abnormal respiratory and sleep patterns and distressed cries have been reported (Corwin et al., 1992; Smith, 1988). Some infants suffer severe effects manifested as seizures and hemiparesis secondary to cerebral infarction. The degree of morbidity is thought to be dose related.

One study has reported characteristics of the child-rearing environment for children whose mothers abused substances prenatally (Free et al., 1990). All 20 children in this study had low scores on the Home Observation for Measurement of the Environment (HOME) scale (Caldwell & Bradley, 1984), which measures the stimulation potential of the home, despite the fact that almost half the children were in the care of a relative other than their mother. The results were affected by the low income and education levels of the mothers and relatives, but also by the chaotic, disorganized pattern of daily life that ensues when the mother uses drugs. When she is not experiencing the effects of her drug of choice, the mother with an addiction is preoccupied with activities that will help her get the drug, which may include stealing (even from her own family) or prostitution. When she is under the drug's influence, her behavior is unpredictable and the care of her child is often neglected. The Free et al. (1990) study showed that mothers scored particularly low on the "Maternal Involvement with the Child" subscale of the HOME scale. When child care is relinquished to a family member, the mother may contribute to continuous emotional upheavals by popping in to visit the child, threatening to snatch the child, and making unkept promises. Consequently, even non–drug-using family members have difficulty providing a consistent, nurturing environment for the child. When a grandmother becomes the caregiver, she often feels physically and emotionally taxed because, having already raised her family, she did not anticipate having to care for an infant again. She may grieve that her daughter (or son) has an addiction, and will be socially stressed by the associated behaviors.

Homeless Families Families comprise at least one third of the homeless population (Damrosch, Sullivan, Scholler, & Gaines, 1988). Homelessness of families in the 1990s has been made worse by the economic recession, reduced government aid programs for families, inadequate low-income housing, and increased numbers of single mothers. Homeless families are those unable to acquire safe and permanent housing without special assistance because of lack of employment, family resources, and/or connections to housing aid programs (Damrosch et al., 1988). Probably most homeless families are also situationally disadvantaged by family distress—domestic violence or parental separation, substance abuse, or mental illness. The children in homeless families are vulnerable to hunger and malnutrition, inadequate health care, and recurrent infections. Uncleanliness and unsanitary living conditions contribute to high incidences of respiratory, parasitic, and skin disorders.

Priorities for homeless parents are the basic needs—food, clothing, and safety —so the developmental needs of the children often go unmet. One study found that one half of preschool homeless children had at least one major developmental delay on the Denver Developmental Screening Test, usually in either the language or the personal–social domain (Bassuk & Rosenberg, 1990). According to their mothers' reports, 35% of all homeless children had serious emotional difficulties and 40% of homeless school-age children had repeated at least one grade. The frequent moves, lesser salient parenting, and greater family violence suffered by homeless children probably contribute to impaired developmental progress (Bassuk & Rosenberg, 1990).

Single Parents Single parents tend to be more socially isolated and have more difficulty providing a consistent, organized, nurturing environment than do married parents. The everyday stressors of single parenthood have mental health ramifications and may result in clinical depression. Hall, Gurley, Sachs, and Kryscio (1991) found that, in one sample of low-income single mothers who had at least one child between 1 and 4 years of age,

59.6% demonstrated a high number of symptoms of depression. Mothers who used avoidance for coping, who experienced high levels of everyday stressors, who had little tangible support, and who were in poorly functioning families were at greatest risk for depression. This study found that high numbers of symptoms of depression and inadequacy in the primary intimate relationship predicted less favorable parenting attitudes. Moreover, less favorable parenting attitudes and high levels of everyday stressors predicted child behavior problems (Hall et al., 1991). The implications are that, when the only parent available to the child is unable to provide an organized, stimulating, stable emotional environment, learning and behavior are affected adversely.

Parents with Mental Retardation Parents who have mental retardation may have difficulty with parenting tasks that require contingent responses, anticipation of events and consequences, organization, and judgment (Keltner & Tymchuk, 1992). The major risks for their children are safety, being deprived of emotional and cognitive stimulation, and child abuse or neglect. Parents who have mental retardation often have special difficulty recognizing illness, anticipating danger, and understanding normal child behavior. Other mediating factors will compound the difficulty a person with mental retardation has in child-rearing. These include poverty, vision or hearing impairment, depression or other mental illness (dual diagnosis), and lack of social supports (Keltner & Tymchuk, 1992).

Despite these risks, it can be assumed that children of parents with mental retardation have the potential for normal intelligence (Keltner & Tymchuk, 1992), provided their environment is supported and enriched. Parents with significant retardation (having IQ scores below 70) require family and community support to compensate their parenting skills. Often, other family members will help a mother with mental retardation care for her child. Special developmentally stimulating day care for children of mothers with mental retardation has been shown to improve the children's IQ scores by 22–30 points (Martin, Ramey, & Ramey, 1990). Interventions by nurses and other health care team members that focus on concrete and consistent health and child care teaching can help mothers and fathers with mental retardation successfully parent their own children (Keltner & Tymchuk, 1992).

Case Finding

Case finding is a term employed in public health practice with reference to identifying persons who need assistance or information. Case finding is usually the domain of the public health nurse; however, more recently others have become involved. Because diseases and disabilities may be prevented or minimized with early identification and treatment, case finding, early identification, and referral have been in the forefront of nursing for many years (Barnard & Erickson, 1976; Krajicek & Tomlinson, 1983). The impact of nurses' skills in early problem identification extends across the life span, because nurses are on the front line in care of young and older adults who have disabilities.

School nurses have a vital role in identifying problems in the school-age child that may have been missed earlier. A holistic approach to care of the child through education, health promotion, disease prevention, and early detection of developmental and health problems characterizes the role of the school health nurse (Parsons & Felton, 1992). The identification of such problems as learning disabilities, attention deficit hyperactivity disorder, impulse control disturbances, and emotional lability permit the nurse to assist the child's integration into classroom situations that promote learning and growth (Roberts, 1983).

Methods of Case Finding Screening for childhood developmental delays has been included in the nursing care of children for many years. When screening results suggest a child has a developmental delay, a referral is made for diagnostic testing or evaluation by a team of health professionals. Nurses have much responsibility as part of the health care team to do case finding. Sometimes it is done informally as part of a health promotion visit or illness care. The Early and Periodic Screening, Diagnosis, and Treatment (EPSDT) program is one formal example of case finding conducted by nurses.

Developmental screening tools now available include the Denver II (Frankenburg et al., 1990a), the Rapid Developmental Screening Test (American Academy of Pediatrics, 1972) and the Battelle Developmental Inventory Screening Test (Newborg et al., 1984). Some communities have implemented a developmental screening program for children using the Denver II. Information for planning such a screening is included in the Denver II Technical Manual (Frankenburg et al., 1990b). Characteristics of effective developmental screening tools are listed in Table 5.

Other tools screen for at-risk conditions, such as biological or environmental situations that place the child at risk for developmental delays. Biological risks such as prematurity and chronic illness always are included when the nurse assesses the health history of a child. An environment that fails to support developmental progress can be screened for on the HOME scale (Caldwell & Bradley, 1984).

With the passage of PL 99-457, Part H, in 1986, each state was required to develop a comprehensive "child find" and referral system, as well as a public awareness program to focus on early identification and intervention. The term *child find* refers to case finding of infants and toddlers with developmental

Table 5. Characteristics of effective developmental screening tools

- Established validity, so that the tool sensitively identifies all those who have a developmental delay and, with specificity, does not falsely identify someone with normal development as having a delay
- Established reliability, so that results of test are consistent if repeated and results are predictive of future performance
- Cost- and time-efficient
- Easy to administer to a child
- Can be administered in a variety of settings—clinic, child care, at home
- Easy to score accurately
- Easy to explain results to other professionals and to parents
- Covers a wide range of ages
- Allows for individual differences within an age range without missing true developmental delays

delays. The public awareness and child find activities may include media announcements, pamphlets, posters, and/or a 1-800 phone number where parents or caregivers may call for information or referral.

Other methods of case finding include mass, selective, or multiple screenings (Roberts, 1983; see Table 6). Because developmental delay leading to disability may be subtle and insidious, it also is necessary for screening and tracking to be part of comprehensive early intervention planning.

Advantages of Early Detection As families are screened for risk factors during antepartum or pediatric assessments, the nurse may identify one or many factors that place the child at risk for delayed development. However, there are no methods for correctly predicting which children will be unable to develop within typical, usual parameters. Sameroff (1985) has noted that even readily identifiable biological and genetic insults do not always result in expected poor outcomes. In many known causes of mental retardation, the child's actual developmental outcome is the result of the interaction of multiple factors. It is the combination of chromosomal disorder and complex environmental factors that promote or limit the child's development. Two examples are children born with phenylketonuria (PKU) and Down syndrome.

PKU is caused by the absence of a single gene necessary for the conversion of phenylalanine into another amino acid, tyrosine. If the child's diet contains phenylalanine, the consequences of the interrupted metabolic conversion sequence are excessive levels of phenylalanine and suppressed brain development. With dietary control of phenylalanine, mental retardation is prevented. It is the combination of factors, the missing gene plus a diet containing phenylalanine levels that cannot be metabolized, that result in abnormal mental development.

Children born with Down syndrome have three chromosomes instead of two

Table 6. Screening methods for case finding

Mass screening	Screening an entire population for a problem (e.g., newborn screening for phenylketonuria or galactosemia)
Selective screening	Screening a given group at higher risk for a condition (e.g., antepartum clients with certain risks will be referred for ultrasonography and those at risk for fetal genetic disorders will be referred for prenatal diagnostic procedures [amniocentesis or chorionic villi sampling]).
Multiple screenings	Screening for more than one condition at the same time (e.g., developmental, hearing, vision, and dental screening performed during an annual health assessment and promotion visit)

for the 21st pair in every cell nucleus or, in the case of mosaicism, in a portion of the cell nuclei. Studies have shown that early intervention with children who have Down syndrome promotes early developmental progress. The child who participates in an early intervention program may gain skills that would not be acquired if learning the skills was not attempted until an older age. Therefore, families who actively participate in such a program with their child affected by Down syndrome and who daily encourage the learning of skills at home are more likely to have children who reach their full potential than are families who do not participate in an early intervention program and do not carry through with skill encouragement in daily routines.

Other factors that mediate the child-rearing environment are socioeconomic status and family mental health (Sameroff, 1985). Impoverished environments, emotional unavailability of a parent, a stress-laden, disorganized home, or family abuse and violence can individually and certainly collectively cripple a child's development. Any model of prediction for future developmental ability would have to include not only biological and genetic status but characteristics of the caregiving environment, including the complex interaction of family functioning, family relationships, mental health of the caregivers, and the intrapersonal perceptions of the child (Sameroff, 1985). It is important to note that environmental risks currently are more amenable to intervention than genetic or biological ones. The impact of meeting the needs of parents with young children and teaching good parenting skills is difficult to measure but should not be underestimated.

For the future of our communities, children with developmental disabilities and children who are clearly at risk for compromised development must be identified as early as possible. Early identification by qualified health and developmental care professionals will allow each child the opportunity to receive those services required to develop to his or her fullest potential.

SUMMARY

Nurses have many opportunities for listening to, assessing, and assisting individuals with developmental disabilities of all ages and their families (or caregivers). All individuals deserve opportunities for developing their full potential and deserve individualized, appropriate health care. The unique contribution of nurses to the habilitation of persons with developmental disabilities is the coordination of family-centered health promotion and care within the context of the major principles of habilitation. Nursing care that promotes independence and a full and healthy lifestyle for such individuals begins with early identification of children at risk of or having developmental disabilities. Recognition of family risk factors and case finding activities by nurses enable the habilitation team to begin preventive and intervention measures designed to provide the best possible outcome for persons with developmental disabilities. The nurse is also an important part of the ongoing service delivery to these persons as their habilitation needs change across the life span.

REFERENCES

Adlin, M. (1993). Health care issues. In E. Sutton, A.R. Factor, B.A. Hawkins, T. Heller, & G.B. Seltzer (Eds.), *Older adults with developmental disabilities: Optimizing choice and change* (pp. 49–60). Baltimore: Paul H. Brookes Publishing Co.

American Academy of Pediatrics, Committee on Children with Handicaps, New York Chapter 3, District 11, M.J. Giannini, Chair: (1972). *Rapid Developmental Screening Test*. New York: American Academy of Pediatrics.

Anderson, D.J., & Factor, A. (1993). Person-centered planning in case coordination. *IM-PACT: Feature Issue on Aging, 6*(1), 4–5. (Minneapolis: University of Minnesota, Institute on Community Integration).

Anderson, D.J., & Moran, P. (1993). Health services for older people with mental retardation–development disabilities. *IMPACT: Feature Issue on Aging, 6*(1), 18–19. (Minneapolis: University of Minnesota, Institute on Community Integration).

Anderson, D.J., & Polister, B. (1993). Psychotropic medication use among older adults with mental retardation. In E. Sutton, A.R. Factor, B.A. Hawkins, T. Heller, & G.B. Seltzer (Eds.), *Older adults with developmental disabilities: Optimizing choice and change* (pp. 61–75). Baltimore: Paul H. Brookes Publishing Co.

Barnard, K.E., & Erickson, M.L. (1976). *Teaching children with developmental problems: A family care approach* (2nd ed.). St. Louis: C.V. Mosby.

Bassuk, E.L., & Rosenberg, L. (1990). Psychosocial characteristics of homeless children and children with homes. *Pediatrics, 85*(3), 257–261.

Bayley, N. (1969). *Manual for the Bayley Scales of Infant Development*. New York: The Psychological Corporation.

Becker, P.T. (1987). Sensitivity to infant development and behavior: A comparison of adolescent and adult single mothers. *Research in Nursing & Health, 10*, 119–127.

Brandt, P.A., & Magyary, D.L. (1989). Preparation of clinical nurse specialists for family-centered early intervention. *Infants and Young Children, 1*(3), 51–62.

Caldwell, B.M., & Bradley, R.H. (1984). *Home observation for measurement of the environment* (rev. ed.). Little Rock: Authors.

Chadsey-Rusch, J., DeStefano, L., O'Reilly, M., Gonzalez, P., & Collet-Klingenberg, L. (1992). Assessing the loneliness of workers with mental retardation. *Mental Retardation, 30*(2), 85–92.

Challela, M.S. (1986). Interdisciplinary practice and education in early intervention. In *Early intervention, concerns of a career in nursing: Proceedings of a symposium in honor of Camille L. Cook* (pp. 16–35). Washington, DC: National Center for Clinical Infant Programs.

Cohen, F.L. (1984). *Clinical genetics in nursing practice*. Philadelphia: J.B. Lippincott.

Consensus Conference Committee. (1993). *National standards of nursing practice for early intervention services*. Maternal and Child Health HRSA Project MCJ-215052. (Available from Dr. Gwen Lee, Project Director, College of Nursing, University of Kentucky, Lexington, KY 40536-0232).

Corwin, M.J., Lester, B.M., Sepkoski, C., McLaughlin, S., Kayne, H., & Golub, H.L. (1992). Effects of in utero cocaine exposure on newborn acoustical cry characteristics. *Pediatrics, 89*(6), 1199–1203.

Crocker, A.C., Yankauer, A., & Conference Steering Committee. (1987). Basic issues. *Mental Retardation, 25*(4), 227–232.

Damrosch, S.P., Sullivan, P.A., Scholler, A., & Gaines, J. (1988). On behalf of homeless families. *MCN, 13*(4), 259–263.

Drash, P.W., Raver, S.A., & Murrin, M.R. (1987). Total rehabilitation as a major goal of intervention in mental retardation. *Mental Retardation, 25*(2), 67–69.

Drotar, D., & Sturm, L. (1991). Mental health intervention with infants and young children with behavioral and developmental problems. *Infants and Young Children, 3*(4), 1–11.

Dudley, J.R. (1988). Discovering the community living arrangements—neighborhood equation. *Mental Retardation, 26*, 25–32.

Frank, A.R., Sitlington, P.L., Cooper, L., & Cool, V. (1990). Adult adjustment of recent graduates of Iowa mental disabilities programs. *Education and Training in Mental Retardation, 25*, 62–75.

Frankenburg, W.K., Dodds, J., Archer, P., Bresnick, B., Maschka, P., Edelman, N., & Shapiro, H. (1990a). *Denver II screening manual*. Denver, CO: Denver Developmental Materials, Incorporated.

Frankenburg, W.K., Dodds, J., Archer, P., Bresnick, B., Maschka, P., Edelman, N., & Shapiro, H. (1990b). *Denver II technical manual*. Denver, CO: Denver Developmental Materials, Incorporated.

Free, T., Russell, F., Mills, B., & Hathaway, D. (1990). A descriptive study of infants and toddlers exposed prenatally to substance abuse. *MCN, 15*(4), 245–249.

Garland, C., Woodruff, G., & Buck, D.M. (1988). *Case management* (White Paper). Reston, VA: Council for Exceptional Children, Division for Early Childhood.

Hains, A.H., Rosenkoetter, S.E., & Fowler, S.A. (1991). Transition planning with families in early intervention programs. *Infants and Young Children, 3*(4), 38–47.

Hall, L.A., Gurley, D., Sachs, B., & Kryscio, R. (1991). Psychosocial predictors of maternal depressive symptoms, parenting attitudes, and child behavior in single-parent families. *Nursing Research, 40*(4), 214–220.

Hauber, F.A., Bruininks, R.N., Hill, B.K., Lakin, K.C., & White, C.C. (1984). *National census of residential facilities: Fiscal year 1982*. Minneapolis: University of Minnesota Center for Residential and Community Services.

Hutchison, D.J. (1978). The transdisciplinary approach. In J.B. Curry & K.K. Peppe (Eds.), *Mental retardation: Nursing approaches to care* (pp. 65–74). St. Louis: C.V. Mosby.

Keltner, B.R., & Tymchuk, A.J. (1992). Reaching out to mothers with mental retardation. *MCN, 17*(3), 136–140.

Kiernan, W.E., McGaughy, M.J., & Schalock, R.L. (1988). Employment environments and outcomes for adults with developmental disabilities. *Mental Retardation, 26*, 279–288.

Kleinert, H.L., Guitinan, S., & Farmer, J. (1991). *Peer tutoring for high school students: A course manual*. Lexington: University of Kentucky, Interdisciplinary Human Development Institute University Affiliated Program.

Krajicek, M., & Tomlinson, A. (Eds.). (1983). *Detec-*

tion of developmental problems in children (2nd ed.). Baltimore: University Park Press.

Lottman, T.J. (1993). Aging and developmental disabilities: State of the art, state of the need. *IMPACT: Feature Issue on Aging, 6*(1), 2. (Minneapolis: University of Minnesota, Institute on Community Integration).

Martinson, M.C., & Stone, J.A. (1993). A national survey of community living options. In E. Sutton, A.R. Factor, B.A. Hawkins, T. Heller, & G.B. Seltzer (Eds.), *Older adults with developmental disabilities: Optimizing choice and change* (pp. 187–198). Baltimore: Paul H. Brookes Publishing Co.

Martin, S.L., Ramey, C.T., & Ramey, S. (1990). The prevention of intellectual impairment in children of impoverished families. *American Journal of Public Health, 80,* 844–847.

Newborg, J., Stock, J.R., Wynek, L., Guidubaldi, J., & Svinicki, J. (1984). *Batelle Developmental Inventory Screening Test.* Allen, TX: DLM Teaching Resources.

Parker, S., Greer, S., & Zuckerman, B. (1988). Double jeopardy: The impact of poverty on early child development. *Pediatric Clinics of North America, 35*(6), 1227–1240.

Parks, P.L., & Arndt, E.K. (1990). Differences between adolescent and adult mothers of infants. *Journal of Adolescent Health Care, 11,* 248–253.

Parsons, M.A., & Felton, G (1992). Role performance and job satisfaction of school nurses. *Western Journal of Nursing Research, 14*(4), 498–511.

Reilly, A.N., Lutz, M.M., Spiegler, B., & Lynn, P. (1987). Head trauma in children: The stages to cognitive recovery. *MCN, 12*(6), 405–412.

Roberts, P. (1983). Nursing assessments: Screening for developmental problems. In M. Krajicek & A. Tomlinson (Eds.), *Detection of developmental problems in children* (2nd ed., pp. 2–40). Baltimore: University Park Press.

Roessler, R.T. (1990). A quality of life perspective on rehabilitation counseling. *Rehabilitation Counseling Bulletin, 34,* 82–91.

Roessler, R.T., Brolin, D.E., & Johnson, J.M. (1990). Factors affecting employment success and quality of life: A one year follow-up of students in special education. *Career Development for Exceptional Individuals, 13,* 95–107.

Roosa, M.W., Fitzgerald, H.E., & Carson, N.A. (1982). Teenage and older mothers and their infants: A descriptive comparison. *Adolescence, 17*(65), 1–17.

Rosenkoetter, S.E. (1992). Guidelines from recent legislation to structure transition planning. *Infants and Young Children, 5*(1), 21–27.

Ruff, C.C. (1987). How well do adolescents mother? *MCN, 12,* 249–253.

Rusch, F.R., Hughes, C., Johnson, J.R., & Minch, K.E. (1991). Descriptive analysis of interactions between co-workers and supported employees. *Mental Retardation, 29*(4), 207–212.

Sameroff, A.J. (1985). Environmental factors in the early screening of children at risk. In W.K. Frankenburg, R.N. Emde, & J.W. Sullivan (Eds.), *Early identification of children at risk: An international perspective* (pp. 21–44). New York: Plenum Press.

Savage, T.A., & Culbert, C. (1989). Early intervention: The unique role of nursing. *Journal of Pediatric Nursing, 4*(5), 339–345.

Shutz, R.P. (1988). New directions and strategies in habilitation services: Toward meaningful employment outcomes. In L.W. Heal, J.I. Haney, & A.R. Novak Amado (Eds.), *Integration of developmentally disabled individuals into the community* (pp. 193–209). Baltimore: Paul H. Brookes Publishing Co.

Smith, J.E. (1988). The dangers of prenatal cocaine use. *MCN, 13*(3), 174–179.

Smull, M.W., & Bellamy, G.T. (1991). Community services for adults with disabilities: Policy challenges in the emerging support paradigm. In L.H. Meyer, C.A. Peck, & L. Broun (Eds.), *Critical issues in the lives of people with severe disabilities* (pp. 527–536). Baltimore: Paul H. Brookes Publishing Co.

Uehara, E.S., Silverstein, B.J., Davis, R., & Geron, S. (1991). Assessment of the needs of adults with developmental disabilities in skilled nursing and intermediate care facilities in Illinois. *Mental Retardation, 29*(4), 223–231.

Urey, J.R., & Bloom, A.S. (1988, May). *Team approaches in the assessment and management of children's developmental problems: A critical review with respect to efficiency and cost-effectiveness.* Paper presented at the 112th Annual Meeting of the American Association on Mental Retardation, Washington, DC.

U.S. Department of Education. (1989, June 22). Early intervention programs for infants and toddlers with handicaps: Final regulations. *Federal Register, 54*(119), 26307–26346.

Walker, V.S. (1988). Presidential address 1988: Conquest of mental retardation. *Mental Retardation, 26,* 251–255.

Wise, P.H., & Meyers, A. (1988). Poverty and child health. *Pediatric Clinics of North America, 35*(6), 1169–1186.

ADDITIONAL READINGS

Aggen, R.L., & Moore, N.J. (1984). *Standards of nursing practice in mental retardation and developmental disabilities.* Albany: State of New York, Office of Mental Retardation and Developmental Disabilities.

Bagnato, S.J., & Neisworth, J.T. (1991). *Assessment for early intervention: Best practices for professionals.* New York: Guilford Press.

Deal, A.G., Dunst, C.J., & Trivette, C.M. (1989). A flexible and functional approach to developing individualized family support plans. *Infants and Young Children, 1*(4), 32–43.

Gottlieb, J. (1990). Mainstreaming and quality education. *American Journal on Mental Retardation, 95*(1), 16–17.

Gray, C.D., & Conley, R.W. (1988). Expanding horizons in services to persons with developmental disabilities. *Mental Retardation, 26,* 59–62.

Guralnick, M.J., & Bennett, F.C. (Eds.). (1987). *The effectiveness of early intervention for at-risk and handicapped children.* New York: Academic Press.

Horner, R.H., Thompson, L.S., & Storey, K. (1990). Effects of case manager feedback on the quality of individual habilitation plan objectives. *Mental Retardation, 28,* 227–251.

Ivey, S.L., Brown, K.S., Teske, Y., & Silverman, D. (1988). A model for teaching about interdisciplinary practice in health care settings. *Journal of Allied Health, 17*(3), 189–195.

Johnson, B.H. (1990). The changing role of families in health care. *Children's Health Care, 19*(4), 234–241.

Mahoney, G., & O'Sullivan, P. (1990). Early intervention practices with families of children with handicaps. *Mental Retardation, 28*(3), 169–176.

National Information Center for Children and Youth with Disabilities. (1991). The education of children and youth with special needs: What do the laws say? *News Digest, 1,* 1–11.

Rubin, I.L. (1987). Health care needs of adults with mental retardation. *Mental Retardation, 25,* 201–206.

Salend, S.J., & Giek, K.A. (1988). Independent living arrangements for individuals with mental retardation: The landlords' perspective. *Mental Retardation, 26,* 89–92.

4

Quality-of-Life Issues

The Nurse's Role

Jacki Miller, Kathlyn J. Steele, and Joyce S. Morse

OBJECTIVES

On completion of this chapter, the reader will be able to:

- Describe the role of the nurse in evaluating quality-of-life outcomes for individuals with developmental disabilities.
- Discuss the role of the nurse as a member of the quality assurance team.
- Apply basic principles of the quality assurance process to service systems for individuals with developmental disabilities.

OVERVIEW

Quality of life (QOL) encompasses physical, care-related, psychological, social, and economic factors that bear on a person's self-esteem (Mueller, 1993). Developmental disabilities may have a significant impact on any or all of the factors that contribute to QOL. This effect is neither a universal nor a static phenomenon. It is the result of the individual's unique, subjective perceptions, and the dynamic changes that the individual undergoes as he or she ages or has life experiences.

This chapter reviews quality assurance concepts and systems that may be utilized by the nurse in order to assure an optimal QOL for individuals with developmental disabilities and their families throughout the life cycle.

QUALITY OF LIFE

Many experts have offered definitions of quality of life. Flanagan (1972) identified

15 life domains that contribute to the quality of life: material well-being and financial security, health and personal safety, relations with a spouse, having and raising children, relationships with other relatives, relationships with friends, helping others, citizenship, intellectual development, self-understanding and planning, job role, creativity and personal experience, socializing, and passive and active recreation. A sample of other definitions highlights some of their commonalities and differences:

the client's satisfaction with care, efficacy of care, technical proficiency and performance of care providers, accessibility and continuity of care, and cost effectiveness. (McElroy & Herbelin, 1984, p. 5)

the degree of satisfaction with present life circumstances as that which makes life worth living. (Padilla & Grant, 1985, p. 45)

a multidimensional concept that includes such things as the ability to participate in activities of daily living, physical comfort, emotional well-being, and the right to self-determination. (Joint Commission on Accreditation of Healthcare Organizations, 1989, p. 5)

Knoll (1990) stated that "the focus on quality of life as a crucial component in quality assurance is only now emerging. There have been a few efforts in the field for people with developmental disabilities to organize quality of life factors, but as yet there has been no systematic presentation of the topic" (p. 249). Knoll (1990) examined 17 sources in an attempt to identify issues concerned with the QOL for individuals with developmental disabilities. The 11 issues most frequently cited were: real choices in all aspects of daily life, functional skills, interaction with a variety of people, use of "generic" services, access to community resources, age appropriateness, use of a range of community environments, living in a typical neighborhood, meaningful daily activity, nonadversive interventions, and relationships with friends.

Access to health services was 22nd and good health was 26th among the 96 QOL topics mentioned.

It is important for the nurse to realize that there is a hierarchy in evaluating QOL issues. The prioritization of QOL indicators may undergo a change as a result of life experience at any stage in the life cycle. Overall, however, individuals with developmental disabilities must have a home and be clean, healthy, and safe from harm before they can learn and grow (Knoll, 1990).

CONCEPT OF QUALITY IN SERVICES TO PERSONS WITH DEVELOPMENTAL DISABILITIES

Nurses who work with individuals with developmental disabilities should be aware of the quality assurance process within the historical perspective of service delivery. It is also important to acknowledge the role that government and funding sources play in the service delivery system, and how these aspects of service delivery and the quality assurance process are interrelated.

Until the late 1950s, the federal government had no role in funding, monitoring, or providing services to individuals with developmental disabilities. At that time there were disturbing revelations of substandard care in state institutions for persons with mental retardation. In 1962 the original Presidential Panel on Mental Retardation was established. Throughout the 1960s and 1970s, there were a series of investigations and exposés that revealed the plight of individuals with mental retardation and other disabilities in these settings. A series of court cases resulted in federal court mandates to the states. Emphasis was placed on improving the quality of residential life for persons living within state institutional systems (Blatt & Kaplan, 1966; *New York State Association for Retarded Children [NYSARC] v.*

Carey, 1975; *Wyatt v. Stickney,* 1971). Once the federal courts became involved in defining minimum acceptable treatment standards, litigation began over the issues of treatment and the constitutional rights of individuals living in state institutions (Chafee, 1990).

The Medicaid program originally was developed in 1965 to provide traditional medical services and health care. In 1971, Congress voted to expand the Medicaid program to include residential care for some individuals with disabilities. Creation of the intermediate care facility for the mentally retarded (ICF/MR) (now known as intermediate care facility for persons with mental retardation) program resulted in a major influx of federal dollars into state services. It also defined minimum standards that facilities were required to meet in order to receive Medicaid funding.

Although the promulgation of these regulations and the infusion of money that accompanied them had profound positive impact on the lives of many persons with developmental disabilities, the ICF/MR program is not a panacea. These regulations have been updated only twice since 1971, and they originally were designed to address only the needs of individuals living in large residential facilities. Additionally, in 1988, combined state and federal spending for the Medicaid and ICF/MR programs was approximately $6.7 billion; the federal share was approximately $3.6 billion (Chafee, 1990). With such large sums of money being spent, both service providers and consumers agree that it is time to deemphasize reliance on large institutional facilities and attempt to develop a comprehensive community-based service delivery system that can deliver person-centered, cost-effective care.

The reality of today's service delivery system calls for a more individualized and nonmedical approach to the lives of individuals with developmental disabil-ities. This is an exciting time for nurses to become involved in implementing and interpreting the ICF/MR regulations in ways that enhance the dignity and quality of life for individuals who reside in ICF/MR licensed and funded settings.

QUALITY ASSURANCE

Quality assurance (QA) is a comprehensive approach for measuring all aspects of service delivery to individuals with developmental disabilities. Bradley (1990, p. 4) stated that there are significant and compelling reasons why quality assurance is an important component of the system of services and supports available to individuals with developmental disabilities:

1. There are an increasing number of individuals with severe disabilities receiving services; they and their families should not be vulnerable to a lack of services or services that are poorly delivered.
2. The development and implementation of QA systems communicates high expectations to service providers.
3. Good QA systems provide feedback to service providers about their performance; this can assist them to accommodate to constantly changing regulatory and funding program expectations.

Nurses, as health care providers, are educated to consider the unique assets and needs of each individual in order to develop and implement an effective plan of nursing care. Nurses have learned that the most successful plans are those that fully engage the individual and his or her family. In the complex service delivery system that characterizes the field of developmental disabilities, it is important to listen actively to the consumers of these services. When providers listen, it is possible to develop programs that build on consumer assets and meet consumers' needs as human beings.

Nurses can act as facilitators for self-advocacy by persons with developmental disabilities. Consumer advocacy groups such as People First, The Association for People with Severe Handicaps (TASH), and The Arc (formerly the Association for Retarded Citizens) have effective programs to assist individuals with developmental disabilities to learn self-advocacy skills in order to receive services that enhance the quality of their lives. At every stage of the life cycle, it is possible to allow the individual with developmental disabilities to participate in his or her health care. Table 1 depicts a continuum of approaches that progressively allow persons with developmental disabilities to assume responsibility for their health and well being.

Families with a member with developmental disabilities may have special concerns about the type and quality of services being offered.

A program that is satisfactory for C.J. and his family meets their standards of quality. These standards may vary from family to family and from time to time.

It is important for families, the individual with developmental disabilities, and the program provider to be open and honest with one another at all times in order to provide a program that enhances QOL for the individual and his or her family (Lehr & Lehr, 1990).

Quality Assurance Information

Every service provider has a management program that identifies standards, monitors compliance with these standards, and gathers, organizes, and acts on data in an effort to achieve compliance with its identified standards. As a result of these activities, the service provider now has QA information that can be used in a variety of ways. The provider can develop and implement new policies and procedures, modify or discard old policies and procedures, take managerial action (e.g., develop an in-service program for all staff members), and expand the range

C.J. is an active 15-year-old boy with a diagnosis of autism and a poorly controlled seizure disorder. He is mainstreamed for some classes in his local high school. Both of his parents hold full-time jobs outside of the home. It is important to all of them that C.J. has an after-school program that meets his needs for leisure/recreational activities and constant supervision. C.J.'s parents also are concerned that the program has an adequate number of well-trained staff on duty, the activities provided are age appropriate, there is a compatible peer group, and there are medical services available in case C.J. has a seizure episode that requires the administration of oxygen or intravenous medication.

As a resource to his after-school program, the school nurse from C.J.'s high school provided a protocol to follow in the event that C.J. experienced a seizure episode. The nurse also provided the name and phone number of the local rescue squad to transport C.J. to the emergency room if necessary. His parents provided an emergency medical information card that described a typical seizure. In addition, they gave detailed information about his medications, including their dosages, routes, and times of administration. The most recent seizure medication blood level results also were noted. This cooperative effort assured C.J.'s health at his after-school program and helped his parents to feel comfortable about his safety.

Table 1. Approaches to health care for persons with developmental disabilities

Approach	Staff responsibility	Individual responsibility
Passive recipient of care	Observation, assessment, intervention, and ongoing evaluation of health status. Represents student in clinic.	Utilizes communication skills to provide information and feedback when prompted by staff.
Active participant in care	Same as above plus informal and/or individual teaching about: signs and symptoms of illness; identification of body parts; appropriate intervention for minor illness.	1) Differentiates between wellness and illness 2) Reports signs and symptoms of illness to appropriate person in a timely manner 3) When questioned, gives feedback about effectiveness of intervention
Advocate for care	All of the above plus participation in group teaching: 1) family life 2) health and hygiene 3) medication self-administration 4) health care provider's role 5) accessing health care 6) payment for health care	1) All of the above plus: 2) Attempts to manage minor problems by symptomatic treatment 3) Determines need for medical services 4) Identifies correct providers of service 5) Arranges appointment 6) Is present at appointment with appropriate information 7) Negotiates treatment regimen 8) Communicates treatment regimen to caregiver 9) Evaluates effectiveness of treatment regimen 10) Provides feedback to provider service

of consumer choices and inputs into its service delivery system.

There are other ways in which this QA information can be utilized. These can include changes in the structure and table of organization to improve service delivery, improving individual program plans, developing new services or service models, and exploring or obtaining funding from new sources.

Our Home is an apartment that houses three young men with cerebral palsy who used to live in a nearby state-operated developmental center. There is a staff member on duty at all times to assist these men with personal care. One of the young men is Arturo. As an individual of Hispanic descent, Arturo feels that the staff member should be able to speak Spanish. This is important to Arturo because his family has been avoiding calling him on the telephone because the staff member on duty cannot converse with them. Arturo brings this concern to the Resident Council of the agency that operates his apartment. A few of the agency's other consumers have similar concerns. The service provider representative on the council proposes two possible solutions. First, the service provider will make an effort to recruit some bilingual personal care assistants. Second, it will make a 1-800 phone number available to Arturo and his family. This will provide translator assistance at no additional cost to the caller. Arturo is pleased with both of these proposals. The service provider has been responsive to his need to have ongoing communication with his family.

Types of Quality Assurance Systems

External QA systems initiate and carry out regulatory or accrediting functions. The auditors are external to the service provider or program. *Internal QA systems* are operated by the employees or consumers within a service provider organization or program. They consider consumer and/or family satisfaction with the services and programs being delivered. Each of these approaches to QA produces information about the degree to which a program or service conforms to identified performance standards. Table 2 identifies eight standards affecting QA.

The Quality Assurance Program

The essential components of a sound QA program should include the following:

- Identification of important or potential problems, or related concerns, in the care of persons with developmental disabilities
- Objective assessment of the cause and scope of the problems or concerns, including the determination of priorities for both investigating and resolving problems; usually, priorities should be related to the degree of impact on program service delivery or personal health/safety that can be expected if the problem remains unsolved.
- Implementation (by appropriate individuals or through designated mechanisms) of decisions or actions that

are designed to eliminate, if possible, identified problems
- Monitoring activities designed to ensure that the desired result has been achieved and sustained
- Documentation that reasonably substantiates the effectiveness of the overall program to enhance the quality of life for persons served and to ensure sound clinical performance (Richards & Rathburn, 1992)

Assessing an Existing Quality Assurance Program The nurse should become familiar with the organization's or agency's QA program in order to understand the nursing role in the QA process. The nurse must understand the changes in program or organizational functioning that may occur as a result of QA program findings. As a member of the interdisciplinary team, the nurse should consider whether the programs planned and implemented for individuals with developmental disabilities within that organization are effective ones. The answers to the following questions will assist the nurse to determine the effectiveness of an existing QA program:

1. Does the program have a clearly written plan based on the organization's philosophy/mission statement?
2. Are the program goals/objectives realistic, measurable, and achievable within available resouces?
3. Does it meet all of the requirements of various external review bodies; i.e., professional organizations such as CARF, ACMRDD, and/or state

Table 2.   Internal and external standards affecting quality assurance

1. Certification for funding based on federal standards (e.g., standards developed by the Health Care Financing Administration [HCFA] for Intermediate Care Facilities for Persons with Mental Retardation [ICFs/MR])
2. Licensure by state departments under established standards for program licensing
3. Accreditation by organizations such as the Accreditation Council on Services for People with Developmental Disabilities (ACDD) and the Commission on Accreditation of Rehabilitation Facilities (CARF)
4. Case management oversight
5. Peer review under which reciprocal review arrangements are worked out with other programs
6. Internal review in which the agency reviews its own programs on a regular basis
7. Consumer review by recipients of services
8. Family/citizen monitoring involving citizen-based visits and a protocol observation

Adapted from Bradley & Bersani (1990).

and national governments i.e., HCFA for ICF/MR's?

4. Does the program articulate a complete cycle that begins with problem identification and ends with sustained problem resolution?

5. Is there appropriate coordination and utilization of all resources and support systems?

6. What program strengths need highlighting?

7. What program weaknesses require change? (Meisenheimer, 1985, p. 104)

An assessment tool such as the one shown in Table 3 may be used to answer these questions.

Establishing a Quality Assurance Program In the service delivery system for individuals with developmental disabilities, the nurse often functions as the health care generalist on the interdisciplinary team. In this role, the nurse identifies the health-related needs of an individual with developmental disabilities. The nurse and other members of the team work collaboratively to ensure that there is an effective plan to meet the individual's identified health care needs. The nurse assures that adequate follow-up care is provided and that the plan results in the desired outcomes.

Table 3.   Checklist for evaluating QA programs

EXTERNAL REQUISITES

____ Does the program meet the requirements of its regulatory agencies (e.g., CARF, state and national government, professional organizations)?

____ Have past surveyed deficiencies been corrected? What is the status of the deficiencies?

INTERNAL REQUISITES (structure, process, and outcome)

____ Is there a written QA plan?

____ Does it include clear and measurable objectives?

____ Does it cover line of authority, coordination, and problem identification and follow-up procedures?

____ Is the program efficient? Efficiency is viewed in terms of the program's cost utilization of mechanisms, activities, staff, and the facility. The following factors may be helpful to evaluate efficiency:

____ Is there an experienced and accountable person to coordinate the program?

____ Is there coordination of accountable staff for various QA functions?

____ Are the data organized and easily retrievable?

____ Do QA mechanisms and activities link with other departments in the organization? Do they facilitate corrective actions that affect, but may be beyond the control of, nursing?

____ Is there a risk management data tracking and control system to ensure appropriate follow up on all identified problems, from the monitoring and evaluation mechanisms in a department to those outside the department?

____ Is there a system for adequate data gathering?

____ Does a component of the program reward and acknowledge the contributions of management and staff (e.g., a creative booklet acknowledging improvements in programs or care)?

____ Is there evidence of support from administration, management, and staff?

____ Are successful problem-solving methods and strategies shared with other organizations?

____ Is the program effective? Does it demonstrate that the desired program outcomes were achieved, including demonstration of improved care and maintenance of outcomes?

____ Are changes and improvements in the organization and program services occurring (behavioral and organizational level)?

____ Are problems being followed to resolution?

____ Do the persons with developmental disabilities, and the services provided, demonstrate evidence of improvement?

____ Are desired program outcomes achieved and maintained?

____ Are monitoring and evaluation activities comprehensive for the scope of services?

____ Are all major functions for persons served by the organization included within monitoring and evaluation activities?

(continued)

Table 3. (*continued*)

_____ Are there scheduled QA monitoring and evaluation activities? (Note: A QA calendar that is disseminated to all levels of staff is helpful to remind them of activities.)

_____ Are there other monitoring mechanisms besides review of the person's record (e.g., observation, interview, staff surveys)?

_____ Are various approaches (such as creative workshops, resource meetings, etc.) used to increase understanding and promote the meaningfulness of the QA program?

_____ Is there any duplication of effort?

_____ Are QA reports streamlined and succinct?

_____ Is there a communication structure that provides feedback to administration, management, and staff?

_____ Are conclusions and recommendations reported to the organization-wide QA program, as specified in the organization's QA plan?

_____ Does the program provide a cost-benefit analysis? The following should be reviewed:

_____ Staff time used for data collection, interpretations, and analysis

_____ Amount of support staff required (secretaries, clerks, administrators)

_____ Need for and use of office equipment and supplies

_____ Cost of duplicating reports and QA information

_____ Costs for resource materials (books, computer literature searches)

_____ Degree of involvement of all levels of staff

Adapted from Sawyer-Richards (1991).

The current emphasis in QA is to examine the actual implementation of care provided and to evaluate the effectiveness of care in meeting the individual's needs. In order to accomplish this, the nurse must observe and interact with the individual as well as the persons implementing the health care plan. The individual with developmental disabilities should be involved in decision making about his or her care. Whenever possible, outcomes should reflect evidence of each client's ability to apply the knowledge and skills he or she has acquired.

Alexandria is an attractive 14-year-old girl who enjoys shopping for pretty clothes. She has a medical diagnosis of cerebral palsy. She uses an adapted power wheelchair for mobility. Alexandria lives at home with her mother and 12-year-old sister. She is mainstreamed in her local middle school. She receives individual speech therapy sessions to improve her oral communication skills.

In November, Alexandria's teacher reported to the school nurse that Alexandria appeared to have been losing weight since the beginning of the school term. The teacher also noted that Alexandria frequently refused snacks in the classroom and she often left 40%–50% of her lunch uneaten.

The school nurse observed Alexandria in the lunchroom. She noticed that Alexandria was experiencing difficulty managing her eating utensils; she would stop eating as soon as she spilled any food. In the classroom, the nurse observed that she was refusing snacks that were difficult for her to manage independently. The nurse then met alone with Alexandria; she also arranged a meeting between Alexandria, her mother, and the teacher.

As a result of the observations and interviews, the nurse initiated a referral for an occupational therapy (OT) evaluation. The purpose of the OT assessment was to determine if Alexandria could benefit from the use of adapted eating utensils. A referral was made to Alexandria's physician for evaluation of her health. In addition,

(*continued*)

the nurse and mother developed a plan to improve Alexandria's food intake to meet her basic nutritional needs.

Over the next 3 months, Alexandria was seen by her physician, who reported that she was in good health and not at risk as a result of her eating habits. The OT recommended the use of adaptive utensils that reduced spillage during mealtime. The teacher allowed Alexandria and her classmates to provide input into the type of snack foods that they would enjoy and that Alexandria could manage independently.

The nurse continued to observe and interact with Alexandria, her mother, and her teacher in order to monitor her progress.

In establishing a QA program for persons with developmental disabilities, the nurse may utilize existing information within the practice setting. Nurses in community-based group homes, adult training sites, early intervention programs, and long-term care facilities have access to a variety of recorded data. Documentation in nurses' notes, health summaries, and/or staff communication books may be a primary source of information. Infection control data, medication error reports, and the nursing component of the individualized program plan also may be used.

Individual client goals should be the primary focus of the nurse in developing the measurement criteria to evaluate nursing care. Outcome-focused approaches to health care should be a part of each individual's active intervention plan. QOL indices such as freedom from injury, restraint, and pain are examples of outcomes that may reflect care based on nursing standards. Evaluating these outcomes is an essential component of the QA program. Although nursing standards and predictable individual outcomes have not been published specific to persons with developmental disabilities, existing standards often apply, or they can be adapted.

Writing a Quality Assurance Program Plan In some situations, the nurse may find that it is his or her role to write a QA program plan. This does not have to be a lengthy document. It must describe the overall nursing QA program, ensure comprehensiveness, and provide guidance in the program's operation. The plan should derive from the philosophy and goals of the service provider. It should describe the program's purpose, scope, and integration with the service provider's QA program, as well as contain an organizational chart that explains responsibilities, levels of authority, and reporting relationships for QA functions (see Table 4).

Table 4.   Writing a quality assurance program plan

1. **State your purpose or goal:** Formulate the answer to the following question: What is the intention of the QA program?
2. **Identify your objectives:** Objectives should define what is to be accomplished by carrying out a QA plan. Some plans include both long-term and short-term objectives. Long-term objectives act as a guide to the overall program—that is, to evaluate compliance with the established standards of client care set by CARF. Short-term objectives reflect the emphasis for the next 1 or 2 years—that is, to revise existing QA reporting tools for consumer-related accidents/incidents.
3. **Describe role responsibilities:** Identify and describe the role of every member of the QA team.
4. **Describe a structure:** The structure should indicate how the work of quality assurance will be completed. It should identify the model of QA that has been chosen. If the model is unique, it should be described. It is

(continued)

Table 4.   (*continued*)

helpful to draw a diagram that shows the structure of the QA process and how it related to the organization as a whole. The reporting relationship between the QA program, the organization's administrator, and the governing body (i.e., the Board of Directors) should be clear.

5. **Describe QA committee functions:** The QA committee will oversee the process of monitoring professional practice and consumer satisfaction. Responsibilities to be described here include: how meetings will be scheduled, conducting an annual evaluation of the QA program, and providing ongoing QA education to staff and consumers.

6. **State how monitoring and evaluation will be accomplished:** For QA monitoring results to be useful, the information must be summarized and evaluated. When there is evidence of any significant problems there must be a plan for follow-up and correction identified.

Adapted from Ducquette (1991).

NURSING STANDARDS OF CARE AND QUALITY ASSURANCE

In 1975, the American Nurses Association (ANA) published a *Plan for Implementation of Standards of Nursing Practice*. This landmark document provided a framework for the nurse to use in the application of standards to the individual work setting. It established a foundation for peer review, which is an essential component of the QA process (American Nurses Association, 1988). Later, the ANA developed a series of standards in specialty practice areas (see Tables 5 and 6). Each practice area addressed a standard for QA that may be applied to nursing practice with persons with developmental disabilities.

Nursing theory, practice, and research, along with the beliefs and values of nurses, all contribute to the formulation of nursing standards. A careful re-

Table 5.   Definitions related to standards and guidelines

These definitions have been adapted by the ANA Board of Directors.

Standard. Authoritative statement enunciated and promulgated by the profession by which the quality of practice, service, or education can be judged.

Standard of Nursing Practice. An authoritative statement that describes a level of care or performance common to the profession of nursing by which the quality of nursing practice can be judged. Standards of nursing practice include both standards of care and standards of professional performance.

Standards of Care. Describe a competent level of care demonstrated by a process of accurate assessment and diagnosis, planning, appropriate interventions, and predicted patient outcomes.

Standards of Professional Performance. Describe a competent level of behavior in the professional role, including activities related to quality assurance education, consultation, research, ethics, resource utilization, accountability, peer review, and interdisciplinary collaboration.

Guidelines. Describe a process of patient care management that has the potential of improving the quality of clinical and consumer decision making; includes assessment and diagnosis, planning, intervention, evaluation, and outcome.

Universal Practice Guidelines. Describe a process of patient care management for nursing diagnoses with recommended interventions to accomplish desired patient outcomes. These guidelines are generally applicable to most areas of nursing and are established through research and/or professional consensus by practitioners.

Specialty Practice Guidelines. Describe a process of patient care management for nursing diagnoses with recommended interventions to accomplish desired patient outcomes for a specific cluster of phenomena within a nursing specialty. These guidelines are established by research and/or professional consensus by practitioners in the specialty. (Note: There may be some overlap between universal and specialty guidelines as they emerge.)

Criteria. Variables known to be relevant, measurable indicators of the standards of practice.

Procedures. Describe a series of recommended actions for the completion of a specific task or function. Procedures may either be specific to an institution or applicable across settings.

Table 6.   Delineation of standards of nursing practice

PURPOSE

To provide broad direction for the overall practice of nursing, including the provision of care and professional role activities.

GOAL

To describe a level of nursing care and professional performance common to all nurses.

Components of Standards of Nursing Practice

Each standard requires general criteria to measure achievement of the standard. In addition, criteria for each standard may be developed to measure compliance with expectations for practice in a specialty area or an advanced level of clinical practice.

Standards of Care	*Standards of Professional Performance*
Assessment	Quality assurance
Diagnosis	Education
Planning	Consultation
Interventions	Research
Evaluation	Ethics
Outcomes	Resource utilization
	Accountability
	Peer review
	Interdisciplinary collaboration

SUBSTANTIVE ATTRIBUTES

- Standards of nursing practice include standards of care and standards of professional performance.
- Standards of care are based on the nursing process.
- Each component of the nursing process is included in the standards of care.
- Standards of professional performance reflect the common activities of the professional nursing role, such as quality assurance, education, consultation, research, ethics, resource utilization, accountability, peer review, and interdisciplinary collaboration.
- Standards are broad statements that describe the full scope of professional nursing practice.
- Standards include general criteria that allow them to be measured. (In previous documents, these criteria may have been labeled as *process criteria* and *assessment factors.*)
- Standards include general criteria and may include additional criteria specific to a specialty area or level of practice.
- Standards are anticipated to remain stable over time, whereas criteria may change over time due to advancements in knowledge and technology.

Reprinted from *Manual of Nursing Quality Assurance* by H.S. Rowland and B.L. Rowland, with permission of Aspen Publishers, Inc., © 1992.

view of these standards shows that the basis for nursing QA guidelines is similar in all settings (Table 7). Developmental nurses must pay particular attention to the need for interdisciplinary collaboration when applying standards (Avillon & Mirgon, 1989).

Nurses must be aware of policies and procedures within their individual practice settings, their state nurse practice act, and state and federal regulations governing the settings in which they work. For example, nurses working in an ICF/MR should be familiar with 42 C.F.R. 483, which is the federal regulation governing care provided in an ICF/MR. Standards are written to apply to a broad population group. When applying these standards, the needs of each individual must be considered and plans to meet their needs developed and implemented.

In addition to standards set forth by the ANA, other external organizational standards influence the care of persons with developmental disabilities. Some of these include federal and state regulations, public health laws, fire and safety codes, and the health standards of the

Table 7.   Standards for organized nursing services

Standard IV. Quality Assurance

ORGANIZED NURSING SERVICES HAVE A QUALITY ASSURANCE PROGRAM

Rationale

Organized nursing services are obligated to provide effective nursing care to society. Standards provide the basis for evaluating care. A quality assurance program is necessary to determine the degree to which the provision of nursing care complies with standards. A quality assurance program provides opportunities to improve care and resolve problems.

Criteria

1. A written plan exists for the ongoing monitoring and evaluation of nursing care.
2. Nurses participate in the monitoring and evaluation of nursing care in accordance with established professional, regulatory, and organizational standards of practice.
3. Actions are taken to resolve problems and improve care; these activities are documented and evaluated for effectiveness.
4. The quality assurance program itself is periodically evaluated to determine its effectiveness.
5. The quality assurance program is an integral part of the risk management and quality assurance effort of the organization as a whole.
6. Recipients of nursing care have the opportunity to express their satisfaction and perceptions of the quality of care they have received.

From American Nurses Association. (1988). *Standards for organized nursing services and responsibilities of nurse administrators across all settings* (p. 6). Washington, DC: Author; reprinted by permission. Copyright © 1988 by American Nurses Association.

Accreditation Council on Services for People with Developmental Disabilities (ACDD), the Commission on the Accreditation of Rehabilitation Facilities (CARF), the Occupational Safety and Health Administration (OSHA), and the Omnibus Budget Reconciliation Act (OBRA).

Evaluation of Nursing Services

The progress made by each individual should be reviewed periodically by the nurse. The review may include: 1) documentation in the individual's record, 2) personal observations, and 3) discussions with other persons involved in providing care to the individual. This information is used to evaluate the effectiveness of the health care plan. If it is determined that the plan of care is being implemented properly and the needs of the individual are being met, the plan probably will continue without modification. However, if the individual's health needs are not being met, the health care plan will need to be revised.

Revisions may include modifying the goals of the plan, changing the intervention strategy, incorporating other caregivers into the plan, retraining the staff or individual involved in the program, or changing the time frames established for successful completion of the plan. The results of the nurse's evaluation and recommendations for revision in the plan are then discussed with the individual, his or her family if appropriate, and other pertinent members of the interdisciplinary team.

The results of the evaluation and decisions made about the health care plan should be documented in the progress notes. Any significant changes also should be documented in the individual's care plan.

THE TRANSITION FROM QUALITY ASSURANCE TO QUALITY IMPROVEMENT SYSTEMS

The process known as quality improvement (QI) is an outgrowth of the older QA methods, which largely focused on data gathering and analysis. QI looks at the organizational environment and the method of communicating the intention to provide quality services throughout the organization. In order to implement a QI program, it is necessary to recognize the various dimensions of the change process and to sequence changes within the organization over time.

In order to implement a QI system, the provider agency staff must:

- *Become process focused*—everyone must understand the way work is performed within the organization.
- *Use statistical thinking*—applying statistical principles and techniques to all phases of operations in order to understand and reduce variation.
- *Become Plan-Do-Check-Act driven*— applying the scientific method to initiate and manage change in all the organization does.

QI methods fall into three major categories:

Group process—Approaches used to facilitate the effective functioning of people when working together. Some examples are: knowledge of basic meeting skills, idea generation, listening, participating, and conflict resolution.

Statistical and scientific thinking— Studies the variations and cause/effect relationships between service delivery methods and outcomes. These can include flow charts, diagrams, and control charts.

Graphic methods—Use visual pictures of data and information to depict trends and changes over time. This makes the steps and thought process used to improve quality visible. (Batalden, 1991, p. 11)

QI is based on the premise that an agency can improve the quality of its services by assessing and improving the component of the agency (i.e., staff, facilities, programs) that most affect consumer satisfaction and program outcomes.

CONTINUOUS QUALITY IMPROVEMENT AND TOTAL QUALITY MANAGEMENT

Continuous quality improvement (CQI) and total quality management (TQM) are industrial/business terms that have found their way into the lexicon of health care and human services providers. They broadly refer to a philosophy and a set of guiding principles that represent the foundation of a continuously improving organization. TQM and CQI are the application of quantitative methods and human resources to improve: 1) the materials and services supplied to an organization, 2) all the processes within an organization, and 3) the degree to which the consumer's needs are met at the present time and in the future (W. Golomski, personal communication, 1991).

Post–World War II changes in business and industry have put an increasing emphasis on consumer satisfaction in order to generate increased company profits. As the service delivery system becomes more consumer oriented, and taxpayers demand more accountability for money spent on program development and implementation, there will be many changes in the methods utilized to assure quality in service delivery.

Although the motivation may be different, there is no doubt that these changes in philosophy are finding their way into the human services sector. Nurses must be professionally proactive and learn about systems that demand accountability to the people they serve.

SUMMARY

The emphasis on the delivery of services to individuals with developmental disabilities continues to shift from large residential settings to more family- and person-centered care. Nurses must become involved in the development and implementation of effective QA programs in order to ensure that individuals with developmental disabilities and their families receive adequate, appropriate, timely, cost-effective care. Factors that especially influence the quality of care to individuals with developmental disabilities and their families include:

- A wide variety of delivery settings, such as the family home, group home, large residential facility, school, workshop, or workplace.
- The inability of the nurse to observe directly individual, family, or staff compliance with program recommendations because of setting or program structure.
- The need for coordinated care by diverse service providers and disciplines.
- The lack of direct supervision of the individual and/or the service providers by the nurse.

In the specialty area of developmental disabilities nursing, the QA process focuses on the outcomes of nursing care provided to an individual with developmental disabilities. It also must consider the impact of those outcomes on the family and the functioning of the interdisciplinary team. The nurse assesses the quality and appropriateness of services being provided to an individual with developmental diabilities and his or her family by participating in the development and implementation of QA plans that reflect administrative, discipline-specific, and team-oriented interventions. All nursing QA activities should be directed toward optimizing the quality of life for an individual with developmental disabilities.

REFERENCES

American Nurses Association. (1975). *Plan for implementation of standards of nursing practice.* Washington, DC: Author.

American Nurses Association. (1988). *Standards for organized nursing services and responsibilities of nurse administrators across all settings.* Washington, DC: Author.

American Nurses Association. (1990). *Task force on nursing practice standards and guidelines: Working paper.* Rockville, MD: Aspen Publishers.

Avillon, A.E., & Mirgon, B.B. (1989). *Quality assurance in rehabilitation nursing: A practical guide.* Rockville, MD: Aspen Publishers.

Batalden, P.B. (1991). Organizationwide quality improvement in health care. *Topics in Health Record Management, 11*(3), 11–17.

Blatt, B., & Kaplan, F. (1966). *Christmas in purgatory: A photographic essay on mental retardation.* Boston: Allyn & Bacon.

Bradley, V.J. (1990). Conceptual issues in quality assurance. In V.J. Bradley & H.P. Bersani (Eds.). *Quality assurance for individuals with developmental disabilities: It's everybody's business* (pp. 3–15). Baltimore: Paul H. Brookes Publishing Co.

Bradley, V.J., & Bersani, H.A. (Eds.). (1990). *Quality assurance for individuals with developmental disabilities.* Baltimore: Paul H. Brookes Publishing Co.

Chaffee, J. (1990). Balancing quality of life and quality of care. In V.J. Bradley & H.A. Bersani (Eds.), *Quality assurance for individuals with developmental disabilities* (pp. 95–101). Baltimore: Paul H. Brookes Publishing Co.

Ducquette, A.M. (1991). Approaches to monitoring practice: Getting started. In P. Schroeder (Ed.), *The encyclopedia of nursing quality: Vol. III: Monitoring and evaluation in nursing.* Rockville, MD: Aspen Publishers.

Flanagan, J.C. (1972). A research approach to improving our quality of life. *American Psychologist, 33,* 138–147.

Joint Commission on Accreditation of Healthcare Organizations. (1989). *Quality assurance in long term care* Chicago: Author.

Knoll, J.A. (1990). Defining quality in residential services. In V.J. Bradley & H.A. Bersani (Eds.), *Quality assurance for individuals with developmental disabilities* (pp. 235–257). Baltimore: Paul H. Brookes Publishing Co.

Lehr, S., & Lehr, R. (1990). Getting what you want: Expectations of families. In V.J. Bradley & H.A. Bersani (Eds.), *Quality assurance for individuals with developmental disabilities* (pp. 61–75). Baltimore: Paul H. Brookes Publishing Co.

McElroy, D., & Herbelin, K. (1984). Assuring quality of care in long term facilities. *Journal of Gerontological Nursing, 15,* 8–10.

Meisenheimer, C.G. (1985). *Quality assurance: A complete guide to effective programs.* Rockville, MD: Aspen Publishers.

Mueller, V. (1993). Quality of life with an ostomy: Building a model for assessment and care. *Progressions, 5*(1), 3–13.

New York State Association for Retarded Children (NYSARC) v. Carey, No. 72-C-356/357 (E.D.N.Y., April 30, 1975); 393 F.Supp. 715 (E.D.N.Y. 1975); 446 F.Supp. 479 (E.D.N.Y. 1978); 466 F.Supp. 487 (E.D.N.Y. 1979), affirmed 612 F.2d 644 (2d Cir. 1979).

Padilla, G.V., & Grant, M.M. (1985). Quality of life as a cancer nursing outcome variable. *Advanced Nursing Science, 8,* 45–60.

Richards, B.P., & Rathburn, K.C. (1992). *Medical risk management: Preventive legal strategies for health care providers*. Rockville, MD: Aspen Publishers.

Sawyer-Richards, M. (1991). Program evaluation and nursing quality assurance. In P. Schroeder (Ed.), *The encyclopedia of nursing care: Vol. 1. Issues and strategies for nursing care quality*. Rockville, MD: Aspen Publishers.

Wyatt v. Stickney, et al. 325 F.Supp. 781 (M.D. Alabama 1971).

5

Self-Care Deficit Nursing Theory and the Care of Persons with Developmental Disabilities

Betty Runion Rice

OBJECTIVES

On completion of this chapter, the reader will be able to:

- Define Orem's Self-Care Deficit Nursing Theory.
- Develop a philosophical approach to nursing care of individuals with developmental disabilities and their families that encompasses self-care agency, autonomy, and client advocacy.
- Incorporate nursing diagnosis into care plans after determining self-care deficits of individuals or families.

OVERVIEW

This chapter addresses the use of Orem's Self-Care Deficit Nursing Theory from a philosophical and practical viewpoint as a basis for nursing practice in developmental disabilities. Nursing diagnosis and nursing process are incorporated into a care plan that utilizes Orem's theory.

DEFINITIONS OF TERMS

Self-Care: The practice of activities that individuals initiate and perform on their own behalf in maintaining life, health, and well-being (Orem, 1991). In its broadest sense, self-care refers to the whole being and is much more than simply performance of activities of daily living.

Self-Care Deficit Nursing Theory: A description of the relationship between an individual's need for self-care and the inability to engage in self-care activities. Thus a deficit, or inability to meet therapeutic demands, results in a need for nursing (Orem, 1991).

Universal Self-Care Requisites: The functional or developmental requirements that are necessary for all human beings. They may be viewed as basic human needs—normal life requirements for everyone regardless of age, developmental state, or functional ability level (Orem, 1991).

Developmental Self-Care Requisites: The specific human needs that are associated with developmental processes of growth and maturation throughout the life span; also includes pregnancy as a normal developmental process (Orem, 1991).

Health Deviation Requisites: The requirements that affect self-care during illness, disease, or disability. Health deviation states can be structural or functional, congenital or acquired. This area also includes self-care needs that arise as a result of treatment or diagnostic measures (Orem, 1991).

Therapeutic Self-Care Demands: The self-care actions needing to be performed by an individual, family, or caregiver in order to meet known self-care requisites (Orem, 1991).

Self-Care Deficit: The inability to engage in beneficial self-care practices because of lack of knowledge or skills. Deficits may occur in one or several of the universal, developmental, or health deviation self-care requisites (Orem, 1991).

Dependent Care Agent: A significant other or caregiver (not the nurse) who cares for a dependent individual (Orem, 1991).

Methods of Assistance: Nursing activities that include acting or doing for another, guiding and directing, providing physical or psychological support, teaching, and providing a developmental environment that facilitates maximum potential (Orem, 1991).

Nursing Process: An orderly and systematic method of designing nursing systems or plans of care. It consists of the five steps of assessment, diagnosis, planning, implementation, and evaluation, with continuing reassessment throughout (Yura & Walsh, 1973).

Nursing Diagnosis: The responses to actual or potential health problems that nurses are able, licensed, and legally responsible and accountable to treat (Moritz, 1982).

CHALLENGE OF DEVELOPMENTAL DISABILITIES NURSING

Providing appropriate nursing care for persons with developmental disabilities often presents a challenge to nurses unfamiliar with the special care and support these individuals sometimes require. Some nurses, because of their own preconceived notions, anxieties, and lack of knowledge or experience, are intimidated by the unique needs of individuals with mental retardation, emotional disorders, severe musculoskeletal problems, or degenerative diseases. When an individual with developmental disabilities is admitted to an acute care hospital, he or she may be ignored or feared by the staff because of their own insecurities in dealing with the unknown. These insecurities may result in inadequate or improper nursing care, and the experience leaves both the individual and the nurse frustrated and eager to avoid such encounters in the future. This situation is complicated by the fast pace and sometimes regimented approach observed in many hospitals during times of nursing shortages and escalating costs.

By contrast, nurses who regularly work with individuals with developmental disabilities have had opportunity to develop expertise and experience that enable them to provide appropriate care and support to these individuals. For example, most public health nurses have experience working with individuals with special needs because of the nature and extent of their practice settings. At the community level, nurses often serve as formal or informal case managers for clients with a variety of disabling conditions. Their caseloads may include individuals of all ages with varying needs and abilities, and the nurse must be able to assess the functional capabilities of these persons as well as the coping abilities of their families. Individual and family advocacy are crucial components of nursing interventions in the community.

School nurses also are seeing increasing numbers of children with developmental disabilities in their practices. With the enactment of PL 94-142 (the Education for All Handicapped Children Act of 1975), children who formerly might have been in hospitals or long-term care facilities now are attending school during the day. Children with complex health care needs, many of whom are dependent on technologies for daily living, are now in the classroom. It is not unusual to see children with gastrostomy tubes, tracheostomies, or oxygen therapy equipment attending school. The nurse's role in school settings will become increasingly important as larger numbers of children with complex health care needs enter school. Interdisciplinary collaboration and cooperation will be essential, with the nurse playing a key part in designing appropriate individualized education programs (IEPs) that meet the unique needs of children with developmental disabilities. In addition to providing direct care to such children, nurses will need to educate teachers, aides, and others regarding the special needs of this population. Screening and case finding of children with actual or potential developmental problems long have been priorities of school nurses and will remain important.

The nurse's role in residential centers, schools, and group homes varies from place to place, and in many cases has been defined rather narrowly as that of "medication giver" or "first aid provider." Titus and Porter (1989) pointed out the need for nurses in residential settings to be well grounded in a solid nursing theoretical framework in order to develop appropriate roles. Without such a framework, even nurses who work daily with individuals with developmental disabilities may lose their focus and fail to utilize their fullest potential as nurses in caring for this population.

Regardless of the setting, nurses who have not developed a philosophical and theory-based approach that they can adapt to a variety of individual needs and abilities may have problems integrating people with disabilities into their practices. Equally important, these nurses may feel insecure and uncomfortable in their interactions with an individual who may not fit society's definition of "normal." Unconditional acceptance of patients "unrestricted by considerations of social or economic status, personal attributes, or the nature of health problems" is the first requirement in nursing's code of ethics (American Nurses Association, 1985, p. 2). Acceptance and understanding are greatly facilitated by a knowledge base of developmental disabilities and a philosophical framework that values the uniqueness of each individual and looks for assets and possibilities rather than limitations.

OREM'S SELF-CARE DEFICIT NURSING THEORY

Dorothea Orem's Self-Care Deficit Nursing Theory provides a model for nursing practice that is particularly suited to allow for the inclusion of persons with developmental disabilities and their families. Orem (1991) stated that the Self-Care Deficit Nursing Theory explains the relationship between the capabilities of individuals and their self-care demands. If the individual is able to meet all self-care requisites without assistance or education, there is no need for nursing intervention. However, if there is a lack of ability to perform self-care activities because of lack of skill or knowledge, a self-care deficit exists and nursing is needed.

Orem views self-care in a much broader context than simply as activities of daily living. Self-care encompasses deliberate acts that facilitate well-being or move an individual toward wellness, independence, or developmental maturation. Orem (1991) defined self-care as acts that "maintain life, healthful functioning, continuing personal development, and well-being" (p. 365).

Orem includes developmental needs in the three major categories of human experience during which nursing care may be required (see Table 1). For some individuals, nursing care is needed in order to meet universal requisites, such as eating or breathing. Others may need nursing care during various developmental stages or life events. Health de-

viation states, such as illness, injury, or disease, require nursing interventions that may range from education or support to intensive care.

Applications to General Nursing Practice

The limitations of Orem's model generally center around the terminology used and its perceived lack of applicability to everyday nursing practice. When viewed in the context of a basic philosophical approach, however, and when unclear terminology can be translated into more general or readily usable terms, Self-Care Deficit Nursing Theory becomes a useful way to organize information, assess clients' abilities and limitations, and plan for individualized care.

Several authors have demonstrated how Orem's theory can be used in a variety of practice settings and with differing age groups (Clark, 1986; Connelly, 1987; Facteau, 1980; Mullin, 1980; Taylor, 1988; Walborn, 1980). Titus and Porter (1989) showed how Orem's theory can be applied in multidisciplinary pediatric residential facilities as a means to define the scope of nursing practice, provide criteria for client admission and assessment, allow for inclusion of family and caregivers, and provide for systematic self-evaluation. Jenny (1991) proposed using Orem's universal self-care requisites as an organizing framework for categorizing nursing diagnoses.

Taylor (1991) also proposed using Orem's theory as a classification system for nursing diagnosis, but based the structure on elements of the theory within levels of specificity. Nursing diagnoses can be determined by calculating the therapeutic self-care demand and the ability of the client, family, or community to meet the demand. If the ability exceeds the demand, this constitutes a positive diagnosis and nursing care is not needed. If the demand exceeds the ability, a self-care deficit results, and nursing care is required. This classifica-

Table 1.   Self-care requisites

Universal self-care requisites	Common to all individuals throughout the life span, regardless of age, developmental state, or health status
Developmental self-care requisites	Arise as individuals proceed through life cycle events or developmental stages
Health deviation self-care requisites	Arise when individuals experience illness, disease, injury, or structural or functional limitations; also may result from treatment measures

tion model also includes a list of action verbs and limiting adjectives that are useful to describe Self-Care Deficit Theory nursing diagnoses.

CASE STUDY: SCHOOL SETTING

Jennie is an outgoing and friendly 15-year-old girl who has a severe seizure disorder. She experienced anoxia at birth with resulting brain damage. Her cognitive abilities are at approximately the third grade level, and her emotional development is at a preadolescent level. She attends a special education class that is mainstreamed into the local high school. Most of her classes are self-contained, but she goes to lunch, general assembly, and home living classes with the regular education groups. Even though she is new to this school, she enjoys interacting with other students and eagerly converses with them.

Attempts to control Jennie's frequent seizures with medication have been partially successful, but she still has an occasional tonic–clonic seizure. She wears a helmet to protect her head from injury, and reports regularly to the clinic to take her prescribed medication. Jennie has an aura prior to her seizures and knows to sit or lie down immediately. When she felt a seizure was imminent during home living class, Jennie reclined on the floor to avoid falling. Other students and the teacher were frightened and unsure of how to respond to the seizure, but the teacher quickly called the school nurse. The episode lasted about 2 minutes and was over by the time the nurse arrived. Jennie was able to accompany the nurse to the clinic, where she napped for an hour and then returned to class.

In this case, Jennie was able to meet her universal self-care requisite of prevention of hazards independently. She was also meeting the requisite of normalcy to the best of her ability, as evidenced by her socialization with others and her capacity to make friends or meet new acquaintances in both special education and regular classes.

A self-care deficit could be identified for Jennie's classmates and teacher, however. They lacked the knowledge of how to respond to someone having a seizure. In addition, if they did not acquire a level of comfort in dealing with Jennie's seizures, their anxieties might transfer to their interactions with her, thus jeopardizing her self-esteem. The nurse determined, therefore, to conduct a follow-up teaching and support session for students who had witnessed the seizure. Some of them had been frightened that she would die, or that they should have started cardiopulmonary resuscitation. Others felt too paralyzed to move but wanted to "do something," without knowing what.

The nurse was able to allay fears and reassure students that in most cases a seizure will be self-limiting and require no interventions other than staying with the person and remaining calm. She reviewed the mechanism of seizures, pre- and postictal states, proper first aid in prevention of injuries, and brief medical management and the necessity of Jennie's taking medications regularly and on time. Then she allowed the students to discuss their feelings about the seizure and what they would do next time. They expressed great relief in being able to ventilate their fears and anxieties, and felt that they could deal with this situation much better in the future. In addition, none of them believed that Jennie should be removed from the mainstream experience because of this incident. They welcomed the opportunity to

(continued)

include her in their class, now that they understood more about her and her unique needs. By looking beyond the "identified patient," the school nurse was able to use a method of assistance that included classmates and teachers and resulted in the provision of a developmental environment for Jennie as well as her classmates.

Application to Persons with Developmental Disabilities

Self-Care Deficit Nursing Theory focuses on the attainment of maximum potential, regardless of level of ability, as the most desirable state of wellness for any given individual. Orem identifies eight universal self-care requisites, or areas of human need, that must be satisfied by everyone in order to achieve beneficial self-care (Table 2). These general areas are basic to survival as well as quality of life for all individuals, regardless of their developmental or health status, and must be met consistently.

Orem's developmental self-care requisites (see Table 1) are particularly important to consider when caring for individuals with special needs. Developmental level must be assessed accurately in order to provide appropriate interventions. For example, nurses who are unfamiliar with cerebral palsy may inappropriately conclude that someone with significant motor involvement also has cognitive limitations. Conversely, an individual who appears "normal" may be held to unrealistic expectations when his or her developmental level does not match his or her chronological age or physical size.

Health deviation states (see Table 1) may occur frequently for some individuals with developmental disabilities because of associated illnesses or physical problems. During times of hospitalization or acute illness, nursing care must be individualized to meet the particular developmental and emotional needs as well as the physical needs of the individual. Attention must be given to universal and developmental requisites simultaneously with the new needs arising from health deviation states.

Orem's model makes provision for inclusion of significant others or caregivers into the nursing care plan when determining the amount and type of nursing care needed. In the case of individuals with developmental disabilities, the deficit relationship can be extended also to caregivers. Caregivers may include significant others, family members, spouses, direct care aides, vocational counselors, volunteers, or teachers. In other words, caregivers, or dependent care agents, are those persons who assist the individual to meet self-care requirements at the point where the individual cannot do so alone. Each person has the right and desire to engage in self-care to the highest extent possible, but caregivers may provide assistance as needed.

When neither the individual nor his or her caregiver (dependent care agent) is able to fulfill the self-care demands of the person being served, a deficit exists and nursing care is needed. For exam-

Table 2.   Universal self-care requisites

1. The maintenance of a sufficient intake of air.
2. The maintenance of a sufficient intake of water.
3. The maintenance of a sufficient intake of food.
4. The provision of care associated with elimination processes and excrements.
5. The maintenance of a balance between activity and rest.
6. The maintenance of a balance between solitude and social interaction.
7. The prevention of hazards to human life, functioning, and well being.
8. The promotion of human functioning and development within social groups in accord with human potential, known human limitations, and the human desire to be normal. *Normalcy* is used in the sense of that which is essentially human and that which is in accord with the genetic and constitutional characteristics and talents of individuals.

From Orem, D. (1991). *Nursing concepts of practice* (4th ed.). St. Louis: C. V. Mosby; reprinted by permission.

ple, during hospitalization, new self-care demands arise related to the hospitalization or illness (health deviation self-care requisites) that the person or dependent care agent is unable to meet, and therefore nursing care is required. In the case of an unconscious patient, nurses provide the universal self-care requisites of air by maintaining a patent airway, or of water by administering intravenous fluids.

Orem does not include nurses in the category of caregiver or dependent care agent; nurses and nursing are separate entities in the theory. Many writers have described ways to use Orem's theory in nursing practice, but few have focused on populations with developmental disabilities. Raven (1989) described the use of Orem's Self-Care Deficit Nursing Theory as a basis for developing a service model for individuals with developmental disabilities in Australia and emphasized the links between principles of normalization and Orem's self-care requisite of normalcy.

CASE STUDY: ACUTE CARE OR AMBULATORY SETTINGS

Anthony Bartolli is an easygoing 9-year-old boy with Down syndrome. Tony receives regular medical care from a private pediatrician. He came into the pediatrician's office with acute asthma and was admitted to the hospital for treatment and observation.

During a previous office visit, the mother had confided to the nurse that she was uncomfortable with and unsure of how to respond to strangers in the waiting room who would stare at Tony. She also shared the fact that once, in a shopping mall, a stranger had stopped her and asked, "What is wrong with that child? He looks funny." Mrs. Bartolli always ignored such comments and told Tony to do likewise, but she felt very hurt that others could be so insensitive. She tried hard not to let Tony know that she was hurt or embarrassed by these incidents and felt guilty at experiencing such emotions.

Even though Mrs. Bartolli did not say anything, the nurse knew that she was feeling anxiety not only about Tony's condition but also about how he would be accepted by the staff in the hospital. Sometimes when he was frightened, Tony exhibited behaviors typical of much younger children such as crying and kicking during procedures. The office nurse assured Mrs. Bartolli that she would contact the nurses on the unit to which Tony would be admitted to facilitate continuity of care, and that she also would keep in touch with Mrs. Bartolli by telephone.

The primary nurse assigned to care for Tony in the hospital had not had much experience working with children with developmental disabilities and was glad the office nurse had contacted her. She was thus able to prepare for the incoming admission more appropriately. Mrs. Bartolli was greatly relieved to see the rapport that the nurse quickly developed with Tony, and the acceptance with which she was greeted. By making positive initial impressions and establishing good communication regarding Tony's special needs, the nurse was able to build a relationship of mutual trust and respect with the family and to devise a nursing care plan that was appropriate and acceptable. During the procedure of venipuncture, when Tony cried and attempted to push the needle away, the nurse was able to reassure him and enlist his cooperation without expecting more of him than he was developmentally able to achieve. In addition, by demonstrating acceptance of Tony and his unique-

(continued)

ness as an individual, the nurse was providing an environment in which the parents could trust that Tony would be respected and given appropriate care. As a result, the parents did not need to resort to defensiveness or other inappropriate coping mechanisms during the hospitalization.

In this case, the nurse recognized that the family had a therapeutic self-care demand to decrease their anxiety about hospitalization and the fear of being rejected by hospital staff because of the special needs or physical appearance of Tony. By conferring and collaborating with hospital staff, the office nurse was acting as client advocate in alerting them to the special needs of both mother and child. Nurses working with individuals with developmental disabilities always must consider the family, not just the "identified patient," as the unit of service. By sharing information regarding the need to provide a developmental and supportive environment for Tony and his mother, the nurse was facilitating the universal self-care requisite of normalcy. An accepting, warm environment in the hospital setting can make a threatening and frightening experience less uncomfortable for both child and family and result in more cooperation and better outcomes for all.

SELF-CARE DEFICIT THEORY AND THE NURSING PROCESS

The nursing process is a well-accepted and systematic way of assessing an individual or family, developing a plan, providing care, and evaluating responses to nursing interventions. Most nurses use the nursing process as a way to solve problems and plan care, whether or not they use specific nursing theories as conceptual models. The Self-Care Deficit Nursing Theory provides a method to calculate deficits (assessment and diagnosis), plan care using appropriate methods of assistance, and evaluate the effectiveness of interventions. However, in order to make the theory more accessible to nurses unfamiliar with the specifics, it also can be incorporated into the five steps of the nursing process: assessment, diagnosis, planning, implementation, and evaluation. Thus it can be used as the organizing framework and philosophical foundation for the process, and can provide direction and meaning to the care plan, as illustrated in the following case studies.

CASE STUDY: COMMUNITY HEALTH PRACTICE SETTING

The Wolsey family was referred to the public health nurse for evaluation as the result of a phone call by Mr. Wolsey to the local Association for Retarded Citizens (The Arc). Mr. Wolsey had called to inquire if there were any services available to help them plan for their 32-year-old daughter Anne when he and his wife were no longer able to care for her at home or in the event of their deaths. Mr. Wolsey was retired but held a part time job; Mrs. Wolsey had never worked outside the home because of the need to provide constant care for Anne. Anne had never received any education or training, and Mr. Wolsey was not aware of any services available for her. The family income was limited. The Arc staff determined that this family had many problems for which further assessment was needed, and contacted the local health department. At first, Mr. Wolsey was suspicious and unreceptive to the idea

(continued)

of a home visit, but after the nurse explained that the purpose of her visit was to assist with finding community resources for Anne, he agreed to the visit.

The Wolseys lived in an older but well-kept neighborhood. On entering the home, the first thing the nurse noticed about the living room was its darkness: all the windows were covered with plywood, and only one lamp was lit. There were no curtains, carpets, or rugs in the room. After a brief introductory discussion, Mr. Wolsey took the nurse to Anne's room. The windows in this room also were covered with plywood, and the room was lit by a ceiling fixture. The only furniture in the room was a single bed that was neatly made. There were some toy blocks and a ball on the floor.

Anne was sitting in the center of the room on the bare floor rocking back and forth. She was dressed in long pants and a shirt, and had a short haircut that was routinely given by her mother. When approached by the nurse, Anne, who had lovely unblemished skin and deep brown eyes, got up, made a loud unintelligible vocalization, and proceeded to slap the nurse on the back. Mr. Wolsey explained that was her way of showing happiness. She then sat back down on the floor and resumed the rocking motions.

Mr. Wolsey did most of the talking on the first visit, and informed the nurse that, when Anne was very young, their family doctor had told them she was "hopelessly retarded" and that they should "put her away in an institution for the good of the family." The parents reluctantly agreed, and did place her in a state institution. They visited her weekly and were very disappointed in the quality of care she received. After an incident of suspected abuse, they took her home and attempted to deal with her increasingly destructive and unpredictable behaviors. The neighbors began to shun the family, several physicians refused to treat Anne, they could find no dentist who would see her after the first visit, and schools would not accept her. As a result of several years of increasing isolation, Mr. and Mrs. Wolsey decided that no one wanted to help them, so they assumed a position of "us against the world" and became as self-sufficient and isolated as possible, caring for Anne alone and dealing with her behavioral problems as best they could.

At about age 12, Anne began punching her fists through the windows, injuring herself several times. In order to keep her from hurting herself further, Mr. Wolsey installed plywood over the windows as a desperate attempt to deal with her behavior. Presently, she still has occasional temper tantrums, especially when forced to go outdoors. She is able to dress herself when there are no zippers or buttons, and she is toilet trained. One skill Anne has mastered is folding linen. Mrs. Wolsey says that she expertly matches corners and seems to enjoy doing this task over and over. Mrs. Wolsey taught her to do this several years ago, and they often give her linen or towels to fold in order to keep her busy.

Mr. and Mrs. Wolsey have not been out together since Anne was a child, because they have been unable or unwilling to leave her with anyone and feel it is unsafe to leave her unsupervised. Mr. Wolsey buys groceries and does all the shopping, and Mrs. Wolsey stays home and cares for Anne. They no longer know any of their neighbors because the neighborhood residents have changed since Anne was young. During leisure time, they watch television.

Anne had numerous grand mal seizures when she was young, and was treated with phenobarbital and Dilantin (phenytoin), the prescriptions for which continue to be refilled by the physician by telephone. The dosage has not been changed for

(continued)

several years, and no blood levels have been checked. Mrs. Wolsey reported that, at the last visit to the physician's office 5 years ago, Anne was unmanageable and the doctor agreed to continue refilling prescriptions by phone without seeing her in the office.

Mrs. Wolsey is still fearful that people do not understand Anne and do not have her best interests at heart, but knows that she and her husband will not always be around to care for her. She and her husband therefore reluctantly have decided to inquire about services.

Assessment

The nurse decided to focus on the family as a whole rather than isolate the "identified patient" because there were several complex family issues that warranted attention. In order to complete the assessment from the perspective of Self-Care Deficit Theory, the nurse categorized data by using the universal self-care requisites as a beginning point. In this case, she decided to address the universal requisite of promotion of normalcy as the most urgent one for the family at this time. She then listed all of the family needs (therapeutic self-care demands) in this category without attempting to prioritize their importance (see Table 3).

Planning

The nurse's next step was to put the list in priority order, and determine what feasible goals could be developed mutually, with the family incorporating their own concerns.

Self-Care Deficit #1: Inability to Trust   Because a decision by the family to seek medical evaluation and use community resources would depend on their ability to trust these services, the nurse decided to focus on the therapeutic need to develop a trusting relationship as the number one priority. Indeed, after listing the therapeutic self-care demands, it became clear that *all* therapeutic needs in this category revolved around the basic issue of reestablishing trust and contact with the community at large. Once trust has been established between the family and the nurse, mutual development of the plan can continue, ensuring a greater probability of follow-through by the family (see Table 4).

Rationale   Based on the family history and their experience with health care providers and individuals in the community in the past, the Wolseys will be reluctant to trust others now. Before any significant gains can be made, it is essential to establish a foundation of trust and respect in order to ensure follow-through by the family. Otherwise, they may be likely to revert to their previous coping methods of shutting out perceived "outsiders" and trying to manage on their own. They need to

---

Table 3.   Universal self-care requisite: Promotion of normalcy

In order to meet therapeutic self-care demands, this family needs to:

* Learn about progress in education and training for individuals with developmental disabilities that has occurred since Anne was young.
* Develop a trusting relationship with the larger community, including health care providers.
* Learn appropriate behavior management techniques for Anne.
* Learn about community resources that may be available to provide services.
* Seek further medical and developmental assessment for Anne.
* Begin to explore plans for Anne's future placement.
* Reorganize the household environment to be more developmentally appropriate for the family.
* Recognize the family strengths and develop or expand coping skills.

(continued)

Table 4. Nursing care plan for Wolsey family: First priority

Self-Care Deficit #1:	Inability of family to trust health care providers or community agencies as a result of past negative experiences
NANDA[a] Nursing Diagnosis:	Impaired health-seeking behaviors related to previous negative experiences with the health care system and resultant lack of trust
Long-Term Goal:	The family will develop a sense of trust in the nurse, the health care system, and the larger community as evidenced by their seeking and using available community resources

Short-term objectives/ desired outcomes	Interventions	Evaluation criteria
Family will permit nurse to make home visits on regular basis	Visit weekly in order to continue assessment and clarify parents' concerns and goals	After three visits, parents freely verbalize concerns and mutually determine time of visit with nurse
Family will seek consultation with social worker regarding financial eligibility for Anne to receive assistance or services from county, state, or federal sources	Provide family with names and telephone numbers of social workers; give examples of resources or assistance that may be available	After four visits, family will make contact with social worker
Family will use respite care services as appropriate	Provide name and telephone number of contact person; arrange for parents and Anne to make observation visit to respite care facility or home	After five visits, family will make observational visit to respite care source and make plan to apply for services

[a]North American Nursing Diagnosis Association.

be able to see successful programs and perhaps meet other parents who can reinforce the value of Anne's venturing out into the community. In addition, they must feel secure in the knowledge that Anne will not be mistreated or misunderstood, as in their earlier experiences.

Self-Care Deficit #2: Inability to Set Behavioral Limits   Because the behavioral problems were identified by the family as being of concern, and because the Wolseys need to be able to take Anne out of the house to facilitate normalization and keep appointments, the nurse chose the therapeutic self-care demand regarding behavior management as the second most important priority (see Table 5).

Rationale   The Wolseys are more likely to participate in activities that they have initiated; therefore, allowing them to make their own appointments will facilitate a successful outcome. By building on the family's successes and strengths, the nurse is enhancing self-esteem of family members and contributing to feelings of family competence. They will be better able to work on areas of weakness if they can recognize their assets. In addition, they may be able to adapt existing coping strategies to assist in their transition back into the community.

Implementation and Evaluation

The nurse visited weekly for 6 weeks, each time continuing the formal and informal assessment of Anne's developmental level and giving the parents some simple behavior management techniques, concentrating on positive reinforcement for appropriate behaviors. She also allowed Mr. and Mrs. Wolsey to discuss their previous experience and concerns for the present, listening in a nonjudgmental and thera-

(continued)

Table 5.   Nursing care plan for Wolsey family: Second priority

Self-Care Deficit #2:	Inability of parents to set behavioral limits for Anne as a result of established patterns and lack of knowledge of behavior management techniques
NANDA Nursing Diagnosis:	Ineffective family coping related to inability of parents to control self-abusive behaviors and violent outbursts of Anne
Long-Term Goal:	Parents will learn methods to deal with Anne's self-abusive behaviors and violent outbursts

Short-term objectives/ desired outcomes	Interventions	Evaluation criteria
Family will seek behavioral management counseling	Give parents names and phone numbers of agencies or specialists who can provide behavior management guidance in the home	Parents will make appointment and meet with behavior management specialist within 1 month
Family will verbalize their strengths and the successes they have had in coping with an individual with severe behavioral problems over many years	Reinforce family's strengths (i.e., they have done the best they could with a difficult situation for many years with almost no outside help, they taught Anne some activities of daily living, and they kept the family unit intact); in addition, note that they live in an area that has services available	Family will discuss their successes and coping mechanisms, sharing with the nurse how these strengths can be used as they begin to expand their interactions with the community and utilize community resources
Anne will be able to keep appointments without having tantrums	Explore parents' anxieties about taking Anne out in public; reinforce behavior management successes; meet family in clinic when they come in for appointment; give positive reinforcement to Anne for appropriate behaviors during visit	Anne will be able to cooperate with physician and nurse during physical examination; she gradually will be able to extend length of attending and participating in evaluations
Self-abusive and violent behaviors will decrease to level set by therapist	Role-model appropriate limit setting with Anne in a firm but caring manner; confer with therapist regarding care plan and therapeutic regimen	Monitor activity/behavior chart kept by parents

peutic way. She showed the parents how toys could be used to facilitate motor development and provide sensory stimulation at a level appropriate for Anne. Although it took more time than the nurse had anticipated, by the seventh week the parents had seen a positive change in Anne and had come to trust the nurse. They were then ready to proceed with seeking community resources, and initiated contact with a university assessment center and respite care facility. As the family came to rely on community providers more, and were satisfied with the quality of respite care received, the nurse decreased the frequency of home visits. She kept the case open to maintain contact, but as the self-care capability of the family increased, the need for nursing interventions decreased.

SUMMARY

Orem's Self-Care Deficit Theory of Nursing can be used as a foundation for providing nursing care to individuals with developmental disabilities. The theory proposes that developmental requirements are as important as universal self-care requirements and health deviation requirements. Orem's framework is a useful model for nurses caring for individuals with developmental disabilities and their families because it provides a general way to organize and deliver care, gives a systematic approach to assessment, addresses the need to provide a developmental environment that fosters achievement of maximum potential, can be used with the nursing process, and allows for the use of nursing diagnosis. In addition, it provides a philosophical approach that recognizes the innate potential in each individual, regardless of physical or mental limitations, and it values the right to self-determination and autonomy insofar as possible. It also provides focus and direction for nurses in role development in working with this population.

REFERENCES

American Nurses' Association. (1985). *Code for nurses with interpretive statements* (ANA Publication Code No. G-56 42M11/86R). Kansas City, MO: Author.

Clark, M.D. (1986). Application of Orem's theory of self care: A case study. *Journal of Community Health Nursing, 3,* 127–135.

Connelly, C.E. (1987). Self-care and the chronically ill patient. *Nursing Clinics of North America, 22,* 621–628.

Facteau, L. (1980). Self-care concepts and the care of the hospitalized child. *Nursing Clinics of North America, 22,* 145–155.

Jenny, J. (1991). Self-care deficit theory and nursing diagnosis: A test of conceptual fit. *Journal of Nursing Education, 30,* 227–232.

Moritz, D. (1982). Nursing diagnoses in relation to the nursing process. In D. Moritz & M. Kim (Eds.). *Classification of nursing diagnoses: Proceedings of the third and fourth national conferences* (pp. 53–57). New York: McGraw-Hill Publishing Company.

Mullin, V. (1980). Implementing the self-care concept in the acute care setting. *Nursing Clinics of North America, 22,* 177–190.

Orem, D. (1991). *Nursing concepts of practice* (4th ed.). St. Louis: C.V. Mosby.

Raven, M. (1989). Application of Orem's self-care model to nursing practice in developmental disability. *The Australian Journal of Advanced Nursing, 6*(2): 16–23.

Taylor, S. (1988, August). Nursing theory and nursing process: Orem's self care theory in practice. *Nursing Science Quarterly,* pp. 111–119.

Taylor, S. (1991, Spring). The structure of nursing diagnosis from Orem's theory. *Nursing Science Quarterly,* pp. 24–32.

Titus, S., & Porter, P. (1989). Orem's theory applied to pediatric residential treatment. *Pediatric Nursing, 15,* 465–468.

Walborn, K.A. (1980). A nursing model for the hospice: Primary and self-care nursing. *Nursing Clinics of North America, 15,* 205–217.

Yura, H., & Walsh, M. (1973). *The nursing process: Assessing, planning, implementing, evaluating* (2nd ed.) Norwalk, CT: Appleton-Century-Crofts.

6

Nursing Assessment and Diagnosis

Marisa C. Brown and Shirley P. Roth

OBJECTIVES

On completion of this chapter, the reader will be able to:

- Identify the essential elements of a nursing assessment.
- Identify considerations for individualizing nursing assessments.
- Use functional health patterns to individualize a nursing assessment.
- Formulate nursing diagnoses based on data obtained from a focused nursing assessment.
- Develop person-centered goals and objectives related to health promotion.

OVERVIEW

This chapter describes the use of a nursing assessment tool and the development of nursing diagnoses relevant to persons with developmental disabilities. Assessment and diagnosis are components of the nursing process that precede planning, implementation, and evaluation. Although this process follows a logical progression, frequently two or more components may occur at the same time (Yura & Walsh, 1987).

DEFINITION OF ASSESSMENT

Carpenito (1987) defined assessment as "the deliberate and systematic collection of data to determine a client's current health status and to evaluate his present and past coping patterns" (p. 40). The assessment (see Table 1) consists of data collected through a review of records, interviews with an individual or his or her family members or personal care assistant, a physical examination, and consultation with other professionals. The assessment phase concludes with the assignment of a nursing diagnosis.

Nursing assessments should capture the essence of nursing practice, which is the "diagnosis and treatment of human responses to actual or potential health problems" (American Nurses Association, 1980, p. 9). Assessments should be formulated in a manner that will assist the nurse in incorporating essential information into a plan of care that meets the needs of the individual being served. In the development of a plan of care that is person centered, nursing assessments should guide the nurse in focusing on the unique needs of the individual.

Assessment data must be comprehensive and must include the individual's strengths. The inclusion of strengths is not simply to mitigate a person's weaknesses. The accurate identification of areas of strength will form the foundation of a plan of care that will involve the individual as an integral part of the habilitation process, along with the case manager and/or team.

The use of a structured format for nursing assessment enables the nurse to gather consistent data on all individuals. This systematic process ensures that adequate information is elicited. The nurse uses this information to identify strengths and problems accurately. Caseload requirements may necessitate the use of abbreviated assessment

tools; therefore, it is important that the nurse analyze the needs of the practice setting in order to develop an appropriate tool.

ASSESSMENT PROCESS

A nursing data base reflects the individual's response to a real or potential problem. Nursing assessments that are based on information compiled only from other disciplines cannot result in an accurate nursing diagnosis. For example, an assessment that only notes special diets, dates of medical consultations, and a listing of prescribed medications fails to document the individual's response to problems associated with diet, medications, or illness. It is within the scope of nursing practice to treat the individual's response to these factors; therefore, a thorough nursing assessment documents the person's eating habits, level of independence in seeking medical care, and need for assistance in taking medication.

When developing an assessment tool to meet specific nursing practice needs, it is helpful to individualize the tool based on two components: the characteristics of the individuals to be assessed and the characteristics of the nurse's practice setting. Individual characteristics that should be considered are age and typical presenting problems. Age variables require a different focus at each chronological stage (i.e., children versus adults). Age variables primarily reflect who will be the informant on issues of confidentiality. For example, in assessing infants, the parents or caregivers will be the primary sources of information for the interview. However, as the child becomes older, he or she should be included in the interview. Confidentiality must be respected for adolescents and adults, particularly when sensitive issues (such as sexuality) are being discussed.

Table 1.   Elements of a nursing assessment

Review of records
Information gathered by interview
—Individual
—Family member
—Personal care assistant
Physical examination
Consultation with other professionals

NURSING DIAGNOSIS

Consideration also must be given to the practice setting and the reason for the assessment. Presenting problems may alter the assessment tool significantly. For example, evaluation of infants in a developmental assessment clinic will focus on developmental milestones and the parenting skills of the family. In contrast, for individuals evaluated at a mental health clinic, emphasis must be placed on the results of a mental status examination and on behavior and coping strategies.

The practice setting defines the time the nurse will have to spend in assessment. Outpatient clinics and acute care settings typically afford the briefest time for assessment. Long-term care settings or school-based health settings provide opportunities for ongoing assessment over time. When the practice setting is such that contact between the individual and the nurse is limited, a concise list of nursing diagnoses is likely to be generated. If the nurse is working with an individual and family over a prolonged period of time, a more comprehensive list of diagnoses will be developed. The nurse then prioritizes the need for intervention.

Assessment also must take into consideration collaboration with other disciplines. Participation as a member of an interdisciplinary team lends itself to a focused approach to health issues. The information from all disciplines is shared at the team meeting. The nurse presents the summary and recommendations of the nursing assessment; this information helps other team members to understand the impact of health issues on the individual's total program. The team meeting is an opportunity to decide how problem areas will be addressed. The nurse or any other team member may use a unidisciplinary approach in resolving some problems. Other issues may be managed more appropriately on a collaborative basis with one or more disciplines.

FUNCTIONAL HEALTH PATTERNS

The focused nursing assessment is divided into sections of functional health patterns. Gordon (1987) defined functional health patterns as those patterns that "contribute to the health, quality of life, and achievement of human potential. These common patterns are the focus of nursing assessment" (p. 92).

The determination of an individual's health patterns acts as a basis for understanding a person's functioning over time. In the event that a health deviation is noted, it can be compared with the individual's usual behavior or health data (blood pressure, pulse, laboratory values). In addition, the comparison of an individual's own patterns over time avoids contrasting that person's pattern with an artificial standard. This is of particular value to persons with developmental disabilities. Prior to the "normalization movement" in the 1970s, individuals with developmental disabilities were viewed within a medical context that only reflected deviance from the norm (Rubin & Crocker, 1989).

Assessment of an individual's health status within the framework of functional health patterns promotes the evaluation of each person as an individual, with comparisons reflected from his or her own baseline. For example, individuals with impaired air exchange resulting from physical deformity and immobilization are not compared to individuals who are ambulatory and participating in athletic activities. The individual's baseline is his or her own pattern of respiratory metabolism. Likewise, individuals with seizure disorders are not compared to individuals who are free of seizures. A measure of successful management may be one seizure per day for one individual, whereas for another it may be one seizure per month. It is important to establish each individual's baseline pattern and track it over time.

Two examples of focused nursing assessments are given at the end of this chapter (see Appendices A and B). This nursing assessment format is based on the work of Levine and Crosley (1986), but has been adapted for persons with developmental disabilities by the authors of this chapter, as further explained in this section. The cues used in these assessments are based on the information needed to plan health care for adults and children with developmental disabilities. In each practice setting, the nurse can adjust the cues within each functional health pattern. For example, sometimes more extensive health history data may be needed; at other times more information about a specific health pattern would be helpful.

If the nurse is responsible for assessing relatively large numbers of individuals within a short time frame, a checklist may be the format that yields the most consistent, comprehensive data. The nurse always should strive to obtain the most comprehensive data base possible. Sufficient information provides the basis for the development of nursing diagnoses. The plan of care then can be determined.

Aspects of Functional Health Patterns Specific to Individuals with Developmental Disabilities

Health Perception and Health Maintenance Patterns Data collected must describe the individual's health concerns and/or the concerns of family members and care providers when appropriate. Information regarding available health care resources and the individual's use of those resources must be substantiated. Data should support each individual's ability to access health services independently. Additionally, health education programs and the individual's response should be documented here.

Nutrition/Metabolic Pattern Data collected here reflect the individual's height, weight, diet, eating skills, and equipment needs. This information may be collected individually or in collaboration with team members from other disciplines such as nutrition, speech-language pathology, or occupational therapy. The potential for food and drug interactions should be reviewed.

Elimination Pattern Data collected here include a description of the individual's typical pattern of elimination, including bowel and bladder continence. An identification of problems such as constipation, diarrhea, and urinary incontinence or retention is done at this time. If the individual is not able to report his or her typical elimination pattern accurately, family members or the individual's support staff may need to provide this information. Accuracy of the assessment will be improved if the reporting individuals are taught how to describe the characteristics and frequency of stools and urine. When needed, a simple system of documentation can be developed. Any information gathered by physical examination (e.g., abdominal palpation) should be included here.

Activity–Exercise Pattern Data collected here should reflect ambulation ability and favorite activities. Special considerations include activity tolerance, the need for special evaluations (i.e., the need for cervical spine radiographs for individuals with Down syndrome), and the use of adaptive equipment. Data obtained from standardized tools, infant motor assessments, and leisure/recreation, occupational, and physical therapy reports can be included. Information that substantiates a typical rate of activity may be needed to assess response to medications for hyperactivity. The nurse may collaborate with psychologists or teachers to gather data.

Sleep/Rest Pattern Data collected on sleep must be very specific if they are to be helpful. Individuals vary widely in their need for sleep. Problems may be reported that are, in fact, inaccurate; for example, Tom is an adult with mental retardation who lives with his parents. Tom needs extensive supports in self-care, home living, health, and safety. Tom's mother reports that he awakens every morning at 4:30 A.M. As part of the assessment process, the nurse learns that Tom is going to sleep at 7:30 every evening. Therefore, he is getting 9 hours of sleep each night. Although this has been reported as a sleep pattern disturbance, in reality the problem is Tom's early bedtime.

Role/Relationship Pattern Data collected here refer to interaction with peers, family members, and others. This pattern looks at the person's role at home and in the community. It is important to consider how the individual communicates with others and the ability of the person to communicate health needs or the presence of pain.

Coping/Stress Tolerance Pattern Data collected here should identify sources of stress for the individual, including how the individual reacts to new experiences. It is important to identify areas of strength in coping skills and examine positive attitudes that reflect the individual's inner strengths. Self-stimulating and/or self-injurious behaviors must be described, along with approaches for management.

Sexuality/Reproductive Pattern Data collected here identify the individual's level of sexual activity and his or her knowledge base, including knowledge of safe sexual practices. For females, the nurse should obtain information about menstruation. This includes the date of menarche, menstrual patterns, and the use of contraceptives. Menopausal issues, including hormonal therapy, should be considered when indicated.

The nurse must respect the private nature of an individual's sexual practices. When there is no need for intervention, documentation should reflect sensitivity to privacy issues. For example, if a person is sexually active and uses appropriate precautions for the prevention of sexually transmitted diseases, the nursing assessment should state: "Personal sexuality discussed, no need for intervention."

Value/Belief Pattern Data collected here reflect individual/family preferences and opportunities to participate in religious activities. Ethnic and cultural practices should be identified and recognized.

EXAMPLE OF NURSING ASSESSMENT PROCESS

A detailed assessment of a woman being evaluated for community-based services is presented here to illustrate the functional health patterns assessment format. The individual's needs and the practice setting of the nurse determine the scope of data collection; a more concise format may be utilized to consolidate information. Each nurse is responsible for making adaptations to the assessment tool that maintain quality and promote efficiency.

CASE STUDY: COMMUNITY HEALTH PRACTICE SETTING

Name: Marilyn Lee
Age: 32 years
SSN: 111-22-3333
Birthdate: 2/19/60
Purpose of Exam: Initial evaluation for services

(continued)

Date of Evaluation: 2/19/92
Informants: Marilyn Lee, Ms. Gray (Ms. Lee's mother, with whom she resides)

Brief Health History

Ms. Lee is a 33-year-old female with a history of kidney transplant (1985), insulin-dependent diabetes mellitus, right leg fracture (1989), right hip replacement (1990), hearing and visual impairments, hypercholesterolemia, and chronic immunosuppressive and steroid therapy.

Current Medications

Cytoxan	25-mg tablet q A.M. PO
Prednisolone	10-mg tablet PO every other day
Bactrim	160-mg tablet PO
Dipyridamole	25 mg t.i.d. PO 1 hr before meals
Catapres	0.2 mg b.i.d. PO
Ultralente insulin	U-40 q A.M. SC

Because of her poor memory and poor visual skills, Ms. Lee relies on her mother to coordinate medication administration. Ms. Gray works with the nurse at the university hospital endocrine clinic regarding insulin dosage. There is much friction about this issue with Ms. Lee. Ms. Lee expresses frustration with her medications and treatments. She has a poor understanding of why they are necessary.

Allergies

Ms. Lee has no known food or medication allergies.

Individual's Health Concerns

Ms. Lee does not understand why she is taking medications. She expresses frustration that she is the only family member with so many health problems.

Family's Health Concerns

Ms. Gray expresses frustration over the constant struggle about diabetes management. She resents the time she must take off from work to accompany her daughter to medical appointments.

Functional Health Patterns

Health Perception and Health Maintenance Pattern   Ms. Lee receives her health care at a university hospital in the following clinics:
   Endocrine Clinic (789-1419): Melissa Terry, M.S./Susan Black, R.N.
   Renal Transplant Clinic (789-2020): David Romain, M.D./Eileen Cummings, R.N.
   Urology Clinic (789-3948): Sees rotating residents/Virginia Patty, R.N.
Mrs. Gray assumes responsibility for scheduling her daughter's appointments. Ms. Lee has signed a release of information form. This permits information from the specialty clinics to be incorporated into this report.

   Nutrition/Metabolic Pattern   The nurse in the Endocrine Clinic provides Ms. Gray with general nutritional guidelines related to her diabetes. The nurse has known and worked with this family over a 10-year period. She reports that some compliance is achieved only with the simplest of regimens. Ms. Lee does not follow any dietary program and often skips meals. She prefers to eat small meals. She states that she would like to learn how to cook.

(continued)

Elimination Pattern   Ms. Lee reports that she has occasional constipation. She denies having any urinary problems. However, the nurse from the urology clinic reports that Ms. Lee has had frequent urinary tract infections.

Personal Care/Bathing Pattern   Ms. Lee wears dentures, which she cleans every day. Ms. Lee attempts to bathe and dress herself independently. She has difficulty completing these tasks without assistance. According to Ms. Gray, when she offers help, her daughter becomes argumentative. When Ms. Lee is asked about menstrual care, she indicates a lack of knowledge.

Cognitive/Perceptual Pattern   A psychologist administered a battery of psychological tests to Ms. Lee within the past 3 months. The Wechsler Intelligence Scale for Children—Revised revealed an IQ of 65. No records of prior tests are available.

Significant limitations exist in the areas of communication, self-care, home living, social skills, community use, self-direction, health and safety, functional academics, leisure, and work. Test results also indicate significant deficits in short-term memory. These results appear to reflect deterioration over time, but it was not possible to determine the etiology or extent of these changes.

Neurological changes can be attributed to the effects of chronic renal disease; however, the most recent report from the renal transplant clinic shows no evidence of renal failure. Another potential source of problems could be vascular changes secondary to her diabetes.

Ms. Lee reports that she is afraid, although she cannot identify the cause of her fear.

Ms. Lee wears eyeglasses to correct presbyopia. She has not had a vision examination in 4 years.

Ms. Lee reports herself to be legally deaf. She states that at one time she had hearing aids. They were lost several years ago and she is not interested in getting them replaced. She did, however, agree to talk to an audiologist.

Ms. Lee uses gestures and a few signs to augment her speech. Her mother does not use any signs.

Activity/Exercise Pattern   Ms. Lee was formerly independent in going out of the home. She can no longer do this because of her decreased physical mobility. Ms. Lee walks very slowly, with a shuffling gait and poor balance. Because of her physical limitations, she tends to be very sedentary. Ms. Lee states that she enjoys coloring and drawing, but her mother discourages these activities because they are "babyish."

Sleep/Rest Pattern   Ms. Lee reports occasional problems falling asleep. She ingests approximately 1 quart of diet sodas with caffeine daily.

Role/Relationship Pattern   Ms. Lee's hearing impairment poses a barrier in communication. She states that she has some friends, but her difficulty in communicating places limitations on reciprocal relationships.

Ms. Lee is employed at Paramount Industries and engages in simple clerical duties. She has been there for 3 years and seldom misses a day of work.

Coping/Stress Tolerance Pattern   Ms. Lee verbalizes anger about things she cannot do and frequently engages in arguments about this. When asked if she feels sad, she replies, "A little bit."

Sexuality/Reproductive Pattern   Ms. Lee expresses an interest in men. She has a boyfriend from work who calls her on the phone. She acknowledges that her hearing impairment makes it difficult to follow his conversation.

(continued)

She indicates that she is not sexually active. Her mother reports that several years ago an incident of rape was suspected but never confirmed. Ms. Lee denies any recollection of the incident.

Value/Belief Pattern   Ms. Lee reluctantly attends the Baptist church with her mother. She reports that she would be more interested in attending the church if she had more friends there. Ms. Gray is very religious, and has difficulty accepting her daughter's lack of enthusiasm for church activities.

Summary

Ms. Lee's complex health needs and past history contribute to the apparent change in behavior and skills noted during the assessment process. Stress and conflict within the home environment may have intensified the problems. The changes in her level of independence are of concern, as are the results of cognitive testing, which reflect a deterioration in her short-term memory capabilities. Neurological assessments may serve to help determine the etiology of these changes. Further evaluations of her neurological, vascular, renal, and diabetic status will need to be performed and coordinated in order to determine the reasons for changes in functioning and behavior.

Ms. Lee's major strengths are in the area of social skills development. Most of the time she is able to communicate her ideas and concerns. She can greet and respond to others appropriately in social settings. She also has demonstrated the ability to perform satisfactorily at work. Support and assistance for the development of more effective stress management and coping strategies will enhance the quality of life for Ms. Lee and her family.

Nursing Diagnoses
1. Altered health maintenance related to inability to make judgments; impaired communication, cognition, and memory; and ineffective family coping
2. Noncompliance with diabetic care regimen related to cognitive impairment
3. Potential for infection related to diabetes and immunosuppressant therapy
4. Potential for injury related to balancing difficulties/decreased mobility
5. Activity intolerance related to decreased mobility
6. Impaired physical mobility related to discomfort secondary to hip replacement
7. Self-care deficit: bathing and dressing, related to cognitive impairment
8. Diversional activity deficit related to lack of age-appropriate activities
9. Anxiety possibly related to chronic illness
10. Altered family processes related to Ms. Lee's chronic illness and her cognitive and emotional functioning

Recommendations

Because of the complex nature of Ms. Lee's situation, the recommendations are divided into those that are short term and those that are long term. The nurse evaluating Ms. Lee for community-based services may not be the person who will work with her on a long-term basis. However, the nurse should make recommendations based on the results of the initial assessment. Future health care providers can consider these recommendations as they plan and implement care for Ms. Lee. In this way, continuity of care can be assured.

(continued)

Short-Term Recommendations

1. Referral to primary care physician for overall health management and coordination of consultant specialists in endocrine, renal transplant, and urology clinics
2. Referral for neurology consultation to evaluate etiology of memory impairment
3. Referral to occupational or physical therapist for evaluation and recommendations to promote safe mobility
4. Referral to audiology clinic for evaluation
5. Referral to speech-language pathologist in order to determine whether Ms. Lee's communication could be improved with further training
6. Referral to therapeutic recreation specialist to assist in the identification of appropriate leisure/recreational activities
7. Referral for respite services in order to support Ms. Gray as a caregiver
8. Referral for individual and family counseling in order to improve stress management skills and coping strategies
9. Consultation with the team psychologist in order to determine Ms. Lee's optimal learning style
10. Development of a comprehensive health teaching plan

Long-Term Recommendations

1. Establishment of nursing case management services to coordinate Ms. Lee's multiple health issues:
    a. To focus on the development and implementation of a comprehensive, integrated health plan that is acceptable to Ms. Lee and her mother.
    b. Utilization of simple medication management and nutrition programs.
2. Exploration of long-term residential options such as respite services, group homes, or supported living apartments.

Incorporating the Assessment into a Habilitation Plan

The nursing assessment and recommendations were shared with Ms. Lee, her mother, and other team members at the interdisciplinary team meeting. At such meetings, the other team members may agree with some or all of the nurse's recommendations. Based on Ms. Lee's nursing assessment, the team agreed to all of the nursing recommendations because they were supported by the findings of the other disciplinary evaluations. The team also agreed that Ms. Lee has a need for health teaching to assist her in understanding the nature of her chronic illness and her role in maintaining her own good health.

Because Ms. Lee was referred for an initial evaluation for services, the interdisciplinary team, including Ms. Lee and her mother, next developed an individualized habilitation plan that incorporates input from all disciplines represented on the team. Determining Ms. Lee's optimal learning style is an essential component of developing an effective health teaching program. However, because the discipline-specific evaluations all support the need for further neuropsychological testing, development of a health teaching program will be coordinated with the psychologist based on the results of further neuropsychological testing to determine more precisely her cognitive limitations and the most effective teaching strategies.

NURSING DIAGNOSIS

Once the nursing assessment data have been systematically collected and documented, the information must be analyzed. A number of factors influence each nurse's approach to this process. These include educational preparation, depth and breadth of clinical experience, specialty preparation, and collaborative opportunities with other nurses or other health professionals. Nurses can supplement their own expertise by consulting reference materials, other nurses, or other members of the interdisciplinary team. By incorporating the assessment data, information from reference materials, and input from colleagues, the nurse is able to draw a conclusion about the existence of a problem that is within the domain of nursing to treat. This conclusion is then stated as a nursing diagnosis.

Many versions of the definition of nursing diagnosis have emerged since the term was first introduced in 1953. Historical accounts of the first conference on nursing diagnosis held in 1973 and the evolving process of the use of nursing diagnoses are available in texts devoted to the subject (Carpenito, 1987; Gordon, 1987). Many definitions of nursing diagnosis have been published. These are reflected in the American Nurses' Association's *Social Policy Statement* (1980) definition of nursing: "Nursing is the diagnosis and treatment of human response to actual or potential health problems" (p. 9). Two widely recognized definitions of nursing diagnosis are:

Actual or potential health problems which nurses, by virtue of their education and experience, are capable and licensed to treat (Gordon, 1976, p. 1299)

A statement that describes the human response (health state or actual/potential altered interaction pattern) of an individual or group that the nurse can legally identify and for which the nurse can order the definitive interventions to maintain the health state or to reduce, eliminate, or prevent alterations (Carpenito, 1987, p. 24)

The North American Nursing Diagnosis Association (NANDA) exists for the purpose of developing, refining, and promoting a taxonomy of nursing diagnostic terminology of general use to professional nurses. Formed in 1982, NANDA has approximately 100 diagnostic categories approved for clinical testing and refining. Each diagnostic category states a definition, contributing factors in or risk factors contributing to the altered state of health, and defining characteristics. These defining characteristics are the data necessary to support the nurse's conclusion or diagnosis. The nursing data must be present in the assessment before that particular diagnosis can be assigned accurately.

Developing a Nursing Diagnosis

An actual nursing diagnosis is written in a three-part statement that includes the diagnosis, the contributing factors, and associated signs and symptoms.

Gerald Schmidt's usual bowel movement pattern is once daily. Staff in the home where Gerald resides report that his stools over the past week have been hard, and he is spending more time in the bathroom but does not defecate. He has not had a bowel movement in 3 days.

Problem statement: Alteration in bowel elimination: constipation.

Problem statement and contributing factors: Alteration in bowel elimination: constipation, related to difficulty with defecation.

(continued)

Problem statement, contributing factors, and signs and symptoms: Alteration in bowel elimination: constipation, related to difficulty with defecation as manifested by hard and infrequent stools.

The nurse develops and implements a bowel regimen to relieve constipation. This is done with the individual, family members, caregivers, and physician as appropriate, depending on the practice setting. Such a program may include nursing orders for increased fluids and fiber on a daily basis. Stool softeners, laxatives, and suppositories are used when indicated. This program must be evaluated on a regular basis and modified as necessary.

A nursing assessment may lead the nurse to conclude that an individual is at risk for potential problems. In this case, the problem statement and contributing factors are preceded by the word *potential*. This then documents the need for the development of a preventive potential problems. This diagnosis is written in a two-part statement.

A third qualifier to a nursing diagnosis is the term *possible*. This is used when an accurate diagnosis cannot be made with the information available, but the nurse suspects that a particular

Mary Day is a 35-year-old woman who has decided to move from her family home to a supervised apartment. Although she feels she is ready for this move, in the past transitions have been difficult for her.

Problem statement: Potential for anxiety.

Problem statement and related factors: Potential for anxiety related to transition from a family home to a semi-independent living arrangement.

The nurse, in conjunction with Ms. Day and the support staff for the apartment, develop a plan that addresses possible short-term stressors during this transition period.

plan. Clearly many health promotion efforts aimed at individuals with compromised physical abilities or chronic illness are directed at prevention of diagnosis is applicable. While assessment data are being gathered or other team members are being consulted, it is acceptable to document the diagnosis.

Cecile Jones is a 30-year-old woman with thick black hair and lively brown eyes who is able to walk independently. She is legally blind, has mentally retardation, and is nonverbal. She had resided in an institution for persons with mental retardation for 20 years. One month ago Ms. Jones and two women from her living unit in the institution moved into a home in the community. The staff who provide services and supports in the community residence have collaborated with the institutional staff to ensure a smooth transition. Ms. Jones is in the initial stages of becoming adjusted and acclimated to her new home, community, and supported work setting. During

(continued)

---

the past week the staff noted that Ms. Jones resumed some former behavior patterns such as rubbing her head to the point of hair loss and being irritable in the early morning hours. While reviewing her records from the institution, the nurse notes some references to possible premenstrual syndrome.

Several problem statements should be considered, such as these for Cecile Jones: data is essential. A variety of reference books and pocket manuals are available

---

Problem Statement: Possible alteration in comfort.

Problem statement and related factors: Possible alteration in comfort related to premenstrual syndrome.

Data will need to be collected and documentation made regarding her menstrual cycle in conjunction with behavioral observations.

Problem Statement: Possible anxiety.

Problem statement and related factors: Possible anxiety related to change in living situation, new caregivers, and new employment setting.

The management of these factors will require collaboration with team members. The nurse also will need to monitor this behavioral pattern as a possible indication of an acute illness.

Problem Statement: Possible alteration in comfort.

Problem statement and related factors: Possible alteration in comfort related to an unknown source of pain.

A thorough physical examination may be needed. Collaboration with a physician and referral for appropriate diagnostic tests should be done as necessary.

It is essential for the nurse to prioritize the list of nursing diagnoses (Table 2). Prioritization is a decision that should be made in conjunction with the individual, family, and support staff as appropriate. Consideration must be given to the practice setting. It must be determined if the plan of care will be carried out by the nurse and the individual, or if the problem is one that requires collaboration with other disciplines.

Use of Reference Materials

The use of a reference manual for the purpose of formulating the diagnosis and validating sufficient assessment

(Table 3). These typically contain tables that cite nursing diagnoses in alphabetical order. They provide a definition of the diagnosis along with its defining characteristics. In order to assure accuracy and standardization in the application of nursing diagnosis, the practitioner must refer to the defining characteristics

Table 2. Factors to be considered when prioritizing nursing diagnoses

- Concerns identified by the individual, family, and/or staff
- Health and safety issues
- Practice setting (e.g., acute care, outpatient clinic, workshop)
- Type and availability of personnel and resources needed to implement the plan of care
- Time considerations

Table 3.   Suggested reference books on nursing diagnosis

Campbell, C. (1984). *Nursing diagnosis & intervention in nursing practice* (2nd ed.). Albany, NY: Deimar.
Carpenito, L. J. (1987). *Handbook of nursing diagnosis* (2nd ed.). Philadelphia: J. B. Lippincott.
Carpenito, L. J. (1987). *Nursing diagnosis: Application to clinical practice* (2nd ed.). Philadelphia: J. B. Lippincott.
D'Argenio, C. (1991). *Implementing nursing diagnosis-based practice: Managing the change*. Gaithersburg, MD: Aspen Publishers.
Doenges, M. E., & Moorhouse, M. F. (1991). *Nurse's pocket guide: Nursing diagnoses with interventions* (3rd ed.). Philadelphia: F. A. Davis.
Duespohl, R. A. (1986). *Nursing diagnosis manual for the well & ill client*. Philadelphia: W. B. Saunders.
Ferri, R. S. (1992). *Care planning for the older adult: Nursing diagnosis in long-term care*. Philadelphia: W. B. Saunders.
Gordon, M. (1982). *Manual for nursing diagnosis*. New York: McGraw-Hill.
Gordon, M. (1991). *Nursing diagnosis: Process & W. B. application*. Philadelphia: W. B. Saunders.
Kim, M. (1990). *Practice guide to nursing diagnosis* (4th ed.). St. Louis: Mosby-Year Book.
Kim, M. J., & Moritz, D. A. (Eds.). (1982). *Classification of nursing diagnosis: Proceedings of the third & fourth national conferences*. New York: McGraw-Hill.
Lederer, J. R. (1988). *Care planning pocket guide: A nursing diagnosis approach*. Redding, MA: Addison-Wesley.
McFarland, F. K. (1989). *Nursing diagnosis: Theory & practice*. St. Louis: Mosby-Year Book.
McFarland, F. K., & Wasli, E. L. (1986). *Nursing diagnosis & process in psychiatric-mental health nursing*. Philadelphia: J. B. Lippincott.
Michael Reese Hospital & Medical Center staff nursing care plans: Nursing diagnosis & intervention No. 2. (1990). St. Louis: Mosby-Year Book.
Miller, E. (1989). *Diagnosis-based nursing practice*. East Norwalk, CT: Appleton & Lange.
Neal, M. C. (1990). *Nursing diagnosis care plans for diagnosis-related groups*. Boston: Jones & Barlett.
Nursing diagnosis care plans for DSM-III-R. (1991). Venice, CA: General Medical Publishers.
Taylor, C. M., & Sparks, S. M. (1993). *Nursing diagnosis cards* (7th ed.). Springhouse, PA: Springhouse Publications.

of each diagnosis before coming to a conclusion. The nurse must determine that sufficient data have been collected to meet the criteria for the defining characteristics of that diagnosis.

Collaborative Nursing Diagnosis

Carpenito (1987) emphasizes that the full range of nursing practice is not limited to the establishment of nursing diagnosis alone. She points out that nursing practice is frequently collaborative.

She defines collaborative problems as "the physiological complications that have resulted or may result from pathophysiological and treatment-related situations. Nurses monitor to detect their onset/status and collaborate with medicine (or other disciplines) for definitive treatment" (p. 24). Collaborative practice is especially relevant for most nurses working with persons with developmental disabilities as part of an interdisciplinary team:

Alicia Sanchez is 14 years old and has juvenile rheumatoid arthritis. She has mental retardation, is nonverbal, and has a limited but functional repertoire of sign language. She receives ibuprofen 400 mg t.i.d. for relief of pain and inflammation. Over the past 2 months, Alicia has refused to participate in many activities that she previously enjoyed. Increasingly, she is spending more time by herself. She becomes very agitated early in the morning and in the later afternoons on school days. She is refusing to get out of bed five mornings out of seven, and her appetite has decreased.

Based on this information, the following nursing diagnosis is made:

(continued)

> *Problem statement and contributing factors:* Alteration in comfort level secondary to chronic inflammation of the joints.
>
> Referrals are made to the following team members for input:
>
>   Primary Care Pediatrician: Reevaluate Alicia's present pain medication regimen and develop strategies for improved pain management.
>
>   Speech-Language Pathologist: Evaluate Alicia's ability to communicate changes in comfort level (see Barks, chap. 9, this volume).
>
>   Physical and Occupational Therapists: Evaluate Alicia for equipment, environmental modification, and positioning and exercise routines to minimize stress on the joints and maintain maximum mobility and independence.
>
>   Leisure/Recreation Therapist: Determination of age-appropriate leisure and recreational activities that accommodate Alicia's interests and do not aggravate her joint pain.

TRANSLATING THE NURSING ASSESSMENT INTO THE PROGRAM PLAN

Once the nurse reviews all of the information gathered as part of the assessment process and formulates the nursing diagnoses, these can be used to identify treatment options that are likely to be successful. As with nursing diagnoses, reference materials may be helpful in developing a treatment program (see Table 4).

In most settings, the nurse working with individuals with developmental disabilities will be part of a team that is responsible for the development of a written habilitation plan (see Russell & Free, chap. 3, this volume). The plan must be written accurately and concisely. Nursing diagnoses form the basis for the nurse's contribution to the individual's plan. Nursing diagnoses must be expressed in terms that are easily understood by all team participants. The language of nursing diagnosis must be "translated" into an education-based format that uses terms such as *goals* and *objectives*.

Goals are expressed in behaviorally stated terms. They reflect the time frame necessary for the individual to achieve the desired outcome. Long-term goals are very broad. They provide an overview of what the individual is hoping to accomplish over time. Short-term goals identify outcomes to be achieved in the near future. Goals must be measurable in order to be implemented and evaluated. Objectives are used to identify specific tasks that must be completed as steps toward the fulfillment of the broader, more encompassing goal.

Goals and objectives must consider the identified strengths and needs of the individual. For purposes of consistency and thoroughness, it is helpful to identify areas of strengths and needs within a framework. The American Association on Mental Retardation (1992), in its *Definition, Classification, and Systems of Supports,* identified the following areas of adaptive functioning: communication, self-care, home living, social skills, community use, self-direction, health and safety, functional academics, leisure, and work.

Health concerns and related nursing issues may occur in any of these areas. Specific goals and objectives should be developed for each need identified by the team:

Table 4. Suggested references for program development

Gardner, J. F., & Chapman, M. S. (1990). *Program issues in developmental disabilities: A guide to effective habilitation and active treatment* (2nd ed.). Baltimore: Paul H. Brookes Publishing Co.

Mager, R. F. (1984). *Preparing instructional objectives* (2nd rev. ed.). Belmont, CA: Lake Publishing Co.

Problem statement and related factors: Knowledge deficit related to information about medication regimen.

Goal: Roger deBoer will be able to state the names of his medications, their purpose, and time of day when they are administered.

Objective #1: Mr. deBoer will state the names of his medications with 100% accuracy.

Objective #2: Mr. deBoer will state the purpose of each of his medications with 100% accuracy.

Objective #3: Mr. deBoer will identify the time of day for medication administration with 100% accuracy.

The progress toward achieving these objectives can be charted in progress notes utilizing the appropriate nursing diagnosis:

in the plan must be evaluated periodically (see Russell & Free, chap. 3, this volume).

Mr. deBoer now is able to name correctly one of the three medications he takes each day. When his personal care assistant asks, "What is the name of the medication that you take to prevent seizures?", he can correctly identify Dilantin 100% of the time. His assistant will continue to work with Mr. deBoer to identify the time of day for medication administration.

Once the team, including the individual, decides on the program plan, data are collected throughout the implementation process. Data collection can be done directly by the person or with the assistance of staff. For example, an individual can learn to monitor fluid intake by using charts that assist him or her to remember when to take fluids. The program plan and the individual's progress toward the goals and objectives

SUMMARY

This chapter has dealt with the use of a focused nursing assessment that leads to the establishment of nursing diagnoses. Functional health patterns form the basis for the collection of health data that reflect the needs of individuals with developmental disabilities. Nursing diagnoses serve as the basis for nursing intervention within the context of an individual's treatment plan.

REFERENCES

American Association on Mental Retardation. (1992). *Mental retardation: Definition, classification, and systems of support* (special 9th ed.). Washington, DC: Author.

American Nurses Association. (1980). *Nursing: A social policy statement.* Kansas City, MO: Author.

Carpenito, L. (1987). *Nursing diagnosis: Application to clinical practice* (2nd ed.). Philadelphia: J.B. Lippincott.

Gordon, M. (1987). *Nursing diagnosis: Process and application* (2nd ed.). New York: McGraw-Hill.

Levine, R.F., & Crosley, J.M. (1986). Focused data collection for the generation of nursing diagnoses. *Journal of Nursing Staff Development, 2,* 56–64.

Rubin, I.L., & Crocker, A.C. (1989). *Developmental disabilities: Delivery of medical care for children and adults.* Philadelphia: Lea & Febiger.

Yura, H., & Walsh, M. (1987). *The nursing process* (5th ed.). Norwalk, CT: Appleton & Lange.

Appendix A. Nursing Assessment of Adults

Name _____   Age _____
Social Security No. _____   Birthdate _____
Medicaid No. _____   Date of report _____
Purpose of Exam _____   Examiner _____

BRIEF HEALTH HISTORY

Hospitalizations _____
_____

Illnesses _____
_____

Changes in medication _____
_____

SIGNIFICANT FAMILY HISTORY

Cardiac problems/hypertension _____
_____

Diabetes _____
_____

Seizures _____
_____

Cancer _____
_____

Known genetic disorders _____
_____

CURRENT MEDICATIONS

Self-administered? _____
_____

Brown, M. C., & Roth, S. P. (1994). Nursing assessment and diagnosis. In S. P. Roth & J. Morse (Eds.), *A life-span approach to nursing care for individuals with developmental disabilities*. Copyright © 1994 by Paul H. Brookes Publishing Co.

(*continued*)

Tablet, crushed, liquid _____

Approach/response _____

ALLERGIES

Food _____

Medications _____

Unusual response/reaction _____

INDIVIDUAL'S HEALTH CONCERNS

Care provider _____

Family member _____

Advocate _____

HEALTH PERCEPTION AND HEALTH MAINTENANCE PATTERN

Consultations _____

Immunizations _____

Listing of lab tests and results _____

Tardive dyskinesia screening results _____

Breast self-exam _____

Vital signs _____

NUTRITION/METABOLIC PATTERN

Height/Weight _____

(*continued*)

(continued)

Underweight/overweight _____

Diet _____

Eating skills _____

Adaptive equipment _____

Precautions (e.g., choking) _____

Positioning _____

ELIMINATION PATTERN

Urinary incontinence (day vs. night) _____

Urinary frequency _____

Bowel frequency _____

Diarrhea _____

Constipation _____

PERSONAL CARE/BATHING PATTERN

Description of self-care skill level _____

Tub/shower _____

Toileting _____

Adaptive needs _____

Toothbrushing (dental care) _____

Skin assessment _____

Lotions/powders _____

(continued)

Hair care _____

Shaving (males) _____

Menstrual hygiene (female) _____

COGNITIVE/PERCEPTUAL PATTERN

Vision screening
—Use of glasses _____

Hearing screening
—Use of hearing aid _____

Unusual reactions to heat, cold, textures _____

Tested level of cognitive functioning _____

Tested level of adaptive
functioning (tests used) _____

Survival skills _____

ACTIVITY/EXERCISE PATTERN

Cervical spine radiograph _____

Use of helmets _____

Swimming precautions (epilepsy) _____

Adaptive equipment _____

Ambulation level _____

Favorite activities
—Appropriate to age _____
—Appropriate to tolerance level _____

Community travel skills _____

(continued)

(continued)

SLEEP/REST PATTERN

Hours of sleep _____

Hour awakens _____

Up at night? _____

Trouble falling asleep? _____

Trouble staying asleep? _____

Use of sleep aids _____

Use of caffeine _____

Naps during day? _____

Bed rails _____

ROLE/RELATIONSHIP PATTERN

Socialization patterns
—Prefers to be alone _____
—Initiates interaction with peers, staff, family _____

Vocational activity _____

Communication patterns _____

COPING/STRESS TOLERANCE PATTERN

Reaction to new experiences _____

Behavior management programs _____

Self-stimulatory behaviors _____

Self-injurious behaviors _____

Strengths in coping _____

History of abuse _____

(continued)

SEXUALITY/REPRODUCTIVE PATTERN

Sexually active? _____

_____

Masturbation
  —Appropriate vs.
   inappropriate behavior _____

Sex education programs _____

_____

_____

Menses
  —Cycle length _____
  —Regularity _____

History of abuse _____

_____

VALUE/BELIEF PATTERN

Religious preference _____

_____

Participation level _____

_____

Preferred site of worship _____

_____

SUMMARY

NURSING DIAGNOSES

RECOMMENDATIONS

_____   /_____
               Signature   /Date

Appendix B. Nursing Assessment of Children

Name _____   Age _____
Social Security No. _____   Birthdate _____
Medicaid No. _____   Date of report _____
Purpose of Exam _____   Examiner _____

BRIEF HISTORY AND NEONATAL PROBLEMS

Prenatal history _____

Type of delivery _____

Condition at birth _____

Illnesses/surgeries _____

Otitis media _____

Respiratory infections _____

SIGNIFICANT FAMILY HISTORY

Cardiac problems/hypertension _____

Diabetes _____

Cancer _____

Known genetic disorders _____

Seizures _____

(continued)

HIV/AIDS _____

Hepatitis A or B _____

CURRENT MEDICATIONS

Tablet (crushed, liquid) _____

Approach/response _____

ALLERGIES

Food _____

Medications _____

Unusual response/reaction _____

INDIVIDUAL'S HEALTH CONCERNS

Care provider _____

Family member _____

Advocate _____

HEALTH PERCEPTION AND HEALTH MAINTENANCE PATTERN

Parent/guardian's concerns _____

Consultations _____

Immunizations _____

Listing of lab tests and results _____

Vital signs _____

Well child exams _____

(continued)

(continued)

NUTRITION/METABOLIC PATTERN

Height/weight _____

Under/overweight _____

Diet _____

Eating skills _____

Adaptive equipment _____

Precautions (e.g., choking) _____

Positioning _____

ELIMINATION PATTERN

History of urinary tract infections _____

Stool consistency/color _____

Toileting issues _____

PERSONAL CARE/BATHING PATTERN

Description of self-care skill level _____

Dressing _____

Toileting _____

Feeding _____

Tooth brushing _____

Visits to dentist _____

Skin assessment _____

Lotions/powders _____

(continued)

COGNITIVE/PERCEPTUAL PATTERN

Vision screening
　—Use of glasses _____

Hearing screening
　—Use of hearing aid _____

Unusual reactions to heat, cold, textures _____

Tested level of cognitive functioning _____
Tested level of adaptive functioning (tests used) _____

ACTIVITY/EXERCISE PATTERN

Typical activity level _____

Adaptive equipment _____

Ambulation level _____

Favorite activities
　—appropriate to age _____
　—appropriate to tolerance level _____
Use of car seats _____

SLEEP/REST PATTERN

Hours of sleep _____

Hour awakens _____

Up at night? _____

Trouble falling asleep? _____

Trouble staying asleep? _____

Naps during day? _____

Crib/rails _____

(continued)

(continued)

ROLE/RELATIONSHIP PATTERN

Parenting skill strengths/needs _____

_____

Socialization patterns _____

_____

Communication patterns _____

_____

Use of toys _____

_____

COPING/STRESS TOLERANCE PATTERN

Reaction to new experiences _____

_____

Self-stimulatory behaviors _____

_____

Strengths in coping _____

_____

Self-comfort level _____

_____

History of abuse _____

_____

SEXUALITY/REPRODUCTIVE PATTERN

Identification of body parts _____

_____

Awareness of own gender _____

_____

Masturbation _____

_____

FAMILY VALUE/BELIEF PATTERN

Religious preference _____

_____

Cultural practices _____

_____

Extended family involvement _____

(continued)

SUMMARY

NURSING DIAGNOSES

RECOMMENDATIONS:

_____ /
              Signature   /Date

7

Health Maintenance and Promotion

Infancy Through Adolescence

Carolyn I. Steadham

OBJECTIVES

On completion of this chapter, the reader will be able to:

- Identify the special needs of the family whose child has a developmental disability, and describe the way in which these needs affect the life of the child and family.
- List at least five common physiological problems that place the child with a developmental disability at risk for impaired health.
- Describe the role of the nurse in maintaining and/or promoting health for the child with a developmental disability.
- Discuss strategies that the nurse can utilize to promote positive, community-based supports that enhance the health of the family with a child who has a developmental disability.

OVERVIEW

A holistic approach is utilized in this chapter to provide guidelines and cues for the nurse providing health maintenance and promotion services from late pregnancy through adolescence. Special emphasis is placed on anticipatory planning for expected developmental changes in the child and in the family. Health issues associated with including the child with delayed physical,

147

language, and social development in community programs are discussed. Interventions are suggested for facilitating healthy family dynamics and supporting individual developmental growth for each member of the family.

HEALTH MAINTENANCE FOR PERSONS WITH DEVELOPMENTAL DISABILITIES

Historically, persons with developmental disabilities were cared for in large public institutions or private residential hospitals. At this time they are increasingly part of society's mainstream. In 1975, the Education for All Handicapped Children Act (PL 94-142) radically changed the community's responsibility for educating children with developmental disabilities. Children with disabilities have become part of the public school system. Motion pictures and television programs featuring persons with developmental disabilities give testimony to the inclusion of individuals with developmental disabilities into all segments of society.

Advances in medicine and allied health disciplines, improved surgical techniques, and the advent of newer technologies have saved and extended the lives of many individuals with developmental disabilities. A generation of babies are alumni of neonatal intensive care units (NICUs), many of whom survive with multiple disabilities. Approximately 18% of very low birth weight infants have severe disabilities (Grogaard, Lindstrom, Parker, Culley, & Stahlman, 1990).

Programs such as Medicaid and Medicare have improved access to acute care. However, it is difficult to obtain health care for children with developmental disabilities. It often is difficult to meet the needs of the families that are associated with the care of these children (Steele, 1990). For this population, there is limited access to services that focus on health maintenance, health promotion,

prevention of illness, and early intervention for identified problems.

Our health care system's focus on the "sick model" of service delivery is partially to blame for this problem. Additionally, most education programs for health professionals lack curriculum content specific to developmental disabilities. When content is included, it usually takes the form of assigned reading or a lecture and does not include clinical experience. Therefore, health professionals caring for individuals with developmental disabilities focus on the pathology of the disability rather than on health promotion/health maintenance activities.

PRENATAL PERIOD

The availability of prenatal diagnosis and genetic counseling gives parents information about their child months before the time of birth. Supporting the parents through the diagnostic procedure is an essential component of the nurse's role. If the parents choose not to have prenatal diagnostic tests performed during pregnancy, the nurse has an equal responsibility to support this decision. Parents who learn that the child they are expecting has a diagnosis associated with developmental disability may choose to have that child. Religious beliefs, difficulty in conceiving, or strong feelings of love for and commitment to the expected child may contribute to such a decision (Benkendorf, Corson, Allen, & Ilse, 1992). Anticipatory counseling regarding the special needs of the child, if known, should be undertaken early in the pregnancy. Parents should be assisted at this time in identifying services the child may need in early infancy to avoid stress and anxiety in trying to arrange for these services following the birth.

The desired outcome for every pregnancy is the birth of a healthy child.

In a high-risk pregnancy, special attention must be given to known potential complications. Prenatal care in a health agency specializing in high-risk pregnancies is optimal. Health professionals in such programs are skilled in preventing and intervening early for problems that may endanger the baby (Korones, 1981). Such a health agency also may be of assistance in securing the services of a pediatrician who has expertise in the care of newborns with special needs.

NEONATAL

The family crisis associated with the birth of a baby with special needs is well documented (Fraley, 1990). The grieving experienced by parents, siblings, and extended family can be acute. It is important to support families by encouraging their participation in support groups. The nurse should assess the coping style within the family and provide emotional support. Referral to social services may be appropriate.

Acute grieving is common and may interfere with bonding between the parents and their infant (Klaus & Kennell, 1982). The nurse can facilitate bonding by encouraging the parents to focus on the characteristics the baby has in common with other infants (Steele, 1990). Formal counseling should be encouraged in dysfunctional grieving to prevent long-term problems.

Infants born with medical problems necessitating prolonged hospitalization following birth have additional risk factors that may complicate bonding and attachment (Lancaster, 1981). Most NICUs now have programs that attempt to offset the intrusive nature of these environments for the infant and family. Many include developmental stimulation as part of the overall plan of care, with specially trained nurses and developmental therapists providing therapeutic touch,

music, rocking, and oral motor stimulation on a regular basis to promote development.

Parents should be taught these techniques and also should be encouraged to touch and hold their infants whenever they are in the NICU. In addition to providing needed stimulation to the baby, these activities help to promote bonding (Healy, Keesee, & Smith, 1985). Visits by siblings and extended family members will facilitate integration of the infant as a part of the family and provide needed support to the parents.

Many communities offer interdisciplinary clinics that provide follow-up care for high-risk infants. When available, referral to such agencies should occur well before discharge. These programs frequently contact the family while the baby is still hospitalized to discuss services to be provided following discharge.

Prior to taking the baby home, the family will need to know the basic care routine for their infant. As discharge approaches, the nurse should begin to work with the family on transition from the NICU to home (Resnick, Armstrong, & Carter, 1988). Parents of newborns with respiratory compromise will need to learn cardiopulmonary resuscitation (CPR) and may need to learn how to use an apnea monitor. For the infant with a poor suck or dysphagia, the speech-language pathologist should be consulted regarding feeding techniques. An occupational or physical therapist can teach the parents how to do therapeutic positioning with the infant. For example, a child with gastroesophageal reflux (GER) needs proper positioning to facilitate the emptying of stomach contents, thus preventing aspiration (see Figure 1) (Sterling, Schaffer, & Jolley, 1993).

Nontraditional Feeding Methods

Infants with congenital structural abnormalities, severe oral motor dysfunc-

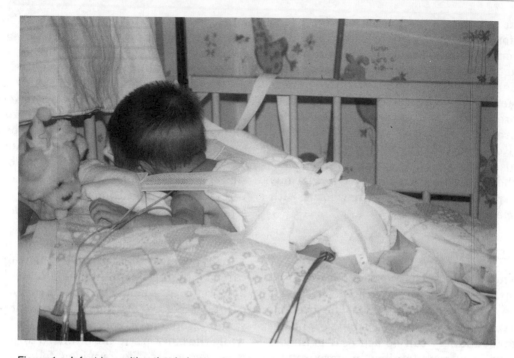

Figure 1.   Infant in position that helps to prevent gastroesophageal reflux (GER).

tion (including dysphagia), and increased vomiting or GER may be at high risk for aspiration. Recurrent aspiration pneumonia and failure to thrive secondary to inadequate caloric intake may result in the decision to utilize nonoral feedings. Although the introduction of nonoral feeding in any form can be a devastating occurrence for parents, emphasis should be placed on the habilitation that will continue despite the introduction of nontraditional feeding methods. It is not a parental failure when a baby needs a non-oral feeding strategy. The nurse can provide instruction in various techniques to assure successful feeding (see Table 1).

The most common nonoral feeding method is tube feeding. A nasogastric tube can be inserted through the nose and down into the stomach via the esophagus, or a gastrostomy tube can be inserted directly into the stomach via the abdominal wall. The nasogastric tube or gastrostomy should be presented

as a method of protecting the baby's lungs and ensuring adequate nutrition.

Gastrostomy tubes may be placed surgically or percutaneously. The surgical route must be utilized when a fundoplication is performed in addition to the gastrostomy tube placement. The percutaneous route avoids the risks of general anesthesia. Gastrostomy buttons may be placed in the gastrostomy opening in lieu of tubes once the stoma is well established. These devices lie flush to the abdomen, promoting a more normalized appearance. They also are less likely to be dislodged by an active infant.

Most infants can be fed a prescribed amount of formula over a 15- to 20-minute period four to six times daily. This is called bolus feeding. Oral motor stimulation, rocking, and socialization should be carried out at feeding times to promote normalized feeding patterns and aid in digestion.

When the inability to feed safely by mouth is further complicated by GER,

Table 1.   Parents' guide to non-oral feeding strategies

1. When oral stimulation is recommended for your child, you can provide the oral stimulation just before or during the tube feeding.
2. Encourage socialization during mealtime. If possible, arrange for your child to eat at regular family mealtimes. If this is not possible, have your child socialize with the rest of the family during the family mealtime. When feeding your child separately, make the feeding time as pleasant as possible. For example, play some soft music that you enjoy. Be sure that your child is clean and comfortable. Don't be afraid to relax and enjoy this special time together.
3. Position your child in as upright a position as possible. This will make it easier for your child to socialize. It also will decrease reflux (the movement of stomach contents into the esophagus). This prevents aspiration, choking, and pneumonia.
4. Report problems to your nurse, therapist, or pediatrician.
5. Remember that eating, in any form, should be a pleasant experience.

delayed stomach emptying, or problems with intestinal motility, feedings may be given by slow drip using gravity or an infusion pump. Some infants may need continuous feedings, whereas others may be able to tolerate intermittent feedings. The nurse can help the family develop a feeding schedule that meets the special needs of the infant while allowing opportunities for the family to be away from home and participate in activities where the pump would be cumbersome. Most pumps have batteries and can accompany the baby on short trips away from home (Howard, 1988).

Therapeutic Positioning

Newborns with hypotonia or hypertonia benefit from proper positioning. For hypotonia the focus is on promoting tone. For hypertonia the emphasis is on relaxation and reduction of muscle tone. For any child with abnormal tone, emphasis is on the prevention of deformities. Parents should practice positioning the baby and doing recommended exercises prior to discharge from the hospital. The physical therapist can assist in developing a positioning program tailored to the needs of the individual baby. Padded supports (see Figure 2) are available to provide more stable seating for the infant.

Impact on Siblings

The homecoming of a brother or sister with special needs can be overwhelming for older siblings (Powell & Gallagher,

1993). The attention always afforded the newest member of the family is further complicated by the stress and anxiety the children see in their parents as they struggle to absorb the enormity of their new baby's needs. Anticipatory guidance about ways to minimize the negative impact on siblings waiting at home is important. Specific suggestions about how to communicate information and answer questions posed by siblings of various ages will be helpful to parents.

Parents should be encouraged to be truthful with their other children and to stress positive and hopeful messages about the new baby. Hiding their own fears and concerns from the older siblings should be discouraged. Children are highly attuned to their parents feelings and behaviors and will sense that there is a secret about the new baby from which they are being excluded. The fantasy young children may conjure up tends to be more frightening than the truth (Powell & Gallagher, 1993).

INFANTS

As the family comes to grips with the reality of the special needs of their newborn, an important role of the nurse is to help the family focus on the wellness needs of their infant. The nurse acts as a role model for the family interactions with the infant. It is important for the nurse's actions to communicate clearly that this baby's needs parallel those of

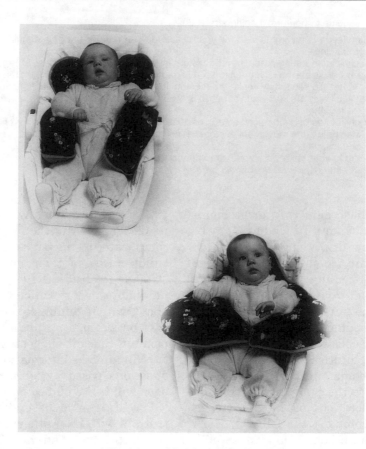

Figure 2. Infant seating can be stabilized by padded supports. (Available from Leachco, 130 East 10th, P.O. Box 717, Ada, OK 74820.)

other infants. The family's interactions with the baby and their ability to provide appropriate stimulation should be assessed. Many useful tools are available to the nurse to carry out these assessments (Bradley & Caldwell, 1988; Quinn, 1991; Zahr, 1991).

Health interventions should follow the guidelines developed by the American Academy of Pediatrics (Table 2, pp. 154–155). Modifications are made, as necessary, depending on the baby's condition. Infants with developmental disabilities should be immunized unless medically contraindicated. For infants with medical problems that necessitate a delay in immunization, separate guidelines should be followed. Tables 3–7 (pp. 156–159) will assist the nurse to implement appropriate and timely immunization practices.

Safety Precautions

It is important to teach parents of infants with developmental disabilities about safety precautions that should be taken to protect the infant. Specific risk factors for the infant should be identified and discussed with the family. When possible, a home visit should be made in order to evaluate the environment for safety hazards. The home should be "baby-proofed." The use of outlet covers, cupboard locks, fences around pools, and gates at the tops and bottoms of stairways are all measures that can protect the infant from harm.

The nurse can advise the parents to select baby furniture and equipment that are safe. A crib that permits the mattress to be elevated at least 30 degrees will help to prevent reflux and promote digestion. Highchairs should have additional straps to provide trunk support for older infants with gross motor delays. Walkers and jumping toys are contraindicated in infants with motor delays (Holm, Harthun-Smith, & Tada, 1983). Infants with poor head and/or trunk support may incur injuries during the use of this equipment. A good rule of thumb for parents is to delay purchase of any devices that equip the infant for movement until health professionals have been consulted.

Car seats usually do not require specialized adaptation to accommodate infants with motor problems. However, in the case of an infant with hypotonia and poor head control, special padding may be used to provide additional support. Devices that provide head support (Figure 3) and trunk support for very young infants (Figure 4) are available commercially. These may be used throughout the time the baby is using the car seat. A physical therapist and/or orthotist can be of assistance in adapting car seats to afford optimal protection for infants with severe postural dystonia.

TODDLERS/PRESCHOOLERS

As the infant enters into toddlerhood, ongoing delays in achieving developmental milestones provide parents with daily evidence of their child's problems. Parents may experience a sense of hopelessness. The concept of chronic sorrow, grieving over the loss of the perfect child, is common in families of children with developmental disabilities (Olshansky, 1962). The nurse can help parents to focus on that which is healthy and whole in their child. Peer support groups can help parents ventilate their feelings in a supportive environment. Such groups also provide a useful network for the exchange of information about special techniques, ideas, and devices to promote development. Many of these organizations also publish newsletters or literature to assist families.

Families should be encouraged to include the child with special needs in family activities. Grandparents and other members of the extended family may be helpful in keeping the family of the child with a developmental disability involved in social activities. Community support networks, such as neighbors, friends, and church members, also can provide opportunities for social interaction with the family. Parents often are reluctant to request respite services. With encouragement from a professional, parents may feel more comfortable asking for assistance. Many agencies providing services to children with developmental disabilities offer in-home or temporary out-of-home respite services. Family members or friends can offer to care for the child with special needs so that parents can spend time alone or with their other children.

The need for updated immunizations should be evaluated regularly. Many preschool programs will deny admission to a child who does not have current immunizations.

Safety Precautions

Safety is of paramount importance in toddlers and preschoolers. There must be a balance between allowing exploration, reasonable risk taking, and developmentally appropriate play and protecting the child from injury. Most preschoolers with developmental delays have learned the relationship between cause and effect, but vulnerability to injury may persist in the preschooler who has developed physical capabilities with-

Table 2.   Recommendations for preventive pediatric health care (Committee on Practice and Ambulatory Medicine)

Each child and family is unique; therefore these **Recommendations for Preventive Pediatric Health Care** are designed for the care of children who are receiving competent parenting, have no manifestations of any important health problems, and are growing and developing in satisfactory fashion. **Additional visits may become necessary** if circumstances suggest variations from normal. These guidelines represent a consensus by the Committee on Practice and Ambulatory Medicine in consultation with the membership of the American Academy of Pediatrics through the Chapter Presidents. The Committee emphasizes the great importance of **continuity of care** in comprehensive health supervision and the need to avoid **fragmentation of care.**

A **prenatal visit** by the parents for anticipatory guidance and pertinent medical history is strongly recommended.

Health supervision should begin with medical care of the newborn in the hospital.

	INFANCY							EARLY CHILDHOOD				LATE CHILDHOOD					ADOLESCENCE[1]			
AGE[2]	By 1 mo.	2 mos.	4 mos.	6 mos.	9 mos.	12 mos.	15 mos.	18 mos.	24 mos.	3 yrs.	4 yrs.	5 yrs.	6 yrs.	8 yrs.	10 yrs.	12 yrs.	14 yrs.	16 yrs.	18 yrs.	20 + yrs.
HISTORY																				
Initial/Interval	•	•	•	•	•	•	•	•	•	•	•	•	•	•	•	•	•	•	•	•
MEASURE-MENTS																				
Height and Weight	•	•	•	•	•	•	•	•	•	•	•	•	•	•	•	•	•	•	•	•
Head Circumference	•	•	•	•	•	•		•	•											
Blood Pressure										•	•	•	•	•	•	•	•	•	•	•
SENSORY SCREENING																				
Vision	S	S	S	S	S	S	S	S	S	S	○	○	○	○	S	○	○	S	○	○
Hearing	S	S	S	S	S	S	S	S	S	S	○	○	S[3]	S[3]	S[3]	○	S	S	○	S
DEVEL./BEHAV.[4] **ASSESSMENT**	•	•	•	•	•	•	•	•	•	•	•	•	•	•	•	•	•	•	•	•
PHYSICAL EX-AMINATION[5]	•	•	•	•	•	•	•	•	•	•	•	•	•	•	•	•	•	•	•	•
PROCEDURES[6]																				
Hered/Metabolic[7] Screening	•																			

154

Immunization[8]

Tuberculin Test[9]

Hematocrit or
Hemoglobin[10]

Urinalysis[11]

ANTICIPATORY GUIDANCE[12]

INITIAL DENTAL REFERRAL[13]

1. Adolescent related issues (e.g., psychosocial, emotional, substance usage, and reproductive health) may necessitate more frequent health supervision.
2. If a child comes under care for the first time at any point on the schedule, or if any items are not accomplished at the suggested age, the schedule should be brought up to date at the earliest possible time.
3. At these points, history may suffice; if problem suggested, a standard testing method should be employed.
4. By history and appropriate physical examination; if suspicious, by specific objective developmental testing.
5. At each visit, a complete physical examination is essential, with infant totally unclothed, older child undressed and suitably draped.
6. These may be modified, depending upon entry point into schedule and individual need.
7. Metabolic screening (e.g., thyroid, PKU, galactosemia) should be done according to state law.
8. Schedule(s) per Report of Committee on Infectious Disease, 1988 Red Book.*
9. For low risk groups, the Committee on Infectious Diseases recommends the following options: (1) no routine testing or (2) testing at three times—infancy, preschool, and adolescence. For high risk groups, annual TB skin testing is recommended.
10. Present medical evidence suggests the need for reevaluation of the frequency and timing of hemoglobin or hematocrit tests. One determination is therefore suggested during each time period. Performance of additional tests is left to the individual practice experience.
11. Present medical evidence suggests the need for reevaluation of the frequency and timing of urinalyses. One determination is therefore suggested during each time period. Performance of additional tests is left to the individual practice experience.
12. Appropriate discussion and counseling should be an integral part of each visit for care.
13. Subsequent examinations as prescribed by dentist.

N.B.: **Special chemical, immunologic, and endocrine testing** are usually carried out upon specific indications. Testing other than newborn (e.g., inborn errors of metabolism, sickle disease, lead) are discretionary with the physician.

Adapted from Committee on Psychosocial Aspects of Child and Family Health. (1988).

* Committee on Infectious Disease. (1988). *1988 red book*. Elk Grove Village, IL: American Academy of Pediatrics.

Key: •, required; S, screening; O, optional, based on history and any presenting symptoms.

Table 3.   Immunization schedules

Children Beginning Series in Early Infancy

Usual Age[*] or Time Interval	Vaccines
Under 1 month	HB
2 months or 1st immunization	DTP, OPV, Hib[1]
4 months or 6–8 weeks after 1st	DTP, OPV, Hib[1]
6 months[8] or 6–8 weeks after 2nd	DTP, Hib[1]
15 months	DTP[2], OPV[2], MMR, Hib[1]
4–6 years	DTP[3], OPV[4]
10–12 years	MMR[5]
14–16 years and every 10 years thereafter	Td

Children Beginning Series at or after Age 15 Months but before Age 7 Years

Age	Vaccines
1st visit	DTP, OPV, MMR, Hib[6]
6–8 weeks after 1st OPV and DTP	DTP, OPV
4–8 weeks after 2nd OPV and DTP	DTP
6–12 months after 3rd DTP	DTP, OPV
4–6 years	DTP[3], OPV[4]
10–12 years	MMR[5]
14–16 years and every 10 years thereafter	Td

Children Beginning Series at Age 7 or Older

Date	Vaccines
1st immunization	Td, OPV, MMR
6–8 weeks after 1st Td and OPV	Td, OPV
6–12 months after 2nd Td and OPV	Td, OPV
10–12 years	MMR[5]
10 years after 3rd Td and every 10 years thereafter	Td[7]

  [*] These recommended ages should not be construed as absolute (i.e., 2 months can be 6–10 weeks, etc.) unless so noted.

1. For HbOC (Lederle) vaccine only. If begun at 2–6 months, give three doses at least 2 months apart. If begun at 7–11 months, give two doses at least 2 months apart. If begun at 12–14 months, give one dose. In all cases, a booster of any type conjugate Hib vaccine should be given at 15 months at an interval not less than 2 months after the previous dose.
2. Administer DTP and OPV providing that at least 6 months have elapsed since 3rd DTP and 2nd OPV.
3. Not necessary if the fourth dose of DTP is given on or after the fourth birthday.
4. Not necessary if the third dose of OPV is given on or after the fourth birthday.
5. Give at entry to 6th grade. May also give to children prior to school entry through 12th grade.
6. If 15–59 months old, should receive one dose. Children 5 years or older may be immunized if they have illnesses or medical conditions placing them at high risk for Hib disease.
7. After previous dose of Td.
8. In some areas of Florida, a dose of single measles antigen vaccine is given at age 6 months followed by the first MMR vaccine administered at the regularly scheduled age of 15 months.

  Source: Department of Health and Human Services, Centers for Disease Control.

  Abbreviations: DTP, diptheria–tetanus–pertussis; HB, Hepatitis B; Hib, *Haemophilus influenzae* type b; MMR, measles–mumps–rubella; OPV, oral polio vaccine; Td, tetanus–diptheria toxoid.

out the cognitive ability needed for self-protection.

Toddlers and preschoolers with gross motor delays may require support to remain properly positioned in car seats and seat belts. Devices such as those pic-tured in Figure 5 can be helpful in providing that support.

Eating and Mealtimes

Eating as an activity is a social as well as a nutritional issue. As infants ma-

Table 4.   Additional information on immunization

Routes of Vaccine Administration

Vaccine	Route	Vaccine	Route
OPV	Oral	IPV	SC
DTP/DT/Td	IM	Influenza	IM
MMR, MR, measles	SC	*Pneumococcus*	IM or SC
Mumps, rubella	SC	Hepatitis B	IM
Hib Conjugate	IM		

Timing Restrictions for Different Vaccines

Live virus vaccines (e.g., MMR, OPV, yellow fever): Can give on same day, but if not given on same day, wait 30 days before giving second live vaccine. No timing restrictions exist between the different inactivated vaccines or between inactivated and live vaccines.

MMR/MR and TB skin test: Can give TB skin test before or on same day, but if 1 or more days have passed after giving MMR/MR, wait 4–6 weeks before giving TB skin test.

MMR/MR/measles and IG (or any other immune globulin preparation): Give MMR/MR/measles either at least 2 weeks before IG or at least 3 months after giving IG. OPV and other currently available childhood vaccines are not affected by IG.

Vaccine Storage and Handling

Storage

1. DTP/DT/TD, Hib, IPV, HB, HBIG, influenza, *Pneumococcus*—Store at 35–46°F (refrigerate but do not freeze). Do not store in door.
2. MMR, MR, measles, mumps, rubella—Store at 35–46°F (refrigerator). **Do not allow to warm up or be exposed to light before use.**
3. OPV—Store in freezer at 7°F or below. Vaccine in liquid state in unopened dispettes may be used for up to 30 days provided it has been stored at 35–46°F. Thaw before using—may be rubbed between hands for rapid thawing. Vaccine may be refrozen, with a maximum of 10 freeze–thaw cycles, provided the total cumulative duration of thaw does not exceed 24 hours, and temperature does not exceed 46°F during the period of thaw.

Instructions in the Event of a Refrigeration Breakdown

Upon discovery of breakdown, determine current refrigerator/freezer temperature and place biologics in equipment that is operational. Do not assume that the vaccines are unserviceable.

Prevention of Vaccine Loss by Refrigeration Breakdown

1. Monitor refrigerator/freezer temperatures at least twice per workday at the start and close of business; post temperature readings on a log sheet attached to the equipment.
2. Install devices to prevent accidental unplugging of equipment and be sure that circuit breaker and power supply switchboxes are secure.
3. To prevent loss by malfunctions during weekends, conduct inspections during weekends or install monitoring/alarm equipment that will alert a responsible party when temperature limits are exceeded.

Source: Department of Health and Human Services, Centers for Disease Control.

Abbreviations: DT, diphtheria–tetanus; DTP, diphtheria–tetanus–pertussis; HB, hepatitis B; HBIG, hepatitis B immune globulin; Hib, *Haemophilus influenzae* type b; IG, immune globulin; IM, intramuscular; IPV, inactivated polio vaccine; MMR, measles–mumps–rubella; MR, measles–rubella; OPV, oral polio vaccine; SC, subcutaneous; TB, tuberculin; Td, tetanus–diphtheria toxoid.

ture, parents usually have become accustomed to dependency needs expressed during infancy. They may need support, guidance, and encouragement to foster independence in the toddler and preschooler. Parents may worry that the child's caloric intake will be inadequate as he or she struggles to acquire new oral motor skills. However, the method of feeding can be just as important as the number of calories consumed. In order for the child to become more than a passive recipient of food, the feeder must relinquish some control. For example, the toddler or preschooler can be encouraged to select the type of

Table 5.   Prophylactic vaccinations

Perinatal Hepatitis B Prevention

Perinatal: Give infants born to HBsAg-positive mothers:
- Within 12 hours of birth: 0.5 ml HBIG and 0.5 ml hepatitis B vaccine[*]
- Then 2 more (0.5 ml) vaccine[*] doses, 1 and 6 months after 1st[**]
  2nd dose can be at age 6–8 weeks along with 1st DTP and OPV doses.
  [*]Recombivax or Engerix-B. Series can include both vaccines.
  [**]If 2nd dose is delayed, give now and 3rd dose 3–5 months after 2nd.
  If 3rd dose is delayed, give as soon as possible.

Susceptible Household Contacts: As above: (a) no HBIG unless person has sexual or needle contact with HBsAg+ person or is infant of HBsAg+ mother; and (b) See vaccine package insert for dosage, which varies with age and with vaccine used.

Tetanus Prophylaxis in Wound Management

Prior Tetanus Doses	Clean, minor wounds		Other wounds[1]	
	Td[2]	TIG	Td[2]	TIG
Uncertain, or <3 doses	Yes	No	Yes	Yes
3 or more doses	No[3]	No	No[4]	No

1. For example, wound contaminated with dirt, feces, saliva, etc.; puncture wound; avulsion wound resulting from missile, crushing, burn, or frostbite; wound extending into muscle.
2. Substitute DTP for children under 7 years.
3. Yes, if > 10 years since last dose.
4. Yes, if > 5 years since last dose.

Source: Department of Health and Human Services, Centers for Disease Control.

Abbreviations: DTP, diphtheria–tetanus–pertussis; HBIG, hepatitis B immune globulin; HBsAg, hepatitis B surface antigen; OPV, oral polio vaccine; Td, tetanus–diphtheria toxoid; TIG, tetanus immune globulin.

Table 6.   Special considerations in immunization

Immunizing Children with HIV Infection

Vaccine	Known asymptomatic	Known symptomatic
DTP/DT/Td	Yes	Yes
OPV	No	No
IPV	Yes	Yes
MMR	Yes	Yes, consider
Hib (conjugate or HbCV)	Yes	Yes
Pneumococcus	Yes	Yes
Influenza	Optional	Yes
Hepatitis B	Yes, if needed	Yes, if needed

Schedule for DT for Infants and Children Who Cannot Take DTP

Infants under age 1 year—Three doses at 4–8 week intervals; a 4th dose 6–12 months after the 3rd, and a 5th dose at age 4–6 years, just before school entry. If 4th dose given after 4th birthday, the 5th dose is not necessary.

Children ages 1–6 years—Two doses 4–8 weeks apart, a 3rd dose 6–12 months after the 2nd, and a 4th dose at age 4–6 years, just before school entry. If 3rd dose given after 4th birthday, the 4th dose is not necessary.

Source: Department of Health and Human Services, Centers for Disease Control.

Abbreviations: DT, diphtheria–tetanus; DTP, diptheria–tetanus–pertussis; HbCV, *Haemophilus influenzae* type b conjugate vaccine; Hib, *Haemophilus influenzae* type b; IPV, inactivated polio vaccine; MMR, measles–mumps–rubella; OPV, oral polio vaccine; Td, tetanus–diphtheria toxoid.

Table 7. Guide to contraindications (valid and invalid) to immunizations[a]

Vaccine[b]	Valid contraindications	Invalid contraindications
General for all vaccines	An immediate anaphylactic reaction following vaccine "Moderate or severe" febrile illness	Local reaction (soreness, redness, swelling) following administration of vaccine Mild acute illness with or without low-grade fever
DTP, OPV, IPV, MMR, Hib, HB		Mild diarrheal illness or gastrointestinal tract disturbance in otherwise well child Current antimicrobial therapy The convalescent phase of illnesses Prematurity: use same dosage and indications as for normal, full-term infants Recent exposure to an infectious disease A history of penicillin or other nonspecific allergies or relatives with such allergies
DTP	Encephalopathy (not due to other identifiable causes) occurring within 7 days of immunization PRECAUTIONS[*] 　Fever of $\geq$ 40.5°C (105°F) within 48 hours of vaccination (not due to other identifiable causes) 　Collapse or shock-like state (hypotonic–hyporesponsive episode) within 48 hours 　Convulsions with or without fever occurring within 3 days 　Persistent, inconsolable crying lasting $\geq$ 3 hours, occurring within 48 hours	Temperature of less than 40.5°C (105°F) following a previous dose of DTP Family history of convulsions Family history of sudden infant death syndrome Family history of an adverse event following DTP immunization
OPV	Infection with human immunodeficiency virus (HIV) Pregnancy Known altered immunodeficiency (hematologic and solid tumors, congenital immunodeficiency, and chronic immunosuppressive therapy) Immunodeficient household contact	Breastfeeding
IPV	Anaphylactic reaction to neomycin or streptomycin	
MMR	Anaphylactic reactions following egg ingestion or to neomycin Pregnancy Known altered immunodeficiency (hematologic and solid tumors, congenital immunodeficiency, and chronic immunosuppressive therapy) Recent (within 3 months) immune globulin administration	Tuberculosis or positive tuberculin skin test Pregnancy in mother of recipient Breastfeeding Immunodeficient family member Infection with HIV Nonanaphylactic reaction to eggs or neomycin

Source: Department of Health and Human Services, Centers for Disease Control.

[*]The events listed as precautions, while not contraindications, should be carefully reviewed. The benefits and risks of administering a specific vaccine to an individual under existing circumstances should be considered. If the risks to the individual are believed to outweigh the benefits, the immunization should be withheld; if the benefits are believed to outweigh the risks (e.g., during an outbreak), the immunization should be given.

[a]DTP, diphtheria–tetanus–pertussis; HB, hepatitis B; Hib, *Haemophilus influenzae* type b; IPV, inactivated polio vaccine; MMR, measles–mumps–rubella; OPV, oral polio vaccine.

[b]Individuals seeking more detailed information should consult the recommendations of the ACIP or *Red Book* of the AAP.

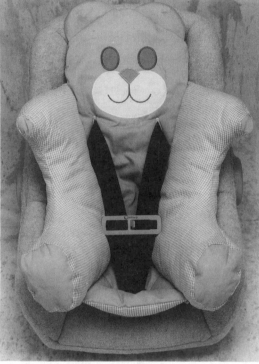

Figure 3.   Head support device for infant in car seat. (Available from Leachco, 130 East 10th, P.O. Box 717, Ada, OK 74820.)

Figure 4.   Trunk support device for infant in car seat. (Available from Teddy Tuckers, Inc., Route 1, Box 47B, Friedens, PA 15541.)

juice they would like to drink. They can also select the order of the food items to be fed.

The toddler or preschooler with a developmental disability should eat with other family members to establish mealtime as a social time. Preschoolers with adequate motor skills can help with setting the table. If motor skills are poor, they can help to set the table by using a yes/no response to indicate where items go on the table. Eating with the rest of the family gives the child an opportunity to socialize and participate as an integral part of the family.

Developing good eating skills may pose significant challenges for the toddler and preschooler with abnormal muscle tone. Parents may need training in order to help the child develop his or her oral motor skills. The goal of an oral motor training program is to promote maximal independence. When there is per-

sistence of tongue thrust, a hyperactive gag reflex, or the presence of a bite reflex, mealtimes may become a frustrating experience for everyone. Special adaptive eating utensils (Figure 6) and proper positioning can be utilized to facilitate independence. The guidelines presented in Table 8 will help parents in their efforts to assist their child in developing good eating habits.

TOILET TRAINING

There are few developmental tasks of childhood as frustrating for parents as toilet training. When the need for diapers continues into preschool years, parents may become despondent. Nurses can be helpful in developing a plan that is both realistic and based on the individual needs of the child.

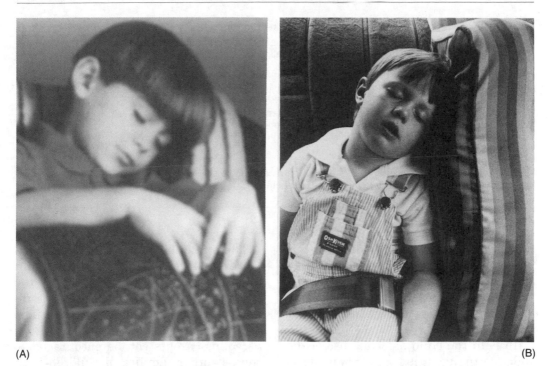

(A)   (B)

Figure 5.   Examples of support devices for toddlers/preschoolers in car seats (A) and seat belts (B). (Car seat device available from Jolly Jumper, Inc., P.O. Box M, Woonsocket, RI 02895; seat belt device available from Teddy Tuckers, Inc., Route 1, Box 47B, Friedens, PA 15541.)

The success of any toilet training program is dependent on four basic principles: physical readiness, a regular toileting schedule, rewards for toileting successes, and an attitude of patience and acceptance by all those involved in the training. If any of these components is missing, the program is in jeopardy.

Unless the child has neurological problems, physical awareness of the need to defecate or urinate is achieved at approximately 15 months of age. The con-

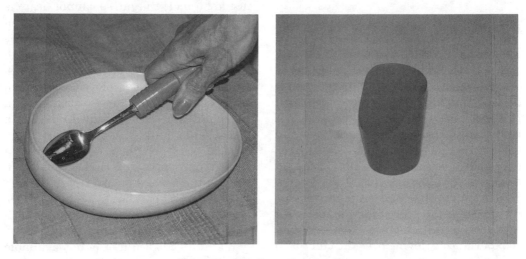

Figure 6.   Adaptive eating utensils.

Table 8.   Feeding guidelines for parents of toddlers/preschoolers

1. Always encourage your child to use the best and safest oral skills during eating and drinking.
2. Encourage your child to use current eating skills well, and introduce new skills slowly. Build on the progress already made.
3. Present a variety of foods in child-size portions.
4. Give your child an opportunity to be as independent as possible. Let him or her assist with meal preparation, eating, and cleanup, to the extent of his or her capabilities.
5. Expect the meal to end in a reasonable period of time.
6. Help your child to eat in as neat and socially acceptable a way as possible.
7. Enjoy mealtimes with your child. Socialize and laugh together.
8. Reduce feeding problems by using
   a. Proper positioning
   b. Food that has a consistency (texture) your child can handle safely
   c. Oral treatment, as prescribed by your child's therapist
   d. Adaptive equipment

cept of toileting can be introduced at this age by placing the child on a potty chair and encouraging its use. Children who have physical disabilities may need adaptive toilet facilities and assistance using the toilet.

To help the child associate use of the toilet with urination and bowel movements, parents can use simple prompts that encourage release of urine and stool while the child is on the toilet. For instance, running water to prompt urination or having the child blow on a whistle to cause bearing down can be incorporated into the toileting routine. Other techniques such as role modeling by the parent of the same sex and social praise for successes can also be helpful.

SCHOOL-AGE CHILDREN

The first day of school has all the qualities of a rite of passage. For the parents of a child with a developmental disability, this may be a bittersweet time (Delp, 1992). School entry kindles hope for opportunities for social experiences and the acquisition of new skills. The mother may now have an opportunity to focus on a job, herself, and the rest of the family. School entry also may act as a stressor by contrasting the child's skills with those of other children. Parents may reexperience grieving over the child who might have been.

The nurse should help the parents explore their feelings of disappointment and ongoing grief. Regression to the emotions experienced at the time of diagnosis is not uncommon at this time. The nurse should accept these feelings as valid. Parents can be encouraged to contact other families of children with developmental disabilities. Participation in groups such as The Arc and the United Cerebral Palsy Association helps parents realize that they are not alone with their emotional pain.

Health Care in the School

Public Law 94-142 ensures an education for all children, regardless of disability. Although the law mandates that medical needs be met, the nurse cannot assume that health issues are an integral part of every curriculum. Parents may have concerns about the safety and health needs of their child during school hours. Nurses may not be employed full time in some schools. The nurse working with the child and family may find that a health aide, parent volunteer, or school clerical staff person is designated as a health care provider (Krier, 1993). In these situations, a school nurse usually visits the school on a regular basis. School districts vary widely in their ability to provide in-school nursing services.

When a school nurse is not available throughout the school day, the community health nurse may be responsible for coordinating the child's health care at school. The school nurse or community nurse, in consultation with the child's primary physician and parents, provides training for school staff and develops written protocols. Bladder catheterization, tube feedings, suctioning, seizure management, and medication administration are some of the skills school staff may learn to master in the absence of professional nursing personnel. State laws and school board policies vary greatly in this area. The nurse must become familiar with the legal and regulatory guidelines that pertain to the delegation of nursing responsibility (see Barks, chap. 9, this volume). In schools where health professional support is limited, a visit with the principal is essential to facilitate communication and gain administrative support.

Children who utilize alternative communication systems should be provided with the means to communicate changes in health status such as pain, nausea, or constipation. Nurses need to give input as communication systems are developed and modified. The nurse can advocate for providing opportunities to express basic needs and emotions through an individualized communication system, including signing, picture boards, or computerized assistive devices (see Morse & Colatarci, chap. 14, this volume). The nurse can advocate for inclusion of these interventions in the child's program when the individualized education program (IEP) is developed by the interdisciplinary team (Opie & Tse, 1988). Parents are advised of these meetings in advance; they should be encouraged to attend and participate actively as members of the team.

School entry is a time for evaluating the child's overall health status. There should be an ongoing review of medications and treatments. Adaptive devices should be repaired and maintained.

Hearing aids and eyeglass prescriptions should be evaluated. Immunizations should be updated as necessary. It is important to ensure that the child is in the best possible health in order to gain the most from the school experience. Parents may be concerned about their child's exposure to communicable diseases when he or she starts school. Most of these fears can be allayed by reassuring the parent that the child's immune system is intact. The relatively benign nature of most communicable diseases encountered in school should be discussed. Preventive measures include adequate immunization prior to school entry; this includes immunization against hepatitis B. Good handwashing practices should be observed at all times.

Integrating Skill Development at School and at Home

The nurse can encourage parents to reinforce new skills as they are taught at school. Incorporation of practice sessions into the family's daily routine will help to diminish the amount of time devoted to these activities during the family's limited hours together at home, preferring to let the experts carry out training and therapy in the school setting. This is especially true when the child resists continuation of school-based programs at home. Although this is understandable, the nurse must assist the parents in remaining involved in their child's training and therapy. The child with a developmental disability benefits most when there is consistency of program at home and at school. Regression or acting out can occur when demands differ from situation to situation.

The nurse can work with parents on techniques that encourage skill attainment and appropriate behavior in their child. A system that emphasizes reward for positive behavior rather than punishment for negative behavior should be developed with the parents. Parents can provide feedback as to the success of various approaches. Their participation also helps to eliminate feelings of helplessness in the face of their child's persistent delay or unacceptable behavior.

Needs of Siblings

The advent of school entry for the child with a developmental disability may pose significant problems for an older sibling, especially if the brother or sister attends the same school (Powell & Gallagher, 1993). Anticipatory guidance prior to the first day of school is essential in such situations. The nurse can help the older sibling develop responses to schoolmates' questions through role playing. Communicating that the sibling's feelings of embarrassment and resentment are normal and do not imply a lack of love for the younger brother or sister will help avoid the guilt associated with these feelings.

School officials may, unintentionally, burden the older sibling with further embarrassment and responsibility. Although complete separation of siblings may be impossible, every effort must be made to ensure the child without developmental delays has a life of his or her own both in school and at home.

the family to take weekends and occasional short vacations away from the child with developmental disabilities in order to work on their own developmental tasks. Respite care can help to make these opportunities a reality. Siblings will benefit from their own special time with parents, without the ever-present possibility that the needs of their brother or sister will divert their parents' attention.

ADOLESCENTS

Adolescence is well known for the challenges it poses to children and their parents. Teenagers who have developmental disabilities and their families face additional challenges during this difficult time.

The adolescent with a developmental disability has the same needs for peer interaction and socialization as do other teenagers. Although creating these opportunities may be more difficult than for teenagers without disabilities, school and community networks are helping to make more activities accessible to individuals who have disabilities. In addition to occasions such as sporting events, school activities, Special Olympics, scouting, and summer camps, parents can plan

James was in third grade when his brother, Joshua, entered the special education program at the same school. Joshua had poor impulse control and would have tantrums whenever he experienced frustration. On these occasions, when the teacher was unable to control this behavior, she would send the aide to get James to calm down his brother. Communications to the parents were routinely sent through James regarding Joshua's seizures, toileting accidents, and missed doses of medications. James became very depressed and began leaving the school grounds soon after he was dropped off by the bus to avoid the pain of having Joshua dominate what had been his only refuge prior to his brother's entry into school.

Time away from the child with a developmental disability is essential for each member of the family, individually and as a unit. The nurse should encourage

parties and outings for groups of teenagers with similar interests. Dancing and basketball both can be accomplished in wheelchairs.

Communication problems may be especially troublesome at this time of life. Teenagers have a language of their own. This "teen-speak" frequently is unintelligible to adults. Private language gives teenagers a sense of belonging and community. An inability to communicate in this special jargon can be painful to the adolescent with a developmental disability. In cooperation with a speech-language pathologist, the nurse can help the adolescent who utilizes an alternative communication device to incorporate special words and phrases into his or her vocabulary.

During the teenage years, physical appearance takes on new importance. Every effort should be made to facilitate choices for the adolescent in clothes, hairstyles, jewelry, and makeup. Parents may have difficulty permitting choices they find unacceptable. The nurse's role is to help them resist the temptation to take control in this area. The teenager's need for self-expression and creation of a personal style are important developmental tasks, and taking these choices away will inhibit growth.

Nutritional Considerations

Obesity can become a problem for some adolescents with developmental delay (Siantz, 1977). Those teenagers who require supervision for outdoor activities, as well as those who have physical limitations that make regular exercise difficult, are at high risk for being overweight. These adolescents may be dependent on others to arrange, supervise, and physically assist with sports, aerobics, swimming, and other forms of exercise. The nurse can be helpful in locating volunteer agencies such as the YMCA to facilitate these activities.

Nutritional counseling should be sought for the teenager who has difficulty making appropriate dietary choices. Although occasional indulgence in "junk food" is standard behavior for most adolescents, consumption of this type of food to the exclusion of a balanced diet may lead to poor health as well as obesity. As with persons who have no disabilities, snacking frequently is employed as a remedy for boredom in teenagers with developmental delays. Many of them work or have allowances, which gives them the capability of purchasing foods outside their homes. Helping them make better choices about the foods they purchase will equip them with important skills needed for their growing independence as well as helping with weight control and good nutrition.

Some teenagers with developmental disabilities may face the opposite health problem. Consumption of adequate calories to maintain the rapid growth and energy needs of adolescence may prove difficult for some teenagers with oral motor dysfunction, gastrointestinal disorders, impaired taste or smell, or depression. The nurse may be helpful to the undernourished teenager by making a referral to a nutritionist. This person can help the adolescent plan meals and snacks that provide optimal caloric and nutritional content. If menu planning and food selection are ineffective alone in improving nutritional status, overnight nasogastric feedings or supplemental feedings of liquid dietary supplements may be indicated.

Constipation is a health problem experienced by many adolescents with developmental disabilities. Causes include diminished intestinal motility secondary to anticonvulsive medication, insufficient intake of fiber and fluids, and motor dysfunction that causes diminished peristalsis (Crump, 1987). The nurse can help the adolescent with a developmental disability to plan a menu, a schedule for the intake of adequate fluids, and a toileting routine that will help reduce the risk of constipation.

Immunizations

Although most immunization series will have been completed prior to school entry, some immunizations are needed throughout life. The diphtheria–tetanus (DT) booster must be administered every 10 years. If a high-risk wound occurs more than 5 years after the DT booster has been administered, a booster of tetanus toxoid is indicated.

The nurse should undertake teaching the teenager about the importance of maintaining up-to-date immunizations. The nurse should ensure that an updated immunization record is part of the individual's health record at school and/or vocational training sites. As the adolescent assumes greater responsibility for his or her own health care, an understanding of the importance of this information is essential.

Puberty and Sexuality

One of the normal changes most parents dread in their child with a developmental disability is the onset of puberty. In order to deal with the ongoing flood of feelings associated with their child's special needs, many parents may adopt a coping mechanism that renders the child forever dependent (Craft & Craft, 1983). Because they perceive that the child always will need their care and supervision, it is understandable that perpetual dependence translates into perpetual infancy in some parents' minds. Although it may seem early to discuss these issues with the parents of a 9- or 10-year-old, many families need time to do the emotional work involved in preparing for this eventuality.

Beginning discussions should focus on the child's physical growth and changing needs. The child's increasing height and weight affect daily care at home, especially if the child is unable to bear weight during transfer activities. One person may no longer be able to lift the child safely. Providing perineal hygiene care may become increasingly difficult. In exploring these realities, the nurse can help the parents plan for normal physiological changes associated with puberty, such as the appearance of pubic hair or breast buds. These discussions can serve as opportunities for the nurse to begin exploration of the parents' feelings about the sexual development of the child.

Historically, because the idea of sexuality in persons with developmental disabilities bordered on the taboo, efforts were directed at rendering the emerging adolescent an asexual being. Saltpeter was given to males because it was thought to diminish sexual urges. Surgical sterilization was performed on women with developmental disabilities in order to prevent pregnancy and the genetic transmission of "feeble-mindedness" (Haller, 1989). Earlier in the 20th century, institutionalization provided social isolation of persons with developmental disabilities.

Such responses to the onset of sexuality in adolescents with developmental disabilities are no longer considered appropriate. Current attitudes reflect acceptance of sexuality as part of the normal behavior pattern of *all* adolescents and young adults, and parents of teenagers with developmental disabilities will require help in achieving a level of comfort and a sense of competence in

---

Margaret entered a large public institution in the early 1960s at the age of 23. When her mother died, there was no family to provide a home for her and she was unable to live independently. On the intake medical history form, many of the items were left blank because the information was unavailable. In the space allocated to describe sexual activity, the physician had written "Normal/None."

dealing with this issue. However, despite anticipatory guidance, the advent of overt sexual activity frequently causes panic in families. Parents may overreact; they may scare the adolescent and communicate negative messages to their child. Parents may fear the possibility of exploitation or sexual aggression. The nurse plays a key role in helping parents to deal with their anxiety and develop an approach that protects the adolescent, respects the parents' personal convictions, and facilitates normal growth and development (see Morse & Roth, chap. 12, this volume).

Teenage girls with significant development disabilities need instruction about personal hygiene measures to be used during menstruation. Uncircumcised boys should be taught care of the foreskin. They should learn socially appropriate behaviors. The concepts of privacy and modesty must be related to personal sexual behaviors. It may be difficult for the teenager to understand why actions previously regarded as cute are now considered to be unappealing or in poor taste. If personal hygiene and privacy were taught during childhood, most of the information needed in adolescence builds on or reinforces this program content.

Adolescents who are sexually active need information about contraceptives and sexually transmitted diseases. These are traditionally areas that parents have difficulty addressing, whether or not their teenager has a developmental dis-

ability. The nurse must assess the needs of the individual and the family before proceeding with a teaching plan. It is important to clarify the issues to be addressed. Parents should be encouraged to ask questions and participate in planning the program where possible.

Aggression

One of the most challenging problems families may face in their child's adolescence is aggressive behavior. Many teenagers with developmental disabilities have the size and physical strength of adults. They may have few options for dealing with their anger and frustration, and may vent feelings through acting out.

In some instances, parents may have chosen not to discipline the child with a developmental disability, or they may have utilized ineffective strategies. Unintentionally, inappropriate behaviors may have been reinforced in an effort to "keep the peace."

Health practitioners may recommend the use of psychoactive medications to control aggressive behavior in persons with developmental disabilities. For some individuals with mental health problems, medication has a limited role as part of a comprehensive program. However, most behaviors respond very well to other interventions. The nurse working with a teenager who is experiencing severe behavior problems should assist the individual and his or her family to access appropriate resources, such

---

Keesha's mealtime behaviors had always been a problem for her family. Beginning in toddlerhood, Keesha had been given cookies and other snack foods throughout the meal to keep her quiet and prevent her from grabbing food off the plates of other family members. When she became a teenager, it was impossible to take her to a restaurant because she would scream, throw dishes of food, and try to take food from the plates of other restaurant patrons. If any attempt was made to restrain her, she would begin to strike family members and others. Many months of intensive behavior modification were necessary to extinguish these behaviors.

as a behavioral psychologist. If necessary, referral can be made to a psychiatrist. The long-term goal of intervention is to help the adolescent develop appropriate ways of dealing with negative feelings and frustrating situations.

Nursing Responsibilities

One of the nurse's roles during this phase is to assist the older adolescent in planning for ongoing access to health care and in making a successful transition from school to work. A comprehensive assessment of the teenager's health status, health-seeking, and health maintenance skills is an essential part of this process. If the adolescent will be moving to a new living situation, the nurse should assist in identifying a new health care provider, if needed. Complete records, including a list of current health problems, immunization dates, allergies, major illnesses and surgeries, and a nursing summary of current health status should be prepared and provided to the new health care practitioner.

Parents may reexperience the fear of letting go that they first had when their child started school as the adolescent moves toward young adulthood. These are feelings shared by all parents as their children move into a more independent time of life. In supporting the parents through this time, the nurse should emphasize the good work they have done in preparing the child for the next stage of life. The nurse can assist the parents in defining their new role. If the older adolescent will be moving to a new residence after graduation, the nurse can help parents identify their visiting times and encourage them to make plans for shared activities.

Siblings of the teenager with a developmental disability may be experiencing or approaching adolescence themselves at this time. Anger toward and resentment of the sibling with a developmental disability are not uncommon emotions (Powell & Gallagher, 1993). Although these feelings may be normal, they are certainly upsetting. The nurse should take time to explore and help the sibling work through these emotions. Referral for formal counseling may be appropriate.

Transition to adulthood can be an exciting time for the teenager with a developmental disability and the family. Ensuring that the older adolescent is equipped with optimal health to move into the developmental tasks of young adulthood is the goal of the nurse providing health services to families.

SUMMARY

The maintenance and promotion of health in the child with developmental disabilities cannot be undertaken without an understanding of the needs of the family and the resources of the community in which that family lives. The nurse can best meet the health needs of the child and family by adapting basic information about normal growth and development.

Throughout this chapter, an effort has been made to emphasize that children with developmental disabilities have more needs in common with other children than they do needs that are different. The challenges for the professional nurse are to help the child and family pace themselves using realistic time frames, plan effectively for anticipated changes, and facilitate each individual's growth and development within the family unit.

REFERENCES

Benkendorf, J., Corson, V., Allen, J.F., & Ilse, S. (1992). Perinatal bereavement counseling in genetics. *Birth defects: Original article series, 26,* 136–148.

Bradley, R.H., & Caldwell, B.M. (1988). Using the HOME inventory to assess the family environment. *Pediatric Nursing, 14,* 97–102.
Committee on Infectious Disease. (1988). *1988 red*

book. Elk Grove Village, IL: American Academy of Pediatrics.

Craft, A., & Craft, M. (1983). Sex education and counseling for mentally handicapped people. Baltimore: University Park Press.

Crump, I.M. (1987). Conditions that require special dietary management. In I.M. Crump (Ed.), Nutrition and feeding of the handicapped child (pp. 69–88). Boston: Little, Brown.

Delp, K.J. (1992). Beyond chronic sorrow: Psychosocial intervention strategies for professionals. Birth Defects: Original Article Series, 28, 75–77.

Fraley, A.M. (1990). Chronic sorrow: A parental response. Journal of Pediatric Nursing, 5, 268–273.

Grogaard, J.B., Lindstrom, D.P., Parker, R.A., Culley, B., & Stahlman, M.T. (1990). Increased survival rate in very low birth weight infants (1500 grams or less): No association with increased incidence of handicaps. Journal of Pediatrics, 117, 139–146.

Haller, J.S. (1989). The role of physicians in America's sterilization movement 1894–1925. New York State Journal of Medicine, 89, 169–179.

Healy, A., Keesee, P.D., & Smith, B.S. (1985). Early services for children with special needs: Transactions for family support. Iowa City, IA: University Hospital School, Division of Developmental Disabilities.

Holm, V.J., Harthun-Smith, L., & Tada, W.L. (1983). Infant walkers and cerebral palsy. American Journal of Diseases of Children, 137, 1189–1190.

Howard, L.H. (1988). Reaction to: Byrne, W.J. Enteral alimentation: Where and for how long? In Enteral feeding: Scientific basis and clinical applications (Report of the 94th Ross Conference on Pediatric Research, pp. 66–69). Columbus, OH: Ross Laboratories.

Klaus, M.H., & Kennell, J.H. (1982). Parent-infant bonding (2nd ed.). St. Louis: C.V. Mosby.

Korones, S.B. (1981). High-risk newborn infants: The basis for intensive nursing care. St. Louis: C.V. Mosby.

Krier, J.J. (1993). Involvement of educational staff in the health care of medically fragile children. Pediatric Nursing, 19, 251–254.

Lancaster, J. (1981). Impact of intensive care on the parent-infant relationship. In S.B. Korones & J. Lancaster (Eds.), High-risk newborn infants (pp. 354–365). St. Louis: C.V. Mosby.

Nehring, W.M. (1991). Historical look at nursing in the field of mental retardation. Mental Retardation, 29, 259–267.

Olshansky, S. (1962). Chronic sorrow: A response to having a mentally defective child. Social Casework, 43, 190–193.

Opie, N.D., & Tse, A.M. (1988). Perceptions of factors influencing individualized educational plan conference outcomes: Implications for health care. Journal of Pediatric Nursing, 3, 2–10.

Powell, T.H., & Gallagher, P.A. (1993). Brothers & sisters—a special part of exceptional families. (2nd ed.). Baltimore: Paul H. Brookes Publishing Co.

Quinn, M.M. (1991). Attachment between mothers and their Down syndrome infants. Western Journal of Nursing Research, 13, 382–396.

Resnick, M.B., Armstrong, S., & Carter, R.L. (1988). Developmental intervention program for high-risk infants: Effects on development and parent-infant interactions. Developmental and Behavioral Pediatrics, 9, 73–78.

Siantz, M.L. deL. (1977). The nurse and the developmentally disabled adolescent. Baltimore: University Park Press.

Steele, S. (1990). Down syndrome: Nursing interventions newborn through preschool age years. Issues in Comprehensive Pediatric Nursing, 13, 111–126.

Sterling, C.E., Schaffer, S., & Jolley, S.G. (1993). Home management related to medical treatment for childhood gastroesophageal reflux. Pediatric Nursing, 19, 167–173.

Zahr, L. (1991). Correlates of mother–infant interaction in premature infants from low socioeconomic backgrounds. Pediatric Nursing, 17, 259–264.

8

Health Maintenance and Promotion in Adults

Donna Rice O'Brien

OBJECTIVES

On completion of this chapter, the reader will be able to:

- Identify nursing roles in health maintenance/health promotion for adults with developmental disabilities.
- Define the terms *health, wellness, health risk,* and *health promotion.*
- Identify and apply the three levels of prevention.
- Develop and apply health promotion techniques through the various stages of the life span.

OVERVIEW

Nurses promote health in adults with developmental disabilities by acting as health advocates. *Webster's Seventh New World Dictionary* (1991) defines **health** as "the condition of being sound in body, mind or soul; especially freedom from physical disease or pain." The pure definition of **advocate** is "one who pleads the cause of another . . . one who speaks or writes in support of something" (*Webster's*, 1991). Too often, health care in the community for persons with develop- mental disabilities focuses on respond- ing to acute health care needs, while basic health promotion activities are neglected. Adults with developmental disabilities truly need a health care advocate who will make health promo- tion a priority and encourage each in- dividual to engage in behaviors that support wellness and minimize health risks.

Wellness is defined as "the condition of being healthy or sound, especially as the result of proper diet, exercise, etc." (*Webster's*, 1991). The definition of **risk**

is "the chance of injury, damage or loss" (*Webster's*, 1991). A **health risk** is any event or behavior that results in the loss of health or results in injury.

Health promotion is the act of furthering the growth and development of *good health* and *wellness*. Edelman and Mandle (1990) described good health as a static state, and wellness as a "dynamic, a condition of change in which the individual moves forward, climbing toward a higher potential of functioning" (p. 9). This chapter focuses on knowledge and strategies that nurses can utilize in a variety of settings to promote good health and minimize health risks in persons with developmental disabilities.

NURSING ROLES IN HEALTH PROMOTION

Health case management is a paradoxically simple yet complex concept. The fundamental focus of health case management is to integrate, coordinate, and advocate for individuals, families, and groups requiring extensive services. Some persons with developmental disabilities require extensive health care services.

Nurses historically have been, and continue to be, the ideal health care provider to offer health case management services. This involves coordinating efforts between clients, their caregivers, their legal guardians, social workers, and other health care professionals. The health promotion activities discussed in this chapter require coordinated case management by a strong client advocate. The role of the nurse as a health care case manager involves advocacy:

Today, nurses play an integral role in all arenas of health care delivery, with care coordination as the hallmark of their practice. Through the efforts of nurse case managers . . . cost effective care can be provided in an atmosphere of patient advocacy. (Cronenwett, 1992, p. v)

Other health promotion roles for nurses include educator, clinician, and researcher. Parents, legal guardians, and direct caregivers must be informed about health risks and how to encourage healthy behaviors. Persons with developmental disabilities need education, at their level of understanding, about their health care needs and behaviors. Nurses may provide direct care activities such as performing health assessments or organizing mass immunization programs.

Nurses also need to be involved in research. There is currently little research published in the area of nursing and developmental disabilities. There is even less research in the area of health promotion and developmental disabilities. In order to be assured that nursing interventions are producing expected results, research must be done. There is a need for the knowledge base in the area of health promotion and developmental disabilities to be expanded with sound, well-structured research.

Roth and Brown (1991) described several areas in which nurses have an important role, including physical examination, screening for visual and hearing defects, dental care, foot care, birth control, testicular screening, and various women's health issues.

Beange (1986) outlined specific health promotion behaviors for persons with developmental disabilities. The activities included an annual physical exam, frequent medication review, appropriate referrals, nutrition counseling, exercise, preventive physical care, preventive mental health care, and behavioral support.

Pamela, a 46-year-old white female with a developmental disability of unknown etiology, recently moved into a supervised apartment. Prior to that, Pam lived with her mother and received her medical care from the family physician. Pam now comes to the clinic for all her medical care.

On the initial visit, the nurse–practitioner interviews Pam and the apartment supervisor to get a complete medical history. There are no records available at this time. Pam indicates that she is on several medications, although she is not sure why she is on them. The nurse–practitioner recognizes the medications as those given for hypertension, diabetes, and hypercholesterolemia. The supervisor also points out that Pam recently was hospitalized for right arm and chest pain. Neither Pam nor the supervisor knows what tests were done or if a final diagnosis was made.

A complete physical exam is performed by the nurse–practitioner, which reveals that Pam is 50 pounds overweight. Also, her blood pressure is slightly elevated, her skin is dry, and she has a quarter-size, dark raised lesion with irregular borders on her back. The remainder of the examination is normal.

Laboratory tests are ordered by the nurse–practitioner, including a serum glucose and glycohemoglobin to determine the status of her diabetes. In an effort to avoid duplicating tests done during her recent hospitalization, the nurse–practitioner arranges to have the medical records released to the clinic.

The lab results indicate that Pam's diabetes is in poor control on her current medication dose and diet. In consultation with the physician, her oral diabetes medication is increased, and a referral is made to the dietitian. The dietitian meets with both Pam and the apartment staff to discuss her diet as it relates to her diabetes and her high cholesterol. The nurse–practitioner will review and reinforce the diet on subsequent visits to the clinic. In addition, the nurse–practitioner counsels Pam on the benefits of exercise. Pam states that she enjoys riding a stationary bike, although she does not use it regularly. A stress test is ordered to be sure there is no contraindication to initiating an aerobic exercise program. Her stress test is normal, and Pam and the apartment staff are counseled by the nurse–practitioner on initiating an exercise program, with written instructions and personalized goals.

The lesion on Pam's back was suspicious because of its size, darkness, and irregularly shaped borders. Pam was referred to a dermatologist, who recommended surgical removal of the lesion. The nurse–practitioner informed Pam's legal guardian and assisted in obtaining the written informed consent. Pam was referred to a surgical clinic, where, under local anesthesia, the lesion was removed. After analysis by the pathologist, it was diagnosed as a benign nevus. Pam will not need any further treatment unless the lesion returns, or similar lesions appear on other areas of her body.

Once Pam's past medical records are received, they are reviewed carefully by the nurse–practitioner and the physician. Pam had extensive testing for her arm and chest pain, and the final diagnosis was viral gastroenteritis. Because Pam is no longer experiencing the pain, and all her tests were negative, there is no need for further workup.

Pam does not remember when she had her last eye examination, and the nurse–practitioner recognizes the importance of at least yearly visits in a client who has diabetes and/or hypertension. The nurse–practitioner refers Pam to an ophthal-

(*continued*)

mologist. The evaluation by the ophthalmologist is unremarkable, and Pam will return to him for yearly examinations.

Pam also does not remember when, or even if, she has ever had a gynecological examination. Although she reports she is not sexually active, an appointment is made by the nurse–practitioner for Pam to have an examination. Pam is quite nervous about the examination. The nurse–practitioner reviews with Pam the equipment used, allowing her to hold the speculum and feel the "cytobrush." A detailed explanation of the procedure is given and Pam is given an opportunity to ask questions. The examination and the Pap smear are normal. The exam will be repeated in 1 year, and, if that is normal, it will be done every 3 years as long as Pam remains sexually inactive and asymptomatic.

Because she has diabetes and hypertension, Pam is evaluated at least every 3 months. On her first visit back to the nurse–practitioner, she reports that she is using her exercise bike fairly regularly, and is trying to keep to her diet. She has lost 3 pounds, her blood pressure is improved, and her glycohemoglobin indicates her diabetes is in better control. She is proud of her accomplishments and looks forward to her next visit. The nurse–practitioner has managed Pam's health care effectively, as a direct care provider, advocate, case manager, and educator.

For all adults with developmental disabilities, the primary focus of all nursing interventions is on attaining and/or maintaining an optimal level of wellness. For persons with developmental disabilities, health education is needed in the areas of alcohol, tobacco, nutrition, exercise, and stress (Brooks-Bertram, 1986). Elderly persons with developmental disabilities were observed to have greater debilitation in self-care and mobility skills than that of the general elderly population. They also were noted to have increased prevalence of cardiovascular, musculoskeletal, and sensory impairments (Janicki & MacEachron, 1984). Nurses are in an ideal position to identify behaviors that increase health risks. They can then counsel and educate individuals in ways to effectively modify these behaviors and promote health.

LEVELS OF PREVENTION

Traditionally, the goal of health promotion has been absence of disease; however, in recent years this view has changed. "Health promotion becomes a broader, more comprehensive area because it includes not just individuals' health, but also family, community and environmental contributions to health" (Benner & Wrubel, 1989, p. 146). In a classic work on health and prevention, Leavell and Clark (1965) described a model based on three levels of prevention. Although written by physicians, this model has provided a comprehensive framework for health promotion and has been used widely by nurses (Edelman & Mandle, 1990; Stanhope & Lancaster, 1992). The three levels of prevention are primary, secondary, and tertiary prevention.

Primary prevention is generalized health promotion and protection from disease. It includes anticipatory guidance, education to reduce health risk behaviors, and motivation to engage in healthy behaviors. Providing immunizations is an example of a primary prevention intervention.

Secondary prevention occurs early in a disease state. It focuses on obtaining a health history and performing a physical examination as well as exam screenings for previously undetected health problems. It includes early diagnosis and prompt treatment to limit disability from the disease process. An example of secondary prevention would be treatment of an individual who has abnormal results from a Pap smear.

Tertiary prevention involves the management of chronic illness to prevent complications and further disability. Monitoring anticonvulsant levels in a person who has seizures would be considered an example of tertiary intervention. For the purposes of this chapter, most discussions involve primary prevention as it relates to health promotion.

Primary prevention includes health education, optimal nutrition, attention to personality developments, and adequate housing, recreation, and vocational opportunities, as well as periodic examinations that have high specificity and sensitivity. Dr. Robert Lawrence, Chair of the U.S. Preventive Services Task Force, has noted that, by modifying behaviors related to tobacco, alcohol, drugs, nutrition, and exercise, 40%–70% of premature deaths could be avoided, in addition to one third of acute disabilities and two thirds of chronic disabilities (U.S. Preventive Services Task Force, 1989). The use of periodic health examinations, immunizations, environmental sanitation, good hygiene practices, protection from occupational hazards, and prevention of accidents are primary interventions. Figure 1 presents age-related guidelines for periodic health screening tests, immunizations, and health education.

PERIODIC HEALTH EXAMINATION

The use of routine health examinations is perhaps the most effective method of early detection of health problems. It also provides the nurse with an opportunity to assess health knowledge and practices. A natural sequela to the examination is a review of current status with the individual and/or his or her caregiver. This is an optimal time to provide effective health teaching and provide health guidance for the coming year.

The Young Adult (Age 21–39 Years)

The young adult should have a yearly blood pressure screening, breast exam, testicular exam, and dental exam (Hoole, Greenberg, & Picard, 1988). Depending on underlying medical problems, laboratory tests are ordered as needed. Cholesterol levels should be monitored every 5 years, and more frequently if a high level previously has been documented. Screening for tuberculosis should be done at least every 10 years, and more frequently in high-risk populations. Some state organizations may have specific requirements. For example, in New Jersey, persons registered with the Division of Developmental Disabilities are required to have tuberculosis screening done every 3 years.

Periodic gynecological exams and Pap smears are recommended for all women. Sexually active women should have annual Pap smears and screenings for sexually transmitted diseases. This is especially important if they have had multiple sexual partners. Persons with developmental disabilities who are sexually active usually will permit an adequate gynecological examination to be performed. It is essential that counseling regarding human immunodeficiency virus and acquired immunodeficiency syndrome be done with any sexually active individual.

In women with developmental disabilities who are not sexually active, it is often not possible to perform an ade-

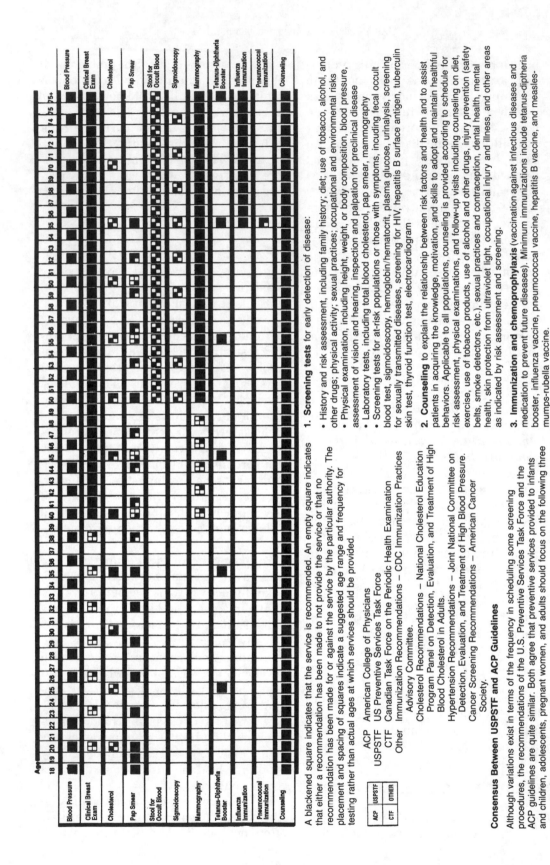

A blackened square indicates that the service is recommended. An empty square indicates that either a recommendation has been made to not provide the service or that no recommendation has been made for or against the service by the particular authority. The placement and spacing of squares indicate a suggested age range and frequency for testing rather than actual ages at which services should be provided.

	ACP	USPSTF
	CTF	OTHER

ACP   American College of Physicians
USPSTF US Preventive Services Task Force
CTF   Canadian Task Force on the Periodic Health Examination
Other   Immunization Recommendations – CDC Immunization Practices
           Advisory Committee.
           Cholesterol Recommendations – National Cholesterol Education
           Program Panel on Detection, Evaluation, and Treatment of High
           Blood Cholesterol in Adults.
           Hypertension Recommendations – Joint National Committee on
           Detection, Evaluation, and Treatment of High Blood Pressure.
           Cancer Screening Recommendations – American Cancer
           Society.

Consensus Between USPSTF and ACP Guidelines

Although variations exist in terms of the frequency in scheduling some screening procedures, the recommendations of the U.S. Preventive Services Task Force and the ACP guidelines are quite similar. Both agree that preventive services provided to infants and children, adolescents, pregnant women, and adults should focus on the following three components:

1. **Screening tests** for early detection of disease:
- History and risk assessment, including family history; diet; use of tobacco, alcohol, and other drugs; physical activity; sexual practices; occupational and environmental risks
- Physical examination, including height, weight, or body composition, blood pressure, assessment of vision and hearing, inspection and palpation for preclinical disease
- Laboratory tests, including total blood cholesterol, pap smear, mammography
- Screening tests for at-risk populations or those with symptoms, including fecal occult blood test, sigmoidoscopy, hemoglobin/hematocrit, plasma glucose, urinalysis, screening for sexually transmitted diseases, screening for HIV, hepatitis B surface antigen, tuberculin skin test, thyroid function test, electrocardiogram

2. **Counseling** to explain the relationship between risk factors and health and to assist patients in acquiring the knowledge, motivation, and skills to adopt and maintain healthful behaviors. Applicable to all populations, counseling is provided according to schedule for risk assessment, physical examinations, and follow-up visits including counseling on diet, exercise, use of tobacco products, use of alcohol and other drugs, injury prevention (safety belts, smoke detectors, etc.), sexual practices and contraception, dental health, mental health, skin protection from ultraviolet light, occupational injury and illness, and other areas as indicated by risk assessment and screening.

3. **Immunization and chemoprophylaxis** (vaccination against infectious diseases and medication to prevent future diseases). Minimum immunizations include tetanus-diptheria booster, influenza vaccine, pneumococcal vaccine, hepatitis B vaccine, and measles-mumps-rubella vaccine.

Figure 1. Recommendations for preventive care guidelines from various North American health organizations. (From American College of Physicians. [1991].)

quate exam. This can be due to patient anxiety and uncooperative behavior, poor positioning as a result of cerebral palsy or other musculoskeletal problem, or the presence of an extremely small introitus. In these cases, if the woman is not sexually active and not at increased risk for cervical cancer, the benefits of a Pap smear must be weighed against the risks of aggressive procedures to obtain one. Low doses of muscle relaxants (Valium) have proven helpful in situations of voluntary or involuntary muscular misalignment. In a small number of cases, general anesthesia may be necessary to ensure an adequate exam and Pap smear. Most individuals can be followed symptomatically. If there is a high index of suspicion because of the presence of positive symptoms or physical findings, a pelvic ultrasound may be a helpful diagnostic tool.

The Middle-Age
Adult (Age 40–59 Years)

In addition to those screening measures outlined for the young adult, the middle-age adult requires screening for other high-risk problems associated with advancing age. Prostate examination as a screening tool for the presence of prostrate cancer should be done yearly. In the individual who cannot cooperate for adequate examination, and in the presence of urinary tract symptoms, measurement of the prostate-specific antigen (PSA) level can be done. A PSA measurement is now recommended annually in all men over age 50 (Abramowicz, 1992).

For women, a baseline mammogram should be made once after age 35, then every other year through ages 40–50. After age 50, low-dose mammography is recommended annually, according to the American Cancer Society (Hoole et al., 1988). Pap smears should be done yearly in sexually active women. Discussion of possible estrogen replacement therapy should take place with high-risk perimenopausal women to reduce the risk of osteoporosis. Rectal exams and stool tests for occult blood should be done on both sexes annually after age 40.

The Older Adult
(Age 60 Years and Older)

Health promotion activities should continue throughout the life span. Awareness of the normal aging process will assist in planning appropriate interventions. As the body ages, the rate of cell division decreases. Organ systems become less efficient as cells die. Between 20% and 40% of neurons die with advanced age. A decrease in nerve conduction substances (neurotransmitters) can result in neurological deficits. There is a decrease in cardiac output as a result of a decrease in muscle mass and strength. The work load on the heart increases as peripheral resistance increases with atherosclerosis. The resulting decrease in cardiac output reduces blood flow to the body, including the kidneys, where there is a 30% decrease in blood flow. A decrease in bladder size predisposes the individual to urinary incontinence and frequency. Less efficient gas exchange occurs in the lungs as a result of a decrease in alveolar surface area and reduced elasticity. A decrease in saliva production may increase swallowing difficulties. There is a decrease in visual acuity and loss of hearing (Edelman & Mandle, 1990). These are just a few of the many physical changes that occur with normal aging. All of them have implications for the nurse who is promoting health activities for older persons with developmental disabilities.

The older adult should continue to have annual physical examinations, including blood pressure screening, vision and hearing screening, a complete skin exam, dental exam, breast, testicular, and rectal/prostate exams, stool test for occult blood, and screening for tuberculosis (Hoole et al., 1988). Cholesterol levels should continue to be monitored. More frequent visits to the health care provider are necessary if the individual has any underlying chronic condition such as diabetes mellitus or hypertension. Yearly examination by an ophthalmologist for glaucoma and cataract screening is recommended for persons over aged 65. Low-dose mammography should continue on an annual basis. Pap smears must be performed yearly in high-risk individuals. The American Cancer Society recommends sigmoidoscopy every 3–5 years after age 50; however, this recommendation is not supported by the U.S. Preventive Services Task Force (1989). Laboratory and ancillary tests should include fasting blood sugar, cholesterol, urinalysis, and electrocardiogram. Underlying medical conditions and medication use would determine what other tests should be done.

Special Considerations in Persons with Developmental Disabilities

Nurses advocating for the health care needs of the person with developmental disabilities must be aware that special health considerations exist in many persons with developmental disabilities, based on the etiology of their disability. They must educate family members as well as all program providers about these needs. In addition to periodic screening, these special considerations in persons with developmental disabilities should be evaluated during their annual exam.

For example, persons with Down syndrome have many health concerns (Table 1). Because thyroid and cardiac disease frequently are found in this population, thorough thyroid and cardiac exams should be performed. Baseline echocardiograms and thyroid function tests also should be obtained. Baseline and follow-up radiographic studies of the cervical spine also should be done to rule

out atlantoaxial subluxation. Mental status exams should start in young adulthood. It has been noted that there is an increased incidence of neuropathological changes consistent with Alzheimers' disease in persons with Down syndrome (Pueschel & Pueschel, 1992). The onset is usually earlier than in the general population. Symptoms include a steady deterioration in memory, language, and motor functions. Bowel and bladder incontinence are common in older persons with Down syndrome, as is an associated new-onset generalized seizure disorder.

Another example of special health considerations is that of persons with the fragile X syndrome. These individuals also have been noted to have an increased incidence of heart disease, and mitral valve prolapse is common (Loehr, Synhorst, Wolfe, & Hagerman, 1986). A baseline echocardiogram should be obtained on these individuals. A third example is persons with neurofibromatosis, who are at risk for hypertension and certain cancers. Health care providers, including nurses, must maintain a high index of suspicion when performing "routine" evaluations on these individuals. If a person with a developmental disability has any other known developmental diagnosis, the associated features of that problem may put the person at risk for other health problems. *Smith's Recognizable Patterns of Human Malformation* (Jones, 1988) is an excellent resource to help identify associated features.

IMMUNIZATIONS

The past 50 years have seen a tremendous decrease in the mortality and morbidity associated with infectious illnesses. This has been largely because of the widespread use of immunizations for preventable diseases. Unfortunately, some individuals never receive their primary immunizations. This can be as a

Table 1. Special health concerns in persons with Down syndrome

Concern	Clinical expression	When seen	Prevalence	Management
Congenital heart disease	Endocardial cushion defect, ventricular septal defect, tetralogy of Fallot	Newborn or first year	34%	ECG, chest X ray, cardiac consultation, surgical repair
Hypotomia	Reduced muscle tone, increased range of joints, motor function problems	Throughout; improvement with maturity	All	Guidance by physical therapy, early intervention
Delayed growth	Typically at or near third percentile	Throughout	All	Early nutritional support; check heart
Developmental delays	Some global delay, variable degrees; special language problems	1st yr; continues	All	Early intervention, special education language therapy
Hearing problems	Serous otitis media, small ear canals, conductive impairment	Check by 1 yr; review regularly	70%	Audiology, tympanometry, ENT consultation
Ocular problems	Refractive errors, strabismus, cataracts	Eye exam by 1 yr, then follow-ups	50%, 35%, 15%	Ophthalmologic consultation
Cervical spine abnormality	Atlantoaxial instability, potential long-track signs	X ray by 3 yr; occasional repeat	10% ±, 1%–2% +	Orthopedic neurologic help; possible restriction, fusion
Thyroid disease	Hypothyroidism (rare hyper-), decreased growth	Some congenital; most 2nd + decade; check 2 yr, repeat	15%	Replacement therapy as needed
Obesity	Excessive weight gain	2–3 yr, 12–13 yr, and in adult life	Common	Caloric restriction activity
Seizure disorders	Primary generalized (also hypsarrhythmia)	Any time	5%–10%	Usual management
Emotional problems	Inappropriate behavior, depression, other emotional disturbances	Mid to late childhood, adult life	Common	Mental health assistance, family guidance
Premature senescence	Behavioral changes, functional losses	4th, 5th decades	Unknown (increased rate)	Special support

From: Rubin, I. L., & Crocker, A. C. (1989). *Developmental disabilities: Delivery of medical care for children and adults* (p. 17). Philadelphia: Lea & Febiger; reprinted with permission.

result of complacency (i.e., "there hasn't been a case of measles here in years"), unwarranted fears (i.e., "pertussis vaccine causes brain damage"), postponement of immunizations because of medical fragility during early childhood, or lack of access to health care services (i.e., "our health insurance only paid for illness-related care; immunizations weren't covered") (Whaley & Wong, 1991).

Adults who were not adequately immunized or infected as children are at increased risk for developing these preventable diseases and their secondary complications. The problem of such childhood diseases as measles, mumps, and rubella occurring in adulthood is well documented (Centers for Disease Control, 1990). The rate of adult cases of tetanus and diphtheria between 1985 and 1989 were 92% and 64%, respectively. In addition, safe and effective adult vaccines that are readily available for influenza and pneumococcal pneumonia are disproportionately underutilized (Centers for Disease Control, 1990).

There has been recent national awareness of this problem, resulting in the formation of the National Coalition for Adult Immunizations in 1988. The Coalition comprises over 50 groups from both the private and public sectors. Its goal it is to improve the immunization status of adults through education of patients and health care providers. National attention to the problem of adult immunizations is expressed in *Healthy People 2000: National Health Promotion and Disease Prevention Objectives* (U.S. Public Health Service, 1990). This document outlines the strategy for improving the health of the nation over the next 10 years. Of the 19 health objectives related to immunizations, 10 are related specifically to adult immunizations (see Table 2).

Special Concerns for Individuals with Developmental Disabilities

In addition to the problems of the general population, such as cost, lack of third-party payment for vaccines, safety concerns, and lack of information about adult immunizations, persons with developmental disabilities have other immunization-related concerns. Incomplete childhood illness and immunization records make it difficult for the health care provider to determine the immunization status of those persons with developmental disabilities who cannot give their own health histories. Persons with developmental disabilities who live primarily in group settings (i.e., institutions, group homes, day and adult training centers and workshops) are at increased risk for various infectious diseases. In particular, individuals with Down syndrome have an altered immune status and therefore are more susceptible to infectious diseases ("The high susceptibility to infections, high risk of malignancies, and increased frequency of autoantibodies have suggested that derangements of humoral and/or cell-mediated immunity may contribute to the clinical picture of Down syndrome" [Pueschel & Pueschel, 1992, p. 218]). If an individual has a cognitive deficit,

---

Table 2.   Healthy People 2000 immunization and infectious diseases objectives

Health Status Objectives

1. Reduce indigenous cases of vaccine-preventable diseases.
2. Reduce epidemic-related pneumonia and influenza deaths among people age 65 and older to no more than 7.3:100,000. (Baseline: Average of 9.1:100,000 during 1980 through 1987)
3. Reduce viral hepatitis.
4. Reduce tuberculosis to an incidence of no more than 3.5 cases per 100,000 people. (Baseline 9.1:100,000 in 1988)
5. Reduce pneumonia-related days of restricted activity.

Risk Reduction Objectives

6. Increased immunization levels.
7. Reduce post exposure rabies treatments to no more than 9,000 per year. (Baseline: 18,000 estimated treatments in 1987)

Service and Protection Objectives

8. Increase to at least 90% the proportion of primary care providers who provide information and counseling about immunizations and offer immunization as appropriate for their patients.
9. Increase to at least 90% the proportion of public health departments that provide adult immunization for influenza, pneumococcal disease, hepatitis B, tetanus, and diptheria.
10. Increase to at least 90% the proportion of local health departments that have ongoing programs for actively identifying cases of tuberculosis and latent infection in populations at high risk for tuberculosis.

Adapted from U.S. Public Health Service. (1990).

he or she may not understand the need for or have adequate knowledge to use methods that decrease the transmission of infectious diseases, such as hand washing. If this person has an accompanying physical disability, he or she may need assistance with such methods.

In addition, the issue of obtaining informed consent for vaccine administration can delay or prevent an individual from being adequately immunized. The National Childhood Vaccine Injury Act (PL 99-660) requires that vaccine materials be given by the health care provider to each adult or legal representative of each person receiving the following vaccines: diphtheria, tetanus, pertussis, measles, mumps, rubella, and poliomyelitis vaccines (Centers for Disease Control, 1991a). Because a significant number of adults with developmental disabilities do not represent themselves legally, either a family member or a representative from a state agency is designated by the courts as legal guardian. In order to obtain informed consent to give a particular vaccine, the health care provider must be willing and able to call or write the legal guardian. The need to comply with PL 99-660 means that often the needed vaccine cannot be administered at the time of the person's regularly scheduled medical visit. This can result in extra visits to the health care provider solely for the purpose of immunization. The nurse who is aware of this issue can attempt to facilitate obtaining the legal consent forms prior to the regularly scheduled health appointment.

When a legal guardian is contacted, there may be resistance or refusal to providing the consent as a result of fear of neurological injury or severe adverse reaction. As a health educator, the nurse can provide information to allay concerns and/or fears. It is important that informed consent be given or withheld on the basis of an understanding of the benefits versus the risks inherent in the immunization process. At the same time, the nurse can provide information about the immunization process to increase awareness and an improved vaccination rate in order to promote health in persons with developmental disabilities.

Recordkeeping and Immunization Schedules

By the time an individual with developmental disabilities has attained adulthood, all of the routine immunizations of childhood should have been received. Nurses in every setting should make it a priority to obtain a thorough immunization history as part of the individual's health history and initial assessment. This will alert the nurse to any omissions in the person's immunization history. The nurse then can develop and implement a program to update immunizations as necessary. If the individual does not have a record of prior immunizations, the nurse should initiate a written record. The adult with developmental disabilities should be encouraged to maintain a complete set of health records that can be shared with any new health care provider. A duplicate set of records may be maintained by the nurse, family, or program provider as appropriate.

The following immunizations should be considered for an adult with developmental disabilities.

Tetanus and Diphtheria If an individual has completed the primary three-dose series of tetanus and diphtheria vaccinations, booster doses of the combined tetanus and diphtheria toxoids should be given once every 10 years. If the immunization history is incomplete, the nurse should inquire about recent lacerations or travel that might provide information about recent vaccination. A primary series of vaccines should be given if one has not been administered previously. This involves giving two doses of a combined tetanus and diphtheria toxoid intramuscularly at least 4 weeks apart, followed by a third dose 6–12 months later (American College of Physicians, 1990).

Measles, Mumps, and Rubella Because of the recent measles outbreaks in the adolescent and young adult populations, it is important to assess whether or not an individual is immune. Persons are considered immune if they were born before 1957, or have had documented physician-diagnosed measles, or have laboratory evidence of immunity (Centers for Disease Control, 1989). If the individual does not meet one of these criteria, then he or she should receive one dose of live attenuated measles vaccine (Centers for Disease Control, 1991b).

Middle-age adults, born before 1957, should be protected against measles through natural immunity, and unlike the young adult should not require additional measles vaccinations. However, 29% of health care workers who developed measles between 1985 and 1989 were born before 1957 (Centers for Disease Control, 1991b). Middle-age adults who will be working in health care facilities or traveling internationally may be at increased risk for measles, and may want to consider having their rubeola titers checked and receiving live measles vaccination if necessary.

Once again, persons with developmental disabilities may not have proof of immunization or childhood illness records. The most cost-effective way to assure immunity is to vaccinate with two doses of live-measles-virus vaccine given at least 1 month apart. However, drawing rubeola titers when performing annual lab tests may be an alternative. For those individuals who do require the measles vaccine, it is suggested that the measles–mumps–rubella (MMR) vaccine be given to protect those who do not have immu-

nity to mumps and especially to protect women of childbearing age against rubella (American College of Physicians, 1990). The MMR vaccine should *not* be given to a woman who is pregnant.

Influenza All individuals over age 65 should receive the influenza vaccine annually. Complications from influenza increase morbidity and mortality, especially in the elderly. Although not traditionally recommended for young adults in the general population, the influenza vaccine is recommended for certain groups of persons with developmental disabilities. Anyone living in a group home or institution, or working in a group setting such as a workshop or activity center, should be considered for vaccination. Persons with underlying medical problems, such as cardiac, respiratory, and metabolic disorders, should receive the influenza vaccine. The vaccine is given annually because the antigen components change every year, depending on what viruses are determined to be dominant in the forthcoming influenza season. The timing of the vaccine is important; it should be administered 4–8 weeks prior to the influenza season in any given region. This allows time for adequate antibody development before the onset of the "flu" season. For example, in the Northeast, influenza vaccines usually are given by the end of November, prior to the winter months' influenza season (American College of Physicians, 1990).

Pneumococcal Pneumonia As with the influenza vaccine, the pneumococcal pneumonia vaccine is not traditionally recommended for young adults. However, persons with developmental disabilities who have chronic respiratory, cardiac, or metabolic diseases should receive the vaccine. It is also recommended for individuals over age 65, anyone who is anatomically or functionally asplenic (i.e., the individual does not have a spleen or has one that functions poorly), or anyone who is immunocompromised (including asymptomatic or symptomatic human immunodeficiency virus infection, Hodgkin disease, lymphoma, multiple myeloma, chronic renal failure, nephrotic syndrome, or recent organ transplantation) (Centers for Disease Control, 1991b). Usually the vaccine is given only once in a lifetime, but individuals in high-risk categories, such as those with asplenia or chronic renal disease, should receive it every 6 years because of the rapid decline of pneumococcal antibody levels in these patients.

Hepatitis B Virus   Vaccination against hepatitis B infection is extremely important in persons with developmental disabilities. If an individual has not been immunized by young adulthood, the three-dose series should be administered. Studies indicate lower seroconversion rates as an individual ages, so it is advantageous to vaccinate as early as possible (Hadler, 1990).

NUTRITION AND WEIGHT

Nutrition is as important for persons with developmental disabilities as it is for persons in the general population, and in many cases more important. The nutritional needs of persons with developmental disabilities should be assessed continually. Discussions regarding nutrition and weight should be conducted at least on an annual basis. Staff members of group homes could benefit from structured nutritional counseling from a nurse or a registered dietitian. Families with an adult member with developmental disabilities living at home also may benefit from this kind of support and counseling.

Obesity

Obesity was found to be the number one medical problem in an outpatient population of persons with developmental disabilities in Australia; 46% were obese as defined by the Body Mass Index (Beange, 1986). Fox and Rotatori (1982) also found obesity to be common in persons with developmental disabilities, regardless of living arrangement (i.e., institution, group home, or family home). They also found obesity in this population to be more common in women than men and more prevalent among those with higher levels of cognitive functioning. Prevalence increases with age, although this finding was not as significant as sex or level of cognitive functioning.

Risk Factors for Obesity   Persons with developmental disabilities are at risk for obesity for many reasons. There may be underlying *chromosomal abnormalities,* such as those found in Down syndrome, Prader-Willi syndrome, Froehlich syndrome, and Laurence-Moon-Biedl syndrome. *Medical conditions* such as Cushings' syndrome, hypothyroidism, and insulin-secreting tumors can cause obesity, although these are infrequent causes. With *advancing age* comes decreased caloric requirements, although caloric intake may remain the same or increase.

More *choice in meal preparation* as a result of new independent living arrangements or group home agency rules forbidding any restrictions on dietary intake may enable persons with developmental disabilities to overeat. An in-home assessment may reveal cabinets full of "goodies" that are high in calories and fat and low in nutritive value. In addition, dinner menus often are high in calories but do not meet the Recommended Daily Allowances (Mercer & Ekvall, 1982).

Many persons with developmental disabilities who live in the community lack any structured exercise program. *Sedentary lifestyles* can lead to obesity. Disabilities that combine impaired mobility with normal hand skills and normal oral motor abilities (e.g., spina bifida) can predispose the individual to inactivity and promote weight gain. Persons with developmental disabilities benefit from encouragement and support in engaging in structured exercise programs.

Persons on certain *medications*, such as the phenothiazines (especially Mellaril), will gain weight as a result of increased appetite. Other medications that can increase appetite include antihistamines, oral contraceptives, insulin, steroids, and antidepressants. *Behavior modification* plans that utilize food as the primary motivator for a person with severe, challenging behaviors can be another source of unwanted weight gain.

Promotion of Ideal Body Weight

Obesity predisposes individuals to other medical problems, such a hypertension, diabetes mellitus, gallstones, and osteoarthritis. To promote optimal health, it is necessary for the individual to work toward ideal body weight. In working with persons with developmental disabilities, it is important to counsel the person or his or her caregivers on how to achieve ideal body weight. The following are general guidelines regarding ideal body weight. For women, allow 100 pounds for the first 5 feet, and add 5 pounds for each inch over 5 feet. Thus, a woman 5'7" tall would have an ideal body weight of 135 pounds. For men, allow 106 pounds for the first 5 feet, and add 6 pounds for each inch over 5 feet. Thus, a man 5'11" tall would have an ideal body weight of 172 pounds. For both men and women, 10% can be added to the total for larger boned individuals and 10% deducted for smaller boned individuals.

Underweight

Being under ideal body weight can be a problem for some individuals with developmental disabilities. Up to 25% of people with mental retardation are underweight (Similia & Niskanen, 1991).

This is more common in those individuals with lower levels of cognitive functioning and those with multiple disabilities and feeding difficulties (e.g., persons with cerebral palsy).

Some persons who have mental health problems have ruminating behaviors and anorexia; as a result, their total caloric intake does not meet their metabolic needs. These individuals may require intervention from a mental health professional as well as careful monitoring of nutritional status. Poor nutrition can lead to debilitation, susceptibility to opportunistic infections, and even death. Behavioral programs can be used to decrease rumination, especially if it is a self-stimulating behavior. Nutritional counseling can be effective only if the individual and a concerned caregiver have the capabilities to understand dietary requirements. They must be willing and able to monitor and document the individual's eating patterns, behavioral episodes, and weight pattern. A good relationship with a dietitian or health care provider in conjunction with the behavioral program may be effective in decreasing or eliminating ruminating activity.

Stimulants given to treat attention deficit hyperactivity disorder or antidepressants used to treat depression are two examples of medications that may cause weight loss. Medical conditions such as diabetes mellitus, endocrine disease, gastrointestinal disease, infection, and malignancies should be considered in the individual with unexplained weight loss or inability to gain weight.

As the individual with developmental disabilities ages, if there is ongoing weight loss, an aggressive approach to the diagnosis of a medical problem may be needed. All of the considerations that pertain to the young adult apply here; however, a higher degree of suspicion should be maintained. Proper nutrition in the older adult with developmental disabilities is just as important as it is at any other time throughout the life span. Caution should be used when assessing intake in relation to the Recommended Daily Allowances because they do not take into consideration special needs for an aging population. Nutritional requirements may be affected by chronic disease or medication use. With a decrease in basal metabolic rate and less physical activity, there is a decrease in energy needs. These factors must be considered when determining nutritional requirements.

Problems with adequate intake in the older adult may result from dental and chewing problems or from gastrointestinal disease. A decreased appetite may result from altered taste sensation or constipation. Side effects of medications given for other medical or psychiatric problems also may contribute to a decline in appetite. Some psychiatric disorders, such as depression, will have anorexia as a main symptom. It is important for the nurse to be aware of any change in appetite and/or nutritional intake and intervene accordingly. Nutritional supplements may be necessary to maintain ideal body weight. Increased fluid intake and regular exercise should be encouraged to prevent constipation.

EXERCISE

Exercise is an important factor in achieving and maintaining ideal body weight and staying healthy. Sedentary lifestyles have been associated with increases in coronary artery disease, diabetes mellitus, and osteoporosis. Although little research has been done to evaluate exercise in persons with developmental disabilities, at least 40% of the general population is considered to be sedentary (U.S. Preventive Services Task Force, 1989). Between 80% and 94% are exer-

cising at a suboptimal level, not obtaining any cardiorespiratory benefits. The U.S. Preventive Services Task Force recommends counseling all individuals regarding regular exercise.

There is support for the claim that minimally supervised exercise programs for adults with mental retardation result in improved cardiovascular fitness (Compton, Eisenman, & Henderson, 1989; Pitetti & Tan, 1991; Tomprorowski & Ellis, 1985). Considerations for young adults with developmental disabilities include preexisting medical illness (e.g., cardiac disease and atlantoaxial subluxation for individuals with Down syndrome). Detection of these conditions may require diagnostic workups, such as stress testing for cardiac disease; their presence (e.g., atlantoaxial subluxation) may result in restrictions on certain types of activities. Working with a physical, occupational, or recreational therapist may be helpful to develop appropriate programs for clients who have severe physical disabilities. Adapted physical education curriculums are available and can be beneficial when implemented properly.

Older adults starting structured exercise programs should have stress tests first, especially if there is any history of cardiac disease. Once it is determined that the individual's cardiac status is stable, an aerobic exercise program (e.g., brisk walking or stationary bicycle riding) can be initiated. Exercise will assist in maintenance of flexibility and increased muscle tone, reducing risks of fractures with the falls that accompany advancing age.

Exercise Programs

Exercise should begin slowly with a gradual increase in intensity. The goal of cardiovascular fitness is to build up, over a period of months, to aerobic exercise lasting 15–45 minutes and done two to four times per week. The target heart rate should be 220 beats per minutes minus age multiplied by 70%. In a man 30 years old, the target heart rate during exercise would be 133 beats per minute ($220-30=190 \times 0.70=133$ beats per minute). Exceeding the target heart rate indicates that the heart is working too hard, and the intensity of the exercise should be reduced (U.S. Preventive Services Task Force, 1989).

Brisk walking is an excellent form of exercise for persons with developmental disabilities. It can be done in groups, if the individual requires supervision or socialization would enhance compliance. In addition, the nurse can assist in locating community recreational resources, such as those sponsored by The Arc (formerly known as the Association for Retarded Citizens) and other organizations such as Special Olympics. Whatever the program, it must be aerobic in nature to reach target heart rates to provide cardiovascular benefit.

TOBACCO, ALCOHOL, AND DRUG USE

An exhaustive review of the literature reveals little research on the use by persons with developmental disabilities of tobacco, alcohol, and other drugs. Although there is a significant body of knowledge about the effects of these substances on the developing fetus in utero and on pregnancy outcomes, very little is known about the epidemiology of these substances in persons with developmental disabilities.

It is well documented that tobacco is a significant human carcinogen, associated with the majority of cancers of the lung, trachea, and bronchus (90%), larynx (80%), oral cavity (92%), and esophagus (78%) (U.S. Preventive Services Task Force, 1989). It is also a leading contributor to atherosclerosis and myocardial infarction (115,000 deaths per year), cerebrovascular disease (27,500 deaths per year), and peripheral vascular disease. Tobacco smoking also is associated with chronic obstructive pulmonary disease (60,000 deaths per year), pneumonia, and influenza. Nonsmokers also are affected and may be at increased risk for lung cancer if they are exposed to secondary cigarette smoke. In utero, cigarette smoking is associated with miscarriages, low birth weight, stillbirth, and retarded growth. In addition to direct medical pathology, 25% of all deaths from residential fires were attributed to cigarette smoking (U.S. Preventive Services Task Force, 1989).

One half of all Americans drink alcohol; 11% do so on a daily basis (U.S. Preventive Services Task Force, 1989). Excessive alcohol consumption contributes to deaths from motor vehicle accidents, drownings, accidents, homicides, suicides, and medical problems such as hepatitis, cirrhosis, pancreatitis, thiamine deficiency, gastrointestinal bleeding, and cardiomyopathy. In pregnancy, 1 of 750 newborns is born with fetal alcohol syndrome (U.S. Preventive Services Task Force, 1989). Illegal use of various drugs, such as cocaine, marijuana, and heroin, is also a serious problem in this country, leading to higher mortality rates in young adults and adolescents.

Risk Assessment and Education

It is prudent to assume that persons with developmental disabilities are at risk for these behaviors. Although the incidence of persons with developmental disabilities using tobacco, alcohol, and drugs is not known, they are at risk for substance abuse. Experience in one clinic for persons with developmental disabilities has indicated that, the higher the individual's cognitive functioning and the more independent his or her living situation, the more at risk the person is for substance abuse.

Gary, a 25-year-old individual who lived in his own apartment with minimal supervision, was evaluated in a clinic after a severe beating. He was beaten because he owed $2,000 in drug money and could not pay it back. Gary had no understanding of the consequences of buying and using illegal drugs.

The nurse must be aware of signs and symptoms of tobacco, alcohol, and drug abuse, and intervene accordingly. Many people believe that a person with a developmental disability has a right to choose to smoke cigarettes, and cigarettes have even been used as a motivator in formal behavior management plans. The nurse must be the health care advocate and educate the person on the benefits of quitting smoking. If there is a true nicotine addiction involved, the person may be a candidate for a nicotine patch. This can be used in conjunction with counseling and/or support groups. If the nurse suspects an alcohol or drug abuse problem, referrals to support groups, counselors, and health care professionals trained in substance abuse may be necessary. It is most important to educate persons with developmental disabilities when they are young, before they start engaging in these behaviors or before they enter high-risk groups (i.e., before placement in an independent living arrangement) (Agran, Marchand-Martella, & Martella, 1994).

SAFETY ISSUES

Accidental injuries are the fourth leading cause of death in the United States in persons under age 45. Of these, half are related to motor vehicle accidents. Males between ages 15 and 24 have the highest mortality rate from motor vehicle accidents. Less than one half of all Americans use seat belts (U.S. Preventive Services Task Force, 1989). The other one half of deaths related to unintentional injuries are due to falls, drowning, fires and burns, poisoning, and firearm injuries. Each year 12,000 older Americans die as a result of falls. There are 172,000 hip fractures each year in the United States that are attributed to falls, seriously increasing mortality rates in the first year after the fracture (U.S. Preventive Services Task Force, 1989).

There is little research specifically examining injuries in the community-based population of persons with developmental disabilities, but common sense can direct interventions. Persons with developmental disabilities are especially at risk as a result of various neurological problems, such as cerebral palsy and disorders of vision and hearing. Increasing numbers of safeguards must be implemented for individuals with lower levels of cognitive functioning.

Environmental assessments should include attention to lighting, floor structures, and possible hazards such as throw rugs, electrical cords, and traction strips on stairs. Handrails should be secure on stairways and in bathrooms. Visual acuity should be evaluated yearly to assure optimal vision. Swimming pools should be enclosed and secured from easy unsupervised access. Smoke detectors should be in place in key positions throughout the home, with frequent fire drills to ensure that everyone knows the escape route. Clients who smoke should not do so in bedrooms or near upholstered furniture. To reduce the possibility of burns, water heater temperature should be reduced to 120°F (U.S. Preventive Services Task Force, 1989). Medications and poisonous substances should be locked and not accessible. Careful assessment of the person's ability to self-medicate should be made prior to initiating a self-medication program. Syrup of ipecac should be available, and the poison control number posted with other emergency numbers. Nurses assessing the home must be aware of all potential dangers and counsel clients and their caregivers accordingly.

OCCUPATIONAL HAZARDS

The Occupational Safety and Health Act of 1970 was designed to protect all employees and guarantee that employers provide a safe and healthful environment for their employees (Levy & Wegman, 1988). Nurses sensitive to this concept can advocate effectively for persons with developmental disabilities in the workplace, working with both employer and employee to assist the individual in reaching optimal health and self-fulfillment.

Chemicals, Toxins, and Physical Hazards

As with the home environment, the workplace also should be evaluated for potential dangers. Certain chemicals and toxins can cause a variety of illnesses, affecting almost every organ system. Lead is a heavy metal that can cause severe neurological impairment, hematological disease (anemia), and renal disease (nephropathy). Although not as available as in the past, glazes containing lead for ceramics and pottery have been the source of acute lead toxicity when ingested. Persons with pica behaviors are especially at risk for ingesting lead-based paint and glazes. Nurses working with individuals in any type of employment setting must be aware of the kinds of chemicals and toxins with which the individual is working and the risks associated with these.

Job-related physical hazards include those involved in outdoor work. Ultraviolet light can cause sunburns and increase a person's risk for skin cancer. Persons on certain medications, especially psychotropic medication, are at even higher risk for sunburn. Outdoor work may expose the individual to extremes of environmental temperature, thereby increasing the risk for heat cramps, heat exhaustion, and heat stroke or, conversely, frostbite and hypothermia. In areas where Lyme disease is epidemic, outdoor workers may be exposed to ticks infected with the spirochete bacteria *Borrelia burgdorferi,* which causes Lyme disease. Epidemic areas in the United States include the Northeast and Atlantic Coast, the Upper Midwest, and the Northwest. Also in the East, animal rabies is epizootic, especially among raccoons. Outdoor workers may find themselves in contact with rabid animals. It is extremely important to educate persons with developmental disabilities, especially if they work or spend time outdoors, to resist the urge to make physical contact with any wild animals.

Lariece is 32-year-old woman with an anxiety disorder and a developmental disability of unknown etiology. She lives in the northern part of New Jersey, where Lyme disease and animal rabies have been epidemic. Along with two other women with developmental disabilities, she resides in a skilled development home and attends an adult training workshop during the week.

One busy morning in the health clinic, one of Lariece's housemates had a scheduled appointment for routine health care follow-up. Lariece did not have work on this particular day and came along for the ride. She was anxiously waiting in the waiting

(continued)

room, constantly talking and mumbling, and picking at sores on her arm. The nurse–practitioner overheard Lariece asking her skilled development sponsor to arrange for her to be evaluated for the rash on her arms. Her sponsor ignored her request and told Lariece she was a "nervous wreck."

At the end of the visit for Lariece's housemate, the sponsor requested that the nurse–practitioner take "just a quick look" at Lariece's arm, "just to make her happy." On examination, the nurse observed that Lariece had two open sores surrounded by a classic erythema migrans rash. In response to questions about previous tick bites, the sponsor replied, "Oh, I pick them off the girls all the time. You can't avoid them in our part of the woods." Additional inquiry revealed that the sponsor actually encourages the women to feed the white-tailed deer that visit their backyard. She also encourages them to feed raccoons on the porch of the house.

The nurse initiated a full course of antibiotic therapy for Lyme disease for Lariece. Her sponsor received information about the dangers involved in feeding wild animals, especially in an area where Lyme disease and animal rabies are prevalent.

Infectious Disease Hazards

In addition to chemicals, toxins, and physical hazards, persons who are employed in large workshops or day training centers may be exposed to a number of infectious agents. These infectious diseases include hepatitis B virus, tuberculosis, rubeola (measles), influenza, *Mycoplasma* pneumonia, scabies, and lice. Nurses in various roles can be active in case finding and encouraging appropriate preventive measures (i.e., vaccination, screening, and industrial hygiene).

Musculoskeletal Injuries

Individuals who engage in repetitive activities, especially those who perform piecework, may be at risk for repetitive motion injury. This type of injury is common in the hands, wrists, shoulders, and neck. Carpal tunnel syndrome, for example, can occur in an individual who stuffs envelopes all day. Other common musculoskeletal injuries include low back pain resulting from poor body mechanics in lifting or moving objects. By direct observation of the person at work, or by carefully questioning job coaches or training staff, the nurse can assess if the job tasks are putting the person at risk for musculoskeletal injury. Once a problem is identified, the nurse can work with the individual and/or work setting to either adjust the individual's body mechanics in performing the task or tasks or substitute other tasks that do not put the individual at risk for these injuries.

Stress

Another occupational hazard worth noting in persons with developmental disabilities is occupational stress. In addition to any stress they may experience in relation to competitive behavior in the workplace, these individuals are susceptible to other stressors that will impact on their health. These stressors include unpleasant working conditions, such as noise, excessive heat and humidity, excessive cold, or smoke-filled air from cigarettes. Also, in workplaces where other individuals have aggressive or assaultive behavior problems, the threat of physical harm can be a constant stressor, even if the physical harm never occurs. All these stressors may contribute to heart disease, peptic ulcers, inflammatory bowel disease, musculoskeletal problems, anxiety, depression, and neuroses. In addition, stress has been associated with altered immune system function, possibly contributing to various cancers (Levy & Wegman, 1988). Again, nurses are in an ideal position to advocate for individuals with developmental disabilities who may be experiencing stress in the workplace. The nurse may need to work closely with a vocational counselor to make changes to reduce stressors, while support is given to the individual to enhance his or her ability to cope with the unavoidable stressors.

MENTAL HEALTH

Persons with developmental disabilities have an increased incidence of mental illness (Stark, Menolascino, Albarelli, & Gray, 1988). It is important to recognize the individual with a "dual diagnosis," one who has a developmental disability as well as mental illness. Collaboration with a mental health professional is essential in these cases. The behavior of these individuals is different than that of individuals responding to stress in the environment.

Mental Health Issues across the Adult Life Span

Entering young adulthood is a stressful period for anyone, but this stage of life poses special concerns for the person with a developmental disability. The security and intense instruction received in school programs sometimes is replaced by overcrowded, noisy workshop programs or a fast-paced "competitive" workplace. Siblings are moving away to school or getting married. Parents are getting older and are less involved in the care of their adult offspring with developmental disabilities, if at all. Death of a parent can elicit an extreme reaction, from anxiety to depression to schizophrenia. Nurses must be aware of any major life changes occurring and provide anticipatory guidance and support. It

may be necessary to refer the individual to a behavior specialist or mental health professional.

There continue to be major life changes through middle adulthood. If parents are still living, they may be ill or in nursing homes. If the person with a developmental disability is not living with his or her biological family, chances are very good that he or she has experienced many changes in residence as well as in residential staff and roommates (significant others). This lack of a strong, consistent support system puts the person at risk for anxiety and depression. The greatest effort must be made at keeping stability in the relationships of persons with developmental disabilities. Nurses may provide the necessary support to assist in these major life changes. Appropriate referral to mental health professionals should be considered when needed.

As with the general population, dementia is a common problem in older persons with developmental disabilities. Data collected by researchers indicate that clinical and subclinical depression is common in persons with developmental disabilities, and that in individuals with Down syndrome it is often associated with dementia (Burt, Loveland, & Lewis, 1992). It is important first to rule out any medical cause for the dementia, which may be treatable and reversible.

Mental Health Promotion

Efforts to promote optimal mental health should include opportunities for socialization and human contact, vocational and recreational activities, and stable living arrangements. The nurse is the ideal professional to advocate for these essential elements that too often are taken for granted.

SUMMARY

Nurses are effective as health advocates, health educators, clinicians, and researchers in developing and implementing programs that promote health in adults with developmental disabilities throughout the life span. The emphasis of all nursing interventions is to promote behaviors that support wellness and minimize health risks. Assuring appropriate periodic health examinations in adults with developmental disabilities is important. It is also imperative to know for what diseases/illnesses each individual is at risk, based on age, underlying medical problems, and especially the nature of their developmental disability.

Promoting healthy behaviors includes assuring that immunizations are current, encouraging appropriate nutritional intake, encouraging regular exercise, and counseling on the avoidance of tobacco and drug use, and excessive alchohol consumption. Other major areas of health promotion include evaluating safety risks in the individual's home environment and occupational hazards at work. Nurses must recognize that encouraging activities that improve mental health and wellness is critical to physical health and wellness.

There has been a trend in recent years to place more emphasis on prevention and health promotion in the general population. Nurses traditionally have been responsible for and have been very effective at teaching prevention and health promotion. In addition, educational and employment opportunities for nurses are expanding. The combination of these factors has created an excellent opportunity for nurses, especially nurses in the field of developmental disabilities. Today, more than ever, nurses in a variety of settings and in numerous roles are in a unique position to promote health and healthy behaviors in adults with developmental disabilities.

REFERENCES

Abramowicz, M. (Ed.). (1992). Prostate specific antigen. *The Medical Letter on Drugs and Therapeutics, 34,* 93.

Agran, M. Marchand-Martella, N.E., & Martella, R.C. (Eds.). (1994). *Promoting health and safety: Skills for independent living.* Baltimore: Paul H. Brookes Publishing Co.

American College of Physicians. (1990). *Guide for adult immunization* (2nd ed.). Philadelphia: Author.

American College of Physicians. (1991). *Preventive care guidelines: Recommendations from various North American health care organizations.* Philadelphia: Author.

Beange, H. (1986). The medical model revisited. *Australia and New Zealand Journal of Developmental Disabilities, 12,* 3–7.

Benner, P., & Wrubel, J. (1989). *The primacy of caring: Stress and coping in health and illness.* Menlo Park, CA: Addison-Wesley Publishing Co.

Brooks-Bertram, P. (1986). Health education and mental retardation (editorial). *Mental Retardation, 24,* 67–69.

Burt, D.B., Loveland, K.A., & Lewis, K.R. (1992). Depression and the onset of dementia in adults with mental retardation. *American Journal on Mental Retardation, 96,* 502–511.

Centers for Disease Control. (1989). Measles prevention: Recommendations of the Immunization Practices Advisory Committee (ACIP). *Morbidity and Mortality Weekly Report, 38*(no. S–9).

Centers for Disease Control. (1990). Public health burden of vaccine-preventable diseases among adults: Standards for adult immunization practice. *Morbidity and Mortality Weekly Report, 39*(no. 41), 725–733.

Centers for Disease Control. (1991a). Publication of vaccine information pamphlets. *Morbidity and Mortality Weekly Report, 40* (no. 42), 726–727.

Centers for Disease Control. (1991b). Update on adult immunization: Recommendations of the Immunization Practices Advisory Committee (ACIP). *Morbidity and Mortality Weekly Report, 40*(no. RR–12).

Compton, D.M., Eisenman, P.A., & Henderson, H.L. (1989). Exercise and fitness for persons with disabilities. *Sports Medicine, 7,* 150–162.

Cronenwett, L.R. (1992). Preface. In K. Bower, *Case management by nurses.* (p. v). Washington, DC: American Nurses Publishing.

Edelman, C.L., & Mandle, C.L. (1990). *Health promotion throughout the lifespan* (2nd ed.). St. Louis: C. V. Mosby.

Fox, R., & Rotatori, A.F. (1982). Prevalence of obesity among mentally retarded adults. *American Journal of Mental Deficiency, 87,* 228–230.

Hadler, S.C. (1990). Immunization in adults, Part I: Vaccines to prevent hepatitis B and hepatitis A virus infections. *Infectious Disease Clinics of North America, 37,* 29–46.

Hoole, A.J., Greenberg, R.A., & Picard, C.G., Jr. (1988). *Patient care guidelines for nurse practitioners* (3rd ed.). Boston: Little, Brown.

Janicki, J.P., & MacEachron, A.E. (1984). Residential, health, and social service needs of elderly developmentally disabled persons. *The Gerontologist, 24,* 128–137.

Jones, K.L. (1988). *Smith's recognizable patterns of human malformation* (4th ed.). Philadelphia: W.B. Saunders.

Leavell, H., & Clark, A.E. (1965). *Preventive medicine for doctors in the community.* New York: McGraw-Hill.

Levy, B.S., & Wegman, D.H. (1988). *Occupational health: Recognizing and preventing work-related disease* (2nd ed., p. 297). Boston: Little, Brown.

Loehr, J.P., Synhorst, D.P., Wolfe, R.R., & Hagerman, R.J. (1986). Aortic root dilatation and mitral valve prolapse in the Fragile X syndrome. *American Journal of Medical Genetics, 23,* 189–194.

Mercer, K.C., & Ekvall, S.W. (1982). Comparing the diets of adults with mental retardation who live in intermediate care facilities and in group homes. *Journal of the American Dietetic Association, 92,* 356–358.

Pitetti, K.H., & Tan, D.M. (1991). Effects of a minimally supervised exercise program for mentally retarded adults. *Medicine and Science in Sports and Exercise, 23,* 594–601.

Pueschel, S.M., & Pueschel, J.K. (Eds.). (1992). *Biomedical concerns in persons with Down syndrome.* Baltimore: Paul H. Brookes Publishing Co.

Roth, S., & Brown, M. (1991). Advocates for health. *Nursing Times, 87*(21), 62–64.

Rubin, I. L., & Crocker, A.C. (1989). *Developmental disablilities: Delivery of medical care for children and adults.* Philadelphia: Lee & Febiger.

Similia, S., & Niskanen, P. (1991). Underweight and overweight cases among the mentally retarded. *Journal of Mental Deficiency Research, 35,* 160–164.

Stanhope, M., & Lancaster, J. (1992). *Community health nursing: Process and practice for promoting health,* St. Louis: Mosby-Year Book.

Stark, J.A., Menolascino, F.J., Albarelli, M.H., & Gray, V.C. (1988). *Mental retardation and mental health: Classification, diagnosis, treatment and services.* New York: Springer-Verlag.

Tomprorowski, P.D., & Ellis, N.R. (1985). The effects of exercise on the health, intelligence and adaptive behaviors of institutionalized severely and profoundly mentally retarded adults: A systemic replication. *Applied Research in Mental Retardation, 6,* 465–473.

U.S. Preventive Services Task Force. (1989). *Guide to clinical preventive services: An assessment of the effectiveness of 169 interventions.* Baltimore: Williams & Williams.

U.S. Public Health Service. (1990). *Healthy people 2000: National health promotion and disease prevention objectives.* Publication No. (PHS) 91-50212. Washington, DC: U.S. Department of Health and Human Services.

Webster's seventh new world dictionary (3rd college ed.). (1991). Cleveland, OH: G. & C. Merriam Co.

Whaley, L.F., & Wong, D.L. (1991). *Nursing care of infants and children* (4th ed.). St. Louis: Mosby-Year Book.

9

Approaches to Medication Administration

Lee Barks

OBJECTIVES

On completion of this chapter, the reader will be able to:

- Identify aspects of developmental disabilities that determine nursing approaches to medication administration for this population.
- Describe influences of medication on the habilitative process.
- Describe the nurse's role as an interdisciplinary team member regarding medication administration.
- Specify legal and licensure aspects of medication administration in the community.

DEFINITIONS OF TERMS

Akathisia—an early-appearing extrapyramidal syndrome associated with the use of antipsychotic medications, characterized by motor restlessness and compulsion to move that is not related to agitation or anxiety.

Akinesia—loss of muscle movement, either complete or partial.

Bolus—an aliquot or portion of a liquid or semiliquid substance, such as a wad of chewed food being swallowed.

Choreiform Athetosis—involuntary writhing or twisting movements, primarily of the extremities, that may be slow or fast and usually result from upper motor neuron injury.

Dystonia—an extrapyramidal syndrome associated with the initiation of antipsychotic medication therapy, characterized by spasm of the muscles of the face, neck, tongue, and/or back, in which facial grimacing and torticollis may be seen; sometimes mistaken for seizures.

Interdisciplinary Team—a group comprising a variety of people, both lay and professional, who are interested in assisting the individual with developmental disabilities in matters of living, learning, working, and playing. The team usually assists in decision making and may be made up of the person, family members, friends, and professionals from many disciplines, so that there is a rich interplay of perspectives, not always alike or initially harmonious.

Oral Motor Specialist—generally, a speech-language pathologist or occupational therapist having formal training in facilitation and inhibition of muscles of the mouth and oropharynx for the purpose of assisting the person to develop functional movement in swallowing, eating, and drinking.

Tardive Dyskinesia—a late-appearing side effect of antipsychotic medication characterized by stereotypic involuntary movements of the lips, tongue, jaw, and extremities. Lip sucking and smacking, lateral jaw movement, and tongue protrusion usually are seen, as well as choreoathetoid movements of the extremities.

APPROACHES TO MEDICATION ADMINISTRATION

When the majority of people with developmental disabilities still lived in large state institutions, service delivery was based on a medical model, which emphasized medicating large numbers of people as efficiently as possible. Nursing staff were available to administer medications to large numbers of people, and in some state institutions unlicensed staff, such as medication aides or attendants, were trained to administer medications with nurse supervision. Since the mid-1970s, there has been a huge movement of people with developmental disabilities out of institutions into the community. People with developmental disabilities now live in a variety of residential settings, are students in schools, and work in competitive employment settings. In each of these places, there may or may not be a nurse to administer medications. There also has been a movement away from the medical, behavioral, and developmental models of service delivery toward a person-centered model, in which the individual with disabilities is the focus of services. His or her needs determine all interventions and dictate the nursing approach.

The nurse is responsible for assessment, planning, intervention, and evaluation of medication administration (Table 1). As the nurse encounters different individuals, he or she must respond with a greater variety of interventions. The nursing process is affected by philosophical issues such as valuing the person and his or her preferences in every situation, as well as special characteristics of the individual's disability (e.g., the person who is tactilely defensive may fiercely resist any form of physical assessment and being touched in any way, such as in taking an apical pulse). The nursing process also is governed by regulatory requirements of the living or work environment; for example, drug and diet reviews are required by state and federal regulations for a specific residential setting, such as an intermediate care facility for persons with mental retardation (ICF/MR).

One hallmark of a person-centered nursing approach to medication administration is a focus on the needs of the person. Using a person-centered approach, the individual program for self-administration of medication begins with a nursing assessment that considers such things as the person's functional movement, ability to swallow, and what texture is easiest for the person to manage. In addition, the nurse considers the individual's ability to understand the

Table 1.   Nursing responsibilities regarding medication

Medication history
History of allergies
Drug information (action, dose, purpose, route, side effects)
Diet history
Problems with perception, coordination
Current condition (e.g., apical pulse rate prior to digoxin dose)
Person's attitudes and knowledge about use of drug
Person's learning needs

The nurse also:

• determines if the person should receive the drug at a specific time and helps to plan schedules
• assesses the person's ability to self-administer
• provides the drug at proper times
• monitors drug effects

Adapted with permission from Potter, P., & Perry, A. (1991). *Basic nursing theory and practice* (pp. 556–559). St. Louis: C. V. Mosby.

medication schedule and to recognize times for self-administration. One important consideration regarding medication administration to the individual with disabilities is whether he or she can reliably identify himself or herself verbally. If not, there should be a recent photo with the medication administration record so that the person administering can correctly identify the person receiving medication. The medication administration system then is tailored to meet the individual's needs.

Where possible, the nurse should work toward increasing the independence of an individual who is taking medication. When medications are necessary, the person has little control over some physical and mental aspects of his or her life. For example, when taking a cathartic medication, a person's bowels do not provide their own stimulus to movement; the cathartic is the stimulus, and the person is dependent on something outside his or her own body to function. Another example is neuroleptic medication. The subdued behavior of an individual taking such medication is brought about by the drug, and is not an expression of his or her own emotional state or personality.

The person-centered approach shifts control to the person as much as possible. Medication still may be necessary,

but the person with intact oral motor function may exert some control by choosing whether the medication is presented whole or crushed, or choosing the vehicle (e.g., applesauce or other food) as long as there is no food–drug interaction. The developmental level of the person is relevant to the type of control he or she is capable of exercising. For example, if the person functions adaptively at the preschool level in the initiative versus guilt stage, he or she may refuse medications that are necessary for health. Rather than allowing the person to "choose" whether or not to take the medication, the nurse may shift control to the person by offering a choice within the medication regimen (e.g., consistency, vehicle). Of course, in cases of medication refusal, the nurse also must assess the person's responses to determine if the refusal is based on some aspect of the medication itself: Does it taste bad? Does it produce some unpleasant side effect, such as local or peripheral anesthesia? Such problems may be remedied by appropriate nursing intervention.

However, it may be difficult for the person with disabilities to perceive accurately the sensations that come from the medications he or she takes, and to interpret whether these are therapeutic or undesired effects. For years, occupational therapists have held the theory that sensory integration is the process by which the brain organizes sensory information for appropriate use (Ayres, 1972, 1979; Scardina, 1986). It follows that persons with the neurological deficits accompanying cerebral palsy or mental retardation may have difficulties with integration of sensory input at the brain level. That is, stimulation may enter through intact sensory nerves into the central nervous system, but if there has been damage of the brain, there may not be a functional interpretation of sensation and response to it. For example, the tactile sensation of something warm and soft actually may be perceived by the person as something cold and prickly. This is a difficult theory to prove, because persons with neurological deficits often are unable to communicate well verbally about their sensations; however, we do know that much of the successful early intervention work with preschoolers with developmental disabilities has involved sensory integration therapy by occupational and other therapists, and we also know, from work with people who have other neurological deficits (e.g., apraxia), that sometimes sensory input is interpreted incorrectly (Ayres, 1985). One of the most difficult aspects of assessment for nurses working with persons with developmental disabilities is assessing the therapeutic versus side effects of medication.

IMPACT OF SELF-CARE DEFICITS

In coordinating administration of medication to persons with developmental disabilities, the nurse must take into account various factors unique to this population. These involve self-care deficits such as communication difficulties, oral motor difficulties, eye–hand coordination difficulties, cognitive difficulties, lack of fine and gross motor control, and possible difficulties with sense of self. The nurse must assess and intervene in these areas in order to adjust the nursing process concerning medication administration to supply needed supports for the person. Table 2 provides examples of nursing diagnoses for drug therapy related to self-care deficits.

Communication Difficulties

In evaluating the effects of medication on, or even the physical status of, an individual, the nurse must be aware of cognitive and communication difficulties that frequently are seen in persons with developmental disabilities. If the person is verbal and is able to communicate somatic experiences, there are far fewer problems in assessment. However, if the person is nonverbal and/or has a very low level of cognitive development, he or she often will not be able to express clearly what he or she is feeling. At least two approaches to these problems are

---

Table 2.   Nursing diagnosis for drug therapy in relation to self-care deficits

- Knowledge deficit regarding drug therapy related to cognitive limitations
- Noncompliance regarding drug regimen related to:
  - limited economic resources
  - client's health beliefs
- Impaired physical mobility related to:
  - upper extremity weakness or paralysis
  - diminished grasp
- Sensory/perceptual alterations: visual related to: blurred vision (visual alteration)
- Impaired swallowing related to:
  - neuromuscular impairment
  - irritated oral cavity

Adapted with permission from Potter, P., & Perry, A. (1991). *Basic nursing theory and practice.* St. Louis: C. V. Mosby.

Figure 1. Wong–Baker Faces Pain Rating Scale. Explain to the person that each face is for a person who feels happy because he has no pain (hurt) or who feels sad because he has some or a lot of pain. Face 0 is very happy because he doesn't hurt at all. Face 1 hurts just a little bit. Face 2 hurts a little more. Face 3 hurts even more. Face 4 hurts a whole lot. Face 5 hurts as much as you can imagine, although you don't have to be crying to feel this bad. Ask the person to choose the face that best describes how he or she is feeling. Recommended for persons age 3 years and older. (From Whaley, L., & Wong, D., [1987]. *Nursing care of infants and children* [3rd ed., p. 1070]. St. Louis: C.V. Mosby; reprinted by permission.)

possible. First, it becomes necessary for the nurse to examine and monitor more aggressively the physical signs of distress, such as elevated blood pressure, flushed skin, and rapid respirations, in order to determine whether the person is in pain or has some other distress. The keeping of reliable data becomes very important. Second, as a member of the person's interdisciplinary team, the nurse can advocate that the person's communication system include items that describe body parts and body sensations, such as "head" and "hurt," so that he or she can communicate his or her feelings as independently as possible. Use of the Wong–Baker Faces Pain Rating Scale (Figure 1) also may be helpful, if the person can make choices and indi-cate them (Wong, Whaley, & Kasprisin, 1990).

Oral Motor Difficulties

Oral motor difficulties are a very significant consideration in medication administration, and the nurse can use several approaches to deal with such difficulties. First, if an individual has immature or abnormal oral patterns, especially if he or she takes food, fluid, or medication orally, the nurse can advocate that the interdisciplinary team refer the person to an oral motor specialist, requesting thorough assessment followed by the development of an oral motor program and instructions for oral intake, as appropriate. Table 3 includes some indicators that assessment by an oral motor spe-

Table 3. Signs of need for assessment by oral motor specialist

The person may show any or all of the following:

- Tonic bite (clamping down on utensils, or biting down when mouth should open)
- Tongue thrust (thrusting forward of tongue when food is taken in)
- Lip purse-stringing (pulling together of lips as though a purse string is being pulled)
- Lip retraction (pulling back of lips as though smiling, usually in response to oral stimulation)
- Jaw retraction
- Coughing, gagging, or any difficulty associated with swallowing
- History of aspiration
- Use of neck extension to hold food, fluid, or medications in the mouth for swallowing, in the absence of sufficient oral control. (In this situation, either the person or staff moves the head back into neck extension. Otherwise, food, fluid, or medication placed in the mouth rolls out, because there is insufficient oral control to keep the substance in. This is often done in the absence of knowledge of other techniques. It is dangerous because it opens the airway, much as is done for intubation or CPR.)

From Barks, L., Beckman, D., Bray, M., & Green-McGowan, K. (1985). *Nutritional management for professional staff* (pp. 31–41). Produced by O'Neal and Associates, Ltd., for the Florida Department of Health and Rehabilitation Services.

cialist is needed. The nurse can use oral intake instructions to decrease the risk of aspiration during administration of oral medications as well as during eating and drinking. To the extent possible, each individual should be encouraged to choose a preferred vehicle for medication administration. Some examples are applesauce, yogurt, pureed fruit, peanut butter, jelly, and cream cheese. However, *it is important to consider food–drug interactions and the amount, texture, temperature, and consistency of the substance swallowed* (Table 4). For example, the person may not be able to swallow a large bolus; however, a small bolus may offer no difficulty. Exact placement within the mouth can be very crucial. Optimum placement can be determined during assessment by the oral motor specialist. In addition, individuals with severe oral motor problems may have some difficulty in mouth opening. Tonic biting on a utensil, delayed swallowing, or loss of food or fluid from the mouth are also common problems. Beckman

and Roberts (1992) have developed helpful techniques for overcoming such difficulties (Figures 2 through 5).

When administering oral medications, the nurse must follow standard practices. Potter and Perry (1991) provided the following guidelines for oral administration of medications:

- Always administer with adequate fluid.
- Never crush or break enteric-coated tablets.
- Mix crushed/powdered drugs with liquids and administer immediately.
- Avoid giving fluids immediately following administration of a syrup.
- Protect against aspiration through positioning in sitting or sidelying and offering medications one at a time (Potter & Perry, 1991, 567).

The nurse also must consider the special needs of persons with developmental disabilities. If the person cannot take a sufficient amount of fluid for the medication to be swallowed and absorbed, the nurse should assist in finding an alternate route. Determining "a sufficient

Table 4.   Considerations in selection of a vehicle for medication administration[a]

	Problem with selected vehicle	Options
Texture[b]	Too coarse	Chop it until it is the right size or select another vehicle.
	Too fine	Don't use it. Get some food that is the appropriate texture.
Consistency[b]	Too sticky	Add liquids, condiments, or fats. For example, add mayonaise to pasta salad; add butter or milk to mashed potatoes.
	Too runny	Fruits and vegetables that are processed are often too runny. Drain off fluids, add unflavored gelatin, add cookie crumbs (to fruit), add bread or cracker crumbs or bran powder.
	Too wet	Blot the food with a paper towel or napkin or add bread or cookie crumbs or bran powder.
	Too dry	Add a binder: liquids, condiments, or fats.
Temperature[c]	Too hot	Stir it, spread it out, wait for it to cool, put it in the refrigerator for a few seconds, or add cooler food.
	Too cold	This is usually not a problem when administering medications.

Adapted from Beckman & Roberts (1992).

[a]Avoid using the individual's food at mealtime as a vehicle for medication administration, unless the individual requests the option. NOTE ALLERGIES AND/OR FOOD–DRUG INTERACTIONS.

[b]These must be appropriate to the individual's eating skills. They should be indicated on the person's mealtime instructions.

[c]Be sure to check that the temperature is pleasant to the person. If the person is senstive to cold temperatures, you may want to warm some refrigerated foods, but do not heat medication without first checking with a pharmacist.

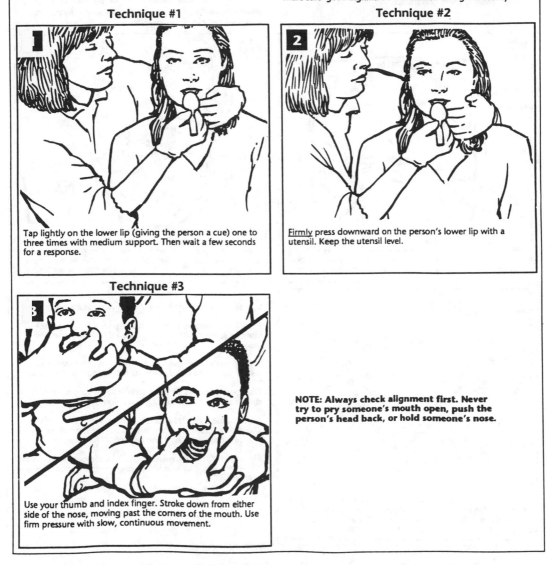

These techniques are for people who cannot open their mouths, not for someone who is just refusing to take oral medicine.

One reason why people may not be able to open their mouths is tonic bite. Tonic bite is an abnormal movement that sometimes happens with increased muscle tone in the jaw. It causes the person to clamp down (with or without something in the mouth) and stay that way.

Different events can trigger a tonic bite. These include other facial movements, head position, and stimulation to the face or mouth.

The techniques here work in several ways. First, they give cues to the person that food is coming and that it is time to open the mouth. Second, they may help relax the muscles around the mouth. Third, you are providing support so that muscles do not have to work so hard. Make sure you monitor constantly to make sure good alignment is maintained during the activity.

Technique #1

Tap lightly on the lower lip (giving the person a cue) one to three times with medium support. Then wait a few seconds for a response.

Technique #2

Firmly press downward on the person's lower lip with a utensil. Keep the utensil level.

Technique #3

Use your thumb and index finger. Stroke down from either side of the nose, moving past the corners of the mouth. Use firm pressure with slow, continuous movement.

NOTE: Always check alignment first. Never try to pry someone's mouth open, push the person's head back, or hold someone's nose.

Figure 2. Techniques: Difficulty opening the mouth. (Adapted from Beckman & Roberts [1992].)

amount" may be a collaborative effort of the nurse, dietitian, oral motor specialist, physician, and pharmacist. Many people with physical disabilities have difficulties with esophageal reflux and erosion. Therefore, enteric-coated tablets should not be crushed, because the esophagus and stomach will be exposed to irritation. If an enteric-coated tablet cannot be taken intact orally, the nurse can assist in finding an alternate route or medication.

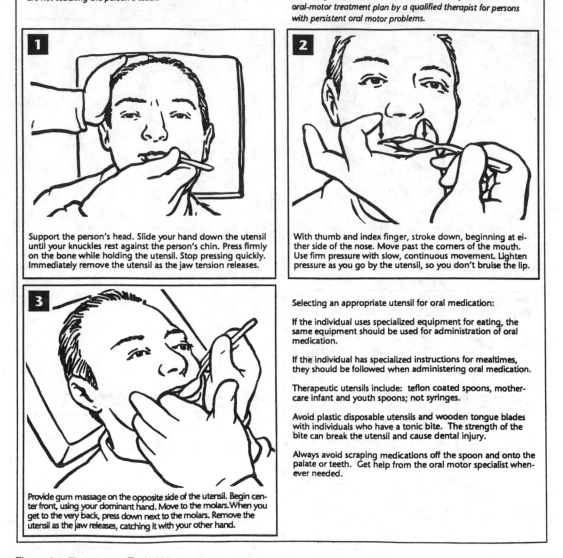

These techniques are for people who cannot control their mouth muscles enough to release their jaws. These people are not voluntarily biting on the utensil; they just can't release it. The techniques here are very similar to those to help people open their mouths, because it is the same problem—the jaw is clenched shut.

Make sure you monitor constantly to make sure good alignment is maintained during mealtime. You should not get bitten, because you are maintaining control of the person's head, and you are not touching the person's teeth.

For #3 below, the key is to apply pressure to the _gums_, not to the teeth or to the place where the lips meet the gums. You are doing a _slow_ stretch.

Do not pull on the utensil-it will only make the muscles clamp down more.

Note: These techniques should be used under the guidance of an oral motor therapist. The Nurse can and should advocate for a thorough oral-motor evaluation and development of an oral-motor treatment plan by a qualified therapist for persons with persistent oral motor problems.

1

Support the person's head. Slide your hand down the utensil until your knuckles rest against the person's chin. Press firmly on the bone while holding the utensil. Stop pressing quickly. Immediately remove the utensil as the jaw tension releases.

2

With thumb and index finger, stroke down, beginning at either side of the nose. Move past the corners of the mouth. Use firm pressure with slow, continuous movement. Lighten pressure as you go by the utensil, so you don't bruise the lip.

3

Provide gum massage on the opposite side of the utensil. Begin center front, using your dominant hand. Move to the molars. When you get to the very back, press down next to the molars. Remove the utensil as the jaw releases, catching it with your other hand.

Selecting an appropriate utensil for oral medication:

If the individual uses specialized equipment for eating, the same equipment should be used for administration of oral medication.

If the individual has specialized instructions for mealtimes, they should be followed when administering oral medication.

Therapeutic utensils include: teflon coated spoons, mothercare infant and youth spoons; not syringes.

Avoid plastic disposable utensils and wooden tongue blades with individuals who have a tonic bite. The strength of the bite can break the utensil and cause dental injury.

Always avoid scraping medications off the spoon and onto the palate or teeth. Get help from the oral motor specialist whenever needed.

Figure 3.   Techniques: Tonic biting on a utensil. (Adapted from Beckman & Roberts [1992].)

In mixing crushed or powdered drugs, it is important to include all of the dose; if the drug must be given in a pureed texture substance, be certain to give the entire amount. Liquid antiepileptic drugs, in particular, are notoriously difficult to dose accurately. In order to attain adequate seizure control, the nurse can work with other interdisciplinary team members, such as the pharmacist,

The most important technique you can use to help a person swallow correctly is to make sure you help the person maintain an aligned position. For some individuals, an inclined sidelying position may afford better oral control for swallowing than an upright position.

Check: Are the head and trunk aligned? Are the lips closed? Is the tongue inside the person's mouth? Is the person positioned in the optimum position for oral intake as identified by the IDT?

You may want to help the person by providing a small sip of a drink after each swallow. Wait to make sure the person has completely swallowed the food. Sometimes, it appears that the person has swallowed, but there is still food in the back of the throat. If the person tries to breathe in, this food can be sucked into the airway. Some people may need to swallow a few times to completely clear the food from their throats.

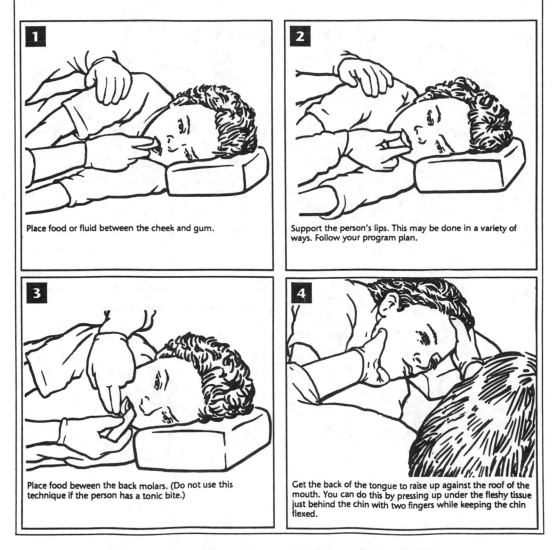

1 Place food or fluid between the cheek and gum.

2 Support the person's lips. This may be done in a variety of ways. Follow your program plan.

3 Place food beween the back molars. (Do not use this technique if the person has a tonic bite.)

4 Get the back of the tongue to raise up against the roof of the mouth. You can do this by pressing up under the fleshy tissue just behind the chin with two fingers while keeping the chin flexed.

Figure 4. Techniques: Delayed swallowing. (Adapted from Beckman & Roberts [1992].)

physician, and oral motor specialist, to ensure precise dosages of these drugs. Syrups and elixirs can exert local anesthetic effects on oral, pharyngeal, and esophageal tissues. If fluid is offered im-mediately after administration of such compounds, the risk of aspiration may be increased. Finally, a person with oral motor difficulties should not be rushed through medication administration. This

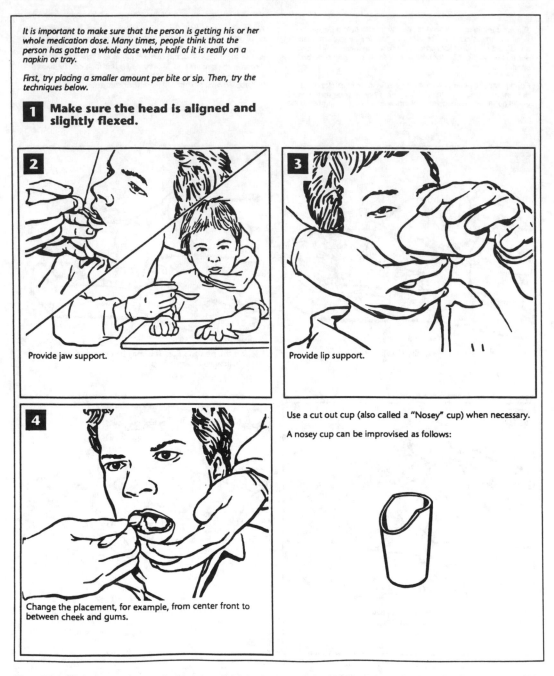

It is important to make sure that the person is getting his or her whole medication dose. Many times, people think that the person has gotten a whole dose when half of it is really on a napkin or tray.

First, try placing a smaller amount per bite or sip. Then, try the techniques below.

1 **Make sure the head is aligned and slightly flexed.**

2 Provide jaw support.

3 Provide lip support.

Use a cut out cup (also called a "Nosey" cup) when necessary.

A nosey cup can be improvised as follows:

4 Change the placement, for example, from center front to between cheek and gums.

Figure 5.   Techniques: Loosening food or fluid from the mouth. (Adapted from Beckman & Roberts [1992].)

is an important learning experience for him or her, whether it concerns opportunities to practice oral motor skills or to remember different medications and their side effects.

Gross Motor Difficulties/Immobility

Many people with developmental disabilities also have physical disabilities that may be accompanied by muscle tone that is either too high (resulting in abnormal movements or postures) or too low (resulting in incoordination and limpness). Abnormal muscle tone can result in difficulty in moving and positioning the body passively or actively for oral intake. Often there are joint contractures and deformity that also make positioning very difficult. For example, persons with severe spasticity and hip and knee contractures may be difficult to seat in an upright position. Persons with very low muscle tone in the trunk often collapse downward when placed in a seated position with insufficient support. These situations can lead to spilling of medications and fluids from the mouth and difficulty in swallowing and keeping swallowed material in the stomach. Alignment and incline are critical components in positioning (Gerber, McAllister, & Tencza, 1991). The person's body must be aligned (arranged around midline) so that optimal muscle function is available for the swallow. Incline is important to allow gravity to assist in the second and third stages of the swallow, in order for food or fluid to move from the mouth down to the stomach. Basic concepts of alignment and the implications of various positions for fluid and food intake are illustrated in Figures 6 and 7, respectively (Beckman & Roberts, 1992). The nurse should ensure that, when in a seated or upright position to take oral medication, the individual is supported so that he or she cannot slump forward or lean backward, thus increasing the chances of aspiration or other swallowing difficulties. Often, inclined sidelying is the best position for oral intake.

If an individual is unable to take medications orally, they may be given through a gastrostomy or jejunostomy tube. Infrequently, a nasogastric tube will be utilized on a temporary basis. For this reason, guidelines for administering medications through enteral tubes are offered in Table 5. Principles of therapeutic positioning are especially important to follow for this person due to increased risks of reflux and aspiration.

Cognitive Difficulties and Eye–Hand Coordination Difficulties

Cognitive difficulties and eye–hand coordination difficulties can combine to have a significant impact on the ability to self-administer medication. For obvious reasons, cognitive difficulties such as knowing how to tell time, to associate activities with particular times, and to recognize and differentiate between various medications, doses, and routes can preclude self-administration of medication. The person also may have difficulty with recording or reporting medication administration. Physical disabilities such as spasticity, low muscle tone, alternating muscle tone, and muscle and joint contractures interfere with ability to reach, grasp, and place or apply medication. However, people with these difficulties still may be able to tell time and track medication administration accurately.

Some persons with developmental disabilities can self-administer medication without difficulty. Many others, with the assistance of teaching programs, can learn to self-administer or can learn to perform some of the steps involved. It is always important for the person to be as independent as possible, so mastery of even some of the steps for self-administration of medication usually can be pursued, even if the person cannot complete the entire process independently. The nurse should support independence in medication administration to enhance the individual's control in and quality of life.

MEDICATION SELF-ADMINISTRATION

Except for pain medication, a review of the literature reveals very little informa-

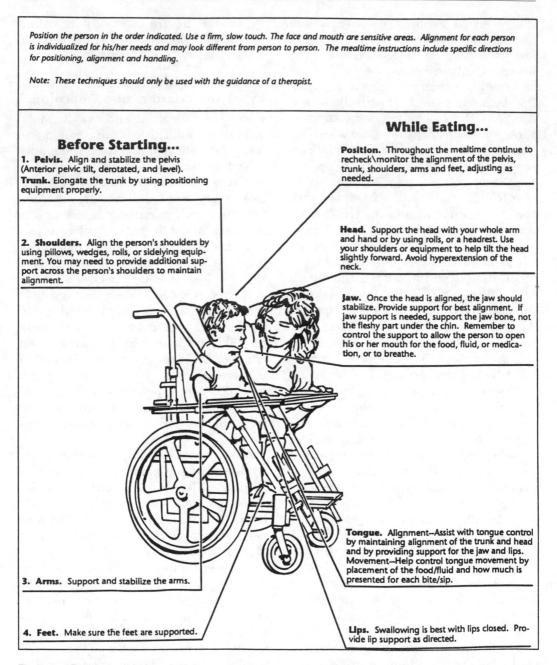

Position the person in the order indicated. Use a firm, slow touch. The face and mouth are sensitive areas. Alignment for each person is individualized for his/her needs and may look different from person to person. The mealtime instructions include specific directions for positioning, alignment and handling.

Note: These techniques should only be used with the guidance of a therapist.

Before Starting...

1. Pelvis. Align and stabilize the pelvis (Anterior pelvic tilt, derotated, and level).
Trunk. Elongate the trunk by using positioning equipment properly.

2. Shoulders. Align the person's shoulders by using pillows, wedges, rolls, or sidelying equipment. You may need to provide additional support across the person's shoulders to maintain alignment.

3. Arms. Support and stabilize the arms.

4. Feet. Make sure the feet are supported.

While Eating...

Position. Throughout the mealtime continue to recheck\monitor the alignment of the pelvis, trunk, shoulders, arms and feet, adjusting as needed.

Head. Support the head with your whole arm and hand or by using rolls, or a headrest. Use your shoulders or equipment to help tilt the head slightly forward. Avoid hyperextension of the neck.

Jaw. Once the head is aligned, the jaw should stabilize. Provide support for best alignment. If jaw support is needed, support the jaw bone, not the fleshy part under the chin. Remember to control the support to allow the person to open his or her mouth for the food, fluid, or medication, or to breathe.

Tongue. Alignment--Assist with tongue control by maintaining alignment of the trunk and head and by providing support for the jaw and lips. Movement--Help control tongue movement by placement of the food/fluid and how much is presented for each bite/sip.

Lips. Swallowing is best with lips closed. Provide lip support as directed.

Figure 6.   Positioning: Alignment before and during meals. (Adapted from Beckman & Roberts [1992].)

tion about self-administration of medication in general. Most articles describe self-administration programs for psychiatric hospital inpatients (Bird, 1990) or rehabilitation inpatients (Johnson, Roberts, & Goodwin, 1970; Reibel, 1969;

Thompson, 1987). Bird's study of a psychiatric population concerned cognitive aspects such as knowledge of drug purpose, potential knowledge of drug side effects, and compliance or tablet counts. One study of rehabilitation populations showed that some people had borderline independence and judgment; however, the inpatients and their families did not perceive problems with judgment and insisted on the patients being discharged to home (Thompson, 1987). This study demonstrated a need for medication administration supervision, used custom adaptive equipment such as coded pill containers, and reported use of various assists with memory, vision, and dexterity problems. The other studies of rehabilitation inpatients showed that omission of medication accounted for the largest number of errors (Johnson et al., 1970; Reibel, 1969), and that mental status, rather than physical impairment, was the major limiting factor in ability to self-administer medication (Johnson et al., 1970). These findings may hold some implications for self-administration of medication by individuals with developmental disabilities, a topic that has received even less coverage in the literature.

In one study (Brown, Smith-Fontaine, Leonard, Wilds, & Aiken, 1992); Smith-Fontaine found that, among the population with developmental disabilities, the following factors were significant components of the nursing process for self-admistration:

Adequate assessment
Interdisciplinary team involvement
Recommendations and a goal in the individualized program plan
Policies and procedures in the agency to determine the ability to self-administer
Periodic monitoring of the consumer to ensure safety for the individual
Quarterly nursing evaluations for continued appraisal of the ability to self-adminster

The study also found that, of the 35 states responding, at least five states had no programs for medication administration in the community; these states claimed that all consumers in their community programs were self-administering their medications. If this is the case, nursing assessments of the ability to self-administer medication have great importance. Some nurses have developed their own assessment forms for this purpose.

Factors to be considered when determining an individual's capability to self-administer medication include:

- Ability to swallow oral medication
- Ability to voluntarily and purposefully move the hand(s) and/or arms
- Ability to identify the correct medication, time, dose, and route
- Ability to follow proper administration procedures for the medication
- Ability to move physically to access the medication at appropriate times
- Ability to store the medications properly
- The range of prompts needed to perform the above (verbal, gestural, physical)
- Performance constraints that may function as contraindications (behavioral, rate or duration, physical or medical)

OTHER CLINICAL PRACTICE ISSUES

Polypharmacy

Most studies have reported that 25%–50% of adults with mental retardation receive psychotropic and antiepileptic medications (Matson & Frame, 1986; Natvig, 1991). The amount and type of medication used varies in different settings (Aman & Singh, 1988), but, as the complexity of the disability increases, the number of medications in use usually increases as well. Although a review of the recent developmental disabilities literature did not reveal information on polypharmacy involving all types of drugs, in the author's experience, polypharmacy is common in many residential care settings. Drugs tend to interact in the blood,

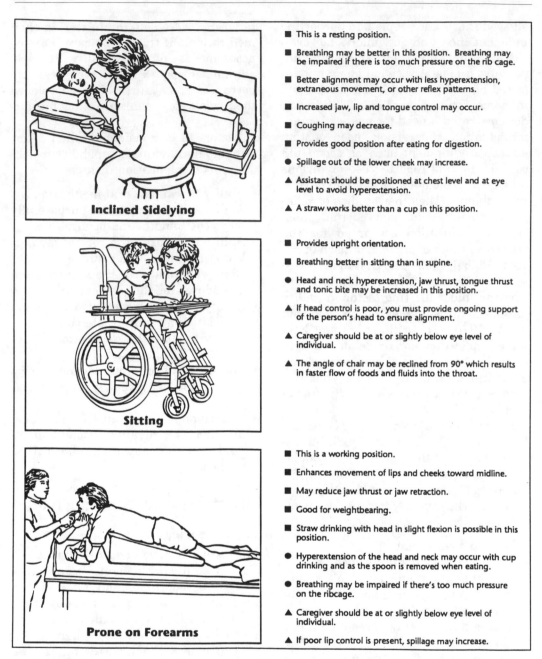

Figure 7. Positioning: Implications of different positions (Key: ■ = a benefit of the position; ● = a potential problem with the position; ▲ = things to consider while assisting.) (Adapted from Beckman & Roberts [1992].)

binding to blood proteins, and to interact with each other. This can alter the body's response to each drug. It is well known among health professionals that use of more than one medication increases the chance of an increase or a decrease in drug action. There is also an increase in drug side effects.

Nurses should strive continually to engage in reducing medication use among

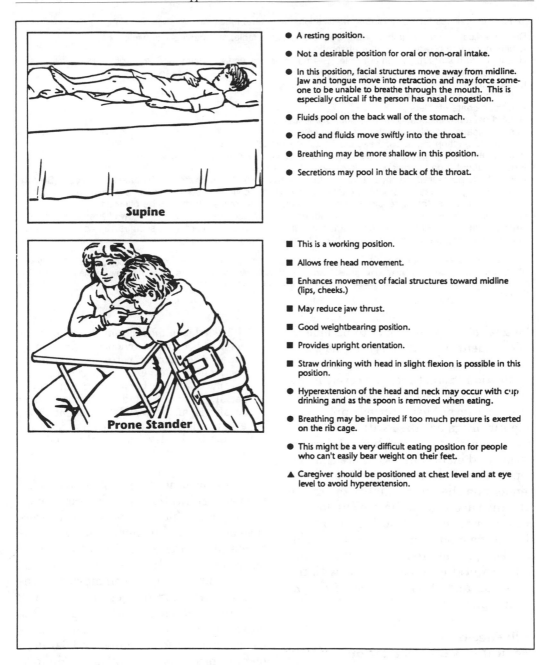

Supine

● A resting position.

● Not a desirable position for oral or non-oral intake.

● In this position, facial structures move away from midline. Jaw and tongue move into retraction and may force someone to be unable to breathe through the mouth. This is especially critical if the person has nasal congestion.

● Fluids pool on the back wall of the stomach.

● Food and fluids move swiftly into the throat.

● Breathing may be more shallow in this position.

● Secretions may pool in the back of the throat.

Prone Stander

■ This is a working position.

■ Allows free head movement.

■ Enhances movement of facial structures toward midline (lips, cheeks.)

■ May reduce jaw thrust.

■ Good weightbearing position.

■ Provides upright orientation.

■ Straw drinking with head in slight flexion is possible in this position.

● Hyperextension of the head and neck may occur with cup drinking and as the spoon is removed when eating.

● Breathing may be impaired if too much pressure is exerted on the rib cage.

● This might be a very difficult eating position for people who can't easily bear weight on their feet.

▲ Caregiver should be positioned at chest level and at eye level to avoid hyperextension.

Figure 7. (*continued*)

persons with developmental disabilities. When appropriate, the nurse should use physical or behavioral interventions to replace pharmacotherapy. For example, laxatives can often be replaced by increased use of gravity in therapeutic positioning and active and passive movement, as well as incorporating more soluble and insoluble fiber in the person's diet. Psychotropic medications sometimes can be replaced by a behavior program. This approach is consistent with

Table 5.   Guidelines for administering medications by enteral tube[a]

• Read medication information carefully before crushing a tablet, or opening a capsule.
• Crush into a fine powder for better absorption.
• Use liquid forms of drug when possible. [Examples are docusate sodium, or theophylline elixir.]
• Use a solution or suspension prepared by the pharmacy whenever necessary.
• Do not crush:
    − buccal or sublingual tablets
    − enteric-coated tablets
    − hard gelatin capsules; open and pour out liquid
    − soft gelcaps; dissolve in water first, then give
    − sustained-action capsules; these can result in stomach irritation
• Avoid bulk-forming agents such as Metamucil; these can occlude the tube.
• Find out about drug interactions before giving drugs together.
• Add water to powdered, crushed drugs and follow with plenty of warm water, or the tube will occlude. [Be sure
    to observe guidelines for stomach capacity for certain individuals, such as people with hiatal hernias or
    thoracic stomachs; these people may have limitations of amounts which may be offered.]
[Use a bolus whenever possible, to maintain normal stomach action and lower bowel flow of alternate filling and
    emptying; it is not normal to ingest a small amount over a long period of time, such as 120 cc over an hour,
    unless there are problems with reflux, hiatal hernia, or thoracic stomach.]

Adapted with permission from Potter, P., & Perry, A. (1991). *Basic nursing theory and practice* (p. 566). St Louis: C. V. Mosby.
  [a]*Note:* Unlicensed personnel may be restricted from non-oral administration of medication by state law, regulations, or policy.
This varies from state to state. The nurse is encouraged to ascertain acceptable practice for the particular state before
delegating.

the goal of helping people to become as independent in their daily lives as possible, including becoming independent of medication. Sometimes, however, medication must be used to treat pathology on a long-term basis. For example, neuroleptic drugs are used with people who are dually diagnosed with mental retardation and mental illness. Increasing independence from medication is often dependent on the nurse's ability to provide less invasive, nonmedical ways for the consumer to secure health and to function in the environment. The nurse is in an ideal position to assist with this process by working collaboratively with the physician and other members of the interdisciplinary team.

Influence of Medications on Habilitation

It is the nurse's unique role to understand how the body and medications function and to *always* assess how medications may be influencing physiological response in the body, which in turn influences adaptive response and skill development. Aman and Singh (1988) have stated:

A knowledge of medication effects is of importance because psychoactive drugs may influence (either for better or worse) the effectiveness of other nonmedical forms of therapy such as behavior modification, special education, and so forth ... drug therapy is an extremely prevalent form, perhaps the single most common mode, of therapy in the developmental disabilities. (p. v)

Drugs need not be psychoactive to influence habilitation. For example, antihistamines, which often are sold as over-the-counter preparations, can cause extreme drowsiness and interfere with learning. These drugs also interact with antiepileptic drugs, which may cause increased seizure frequency. In addition to lessening alertness, drugs can affect muscle tone and can alter sensory experiences needed for learning and developmental progress. For example, dantrolene sodium (Dantrium), which often is used to decrease spasticity, can interfere with swallowing and oral motor function. Chlorpromazine (Thorazine) can locally anesthetize the oral area and interfere with taste and other sensation. Collection of data about an individual's response to medication is a traditional nursing role, which is interdependent with the physician's role. The evaluation of physiological response as a foundation for health, development, independence, and skill development is an ongoing part of the nursing process.

Drugs Typically Used by Persons with Developmental Disabilities Many persons with developmental disabilities have seizure disorders and take antiepileptic medications (see Frank, chap. 10, this volume). Others have severe behavior disorders and/or psychiatric diagnoses; neuroleptic medications may be used as part of their treatment plans. People with severe physical disabilities may utilize medications for respiratory and gastrointestinal problems. The nurse must be familiar with specific drugs, their uses and side effects, and special considerations for this population. Table 6 lists drugs typically used by persons with developmental disabilities and the adverse effects often noted with these drugs.

The nurse should use a drug reference source book (e.g., American Society of Hospital Pharmacists, 1993; Barks, Capozzi, Smith, & Tencza, 1991) to learn about every medication a person receives. Each drug's desired effect should be compared to the person's response. The nurse brings this information to the interdisciplinary team.

Side Effects of Psychotropic Medications Use of psychotropic medications often is associated with side effects such as movement disorders. Some movement disorders, such as *acute dystonia, pseudoparkinsonism, akinesia,* and *akathisia,* have an early onset, within the first days or weeks of therapy. These disorders usually are reversible with reduction or discontinuation of the drug. Probably the best known side effects of psychotropic drugs are those of *tardive dyskinesia,* which have a late onset, are associated with prolonged use of psychotropic medication, and often are irrever-

sible. The movements are involuntary, repetitive, and choreiform, athetoid, or dystonic (Rinck & Rinck, 1991). Rinck and Rinck also stated that approximately 80% of the individuals with tardive dyskinesia have movements of the face or mouth. Practitioners who fail to inform individuals or their guardians of the risks of psychotropic medications and to allow them to assist in the decision to use the medication, to monitor and alter treatment, or to consult a specialist may be sued by persons who experience severe side effects (Rinck & Rinck, 1991). In litigation of cases of tardive dyskinesia, plaintiffs have been awarded substantial sums of money, in or out of court. In a recent class action suit, *Thomas S. v. Flaherty,* it was shown that at least some of the members of the class had suffered harm through use of psychotropic medication that resulted in the development of movement disorders. When one potential class member in the *Thomas S.* case was asked whether the writhing movements of his left hand bothered him, he replied, "Sometime, I wished I could just cut it off."

Persons with developmental disabilities may be less aware of or bothered by abnormal movements caused by such drugs. In order to monitor or to detect whether harm is being done in ongoing treatment with psychotropic medications, several assessment scales have been devised. Probably the best known is the Associated Involuntary Movement Scale (AIMS), developed by the National Institute on Mental Health. Other scales intended specifically for use with people with developmental disabilities are the Dyskinesia Identification System—Coldwater (DIS-Co) and the Dyskinesia Identification System: Condensed User Scale (DISCUS). The Monitoring of Side Effects Scale (MOSES) is a scale that rates selected general side effects and is not limited only to movement disorders. These are screening instruments and

Table 6.   Drugs typically used by persons with developmental disabilities

Class	Drug	Problems associated with use (by class)[a]
Antacids	Amphogel Gelusil Maalox Mylanta	• Most drugs in this class are constipating. • Antacids containing aluminum salts can interfere with absorption of calcium and phosphorus
Antianxiety drugs	Ativan Buspar Librium Tranxene Valium Xanax	• Sedation • Weakness/dizziness • Restlessness • Hearing loss • Blurred vision • Difficulty swallowing
Anticholinergics	Artane Cogentin Urecholine	• Often used with psychotropic medication to prevent dyskinesia or extrapyramidal signs • Dry mouth, nose • Constipation • Slow stomach emptying, contributing to gastro-esophageal reflux • Sleepiness, lethargy • Rapid heart rate • Uncoordinated movement • Urinary retention • Decreased control of temperature regulation
Antidepressants[b]	Elavil Norpramin Pamelor Sinequan Tofranil Triavil	• Extrapyramidal effects • Sun-sensitive skin • Headaches • Loss of appetite • Blurred vision • Constipation • Lowering of seizure threshold • Neck stiffness • High blood pressure
Antiemetics/GE reflux control agents	Emetrol Phenergan Reglan Thorazine	• Reglan lowers seizure threshold, possibly increasing seizure frequency • Nausea and vomiting • See other classes for specific effects
Antiepileptics	Depakene Depakote Dilantin Klonopin Mysoline Phenobarbital Tegretol Zarontin	• Toxicity; lethargy or drowsiness • Constipation • Gingival hypertrophy • Poor appetite • Nausea or vomiting • Elevated liver enzymes or liver failure • Anemias • Osteoporosis (These vary by medication; for specific effects of medications, see individual medications)
Bronchodilators	SloPhyllin Theo-Dur Theophylline	• Stomach irritation/nausea • Arrhythmias/tachycardia • Insomnia • Jitteriness • Seizures • Relaxation of smooth muscle, including the lower esophageal sphincter, which may lead to gastro-esophageal reflux
Histamine blockers	Tagamet Zantac	• Constipation • Drowsiness • Slowing of gastric emptying due to decreased secretion of acid and enzymes (stomach pH must be sufficiently low for emptying to occur)

(continued)

Table 6.   (*continued*)

Class	Drug	Problems associated with use (by class)[a]
Laxatives/Cathartics & bowel preparations	Castor oil Colace Dulcolax Fleet enema Glycerine suppositories Metamucil Modane Senokot Surfak	• Dependence (for any bowel flow) • Abdominal cramping • Rectal irritation and sloughing of mucosa • Loss of electrolytes
Muscle relaxants	Dantrium Lioresal Valium	• Weakness/tiredness/difficulty with voluntary movements, including swallowing • Severe respiratory failure • Increased sun sensitivity • Irritability
Psychotropics	Ativan Haldol Inderal Lithium Mellaril Moban Navane Prolixin Ritalin Seretil Stelazine	• Blurred vision • Constipation • Increased appetite • Dry mouth • Nasal stuffiness • Skin rash • Increased sun sensitivity • Orthostatic hypotension • Extrapyramidal effects/tardive dyskinesia • Jaundice or skin discoloration
Stimulants	Cylert Dexedrine Ritalin	• High blood pressure • Tachycardia • Insomnia • Nausea or vomiting • Headache • Weight loss • Arrythmias • Restlessness • Skin rashes

From Barks, L., Capozzi, L., Smith, C., & Tencza, C. (1991). *Health building: Medications reference manual.* Produced for the Oklahoma Department of Human Services. Winter Park, FL: Therapeutic Concepts, Inc.

[a]*Note:* Not every medication in each class is associated with the effects listed; see individual drug information.

[b]*Note:* Monoamine oxidase inhibitors (MAOIs) are also antidepressants. When taken with some other medications and foods, MAOIs can cause hypertension, liver damage, and death. MAOIs are usually not used for people with developmental disabilities.

can be used for early detection, which is associated with reversibility of side effects. A baseline should be established prior to the beginning of treatment, using a scale scored by a trained rater, and the person should be monitored with the scale at least every 6 months thereafter. Each scale has unique features that should be considered when selecting a monitoring instrument. For a full discussion of monitoring procedures, the reader is referred first to Supporting Positive Behaviors (Toleman, Brown, &

Roth, chap. 11, this volume) and then to Kalachnik (1988).

With all medications, particularly psychotropic medications, the nurse functions as an integral member of the interdisciplinary team. Natvig (1991) has stated the following:

1. The team as a whole is responsible for development of an appropriate active treatment plan.
2. Ideally, psychotropic medication is used for behavioral management only

after less restrictive programmatic alternatives have been exhausted, and then only in conjunction with a behaviorally based training program.

3. Attitudes and beliefs of individual team members will contribute to the success or failure of the interdisciplinary team process.

INTERDISCIPLINARY TEAM ISSUES

The work of the interdisciplinary team is to teach the person skills to help him or her become more functional in his or her environment. The nurse is perhaps the team member best prepared to understand the relationships between health, medications, independence, and function. No other discipline represented on the interdisciplinary team has as much experience with health, employing both medical *and* nonmedical approaches. The nurse, because of education about drugs, ways of facilitating health, and understanding how the person functions in the environment, often is an interpreter for the nonmedical team members about the effects of medications and the ways in which they affect habilitation. The nurse has a unique role in facilitating independence from medical treatments, when warranted, by focusing on increasing the independence of the consumer.

Within this role, the nurse's responsibility is to share changes in the drug regimen with the interdisciplinary team. For example, if a person with a seizure disorder has had Reglan prescribed to reduce gastroesophageal reflux, the nurse's role is to communicate that Reglan can lower the seizure threshold. The person could begin to experience more seizures, which would interfere with alertness. There will be an increased need for the whole team to document seizures. In addition, the nurse will guide the team to increase align-

ment and incline in therapeutic positioning, and increase texture and fiber in the diet to improve bowel function and reduce reflux. Then the person may not need the Reglan any longer. Another example is the immobile person who must receive pain medication such as codeine after surgery. In this situation, the usually "benign" side effect of codeine, constipation, may be quite severe, and the whole team may want to give some thought to ways to avoid further health risk by maintaining bowel function.

In the 1988 ICF/MR standards, there is no specific requirement for monthly drug and diet reviews. However, most ICFs/MR continue to find an ongoing need for review of the medication and dietary regimens of their residents. For example, there are specific interactions, such as the interaction between tube feeding formula and Dilantin suspension, that must be planned for and avoided at medication administration times. In many residential programs, this planning with the nurse, dietitian, physician, and pharmacist is formalized by designating a specific time for it to occur on a regular basis, such as monthly. In order for the nurse to prepare for a drug and diet review, he or she should be thoroughly familiar with the current medications for all the people for whom he or she is responsible and ready to discuss the therapeutic and undesired effects, as well as the individual's current health status.

Another role of the nurse on the interdisciplinary team is to understand medication schedules and their impact on activities and learning. The nurse should avoid giving medications that may result in weakness of voluntary muscles, such as Dantrium, at times that will interfere with teaching programs for upper extremity control. In individuals who experience gastroesophageal reflux (especially with bleeding), the nurse should be aware of appropriate positioning. There are times when the person must be placed in therapeutic positions that may exacerbate reflux. The nurse teaches all persons who work with the individual to avoid giving any food, fluids, or medications at those times. This limits the possibility of aspirations.

Another important role of the nurse on the interdisciplinary team is to understand licensure issues, particularly nurse licensure issues, and to guide the team to find ways to deliver health care that are legitimate as well as useful to the consumer and to the team. These issues are discussed more fully in the next section. No other interdisciplinary team member can be expected to understand licensure issues concerning nursing better than the nurse. In some settings, the nurse may be asked to do things that are illegal under the nurse practice act for that state.

LICENSURE AND LEGAL ASPECTS OF MEDICATION ADMINISTRATION

It is important for the nurse to understand licensure issues related to the administration of medication. Nurse practice acts are not uniform from state to state, and often only one nurse is employed by an agency that provides services to persons with developmental disabilities. Based on the information agencies have, they may unknowingly make requests of the nurse that make sense within the agency but may not conform to licensure requirements in the state, or may in fact be illegal. It is the nurse's responsibility to be aware of legal requirements for nursing practice in the state. The nurse must be familiar with the regulations governing medication administration, and communicate these courteously, responsibly, and without indignation. It is important to identify professional concerns in a calm manner without becoming self-righteous. At the same time, the nurse must work

with the agency to provide cost-effective health care and to protect the health interests of the individuals served. The goal always should be to find a solution that does not compromise care of the individual, the interdisciplinary team's effort, the agency, or the nurse's license.

Service delivery is not consistent from state to state for people with developmental disabilities. In most states, only nurses, birth parents, foster parents, and legal guardians are legally allowed to administer medication. In some states, nonlicensed hired personnel may administer medications. Regulations and restrictions vary widely, and legal responsibility may reside with the nurse, whether or not the nurse actually administers medication. A recent survey conducted in Maryland and involving all 50 states' developmental disabilities program offices (Smith-Fontaine in Brown et al., 1992) was the first to look at national trends in medication administration to people with developmental disabilities. It surveyed the type of personnel used, tasks, supervision, training, trainee monitoring, values, and other aspects. The response rate was 70%. Among states responding, 51% stated that medication administration is done by licensed personnel and 46% that it is delegated to unlicensed personnel. The remaining 3% stated that only people who can self-administer medications are placed in community programs in their states. Among states, there were no consistent definitions of *self-administration* and *delegation,* and there were significant differences in staff preparation programs. This study is important because it is the first to identify many issues of concern about medication administration to persons with developmental disabilities in the community.

There are many rsponsibilities that go along with medication administration. Potter and Perry (1991) stressed the "five rights": the right drug, in the right dosage, given to the right person by the right route and at the right time. In addition to safe delivery of the drug by the appropriate route, there are responsibilities for safe storage, documentation, and assessment of the person for therapeutic and undesired or side effects (Potter & Perry, 1991). The nurse must be aware of these other responsibilities, in order to assure that they are fulfilled. The nurse also must take responsibility for becoming informed about all regulations that apply to individuals with developmental disabilities in each practice setting. For example, the guidelines for narcotics administration represented in Table 7 often are applied to professional nursing practice in general, but they may not apply in all settings (e.g., group homes or public schools). In those settings, there may be additional pertinent, and sometimes conflicting regulations.

It is important to know which regulatory authority supersedes others. The nurse should try to create "win/win situations" with administrators and policy makers while observing legal and professional practice standards. Each nurse has the individual professional responsibility to be familiar with the state nurse practice act, including the hiring of an attorney to educate oneself, if necessary. Where difficult situations are encountered, nurses can work collaboratively with their state board of nursing and other consumer protection groups to assure safety in the medication administration process. In recent years, there

has been at least one lawsuit that stemmed from these issues. In *Ellen Johnsen v. Broken Arrow Public Schools* (*Northern District of Oklahoma*), a nurse who insisted on following established professional standards for medication administration in the school setting was fired. She sued the schools and lost her case on appeal.

Personnel for Medication Administration

In most states, however, licensed personnel are the only ones authorized by law to administer medication in exchange for payment. Although fees are not involved, natural and foster parents also have the legal authority to administer medication. The use of registered nurses and licensed practical/vocational nurses to administer medications directly is more economical in institutional settings, where many individuals are receiving services in one place. It is often not feasible to employ professional nurses in many community settings because of the high costs involved (Brown et al., 1992). Because of these economic constraints, it is becoming accepted practice to use unlicensed personnel to administer medication in community settings. There are various legal mechanisms that provide for the use of unlicensed personnel in certain settings, and these vary from place to place. The nurse must be cognizant of the legal guidelines for practice in his or her jurisdiction, and should know which personnel are allowed to ad-

---

Table 7.   Guidelines for safe narcotic administration and control

1. Store all narcotics in a locked, secure cabinet.
2. The nurse[a] carries the keys to the cabinet.
3. At change of shift, oncoming and outgoing nurses count controlled drugs.
4. Discrepancies are reported immediately.
5. A special inventory record is used each time a drug is taken from the supply and administered.
6. This record documents name, date, time, drug name, dose, and nurse's signature.
7. This form provides an ongoing count.
8. If only one part of the dose is given, disposal is witnessed by a second person and documented, then cosigned.

Adapted with permission from Potter, P., & Perry, A. (1991). *Basic nursing theory and practice* (p. 566). St Louis: C. V. Mosby.
    [a]Or, in some states, persons designated by the agency/facility (e.g., group home manager).

minister medications in each community setting. This will enable the nurse to ensure good health for all persons with developmental disabilities living and working in the community.

Although physicians and pharmacists are legally entitled to administer medications, they rarely routinely provide direct medication administration services to individuals. Nurses have knowledge of drug action, absorption, and half-life. They also have access to other sources of information about drugs. The nurse can assist families and/or staff to assess ways that drugs may be behaving in the body. Potential or suspected problems then can be referred to the pharmacist or physician for intervention. The role of the professional nurse is to provide support and teaching where knowledge deficits exist regarding medications.

the constitutional right to protection from harm, so as to protect society against ignorance, incapacitation, deception, and fraud. For these reasons, professional practice acts have been created in each state to protect recipients of care. The practice acts define boundaries of and criteria for practice; they are designed to protect not licensed nurses but the public (recipients of care) (Brown et al., 1992). The nursing license is a sign to the public that its holder possesses the minimum qualifications to practice nursing safely.

In addition, administrative agencies are authorized by law in all states to make rules in order to implement state laws. One such administrative agency is the State Board of Nursing, and an example of a ruling might be one governing procedures for offering continuing edu-

---

Keiko is a vibrant 22-year-old woman who has cerebral palsy, spastic quadriplegia, and a seizure disorder that is well controlled by medication. She receives medications via nebulizer four times a day to treat chronic reactive airway disease. Recently, Keiko had symptoms of a urinary tract infection and she is now completing a course of antibiotic therapy. Keiko resides in a community-based ICF/MR. The nonlicensed staff administer medications to Keiko under the supervision of a nurse consultant to the agency that operates her residence.

Because Keiko receives multiple medications on a daily basis, there is always the potential for drug interaction. In this situation, the nurse assumes a case manager role and coordinates the ordering, storage, administration, and documentation of Keiko's medications. The nurse educates Keiko and her caregivers so that they are aware of the actions, indications, and side effects of each medication. The nurse assists them to collect and share information about Keiko's response to her medications with other members of the interdisciplinary team. By maintaining good records and open communication with the various medical specialists who ordered the medications, it may be possible to reduce the need for polypharmacy for Keiko.

Rights of the Individual, Professional Licensure, and Administrative Authority

The welfare of society depends on safeguarding the public's safety, life, morals, and general welfare (Brown et al., 1992). Each U.S. citizen is considered to have

cation to nurses in the state. The State Board may be asked by another administrative agency, such as the Developmental Disabilities Division or Program office in the state, to make a *declaratory ruling*. This is an official interpretation of the practice act or of a ruling by the Board, made in order to clarify implementation of the practice act. The courts respect these rulings as expert opinions (Brown et al., 1992).

According to Brown et al. (1992), other administrative agencies may make policies that may conflict with the State Board's rulings or declaratory statements (e.g., that unlicensed residential provider staff in the community may give medication). As long as these policies do not violate the law or rules, or require that providers do so, they are considered part of the legal framework. If they do conflict with rules or practice acts, usually state law or a declaratory ruling supersedes them and they are rescinded.

Delegation

Brown et al. (1992) stated that the National Council of State Boards of Nursing has defined *delegation* as "nurses entrusting performance of selected nursing tasks to competent subordinate persons in selected situations." Performance of the task is delegated, but the nurse retains accountability for the total nursing care of the individual. Brown et al. also noted the following:

1. There must be statutory authority [in the practice act] for the nurse to delegate.
2. The nurse must have a documented assessment in order to delegate, to show that the situation is appropriate.
3. The nurse must establish that the person to whom tasks are delegated is competent to perform the task. Thus, the nurse has an obligation to determine the competence of the delegate and to supervise performance of the task. If the task changes, delegation may also need to change. (Brown et al., 1992)

Unlicensed staff increasingly are being used to administer medication. In many states, this is not new. Mental health and developmental disabilities institutions in these states long have had medication aides (or attendants) who were trained to administer medications only in the institution where they worked. In these institutions, it is usual for unlicensed staff to be supervised directly by nurses. The nurse then retains responsibility for the acts of the unlicensed staff. In some states, such as Louisiana, a separate state statute authorizes the medication attendants to administer medications. However, nurses remain responsible for the supervision of such attendants. There is no delegation of nursing responsibility in that situation (Brown et al., 1992). Clearly, in order to assume responsibility appropriately in each state, the professional nurse must be aware of practice acts, administrative rulings, agency policies, and other aspects of medication administration.

Nurses have a professional responsibility to be flexible in planning and devising ways for people in community settings to get the care they need. However, it is unfair to demand that any nurse assume responsibility for the delegation of tasks to another without allowing that nurse to control competency and supervision. The nurse has an important interest in the competence of the delegate, because the nurse is liable for any errors committed by an unlicensed giver of medications in a situation in which the nurse has delegated that task. If the nurse is delegating tasks to unlicensed staff and they are incompetent, there is improper delegation and the nurse is still liable for the acts of the staff (Brown et al., 1992). Brown et al. also stated that the nurse can require the staff member to undergo additional training, if he or she is not competent to perform the particular task.

Training and Competency

Didactic, or lecture-type, training gives trainees the knowledge they need to perform the skills required at exit from training, but there are no opportunities to practice the skills being taught. Generally, a didactic or lecture method used alone in training cannot develop competence in medication administration for unlicensed staff. In competency-based or skills-based training, the focus is on what the trainee must be able to *do* on the job, rather than only on what he or she must *know*. On completion of competency-based training, the trainee must demonstrate competence (be tested) in particular skills taught to acquire a certificate.

In the Smith-Fontaine study (Brown et al., 1992), all responding states that designated a training program for medication administration had enforcement mechanisms to ensure that unlicensed staff are trained. In some states, control of training by licensed personnel may be an issue. This is true when the administrator of the program (such as a state Developmental Disabilities Program) expects the trainer to accomplish delegation as a function of the training. It is unrealistic to expect the trainer to train unlicensed staff, and be responsible for establishing their competence, unless the trainer also has the opportunity to supervise the trainees in the task to be performed on the job. Nurses training unlicensed staff should clarify their responsibility for delegation, supervision, and follow-up performance monitoring of trainees before accepting responsibility for training.

Problems also exist in those state programs that do not assume responsibility for monitoring of trainee performance after completion of training. Responsibility for ongoing performance monitoring may be the role of the nurse employed by an agency providing residential program services. This nurse becomes responsible for delegation of the medication administration task and for establishing competence of the delegate. In evaluating competence, the nurse should look at the person's training program and at any certificate showing comeptence, as well as at the person's actual skills.

SUMMARY

Persons with developmental disabilities receive medications to relieve symptoms, treat illness, or promote health and prevent disease as part of the active treatment process. As a member of the interdisciplinary team, the nurse is responsible for developing and implementing medication administration programs that support health, safety, and independence for these individuals. The clinical practice issues as well as the legal, regulatory, and training issues in medication administration are complex and interrelated. Not long ago, the majority of people with developmental disabilities lived in large state institutions where administration of medications to those persons emphasized efficiency and accuracy. As large numbers of people with developmental disabilities have moved to community residences, many other issues began to surface. Consideration in the nursing process is now given to the supports needed by the individual, such as the needs for modification of textures given orally, therapeutic positioning, and individualized sensory stimulation. The nurse also plays a key role in understanding ways that medications influence physiological responses in the body, which in turn influence development of adaptive skills. In particular, persons with developmental disabilities who receive psychotropic drugs additionally need monitoring every 6 months for signs of movement disorders, which develop usually as irreversible side effects of the drugs. Finally, the nurse must understand licensure and legal aspects of medication administration, specifically training of and delegation to unlicensed personnel and provisions of the state nurse practice act.

REFERENCES

Aman, M., & Singh, N. (1988). *Psychopharmacology of the developmental disabilities* New York: Springer-Verlag.

American Society of Hospital Pharmacists. (1993). *AHFS drug information.* Bethesda, MD: Author.

Ayres, A.J. (1972). *Sensory integration and learning disorders.* Los Angeles: Western Psychological Services.

Ayres, A.J. (1979). *Sensory integration and the child.* Los Angeles: Western Psychological Services.

Ayres, A.J. (1985). *Developmental apraxia and adult-onset apraxia.* Torrance, CA: Sensory Integration International.

Barks, L., Capozzi, L., Smith, C., & Tencza, C. (1991). *Health building: Medications reference manual.* Produced for the Oklahoma Department of Human Services. Winter Park, FL: Therapeutic Concepts, Inc.

Beckman, D., & Roberts, L. (1992). *Mealtime challenges; eating assistance for individuals with severe oral motor challenges.* Produced for the Oklahoma Department of Human Services. Winter Park, FL: Therapeutic Concepts, Inc.

Bird, C. (1990). Drug administration, a prescription for self help. *Nursing Times, 86*(43), 52–55.

Brown, M., Smith-Fontaine, S., Leonard, L., Sr., Wilds, T., & Aiken, T. (1992, May 27). *Medication issues in the community.* Panel presentation at the annual conference of the American Association on Mental Retardation, New Orleans.

Ellen Johnsen v. Independent School District No. 3 of Tulsa County, Oklahoma, 891 F.2d 1485 (Tenth Cir. 1989).

Gerber, D., McAllister, S., & Tencza, C. (1991). *Challenges in physical management.* Produced for the Oklahoma Department of Human Services. Winter Park, FL: Therapeutic Concepts, Inc.

Johnson, E., Roberts, C., & Goodwin, H. (1970). Self medication for a rehabilitative ward. *Archives of Physical Medicine and Rehabilitation, 51,* 300–303.

Kalachnik, J.E. (1988). Medication monitoring procedures: Thou shall, here's how. In K.D. Gadow & A.G. Poling (Eds.), *Pharmacotherapy and mental retardation* (pp. 231–268). Boston: Little, Brown.

Matson, J., & Frame, C. (1986). *Psychopathology among mentally retarded children and adolescents.* Beverly Hills, CA: Sage.

Natvig, D. (1991). The role of the interdisciplinary team in using psychotropic drugs. *Psychosocial Nursing and Mental Health Services, IX*(10), 3–8.

Potter, P., & Perry, A. (1991). *Basic nursing theory and practice.* St. Louis: C.V. Mosby.

Reibel, E. (1969). Study to determine feasibility of self-medication program for patients at a rehabilitation center. *Nursing Research, 18,* 65–68.

Rinck, W., & Rinck, O. (1991, January–March). Drug-induced movement disorders. *Dialogue on Drugs, Behavior, and Developmental Disabilities, 3,* 1.

Scardina, V. (1986, August 16 and 17). *Sensory Integration Symposium: Sensory integration: Its relationship to development and performance.* Orlando Regional Medical Center, Orlando, FL.

Thomas S. v. Flaherty, 699 F.Supp. 1178, 1188–1189 (W.D.N.C. 1988).

Thompson, T. (1987). A self-medication program in a rehabilitation setting. *Rehabilitation Nursing, 12*(6), 316–319.

Whaley, L., & Wong, D. (1987). *Nursing care of infants and children* (3rd ed.). St. Louis: C. V. Mosby.

10

The Role of the Nurse in Seizure Management

Jeannie Frank

OBJECTIVES

On completion of this chapter, the reader will be able to:

- Identify different types of seizures according to the International Seizure Classification System.
- Identify the major antiepileptic drugs, including dosage, advantages, and side effects.
- Recognize the normal laboratory values used to monitor antiepileptic drugs.
- Describe safety and protection from injury considerations for persons with epilepsy.
- Discuss components of a seizure management program that promotes an optimal quality of life for the individual who has a seizure disorder and developmental disabilities and his or her family.

OVERVIEW

This chapter provides the nurse with an understanding of seizures as well as the medications, interventions, and monitoring strategies used to control seizures and minimize their negative impact on the quality of life for the individual with a seizure disorder. This information will enable the nurse to assist individuals who have seizure disorders and developmental disabilities to optimize their potential and to live full, productive lives.

The first step in the treatment of seizures for a person with developmental

The author would like to thank Joan Keller for her contribution of the artwork for Figure 1 and Figure 2 of this chapter.

disabilities (as with all persons) is to define and classify seizure types and symptoms and establish appropriate pharmacotherapy. It is equally important to identify the psychosocial effects of seizures for the individual and his or her family. The interdependence of physiological and psychological components is an essential consideration in determining the individual's perception of symptoms, his or her ability to communicate these symptoms, and the coping methods utilized by individuals and their families. The degree of disruption in daily living activities that a seizure disorder is perceived to have by individuals and families has significant impact on the effectiveness of the overall treatment plan.

DEFINITIONS

A **seizure** is a discrete event characterized by a sudden, excessive, and disorderly (abnormal) discharge of electrons in the brain that is accompanied by an abrupt alteration in motor and/or sensory function and/or consciousness (Aicardi, 1986). Repeated episodes of seizures are referred to as **epilepsy** (Batshaw & Perret, 1992; Commission on Classification and Terminology of the International League against Epilepsy, 1981, 1985; Dreifuss, 1989).

INCIDENCE AND PREVALENCE

The incidence of epilepsy in the United States ranges from 0.5% to 2%, with approximately 100,000 new cases reported annually (Engel, 1992; Epilepsy Foundation of America, 1991). The incidence is usually higher in persons with developmental disabilities. Batshaw and Perret (1992) reported that about 50% of children with a seizure disorder have varying degrees of mental retardation. In addition, among children with developmental disabilities, the prevalence of seizures is as follows: 16% in children with mental retardation; 25% in children with spina bifida and hydrocephalus; and no increased risk of seizures for children with learning disabilities. Epilepsy affects approximately 21% of persons with mental retardation who do not also have cerebral palsy. It is more common in those individuals who have a measured IQ below 50. Epilepsy affects approximately 50% of the individuals with mental retardation who do have cerebral palsy (Hauser & Hesdorffer, 1990). The rate of occurrence depends on etiological considerations such as congenital malformations of the brain, metabolic disorders, trauma, infections of the nervous system, and brain tumors. In general, seizures in persons who also have mental retardation are more difficult to control with medications (Goulden, Shinnar, Koller, Katz, & Richardson, 1991).

ETIOLOGY

The brain consists of over 14 billion nerve cells, many of which are connected by tiny junctions, with electrical impulses being sent along the chain by chemical neurotransmitters. Each electrical impulse releases neurotransmitters that then activate the next neuron. These electrical impulses normally fire in regular patterns known as brain waves. However, when there is abnormal firing, a seizure may result. Sudden, rapid, excessive firing of the neurons in the cortex of the brain is like an electrical storm. The seizure is the body's visible response to the storm (Clancy, 1990).

Etiological considerations in the development of seizures include both genetic and acquired factors. Genetic factors may contribute to the development of seizures in three ways: 1) a low threshold for seizure activity may be inherited, 2) genetic traits underlie some specific primary epileptic conditions, and

3) many inherited diseases of the brain are associated with structural disturbances that produce seizures (Engel, 1992). The most common example of a seizure caused by a low threshold for seizure activity is the benign febrile convulsion, which often is seen during infancy and early childhood. A single isolated generalized seizure also may be seen as the result of physiological stress such as sleep deprivation, alcohol or sedative drug reaction, or acute head trauma, or in response to toxic, metabolic, and infectious processes. Inherited primary epilepsies account for 30% of chronic epileptic disorders. Primary epilepsies are generally benign and usually remit spontaneously in adolescence or early adulthood (Janz, Beck-Mannagetta, & Sander, 1992). Inherited diseases of the brain that are associated with structural disturbances may include inborn errors of metabolism such as phenylketonuria, the lipidoses, and the leukodystrophies. Syndromes such as tuberous sclerosis and neurofibromatosis are associated with the development of abnormal cerebral tissue.

Acquired factors also may be pivotal in the development of seizures. Congenital lesions resulting from prenatal and perinatal injuries are common in persons with epilepsy. Partial seizures can be the result of minor focal lesions such as microgyria, porencephalic cysts, and areas of calcification and atrophy. Secondary generalized seizure disorders may be seen as the result of more severe trauma, anoxia, and infections such as toxoplasmosis, cytomegaloviral inclusion disease, rubella, and acquired immunodeficiency syndrome.

Head trauma, infectious processes, and brain tumors also can produce seizure activity at any stage of the life cycle. In older individuals, cerebrovascular disease such as cerebral venous thrombosis, cerebral arteritis, and scar tissue formed after a stroke all may result in seizure activity. At any age, systemic toxic and metabolic disturbances (e.g., lead poisoning or ketoacidosis) can cause seizure activity (Schapiro, Haxby, & Grady, 1992). In persons with developmental disabilities, there is a higher incidence of instability of the brain cells that contributes to seizure activity (Engel, 1992). Some types of seizures, such as absence seizures, may go into remission spontaneously during adolescence. Seizures caused by underlying brain lesions may continue indefinitely without medication. Seizures tend to become less frequent for the individual with developmental disabilities as the brain matures (Batshaw & Perret, 1992).

INTERNATIONAL CLASSIFICATION OF SEIZURES

There are many types of seizures. Seizures are defined as either partial or general and are classified according to the International Classification System (Commission on Classification and Terminology of the International League against Epilepsy, 1981, 1985). Partial seizures may spread to become generalized seizures. The term *mixed seizure disorder* is used to describe the presence of both partial and generalized seizures in the same individual. Understanding the seizure classification system (Table 1) permits selection of an appropriate antiepileptic medication and optimal seizure management.

Partial (Focal) Seizures

Partial (focal) seizures involve part of one hemisphere of the brain (Pellock, 1990). The symptoms of partial seizures depend on the part of the brain that is involved and include the following types.

Simple Partial Seizures During simple partial seizures there is no loss of consciousness. However, the seizure may cause jerking in one part of the body. A seizure in the sensory cortex of the brain

Table 1.   International classification of epilepsies and epileptic syndromes

I. **Partial (focal, local) seizures**
   A. **Simple partial seizures** (consciousness not impaired)
      - Motor (abnormal movement of arm, leg, or both; Jacksonian march; versive, postural, phonatory)
      - Somatosensory or special sensory (gustatory, olfactory, auditory, visual, vertiginous)
      - Autonomic (tachycardia, increased respiration, flushing, pallor, sweating, piloerection, & pupillary dilation)
      - Psychic (dysmnesic, e.g., deja vu; dysphagic, affective, e.g., fear, anger; illusions, structured hallucinations, e.g., music; structured scenes)
   B. **Complex partial seizures** *(with impaired consciousness)*
      - Beginning as simple partial seizure and progressing to impairment of consciousness
      - No other symptoms
      - Motor, somatosensory, special sensory, autonomic, or psychic symptoms
      - Automatisms
   C. **Partial seizures evolving to secondarily generalized seizures**
      - Simple partial leading to generalized seizures
      - Complex partial leading to generalized seizures
      - Simple partial leading to complex partial leading to generalized seizures
II. **Generalized seizures (convulsive or nonconvulsive)**—*All have loss of consciousness*
   A. **Absence seizures** (petit mal)
      - Onset in childhood; approximately 40% ending in adolescence and 50% supplanted by tonic–clonic seizures
      - Symptoms include altered awareness or attention and blank stare; may include eye blinking lasting 5–30 seconds
      - Can be mistaken for learning disabilities or behavior and coordination problems
   B. **Myoclonic seizures**
      - Characterized by short, abrupt muscular contractions of arms, legs, and/or torso
      - Symptoms include symmetrical or asymmetrical, synchronous or asynchronous, single or multiple jerks; possible brief loss of consciousness
   C. **Clonic seizures**
      - Symptoms include muscular contraction and relaxation, usually lasting several minutes
      - Distinct phases may not be observable
   D. **Tonic seizures**
      - Symptoms include an abrupt increase in muscle tone (contraction), loss of consciousness, and autonomic signs, lasting from 30 seconds to several minutes
   E. **Tonic–clonic seizures** (grand mal)
      1. **Tonic**
         - May begin with a shrill cry caused by secondary expulsion of air due to the abrupt closure of the epiglottis
         - Characterized by rigidity, opisthotonos, and extension of the arms and legs
         - Jaws may snap shut
         - Respiration may decrease or cease
         - Pupils are dilated and unreactive
         - Heart rate is decreased
         - Episode is brief—up to 1 minute
      2. **Clonic**
         - Begins suddenly and ends gradually
         - Characterized by quick, bilateral severe jerking movements
         - Stertorous breathing
         - Autonomic symptoms
         - Usually lasts less than 1 minute
      3. **Postictal**
         - Muscles become flaccid
         - Consciousness gradually returns
         - Amnesia related to the seizure
         - May need to sleep few minutes to 1 hour
   F. **Atonic seizures**
      - Characterized by abrupt loss of tone
      - May be followed by postictal confusion
      - Injury likely

(continued)

Table 1. (*continued*)

III. Unclassified epileptic seizures—Such seizures cannot be classified because of inadequate or incomplete data; they include some neonatal seizures (e.g., rhythmic eye movements, chewing, and swimming movements)

IV. Addendum
  A. Repeated epileptic seizures occur under a variety of circumstances:
    • As fortuitous attacks, coming unexpectedly and without any apparent provocation
    • As cyclic attacks, at more or less regular intervals (e.g., in relation to the menstrual cycle, or the sleep–waking cycle)
    • As attacks provoked by: a) nonsensory factors (fatigue, emotions, alcohol, etc.), or b) sensory factors, sometimes referred to as "reflex seizures"
  B. The term **"status epilepticus"** is used whenever a seizure persists for a sufficient length of time or is repeated frequently enough that recovery between attacks does not occur. Status epilepticus may be divided into partial (e.g., Jacksonian) or generalized (e.g., absence status or tonic–clonic status). When very localized motor status occurs, it is referred to as "epilepsia partialis continua" (Farley, 1992).

Adapted from Commission on Classification and Terminology of the International League against Epilepsy (1985); Engel (1992).

will produce abnormal sensations, such as abnormal visual phenomena. If the temporal lobe of the brain is involved, feelings of unreality or abnormal psychic sensations or memory disturbances may be reported (Batshaw & Perret, 1992). Figure 1 shows a typical posture during a simple partial seizure.

Complex Partial Seizures Complex partial seizures are like simple partial seizures except that the electrical discharges affect the level of consciousness. Consciousness will be lost or at least disturbed during a complex partial seizure.

Secondary Generalization Partial seizures may spread and evolve into a generalized tonic, clonic, or tonic–clonic seizure (Engel, 1992).

Generalized Seizures

During generalized seizures, the entire cortex of the brain is affected. Seizures start bilaterally and may be convulsive or nonconvulsive. There is immediate loss of consciousness at the onset of the seizure. The following are types of generalized seizures.

Absence Seizures During an absence seizure, impairment of consciousness may be the only symptom. The person suddenly stops what he or she is doing, and stares blankly or occasionally blinks for 5–20 seconds. Hundreds of these episodes may occur daily before a diagnosis of absence seizures is made and treatment is initiated.

Atypical Absence Seizures Atypical absence seizures occur when the absence seizure also involves an automatism (a mild involuntary motor component, such as lip smacking) (Farley, 1992).

Figure 1.   Typical posture during simple partial seizure. (Produced by Therapeutic Concepts, Inc., for the Oklahoma Department of Human Services.)

Tonic–Clonic, Clonic, or Tonic Seizures Tonic–clonic, clonic, or tonic seizures, previously referred to as "grand mal seizures," are major motor convulsive seizures. Tonic seizures involve stiffening and increased tone; clonic seizures involve bilateral rhythmic jerking of the extremities (Figure 2). These may be combined as tonic–clonic seizures, with the tonic phase appearing first and lasting for several seconds to several minutes, followed by the clonic phase. Bladder control may be lost during the seizure. Following the seizure, sleep or temporary confusion may occur; the person also may complain of a headache (Batshaw & Perret, 1992).

Myoclonic Seizures Myoclonic seizures involve quick jerking of body parts or the trunk. These seizures are seen alone or may be part of a mixed seizure disorder. This type of seizure often carries a prognosis of worsening condition. Although myoclonic seizure is uncommon in the general population, it occurs fairly frequently in persons with developmental disabilities (Lockman, 1989).

Infantile Spasms Infantile spasms are a type of myoclonic seizure that may involve nodding of the head, crying, flexor and/or extensor spasms, and clustering of groups of spasms. It commonly starts at about 6 months of age and usually resolves by 24 months (Bobele & Bodensteiner, 1990). Infantile spasms may be misdiagnosed as colic in young infants. This is a very severe form of epilepsy that benefits from early detection and aggressive treatment with an adrenocortical-stimulating hormone (adrenocorticotropic hormone; ACTH). Neurodevelopment appears to stop at the onset of infantile spasms, and the prognosis is variable. Even with treatment, mental retardation frequently is seen in children who experience infantile spasms (Glaze, Hrachovy, Frost, Kellaway, & Zion, 1988). An increased incidence of infantile spasms is associated with some other disorders, such as tuberous scle-

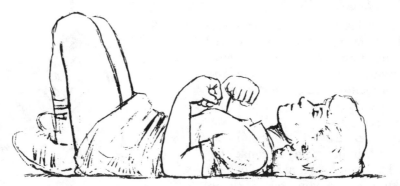

Figure 2.   Tonic seizures involve stiffening and increased tone (top); clonic seizures involve bilateral rhythmic jerking of the extremities (bottom). (Produced by Therapeutic Concepts, Inc., for the Oklahoma Department of Human Services.)

rosis, Tay-Sachs disease, and Down syndrome (Batshaw & Perret, 1992).

Lennox-Gastaut Syndrome Lennox-Gastaut syndrome often develops in children ages 1–8 years, as a sequel to infantile spasms. This syndrome is associated with severe mental retardation in about 80% of individuals who are diagnosed with the disorder. It is characterized by a mixed seizure pattern that includes atypical absence, tonic–clonic, myoclonic, and atonic seizures. These seizures are difficult to control. Valproic acid is the drug of choice, with the benzodiazepines as secondary medication. A ketogenic diet also has been found to be helpful (Batshaw & Perret, 1992).

Atonic Seizures Atonic seizures (also referred to as "drop attacks") begin almost exclusively in childhood and usually reflect diffuse lesions of the brain. This disorder is characterized by a sudden loss of muscle tone. In its simplest form, the child's head drops for a second or less. More severe forms cause the tone to disappear from the entire body, causing the person to collapse to the floor. Serious injuries such as concussion, broken bones, and lost teeth are not uncommon. Atonic seizures usually occur many times a day and are refractory to drug therapy (Engel, 1992). In an individual who has atonic seizures, the primary goal is to prevent injuries. These individuals should be advised to wear protective headgear. As a member of the interdisciplinary team, the nurse can teach family members and other caregivers how to assess the individual for injury following the seizure (Farley, 1992).

Status Epilepticus

Major motor status epilepticus occurs when there is continuous, generalized tonic–clonic seizure activity. When status epilepticus involves partial motor seizures, it is known as *continuous partial epilepsy*. Status epilepticus can occur with the generalized disorders, but,

more commonly, it is the result of partial seizures that secondarily generalize (Engel, 1992). Although most seizures do stop within 5 minutes, status epilepticus is a medical emergency that is potentially life threatening and requires immediate medical intervention. Table 2 describes the etiology of status epilepticus episodes. Table 3 describes pharmacological interventions during status epilepticus. Table 4 delineates the treatment protocol in status epilepticus, emphasizing the time frames for intervention.

Febrile Convulsions

One or more febrile convulsions occur in 3%–4% of otherwise healthy children between the ages of 6 months and 5 years. In this age group, there is a low seizure threshold (Batshaw & Perret, 1992). These convulsions manifest as brief tonic–clonic reactive generalized seizures. Febrile convulsions can be recurrent, but the syndrome is considered to be benign, and often no intervention is necessary. There seems to be evidence of a genetic predisposition, but it is poorly defined (Engel, 1992). About 6% of families have more than one member who has experienced a febrile convulsion in childhood (Batshaw & Perret, 1992).

Affected children usually outgrow their tendency to have febrile convulsions at between 3 and 5 years of age. In affected children, the most likely time for a febrile convulsion to occur is when a fever is rising; therefore, febrile convulsions

Table 2. Etiology of status epilepticus episodes

Idiopathic	24%–37%
Tumors	1%–25%
Trauma	1%–26%
Cerebrovascular	4%–28%
Infection	5%–15%
Febrile	3%–28%
Congenital abnormalities	3%–17%
Other	2%–26%

Adapted from Leppick (1990).

Table 3.   Drugs used to treat status epilepticus

Diazepam	Allows rapid control of status but brain concentration decreases rapidly as a result of redistribution; therefore, seizures commonly recur 20–40 min after administration Dose: 5–10 mg IV and repeat prn till reach 20 mg
Ativan	Dose: based on mg/kg of body weight
Phenytoin	Loading dose: 18–20 mg/kg; maintains concentrations for 24 hr IV rate <50 mg/min; minimum effective dose is 3–5 mg/kg
Phenobarbital	Second-line agent (can cause respiratory depression) Loading dose: 15–20 mg/kg Continue IV at rate of 60–100 mg/min until seizure stops
Other agents	Paraldehyde Lidocaine Valproic acid Pentobarbital coma

Adapted from Leppick (1990).

often are seen in conjunction with upper respiratory infections, ear infections, or those viral and/or bacterial illnesses that are common in young children. A child who has had one febrile convulsion has an increased risk of having another febrile seizure before age 4 (Berg, Shinnar, Hauser, & Leventhal, 1990). If the first seizure occurs before the child's first birthday, the recurrence rate is 50%; if the first febrile convulsion occurs after the child's first birthday, the risk of recurrence is 11% (Berg et al., 1990).

After a child has had multiple febrile convulsions, prophylactic treatment with antiepileptic drugs sometimes is considered. Phenobarbital is the drug most commonly used. In order to be effective,

Table 4.   Treatment protocol in status epilepticus in adults

Time frame for intervention	Protocol
0–5 min	Assess cardiorespiratory function Obtain history, perform neurological and physical examination Obtain blood specimen for antiepileptic seizure medication levels, glucose, BUN, electrolytes, metabolic screen, and drug screen Insert oral airway and administer oxygen if needed Have someone explain treatment protocol to family or caregivers
6–9 min	Start IV infusion with normal saline Administer 25 g of glucose and B vitamins if cause of status is elusive
10–30 min	Begin infusion of phenytoin (20 mg/kg at a rate no faster than 50 mg/min); this may take 20–40 min Monitor ECG and blood pressure Give diazepam (5–20 mg) or lorazepam (4–6 mg) if seizures occur while phenytoin is being given Provide family or caregivers with information about the person's condition
31–60 min	If seizure persists, administer phenobarbital 10 mg/kg at 100 mg/min intravenously Continue to monitor ECG and blood pressure Check neurological status Suction airway prn Maintain communication with family or caregivers
1 hr	If seizure persists, barbiturate coma should be induced using an agent with which the agency is familiar; alternatively, general anesthesia can be utilized Continue to monitor vital signs, ECG, and airway status Maintain patent IV line Provide ongoing emotional support to family and/or caregivers

Adapted from Leppick (1990).

Abbreviations: BUN, blood urea nitrogen; ECG, electrocardiogram.

it must be taken daily. The side effects of the drug include fatigue secondary to sedation. The child also may experience alterations in activity, behavior, and/or cognition while taking phenobarbital. Therefore, drug therapy is not usually recommended unless there have been many recurrences of febrile seizures, the child has developmental disabilities, or the parents are very anxious about the possibility of future seizures (Berg et al., 1990).

FOCUSED SEIZURE ASSESSMENT AND POSTSEIZURE CARE

The mnemonic "Rapid Seizures Make Doctors And Nurses Contemplate Diazepam" provides a guide to nursing assessment and care of the person experiencing a seizure (Ellis, 1993). The steps involved include assessing the *r*esponsiveness, *s*afety, *m*emory, *d*escription, *a*irway, *n*eurological assessment, comfort, and *d*ocumentation. Nurses must adapt all of the baselines to reflect the specific needs of an individual with developmental disabilities. Age-appropriate memory cues must be utilized when a child experiences a seizure. The nurse should communicate the results of the assessment to the interdisciplinary team, and assist them in learning to gather assessment information and care for the person during and after a seizure.

Steps in Assessment and Care

Responsiveness Some seizures are characterized only by changes in the individual's behavior. When seizure activity is suspected, the nurse can assess responsiveness to verbal stimuli by asking "Are you having a seizure?" and then giving a simple verbal command such as "Look at my hand." This may help to describe the responsiveness of the individual, at least during the initial phase of seizure activity. This is obviously more difficult in persons who are nonverbal. Tickling them to assess responsiveness is often helpful.

Safety There is always the potential for injury during seizure activity. The person experiencing the seizure is at risk for trauma secondary to contact with furniture and other objects in the environment. There is also a risk of falling during a seizure. Aspiration of food or mucous secretions can occur if the individual loses consciousness. The nurse can instruct the individual with developmental disabilities, his or her family or caregivers, and other interdisciplinary team members to provide a safe environment during any seizure event. Table 5 lists first-aid steps to promote safety during seizure activity.

Table 5. First aid during tonic–clonic seizure activity

The following steps should be taken when administering first aid to an individual having a generalized tonic–clonic seizure:

- Unless he or she is in danger, do not move the person.
- Protect the person from injury.
- Loosen any tight clothing.
- Turn the individual on his or her side so that secretions can drain.
- Do not attempt to place anything in the mouth.
- Observe the seizure. Note how it started, how it progresses, the duration of each phase, level of consciousness, motor and ocular activity, and respiratory difficulty.
- Call for medical/rescue assistance if the seizure is a generalized tonic–clonic seizure and lasts longer than 5 min.

Adapted from Commission on Classification and Terminology of the International League against Epilepsy (1981); Santilli (1993).

Memory   For an individual who has developmental disabilities, it is important to acquire baseline information about memory from family members or caregivers in order to provide adequate assessment. Existing memory deficit disorders can impair postictal memory assessment.

Description   Ellis (1993) recommends describing all observations out loud while the seizure is occurring. This provides an opportunity to reinforce details that then can be recalled for inclusion in the written seizure record.

Airway   Positioning is the most effective way to maintain an adequate airway during a generalized seizure. If the person is unresponsive, he or she should be turned to the side in order to facilitate the drainage of secretions. All interdisciplinary team members should be familiar with correct positioning, and should know that nothing should be inserted into the mouth of a person who is having a generalized seizure. Trauma to the teeth or oral mucosa could result (Ellis, 1993; Farley, 1992).

Neurological Assessment   In individuals with developmental disabilities, it is important to establish the neurological baseline prior to the onset of a seizure episode (Engel, 1992). This can avoid serious errors in the postictal assessment. Assessment should include the individual's responsiveness, orientation, pupillary reactivity, motor strength, reflexes, ability to follow instructions, memory, any episodes of incontinence, and any injury sustained. It is important to note when specific deficits resolve. This provides information about the extent of the seizure and establishes a postseizure pattern base for future reference.

Comfort   Many individuals complain of fatigue and/or headache after a seizure. Providing an opportunity to rest and using a nonnarcotic analgesic such as Tylenol will be helpful (Ellis, 1993).

Specific comfort measures such as changing wet or soiled clothing should be offered as appropriate.

Documentation   A seizure tracking sheet can be utilized to provide uniform and consistent information that should be communicated to the health care provider. Tracking sheets can be adapted for most family, group home, and program settings, and the nurse can teach interdisciplinary team members how to use them. Figure 3 is a sample of a typical seizure tracking sheet. Documentation should be completed as soon as the seizure is over and the individual is stable.

Specific Steps for Tonic–Clonic Seizures

The above steps are guides for the nurse in assessing all seizures. However, specific steps have been identified in providing first-aid treatment to a person experiencing a tonic–clonic seizure. Table 5 outlines these procedures.

DIAGNOSTIC CONSIDERATIONS IN SEIZURE MANAGEMENT

Seizure identification and diagnosis are critical if epilepsy is to be diagnosed accurately and controlled. Up to 20% of children who experience seizures are misdiagnosed as having epilepsy (Ferry, Banner, & Wolf, 1986). Table 6 lists conditions that mimic seizure activity.

The following information is needed to help differentiate and establish a diagnosis of epilepsy:

- A detailed seizure history
- A description of seizure activity
- The time when seizures most often occur
- A description of the behavior
- The length of the seizure
- The length of the postictal period (length of time before return to previous state of alertness)

Name _____ DOB: _____ Type _____ Description: _____ Duration _____
Date of last seizure before tracking sheet begun: _____

Directions: Complete pertinent information for each seizure observed. Be sure this sheet is taken to health care provider on each visit

Description	Day
	Month
	Conscious
	Unconscious
	Confused
	Fell
	Became limp
	Became stiff
	Flush
	Pale
	Cyanotic/blue
Body Movements	Jerking
	Twitching face
	Chewing motion
	Tongue biting
	Excess drooling
	Eyes rolled back
	Eyes staring
	Eyes blinking
	Incontinent of urine
	Incontinent of feces
Behavior Post Seizure	Sleepy/tired
	Alert
	Confused post seizure
	Headache
	Temporary paralysis
	Unsteady walking
	Slurred speech
	Drowsiness
	Increased activity
	Unusual activity
	Time of day
	Duration (#min.)

Figure 3.   Sample seizure tracking sheet. (Adapted from *Nursing Department Policy and Procedure Manual* [1993b]. Matheny School and Hospital, Peapack, NJ.)

229

Table 6.   Conditions that mimic seizures

Systemic
 Syncope (fainting)
 Breath-holding spells
 Hyperventilation attacks
 Hypoglycemia
 Tetanus
 Gastroesophageal reflux (may manifest as an increase in extensor tone in children with cerebral palsy, as the
  child tries to assume a position of increased comfort; this may be mistaken for a tonic seizure)

Neurological
 Sleep disorders (night terrors, sleepwalking, nightmares, sleep apnea, bruxism, head banging)
 Tics
 Migraine headaches
 Transient ischemic attacks in older individuals or those with hypertensive cardiac disease
 Paroxysmal vertigo
 Tourette syndrome
 Extrapyramidal disorders (e.g., chorea, athetosis)
 Dyskinesias (may be secondary to antipsychotic medications)

Behavioral
 Episodic dyscontrol syndrome (rage attacks)
 Pseudoseizures
 Panic attacks
 Hysteria
 Attention deficit hyperactivity disorder
 Self-stimulatory behaviors (particularly masturbation in children)
 Self-injurious behaviors

Developed by Joyce S. Morse (1993).

A careful physical assessment and neurological examination are performed, and a detailed neonatal and family history and a history of past trauma or infections is obtained (Hirtz, 1989).

Electroencephalogram (EEG) verification is done to assist in diagnosing the type of seizure and to help delineate the treatment plan. The EEG is a written record of the brain's electrical activity. Electrodes are placed on the individual's head, and wires lead from the electrodes to the EEG machine in order to record electrical impulses from the brain. Preparation for the EEG may include seizure activation procedures such as hyperventilation, photic stimulation, sleep deprivation, sleep, and reduction or withholding of medication in order to reduce the seizure threshold and stimulate seizure activity. This permits observation of the brain's activity during an actual seizure. Occasionally the EEG may be combined with videotelemetry, allowing simultaneous correlation of behaviors and the written EEG record (Batshaw & Perret, 1992).

Brain imaging techniques may be used in addition to a careful history and physical examination to determine the etiology of seizure activity. These techniques include computerized tomography (CT) scanning, magnetic resonance imaging (MRI), and positron emission tomography (PET) scanning. The MRI is preferred over the CT scan in adults unless a small calcified lesion is suspected (Engel, 1992). These modalities are utilized to identify or rule out tumors, malformations, blood clots, enlarged blood vessels, enlarging ventricles, and problems with the brain or surrounding tissue. Discrete areas of brain abnormality are identified in about 5% of children with seizure disorders (Batshaw & Perret, 1992).

Psychometric studies, including standardized tests for attention, verbal IQ, memory, language, and personality, may be utilized, as appropriate, with individuals who have developmental disabilities and a seizure disorder. Such tests can verify the presence of a focal or diffuse brain disturbance. Serial testing can be utilized to document progressive deterioration or the effectiveness of interventions (Engel, 1992).

Laboratory studies are useful in detecting metabolic problems that can cause seizures. Therefore, measurements of serum glucose, electrolytes, and calcium, renal function tests, and liver function tests may be performed. A septic workup, including a lumbar puncture, may be indicated when bacterial meningitis is present or if other infections are suspected. A urine screen for toxins is helpful if drug ingestion is suspected (Sargraves, 1990), and a complete blood count, liver function tests, blood urea nitrogen measurement, and urinalysis are necessary for all individuals about to begin antiepileptic drug therapy in order to establish a baseline for evaluating possible subsequent toxic side effects (Engel, 1992; Wagner, 1993).

PHARMACOLOGICAL THERAPY FOR SEIZURES

The goal of pharmacological therapy is to utilize the least number of medications while maintaining the maximum level of alertness with the fewest number of seizures. Ideally, the person should be fully alert and functional, with no seizures and taking only one medication (Garnett, 1989). However, individuals with developmental disa-

bilities may have more than one neurological problem, making seizure management more complex. Management protocols may have to achieve a balance between an individual's frequency of seizure activity and alertness by utilizing multiple medications.

Common Antiepileptic Medications

Each type of seizure is most responsive to a specific antiepileptic drug. Factors that influence the selection of a medication are seizure type; the individual's age, sex, weight, and physical condition; and the individual's response to medication. A careful history must be taken regarding drug allergies before initiating antiepileptic medication treatment. Table 7 lists commonly used antiepileptic drug choices based on seizure classification. Table 8 describes some idiosyncratic side effects of such drugs, and Table 9 summarizes the interactions between these drugs and other commonly used medications. Table 10 is a summary of the dosage forms, therapeutic levels, and common side effects of some commonly used antiepileptic drugs.

Phenobarbital Phenobarbital, one of the most common and least expensive anticonvulsants, has been used for more than 75 years. The major advantage of phenobarbital is that it has a relatively long half-life of 37–73 hours; thus, it needs to be given only once or twice a

Table 7. Antiepileptic drugs of choice based on seizure classification

Seizure type	Drugs of choice	Primary alternative	Secondary alternative
Partial[a]	Carbamazepine	Phenobarbital Valproate Primidone	
Absence	Ethosuximide Valproate	Clonazepam	Acetazolamide
Myoclonic	Valproate	Clonazepam	
Generalized tonic–clonic	Valproate[b] Carbamazepine	Phenobarbital Primidone	

Developed by Joyce S. Morse (1993).

[a]Includes simple partial seizures, complex partial seizures, and partial seizures that secondarily generalize.

[b]Probably the drug of choice for primary (generalized-onset) tonic–clonic seizures.

Phenytoin, although used rarely in children, may be used as the drug of choice in adults to treat both partial and generalized tonic–clonic seizures.

Table 8. Idiosyncratic antiepileptic drug side effects

Phenytoin	Phenobarbital	Carbamazepine	Valproic acid
Gingival hyperplasia	Cognitive impairment	Cardiac conduction disturbance	Nausea
Coarsening of facial features	Hyperactivity	SIADH (syndrome of inappropriate adrenal hormone secretion)	Weight gain
Hirsutism		Decreased white blood cell count	Hair loss and texture change
Acne			Decreased platelets Increased bleeding time Increased bruising

Adapted from Wagner (1993).

day (Wagner, 1993). Side effects are relatively uncommon. The major side effect is drowsiness in the first few weeks of use. Occasionally, hyperactivity has been noted in young children. Allergic reactions, although rare, can be serious. They usually appear during the first 2–4 weeks of drug use and manifest as a fine red rash over the body, with blisters in the mouth or eyes.

The usual pediatric dosage of phenobarbital is 2–4 mg/kg/day; adults may need 150–200 mg/day (Livingston, 1989). Children usually receive phenobarbital in twice-daily evenly divided doses. Adults generally take phenobarbital once a day. The therapeutic blood level for phenobarbital is 15–40 µg/ml. Phenobarbital is available in 15-, 30-, 60-, and 100-mg tablets, or in liquid form (20 mg/5 ml). It is also available in parenteral form for treatment of status epilepticus (*Physicians' Desk Reference*, 1993).

Carbamazepine (Tegretol) Carbamazepine is very effective for controlling several types of seizures, including partial seizures, partial complex seizures, and partial complex seizures with secondary generalization. It usually does not cause behavioral changes. Deleterious effects of carbamazepine on the

Table 9. Common drug interactions with antiepileptic drugs

Antiepileptic drug	Altered by	Results	Alters	Results
Phenytoin	Antacids	↓ absorption	Oral contraceptives	↓ efficacy
	Disulfiram	↑ concentration	Bishydroxycoumarin	↓ anticoagulation
	Isoniazid	↑ concentration	Quinidine	↓ concentration
	Chloramphenicol	↑ concentration	Vitamin D	↓ concentration
	Propoxyphene	↑ concentration	Folic acid	
	Cimetidine	↓ concentration		
	Ethanol			
Phenobarbital			Oral contraceptives	↓ efficacy
Primidone			Quinidine	↑ metabolism
			Tricyclics	↑ metabolism
			Corticosteroids	↑ metabolism
			Chlorpromazine	↑ metabolism
			Furosemide	↓ renal sensitivity
Carbamazepine	Propoxyphene	↑ concentration	Warfarin	↓ concentration
	Cimetidine	↑ concentration	Theophylline	↓ concentration
	Isoniazid	↑ concentration	Doxycycline	↓ concentration
	Erythromycin	↑ concentration		

Adapted from Wagner (1993).

Table 10.   Pharmacokinetics of antiepileptic drugs

Drug	Daily dose (mg/kg)	Bioavailability (%)	Time to peak absorption (hr)	Plasma half-life (hr)	Therapeutic plasma level (µg/ml)
Carbamazepine	5–25, b.i.d.–q.i.d.	75–85	4–8	25–45 (single dose) 8–24 (chronic therapy)	4–12
Clonazepam	0.1–0.3, q.d.–t.i.d.	80–90	1–4	30–40	5–70 mg/ml
Clorazepate	0.3–1.3, q.d.–t.i.d.	—	0.5–2	55–100	—
Ethosuximide	15–40, q.d.–b.i.d.	90–95	1–7	20–60	40–100
Phenobarbital	2–4, q.d.–b.i.d.	95–100	1–4	72–144	15–40
Phenytoin	5–10, q.d.–b.i.d.	85–95	4–8	9–40	10–20
Primidone	10–25, b.i.d.–t.i.d.	90–100	1–3	5–18	5–15
Valproate	15–60, b.i.d.–t.i.d.	100	2–8	20–60	50–150

Sources: Brodie (1990); Levy, Dreifuss, Mattson, Meldrum, & Penry (1989); *Physicians' desk reference* (1993).

blood are rare but can be serious, and include a reduction in the number of platelets, red blood cells, or white blood cells. Effects on the liver are also rare but potentially serious. Side effects of carbamazepine include sleepiness and/ or mild dizziness. This is usually transient and most often observed when the medication is first started. It can be avoided or diminished by starting the medication with a low dose and increasing the dose gradually until the desired protocol is achieved. Allergic reactions may appear 2–4 weeks after starting the medication in the form of a fine red rash over the body (*Physicians' Desk Reference*, 1993).

Persons taking carbamazepine should never take erythromycin (Ilosone, Pediazole, EES) because it interferes with the metabolism of carbamazepine, resulting in increased blood levels of carbamazepine, drowsiness, and unsteadiness. Other medications that alter or affect the metabolism of carbamazepine include: theophylline, isoniazid, doxycycline (Vibramycin), propoxyphene (Darvon), lithium, and cimetidine (Tagmet) (Wagner, 1993). Carbamazepine may low-er serum ethinyl estradiol levels in females who utilize birth control pills. There may be spotting and breakthrough bleeding during the menstrual cycle unless tablets with 50 µg of ethinyl estradiol are used (Frank & Fischer, 1987).

The usual dosage of carbamazepine is 10–15 mg/kg/day given in two or three divided doses (Dodson, 1989; Holmes, 1987). A maximum of 800 mg/day is prescribed for adults (Livingston, 1989). The therapeutic blood level for carbamazepine is 4–12 µg/ml. Carbamazepine is available as a chewable, cherry-flavored 100-mg tablet, a 200-mg nonchewable tablet, and in liquid form (100 mg/5 ml). Carbamazepine is not provided in a parenteral form. Carbamazepine can be ordered as a generic drug. However, switching to a generic form or trying different generic forms should be done with great caution because of differing bioavailability among forms. An increase in seizure activity and altered blood levels can occur when different generic forms are utilized (Levy, Dreifuss, Mattson, Meldrum, & Penry, 1989).

Valproic Acid (Depakene/Depakote)
Valproic acid can be used to control several types of seizures that do not re-

spond to other types of medication. It is also very effective for persons who have a mixed seizure disorder. It is unlikely to cause sedation or behavior problems (Wagner, 1993). Valproic acid always should be given with food in order to avoid indigestion, nausea, and vomiting. These symptoms are less pronounced with Depakote than with the liquid form of Depakene. Another possible side effect is mild thinning of hair. Hair growth resumes when the medication is discontinued. Mild tremors may occur when high doses of valproic acid are given. Sedation may be seen if valproic acid is used in combination with other antiepileptics. Hematologic effects, including platelet dysfunction, thrombocytopenia, neutropenia, and bone marrow suppression, are rare, but the individual should be monitored regularly for their occurrence. Prior to beginning treatment, a baseline complete blood count and liver function studies should be done. They should be repeated periodically thereafter for monitoring purposes. Monitoring also should be done for pancreatitis and hyperammonemia, which occur on rare occasions with valproic acid use (Holmes, 1987).

The usual dosage of valproic acid is 15–60 mg/kg/day given in two to three divided doses. Depakote has a long half-life (14 hr); therefore, it is given twice a day. Depakene may have a half-life as short as 4 hours; therefore, it is given three times per day. The therapeutic range of valproic acid is 50–100 μg/ml; a level as high as 150 μg/ml may be acceptable under certain clinical conditions when closely monitored. Depakene is available in soft gelatin capsules of 250 mg and as a liquid (250 mg/5 ml). Depakote is available as enteric-coated 125-, 250-, and 500-mg capsules and 125-mg sprinkle capsules (Garnett, 1989; *Physicians' Desk Reference*, 1993).

Phenytoin (Dilantin) Phenytoin has been used for more than 50 years. Its side effects are well known, and it is an inexpensive drug. It has a relatively long half-life, and therefore can be given once or twice a day. After the first few days, phenytoin rarely causes a sedation effect, nor does it cause hyperactivity. One of phenytoin's major side effects is gum hypertrophy. Dental care and oral hygiene are essential because of problems with gingival hyptertrophy. Other side effects include coarsening of the facial features and hirsutism, which is noted occasionally in children, but rarely in adults. Allergic reactions, although rare, are manifested as a fine rash that appears 2–4 weeks after drug therapy is initiated.

The usual pediatric dosage of phenytoin is 5–10 mg/kg/day; the maximum adult dosage is 400 mg/day (Livingston, 1989). The therapeutic range is 10–20 μg/ml. Signs of toxicity include confusion, blurred speech, and loss of coordination. Phenytoin is available as 30- and 100-mg capsules and as 50-mg chewable tablets. A suspension is available in two strengths: 30 mg/5 ml and 125 mg/5 ml. Phenytoin also is available as injections for parenteral use. Suspensions are not recommended because of problems with incomplete mixing, resulting in variable dosing (Sarkar, Karnes, & Garnett, 1987). It is important to note that chewable tablets and capsules should not be mixed because each form has a different half-life.

Ethosuximide (Zarontin) Ethosuximide is the drug of choice for the control of absence seizures. It is less likely to cause drowsiness than some other antiepileptic drugs. The side effects of ethosuximide include occasional gastric distress, such as nausea, vomiting, or loss of appetite. Irritability, sleep disturbances, or changes in behavior may occur in children. Allergic reactions are rare. Blood dyscrasias are rare, but can be very serious if they occur. These include reduced numbers of platelets, red blood cells, or white blood cells.

The usual pediatric dosage of ethosuximide is 15–35 mg/kg/day given once or twice per day. For adults, the maximum dosage is 1,000 mg/day, which is given in four divided doses (Livingston, 1989). The therapeutic range for ethosuximide is 40–100 μg/ml. Ethosuximide is available in 250-mg capsules or as a liquid containing 250 mg/5 ml (*Physicians' Desk Reference*, 1993; Wagner, 1993).

The Benzodiazepines The benzodiazepines—Clonazepam (Klonopin), Clorazepate (Tranxene), and Diazepam (Valium)—are a group of medications that may be used to control seizure activity. Side effects from the benzodiazepines are most likely to occur during the initial doses of the medication. Sedation, impaired mentation, and hyperactivity may occur with the benzodiazepines. Therefore, these medications are begun at a low dose with gradual increases until any problems noted can be resolved. Over time, the benzodiazepines tend to lose effectiveness as the individual develops tolerance for the drug. Therefore, it is not uncommon to see one of these medications used in combination with other antiepileptic drugs (Engel, 1992).

Diazepam also can be given parenterally to manage status epilepticus. Parenteral diazepam must be administered cautiously because of the potential for serious respiratory problems resulting in cardiac arrest (Wagner, 1993). Clonazepam may cause an increase in salivation and bronchial secretions. Allergic, hematological, and hepatic problems are rare with any of the benzodiazepines (Engel, 1992).

All of the benzodiazepines are available as tablets in a variety of dosages. There are no established therapeutic levels. Dosage schedules vary; for example, with children, Klonopin may be started at 0.25 mg b.i.d. and gradually increased. Slow tapering is necessary when discontinuing these medications because of the potential problems of irritability and/or seizures (Lockman, 1990).

Primidone (Mysoline) Primidone is a barbiturate that may be used to control generalized tonic–clonic seizures. Adverse reactions to primidone include nausea, vomiting, sedation, ataxia, sleep disturbances, and hyperactivity. The incidence and severity of side effects usually decrease as tolerance for the drug develops.

The usual maintenance dose is 10–25 mg/kg/day given in two or three divided doses. The maximum dosage for adults is 2,000 mg given in four divided doses (Livingston, 1989). The medication usually is started at one fourth of the projected maintenance dose, and the dosage is gradually increased over several weeks. If the individual also is taking phenobarbital, its level should be monitored because primidone is metabolized to phenobarbital and phenylethylmalonamide (PEMA) (Holmes, 1987). The therapeutic range for primidone is 5–15 μg/ml. Primidone is available as 50- and 250-mg tablets and as a suspension containing 250 mg/5 ml (*Physicians' Desk Reference*, 1993).

Monitoring Blood Levels during Antiepileptic Drug Use

Baseline values for various laboratory tests must be obtained prior to starting an antiepileptic drug so that drug effects can be monitored. After 1 month of medication therapy, the baseline laboratory tests are repeated and drug levels obtained. The medication administration schedule then can be adjusted as necessary. Laboratory monitoring protocols for various antiepileptic drugs are shown in Table 11.

In children, laboratory tests may be repeated in 1 month and every 3–4 months thereafter. If the individual is doing well, and seizures are in control, the amount of medication does not have to be changed. The laboratory monitor-

Table 11.   Laboratory monitoring protocols for persons taking antiepileptic medications

Medication	Laboratory tests	Frequency
Phenobarbital	CBC Phenobarbital level	Baseline; every 6 months or to check compliance
Carbamazepine	CBC SGOT Carbamazepine level	Baseline, at 1 month, then every 3–4 months
Valproic acid	CBC SGOT Valproic acid level Blood ammonia Serum carnitine, lactate, pyruvate	Baseline, at 1 month, then every 3 months
Phenytoin	CBC SGOT Phenytoin level	Baseline, at 1 month, then every 3–4 months
Clonazepam	Baseline CBC Blood level only to check compliance	Baseline; every 6 months or to check compliance
Clorazepate	Baseline CBC Blood level only to check compliance	Baseline; every 6 months or to check compliance

Adapted from Matheny School and Hospital (1993a).
Abbreviations: CBC, complete blood count; SGOT, serum glutamic oxaloacetic transaminase.

ing protocols may be different for adults; less frequent monitoring may be indicated if there is no problem with compliance and seizures are well controlled. When monitoring valproic acid levels, blood ammonia as well as lactate and pyruvate levels may be utilized in order to monitor hepatic function.

Discontinuing Antiepileptic Medications

There are no rigid guidelines about the duration for drug therapy after seizures are well controlled. When an individual has been seizure free for at least 2 years, an EEG is the first step in reevaluation. The presence of abnormalities is assessed in order to determine the probability of successful withdrawal from medication (Freeman, Vining, & Pillas, 1990). Many physicians recommend a seizure-free period of 2 years before starting to taper medication dosages. The term *taper* refers to a gradual reduction in seizure medication dosages, usually over a protracted period of time. During the time when medications are being tapered, the person will have subtherapeutic blood levels of the drug. Therefore, seizure activity may reap-

pear at any time. As the use of medication decreases, it is important to maintain careful monitoring for seizures. Safety measures must be followed throughout the medication tapering process (Wagner, 1993). These include water safety and safety with heights.

Suggestions to Ensure Medication Compliance

It is important to achieve a balance in drug therapy between the rapid control of seizures and the avoidance of side effects. Medication compliance is enhanced when the person taking medication is actively involved in the process on an ongoing basis. When a new drug regimen is introduced, it is helpful for the individual to take the medication with meals if nausea is an anticipated side effect. Higher doses can be given at bedtime when sedation is expected. Drug doses can be reduced temporarily if untoward side effects occur. Most of the unpleasant side effects are transient, and eventually a therapeutic regimen can be established (Engel, 1992).

Medication administration can be related to a familiar, everyday activity such as mealtime. A 7-day pillbox that is filled once per week may be helpful, especially when the individual self-administers medication. Children, older adults, or persons with cognitive disabilities should have assistance from a responsible adult to ensure compliance. When medication is in tablet form, if it cannot be swallowed whole, it should be crushed and put in a small spoonful of a favorite food, such as applesauce or ice cream. Medication should never be mixed into an entire serving of food or container of fluid because, if the food or fluid is not finished, the entire dose of medication may not be received.

Future Antiepileptic Drugs

Felbamate (Wallace Laboratories) is the first antiepileptic drug to be introduced since 1978, when valproate became available. Gabapentine (Parke-Davis), lamotrigine (Burroughs-Wellcome), vigabatrin (Merrell-Dow), and topiramate (McNeil) are presently under consideration for approval by the Food and Drug Administration. These drugs are similar in action to the present antiepileptic drugs; however, they may be more powerful and have fewer side effects. They have the potential to aid in the control of seizure disorders that do not respond favorably to the medications currently in use (Batshaw & Perret, 1992; Wagner, 1993). Table 12 presents a comparison of three of these new drugs: felbamate, gabapentin, and lamotrigene.

OTHER APPROACHES TO THE TREATMENT OF SEIZURES

Surgical Interventions

When seizures prove resistant to pharmacological intervention and are interfering with the life of the individual, surgical intervention may be considered. Resective surgery is limited to those individuals with intractable seizures. A thorough presurgical workup is performed. An individual is considered to be a candidate for surgery is he or she has a documented partial seizure disorder, seizures are occurring at a frequency that seriously interferes with daily living even though the person is taking adequate levels of appropriate antiepileptic drugs, and there is no substantial interictal mental retardation or psychosis (Engel, 1992). There are three basic types of surgical procedures currently in use.

Focal Excision This is a technique that removes a seizure focus that can be localized to one region of the brain. The most commonly performed surgery is the excision of an abnormal region of one temporal lobe of the brain (Batshaw & Perret, 1992; Engel, 1992).

Corpus Callosotomy This procedure involves excision of the tissue of the corpus callosum. It has been particularly effective in controlling otherwise intractable drop attacks (Engel, 1992). It also has proven to be useful in Lennox-

Table 12. Pharmacokinetics and side effects of selected new antiepileptic drugs

	Felbamate	Gabapentin	Lamotrigine
Absorption	Rapid T_{max} 2–4 hr	Rapid T_{max} 2–3 hr	Rapid T_{max} 1.5–4 hr
Protein binding (%)	22–25	<3	55
Plasma half-life (hr)	20–23	5–8	25
Therapeutic range (μg/ml)	a	≥2	1–5
Enzyme inducer	No	No	No
Side effects	Headache, nausea, anorexia, insomnia, weight loss	Fatigue, somnolence, nausea, unsteady gait	Drowsiness, headache, nausea, tremor

From Sierzant, T. (1993). Patient and nurse: Partners in medication management. *Clinical Nursing Practice in Epilepsy, 1*(3), 12. Copyright © 1993, Churchill Radius Inc., Clifton, NJ. Reprinted by permission.

a The value of monitoring felbamate blood levels is not established.

Gastaut syndrome (Batshaw & Perret, 1992).

Hemispherectomy   This is the most radical of the surgical techniques. It involves the removal of one of the cerebral hemispheres (Batshaw & Perret, 1992). It is the most effective surgical procedure for epilepsy, but it should be considered only in children who experience severely incapacitating unilateral seizures and have a hemiparesis that indicates damage has already occurred to that hemisphere of the brain.

Ketogenic Diet

Another treatment modality that occasionally is considered when a person has intractable seizures is the ketogenic diet. The ketogenic diet is high in fats and low in carbohydrates. The exact mechanism of antiepileptic action is unknown. In order to compensate for the deficiency in carbohydrates, the body breaks down the fats. This leads to metabolic ketosis. The fat in the diet is provided in the form of butter and heavy cream. The diet is quite unpalatable and difficult to administer, particularly to older children and adults who have access to candy and other carbohydrate treats (Batshaw & Perret, 1992). However, if successful, antiepileptic drugs may be able to be reduced or eliminated in about half of the persons treated with this diet (Freeman et al., 1990).

IMPACT OF SEIZURES ON QUALITY OF LIFE

The impact of seizures or epilepsy on the quality of life for an individual with developmental disabilities varies widely because each individual's needs are unique.

Categories of Impact

Descriptive categories are useful to aid individual assessment and target persons at high risk of experiencing difficulty coping with their seizures. Marshall and Cupoli (1986) identified three categories of quality of life for persons with seizure disorders: uncomplicated, compromised, and devastated. Because epilepsy is a chronic health condition and life is a dynamic process, individuals may move in and out of these categories. Also, these groupings are not mutually exclusive (Santilli, 1993).

Uncomplicated   The majority of individuals with seizures fall into this category. Their seizures are well controlled and their medication causes few or no side effects. They have support from family and friends. Academic, vocational, or psychological problems secondary to their epilepsy are rare. Most of these individuals see a specialist only during the diagnostic workup or when pathophysiological or psychological changes threaten their functioning status and thereby affect their categorization (Santilli, 1993).

Luis is a 13-year-old avid baseball fan with a medical diagnosis of cerebral palsy and partial complex seizures. Luis takes carbamazepine (Tegretol), and his seizures have been well controlled. Luis' family moved to another state when his father had a job transfer. Luis is now anxious about his new school, and he misses his old friends. He begins to have difficulty sleeping and his appetite is diminished. These changes alter his seizure threshold and he experiences an increase in seizure activity. His carbamazepine dose is increased with good results during this stressful time. Once Luis becomes comfortable in his new environment, his seizure control regimen can be readjusted back to his baseline. Thus, the fluctuation in his status is brief and, with appropriate interventions and supports, Luis returns to his baseline functional state.

Claudine is a 33-year-old computer data entry specialist. She has a medical diagnosis of Down syndrome and benign partial epilepsy. She has not experienced any seizures for almost 16 years. Six months ago, Claudine began a new job. One of her roommates got married and moved out of the apartment they shared for more than 8 years. Recently, Claudine has begun to complain that she feels "spacey" and tired. She says she keeps forgetting things. At her insistence, Claudine was referred to a neurologist. A complete neurological workup revealed focal brain atrophy. There were also EEG changes, as well as visual and fine and gross motor changes on physical examination. Thus, a pathophysiological basis for Claudine's difficulties has been identified and appropriate interventions can be developed. For Claudine, it was not the life changes that were causing her problems; however, they made her problems more apparent.

Compromised Individuals in this category have seizures that are well controlled. They are free of serious cognitive and motor problems. However, they can experience difficulties that affect their functional, social, and emotional status. The general quality of the individual's life, including cognition and health perceptions, may be negatively affected. Often, health professionals overestimate how well these individuals are doing because, on the surface, everything may appear to be fine (Santilli, 1993).

Devastated Individuals who experience multiple problems as a result of their seizure disorder combined with impaired learning, motor, and emotional functioning comprise this category. The person may have mild to severe cognitive limitations because of the pathology of his or her seizure disorder, the frequency of seizures, and/or overmedication. Overmedication may occur in an effort to increase seizure control. These individuals require continuous intervention and reassessment in order to maintain good seizure control (Santilli, 1993).

Tobias is a 67-year-old man who resides with his younger sister and her husband. He has mild cognitive limitations and, until he became ill, worked in a dress factory. He was diagnosed with epilepsy following a mild cerebral vascular accident at the age of 65. Presently, his seizures are uncontrolled. Tobias has generalized tonic–clonic seizures four or five times a day; occasionally he experiences myoclonic seizures as well. Tobias has chronic fatigue as a result of his antiseizure medications and postictal lethargy. He no longer travels independently, and this has caused him to lose contact with many of his friends and co-workers. His sister and her husband have decreased the time they spend away from Tobias. They feel that he requires constant supervision and monitoring to prevent injury during a seizure. Epilepsy is dominating the activities of Tobias and his family. A comprehensive seizure management program, including transportation and respite services, is needed to assist all of them in dealing with the impact of epilepsy on their lives.

Living with Epilepsy in Childhood

Sharon is an attractive 6 $\frac{1}{2}$ –year-old girl with blond curls and bright green eyes. She has a longstanding history of staring spells. Initially, these were first noted when she was tired or sick. Her teacher became very concerned and reported frequent episodes in class of what looked like daydreaming. Sharon's performance was declining. The teacher noted that it might be necessary to retain Sharon in first grade.

During an initial assessment by the primary health care provider, Sharon's mother reported that Sharon was born after a normal pregnancy and labor. Delivery was complicated by the use of forceps, but the neonatal period was uneventful. Her developmental milestones were somewhat delayed. She did not sit until 9 months of age, and did not walk independently until she was 18 months old. She did not talk in sentences until after age 2. There is a strong family history of epilepsy: two maternal cousins have absence seizures and a maternal aunt has generalized tonic–clonic seizures.

During the physical examination, Sharon was cooperative and pleasant but somewhat shy. Cranial nerve function was unremarkable. Muscle strength, tone, reflexes, and sensation were also within the normal range. However, on hyperventilation, after approximately 2 minutes she began staring and smacking her lips. When asked to begin hyperventilation again, she did so without any awareness that she had stopped.

A 24-hour video EEG was done to obtain a baseline frequency of Sharon's seizures. She was found to have 90 seizures. Over half of the seizures occurred while she was awake and 20 occurred while she was working on her homework. Results of other tests, including blood chemistry and hematology, were normal.

Sharon also was evaluated by a psychologist to further assess her school problems. Her attention and effort during the evaluation were appropriate. No seizures were detected during the testing. She was found to be at the sixth percentile on a Peabody Picture Vocabulary Test. Results on a Woodstock-Johnson Battery placed her reading and written language at age level, with math and general knowledge below average. Because performance in many areas was average, retention in first grade was not recommended. However, it was recommended that Sharon be given extra time for classroom assignments and tests. She also should have extra help from the resource specialist in gaining difficult concepts.

The primary health care provider reviewed these results with Sharon's family and recommended ethosuximide (Zarontin) 250 mg b.i.d. The side effects of the medication were discussed with the family. One month later, Sharon's teacher reported that, during the past several weeks, Sharon seemed more alert, with far fewer episodes of "being out of it." Two months after beginning medication, Sharon was doing much better in school. Her mother felt she was more alert and less clumsy. Neither her family nor the school staff had observed any seizures in the last month. An EEG done 6 months after medication was started showed normalization of the brainwave patterns. Three minutes of hyperventilation did not evoke any seizure activity.

A child's ability to perform desired tasks competently and control situations is an important factor in building his or her self-esteem and sense of self-worth. The loss of control associated with a seizure undermines the child's confidence. Children who have seizures feel vulnerable because of the unpredictability of when a seizure may occur. There is often a sense of helplessness to prevent seizures. The limitation of recreational or sports activities available to children with epilepsy because of safety considerations also may contribute to the child's feelings of inadequacy. Nurses can assist parents and other members of the interdisciplinary team to understand the child's feelings and develop strategies for interventions. This will enable them to help increase the child's sense of self-worth (Sixtrud, 1988). The child should be involved, as appropriate, in important decisions about him- or herself.

Living with Epilepsy in Adolescence

Self-esteem is extremely important for adolescents. Their relationships with peer groups are of vital importance. Seizures represent the ultimate in loss of control because the adolescent may not be able to predict when or if they will occur. The nurse can be instrumental in helping an adolescent who has developmental disabilities and a seizure disorder try to maintain or regain control by empowering him or her to manage his or her own medication regimen. The nurse also can help the adolescent to gain some control over his or her life by encouraging a healthy lifestyle that includes a nutritionally adequate diet and adequate sleep. The adolescent needs information about the effects of poor nutrition, sleep deprivation, and alcohol and/or drug use on the seizure threshold.

The school or vocational program should

Carlos, age 14, is a friendly teen with an engaging smile who has Lennox-Gastaut syndrome. Carlos is in special education but he is mainstreamed for some of his classes. His seizures started with myoclonic jerks at 6 months of age. Since that time, his developmental progress has slowed. At age 3, he began having atonic and absence seizures. At age 5, he had generalized tonic–clonic seizures about once a month. His seizures have never been well controlled. Carlos has been treated with valproate, carbamazepine, phenytoin, and phenobarbital, alone and in combination; he has been chronically overmedicated in an effort to increase seizure control.

Extensive metabolic workups have included blood and urine tests as well as skin biopsies, all of which are normal. EEGs revealed spike-and-wave discharges. CT scans as well as MRI demonstrate no abnormalities.

Current seizure types and frequencies are as follows: generalized tonic–clonic, 3–5/day; atonic, 10/day; tonic, 10/day; and absence, 15–20/day. On a bad day, Carlos may experience as many as 10 generalized tonic–clonic seizures and 15–20 atonic seizures. Although these seizures last only a few seconds, they can go on for hours and be too numerous to count, disrupting both his day and that of his family, teacher, and class. Presently Carlos' medication is valproate 500 mg t.i.d., clonazepam 0.5 mg b.i.d., and ethosuximide 250 mg b.i.d. Carlos' only significant past medical problem has been thrombocytopenia related to high doses of valproate. His platelet count has been observed to decrease when his dose of valproate exceeds 1,725 mg/day.

be informed if any individual has a history of seizures. As a member of the interdisciplinary team, the nurse should instruct all involved school personnel about what procedures to follow if a seizures occurs, and should familiarize them with the person's medication schedule. Sedation and the effects of medication on learning should be monitored by appropriate team members and reported to the physician as appropriate. Sports activities, except those that involve heights or water, should be encouraged.

Living with Epilepsy in Adulthood

Yolanda, a 34-year-old receptionist, is a diligent, conscientious worker. She was found slumped over her desk one day by another secretary. She exhibited tonic activity followed by mild jerking that was limited to the left side of her body, lasting 3 minutes. Within seconds after the seizure activity ceased, Yolanda appeared confused, lethargic, and mildly disoriented. There was no associated bladder or bowel incontinence. Yolanda had been home the day before with the flu. Yolanda's boss strongly recommended that she be seen by her doctor for a complete evaluation. Arrangements were made for a co-worker to accompany her to the physician's office.

Yolanda began having seizures following a car accident at the age of 2. A depressed left posterior skull fracture caused paralysis on the right side of her body, and surgery was required to relieve the pressure. The right-sided paralysis resolved except for Yolanda's preference of the use of her left hand for activities such as eating and writing. She progressed well until, at age 2 1/2 years, she had a generalized seizure associated with a fever. Phenobarbital was started, but her mother gave it inconsistently. Her mother finally stopped the phenobarbital completely because Yolanda appeared sluggish when taking it.

Yolanda has no other major health problems. Her family history is negative for any neurological problems or epilepsy. Yolanda lives at home with her mother and is somewhat of a loner; she has few friends. Results of a neurological exam were normal except for the following: 1) motor examination revealed mild asymmetries with minimal weakness of the right hand; 2) reflexes on the right side were slightly brisker than those on the left; 3) the Babinski reflex was neutral on the right foot, with plantar flexion on the left; and 4) fine motor coordination showed subtle slower movements on the right when compared to the left. The blood chemistries and the toxic screening results were normal. The CT scan showed focal brain atrophy in the left occipital region. An EEG showed an occasional seizure coming from the left temporal region and generalizing. It was determined that Yolanda had partial seizures with secondary generalization.

Yolanda met with the physician to review these findings. After discussing the diagnosis and advantages and disadvantages of treatment, it was decided to begin monotherapy with Dilantin 100 mg b.i.d. Yolanda was advised to avoid tub baths and automobile driving. The importance of taking the medications as ordered was discussed. Serum phenytoin was measured at 1 week and at 2 weeks. These levels were 6 and 3.2 μg/ml, respectively. It was recommended to increase the medication to 300 mg daily with blood levels to be measured in 1 week. At the higher dosage, the medication level remained subtherapeutic. Yolanda admitted that it was difficult

(continued)

for her to remember the medication. Use of a 7-day pillbox was recommended, with all medication to be taken at bedtime. Medication was increased to 400 mg at bedtime.

Several weeks later Yolanda experienced a seizure similar to the one at work. It occurred after spending several days with her boyfriend, during which time she had forgotten to take her medication. At this point Yolanda was seen by a neurologist. She reported problems with job performance, clumsiness, and feeling sluggish. Her phenytoin level was found to be 36 μg/ml and her medication was reduced to 300 mg/day. She felt extremely frustrated because she had to depend on friends to drive her places or take the bus. Yolanda related her problems with job performance to reading difficulty possibly caused by headaches and blurred and double vision. Although these symptoms might have been related to phenytoin toxicity, it was pointed out that these problems predated the period of phenytoin toxicity.

Several months following the medication change, although somewhat improved, the symptoms of clumsiness and difficulty with her job remained. A medication change was suggested. Although most of her difficulty was thought to be based on a structural lesion, her physician hoped to maximize her potential by switching from phenytoin to carbamazepine. A very slow transition was planned, with Yolanda starting on carbamazepine 100 mg b.i.d. for 1 week, followed by 200 mg t.i.d., with blood counts and carbamazepine levels measured at 2 weeks and 1 month. Once a therapeutic carbamazepine level was reached, the phenytoin dose would be reduced by 100 mg monthly. Yolanda was warned about the possibility of breakthrough seizures.

Every effort should be made to help adults be as independent as possible in terms of daily living. This includes opportunities for self-administration of medications. Each individual should be taught the name, action, and side effect of every medication that they use. Individuals with severe epilepsy should wear some form of medical identification, such as a Medic Alert bracelet.

Persons with seizures may face job discrimination unless employers are advised of the nature and frequency of the person's seizures. Employers also must be aware of appropriate actions to take should a seizure occur. It may be difficult for individuals with epilepsy to tell their employers for fear they will lose their job or "feel different" from their co-workers. The nurse can help by educating employers and co-workers about seizures and seizure medication.

In general, persons must be seizure free for a period of 6 months to 2 years to be able to drive an automobile. Often this means that they are dependent on others or on public means of transportation. It may be necessary for them to consider living near public transportation arrangements that facilitate independence.

Medication dosages may need to be adjusted with advancing age because older adults, in general, need less medication and are more subject to sedation and confusion as side effects of medication. Decreased activity, a natural occurrence in advancing age, also alters the person's need for and metabolism of antiepileptic medications (Wagner, 1993). However, increased somnolence and decreased activity should not be shrugged off as "normal" until a determination of drug serum levels has been made. Routine evaluations that focus on possible drug toxicity or increasing numbers of seizures will be necessary throughout older adulthood. In addition, the use of multiple medications, which often occurs in older adults, increases the risk of drug interactions. It is helpful if the person uses the same pharmacy to obtain all medications, so that the pharmacist can review the medication records to lessen the chance of drug interactions.

SAFETY ISSUES

In persons with uncontrolled seizures, safety issues must be addressed by all members of the interdisciplinary team, including the individual, his or her family and caregivers, school or program personnel, and his or her employer. The individual must avoid (or be closely supervised during) any activity that could result in death if the person had a seizure. Foremost among such activities are those that involve water, heights, power tools, and driving. For example, showers should be taken in preference to tub baths because, during a seizure, it is possible to drown in the tub. The person may swim, but only with qualified supervision and/or while wearing a life jacket. For children and adults, height safety precautions limit climbing to a height no higher than the individual is tall. For adults, this precludes working on a ladder or roof.

Power tool safety must be evaluated carefully. Driving is forbidden unless seizures have been under complete control. State licensing requirements vary, but most require 6 months to 2 years of total absence of seizure activity. Some states require a physician's certification stating seizures are well controlled. For many teens, this may be a motivating factor to help ensure compliance. Individuals who use a power wheelchair for mobility may need extra supervision. There should be a readily accessible "on–off" switch so that the power source for the wheelchair can be turned off if the person experiences a seizure while mobile. Postictally, if the person is drowsy, he or she should use a manual wheelchair if possible until full alertness returns. Helmets rarely are used by persons who have seizures except for those who have atonic (drop) seizures that are poorly controlled and can result in injury. Helmets are extremely hot and uncomfortable to wear, and they can act as a barrier to the person's ability to function in the community. However, if the person with atonic seizures has many episodes per day with resultant trauma to the mouth and face, a helmet with a face guard may be necessary.

WOMEN'S HEALTH ISSUES

Menses

Females with epilepsy experience the same physiological changes as do other females during their menstrual cycles. However, the hormonal changes associated with menstruation sometimes precipitate changes in seizure threshold as well. The water retention, weight gain, and decrease in estrogen levels that precede menstruation stress the system. A female who is relatively seizure free may have several breakthrough seizures during the days preceding and following the onset of her menstrual period. If serum levels of her antiepileptic medications are within therapeutic range, changes in usual dosages are generally unnecessary.

Seizure frequency in relation to menses should be closely monitored. Medication such as acetazolamide (Diamox) may be given prior to and during menses to help control seizures. If seizure activity is severe, or results in status epilepticus, these episodes usually are managed by a physician with diazepam or lorazepam. Of course, anytime breakthrough seizures occur, the individual should be interviewed about adherence to the prescribed dosing schedule, life-style changes (e.g., less sleep, more stress), and recent illnesses.

Pregnancy

During pregnancy, about 33% of women with epilepsy experience an increase in seizure activity. The treatment plan during pregnancy should include starting multivitamins with folic acid prior to conception in order to decrease the possibility of having a baby with a neural tube defect such as myelomeningocele or spina bifida (Yerby, 1991). It is also important to establish baseline data regarding the frequency of seizures and antiepileptic drug blood levels prior to conception. The lowest effective anti-epileptic drug dose should be used throughout the entire pregnancy, but dosage is most critical during the first trimester. There is an increased risk of bleeding for approximately 10% of women, and an estimated 4%–6% chance of teratogenicity (Wagner, 1993). The risk of malformation in children born to mothers on antiepileptic drugs is approximately twice that of untreated epileptic mothers. This difference may be due to the severity of the maternal disorder as well as to the teratogenic nature of the drugs themselves (Engel, 1992). Women considering pregnancy should be counseled regarding the teratogenic effects of some of the medications used to manage epilepsy. Valproate is implicated in the production of neural tube defects. The use of Dilantin may result in the birth of a child with developmental delays (Pugh & Garnett, 1991).

Pregnancy also may result in an increase in seizures for women who usually have few seizures. Increased weight, hormonal changes, increased fluid load, and changes in activity all contribute to destabilizing the metabolic system. Uncontrolled seizures also are considered to be potentially damaging to the developing fetus (Yerby, 1991). Although most women with epilepsy give birth to perfectly healthy children, prenatal care through a high-risk pregnancy program is advised.

During the last 2–4 weeks of pregnancy, vitamin K 20 mg/day is recommended (Wagner, 1993). Once the baby is born, the new mother should try to space her medication times and breast feeding as far apart as possible because anti-epileptic medications will appear in the milk during lactation (Yerby, 1991). The baby should be monitored carefully for any signs of lethargy or behavioral changes (Engel, 1992; Wagner, 1993).

Osteoporosis

Recent studies have uncovered a link between lifelong Dilantin use and osteoporosis in female adults with epilepsy. This risk appears to be particularly high in nonambulatory and sedentary individuals. Many physicians routinely supplement the diets of individuals at risk with vitamin D. It is recommended that regular periods of sunlight be part of the activity schedule to offset the effect of Dilantin on bone loss (Wagner, 1993).

EPILEPSY EDUCATION RESOURCES

Nurses have the skills and knowledge needed to teach the individual with a seizure disorder, his or her family, and those involved with the person on a regular basis so that they are as knowledgeable as possible about epilepsy and its management. The Epilepsy Foundation of America (4531 Garden City Drive, Landover, MD 20785) is an excellent resource. The Foundation has many useful materials for parents and professionals that are free, are available on loan, or can be purchased at a very low cost. These include pamphlets, books, movies, videotapes, slides, and computer programs. *Students with Seizures: A Manual for School Nurses* (Santilli, Dodson, & Walton, 1991) was developed by the Epilepsy Foundation of America in collaboration with the National Association of School Nurses. There is continuous printing of new materials as new information becomes available. In addition, speakers are available to organizations through a regional network. There are also numerous support groups and summer camping programs to assist individuals and support families.

SUMMARY

The prognosis for an individual with developmental disabilities and a seizure disorder varies. It is dependent on many complex and interrelated variables, including, but not limited to, the type of developmental disabilities, the type and severity of the seizure disorder, the presence of coexisting medical conditions, and the type and success of medical, surgical, and/or nutritional interventions. Coulter (1993) noted that, although the primary care physician and neurologist are principally responsible for the diagnosis and the prescription of medications, the rest of the interdisciplinary team—consisting of the individual with epilepsy, the family, nurse, pharmacist, social worker, psychologist, physical and occupational therapists, nutritionist, educator, vocational counselor, and others—have important input into the various aspects of management.

The nurse can assist the individual and his or her family to cope with the stressors associated with living with developmental disabilities and seizures. An optimum quality of life for the person with developmental disabilities and seizures is possible when the individual and/or those responsible for his or her care are knowledgeable about seizures, antiepileptic drug therapy, and management during active seizures. The nurse can support these efforts through assessment, implementation of plans, coordination of services, and reassessment of the effectiveness of the interventions throughout the life span.

REFERENCES

Aicardi, J. (1986). *Epilepsy in children*. New York: Raven Press.

Batshaw, M.L., & Perret, Y.M. (1992). *Children with disabilities: A medical primer* (3rd ed.). Baltimore: Paul H. Brookes Publishing Co.

Berg, A.T., Shinnar, S., Hauser, W., & Leventhal, J.M. (1990). Predictors of recurrent febrile seizures: A metaanalytic review. *Journal of Pediatrics, 116,* 329–337.

Bobele, G.B., & Bodensteiner, J.B. (1990). Infantile spasms. *Neurologic Clinics, 8,* 633–645.

Brodie, M.J. (1990). Established anticonvulsants and treatment of refractory epilepsy. *Lancet, 1,* 350–354.

Clancy, R.R. (1990). Valproate: An update—the challenge of modern pediatric seizure management. *Current Problems in Pediatrics, 20,* 161–223.

Commission on Classification and Terminology of the International League against Epilepsy. (1981). Proposal for revised clinical and electroencephalographic classification of epileptic seizures. *Epilepsia, 22,* 489–501.

Commission on Classification and Terminology of the International League against Epilepsy. (1985). Proposal for classification of the epilepsies and epileptic syndromes. *Epilepsia, 26,* 268–278.

Coulter, D. (1993). Epilepsy and mental retardation: An overview. *American Journal on Mental Retardation, 98* (suppl.), 1–11.

Dodson, W.. (1989). Medical treatment and pharmacology of antiepileptic drugs. *Pediatric Clinics of North America, 36,* 421–433.

Dreifuss, E.F. (1989). Classification of epileptic seizures and the epilepsies. *Pediatric Clinics of North America, 36,* 265–279.

Ellis, C. (1993). Nursing assessment and intervention for the patient experiencing seizures: A structured approach. *Clinical Nursing Practice in Epilepsy, 1*(2), 4–7.

Engel, J. (1992). The epilepsies. In J.B. Wyngaarden, L.H. Smith, & J.C. Bennett (Eds.), *Cecil textbook of medicine* (19th ed., pp. 2204–2213). Philadelphia: W.B. Saunders.

Epilepsy Foundation of America. (1991). *Epilepsy fact sheet.* Landover, MD: Author.

Farley, J. (1992). Epilepsy. In P.L. Jackson & J.A. Versey (Eds.), *Primary care of the child with a chronic condition* (pp. 268–285). St. Louis: Mosby-Year Book.

Ferry, P.C., Banner, W., Jr., & Wolf, R.A. (1986). *Seizure disorders in children*. Philadelphia: J.B. Lippincott.

Frank, J., & Fischer, R. (1987). Drug interactions with carbamazepine. *Pediatric Nursing, 13,* 545.

Freeman, J., Vining, E., & Pillas, D. (1990). *Seizures and epilepsy in childhood: A guide to parents.* Baltimore: Johns Hopkins University Press.

Garnett, W.R. (1989). Epilepsy. In J.T. DiPiro, R.L. Talbert, P.E. Hayes, G.C. Yee, & L.M. Posey (Eds.), *Pharmacotherapy: A pathophysiological approach* (pp. 107–140). New York: Elsevier.

Glaze, D.G., Hrachovy, R.A., Frost, J.D., Kellaway, P., & Zion, T.E. (1988). Prospective study of outcome of infants with infantile spasms treated during controlled studies of ACTH and prednisone. *Journal of Pediatrics, 112,* 389–396.

Goulden, K.J., Shinnar, S., Koller, H., Katz, M., & Richardson, S.A. (1991). Epilepsy in children with mental retardation: A cohort study. *Epilepsia, 32,* 690–697.

Hauser, W.A., & Hesdorffer, D.C. (1990). *Epilepsy: Frequency, causes and consequences.* New York: Demos.

Hirtz, D.G. (1989). Generalized tonic–clonic and febrile seizures. *Pediatric Clinics of North America, 36,* 365–382.

Holmes, G.L. (1987). *Diagnosis and management of seizures in children.* Philadelphia: W.B. Saunders.

Janz, D., Beck-Mannagetta, G., & Sander, T. (1992). Do idiopathic epilepsies share a common susceptibility gene? *Neurology, 42*(4, suppl. 5), 48–55.

Leppick, I.E. (1990). Status epilepticus in perspective. *Neurology,* 40 (Suppl. 3), 1–42.

Levy, R.H., Dreifuss, F.E., Mattson, R.H., Meldrum, B.S., & Penry, K. (1989). *Antiepileptic drugs* (3rd ed.). New York: Raven Press.

Livingston, S. (1989). *Comprehensive management of epilepsy in infancy, childhood, and adolescence.* Springfield, IL: Charles C Thomas.

Lockman, L.A. (1990). Absence, myoclonic, and atonic seizures. *Pediatric Clinics of North America, 36,* 331–341.

Marshall, R.M., & Cupoli, J.M. (1986). Epilepsy and education: The pediatrician's expanding role. *Advances in Pediatrics, 33,* 159–180.

Matheny School and Hospital. (1993). *Medical department policies and procedures manual.* Peapack, NJ: Author.

Matheny School and Hospital. (1993). *Nursing department policy and procedures manual.* Peapack, NJ: Author.

Pellock, J.M. (1990). The classification of childhood seizures and epilepsy syndromes. *Neurologic Clinics, 8,* 619–632.

Physicians' desk reference (47th ed.). (1993). Montvale, NJ: Medical Economics Data.

Pugh, C.B., & Garnett, W.R. (1991). Current issues in the treatment of epilepsy. *Clinical Pharmacy, 10,* 335–393.

Santilli, N. (1993). The spectrum of epilepsy. *Clinical Nursing Practice in Epilepsy, 1*(1), 4–7.

Santilli, N., Dodson, W.E., & Walton, A.V. (1991). *Students with seizures: A manual for school nurses.* Cedar Grove, NJ: Healthscan, Inc.

Sargraves, R. (1990). Childhood epilepsies and febrile seizures: A pathophysiologic and therapeutic overview. In R.J. Kuhn, J.J. Piecoro, & M.C. Shannon (Eds.), *Pediatric pharmacotherapy.* Lexington, KY: University of Kentucky Press.

Sarkar, M.A., Karnes, H.T., & Garnett, W.R. (1987). Effects of storage and shaking on the settling properties of phenytoin suspension. *Neurology, 39* (suppl. 1), 207–209.

Schapiro, M.B., Haxby, J.V., & Grady, C.L. (1992). Nature of mental retardation and dementia in Down syndrome: Study with PET, CT, and neuropsychology. *Neurobiology of Aging, 13,* 723–734.

Sierzant, T. (1993). Patient and nurse: Partners in medication management. *Clinical Nursing Practice in Epilepsy, 1*(3), 12.

Sixtrud, W.R. (1988). Helping your child develop high self-esteem. In H. Reisner (Ed.), *Children with epilepsy: A parent's guide.* Rockville, MD: Woodbine House.

Wagner, M.L. (1993, May 18). *Pharmacotherapy of seizures.* Paper presented at the College of Pharmacy, Rutgers–The State University of New Jersey, New Brunswick.

Yerby, M.S. (1991). Pregnancy an depilepsy. *Epilepsia, 32*(suppl. 6), 551–559.

11

Supporting Positive Behaviors

The Nurse's Role

Brent C. Toleman, Marisa Cenci Brown, and Shirley P. Roth

OBJECTIVES

On completion of this chapter, the reader will be able to:

- Define a problem behavior and its relative significance in persons with developmental disabilities.
- Identify the functional and environmental variables that cause problem behavior.
- List several positive approaches in the prevention and remediation of problem behavior.
- Describe the role of the nurse in monitoring psychotropic medications.

OVERVIEW

Supporting positive behaviors is an ongoing process of assessment and response to the changing conditions in which individuals live, and the actions that they take to have their needs met. This chapter provides basic principles and case examples in the assessment of and response to problem behavior. It offers a perspective on how positive programming can make a long-term difference in the productivity, independence, and involvement of persons with developmental disabilities in their communities. The nurse's role in reviewing and monitoring psychotropic medications is addressed.

PROBLEM BEHAVIOR

It is common for nurses working in the field of developmental disabilities to encounter unusual or harmful behavior in the individuals they assist. Understanding the significance of these behaviors and ways to approach individuals who exhibit them can enhance the safety of the living environment and significantly improve the quality of life. As members of interdisciplinary teams, nurses have the responsibility to include behavioral observations in their nursing assessments, monitor and advise on the management of behaviors, and advocate for the best interests of the individual. In addition, nurses may develop interventions in consultation with psychologists and/or psychiatrists.

Terminology

The words used to describe the kind of behavior that may need corrective attention in community settings are the subject of ongoing controversy. Like many of the diagnostic labels that have faded into ignominious history (e.g., idiot, imbecile, moron), words such as *abnormal, deviant, aberrant, maladaptive, dysfunctional,* and *inappropriate* have been attached to behavior to describe a class of actions that generally are seen as incompatible with normal, healthy, functional, adaptive, acceptable, and appropriate standards of conduct. These terms are not at all well defined or agreed on. They often are used interchangeably, or are distinguished by concern for the image they might attach to persons with disabilities rather than for clarifying the kind of behavior being discussed.

Some behaviors, such as assault, are illegal or dangerous and would lead to criminal prosecution of a person competent to stand trial. Other behaviors, such as the use of lewd or obscene language, may be viewed as morally repugnant. Still others are merely an annoyance or embarrassment to people who must endure such behavior; loud talking, sloppy eating or toileting habits, and incessant complaining are examples of these. Finally, some behavior is injuri-

ous or even life-threatening to the individual himself or herself.

Few, if any, terms adequately encompass this array of behaviors, but each term carries with it an implicit message about how one is to respond. Whether an individual who is screaming, grabbing, and spitting is seen as sick, frustrated, or manipulative makes a critical difference in the family's or staff's attitude and approach toward discovering and resolving the issue at hand. With this in mind, the use of a term that avoids prejudging either the behaviors or the person who exhibits them has importance beyond semantics. For this chapter, the word *problem* has been chosen to convey the perplexing nature of the behaviors encountered and the need for a solution. In addition, the terms *constructive* and *destructive* have been used to distinguish between the likely results of a person's behavior on his or her quality of life, and not as a description of the behavior itself.

Defining the Problem

An interdisciplinary team approach that includes the individual and his or her family members along with staff members most directly involved with the individual is vital in the identification of problem behaviors. The general rule of thumb in defining a behavior as problematic is that it presents a physical danger to the individual or others, or prevents an individual from engaging in meaningful activity. Some behaviors may be interpreted by the nurse or other professionals as problematic but are not perceived by the individual or his or her family in the same manner. With regard to behaviors that do not have significant safety implications for the individual, it is best to target change only for those about which the team can reach consensus.

The nursing assessment of problem behavior should include:

- A detailed description of the behavior of concern (target behavior)
- A description of the environment in which the behavior is likely to occur
- Any correlation between behavior and recent chronic illnesses
- Past successful interventions
- Medications in use and medication history (when available)

For purposes of assessment, problem behaviors often are referred to as target behaviors. A **target behavior** is defined as the behavior that will be measured and for which programs will be developed to elicit change (Kalachnik, 1988).

The first step for nurses in assessing problem behavior, formulating a detailed description of the behavior of concern, is the most important. This description must be a clear, accurate statement of the problem reported in observable, measurable terms. Behavioral descriptions should form a picture of the setting and actions of the individual that could be easily understood by anyone hearing or reading them. Data on the frequency, duration, or intensity of behavior help to quantify the problem. Without such clarity, a concrete statement of the result that the team plans to achieve through behavior management is difficult to create.

Nurses can be instrumental in assisting family members or staff to formulate statements and opinions that avoid being imprecise, mentalistic, or judgmental. Such opinions often are based on myths (e.g., individuals with Down syndrome are always passive). These beliefs also may represent lost objectivity that has resulted from frustration or fatigue. In contrast, terms that are precise, observable, and realistic provide much information that is needed in understanding the problem behavior's impact on the individual (Table 1).

Determining the Severity of Problem Behaviors

Problem behaviors in individuals with developmental disabilities can be thought of as ranging along a hierarchy of severity from those that can be ignored without serious consequences to those that must be dealt with immediately and with all available resources. Of lesser significance are those behaviors that present obstacles to learning, including wandering, inattention, with-

Table 1. Examples of meaningful and nonmeaningful ways to describe behavior

Nonmeaningful terms	Meaningful terms
Imprecise	Precise
• Jake is **aggressive** all the time.	• Jake **hits** other students when they are receiving one-to-one assistance from the teacher.
• Sally engages in episodes of **self-injurious behavior.**	• Sally **bites** her wrist 10–20 times daily at home, but not while riding on the bus.
Mentalistic	Observable
• Richard throws his shoes when he **knows** staff are leaving.	• Richard throws his shoes when **staff say good-bye to each other at the end of the workshop day.**
Judgmental	Realistic
• Laura is **stubborn** and **willful.**	• Laura's safety needs often conflict with her need for **independence.**
• Bob is **noncompliant.**	• When requested to complete a task, Bob **does not respond immediately and consistently to** the request before taking action.
• Helen cries because she is **spoiled.**	• Helen cries any time she is left **alone.**

A classroom teacher reported that periodically Derek tapped persistently on his desk. On further observation, the teacher noted that this behavior occurred when Derek engaged in any activity for longer than 15 minutes. The teacher postulated that she should introduce another activity every 15 minutes in order to keep Derek interested in an activity. Once this was initiated, the tapping behavior ceased.

Nikki had once-a-week outbursts of aggression that involved throwing anything movable in her environment. The teacher requested assistance from the school's psychologist, social worker, and nurse to evaluate the behavior and to seek possible solutions. Based on the team's assessment, physical causes were ruled out. It was hypothesized that Nikki could benefit from an increase in transition time from one activity to another, along with more one-to-one assistance. When Nikki was given the opportunity to work in a study cubicle with reduced distractions, and an aide was assigned to give her more individualized assistance, the aggressive outbursts decreased significantly.

drawal, and refusal to respond. Resolution of these behaviors will be helpful to the individual concerned and to others in his or her class or program.

Of greater importance are behaviors that may result in exclusion from the community or from employment, such as property destruction, inappropriate sexual expression, theft, repeated use of obscenities, and tantrums. These behaviors must be addressed with the necessary resources to enable the individual to function more effectively.

Problem behaviors that involve physical injury to the individual and/or others are the most serious and require prompt attention with full allocation of resources. Such behaviors include pica, regurgitation, biting, hitting, and kicking.

Selecting Appropriate Interventions

There is a range of available interventions in dealing with problem behaviors, from the relatively benign to those so intrusive or restrictive as to require regulatory approval:

Least restrictive or intrusive are those interventions utilizing natural reinforcement and environmental accommodations, such as interaction that is compassionate and enjoyable, preventive counseling, and modifications in settings and schedules.

More restrictive and intrusive are extinction programs and artificial rewards, such as timeout and token economies.

Most restrictive and intrusive are those interventions that involve restraint,

Marcus was engaging in escalating self-injurious behavior that consisted of hitting his right eye. His family had been working with an in-home therapist to address some problem behaviors, and a one-on-one classroom aide had been assigned since the beginning of the school year. The school nurse referred Marcus for a
(continued)

physical exam and an ophthalmalogical exam to rule out any medical causes for the behavior. Although no medical cause was identified, the ophthalmologist expressed concern because of noted cornea trauma. Because of the risk of permanent injury, and the family and school's exhaustion of resources, Marcus was referred for inpatient treatment at a University Affiliated Program that specialized in the treatment of severe behaviors. Round-the-clock nursing and medical care were available. Electronic monitoring and a high staff-to-student ratio allowed for implementation of medical and behavioral regimens with close follow-up and adjustments to the treatment plan. Within 4 weeks, Marcus was able to begin having weekend passes to his home. The family members and staff worked closely together, so that new approaches for supporting positive behavior changes could be transitioned to the home setting. A teacher and nurse from the school also met with university staff and family members to discuss and coordinate transition plans for the school setting.

whether physical, mechanical, or chemical.

This description of various levels of intervention indicates nothing about the difficulty that may be involved in changing an individual's behavior. The importance of dealing successfully with self-injury or aggression is obvious, but the rationale for resisting the urge to change more idiosyncratic behavior may not be. Too often, practitioners engage in "power struggles" with individuals whose behavior, although less than ideal, is insufficiently extreme to warrant the risk that the struggle itself will yield more destructive behavior.

Severe problems may be resolved by an interested staff member's investment of time and effort in very ordinary ways with an individual needing such focused attention. Conversely, countless hours of professional intervention for relatively insignificant problems may produce nothing more than frustration. Not every battle can be fought when technical, fiscal, and personal resources may be limited. Not every battle *should* be fought, when the cost to the relationship between the professional or parent and the individual could be greater than the convenience gained by unexamined conformity to rules and appearances.

Punishment In their role as health care monitors, nurses must be vigilant in recognizing and reporting any excesses or abuses in behavior management approaches. The most common of these is the unauthorized or unplanned use of punishment to suppress undesirable behavior. Most people would recognize a painful slap as an unacceptable type of punishment, but the use of threats, humiliation, and yelling often goes unrecognized as a form of punishment. These approaches not only may expose staff to

Sam insists on waiting in the office for his ride home from his work setting, instead of in the designated waiting room. This behavior is not hurting anyone, until a verbal request is made for him to leave the office. He then strikes out at the person making the request or hits himself. In this case, it may be better to accommodate Sam's refusal to stay in the waiting room than to provoke more problematic behavior by attempting to overcome his insistence.

allegations of abuse, but are typically ineffective as long-term solutions to behavior problems.

Because the use of punishment and other aversive consequences to "correct" problem behavior presents potential conflict with the concept of least restrictive environment as well as an individual's rights, during the 1980s, several national organizations promulgated resolutions on the use of aversive interventions (American Association on Mental Retardation, 1986; Arc/US, 1985; The Association for Persons with Severe Handicaps, 1986; National Association of School Psychologists, 1986). Regulations such as those for intermediate care facilities for persons with mental retardation (ICFs/MR) (U.S. Department of Human Services, 1988) and professional standards such as those of the Accreditation Council on Services for People with Developmental Disabilities (1987) provide guidelines for the use of behavioral interventions and the use of psychotropic medications. Regulations include the utilization of Human Rights Committees to evaluate behavioral plans, particularly those that recommend the use of medications, or any intervention that intrudes on the rights of an individual. Nurses must ensure that the use of aversive consequences to reduce destructive behavior is always part of a systematic and holistic approach that has met all the legal and regulatory requirements for the jurisdiction within which he or she works.

CAUSES OF PROBLEM BEHAVIOR: ASSESSMENT AND INTERVENTION

When persons with developmental disabilities exhibit problem behavior, the possibility exists that they may have concomitant mental disorders that are causing the problem behavior. In fact,

over the past 10 years, there has been increased recognition of the incidence of both mental illness and mental retardation in the same individual (Reiss, Levitan, & Szyszko, 1982; Stark, Menolascino, & Albarelli, 1987). However, many behaviors, including those that are destructive, are learned rather than diagnostic indicators of mental illness in persons with developmental disabilities.

Individuals learn by reacting to some specific stimulus and by experiencing the desirable or undesirable consequences of his or her actions. When these consequences make it likely that a person will react in the same way to the same stimulus when it is presented again, the behavior is reinforced. Consequences thus form the motivation or functional cause of behavior, while the stimuli to which the person responds form the antecedent or environmental cause. Both must be taken into account in an examination of problem behavior as a conditioned response. In addition, it is useful to think of problem behavior not only as a conditioned response, but also as a communication about what the individual needs and wants (Carr & Durand, 1985; Donnellan, Mirenda, Mesaros, & Fassbender, 1984). It is another reminder that, ultimately, there is a person behind the problem.

The function of behavior is to satisfy one's needs. The range of needs, and therefore the functions of the behaviors that individuals exhibit in response to their needs, is highly variable. It is helpful to conceptualize an individual's needs as always legitimate, although the strategies a person may develop to satisfy his or her needs may be either constructive or destructive. Needs are satisfied in a destructive manner, when the nature of that behavior is likely to impact negatively on a person's future choices, experiences, and relationships.

Tomas, a likable 25-year-old, has severe cerebral palsy and requires the help of a personal care assistant during the day. He is attending college and living at home with his parents. As Tomas has begun to see his younger siblings complete their education and move away from home, he has responded by expressing a desire for increased independence; on occasion, Tomas is reluctant to go home after his classes end. This struggle for increased independence has placed strenuous demands on his parents, and conflict has erupted between Tomas and his parents as to what Tomas' future living arrangements should be. Tomas has a legitimate need for independence. However, he is selecting a destructive means of achieving it.

Nursing Assessment of Behavior Functions and Environmental Antecedents

An analysis of both the function of problem behaviors and their environmental antecedents is essential to assessing the reason such behaviors occur, so that methods for change can be developed. Identifying environmental antecedents to problem behaviors is the first step in the development of a therapeutic approach. Therefore, a systematic review of possible antecedents must be included in a comprehensive nursing assessment of problem behavior. The analysis of environmental antecedents begins with an attempt to capture a complete and unbiased description of conditions preceding and following the behavior at issue. Data regarding the day, time, and place of the behavior, other persons present, and activities occurring at the time are often critical in establishing the relevant setting events for behavior problems.

Interviews with other persons familiar with the individual, and with the individual himself or herself, may shed light on the precise conditions in which the behavior occurs (Durand & Crimmins, 1988). Changes in the pattern of sleeping, eating, or elimination may correlate with problem behavior and serve as an indicator of a physiological event that is contributing to problem behavior. Plotting behavior incidents on a graph along with sleep, eating, or elimination data may assist in the identification of a physiological antecedent.

Assessing the function of problem behavior is also central to the determination of the appropriate method of intervention. A clear record of the typical consequences to a problem behavior often provides one indication of the function of the behavior in the individual's life. Frequently, psychologists and psychiatrists are responsible for coordinating data collection regarding such behavioral issues. However, if physiological events (e.g., pain, disease) are affecting behavior, nurses may be the initiators of data gathering.

For example, some behaviors may be the result of an attempt to increase or reduce physical sensation. Self-stimulatory behavior—stereotypical hand-waving, rocking, and so forth—is, by definition, a type of behavior that has positive sensory consequences. Even self-injury may have a sensory function (Favell, McGimsey, & Schell, 1982; Rincover & Devaney, 1982).

Self-injurious behaviors require a careful nursing assessment because they frequently yield a physical component that is at the root of the problem behavior. A thorough medical history and examination, including a review of all medications currently prescribed, is essential to rule out injury, disease, or drug side effects as the cause of the problem. Other physical problems that

Gertrude is a 54-year-old woman who lives with three other women in a community residence. She is a nonverbal woman with mental retardation and a long history of self-injury to the skin near her right ear, which she rubbed with her knuckles for long periods of time. A cursory ear, nose, and throat exam was negative for an ear infection and she was referred to a behavioral specialist, who tried rubbing the spot for her, with the result that she relaxed her hand and allowed him to rub the affected area. Rubbing other areas of the face and hands did not produce this result, leading to the strong suspicion of physical symptoms. The nurse referred Gertrude for a dental consultation. The dentist diagnosed an impacted wisdom tooth. Following the removal of the affected tooth, Gertrude no longer rubbed her skin near her right ear.

nurses should consider as possible instigating factors in cases of self-injury include rashes (with resultant urticaria), insect bites, hemorrhoids, headaches, and menstrual cramps.

Nurses assessing individuals with developmental disabilities may encounter a number of barriers, including the person's impaired ability to communicate verbally, the unavailability of precise laboratory tests, and the fact that behavior, by its nature, usually is open to interpretation (Kalachnik, 1988). Typically, the nurse would work with support staff and family members, in addition to the individual, to help overcome these barriers in collecting data. Meyer and Evans (1989) identified data collection strategies that are adaptable to community settings, and Table 2 describes some commonly used methods of data collection that are particularly adaptable to nursing practice.

Finally, nurses must know efficient means for organizing relevant data and determining exactly what services are desired. This may include evaluation of possible contributors to problem behavior, initiation of medication to treat problem behavior, and a review of ongoing treatment. Nurses can ensure that data are current, complete, and descriptive, and that the individual's or family's concerns are addressed.

Table 2.   Commonly used methods of data collection

Method	Definition
Frequency counting	Recording every instance of the target behavior.
Duration recording	A record of the length of time a behavior occurs.
Counting permanent products	Tabulating the number of objects or products that result from the individual's activities (e.g., number of broken windows, number of dishes washed, number of items left on the floor).
Time sampling	Dividing a period of time into equal segments, and recording target behavior as occurring or not occurring during a very short time interval at the end of each time segment.
Interval recording	Dividing a period of time into equal segments and indicating whether the target behavior occurred at any time within each segment.
Rating scale	Requires the respondent to select one response from a series of defined numerical values (e.g., not at all = 0, very often = 3).
Combining techniques	Measurement techniques often can be combined to meet the needs of a particular situation.

Adapted from Kalachnik (1988).

Behavior Management Techniques

In general, the techniques of behavior management can be thought of as responsive or preventative. Response techniques rely on an understanding of the function of behavior and typically fall into one of the following categories:

- Tangible (material) rewards
- Intangible rewards
- Escape/avoidance (negative reinforcement).
- Extinction

Tangible Rewards Tangible rewards, such as food, personal items, activities, and tokens that can be exchanged for other tangibles, are valuable behavior reinforcement tools and should reflect the choice of the individual receiving them, but the intrinsic benefits of and access to such rewards must be considered in light of their potential risks. For example, the use of food and liquids in a systematic approach to behavior management can negatively affect nutrition, because eventually quantities provided in the course of rewarding appropriate behavior may exceed reasonable amounts. In addition, family members or staff may unwittingly reinforce increasingly extreme behavior through poor timing of the delivery of rewards.

When a reinforcement system uses food or liquids in a preventive fashion, or allows these rewards to be given in excessive quantities every day, issues of nutrition and health, as well as the effectiveness of the reward as a reinforcement, must be considered. Tailoring the use of food rewards to account for such factors means that staff and/or family members usually are forced into withholding the items for intervals longer than the person can maintain appropriate behavior. Edibles should be earned in reasonable quantities, and self-administered if possible, so that reinforcement procedures do not degenerate into continuous feeding programs. A reinforcement system that orders pizza for an accumulation of points or tokens is more realistic, more easily implemented, more transferable to other staff and settings, and more fun than one that provides two ounces of coffee every hour for "good" behavior.

Cosmetics and toiletries, cassette tapes, special clothing, favorite activities, or anything that is *not* part of an individual's daily needs are better tangible rewards. Money is a good tangible reward in that it allows the individual a choice in how to use it and the potential for learning about the relative cost of items. However, where easy access and inappropriate requests for money are problematic; the use of a token economy may be a more practical alternative for some individuals. When using such rewards, care providers must ensure that the individual's specific preferences are taken into account, so that the reward has special meaning for its recipient.

Frank, a tall, lanky blond, has a long history of scratching and biting himself and others. Day care staff can anticipate these episodes as he starts searching the lunch room for food and then crying when he doesn't find any. In the past, he was given sodas and candy when he began searching, but staff were asked to discontinue these treats because Frank was overweight and because his searching/crying behaviors were becoming more frequent. Now his behavior has escalated and staff confess that, when the situation becomes too violent, they can calm him quickly by giving him a can of soda. It is the staff's inconsistency that has unwittingly reinforced Frank's behavior.

In a print shop, support staff and co-workers were spending a good deal of time ignoring Dimitri's "off-color" comments, frequent practical jokes, and occasional overbearing physical interaction with others. Although some individuals found him funny, such behaviors were interfering with Dimitri's and his co-workers' productivity. Dimitri's case manager tried a multitude of warnings and restrictions without achieving long-term behavioral changes. Finally, an "Employee of the Week" system was implemented. The winner was given an interview with the agency director before an applauding, assembled staff and clientele, and his or her photo was displayed in the office. At the same time, Dimitri was enrolled in a drama workshop to provide an outlet for his exuberances. After several weeks of the award going to his quieter, more productive peers, Dimitri's behavior was sufficiently improved for him to win.

Intangible Rewards Rewards also can be based on the need for social attention, affiliation, status, excitement, competition, and a great variety of other human needs beyond the basics of hunger and sensory stimulation. In addition to their effectiveness, such rewards have the advantages of building relationships, expanding the person's repertoire of constructive action, and enabling individuals to gain self-respect and social acceptance. Ensuring that individuals receive personal attention, affection, and status can be an important motivator in eliciting appropriate behavior.

Attention Positive regard for an individual's concerns, efforts, and achievements may be both the easiest and the most effective intervention in preventing problems and maintaining constructive behavior. Yet, too often, staff are lulled into the rather puritanical belief that withholding attention will encourage individuals to greater effort, or that too much attention will "spoil" an individual who will "never get enough." The question should be not "How much attention?" but "How can this person satisfy his or her need for attention constructively?" Such person-focused programs raise the level of personal attention received by the individual. Providing an alternate, more appropriate forum in which to express behavior that is inappropriate within a particular setting allows the person to experience rewards for those behaviors as well.

Affection Emphasis often is placed on not encouraging the affectionate hugging and kissing some individuals engage in with familiar individuals and strangers alike. This powerful need for

Hassan is a young man who, when frustrated, threatens violence against others. These threats initially were handled by placing Hassan in time out when they occurred. After months without progress, the day program staff observed that, although he continued to curse and struggle when placed in time out, his affect lacked real anger or fear and he was friendly and personable between episodes. The staff felt that Hassan's outbursts might reflect his need for physical interaction with others. After ruling out the possibility of seizures, a program of affectionate "roughhousing" with Hassan was instituted on a daily basis by the male staff. After 3 weeks of resistance and confusion on his part, Hassan's participation in this activity began to build, with a concurrent drop in the behavior that led to time out.

Roger, who has dual diagnoses of mental retardation and schizophrenia, engaged in occasional outbursts that frequently resulted in hitting another person. The nursing assessment indicated that most such incidents occurred at work, and that Roger had verbally expressed dissatisfaction with the routine aspects of his job. Although he was referred for a vocational assessment to determine other employment possibilities, a temporary solution was identified: Roger was promoted and became an assistant to the secretarial staff. His status was contingent not on job performance, but simply on the absence of the violent attacks for which he was referred. After Roger's promotion, these incidents dramatically decreased without the need for tangible rewards.

touch should not be ignored because some individuals may discover destructive ways to meet this drive for closeness.

Status Rarely do persons, regardless of ability, fail to distinguish between staff and peers. The need to be like the people who have the power and the perks can be a real motivator for meeting higher behavioral expectations.

Escape and Avoidance Some persons find their environment threatening, restrictive, or simply too demanding. They may exhibit destructive behavior in an attempt to disengage themselves from the persons, places, and activities that create so much stress (Carr & Newsom, 1985; Carr, Newsom, & Binkoff, 1980). When this occurs, the behavior may be reinforced not by positive rewards but negatively, by the escape from or avoidance of undesirable stimuli.

Changing problem behavior that receives negative reinforcement is a complex process (Iwata, 1987). The following case studies illustrate two options. The first is a compliance training procedure and the second, a desensitization technique.

Harold is an outgoing, middle-age man who lives in a group home with four other men. When Harold is required to return his dirty dishes to the kitchen after meals, he strikes out at others with his fist. A compliance training procedure is utilized in which staff will ignore this behavior and prevent Harold from exiting the dining room until he takes his dishes, and then thank him for doing so and allow him to leave. The behavior escalates for several days, then suddenly stops.

Renee, a shy girl who has spina bifida and mental retardation, cries intensely whenever anyone attempts to touch or talk with her at any length, but otherwise sits quietly in her wheelchair. A psychologist hypothesized that Renee has difficulty tolerating more than minimal sensory input. To help her manage this problem, teachers begin to say only "Hi" to her as they pass, touching her shoulder momentarily without stopping. She alerts to this but does not cry. Very gradually (over months) the verbal and physical interaction time is lengthened as Renee's tolerance increases.

Extinction   Although the emphasis in behavior management always should be on reinforcing people for constructive behavior, there are many times when one must limit an individual's access to reinforcement in order to reduce problem behavior. Extinction procedures are designed to deny individuals reinforcement whenever destructive behavior occurs. However, care must be taken that such procedures do not entail denial of anything to which the individual is entitled by fundamental right, law, policy, or common sense.

Person, Place, and Time   The most obvious and often the most easily manipulated antecedent variables affecting behavior revolve around staffing, furniture, activities, and scheduling. It is common for supposedly unpredictable and unprovoked behavior to be correlated, on closer examination, with the presence of certain personnel, proximity to other individuals, environmental noise (including television and radio), time of day, day of the week, holidays, and specific vocational, recreational, or personal care activities. Environments

---

Tabitha complains chronically, and is critical and accusatory toward others as a means of seeking attention and control. Previously, the staff in her group home would attend to her complaints and intercede when she criticized another resident or a staff member, thus reinforcing her behavior. In an attempt to reduce Tabitha's complaining and criticizing, the group home staff decide to ignore the tone and content of her remarks and direct their attention to unrelated items or events to which they can respond positively, such as Tabitha's clothes, preferences in food, or favorite television programs. When staff find something that redirects Tabitha's behavior, they lavish her with compliments and praise. Over time, Tabitha's destructive complaining and criticizing are diminished as the attention she received for these behaviors is withdrawn.

Environmental Interventions

Environmental interventions are preventive techniques that rely on an understanding of the antecedents to problem behavior. They redesign the conditions that trigger destructive behavior into opportunities for more constructive activity. Ideally, a comprehensive approach to behavior change will include both responsive and preventive strategies that may be adjusted as the individual's behavior improves.

Environmental interventions can be grouped into three primary categories: 1) person, place, and time; 2) precorrection; and 3) self-control. Medications may be used as an adjunct intervention to any of these three, but should never be used alone.

are complex by nature, and sifting through them for the one or two relevant stimuli that are affecting behavior, although time consuming, may be very productive.

Function, of course, plays a role in any type of problem behavior. For example, the function of Juan's behavior was to communicate hunger, since Juan was unable to signal his need clearly simply by obtaining a meal when he wanted it. In the second case study, teachers had attributed Laura's behavior to hunger despite her obvious lack of interest in eating. A more plausible explanation is that Laura eats rapidly and then wants to leave the cafeteria, and has discovered accidentally that snatching food will get staff to remove her—an exception that was daily reinforced.

Juan, an amiable 10-year-old, reportedly became agitated in the mornings, wandering away from his seat and disturbing his class at school. His parents reported similar behavior in the afternoon at home. Praise was lavished on Juan for remaining in his seat, but to no avail. A request for more precise data revealed that nearly all these behaviors occurred in the hours preceding lunch and dinner. Juan's lunch and dinner times were moved up an hour and the behavior stopped.

Laura, a quiet brunette, reportedly snatched food from others' plates during lunch in the school cafeteria. Her lunch was determined to be of sufficient amount because she seldom finished it. A single mealtime observation revealed that, of the four students who sat at Laura's lunch table, she finished first; she then took food from the others' plates before the lunchroom monitor could escort her from the table. Laura was moved the next day to a table with students who ate faster. By the time she finished, the others also were ready to leave, and no further incidents of food snatching occurred.

Precorrection A correction demonstrates the right way to perform during or after a given behavior. Precorrection shows the right way before the behavior occurs. Although rehearsals and prompts may be used, precorrection typically takes the form of rule reviews or role plays.

Rule reviews are responsive question-and-answer dialogues about one's expectations for the individual just prior to entering the setting where destructive behavior is more likely to occur. They provide a valuable reminder of the contingencies associated with behavior without the distraction of the stimulus for the problem behavior.

Role plays involve acting out constructive responses to troublesome situations outside the natural setting. They provide valuable practice and feedback for those individuals who can imagine themselves in the target setting.

When role plays are too abstract, *rehearsals* in the natural setting allow an opportunity to practice constructive behavior prior to the time when the behavior is needed. Finally, verbal, gestural,

Before getting on the bus, Eric recites the rules for travel, such as no waving of arms out the window and no yelling. Boarding the bus is the reward for getting the rules right, and he is asked to repeat them occasionally on long rides, for which he receives a "thumbs up."

Jody does a 30-second role play twice daily with a day program staff member playing the role of a person who especially annoys her. She practices her standard response—to walk away—on hearing a variety of taunts. Jody is praised lavishly for her success in the role play. Later she is observed walking away from the troublesome peer while mumbling, "Just walk away."

or physical *prompts* during events in the natural setting may be used just prior to the point in the event at which destructive behavior usually occurs.

Self-Control The ideal antecedent intervention provides the individual with the tools needed to manage his or her own behavior. Three such tools are self-monitoring, stress reduction, and choices.

Self-monitoring allows an individual to record his or her own behavior in whatever way is meaningful. Precision is less important than the visual display of progress, so thermometer charts that fill up or calendars with happy faces are acceptable. A "bad day" in a self-monitoring system is seen merely as a temporary setback to the accumulation of "good days," and, even on a bad day, the individual can be praised for recording his or her data correctly.

Stress reduction strategies help persons regain control by reducing their level of anxiety or providing alternate constructive behaviors. Both antecedent physical exercise (Bachman & Fuqua, 1983; Baumeister & MacLean, 1984) and relaxation techniques (Steen & Zuriff, 1977) have been shown to have a calming effect, although there is no way to predict with certainty who will benefit from each technique. Meyer and Evans (1989) have provided a summary of methods used to teach relaxation and anger control that nurses can employ as intervention methods.

Choices provide people, regardless of ability, with the freedom and power one associates with being human. Choice is an inherent right of each human being, and being able to choose among options is central to a sense of self-control for all persons. Yet it is probably choice that persons with developmental disabilities most frequently are denied. Without freedom of choice, such individuals lack the capacity to be self-determining to the fullest extent possible, which con-

strains their ability to function fully in the community. However, many persons with developmental disabilities have little experience in choice making, and may have difficulty understanding the concept of choice. They need supportive assistance to enable them to make choices about daily living tasks.

In terms of behavior management, the rationale for providing greater choices is fairly straightforward. First, it may be naive to expect persons with developmental disabilities to make constructive choices without practice. An individual who is not allowed to choose the clothes he or she will wear, the foods he or she will eat, or with whom he or she lives, works, and plays is unlikely to understand that he or she has a choice between aggression and discussion. Second, the natural consequences, both positive and negative, to behavior resulting from safe choices provide valuable learning to the individual about the risks and rewards of various courses of action, and to the care provider about the individual's abilities and preferences. Third, the more aspects of another's life one tries to control, the more opportunities there are for conflict. Finally, most opportunities for choice are between options that, although not equally constructive, are relatively benign either way. Protecting individuals from harm is not the same thing as protecting them from risk. A person's choice to behave in ways that might lead to failure, embarrassment, delay, or extra effort is preferable to the conflict and dependency engendered by well-intentioned but unnecessary manipulation of the individual or his or her options.

MEDICATIONS AS PART OF THE TREATMENT PLAN

Psychotropic medications provide an adjunct to behavior management techniques and environmental interventions in supporting positive behavior in individuals with developmental disabilities.

The use of neuroleptic medications to treat individuals with mental retardation rose dramatically during the 1960s and 1970s, along with documentation of misuse (Rinck, Guidry, & Calkins, 1989). Litigation has increased sharply over the past 10 years in response to the overuse of psychotropic medications, failure to obtain informed consent, and failure to monitor for deleterious side effects (Blair & Dauner, 1993; Ciccone, Tokoli, Gift, & Clements, 1993; Clayton, 1987; Hargreaves, Shumway, Knutsen, Weinstein, & Senter, 1987; McKinnon, Cournos, & Stanley, 1989).

The judicious use of medication treatment for problem behaviors must ensure that medication therapy is used as part of an individualized program plan in which the following are carefully considered: the benefits of treatment in light of potential risks, utilization of the lowest effective dose, and monitoring of side effects in a consistent manner by trained personnel. Medications are never to be used as punishment, for the sake of staff convenience, as a substitute for appropriate programming, in excessive quantities, or in the absence of specific supporting data.

The Nursing Role

Nurses are in an excellent position to assume a proactive stance in the use of medications. Nurses have a solid foundation in psychiatric illness as part of their basic preparation. They can assist in the identification of symptoms that aid the physician in the establishment of a psychiatric diagnosis. The nurse's ability to assess an individual holistically adds an essential perspective in deciding when to treat an individual with psychotropic medications. Nurses can monitor health patterns in conjunction with target behaviors to determine if sensory events are triggering behavioral responses. Nurses

can monitor for side effects of medications and assess progress to determine if minimally effective doses are being employed.

The role of the nurse in the assessment and treatment of problem behaviors within the interdisciplinary team is multifaceted. The nurse contributes expertise regarding mental illness, the psychosocial aspects of illness, and observational skills. In addition, the nurse, pharmacist, and physician all contribute knowledge of medications and their side effects, and can determine instructional strategies for the individual and family members regarding medication administration, the monitoring of side effects, and the importance of follow-up.

Nursing Assessment

Least intrusive methods of treating problem behaviors with medication begin with a thorough nursing assessment that reviews multiple factors and establishes a baseline of health patterns and responses to illness. With continued monitoring, the nurse can assist the individual and family in reaching a decision to utilize medications appropriately to achieve maximum benefit, and to reduce or eliminate medications given unnecessarily.

As discussed earlier in this chapter, assessment techniques usually involve a variety of data collection techniques. Even if the nurse is not responsible for the coordination of data collection, he or she must have a working knowledge of these techniques so that a health perspective can be added. How aggregate data are handled will depend on the practice setting. There may be a need to consolidate data on a daily, weekly, monthly, quarterly, or annual basis.

Informed Consent

Either written or verbal informed consent should be obtained prior to initiation of psychotropic therapy. Consent must be voluntary, and must be obtained from an individual or guardian who is capable of giving consent. Information that is understandable to the individual giving consent must be provided regarding diagnosis, available treatments, risks versus benefits of treatments, and an explanation of all significant risks (DeVeaugh-Giess, 1982).

Medication Review and the Minimal Effective Dose

An individual's psychotropic medications should be reviewed on a regular basis by his or her interdisciplinary team. Natvig (1991) presented a comprehensive review of this process. Table 3 identifies the roles of various team members in the review of psychotropic medications, and a sample psychotropic medication review form, as developed by Kalachnik and Nord (1990) is shown in Figure 1.

ICF/MR regulations (U.S. Department of Human Services, 1988), and professional standards (Accreditation Council, 1987) have established the standard of interdisciplinary review of psychotropic medications every 3 months. In addition, state and federal regulations dic-

tate minimum standards for review. However, the frequency of review of psychotropic medications always should be dictated by individual need. For example, new psychotropic treatments may require weekly or monthly review.

Various methods employing an interdisciplinary team review have been shown to be effective in reducing psychotropic medication use in some settings (Briggs, 1989). Fielding, Murphy, Regan, and Peterson (1980) are credited with developing the concept of the minimal effective dose (MED). The MED is the lowest dose of medication that can be given that still produces the desired effect on the individual's behavior. This concept is now stressed by clinicians in terms of both safety for the individual and avoidance of potentially irreversible side effects, and it also fits within the concept of least intrusive behavior management. A sample planning sheet for the MED procedure is shown in Figure 2.

Kalachnik (1988) described three phases of the MED procedure: the review phase, the preparation phase, and the evaluation phase. In the review phase, the interdisciplinary team may

Table 3. Psychotropic review team members and roles

Team member	Role
Qualified mental retardation professional	A professional working with persons with mental retardation, often as a case manager or service coordinator
Pharmacist	Has in-depth knowledge of the action of medications, interactions with food and other drugs, and medication side effects
Psychologist	Offers expertise in behavior analysis, the development of treatment programs, and data analysis
Registered nurse	Possesses knowledge of an individual's overall health status and his or her reaction to treatment procedures
Physician	Evaluates medication status, particularly related to the history of disease or illness, and possesses the legal authority to prescribe medication
Individual receiving treatment	States his or her needs and desire to continue or discontinue treatment; describes his or her experience with medication side effects; an advocate may be needed to assist the individual in articulating his or her needs

Adapted from Natvig (1991).

PSYCHOTROPIC MEDICATION REVIEW	INDIVIDUAL		I.D.	
	DATE OF REVIEW	TYPE OF REVIEW ☐ Monthly ☐ Other ☐ Quarterly	NEXT REVIEW DATE	

PSYCHOTROPIC MEDICATION(S) AND MEDICATIONS USED TO TREAT SIDE EFFECTS. See specific physician orders for dosing schedule. Under route indicate oral, injection, decanoate, elixir, etc. Include P.R.N. orders. If decanoate cross off "day" and enter dosing schedule. Example: "37.5 mg every 21 days." Cross reference additional information or comments.

BEFORE REVIEW			AFTER REVIEW		
Medication	Dose	Route	Medication	Dose	Route
	mg/day			mg/day	
	mg/day			mg/day	
	mg/day			mg/day	
	mg/day			mg/day	
	mg/day			mg/day	

MINIMAL EFFECTIVE DOSE (M.E.D.) (check one)

☐ Currently participating in formal reduction program.

☐ At M.E.D. The next formal M.E.D. review date is specified in the chart.

☐ Deleted. The reasons for deletion and the next formal M.E.D. review date are specified in the chart.

☐ Acute use status : on drug six months or less.

PERTINENT DIAGNOSES

SIDE EFFECTS. See other chart locations for actual side effects data (such as Medical Section, Lab Section, etc.) and an in-depth list of possible side effects. Cross reference additional comments.

MONITORING METHODS (check one or more)

☐ Monitoring of Side-Effects Scale (MOSES).

Last exam date: _____

☐ Dyskinesia Identification System: Condensed User Scale (DISCUS). (Neuroleptics/Amoxapine only).

Last exam date: _____

☐ Other (specify): _____

SIDE EFFECTS PRESENT (check one)

☐ No   ☐ Yes (specify)

POSSIBLE SIDE EFFECTS. An in-depth list is provided in the chart (check one).

☐ Yes
☐ No (provide list in comments below)

COMMENTS

SIGNATURE AND TITLE	SIGNATURE AND TITLE	SIGNATURE AND TITLE

Note. While variations will occur depending on staff and applicable regulations, typical psychotropic review signatures should include the physician, pharmacist, nurse, and psychologist/behavior analyst.

Figure 1. Psychotropic medication review form. (Reprinted from Kalachnik, J.E., & Nord, G.B. [1985]. *Psychotropic medication monitoring.* St. Paul: Minnesota Department of Human Services.)

recommend proceeding with the MED procedure or may determine that a MED procedure is not in the best interests of the individual at this time. If the latter option is selected, the team's rationale is documented (Figure 3) and a date for an-

MINIMAL EFFECTIVE DOSE (M.E.D.) WORKPLAN	INDIVIDUAL		I.D.
	DATE	PROPOSED DATE OF FIRST REDUCTION	

PSYCHOTROPIC TO BE REDUCED | **REVISIONS (date and specify)**

REDUCTION AMOUNT

Current
Dose: _____ mg/day   Step 9: _____ mg/day

Step 1: _____ mg/day   Step 10: _____ mg/day

Step 2: _____ mg/day   Step 11: _____ mg/day

Step 3: _____ mg/day   Step 12: _____ mg/day

Step 4: _____ mg/day   Step 13: _____ mg/day

Step 5: _____ mg/day   Step 14: _____ mg/day

Step 6: _____ mg/day   Step 15: _____ mg/day

Step 7: _____ mg/day   Step 16: _____ mg/day

Step 8: _____ mg/day   Step 17: _____ mg/day

REDUCTION FREQUENCY (check one) (note: may vary depending upon data)
☐ Weekly   ☐ Every two months   ☐ Other (specify)
☐ Monthly   ☐ Every three months

TARGET BEHAVIOR	RATE	DETERIORATION LEVEL	WAS PREREDUCTION DATA COLLECTED USING RECOGNIZED METHODS?
TARGET BEHAVIOR	RATE	DETERIORATION LEVEL	☐ Yes ☐ No
TARGET BEHAVIOR	RATE	DETERIORATION LEVEL	PROGRAMS IN PLACE? ☐ Yes ☐ No

COMMENTS/POSSIBLE PROBLEMS/OTHER BEHAVIORS BEING MONITORED/ADDITIONAL REVISIONS/ETC.

SIGNATURE AND TITLE	SIGNATURE AND TITLE	SIGNATURE AND TITLE
SIGNATURE AND TITLE	SIGNATURE AND TITLE	SIGNATURE AND TITLE

Figure 2.   Minimal effective dose planning form. (Reprinted from Kalachnik, J.E., & Nord, G.B. [1985]. *Psychotropic medication monitoring*. St. Paul: Minnesota Department of Human Services.)

MINIMAL EFFECTIVE DOSE (M.E.D.) DELETION	INDIVIDUAL		I.D.
	DATE	DATE OF NEXT FORMAL M.E.D. REVIEW (not to exceed one year)	

CHART LOCATION(S) AND DATE(S) WHERE INFORMATION IN THIS SECTION MAY BE FOUND (Check one or more; list date)	IS THERE QUANTIFICATION OF THE TARGET BEHAVIOR SINCE THE LAST M.E.D. ATTEMPT, REVIEW, OR MEDICATION INITIATION? (check one)
☐ Monthly/Quarterly Psychotropic Review	☐ Yes ☐ No
☐ Annual	IS A NON-PHARMACOLOGICAL PROGRAM IN PLACE TO ADDRESS THE CONDITION OR TARGET BEHAVIORS OF CONCERN? (check one)
☐ Other (specify)	☐ Yes ☐ No
IS THE CURRENT PSYCHOTROPIC MEDICATION, DAILY DOSE, MAXIMUM DOSE, AND ROUTE OF ADMINISTRATION SPECIFIED? (check one) ☐ Yes ☐ No	DATE(S) OF PRIOR M.E.D. ATTEMPTS
IS THE PSYCHOTROPIC TARGET BEHAVIOR(S) SPECIFIED? (check one) ☐ Yes ☐ No	
IS THE TARGET BEHAVIOR DATA COLLECTION METHOD SPECIFIED? (check one) ☐ Yes ☐ No	

SPECIFIC REASONS IN THE FORM OF RISK-BENEFIT ANALYSIS WHY A M.E.D. ATTEMPT CANNOT BE DONE AT THIS TIME. (If additional space needed, cross-reference location.)

SIGNATURE AND TITLE	SIGNATURE AND TITLE	SIGNATURE AND TITLE

Figure 3. Minimal effective dose deletion form. (Reprinted from Kalachnik, J.E., & Nord, G.B. [1985]. *Psychotropic medication monitoring.* St. Paul: Minnesota Department of Human Services.)

other review is set. MED procedures may be postponed based on an individual's past reaction to reduction attempts, or current environmental or physical circumstances. However, the nurse should assess carefully whether past failed attempts were due to large dose reductions, lack of quality programming in conjunction with the medication reduction, poor data collection, or insufficient trial period at the reduced dose (Kalachnik, 1988).

If a MED procedure is warranted, the interdisciplinary team must prepare a plan that specifies the target behavior(s), data collection methods, and baseline requirements. Once the plan is ready, the evaluation phase is implemented, wherein drug response data are collected for a 1-month period. Based on the evaluation of the data, medication is further reduced, other interventions are introduced, or the medication is reinstated at the original dose.

Rating Scales to Monitor Side Effects

The side effects of psychotropic medications range from mild temporary lethargy upon initiation of medications to a life-threatening, malignant neuroleptic syndrome. Often, individuals with developmental disabilities have difficulty communicating their subjective reactions to medications. This underscores the need for nurses to be vigilant in monitoring for possible side effects of psychotropic medications. Training caregivers how to monitor and report their observations is also of utmost importance.

A number of rating scales for monitoring side effects have been developed. Of course, no checklist can ever substitute for the observation of changes from an individual's usual health pattern, which is why a comprehensive nursing assessment is so important (as detailed in Brown & Roth, chap. 6, this volume). Because individuals with developmental disabilities may have impaired communication abilities, and because of the potential for idiosyncratic reactions, a

baseline of the individual's typical response patterns is critical.

The Monitoring of Side Effects Scale (MOSES), developed by Kalachnik and Nord (1985), is intended for utilization by Registered Nurses, Licensed Practical Nurses, or other individuals trained and supervised by nurses. This checklist was developed for use with individuals with developmental disabilities or mental illness or geriatric populations who are or may be receiving psychotropic or anticonvulsant medication. The MOSES checklist (see Appendix A) does not provide a specific diagnosis, but rather presents specific data that can be evaluated by the physician in conjunction with the nurse or other team members.

Tardive Dyskinesia Tardive dyskinesia is a syndrome of side effects associated with the long-term use (usually 1–2 years or more) of antipsychotic medication (American Psychiatric Association, 1979). It consists of a variety of involuntary movements of the face, eyes, mouth, tongue, head, neck, and upper and lower limbs; respiratory interference; difficulty in standing or walking; severe weight loss; and severe social and psychological implications. The drugs most often associated with tardive dyskinesia include Mellaril, Thorazine, Navane, Haldol, and Prolixin. Less commonly, L-dopa, Reglan, and Amoxapine may cause tardive dyskinesia (Kalachnik, 1988). Much has been written regarding tardive dyskinesia, including the results of some studies that involve the presence of tardive dyskinesia in individuals with mental retardation (Casey, 1987). A review and summary of tardive dyskinesia issues for persons with mental retardation can be found in Kalachnik (1988).

Tardive dyskinesia can be confused with other movement disorders, including cerebral palsy, hyperthyroidism, hypoglycemia, extrapyramidal system side effects, Huntington's chorea, Parkinson disease, Wilson's disease, and the tremor of advanced age. Table 4 provides a

Table 4. Extrapyramidal system (EPS) side effects associated with neuroleptic medication and differential diagnosis with tardive dyskinesia

EPS side effect	Clinical signs	Incidence	Onset after drug Rx or dose increase	To anticholinergics	Response To neuroleptic increase	To neuroleptic decrease	Tolerance over time
Acute dyskinesia	Tics/grimaces Writhing limbs Blinking Tongue protrusion	2%	Early: 1–5 days	Yes	No	Yes	Yes
Akathesia	Pacing Restlessness Restless legs Inability to sit Verbal complaints: "jitters" "crawling out of my skin" Foot tapping Rocking (standing) Shift weight (standing)	21%	Early: 5–60 days	Yes, but some experts say minimally responsive	No	Yes	Little
Dystonia	Head snapped back Rigidity Back arching Lock jaw Contorted face Eyes rolled up	2%	Early: 1–5 days	Yes	No	Yes	Yes, but anti-cholinergics preferred

(continued)

Table 4. (continued)

EPS side effect	Clinical signs	Incidence	Onset after drug Rx or dose increase	To anticholinergics	Response		
					To neuroleptic increase	To neuroleptic decrease	Tolerance over time
Pseudoparkinsonism	Drooling No movement Tremor Shuffling gait Pill rolling Lack of expression Cogwheel rigidity	45%	Early: 5–30 days	Yes	No	Yes	Yes
"Rabbit" syndrome	Lip tremor/ perioral tremor	?	Mixed: some experts say early, some late	Yes: but some experts say no	No	Yes	No
Tardive dyskinesia	Tics/grimaces Writhing limbs Blinking Tongue protrusion	20%	Late: 1–2 years or more	No: may worsen	Yes	No	No, but may improve in some cases

Reprinted from Kalachnik, J.E., & Nord, G.B. (1985). *Psychotropic medication monitoring*. St. Paul: Minnesota Department of Human Services.

270

guide for differentiating between extra-pyramidal system side effects associated with neuroleptic medication and tardive dyskinesia.

There are several types of tardive dyskinesia. Tardive dyskinesia can manifest itself on withdrawal of a neuroleptic drug and then dissipate, or it can be masked by the neuroleptic agent. Tardive dyskinesia also can be transient or persistent. In order for an individual to be diagnosed as having tardive dyskinesia, he or she must have at least 90 days of cumulative neuroleptic exposure, he or she must meet the criteria for tardive dyskinesia using a standardized rating scale, and other conditions that could cause abnormal movements must be ruled out (Schooler & Kane, 1982).

The Dyskinesia Identification System: Condensed User Scale (DISCUS) is the only instrument for which psychometric data on persons with mental retardation are available (Sprague, Kalachnik, & White, 1984, 1985). Although the complete rating scale is included in Appendix B, readers must be cautioned that reliability in the administration of the DISCUS is adversely affected if the rater does not receive formal training (Kalachnik & Nord, 1985). Each agency or practitioner should adhere to a formal system of periodic review by qualified raters.

SUMMARY

Problem behavior is an umbrella term for a wide range of learned responses that damage individuals or create serious conflicts between them and others. It is vital for nurses to be able to define the problem correctly, to assess its cause, to evaluate current and proposed interventions, and to help implement intervention procedures. Assessment focuses on the function of the behavior and the setting in which it occurs. Interventions focus on creative, proactive, and nonaversive procedures that respect personal preferences and individuality. When medications are indicated, their use must be justified by diagnosis, ongoing monitoring, and balancing the expected benefits and risks.

As individuals learn new, more constructive ways to behave, they also are developing expectations about their environment that will have to be met routinely, if not continuously, in order to maintain that new learning. The maintenance of problem-free behavior depends on reformed environments, improved relationships, and physical wellness.

REFERENCES

Accreditation Council on Services for People with Developmental Disabilities. (1987). *Standards for services for developmentally disabled individuals.* Washington, DC: Author.

American Association on Mental Retardation. (1986). *AAMR position statement on aversive therapy.* Washington, DC: Author.

American Psychiatric Association. (1979). *Task force report 18: Tardive dyskinesia.* Washington, DC: Author.

Arc/US. (1985). *Arc/US resolution on use of aversives.* Arlington, TX: Author.

Bachman, J.E., & Fuqua, R.W. (1983). Management of inappropriate behaviors of trainable mentally impaired students using antecedent exercise. *Journal of Applied Behavior Analysis, 16,* 477–484.

Baumeister, A.A., & MacLean, W.E. (1984). Deceleration of self-injurious and stereotypic responding by exercise. *Applied Research in Mental Retardation, 5,* 385–393.

Blair, D.T., & Dauner, A. (1993). Neuroleptic malignant syndrome: Liability in nursing practice. *Journal of Psychosocial Nursing and Mental Health Services, 31,* 5–12.

Briggs, R. (1989). Monitoring and evaluating psychotropic drug use for persons with mental retardation: A follow-up report. *American Journal on Mental Retardation, 93,* 633–639.

Carr, E.G., & Durand, V.M. (1985). The social-communicative basis of severe behavior problems in children. In S. Reiss & R. Bootzin (Eds.), *Theoretical issues in behavior therapy* (pp. 219–254). New York: Academic Press.

Carr, E.G., & Newsom, D.D. (1985). Demand-related tantrums: Conceptualization and treatment. *Behavior Modification, 9,* 403–426.

Carr, E.G., Newsom, C.D., & Binkoff, J.A. (1980). Escape as a factor in the aggressive behavior of two retarded children. *Journal of Applied Behavior Analysis, 13,* 101–117.

Casey, D.E. (1987). Tardive dyskinisia. In H.Y. Meltzer (Ed.), *Psychopharmacology: The third generation of progress* (pp. 1411–1420). New York: Raven Press.

Ciccone, J.R., Tokoli, J.F., Gift, T.E., & Clements, C.D. (1993). Medication refusal and judicial activism: A reexamination of the effects of the *Rivers* decision. *Hospital and Community Psychiatry, 44,* 555–560.

Clayton, E.W. (1987). From *Rogers* to *Rivers:* The rights of the mentally ill to refuse medication. *American Journal of Law and Medicine, 13,* 7–52.

DeVeaugh-Geiss, J. (1982). Informed consent for neuroleptic therapy. In J. DeVeaugh-Geiss (Ed.), *Tardive dyskinesia and related involuntary movement disorders* (pp. 185–189). Littleton, MA: John Wright.

Donnellan, A.M., Mirenda, P.L., Mesaros, R.A., & Fassbender, L. (1984). Analyzing the communicative functions of aberrant behavior. *Journal of The Association for Persons with Severe Handicaps, 9,* 201–212.

Durand, M.V., & Crimmins, D.B. (1988). Identifying the variables maintaining self-injurious behavior. *Journal of Autism and Developmental Disorders, 18,* 99–117.

Favell, J.E., McGimsey, J.F., & Schell, R.M. (1982). Treatment of self-injury by providing alternate sensory activities. *Analysis and Intervention in Developmental Disabilities, 2,* 83–104.

Fielding, L.T., Murphy, R.J., Reagan, M.W., & Peterson, T.L. (1980). An assessment program to reduce drug use with the mentally retarded. *Hospital and Community Psychiatry, 31,* 771–773.

Hargreaves, W.A., Shumway, M., Knutsen, E.J., Weinstein, A., & Senter, N. (1987). Effects of the Jamison-Parabee consent decree: Due process protection for involuntary psychiatric patients treated with psychoactive medication. *American Journal of Psychiatry, 144,* 188–192.

Iwata, B.A. (1987). Negative reinforcement in applied behavior analysis: An emerging technology. *Journal of Applied Behavior Analysis, 20,* 361–378.

Kalachnik, J.E. (1988). Medication monitoring procedures: Thou shall, here's how. In K.D. Gadow & A.G. Poling (Eds.), *Pharmacotherapy and mental retardation* (pp. 231–268). Boston: Little, Brown.

Kalachnik, J.E., & Nord, G.B. (1985). *Psychotropic medication monitoring.* St. Paul: Minnesota Department of Human Services.

McKinnon, K., Cournos, F., & Stanley, B. (1989). *Rivers* in practice: Clinicians' assessments of patients' decision-making capacity. *Hospital and Community Psychiatry, 40,* 1159–1162.

Meyer, L.H., & Evans, I.M. (1989). *Nonaversive intervention for behavior problems: A manual for home and community.* Baltimore: Paul H. Brookes Publishing Co.

National Association of School Psychologists. (1986). *NASP resolution on corporal punishment.* Washington, DC: Author.

Natvig, D. (1991). The role of the interdisciplinary team in using psychotropic drugs. *Journal of Psychosocial Nursing, 29,* 3–8.

Reiss, S., Levitan, G.W., & Szyszko, J. (1982). Emotional disturbance and mental retardation: Diagnostic overshadowing. *American Journal of Mental Deficiency, 86,* 567–574.

Rinck, C., Guidry, J., & Calkins, C.F. (1989). Review of states' practices on the use of psychotropic medication. *American Journal on Mental Retardation, 93,* 657–668.

Rincover, A., & Devaney, J. (1982). The application of sensory extinction procedures to self-injury. *Analysis and Intervention in Developmental Disabilities, 2,* 67–81.

Schooler, N.R., & Kane, J.M. (1982). Diagnoses for tardive dyskinesia. *Archives of General Psychiatry, 39,* 486–487.

Sprague, R.L., Kalachnik, J.E., & White, D.M. (1984). The Dyskinesia Identification System—Coldwater (DIS-Co): A tardive dyskinesia rating scale for the developmentally disabled. *Psychopharmacology Bulletin, 20,* 328–338.

Sprague, R.L., Kalachnik, J.E., & White, D.M. (1985). *Dyskinesia Identification System: Condensed User Scale* (DISCUS). Champaign, IL: Institute for Child Behavior and Development.

Stark, J.A., Menolascino, F.L., & Albarelli, M. (1987). *Mental retardation and mental health: Classification, diagnosis, treatment, services.* New York: Springer-Verlag.

Steen, P.L., & Zuriff, G.E. (1977). The use of relaxation in the treatment of self-injurious behavior. *Journal of Behavior Therapy and Experimental Psychiatry, 8,* 447–448.

The Association for Persons with Severe Handicaps (1986). *TASH resolution on the cessation of intrusive interventions.* Seattle: Author.

U.S. Department of Human Services. (1988). Standards for intermediate care facilities for the mentally retarded. *Federal Register, 53,* 20448–20505.

Appendix A. Monitoring of Side Effects Scale

MONITORING OF SIDE-EFFECTS SCALE (MOSES)	INDIVIDUAL		I.D.	
	DATE	RATER SIGNATURE AND TITLE		
	INSTRUCTIONS: See other side. **Bold items are primarily observable.** Regular print items are primarily client verbalization, staff input, and/or chart review.			

SCORING: See other side for details

0 = None	2 = Mild	4 = Severe
1 = Minimal	3 = Moderate	NA = Not Assessable

EXAM TYPE (check one; if * specify in comments)

☐ 1. Admission   ☐ 4. Drug D/C (*)   ☐ 7. Other (*)
☐ 2. Baseline   ☐ 5. Drug Initiation
☐ 3. Dosage Increase   ☐ 6. Six Month Assessment

EYES/EARS/HEAD

01. **Blink Rate: Decreased**   0 1 2 3 4 NA
02. **Eyes: Rapid Vert/Horz.** 0 1 2 3 4 NA
03. **Eyes: Rolled Up**   0 1 2 3 4 NA
04. **Face: No Expression/ Masked**   0 1 2 3 4 NA
05. **Tics/Grimace**   0 1 2 3 4 NA
06. blurred/double vision   0 1 2 3 4 NA
07. ear ringing   0 1 2 3 4 NA
08. headache   0 1 2 3 4 NA

MOUTH

09. **Drooling**   0 1 2 3 4 NA
10. **Dry Mouth**   0 1 2 3 4 NA
11. **Mouth/Tongue Movement**   0 1 2 3 4 NA
12. **Speech: Slurred/ Difficult/Slow**   0 1 2 3 4 NA

NOSE/THROAT/CHEST

13. **Nasal Congestion**   0 1 2 3 4 NA
14. **Sore Throat/Redness**   0 1 2 3 4 NA
15. **Breast: Discharge**   0 1 2 3 4 NA
16. **Breast: Swelling**   0 1 2 3 4 NA
17. **Labored Breathing**   0 1 2 3 4 NA
18. **Swallowing: Difficult**   0 1 2 3 4 NA

GASTROINTESTINAL

19. Vomiting/nausea   0 1 2 3 4 NA
20. appetite: decrease   0 1 2 3 4 NA
21. appetite: increase   0 1 2 3 4 NA
22. constipation   0 1 2 3 4 NA
23. diarrhea   0 1 2 3 4 NA
24. flatulence   0 1 2 3 4 NA
25. thirst: increased   0 1 2 3 4 NA
26. abdominal pain   0 1 2 3 4 NA
27. taste abnormally: metallic, etc.   0 1 2 3 4 NA

MUSCULOSKELETAL/ NEUROLOGICAL

28. **Arm Swing: Decreased** 0 1 2 3 4 NA
29. **Contortions/Neck-Back Arching**   0 1 2 3 4 NA
30. **Gait: Imbalance/ Unsteady**   0 1 2 3 4 NA
31. **Gait: Shuffling**   0 1 2 3 4 NA
32. **Limb Jerking/Writhing** 0 1 2 3 4 NA
33. **Movement: Slowed/ Lack Of**   0 1 2 3 4 NA
34. **Pill Rolling**   0 1 2 3 4 NA
35. **Restlessness/Pacing/ Can't Sit Still**   0 1 2 3 4 NA
36. **Rigidity**   0 1 2 3 4 NA
37. **Tremor/Shakiness**   0 1 2 3 4 NA
38. fainting/dizziness/upon standing   0 1 2 3 4 NA
39. seizures: increased   0 1 2 3 4 NA
40. complaints of jitteriness/jumpiness   0 1 2 3 4 NA
41. tingling/numbness   0 1 2 3 4 NA

SKIN

42. Acne   0 1 2 3 4 NA
43. Bruising: Easy/ Pronounced   0 1 2 3 4 NA
44. Color: Blue/Coldness   0 1 2 3 4 NA
45. Color: Pale/Pallor   0 1 2 3 4 NA
46. Color: Yellow   0 1 2 3 4 NA
47. Dry/Itchy   0 1 2 3 4 NA
48. Edema   0 1 2 3 4 NA
49. Hair: Abnormal Growth 0 1 2 3 4 NA
50. Hair: Loss   0 1 2 3 4 NA
51. Rash/Hives   0 1 2 3 4 NA
52. Sunburns/Redness   0 1 2 3 4 NA
53. Sweating: Decreased   0 1 2 3 4 NA
54. Sweating: Increased   0 1 2 3 4 NA

MEASURES (enter under OTHER)
Temperature   Pulse   Blood Pressure

URINARY/GENITAL

55. menstruation: absent/ irregular
56. sexual: continual erection
57. urinary retention
58. urination: decreased
59. urination: increased (includes nocturnal)
60. sexual: activity decreased
61. sexual: activity increased
62. sexual: erection inability
63. sexual: orgasm difficult
64. urination: difficult/ painful

WHILE THE SIDE-EFFECTS IN THESE TWO AREAS ARE OFTEN DIFFICULT TO DETERMINE, PLEASE BE AWARE THEY MAY OCCUR DEPENDING ON THE SPECIFIC DRUG PROFILE. BE CERTAIN TO INQUIRE ABOUT THESE IF THE CLIENT IS VERBAL.

PSYCHOLOGICAL

65. agitated
66. **Drowsiness/Lethargy/ Sedation**   0 1 2 3 4 NA
67. attention difficulty
68. confusion
69. irritability
70. morning "hangover"
71. perceptual: hallucinations/ delusions
72. sleep: excessive
73. sleep: insomnia
74. withdrawn
75. feelings of sadness/Crying
76. nightmares/vivid dreams

IF SEEN:
• CIRCLE ITEM
• ENTER UNDER "OTHER"
• ASSIGN INTENSITY SCORE

OTHER

_____
_____
_____
_____
_____
_____
_____
_____

Reprinted from Kalachnik, J.E., & Nord, G.B. (1985). *Psychotropic medication monitoring.* St. Paul: Minnesota Department of Human Services.

CURRENT PSYCHOTROPICS/ANTICHOLINERGICS/ANTIEPILEPTICS/OTHER DRUGS OF IMPORTANCE
(e.g., stool softeners, etc.) AND TOTAL MG/DAY. ASTERISK OR INDICATE A NEW DRUG OR DOSE INCREASE.

_____ _____ mg/day   _____ _____ mg/day

_____ _____ mg/day   _____ _____ mg/day

_____ _____ mg/day   _____ _____ mg/day

_____ _____ mg/day   _____ _____ mg/day

COMMENTS (cross-reference if more space needed)

INSTRUCTIONS

1. Observe the client for 5 to 15 minutes in a quiet area.
2. Perform procedures to ascertain items. For example, flex arm for rigidity, open mouth to check throat and saliva, watch arm swing while walking, etc.
3. If client is verbal, inquire as to problems on items. For example, "Are you having trouble seeing what you read? Describe this to me."
4. Review data such as seizure counts. Talk to and review comments by reliable staff especially on items which cannot be observed during the exam such as sleeping or eating.
5. If an item is scored and a logical explanation exists, be sure to explain this in COMMENTS (for example, the client tremors, but is 80 years old and had tremor before the drug was started.)
6. Provide copy to physician and place a copy in the chart. Refer to exam and summarize results in regularly scheduled medication reviews.
7. Attempt to coordinate with physician appointments so the assessment is available to the physician such that further inquiry, if needed, may occur.

SCORING

Bold items are primarily observable. Regular print items are primarily client verbalization, staff input, or chart review.

NOT PRESENT (0): The item is not observed or is within the range of normal.

MINIMAL (1): The item is difficult to detect. It is questionable if it is in the upper range of normal. The client does not notice or comment on the side effect.

MILD (2): The item is present, but does not hinder the client's normal functioning level; i.e., his or her level at pretreatment. While the client is in no extreme discomfort, it is an annoyance to the client or may progress to future severity and problems if ignored.

MODERATE (3): The item is present and produces some degree of impairment to functioning, but is not hazardous to health. Rather it is uncomfortable and/or embarassing to the client.

SEVERE (4): The item is a definite hazard to well being. There is significant impairment of functioning or incapacitation.

NOT ASSESSED (NA): Appropriate data is not available, the client will not cooperate for certain items, etc.

Appendix B.
Dyskinesia Identification System: Condensed User Scale

NAME		I.D.

Dyskinesia Identification System: Condensed User Scale (DISCUS)

_____
(facility)

CURRENT PSYCHOTROPICS/ANTI-CHOLINERGIC AND TOTAL MG/DAY

_____ _____ mg

_____ _____ mg

_____ _____ mg

_____ _____ mg

See Instructions On Other Side

EXAM TYPE (check one)
- ☐ 1. Baseline
- ☐ 2. Annual
- ☐ 3. Semi-Annual
- ☐ 4. D/C — 1 Month
- ☐ 5. D/C — 2 Month
- ☐ 6. D/C — 3 Month
- ☐ 7. Admission
- ☐ 8. Other

COOPERATION (check one)
- ☐ 1. None
- ☐ 2. Partial
- ☐ 3. Full

SCORING

0 — **Not Present** (movements not observed or some movements observed but not considered abnormal)

1 — **Minimal** (abnormal movements are difficult to detect or movements are easy to detect but occur only once or twice in a short non-repetitive manner)

2 — **Mild** (abnormal movements occur infrequently and are easy to detect)

3 — **Moderate** (abnormal movements occur frequently and are easy to detect)

4 — **Severe** (abnormal movements occur almost continuously and are easy to detect)

NA— **Not Assessed** (an assessment for an item is not able to be made)

ASSESSMENT
DISCUS Item and Score (circle one score for each item)

FACE
- 1. Tics . . . . 0 1 2 3 4 NA
- 2. Grimaces . . . . 0 1 2 3 4 NA

EYES
- 3. Blinking . . . . 0 1 2 3 4 NA

ORAL
- 4. Chewing/Lip Smacking . . 0 1 2 3 4 NA
- 5. Puckering/Sucking/ Thrusting Lower Lip . . : . . 0 1 2 3 4 NA

LINGUAL
- 6. Tongue Thrusting/ Tongue in Cheek . . . . 0 1 2 3 4 NA
- 7. Tonic Tongue . . . . 0 1 2 3 4 NA
- 8. Tongue Tremor . . . . 0 1 2 3 4 NA
- 9. Athetoid/Myokymic/ Lateral Tongue . . . . 0 1 2 3 4 NA

HEAD/NECK/TRUNK
- 10. Retrocollis/Torticollis . . . . 0 1 2 3 4 NA
- 11. Shoulder/Hip Torsion . . . . 0 1 2 3 4 NA

UPPER LIMB
- 12. Athetoid/Myokymic Finger-Wrist-Arm . . . . . . 0 1 2 3 4 NA
- 13. Pill Rolling . . . . 0 1 2 3 4 NA

LOWER LIMB
- 14. Ankle Flexion/ Foot Tapping . . . . 0 1 2 3 4 NA
- 15. Toe Movement . . . . 0 1 2 3 4 NA

COMMENTS/OTHER

_____

_____

_____

_____

_____

TOTAL SCORE (items 1-15 only)

EVALUATION (see other side)

1. Greater than 90 days neuroleptic exposure?   : YES   NO

2. Scoring/intensity level met?   : YES   NO

3. Other diagnostic conditions?   : YES   NO
(if yes, specify)

_____
_____
_____

4. Last exam date : _____
   Last total score : _____
   Last conclusion : _____

Preparer signature and title for items 1-4 (if different from physician):

5. Conclusion (circle one):

A. No TD (if scoring prerequisite met, list other diagnostic condition or explain in comments)

B. Probable TD

C. Masked TD

D. Withdrawal TD

E. Persistent TD

F. Remitted TD

G. Other (specify in comments)

6. Comments:

_____
_____
_____
_____
_____
_____
_____

EXAM DATE

RATER SIGNATURE AND TITLE	NEXT EXAM DATE	PHYSICIAN SIGNATURE	DATE

Reprinted from Kalachnik, J.E., & Nord, G.B. (1985). *Psychotropic medication monitoring.* St. Paul: Minnesota Department of Human Services.

Simplified Diagnoses for Tardive Dyskinesia (SD-TD)

PREREQUISITES. — The 3 prerequisites are as follows. Exceptions may occur.

1. A history of at least three months' total cumulative neuroleptic exposure. Include amoxapine and metoclopramide in all categories below as well.

2. **SCORING/INTENSITY LEVEL.** The presence of a **TOTAL SCORE OF FIVE (5) OR ABOVE.** Also be alert for any change from baseline or scores below five which have at least a "moderate" (3) or "severe" (4) movement on any item or at least two "mild" (2) movements on two items located in different body areas.

3. Other conditions are not responsible for the abnormal involuntary movements.

DIAGNOSES. — The diagnosis is based upon the current exam and its relation to the last exam. The diagnosis can shift depending upon: (a) whether movements are present or not, (b) whether movements are present for 3 months or more (6 months if on a semi-annual assessment schedule), and (c) whether neuroleptic dosage changes occur and effect movements.

*   **NO TD.** — Movements **are not** present on this exam **or** movements are present, but some other condition is responsible for them. The last diagnosis must be NO TD, PROBABLE TD, or WITHDRAWAL TD.

*   **PROBABLE TD.** — Movements **are** present on this exam. This is the first time they are present **or** they have never been present for 3 months or more. The last diagnosis must be NO TD or PROBABLE TD.

*   **PERSISTENT TD.** — Movements **are** present on this exam **and** they have been present for 3 months or more with this exam or at some point in the past. The last diagnosis can be any except NO TD.

*   **MASKED TD.** — Movements **are not** present on this exam **but** this is due to a neuroleptic dosage increase or reinstitution after a prior exam when movements were present. Also use this conclusion if movements are not present due to the addition of a non-neuroleptic medication to treat TD. The last diagnosis must be PROBABLE TD, PERSISTENT TD, WITHDRAWAL TD, or MASKED TD.

*   **REMITTED TD.** — Movements **are not** present on this exam **but** PERSISTENT TD has been diagnosed **and** no neuroleptic dosage increase or reinstitution has occurred. The last diagnosis must be PERSISTENT TD or REMITTED TD. If movements re-emerge, the diagnosis shifts back to PERSISTENT TD.

*   **WITHDRAWAL TD.** — Movements **are not seen while** receiving neuroleptics or at the last dosage level **but are seen within** 8 weeks following a neuroleptic reduction or discontinuation. The last diagnosis must be NO TD or WITHDRAWAL TD. If movements continue for 3 months or more after the neuroleptic dosage reduction or discontinuation, the diagnosis shifts to PERSISTENT TD. If movements do not continue for 3 months or more after the reduction or discontinuation, the diagnosis shifts to NO TD.

INSTRUCTIONS

1. The rater completes the Assessment according to the standardized exam procedure. If the rater also completes Evaluation items 1-4, he/she must also sign the preparer box. The form is given to the physician. Alternatively, the physician may perform the assessment.

2. The physician completes the Evaluation section. The physician is responsible for the entire Evaluation section and its accuracy.

3. IT IS RECOMMENDED THAT THE PHYSICIAN EXAMINE ANY INDIVIDUAL WHO MEETS THE 3 PREREQUISITES OR WHO HAS MOVEMENTS NOT EXPLAINED BY OTHER FACTORS. NEUROLOGICAL ASSESSMENTS OR DIFFERENTIAL DIAGNOSTIC TESTS WHICH MAY BE NECESSARY SHOULD BE OBTAINED.

4. File form according to policy or procedure.

OTHER CONDITIONS (partial list)

1. Age
2. Blind
3. Cerebral Palsey
4. Contact Lenses
5. Dentures/No Teeth
6. Down Syndrome
7. Drug Intoxication (specify)
8. Encephalitis
9. Extrapyramidal Side-Effects (specify)
10. Fahr's Syndrome
11. Heavy Metal Intoxication (specify)
12. Huntington's Chorea
13. Hyperthyroidism
14. Hypoglycemia
15. Hypoparathyroidism
16. Idiopathic Torsion Dystonia
17. Meige Syndrome
18. Parkinson's Disease
19. Sterotypies
20. Sydenham's Chorea
21. Tourette's Syndrome
22. Wilson's Disease
23. Other (specify)

Item Definitions

I. Facial movements

1. Tics .... Brief muscular contractions of small sections of the face.

2. Grimaces .... Brief muscular contractions of large sections of the face or the forehead area ("brow arching").

II. Ocular movements

3. Blinking .... Rapid opening and closing of the eyelids increasing the frequency or resulting in "bursts" of blinking.

III. Oral movements

4. Chewing .... Circular or up and down jaw movements similar to chewing gum.

and/or

   Lip smacking .... Quick parting of the lips which usually produces a smacking sound.

5. Puckering .... Pursing the lips similar to movements when kissing or pulling a drawstring.

and/or

   Sucking .... Drawing in of one or both lips similar to movements when drinking with a straw.

and/or

   Thrusting lower lip .... Extending movements of the lower lip similar to a child's pout.

IV. Lingual movements

6. Tongue thrusting .... Abrupt (similar to a frog catching a fly) or rhythmic movement of the tongue in and out of the mouth beyond the lips.

and/or

   Tongue in cheek .... Pressing the tongue against the inside of the cheek OR lips producing a noticeable bulge similar to a piece of large candy or a wad of tobacco.

7. Tonic tongue .... A hanging flaccid tongue extending beyond the lips (similar to the tongue of a hot panting dog or a Down syndrome tongue).

8. Tongue tremor .... A fine rhythmic quivering of the tongue observed with the mouth open and the tongue inside or outside of the mouth.

9. Athetoid tongue .... Worm-like rolling and twisting movements of the tongue observed with the mouth open and the tongue inside or outside of the mouth.

and/or

   Myokymic tongue .... Jerking or twitching movements of the tongue observed with the mouth open and the tongue inside or outside of the mouth.

and/or

   Lateral tongue .... Side-to-side movements of the tongue observed with the mouth open and the tongue inside or outside of the mouth.

V. Head/neck/trunk movements

10. Retrocollis .... Contractions of the neck muscles tilting or bending the head back (similar to looking up at the ceiling).

and/or

Torticollis .... Contractions of the neck muscles twisting the head to one side (similar to a stiff neck).

11.   Shoulder/hip torsion .... Twisting rolling movements of the shoulders and/or hips involving large sections of the body.

VI.   Upper limb movements

12.   Athetoid finger–wrist–arm .... Worm-like writhing, vermicular rolling, and twisting movements of the fingers, wrists, and/or arms. DO NOT include tremor which is rhythmic.

and/or

Myokymic finger–wrist–arm .... Twisting or jerking movements of the fingers, wrists, and/or arms. DO NOT include tremor, which is rhythmic.

13.   Pill rolling .... Circular movements of the thumb against the fingers of the same hand.

VII.   Lower limb movements

14.   Ankle flexion .... Circular, up and down, and/or back and forth bending or twitching movements of the ankle or foot.

and/or

Foot tapping .... An alternate contact–noncontact tapping or striking movement of the heel, toe, and/or entire foot with the floor.

15.   Toe movement .... Bending or jerking movements of the toe(s). DO NOT include tremor.

Other movements

List and score any other movements that do not fit defined items provided, but that are thought to be of importance. There are three types of "other" items. DO NOT COUNT THESE ITEMS IN THE TOTAL SCORE.

Dyskinesia related .... Items such as lateral jaw movements, throat movements, breathing difficulty, "restless" or jiggling legs, and so forth that MAY be related to dyskinesia.

Non–dyskinesia related .... Items such as rocking, picking finger nails, rolling lint, teeth grinding, noises, etc. that USUALLY are self-stimulatory or stereotypic in nature and that may help in preventing misinterpretation of movements.

Other side effects .... Items such as tremor, rolling the eyes, rigidity, excessive perspiration, etc. that MAY be of importance or that may assist in preventing misinterpretation of movements.

Examination Procedure

A.   There are 12 steps in the examination procedure. The examination normally takes 5–10 minutes. More or less time may transpire depending on the specifics of the client.

1.   The client walks into a quiet room or area and stands with his or her hands at the side for approximately 15 seconds. The rater stands directly across from the client above 5 feet away.

2.   The client extends his or her arms straight out in front horizontal to the floor with the palms down for approximately 10 seconds. The client lowers the arms to the

sides and after approximately 10 seconds the procedure is repeated once. A cognitive activation task such as the rater telling the client to "name five animals," "name four presidents," etc. may be added.

3. The client opens his or her mouth wide for approximately 10 seconds. The client closes the mouth, and the procedure is repeated once.

4. The client opens his or her mouth and sticks out the tongue for approximately 10 seconds. The client closes the mouth, and the procedure is repeated once.

5. The client sits in a chair directly across or slightly off center from the rater. The client takes his or her shoes and socks off.

6. The client raises his or her right arm in the air and touches the thumb with each finger one at a time in rapid succession several times. The client lowers the right hand, and the procedure is repeated with her left hand. The client lowers the left hand, and the procedure is repeated with both hands in the air.

7. The client writes his or her name and/or draws a picture on a piece of paper on a clipboard handed to him/her by the rater. Alternatively, this can be performed on a table located to the side of the chair.

8. The client opens his or her mouth wide for approximately 10 seconds. Repeat the procedure once (same as Step 3).

9. The client opens his or her mouth and sticks out the tongue for approximately 10 seconds. Repeat the procedure once (same as Step 4).

10. The client puts on his or her socks and shoes.

11. The client stands with his or her hands at the side for approximately 15 seconds. The rater stands directly across from the client about 5 feet away (same as Step 1).

12. The client extends his/her arms straight out in front horizontal to the floor with the palms down for approximately 10 seconds. Repeat the procedure once (same as Step 2).

B. If a client is resistive to an examination step, *skip* the resistive step and go to the next step. Similarly, if a client is unable to perform an examination step due to his/her developmental level, skip the step unless prompting the step will help.

C. If a client is resistive to the point of aggression or completely noncompliant (runs away, constant yelling, etc.), *cancel* the exam and schedule it for another day.

D. If complete resistance occurs several times, observe the client from a distance from across the room. Save any interactions until observation is complete. Document the noncompliance and the reasons for the compromised examination.

E. Provide specific instructions to the client for each step and *model* each step for the client. For example, say, "Open your mouth," and then open your mouth.

F. Be sure there are no objects such as gum in the mouth. Also be sure there is no stickiness from candy, soda pop, or food from a recent meal.

G. If the floor is cold and the shoes and socks are off, be sure a towel or small rug is placed on the floor.

H. When the client does such things as touch his/her fingers and write his/her name, these are referred to as "activation" or "recruitment" procedures. Be sure to look at other body areas and not the body part being used.

I. In conducting the examination steps, the rater must continually shift his/her observation from body area to body area. The rater should not stare at one area to the neglect of other areas.

J. At the end of the examination the client should be provided an item of his/her liking such as candy, soda, a cigarette, etc. This aids in the likelihood of future cooperation.

12

Sexuality

The Nurse's Role

Joyce S. Morse and Shirley P. Roth

OBJECTIVES

On completion of this chapter, the reader will be able to:

- Describe strategies that promote healthy sexual development and expression throughout the life span of persons with developmental disabilities.
- Discuss the components of sexuality education and counseling programs that address the needs of persons with developmental disabilities.
- Identify factors that increase the risk of sexual abuse for individuals with developmental disabilities, and describe nursing interventions to decrease these risks.

SEXUALITY IN INDIVIDUALS WITH DEVELOPMENTAL DISABILITIES: A CHANGING VIEWPOINT

Wolfensberger (1972, 1983) has described the negative perceptions by society of any individual who is "different" by virtue of appearance or intellect. The term *deviant* was utilized in the past to describe such individuals. Because individuals labeled as deviant were perceived to be less than human, they were likely to be held blameless for their condition, unaccountable for their behavior, and exempt from normal social responsibilities (Knopp, 1990). Seen as a potential public menace because of their contribution to genetic decline (Dee, 1977),

The authors express their gratitude to Sally L. Colatarci, R.N., for her assistance in preparing this chapter.

individuals labeled as deviant were ostracized in the name of protecting society. Society attempted to restrict such persons by segregating them in institutions, thereby removing them from interactions with their families and the community (Dee, 1977; Wolfensberger, 1972, 1983). Because of such attitudes and segregation tactics, these individuals were stripped of their rights and privileges as human beings (Batshaw & Perret, 1992).

Historically, individuals with developmental disabilities were denied the freedom to experience their own sexuality in virtually all forms of need and expression. Many misconceptions and fears developed about sexuality in individuals with developmental disabilities (Table 1). Problems of sexual and social behavior were largely ignored, except for pregnancy, in which case an abortion or sterilization was performed (Rivet, 1990).

However, the presence of developmental disabilities does not destroy or negate an individual's sexuality. It may alter a person's perception of himself or herself as a sexual being, or it may affect the ways in which the person expresses his or her sexuality, but it does not alter the universal, lifelong need to be close to others, to be touched, and to communicate one's feelings (Batshaw & Perret, 1992). Table 2 provides facts and information about the sexuality of individuals with developmental disabilities.

Table 1. Misconceptions and fears about the sexuality of individuals with developmental disabilities

Because of differences in intellectual, social, and/or physical development, persons with developmental disabilities:

- Are incapable of learning sexually and socially appropriate behaviors.
- Are either asexual or hypersexual.
- Are incapable of heterosexual relationships.
- Are sexually aggressive and dangerous.
- Are always vulnerable to exploitation by immoral people in the community.
- Should not be allowed to marry.
- Should never be allowed to reproduce.

Adapted from Dee (1977) and Knopp (1990).

Gordon (1976) proposed a bill of sexual rights to ensure sexual freedom for all individuals, regardless of their abilities or disabilities. These rights included:

- Freedom from sexual stereotyping
- Freedom from sexual oppression
- Freedom of information
- Freedom from research nonsense and sex myths
- Freedom to control one's own body
- Freedom to express affection

In an attempt to affirm and implement Gordon's Bill of Sexual Rights, efforts to restrict the sexuality of individuals with developmental disabilities have been replaced by a growing commitment to fostering satisfying social and sexual development as well as relationships (Koegel & Whittemore, 1983). There also has been an increase in the availability of educational curricula to support families, agencies, and program staff in their efforts to learn about socialization, sexuality, and reproductive health care for individuals with developmental disabilities (Acton, 1992).

At the same time, establishing the consequences of sexual behavior and recognizing the individual's right to determine his or her sexual lifestyle implies that the individual accepts responsibility for those choices. The issue of accountability is an integral component of the normalization principle (Ward et al., 1992; Wolfensberger, 1972). Individuals with developmental disabilities must be assisted to make informed, responsible choices about sexual behaviors with the understanding that society has rules and penalties for noncompliance. The primary rule is that appropriate sexual behavior occurs privately between consenting adults without injury or harm to either person (Ward et al., 1992); the most severe penalty is lengthy incarceration. Table 3 summarizes the sexual rights and opportunities of individuals with developmental disabilities.

Table 2.   Sexuality of individuals with developmental disabilities

Differences in biological, social, intellectual, and physical function or family living situations may delay or limit the extent of sexual and/or social maturation in persons with developmental disabilities.

These individuals:

• Have sexual drives and interest in persons of the opposite sex (sexual interest decreases proportionally as the level of general intellectual functioning decreases).
• May not receive appropriate sexual education and age-appropriate social behavior guidelines.
• May exhibit social/sexual behaviors that are characteristic of younger individuals.
• May experience psychosexual maturation at a later chronological age than persons without developmental disabilities.
• May experience delay in the onset of puberty when the etiology of the disability is genetic or prenatal in origin.
• Have difficulty foreseeing the consequences of their actions.
• Use genital manipulation and masturbation in situations in which there is boredom, lack of activities, and a failure to establish acceptable standards of social conduct.
• Express an interest in dating, seeking out companionship, and learning about sex.
• Are capable of initiating and sustaining a meaningful relationship with a "significant other."
• Can sustain a marital relationship and succeed at parenting with appropriate supports.

Adapted from Acton (1992) and Ward, Heffern, Wilcox, McElwee, Dewriek, Brown, Jones, & Johnson (1992).

DEVELOPMENTAL ASPECTS OF HUMAN SEXUALITY

Human sexuality is present from conception through old age. The sex of an individual is genetically determined. The human need for touch and body contact, as well as love and intimacy, begins in utero and is nurtured throughout the life span (Montague, 1971). Sexuality is a natural part of each individual's life. It is a basic element of self-identity, and is intrinsically integrated with the concepts of self-esteem and body image. Sexuality involves the whole person. It is greater than the sum of personality traits, behaviors, physical functioning, and communications (Flodberg, 1990). Sexuality incorporates an individual's attitudes, behaviors, culture, and religious or moral values.

The development of sexuality in any individual occurs in a series of stages across the life span. At each stage of the life cycle, specific developmental milestones are achieved as an individual progresses through the various psychosocial–sexual tasks related to that stage. These life-cycle tasks are interdependent, and failure to complete the tasks of any stage interferes with healthy adaptation and slows personal growth (Erickson, 1963). For persons with developmental disabilities, chronological age is not an accurate basis for determining either life cycle stage or expected level of development. In devising educational programs, parents and service providers should consider an individual's growth patterns and achievements in order to select those interventions that are most appropriate to foster healthy psychosocial–sexual de-

Table 3.   Sexual rights and opportunities of individuals with developmental disabilities

• The right to develop and relate to others as a sexual being
• The right to privacy
• The right to be informed about matters of sexuality
• The right to be given all facts and information so that informed consent can be given
• The right to marry, procreate, and raise children unless determined incompetent in a judicial proceeding.
• The opportunity to express sexuality within the framework of acceptable behavior
• The opportunity to have access to needed services such as competent medical services, obstetrical and gynecological care, family planning information, parent training, genetic counseling, acquired immunodeficiency syndrome education and screening, day care for children, and counseling for individuals, couples, and family members

Adapted from Gardner & Chapman (1992).

velopment at each stage of the life cycle. Appendix A identifies the psychosocial–sexual developmental milestones of various life cycle stages, the impact of developmental disabilities, and potential interventions to promote/facilitate healthy sexuality from birth through older adulthood for persons with developmental disabilities.

EDUCATION IN HUMAN SEXUALITY

The term *sex education* is used to describe the provision of information about human sexuality. This includes the ongoing process of learning about being male or female, self-identity, self-concept, and self-esteem. Gardner and Chapman (1992) stated that the attitudes people have about their own sexuality are a more important outcome of sex education than their ability to name body parts. The education process can be formal and take place in a classroom setting, or it can be informal, learned through role-playing, observation of family and staff, and experiences in the community. Table 4 describes the basic content of a human sexuality program.

Many individuals with developmental disabilities receive little or no appropriately planned sex education. Attempts at sexual expression are either punished or ignored. Much of what is

Table 4.   Basic content of a human sexuality education program

- Anatomy and physiology
- Maturation and body changes
- Birth control
- Sexually transmitted diseases and their prevention
- Masturbation
- Responsibility for sexual behavior
- Inappropriate sexual behaviors and sex offenses
- Same-sex and opposite-sex activities
- Psychosocial–sexual aspects of behavior and psychosocial development
- Marriage and parenthood

From Monat-Haller, R. K. (1992). *Understanding and expressing sexuality: Responsible choices for individuals with developmental disabilities* (p. 42). Baltimore: Paul H. Brookes Publishing Co.; reprinted by permission.

learned is inaccurate, potentially harmful, and couched in secrecy (Crocker, Cohen, & Kastner, 1992). Factual sex education provided appropriately at each developmental stage is necessary in order to dispel myths, superstition, and ignorance, to prevent abuse, and to establish criteria for appropriate social/sexual behaviors. Society, in general, is reluctant to acknowledge the sexuality of individuals with developmental disabilities and to provide appropriate sex education. Thus, there is often little opportunity to learn appropriate behavior.

Nurses have many opportunities to educate and counsel individuals with developmental disabilities and their families across the life span about sexuality issues. In many community settings, it is the nurse who has the primary responsibility for teaching individuals with developmental disabilities about sexuality. Persons should have the opportunity to discuss relationships, physical sexual activity and preferences, contraceptives, family planning, and sexually transmitted diseases (Cookfair, 1991). Nurses also have a role in providing information to parents concerning the normal sexual desires of a child with developmental disabilities and to persons with developmental disabilities at all ages about many aspects of sexuality. Finally, the nurse is a resource to other members of the interdisciplinary team regarding sexuality issues.

It is important for the nurse (or any sexuality educator) to have a positive and open attitude about human sexuality; to be able to talk honestly and openly about sexuality, alone or in a group setting; and to have correct information to meet an individual's needs (Gardner & Chapman, 1992). It is also important to understand that impromptu teaching may occur at unexpected times. A sexuality educator must make the most of these "teachable moments" when a person with developmental disabilities is receptive to learning. It is important to avoid overreaction or panic if a question or situation is unexpected or uncomfortable. The safest response is always one that is simple and nonjudgmental. The nurse can bolster an individual's self-esteem by using humor and by acknowledging honest feelings of embarrassment in awkward situations (Carmody, 1992). By promoting respect for the normal sexual needs of each individual, the nurse influences the attitudes of all persons who interact with an individual with developmental disabilities.

Assessing Sexuality Education Needs

Individuals with developmental disabilities have a wide variety of needs and interests concerning sexuality. An effective sex education program based on adequate assessment provides the groundwork for effective individualized program interventions (Huntley & Benner, 1993). Assessment information is obtained by the nurse during interviews with the individual, his or her family, and/or program staff, and from case records, incident reports, and objective diagnostic tests. The Socio-Sexual Knowledge and Attitudes Test (Wish, McCombs, & Edmonson, 1980) or similar tools are available to assess understanding and attitudes of anatomy terminology, menstruation, dating, marriage, intimacy, intercourse, pregnancy/childbirth, birth control, masturbation, homosexuality, venereal disease, alcohol and other drugs, and community risks/hazards. A human sexuality assessment form such as that provided in Figure 1 on page 287 is also helpful in obtaining baseline information that can be incorporated into a teaching plan. The purpose of using an assessment tool is to identify an individual's strengths and learning needs in each area. It provides guidelines for training topics to be emphasized.

When possible, interviews with the individual and his or her family should occur in the person's home environment. The nurse can observe the relationships within the family and also note what supports are currently in place. In addition, most people feel more secure and comfortable in familiar surroundings. A home-based interview also provides the nurse with an opportunity to communicate with parents or caregivers and assist them to identify their own attitudes and expectations about sex education. It is also a time to discuss the sexual and social behaviors of their child, and how their own feelings, values, and beliefs are being communicated to their child and his or her program providers.

Abe Green is a friendly 23-year-old man with Down syndrome. He was referred to an adult day program by his parents. Prior to admission, the nurse made a home visit to meet Abe and his family. During the sexuality assessment, a part of the nursing assessment, the Greens stated that Abe masturbates frequently and they have been hesitant to allowing him to participate in a day program because of this. The nurse assured the Greens that, although this is a normal activity, it is important for Abe to learn appropriate settings for engaging in this activity. She stated that she and the staff would assist Abe in learning this.

The following week, Abe started at the center. The nurse noticed that, whenever he was in a situation that caused him anxiety, he would begin to masturbate. While he was sitting at a table, the nurse went over to Abe and, in a quiet, nonthreatening manner, asked him to put his hands on the table. She then explained to him that such activity was okay as long as it was done in a private area such as in the bathroom or his bedroom. Abe complied with this request.

(continued)

At the staff meeting that day, the nurse discussed strategies with the staff for assisting Abe in expressing his sexuality in appropriate settings in private. The nurse encouraged staff members to utilize positive direction such as "Put your hands on the table," as opposed to a negative approach ("Don't do that").

As time went on, Abe's inappropriate masturbation behavior decreased during the day program. The Green family reported that they gave Abe time alone in the bathroom or his bedroom to "do private things." They also reported that Abe occasionally goes into his room during stressful times to be "private" for awhile. His family was relieved that a satisfactory solution had been found for this behavior. They stated that they now feel more relaxed about including Abe in family outings.

The nurse also needs to consider the influence mass media may have on an individual's perceptions of sexuality.

The nurse may have an opportunity to observe an individual's social interactions during the school, workshop, or day program. These observations can provide information about the individual's social skills, the extent of limitations relating to his or her disabilities, and the responses of others to his or her behavior. Case record reviews of services received from program providers such as schools, workshops, and medical and mental health centers yield information about physical, emotional, psychological, and personality characteristics. If the individual has had encounters with the legal system, these reports provide details about the specific incidents.

Factors in Effective Program Interventions

Bopp and Lubkin (1990) described six factors that have significant impact upon the ability of an individual to learn and that directly affect the success of program interventions. These factors must be considered by the nurse in developing programs to promote healthy sexual development in individuals.

Lack of Readiness Physical readiness depends primarily on the state of an individual's neuromuscular system and is relevant to learning physical skills. Mental readiness depends on the state of the learner's intellectual development. The learner must have sufficient capacity for the learning task, as well as adequate ability to perceive ideas, communicate thoughts, and conceptualize information (Bopp & Lubkin, 1990). The teaching process must be modified and adapted to engage fully the competencies of an individual with developmental disabilities.

Physical Obstacles Discomfort, energy limitations, and decreased physical mobility are among the obstacles that can impede learning in any individual. The nurse works with other members of the interdisciplinary team to identify

While discussing appropriate social interactions with a group of 12- to 14-year-olds with developmental disabilities, the nurse asked the group, "What do you do on a date?" The immediate response of a 12-year-old girl was, "You meet somebody, you drink, and then you go to bed with your clothes off." When the nurse inquired about how the girl knew this, the girl continued, "That's how they do it on the soap operas." The nurse then discussed dating and other ways of developing friendships and expressing sexuality that do not involve sexual intercourse.

NAME: _____

Does this person...

	Yes	No	N/A
1. Respond to his/her own name?	Yes	No	N/A
2. Tolerate, at a passive level, contact from others (e.g. eye contact/physical contact)?	Yes	No	N/A
3. Recognize that others can help meet his/her own wants or needs?	Yes	No	N/A
4. Respond, at an active level, to the presence of others (e.g. accepts an object offered by another, takes turns)?	Yes	No	N/A
5. Recognize the difference between familiar and unfamiliar careproviders (e.g. staff/family members)?	Yes	No	N/A
6. Engage in interactions with familiar care providers?	Yes	No	N/A
7. Maintain contact with familiar care providers?	Yes	No	N/A
8. Seek out familiar care providers?	Yes	No	N/A
9. Exhibit specific peer preferences?	Yes	No	N/A
10. Engage in interactions with familiar peers?	Yes	No	N/A
11. Maintain contact with familiar peers?	Yes	No	N/A
12. Seek out familiar peers?	Yes	No	N/A
13. Identify him/herself as male/female, boy/girl or man/woman?	Yes	No	N/A
14. Identify others as male/female, boy/girl or man/woman?	Yes	No	N/A
15. Name/identify basic body parts (e.g. head, feet, hands, legs, arms) on self?	Yes	No	N/A
16. Name/identify basic body parts (e.g. head, feet, hands, legs, arms) on others?	Yes	No	N/A
17. Name/identify sexual body parts (e.g. genitals, buttocks, breasts) on self?	Yes	No	N/A
18. Name/identify sexual body parts (e.g. genitals, buttocks, breasts) on others?	Yes	No	N/A
19. Masturbate?	Yes	No	N/A
20. Masturbate in private and appropriate places (e.g. bathroom, bedroom)?	Yes	No	N/A
21. Masturbate at appropriate times (e.g. not during activities/programming)?	Yes	No	N/A
22. Masturbate to climax/ejaculation?	Yes	No	N/A
23. Masturbate without causing injury to him/herself?	Yes	No	N/A
24. Make decisions, with a yes or no when given a choice?	Yes	No	N/A
25. Decline (say "no") to engage in sexual activity with others?	Yes	No	N/A
26. Understand the basic functions/concepts of sexual intercourse?	Yes	No	N/A
27. Talk/ask questions appropriately concerning sexual matters?	Yes	No	N/A
28. Speak appropriately when discussing the desire to have sex with others or a desired partner?	Yes	No	N/A
29. Understand that it is inappropriate to touch another person's sexual body parts without their consent?	Yes	No	N/A
30. Demonstrate affection to others in an appropriate manner?	Yes	No	N/A
31. Indicate knowledge that others have a right to privacy (e.g. does not climb in bed with others)?	Yes	No	N/A
32. Refrain from attempting to engage "passive" clients in sexual activity?	Yes	No	N/A
33. Have knowledge that sexual intercourse is only appropriate with mutually agreeing others and in private?	Yes	No	N/A
34. Date/show interest in a member of the opposite sex?	Yes	No	N/A
35. Date/show interest in a member of the same sex?	Yes	No	N/A
36. Understand the staff-client relationship?	Yes	No	N/A
37. Understand the client-client relationship?	Yes	No	N/A
38. Know that every act of heterosexuality intercourse can result in pregnancy?	Yes	No	N/A
39. Understand the responsibility of being a sexually active adult?	Yes	No	N/A
40. Know that specific diseases can only be transmitted through sexual activity?	Yes	No	N/A

Recommendations

Date: _____   Signature: _____
                    Title: _____

Figure 1.   Human sexuality assessment form. (Reprinted with permission of The Matheny School and Hospital, Peapack, New Jersey.)

287

and take advantage of periods of increased physical comfort and high energy levels to facilitate learning. Adaptive equipment can be utilized to compensate for decreased physical capabilities.

Emotional Obstacles Anger, depression, denial, withdrawal, anxiety, and diminished self-esteem must be dealt with in order for interactive learning to occur. The nurse can collaborate with other team members to prioritize learning needs so that the teaching plan addresses the individual's emotional needs (Bopp & Lubkin, 1990).

Communication Barriers Communication barriers can occur on a variety of levels. There may be a difference in primary language between the individual and the nurse; teaching terms may be too medical or sophisticated for the individual to comprehend. For some persons with developmental disabilities, receptive language skills may be better than expressive language skills. This can cause problems if the individual wants to ask questions or express his or her thoughts or feelings (Bopp & Lubkin, 1990).

Motivation Motivation is an essential component of the learning process. Motivation increases when the individual develops an interest in the subject and wants to know more about his or her role as a sexual being. Motivation can be increased in situations in which the learner is able to experience success as a result of learning (Bopp & Lubkin, 1990).

Age-Related Differences In some situations it is appropriate to involve the parent or primary caregiver in addition to the individual with developmental disabilities. The decision to involve others in the teaching/learning program should be based on the individual's age; developmental status in terms of communication ability, level of understanding, attention span, and memory; and capability to perform physical tasks. For older adults with developmental disabilities, consideration should be given to the normal physiological changes that accompany aging, such as loss of visual and auditory acuity. Endurance and muscle strength also diminish with aging, as do cardiovascular tolerance, balance, and some memory functions (Schuster & Ashburn, 1980).

Dealing with Inappropriate Sexual Behaviors

When an individual with developmental disabilities exhibits "inappropriate" sexual behavior (e.g., genital manipulation in public), the behavior is amenable to change. Sexual expression can be redirected and appropriate behavior can be reinforced. Partner discrimination, sex education, and social skills training can be provided as part of a person's program plan. Access to privacy and social opportunities to meet appropriate partners can be increased. Living and work environments can be restructured, when necessary, to encourage appropriate sexual expression (Griffiths, Quinsey, & Hinsburger, 1989).

Ward et al. (1992) stated that research regarding sexual deviance among persons with developmental disabilities shows that deviant sexual behavior stems from several variables. These may include inappropriate arousal or ways of expressing sexual feelings, social skills deficits, lack of sexual knowledge, and distorted thinking. It has been postulated that the treatment needs of individuals with developmental disabilities who exhibit deviant sexual behavior are similar to those of individuals without developmental disabilities. A multidimensional approach to decrease inappropriate arousal, increase appropriate arousal, increase psychosocial–sexual skills and knowledge, and teach self-management skills includes a variety of components that must be tailored to the needs of each individual in order to achieve optimal outcomes (Griffiths et al., 1989; Knopp, 1990; Pithers, Martin, & Cumming, 1989).

Regardless of the etiology of inappropriate sexual behavior, families and program providers must take the behavior seriously. The individual who expresses inappropriate sexual behavior should be held accountable for this behavior and provided with appropriate education and treatment in the least restrictive environment possible (Knopp, 1990). Nurses, as members of the interdisciplinary team, have a responsibility to foster healthy personal growth in the individual with developmental disabilities as well as to protect others in the community from potential harm.

Parental Concerns about Sexuality and Sex Education

Parents of all children, with or without disabilities, must deal with their personal, moral, and religious values about sexual behaviors such as masturbation, homosexuality, contraception, sex out of wedlock, and fear of acquired immunodeficiency syndrome (AIDS). This is a challenging undertaking, and parents (including those with developmental disabilities) may be so overwhelmed by their own fears and anxieties that they are not aware of the impact of their attitudes and behaviors on their children. As a result, the individual with developmental disabilities becomes the victim of both parental and societal attitudes (Kempton, 1988). Sometimes, parents of individuals with developmental disabilities are unable to acknowledge their child's potential for adulthood and independence. This reluctance to perceive their child's sexual needs makes them unable to prepare a son or daughter for a happy, healthy sexual future (Turnbull, Turnbull, Bronicki, Summers, & Roeder-Gordon, 1989).

According to Ames, Hepner, Kaeser, & Pendler (1988), parents sometimes become dependent on their child's dependence; consequently, they refuse to give a child opportunities for social/emotional development. Parents may worry about vulnerability and exploitation of their offspring with developmental disabilities. Concerns often are expressed that their child, as an adult, may embarrass them or get into trouble with the law.

Refusing to "let go" during adolescence can take the form of overprotection. Parental overprotection can hinder the efforts of the young adult with developmental disabilities to obtain the information and guidance needed to succeed as a sexually responsible citizen (Walker-Hirsch & Champagne 1983).

Inez is a personable 18-year-old who has cerebral palsy and cognitive disabilities. At an evening recreation center, she became attracted to Leroy, who is 22 years old. Inez flirted with Leroy over the course of a few months. She told her mother that she had a boyfriend, and asked for information about birth control pills. Her mother brushed off this request and told Inez that she was too young to know about such things. One evening, Inez and Leroy had sexual intercourse in an empty room at the recreation center. They were discovered in the room by a staff member. He reported the situation to his supervisor, who spoke privately with both Inez and Leroy. Inez insisted that her family be notified immediately. Inez's parents and her three brothers came to the center intent on avenging the honor of their sister. They demanded to know the identity of the man who had taken advantage of Inez.

(continued)

The recreation center nurse met with the family and provided emotional support for them by encouraging expression of their feelings. She also offered information about sexuality development and Inez's emerging feelings for Leroy, including her previous request for contraceptive information. Inez's family had many issues to discuss. They had not previously consented to teaching Inez about sexuality issues because they thought it was unnecessary since she had cerebral palsy. They also had not permitted her to learn about birth control because of their own religious beliefs. Together, the nurse and social worker helped this family come to terms with Inez's sexual needs and feelings.

By the following week, after listening to all sides of the issue, it was determined that Inez and Leroy had mutually consented to sexual relations. Both Leroy and Inez received counseling about safe sex and appropriate settings for engaging in sexual activities. Both expressed feelings of surprise that sexual activity could lead to pregnancy, even though Inez had previously requested birth control pills.

Inez's mother and father attended a parent support group meeting at the recreation center. They were relieved to hear that they were not the only family with concerns regarding sexuality issues. They were amazed that the focus of an entire meeting was related to sexuality issues of young people. At the end of the meeting, Inez's mother stopped the nurse and told her that, after she had gotten over the initial shock, she realized that she had something for which to be thankful: "My daughter is like all other girls in one aspect of her life. After all, I married her father when I was 17."

In these kinds of situations, it is important to remember that it is counterproductive to challenge parents in a judgmental manner, to deny the validity of their feelings, or to prevent their involvement in the sex-related program issues of their adolescent or adult child (Johnson & Kempton, 1981). Huntley and Benner (1993) stated that the feelings and opinions of parents regarding their child's sexuality are best dealt with through sensitivity and respect. However, when sexuality-related issues cause conflict between parents and their legally competent adult children, the nurse and the provider agency's first responsibility is to the individual with developmental disabilities. States vary widely in their definitions of legality and appropriateness. Thus, nurses and other service providers should be familiar with the relevant legal perspectives in their locale (Young, 1993).

Parents need access to information and support groups that provide opportunities for them to be involved in sexuality education for their children with developmental disabilities. It is critical for parents to realize that sexuality education does not create sexual feelings. Those feelings are already there. By providing appropriate and timely sexual information to their children with developmental disabilities, parents become involved in the process of fostering genuine, caring, warm, touching, wonderful relationships (Ames et al., 1988).

Nurses can support parents by helping them to appreciate the fact that "sexuality encompasses not only intercourse, but also love given and received in many ways" (Thompson, 1986, p. 135). Some individuals with developmental disabilities may need to learn about the many socially appropriate ways to express caring and loving feelings. Nurses can assist parents of individuals with developmental disabilities to act as advocates for and support privacy issues in group homes. They also have an important role in developing sexuality policies, proce- dures, and training programs for staff in agencies that provide services to people with developmental disabilities (Ames et al., 1988).

PREVENTION OF ABUSE

Sexual abuse of persons with develop- mental disabilities is a serious and wide- spread problem. Sobsey (1994) identified the basic components of abuse preven- tion education for individuals with de- velopmental disabilities as being the same as those for all persons in society. These include personal skills safety training, personal rights education, as- sertiveness and self-esteem training, communication skills training, social skills training, sex education, and self- defense training. These strategies repre- sent some traditional and nontraditional areas of training for persons with devel- opmental disabilities in order to help re- duce their risk of abuse and victimiza- tion.

Nurses are in a unique position to as- sist in the prevention of abuse of indi- viduals with developmental disabilities. They must be familiar with the strate- gies described here and work to incorpo- rate them into both formal and informal teaching opportunities. However, spe- cific training in risk management must be approached cautiously. Table 5 lists the principles for establishing a risk management program for individuals with developmental disabilities. These

Table 5. Principles for establishing risk management programs for persons with developmental disabilities

- Individualizing content and instructional delivery
- Providing activity-based instruction
- Ensuring ecological validity
- Coordination of team efforts
- Facilitating active participation
- Accepting and encouraging reasonable risks
- Drawing on a variety of resources and techniques
- Assessing progress and revising programs

Adapted from Sobsey (1994).

must be applied to all content areas be- fore developing a curriculum.

Components of an Abuse Prevention Training Program

Personal Skills Safety Training This component teaches patterns of behavior that are intended to reduce a person's risk of abuse, exploitation, and violence. The curriculum content could include training the individual to recognize abuse, to say "no," to avoid or escape abuse, and how to seek assistance. Cur- riculum should be modified to take into consideration the individual's age, abili- ties, level of independence, activities, su- pervision, and any history of victimiza- tion.

Personal Rights Education Indivi- duals with developmental disabilities may lack experiences from which one learns about specific human rights as a citizen of a particular community. Teaching materials specific to the indi- vidual's living situation must be pre- sented in understandable terminology. The individual must be encouraged and supported in attaining his or her rights. Opportunities for exercising human rights can occur in the simple right to live in the community and to participate in the election of public officials.

Assertiveness and Self-Esteem Train- ing For an individual with develop- mental disabilities who has low self- esteem, assertiveness is often difficult. Uncertainty may result in overly aggres- sive and/or negative attempts at self- assertion that can result in retaliation. The building of a positive sense of self- esteem is a lifelong process. Families and care providers can enhance positive self-esteem by supporting and encourag- ing positive nurturing and learning ex- periences. Acceptance of the individual with developmental disabilities and fo- cusing on assets rather than deficits supports positive self-perception. It is also important to promote self-direction, support decision making, and avoid scapegoating. When an individual has a healthy sense of self-esteem, it is easier for him or her to be assertive about wants and needs. Real-life experiences should allow for opportunities for the individual to practice assertiveness and have his or her choices respected.

Communication Skills Training Communication skills are necessary for any individual to be able to assert his or her rights. The person who is unable to communicate will appear to be more vulnerable to offenders and may become a victim of abuse more often than those who can communicate effectively. Taking the initiative in communication and making sure that each person has an effective mode of communicating should be a priority within the interdisciplinary team. The nurse can advocate for the inclusion of symbolic language related to sexuality, as described by Steadham (chap. 7, this volume), for those persons who are nonverbal.

Social Skills Training Individuals with developmental disabilities need to use socially appropriate skills in naturally occurring situations in order to reduce the risk of abuse, victimization, or the perception of deviance (Ward et al., 1992).

Sex Education Sex education for individuals with developmental disabilities should focus on providing age-appropriate, understandable content that reinforces socially acceptable behaviors and does not eliminate those inhibitions that might result in increased vulnerability to sexual abuse (Monat-Haller, 1992; Sobsey, 1994).

Self-Defense Training Sobsey (1994) discussed the need for physically capable individuals with developmental disabilities to gain experience in self-defense strategies such as yelling or running to escape an adversary. Such techniques require individualization and opportunities for practice in order to be utilized appropriately.

DEVELOPING SEXUALITY POLICIES AND PROCEDURES

Sexuality is much more than the sexual act. It refers to the whole identity of a person, including personality, self-esteem, and the biological, psychological, sociological, and spiritual aspects of personhood. Respect for sexuality through the development and implementation of sexuality policies and procedures demonstrates a commitment to provide and foster life experiences that increase an individual's sense of self-worth and dignity. It fosters opportunities for individuals with developmental disabilities to develop relationships of their own choosing that are meaningful and satisfying (Acton, 1992).

Nurses who work in agencies that provide services to individuals with developmental disabilities and their families understand the need to have clear sexuality policies and procedures (Acton, 1992). These promote positive feelings about the normalcy of sexuality as part of the continuum of human growth and development. By identifying operational guidelines for individuals, families, and staff, it is possible to reduce confusion about the sexuality needs of individuals with developmental disabilities. It creates opportunities for consumers to act as self-advocates and take responsibility for their social and sexual behaviors. The use of an accepted agency-wide policy and procedures plan ensures staff consistency by defining staff responsibilities related to various aspects of an individual's sexuality.

Incorporating guidelines that address sexuality concerns into agency policy and procedures also serves to acknowledge that developing skills to achieve a personal identity as male or female and gain life skills in getting along with others, making and keeping friends, and developing relationships that make a person feel good are at least as important as other areas that are addressed through

At one community agency, it was decided that developing a comprehensive sexuality program would become a function of the human rights committee. Several individuals with developmental disabilities were asked to be members of this committee. The rights of consenting adults within the agency became a subject of intense interchanges. One of the individuals with developmental disabilities stated, "Without the ability to express myself in a sexual manner, I would not feel like a whole person." Some of the community and staff members emphasized the idea that one can express one's sexuality in many ways without engaging in sexual intercourse. The individual responded, "Yes, but I want to be able to choose how to express my sexuality, not have someone decide it for me." In spite of individual staff members' objections, the agency's sexuality program was developed to protect the rights of the adults with developmental disabilities.

programmatic interventions (e.g., shopping, cooking, traveling independently) (Hingsburger, 1990). Table 6 describes steps that can be taken as an agency develops its own policies and procedures about human sexuality. Appendix B is a sample human sexuality policy that was developed within an agency utilizing individual, family, staff, and community input.

SUMMARY

Concern for the healthy sexual development of persons with developmental disabilities should begin at the time of birth and continue throughout the life span. There is a close correlation between healthy self-esteem and an individual's positive sense of his or her sexuality. The collaboration of parents/caregivers and professionals is helpful in dealing with sexuality issues. Ongoing interaction between the nurse, other members of the interdisciplinary team, the individual with developmental disabilities, and his or her family should be focused on the sharing of feelings, values, and concerns about human sexuality in an open and thoughtful manner.

Sexuality education for persons with developmental disabilities should be based on the same knowledge base and factors as those for individuals without developmental disabilities. Each person must be encouraged to make responsible

Table 6.   Considerations in developing agency policies and procedures for human sexuality

- Determine the agency's readiness to address the issues. Identify resources within the agency to get the job done. Review any existing policies and procedures.
- Select a committee to develop policies and procedures for the agency. Be sure consumers, family, community, clergy, and paraprofessional and professional staff from each discipline are represented. The more divergent the views represented by the committee, the more likely it is that the end result will reflect the divergent cultures and beliefs of the people served by the agency.
- Collect policies and procedures about human sexuality from other agencies. If possible, utilize a sexuality educator or consultant. Planned Parenthood can be a good resource for easy-to-read information.
- Review sexuality policies and procedures as a team. Be sure to consider: provisions for consumer and staff training; a human rights group to address individual or special concerns that may arise; policies on sexual expression, privacy, contraception, and sexually explicit materials; acknowledgment of differences in personal and religious beliefs; acceptance of expressions of sexuality for all individuals with developmental disabilities; and a statement that affirms the belief that each individual is entitled to express his or her sexuality as part of normal human growth and development.
- Write the policy in draft form. Have all committee members review it for consensus and approval. Keep the agency's administrator and board of directors apprised of the group's status and progress. Submit draft proposals to administration and the board for feedback. When the committee has the policies and procedures in final draft format, submit them to the board of directors for final approval and adoption.

Adapted from Acton (1992).

decisions regarding sexual issues on the basis of appropriate information. Primary prevention and proactive measures can be used to enhance an individual's knowledge and understanding, enabling him or her to make informed choices to protect himself or herself from unwanted or abusive sexual contact. Agen-

cies that provide services to individuals with developmental disabilities should develop policies and procedures that reflect the sexuality needs of these individuals, promoting responsibility and acknowledging the importance of every person's sexuality.

REFERENCES

Acton, G. (1992). Comprehensive sexuality policy, procedures, and standards. In A.C. Crocker, H.J. Cohen, & T.A. Kastner (Eds.), *HIV infection and developmental disabilities: A resource for providers* (pp. 133–139). Baltimore: Paul H. Brookes Publishing Co.

Ames, T.R., Hepner, P., Kaeser, F., & Pendler, B. (1988). *The sexual rights of persons with developmental disabilities: Guidelines for programming with severely impaired persons.* New York: Members of the Committee on Legislative and Legal Issues of the Coalition on Sexuality and Disability, Inc.

Batshaw, M.L., & Perret, Y.M. (1992). *Children with disabilities: A medical primer* (3rd ed.). Baltimore: Paul H. Brookes Publishing Co.

Bopp, A., & Lubkin, I. (1990). Teaching. In I. M. Lubkin (Ed.), *Chronic illness: impact and intervention* (2nd ed., pp. 279–298). Boston: Jones & Bartlett, Publishers.

Carmody, M.A. (1992). Planning a sexuality education curriculum. *Active Treatment Solutions, 3*(2), 3.

Cookfair, J.M. (1991). *Nursing process and practice in the community.* St. Louis: Mosby–Year Book.

Crocker, A.C., Cohen, H.J., & Kastner, T.A. (Eds.). (1992). *HIV infection and developmental disabilities: A resource for providers.* Baltimore: Paul H. Brookes Publishing Co.

Dee, V. (1977). Sex education. In M. L. deLeon Siantz (Ed.), *The nurse and the developmentally disabled adolescent* (pp. 187–211). Baltimore: University Park Press.

Erickson, E. (1963). *Childhood and society.* New York: W.W. Norton.

Evans, J., & Conine, T. (1985). Sexual habilitation of youngsters with chronic illness or disabling conditions. *Journal of Allied Health, 14,* 79–87.

Flodberg, S.O. (1990). Sexuality. In I.M. Lubkin (Ed.), *Chronic illness: Impact and interventions* (pp. 232–257). Boston: Jones & Bartlett, Publishers.

Gardner, J.F., & Chapman, M.S. (1992). *Developing staff competencies for supporting people with developmental disabilities: An orientation handbook* (2nd ed.). Baltimore: Paul H. Brookes Publishing Co.

Gordon, S. (1976). Counselors and changing sexual values. *Personnel and Guidance, 54*(7), 363.

Griffiths, D., Quinsey, V., & Hingsburger, D. (1989). *Changing inappropriate sexual behavior:*

A community based approach for persons with developmental disabilities. Baltimore: Paul H. Brookes Publishing Co.

Hingsburger, D. (1990). *I contact: Sexuality and people with developmental disabilities.* Mountville, PA: VIDA Press.

Huntley, C.F., & Benner, S.M. (1993). Reducing barriers to sex education for adults with mental retardation. *Mental Retardation, 31*(4), 215–220.

Johnson, W., & Kempton, W. (1981). *Sex education and counseling of special groups.* Orwell, VT: The Safer Society Press.

Kempton, W. (1988). *Sex education for persons with disabilities that hinder learning.* Santa Barbara, CA: James Stanfield Publishing Company, Inc.

Knopp, F.H. (1990). Introduction. In J. Haven, R. Little, & D. Petre-Miller (Eds.), *Treating intellectually disabled sex offenders* (pp. 2–9). Orwell, VT: The Safer Society Press.

Koegel, P., & Whittemore, R. (1983). Sexuality in the ongoing lives of mentally retarded adults. In A. Craft & M. Craft (Eds.), *Sex education and counseling for mentally handicapped people* (pp. 213–240). Baltimore: University Park Press.

Maksym, D. (1990). *Shared feelings: A parent's guide to sexuality education for children, adolescents, and adults who have a mental handicap.* Downsview, Ontario, Canada: G. Allan Roeher Institute.

Monat-Haller, R.K. (1992). *Understanding and expressing sexuality: Responsible choices for individuals with developmental disabilities.* Baltimore: Paul H. Brookes Publishing Co.

Montague, A. (1971). *Touching: The human significance of the skin.* New York: Columbia University Press.

Pithers, W., Martin, G.R., & Cumming, G.F. (1989). Vermont treatment program for sexual aggressors. In R. Laws (Ed.), *Relapse prevention with sex offenders* (pp. 292–331). New York: Guilford Press.

Rivet, M. (1990). Sterilization and medical treatment of the mentally disabled: Some legal and ethical reflections. *Medicine and Law, 9*(5), 1150–1171.

Schuster, C.S., & Ashburn, S.S. (1980). *The process of human development: A holistic approach.* Boston: Little, Brown.

Sobsey, D. (1994). *Violence and abuse in the lives of people with disabilities: The end of silent acceptance?* Baltimore: Paul H. Brookes Publishing Co.

Taylor, M. (1989). Teaching parents about their impaired adolescent's sexuality. *American Journal of Maternal and Child Nursing, 14,* 109–112.

Thompson, C. (1986). *Raising a handicapped child.* New York: Morrow.

Tse, A.M., & Opie, N.D. (1986). Menarche in the severely disabled adolescent: School nurses' attitudes, perceptions, and perceived teaching responsibilities. *Journal of School Health, 56*(10), 443–447.

Turnbull, H.R., Turnbull, A.P., Bronicki, G.J., Summers, J. A., & Roeder-Gordon, C. (1989). *Disability and the family: A guide to decisions for adulthood.* Baltimore: Paul H. Brookes Publishing Co.

Vahldieck, R., Renes, S., & Schmelzer, M. (1993). A framework for planning public health nursing services to families. In G. Wegneer & R. Alexander (Eds.), *Readings in family nursing* (pp. 131–140). Philadelphia: J.B. Lippincott.

Walker-Hirsch, L., & Champagne, M. (1983). *Circles 1 (Intimacy and relationships).* Santa Barbara, CA: James Stanfield Publishing Co.

Ward, K.M., Heffern, S.J., Wilcox, M.S., McElwee, D., Dewriek, P., Brown, T.D., Jones, M.J., & Johnson, C.L. (1992). *Managing inappropriate sexual behavior: Supporting individuals with developmental disabilities in the community.* Anchorage: Alaska Specialized Education and Training Services.

Wilson, N., & Trost, R. (1993). A family perspective in aging and health. In G. Wegner & R. Alexander (Eds.), *Readings in family nursing* (pp. 141&148). Philadelphia: J.B. Lippincott.

Wish, J.P., McCombs, K.R., & Edmonson, B. (1980). *The socio-sexual knowledge and attitude test.* Wooddale, IL: Stoelting Company.

Wolfensberger, W. (1972). *The principle of normalization in human services.* Toronto, Ontario, Canada: National Institute on Mental Retardation.

Wolfensberger, W. (1983). Social role valorization: Proposed new term for the principle of normalization. *Mental Retardation, 21,* 234–239.

Young, J.B. (1993). Legal perspectives on sexuality and people with developmental disabilities. *Healthy Times, 5*(2).

Appendix A. Impediments to and Interventions for the Development of Healthy Sexuality in Persons with Developmental Disabilities

Infancy: Period of establishing a basic sense of trust or mistrust of others based on attainment of pleasure and relief of discomfort. Infant learns to differentiate between "self" and others.

Potential impediments to development of healthy sexuality	Suggested actions for fostering healthy development
• Immobilization and decreased or ambivalent handling may lead to delay in acquisition of body schema and therefore concept of self.	• Instruct parents on confident, competent handling. Provide tactile, vestibular, and proprioceptive input: hug, hold, caress, touch the infant.
• Separation from primary caregivers may lead to confusion, withdrawal, fear of abandonment.	• Keep parents as involved in the infant's care as possible. Maintain consistency in professional caregivers.
• Pain, feeding problems, or digestive problems, such that the association between nurturing and pleasure is disrupted.	• Manage medical problems. Use tactile and vestibular stimuli to produce pleasure response. Use non-nutritive sucking for oral gratification.

Toddlerhood: Period of establishing a sense of gender identity, autonomy, mastery of own body and the environment. Toddler learns limits and societal expectations.

Potential impediments	Suggested actions
• Immobilization resulting from disability or absent or diminished sensation or motor control, and inability to explore own body and fondle genitals.	• Minimize immobilization. Provide for tactile stimulation of all body parts in natural setting (e.g., while bathing). Allow for sensual play (e.g., rocking, swinging), and affection (e.g., hugging).
• Lack of sphincter control or pain or discomfort on elimination.	• Avoid strict toilet training but begin early to prepare incontinent child for management of elimination needs.
• Overpermissiveness and lack of limit setting. Necessary restriction on activity or needless overprotection as a result of parental guilt or anxiety.	• Set limits on behavior that is self-destructive or socially unacceptable. Convey limits in ways that avoid destroying child's self-esteem. Encourage child in areas of ability to support need for autonomy.
• Communication of disgust or dirtiness of bodily parts, products, or functions.	• Teach child names of all body parts. Use appropriate terms (e.g., penis, vagina, breast). Help explore body parts. Be matter-of-fact.

(*continued*)

(continued)

Preschool Age: Child establishes a sense of initiative. Language, motor behavior, and fantasy are the child's own creations.

Potential impediments	Suggested actions
• Immobilization or social restrictions prevent masturbation and sex play involving playmates.	• Do not punish for sexual activity or portray sex as evil.
• Intellectual curiosity not supported. Fantasy ideas scorned. Misinformation given.	• Answer questions honestly and frankly, particularly sexual questions. Provide simple factual answers. Allow for fantasy play.
• Isolation from peers.	• Facilitate peer relationships through play groups or preschool program.
• Limited opportunity to identify with same-sex parent and develop attachment to opposite-sex parent.	• Provide sex role models through selection of health caregivers. Refer to Big Brothers/Big Sisters program if indicated.
• No communication of expectations for future sex role (e.g., children infrequently hear "when you are a mommy"), or negative communication.	• Communicate reasonable expectations for future. Encourage working and parenting fantasy play as with all children.
• Concrete cause–effect reasoning leads child to see disability as punishment for "bad" behavior.	• Explain the disorder and any medical interventions in age-appropriate terms. Use play therapy to express concerns.

School Age: Period in which child achieves in social and academic areas.

Potential impediments	Suggested actions
• Social isolation; lack of same-sex friends and peer group to develop social skills or compare ideas about sexuality; delay or lack of shift from family emotional support.	• Organize social and recreational activities. Facilitate communication among children with speech disorders. Encourage parents to facilitate typical activities such as overnight visits and allow for privacy. Assist child to develop those abilities that make him or her an attractive companion. Involve in Special Olympics, YMCA swimming programs, or other athletic outlet.
• Lack of information about sex and sexuality.	• Encourage parents and school to provide information about menarche and nocturnal emissions. Teach management of menstrual needs and masturbatory techniques when needed. Address concepts of privacy and personal safety.
• Fear or guilt about same-sex relationships.	• Establish communication and trust. Teach self-control and behavior limits to develop a sexual value system. Explain homosexuality.

Adolescence: Period of establishing a unique self-identity.

Potential impediments	Suggested actions
• Precocious or delayed acquisition of secondary sex characteristics. Physical development altered by disease, disability, medication, or surgical intervention.	• Provide detailed, explicit information about both disorder and treatment. Discuss concerns about sexual development without waiting for child to ask.
• Reaction to cosmetic problems or disfigurement complicated by normal adolescent narcissism.	• Provide aggressive medical intervention if desired by adolescent. Emphasize attractiveness of character attributes or other nonphysical aspects of child. Offer opportunities to express feelings.

(continued)

(continued)

Potential impediments	Suggested actions
• Limited opportunity for opposite-sex friendships, dating, petting, taking responsibility for sexual activity, and experimentation with social skills.	• Involve in social activities with peers of both sexes. Counsel parents to allow privacy and facilitate dating without usurping the teen's decision-making role.
• Delay in acquisition of skills and attitudes necessary for taking on adult role as a result of enforced dependency, lack of experience, or overprotection. Overprotection may lead to depression and withdrawal or to rebellion and self-destructive behavior.	• As appropriate, prepare teen to take on management of his or her own disease/disability. Allow him or her to become actively involved in informed decision making about care. Teach to administer all possible medications/treatments for which parents or caregivers have been responsible. Encourage parents or caregivers to begin "letting go" of the adolescent. Provide prevocational skills and work experience with appropriate supports, such as a job search, if necessary.

Young Adulthood[a]: Period of forming intimate relations with others of both sexes based on mutual sharing, respect, and love, or of increasing feelings of isolation and emptiness.

Potential impediments	Suggested actions
• Lack of information about sexual response cycle, intercourse, reproductive capabilities, and risk of passing on genetic deficiencies resulting in inhibition of sexual activity. Inability to manage physiological aspects of sexual activities.	• Discuss the effects of the disorder on all aspects of sexuality; provide genetic counseling and intervention in organic and psychogenic sexual dysfunctions. Provide for adaptive equipment and exploration of alternatives in sexual expression and intimacy. Provide information about contraceptives and sexually transmitted diseases.
• Failure to acquire a system of values or a code by which to guide sexual and other behavior as a result of limited exposure to ideas or limited experience and stereotypic and rigid sexual beliefs.	• Facilitate values and attitudinal clarification by discussions within peer support group. Expose to a variety of ideas and mores. Emphasize mutual rights and responsibilities of sexual behavior.
• Reactions to self-doubt and feeling different resulting in promiscuity, depression, sexual obsession, or paraphilia. Homosexual arousal that is unwanted, distressing, or unacceptable to the youth (i.e., ego-dystonic).	• Secure individual or group counseling or psychotherapy. Accept homosexuality that is ego-syntonic (acceptable to self). Continue to reinforce adult status.

Middle Adult Years: Period of adjustments to or frustration with one's state in life. Coping with declining health of one's parents. Experiencing menopause and other midlife crises.

Potential impediments	Suggested actions
• Social isolation resulting from living arrangements, lack of transportation, declining physical resources of parents, independence/geographic isolation from siblings.	• Encourage participation in group social activities, use of community-based resources. Identify optimal living situation.
• Poor social skills resulting from overprotection by family, caregivers.	• Teach peer interaction skills as necessary.
• Physical changes that are normal for biological aging (e.g.,diminished vision, hearing). Onset of some chronic health problems, such as arthritis.	• Promote wellness through health supervision and teaching, particularly about safe versus risky sexual behaviors.
• Inappropriate sexual behaviors may have become habit.	• Set limits on inappropriate behaviors. Encourage appropriate behaviors. Use tangible reinforcers, consistency, repetition, positive role modeling, and the use of consequences.

---

[a] Adapted from Conine & Evans (1985).

(continued)

(*continued*)

Older Adult Years: Challenge to maintain a sense of well-being and control over one's life. Declines in health status, loss of loved ones and friends.

Potential impediments	Suggested actions
• Alterations in physical condition (i.e., deterioration of the immune and nervous system). Recovery from illness may be prolonged.	• Facilitate expression of feelings related to these changes. Provide for privacy during physical care. Encourage continued support from family and significant others.
• Decreased mobility and/or activity tolerance.	• Assist person to find new ways to spend leisure time. Explore plans for retirement from job or day program.
• Declining opportunities for sexual outlet or expression.	• Emphasize socialization and rewarding use of leisure time.

Sources: Vahldieck, Renes, & Schmelzer (1993); Wilson & Trost (1993).
Adapted from Conine & Evans (1985).

Appendix B. A Sample Human Sexuality Policy

I. Sexuality Policy—Overall Philosophy

Matheny School/Hospital recognizes the rights of persons with developmental disabilities to grow to their maximum potential in all areas of human development. In keeping with this policy, Matheny acknowledges that all persons residing within the facility have the right to develop as sexual human beings and that each person's knowledge in this area should be assessed annually by the social worker and included in his or her individual treatment plan if it is age applicable.

II. Sexuality Awareness Assessment

Policy   It is the policy of the Nursing Department at the Matheny School and Hospital to do a human sexuality assessment on each client admitted into the program, and on each resident yearly.

Procedure   The primary nurse will meet with the resident, family, and caregivers to assess the resident's ability to participate in the family life education program. The nurse will complete the human sexuality assessment form (see Figure 1) within 30 days of admission to the Matheny School Intermediate Care Facility or within 90 days of admission to the Special Hospital. The completed form will remain on file in the resident's program record under the functional assessment section of the chart.

The completed form will be used by staff in implementing the family life program in accordance with the resident's cognitive, psychosocial, and developmental status.

The assessment will be updated at the time of the resident's annual review by the Nursing Department.

III. Sexuality Education for Residents

The assumption of a right to human sexual expression is one of the developmental hallmarks. It is accompanied by developments in many other areas, including self-esteem and responsibility toward others. Assuming the responsibility for sexuality implies understanding of all topics covered in the family life program to the extent of the individual's cognitive level.

Policy   All residents have the right to clinically sound information and education on the topic of sex-uality and family planning services. This information or education should focus on assisting the resident in making responsible choices regarding the acceptable expression of his or her sexual needs and desires as limited by consensual ability. Based on the resident's level of awareness and functioning, appropriate training and instruction should be provided.

Procedure: The resident has the ocpportunity to discuss issues of sexuality with the social worker as needed.

1. Prior to the annual or quarterly meeting, the resident can have a private meeting with an appropriate team member to discuss his or her current concerns, which can be included in the meeting as necessary.
2. Based on team recommendations, a designated professional staff member should assess the resident's level of awareness and functioning concerning sexuality. Where indicated, the Sexuality Awareness Assessment Form (see Figure 1) could be administered.
3. Based on assessment findings and coupled with the resident's level of awareness and functioning, the team, where appropriate, should:
   a. Develop an individualized sexuality program.
   b. Develop an individualized counseling program.
   c. Recommend the resident's participation in a sexuality awareness program.
   d. Recommend referral for family planning services.
   e. Set individualized criteria for the resident within which sexual behavior or activity may occur.
   f. Document decision making and rationale in the minutes of an interdisciplinary treatment team meeting.

Any hands-on sexuality training must be presented to the Human Rights Committee for approval prior to implementation.

Program Plan   The resident will receive training and instruction from a professional staff member des-

Adapted from Matheny Human Rights Committee (1993).

ignated as responsible for the development, implementation, and monitoring of the program.

On a resident-by-resident basis, staff should receive training and instruction on any individually designated sexuality program, including parameters within which sexual activity may be allowed to occur (see XIII. Staff Training in Human Sexuality). This training will be provided by a designated professional staff member responsible for the development, implementation, and monitoring of the program. Training records should be maintained in the general program book as well as on the program site.

IV. Adult Sexual Activity

Policy *Adult sexual activity* refers to sexual interactions between persons of the same or opposite sex. Sexual activity is considered a normal form of social expression between *consenting* adults. Individuals who have cognitive delays or developmental disabilities are entitled to the opportunity to express their sexuality and experience sexual activity within their established relationships as long as they are not hurting themselves or others and appropriate privacy and health factors are adhered to.

An individual's sexuality is enhanced and made more meaningful when he or she is in a position to apply what has been learned in acceptable experiences. This requires that residents, parents, and staff be prepared to acknowledge and accept that reasonable risks are a prerequisite to personal development. Matheny's interdisciplinary treatment team, including the resident and his or her family member or legal guardian if this person so chooses, are charged with addressing the individual's needs regarding sexual activity.

Procedure Based on the results of a sexuality questionnaire, the social worker, in conjunction with other staff as appropriate, must ensure that the resident demonstrates an understanding and accepts responsibility for his or her actions. Criteria may include, but need not be limited to, the following:

1. *Consenting adult:* persons 18 years or older who are capable of understanding their sexual actions and the consequences of those actions.
2. *Consenting partner:* a consenting adult in a relationship with another person who is also a consenting adult.
3. *Acceptable locations:* this refers to a private location (e.g., bedroom) that does *not* disturb or infringe on the rights of others.
4. *Acceptable time periods:* sexual activity should not interfere with other scheduled activities and programs that are a part of the resident's individualized program plan.
5. *Health and safety practices:* provision of birth control and health information to residents; prevention of sexually transmitted diseases through training in safe sexual practices.
6. Ongoing participation in or completion of a sexuality awareness program or participation in individual counseling.

V. Requests for Sexual Information

Policy When a resident requests sexuality information about dating, marriage, contraception, sexually transmitted diseases, and the like, staff should respond with accurate information suitable to the resident's level of understanding in a sensitive and dignified manner.

Procedure

1. All staff should receive in-service training in the area of human sexuality (see XIII. Staff Training in Human Sexuality).
2. If a resident approaches a staff member with questions about sexuality, his or her questions must be answered in a respectful and nonjudgmental manner. If a resident requires additional information, the question should be referred to the supervisor or appropriate team member.

VI. Family Planning

Policy All residents age 18 and older have the right to family planning services. Those residents receiving family planning services or birth control will be provided access to sexuality counseling.

Procedure If need for birth control exists, the resident will be seen by a primary care physician who will: 1) for female residents, refer to a gynecology clinic or prescribe contraception if indicated; and 2) for male residents, examine resident and prescribe use of condoms.

The client will be referred to designated clinicians for individual or group sexuality counseling.

VII. Nudity

Policy Nudity shall be considered a normal occurrence only when a resident is preparing for bathing, dressing, sleeping, or engaged in private sexual activity. Nudity outside of these settings is in our society considered to be socially unacceptable behavior.

Procedure If a resident is found to be nude or exhibiting his or her body inappropriately, the staff person will:

1. Direct the resident to dress self or assist the resident in dressing.
2. Discuss the behavior with the resident as appropriate.
3. Notify the social worker of the resident's specific behavior.
4. If the resident refuses to get dressed, interact with him or her in a manner described in the individual's program. If this behavior occurs for the first time and no program has been written to discuss the interventions for such behavior, the staff persons should contact the social worker or nurse in charge for assistance.

VIII. Masturbation

Policy Masturbation is an acceptable means of sexual expression. Residents shall be permitted to engage in masturbation in a private area as long as it does not infringe on the rights of others, is not self-injurious, and does not interfere with activities of daily living.

Procedure

1. The staff are not to interfere if a resident is masturbating in a private area at a time that does not

interfere with daily activities, infringe on the rights of others, or cause self-injury.

2. If a resident is masturbating in a public area, infringing on the rights of others, or causing self-injury, the staff person should interrupt the activity in a nonpunitive manner and discuss the issue of privacy in a manner appropriate to the resident's level of understanding or move the resident to a private area. In addition, the staff person should notify the nurse and obtain medical attention if necessary.

3. Residents with specific physical needs should direct their concerns to the nurse, who will direct these to a human sexuality consultant.

IX. Sexually Explicit Materials

Policy   Residents 18 years and older have the right to possess sexually explicit materials, including but not limited to books, films, and photographs.
Procedure

1. If sexually explicit material is found in the possession of a resident 18 years or older, the staff person should allow the resident to keep the material if its use is determined not to be infringing on the rights of others or interfering with the provision of active treatment services for that individual.

2. If sexually explicit material is in the possession of a resident 18 years or older and it is interfering with the rights of others or provision of treatment, the staff person should advise the social worker, who should meet with the resident to discuss the situation.

3. If sexually explicit material is found in a common living area, the staff person should remove the material from that area and determine ownership, return the material to the owner, and explain to the resident the reason for its removal.

4. For residents under 18, parents or guardian must approve of the possession of sexually explicit material.

X. Dating

Policy   All residents have the right to date persons of their choice. Dating is a form of socialization that is an appropriate interaction between two persons who have expressed an interest in being in each other's company. Dating can occur within Matheny itself or can be an outside activity. One member of the couple can come from outside Matheny. Dating can occur when two people are alone together or when they are within a larger group. Depending on a resident's level of disability, certain individuals might require assistance to protect their safety and welfare.
Procedure

1. In most cases, the residents will arrange their dating activities themselves. Residents have the right to date. If they need assistance with making arrangements, a staff member of their choice can help them.

2. The staff member will offer assistance in arranging a date as appropriate (e.g., transportation, financing, possible sites for this occurrence, notification of other parties involved).

3. If residents are on a date within the facility itself, staff are expected to respect residents' privacy and not impose their presence unnecessarily.

XI. Marriage

Policy   All residents who have reached 18 years of age and have not been adjudicated mentally incompetent have the right to be married. It is the responsibility of an interdisciplinary team to ensure that these people have been made aware of marital life and its responsibilities and to recommend and facilitate premarital counseling if appropriate. The current Matheny policy is that married couples will live off campus.

Procedure: The designated clinician will meet with the couple following the team meeting and discuss the team's recommendations as well as their concerns. Based on the team's recommendations, the designated clinician may initiate the following:

1. Counseling sessions with both persons regarding family planning, housing, finances, etc.

2. Where appropriate, arranged meetings with outside parties such as the family, etc.

3. Seek out any appropriate local support services in which the resident can participate to assist him or her in preparation for marriage (e.g., wedding planners).

4. Resident's manager/coordinator will keep the program director and the President informed of the resident's progress.

5. After the wedding, support services will be provided on an as-needed basis.

6. If pregnancy occurs, the appropriate government agencies will evaluate the ability of the mother and father to raise the child and, if necessary, assume responsibility for the child.

XII. Sexual Abuse

Policy   Sexual abuse includes any sexual activity to which the resident has not consented, as well as sexual activity that involves a resident who does not have the capability to differentiate.

Examples of sexual activity considered abuse include but are not limited to unwanted touching and fondling, directly or through clothing, as well as unwanted direct sexual contact. Encouraging or using verbal or physical expression for the purpose of arousal or gratifying sexual desires is considered sexual abuse.

Sexual contact between an employee, consultant, contractor, or volunteer and a resident is *always* considered sexual abuse.
Procedure

1. If sexual abuse is suspected, a staff member should be notified immediately. Staff should interrupt immediately and with sensitivity to the situation when: a) a staff member is involved; b) a stranger is involved, c) a minor is involved, d) the resident is a nonconsenting adult, e) it is obvious that a resident is being coerced into a sexual act, or f) it is obvious that a resident is being abused.

2. Staff members always should explain to the resident the purpose of the interruption, using an extreme amount of sensitivity.

3. The staff member discovering the situation will immediately notify both the social worker and the nurse in charge during that particular shift.
4. In a case in which a crime has been committed or a minor is involved, policies outlined in the Policies and Procedures Manual of Matheny should be invoked.
5. The social worker will notify within 24 hours of the occurrence the President of the facility, the chair of the Incident Review Committee, the referral agent, and the family or guardian of all residents involved.
6. The social worker will ensure that a thorough investigation is conducted in a timely manner and inform the President.
7. Appropriate forms will be submitted to the state within 24 hours of the occurrence and contain as much information as is known. Appropriate reporting requirements of the state of New Jersey will be followed.

The Incident Report will be submitted to the Incident Review Committee for review and should include all corrective measures to ensure resident safety.

XIII. Staff Training in Human Sexuality

Policy All staff must receive training in human sexuality during a preservice orientation and annually thereafter. This training should provide staff with an understanding and knowledge of Matheny's policies regarding sexuality and must emphasize the development and support of positive attitudes and respect for the dignity and individual rights of each and every resident.

Procedure

1. All newly hired staff should be trained in human sexuality within the first 3 months of employment. Attendance at these sessions must be documented and, should staff miss any of these sessions, arrangements for makeup sessions must be made at a later time.
2. On at least an annual basis, all staff should receive training in topics related to human sexuality. Additional staff training will be provided on an as-needed basis. If at all possible, training

should be conducted in small group sessions by designated professional staff members.
3. Staff may receive additional training on issues related to sexuality on a resident-by-resident basis. This training may include such topics as sexual education, sexual awareness programs, criteria for adult sexual activity, and guidelines and procedures for staff interventions.

Staff in-service training in human sexuality and resident sex education training or counseling programs must be conducted by professionally trained staff.

Staff Responsibilities

When a resident engages in sexual activity in accordance with the guidelines set, staff will respect the privacy of the individual and respond in a nonjudgmental manner.

When a resident engages in sexual activity that is not in accordance with guidelines set, staff will intervene immediately and interrupt the activity in a nonthreatening manner, utilizing sensitivity and making every effort to maintain the dignity of the individual.

The staff person will discuss with the individual the reason for the interruption in a manner appropriate to his or her level of understanding. The staff member will document any and all such occurrences and notify appropriate team members, such as the nurse, applied behavioral science specialist, or social worker.

Other situations that warrant immediate interruption of sexual activity include:

1. When it is apparent that a resident is being coerced into a sexual act or being abused.
2. If a minor child is involved.
3. If a staff member is involved.
4. If an individual unknown to staff and/or to the resident is involved.

If any of the situations described above occurs, staff members must *immediately* notify their direct supervisor or the administrator on call. The staff member discovering the situation must initiate an incident report. All procedures for reporting and investigating allegations of sexual abuse are to be followed. These procedures are documented in the Policy and Procedure Manual under Child Abuse.

13

The Role of the Nurse in Infection Control

Shirley P. Roth and Patricia W. Clausen

OBJECTIVES

On completion of this chapter, the reader will be able to:

- Identify factors that contribute to the transmission of disease.
- List the characteristics that increase vulnerability for infection and/or transmission of diseases for persons with developmental disabilities.
- State strategies that will reduce and/or control infection.
- Define the role of the nurse in the education of individuals, family, and staff in principles of infection control.
- Identify factors to be incorporated into the development and implementation of effective policies and procedures for infection control.

OVERVIEW

Nurses who work with individuals with developmental disabilities often face a challenge in the prevention, early detection, and management of infectious diseases. Certain general and disease-specific infection control procedures in homes, community residences, and program settings can reduce significantly the acquisition and transmission of in-fectious diseases. This chapter explores the components of the infectious disease process and describes appropriate nursing interventions.

An important role for nurses is to assume responsibility for policy development in establishing and maintaining a healthful environment for all persons. Each nurse must become familiar with the federal, state, and local regulations that govern his or her practice setting.

INFECTIOUS DISEASE PROCESS

There is a need to understand the chain of events that occurs in the infectious disease process in order to develop appropriate prevention and control programs in settings where persons with developmental disabilities live and work. In its simplest form, the infectious disease process can be reduced to the interaction of three components:

- The infectious agent
- The environment
- A susceptible host

The infectious agent is any organism whose presence or excessive presence is capable of causing disease in an individual. The environment may be defined as the external conditions that contribute to or interfere with the organism's ability to survive and multiply in its reservoir. A susceptible host is a person who provides a place for the infectious agent to grow and who is likely to develop disease when exposed to a specific infectious organism.

A number of other factors also must be present to link these three components in order for a specific communicable disease to infect a population. Figure 1 shows the links in the "chain" of disease transmission. By intervening at any point, the nurse can interrupt the cycle of disease transmission. These links (components) are described in Table 1, along with corresponding interventions for interrupting the cycle of disease transmission.

COMMUNICABLE DISEASES OF SPECIAL CONCERN

In the past century, there has been remarkable progress in the control of infectious diseases, with an associated reduction in morbidity and mortality. In the early 1900s, diseases such as measles, diphtheria, and tuberculosis were commonplace. They were associated with periodic epidemics that resulted in high mortality rates (U.S. Bureau of the Census, 1975). Although these diseases have not been eliminated, their impact on the population in this country has been reduced greatly. This change came about as the result of advances over the past 150 years.

The introduction of such practices as routine hand washing between contact with sick persons, the relief of overcrowded living and working conditions, and the quarantining of persons with certain infectious diseases reduced the impact of these diseases on the community long before the advent of effective vaccines or the discovery of antibiotics. Persons with developmental disabilities benefited from these changes because they often were at greater risk for infectious diseases as a result of the practice of institutionalization.

The second half of this century has seen still more progress in reducing the morbidity and mortality associated with infectious diseases. Antibiotics to treat previously incurable diseases have been discovered; safe and effective vaccines to prevent a variety of communicable diseases have been developed. Although these are powerful tools, reliance on them alone to control infectious diseases is not enough. The increase in hepatitis B infection during the 1980s (Kane, Alter, Hadler, & Margolis, 1989), the rise in tuberculosis cases since 1986, along with the development of new strains of tuberculosis that are multidrug resistant (Centers for Disease Control, 1992c); and the development of the new disease threat of human immunodeficiency virus (HIV) (Crocker, Cohen, & Kastner, 1992) all point to the fact that infectious diseases have not yet been conquered.

Hepatitis B

Viral hepatitis is a general term used for several different diseases that are simi-

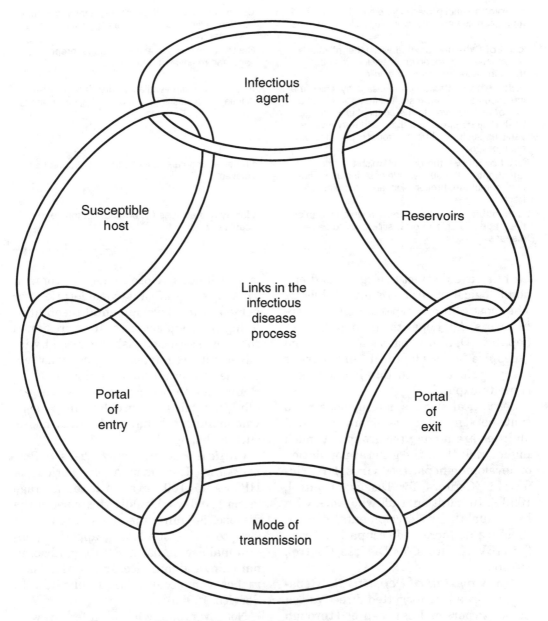

Figure 1.   The chain of disease transmission.

Table 1.   Components of the infectious disease cycle with suggested interventions/strategies

Components of the infectious disease cycle	Interventions/strategies
Infectious Agent—an organism (i.e., virus, bacterium, fungus) capable of causing disease in humans	Rapid identification for specific treatment and appropriate interventions
Reservoirs—those places where an infectious agent can live and multiply; may include humans	Use of sanitary practices, disinfectants, and sterilization to limit the number of organisms in a specific reservoir
Portal of Exit—the point at which the infectious agent leaves its reservoir or habitat; may be through secretions from any orifice	Control of excretions and secretions; proper storage and removal of trash
Mode of Transmission—the means by which the infectious agent is transmitted from the portal of exit of the reservoir to the portal of entry of the host; may be direct or indirect and may involve vehicles such as airborne droplets, particles of dust, or food	Attention to room ventilation, disinfection of surfaces, hand washing, and other hygiene practices
Portal of Entry—the point at which the infectious agent enters the susceptible host; includes mucus membrane, broken skin, and gastrointestinal tract	Proper wound care, aseptic technique, and use of gloves
Susceptible Host—the person in which the infectious agent is able to grow sufficiently to cause disease	Identify and address factors that contribute to susceptibility

lar but have distinct etiological and epidemiological characteristics (Table 2). The most common types of hepatitis are hepatitis A, hepatitis B, hepatitis C, hepatitis D, and hepatitis E. Additional types are being identified, and there is every indication that this list will continue to expand.

Serological surveys have demonstrated that persons with developmental disabilities are among the groups at much higher risk than the general population of developing hepatitis B virus (HBV) infection (Centers for Disease Control, 1990b). In addition, staff who work with individuals with developmental disabilities are at increased occupational risk for HBV (Centers for Disease Control, 1990b).

Transmission of Hepatitis B Hepatitis B virus is transmitted directly from person to person. It is not spread through the air by droplets, such as by coughs or sneezes. Direct contact with infected blood, saliva, semen, and vaginal fluids is the most common form of transmission (Benenson, 1990). Infection can occur in living environments where there

is continuous, close personal contact. This is a significant consideration for persons with developmental disabilities living in group settings. It is presumed that this increased risk is caused by inadvertent exchange of secretions via skin lesions or mucous membranes (U.S. Public Health Service, 1990b). Occasionally, this can be a problem in persons who manifest behavioral impairments such as biting.

Clinical Features and Disease Progression The incubation period of HBV is 45–160 days, with the average being 120 days. Usually the onset of the disease is quite insidious. Signs and symptoms include loss of appetite, general malaise, nausea, vomiting, abdominal pain, and jaundice. In addition, skin rashes can occur (U.S. Public Health Service, 1990b).

Not everyone who is infected with HBV will become chronically infected with the virus (such an individual is referred to as a *carrier*). There appears to be great variability in infectivity rate (Table 3). However, the younger age groups are infected at a proportionately

Table 2. Basic features of viral hepatitis

	Hepatitis A	Hepatitis B	Hepatitis C	Hepatitis D	Hepatitis E
Incubation period (days)	15–45 (mean 30)	45–180 (mean 60)	15–180	15–60	15–60 (mean 42)
Transmission	Fecal–oral	Blood borne, sexual	Blood borne, sexual	Blood borne, sexual	Fecal–oral
Progression to chronicity	No	Occasionally	Occasionally	Occasionally	No
Etiological agent	Hepatitis A virus (HAV)	Hepatitis B virus (HBV)	Hepatitis C virus (HCV)	Hepatitis D virus (HDV)	Hepatitis E virus (HEV)
Comments	During period of communicability, persons should be restricted from food preparation	Vaccine universally recommended	Blood banks screen for hepatitis C	Occurs only as coinfection with HBV or as superinfection of HBV carrier	To date no cases in United States; no serologic test available

Adapted from Centers for Disease Control (1990b).

Table 3. Likelihood of becoming chronically infected with HBV

Newborns with HBsAg-positive mothers[a]	Up to 90%
Children 5 years and younger	25%–50%
Adults	6%–10%

[a]HBsAg, hepatitis B surface antigen.

higher rate (U.S. Public Health Service, 1990a).

Hepatitis B virus infection is a significant health problem, and may result in long-term health impairments. In the United States, some 300,000 persons (primarily young adults) are infected each year. Approximately 25% of these persons develop symptoms, which may include jaundice. More than 10,000 persons become ill enough to need hospitalization. About 250 persons die each year as a result of HBV infection. As of 1990, it is estimated that 750,000 to 1 million persons in the United States are infectious carriers. Of these carriers, approximately one quarter will develop chronic active hepatitis, which frequently progresses to cirrhosis and/or other hepatic illnesses. For example, HBV carriers are at significant risk for developing primary liver cancer at a rate 12–300 times higher than that in the general population. Each year there are an estimated 4,800 deaths—4,000 from hepatitis B–related cirrhosis and 800 from hepatitis B–related liver cancer. The fatality rate for persons of all age groups reported to be carriers is approximately 1.4% (U.S. Public Health Service, 1990b).

Infection Control Measures As part of an infection control program, the nurse should carefully and regularly assess the daily living routines of the individuals being served. It is essential that grooming instruments not be shared. Each person should have a personal razor and toothbrush stored in an individual container. Communally used razors and toothbrushes have been found to be occasional transmitters of hepatitis B

because of cuts to the skin and/or mucosal tissues (Benenson, 1990).

Females should be taught simple, step-by-step approaches for the handling and disposal of sanitary pads. Proper hand washing technique must be emphasized and become incorporated into the individual's personal hygiene routine.

Staff should be encouraged to wear latex or vinyl gloves when working with persons who need assistance in such activities as eating and drinking and personal hygiene care. Such gloves also should be worn when the staff member has a break in his or her skin and is being exposed to blood and body secretions. Appropriate use of vinyl or latex gloves may effectively reduce the spread of infection to staff. Staff infection control procedures also should incorporate universal precautions such as hand washing and care in the use and disposal of needles and sharp instruments (refer to the universal precautions guidelines discussed later in the chapter [see Table 12]).

Simply using vinyl or latex gloves may give staff a false sense of security. Unless they are used for a specific task and then properly discarded, the gloves may aid in the transmission of various organisms. For example, when assisting participants in day treatment programs with eating or drinking, staff often touch secretions and areas around the mouth. When a number of persons need assistance, staff frequently move from one individual to the next without changing gloves or giving thought to the spread of disease.

All surfaces that may become contaminated by body fluids (e.g., tubs, sinks, toilets, dining tables and chairs, diaper changing areas) must be cleaned regularly with a germicidal cleaning solution. Chlorine disinfectants are indispensable in cleaning areas contaminated by body fluids because of their effectiveness against HBV and their relative inexpensiveness (Ching & Seto, 1989). However, the effectiveness of chlorine disinfectants is only good if proper dilution is maintained. Sodium hypochlorite (also known as Clorox or Purex bleach) is an effective disinfectant when one half cup of sodium hypochlorite is used per gallon of water. A fresh solution should be prepared daily because its strength is known to decompose rapidly. Spilled blood or other body fluids should be cleaned up quickly using soap and water, followed by use of a chlorine disinfectant solution. This solution should remain on the treated area for 30 minutes. It is then rinsed off with water (Table 4).

Ching and Seto (1989) surveyed 149 areas in hospitals in Hong Kong and found that a high proportion of chlorine disinfectant users were not using the proper dilutions. Although comparable data from U.S. facilities could not be found, it can be speculated that there is a great likelihood of incorrect dilutions of chlorine disinfections (or other less effective solutions) being used in many community and residential facilities. Nurses must be cognizant of this and develop and implement effective procedures against infection.

Hepatitis B Vaccines Hepatitis represents a significant health risk. An estimated 10,000–15,000 health care workers become infected with HBV each year. Of these, an estimated 300 individuals eventually will die of hepatitis-related causes (Blumberg, 1989).

The U.S. Department of Labor Occupational Safety and Health Administration (OSHA), (1991) issued standards to protect workers against blood-borne infections. Hepatitis B vaccinations are to be made available to all employees who have potential for occupational exposure to blood.

Two types of hepatitis B vaccines, plasma-derived vaccine and recombinant hepatitis B vaccine, currently are licensed in the United States. The recombinant vaccine is made with Baker's yeast. The administration of plasma-derived vaccine now is generally limited to persons with known yeast allergy and persons with immunocompromised conditions (Centers for Disease Control, 1990b).

For adequate antibody protection, each individual should receive a series of three intramuscular (IM) doses of hepatitis B vaccine given in the deltoid muscle. This produces adequate antibody response in greater than 90% of healthy adults and in greater than 95% of persons from birth to 19 years of age. For persons who are immunocompromised or receiving hemodialysis, two to four times the usual dose and up to four doses may be required to obtain an adequate antibody response (Centers for Disease Control, 1990b). Table 5 presents the recommended doses and schedules of hepatitis B vaccines.

Considerations for Follow-Up of Exposure to Blood If an accidental needlestick, laceration, or human bite (which breaks the skin) occurs, the decision to give prophylactic treatment must include consideration of the following factors:

- Whether the source of the blood is known and/or available
- The hepatitis B antibody status of the source
- The hepatitis B vaccination status (and response, if known) of the exposed person

For any exposure of an individual who has not previously received the hepatitis

Table 4. Steps for proper use of chlorine disinfectants to reduce environmental spread of hepatitis B virus

1. Mix one-half cup of sodium hypochlorite (Clorox or Purex) per gallon of water.
2. Prepare a fresh solution daily because its strength decomposes rapidly.
3. Leave sodium hypochlorite solution on contaminated surface for 30 minutes and then thoroughly rinse with water.

Table 5.   Recommended doses and schedules of hepatitis B vaccines[a]

Recipients	Recombivax HB[b] dose	Engerix-B[b,c] dose
Infants of HBV carrier mothers	0.5 ml	0.5 ml
Children <11 years	0.25 ml	0.5 ml
Youth 11–19 years	0.5 ml	1.0 ml
Adults >19 years	1.0 ml	1.0 ml
Persons on dialysis or immunocompromised	1.0 ml[d]	2.0 ml[e,f]

Adapted from Centers for Disease Control (1990b).

[a] Heptavax B vaccine is available only for persons who are immunocompromised and/or have known allergy to yeast, and is seldom given.

[b] Usual schedule: three doses at birth, 1 month, and 6 months.

[c] Alternate schedule: four doses at birth and 1, 2, and 12 months.

[d] Special formulation for persons receiving dialysis.

[e] Two 1.0-ml doses given at different sites.

[f] Four-dose schedule recommended at birth and 1, 2, and 6 months.

B vaccine, a single dose of hepatitis B immune globulin (HBIG),0.06 ml/kg IM for children or 5 ml IM for adults, should be given as soon as possible but at least within 24 hr. The hepatitis B vaccine series also should be started at that time (Benenson, 1990; Centers for Disease Control, 1991).

Final Comments The nurse must become knowledgeable and assist in the development and implementation of guidelines and procedures, as previously described, to protect all individuals from hepatitis B. Hepatitis B continues to be a significant public health menace. If principles of infection control and immunization guidelines are not followed, the health of all persons may be threatened.

Tuberculosis

Tuberculosis once was feared as an insidious disease that frequently resulted in death. By the early 1900s, it had reached epidemic proportions and was one of the leading causes of death in the United States (U.S. Bureau of the Census, 1975). By this time, the causative agent had been identified but there was no known cure. The standard treatment was to place individuals with tuberculosis in special isolation hospitals called *sanatoria*. Often they remained isolated from family and community for years. The sanatorium remained an im-

portant part of the treatment for tuberculosis until the discovery of effective drug therapy made such long-term isolation unnecessary.

With the advent of effective drug therapy in the 1950s, there was a steady decline in the case rate of tuberculosis until 1985 (Centers for Disease Control, 1989). This led to the closing of the sanatoria and a decreased emphasis on tuberculosis control efforts. There was a false sense of security that tuberculosis had become a disease of the past. However, since 1986 there has been a gradual increase in the incidence of tuberculosis in this country. This is due, in part, to the impact of the acquired immunodeficiency syndrome (AIDS) epidemic, the increase in homelessness and poverty, and the increase in immigrant and refugee populations. It presents a particular problem for those who live or work in group settings or with individuals who already may have an impaired immune system. It is important for the nurse working with individuals with developmental disabilities to know the principles of tuberculosis prevention and control and how these apply to a specific work setting.

Transmission of Tuberculosis The tubercle bacillus is transmitted through airborne droplet nuclei (1–5 microns in size) that are produced when a person with active pulmonary disease coughs, speaks, sneezes, or sings. These microscopic droplets containing the tubercle bacilli must reach the alveoli of the lungs in order to cause infection. Tuberculosis has a low rate of infectivity. This means that frequent, prolonged exposure usually is required for transmission to occur. As with other infectious diseases, transmission occurs when there is an interaction between the infectious agent, the environment, and a susceptible host. For transmission to take place, the following conditions must exist:

• Virulent *Mycobacterium tuberculosis* present in the patient's sputum
• Sputum aerosolized as droplet nuclei
• A large concentration of the infectious droplet nuclei in the air
• A susceptible host
• Sufficient exposure of the host to the air contaminated with the droplet nuclei

Clinical Features and Disease Progression Once the droplet nuclei reach the alveoli, *M. tuberculosis* is able to grow and spread throughout the body with no initial resistance from the host. At this stage of primary infection, the immune system usually requires 2–10 weeks to respond and limit further progression of the disease. Only a small number of those persons newly infected (less than 5%) go on to develop active tuberculosis within the first year after exposure (Centers for Disease Control, 1990c). The vast majority of individuals have immune systems that are able to contain the infection at this point, and these persons enter a period of latent infection. In this stage, the host experiences no symptoms and the only evidence of exposure to *M. tuberculosis* is a significant reaction to the tuberculin skin test.

Most of those persons infected with tuberculosis are able to contain the disease in this latent or dormant state for a lifetime. About 5% will advance to active disease within 1–2 years following the initial infection. Another 5%–10% will develop active disease at some point in the future, within a few years or a few decades (Centers for Disease Control, 1990c). Those co-infected with HIV have a greater risk (up to 10% per year) of developing active tuberculosis disease. Active disease occurs when bacilli that have been dormant begin to grow. At this point the infected individual is said to have active disease, and is able to transmit the disease to others. Table 6 lists the differences between latent and active tuberculosis.

It should be noted that pulmonary tuberculosis accounts for approximately 85% of the cases of tuberculosis in those *not* co-infected with HIV. Although the tubercle bacilli can cause disease in other organs, such as the kidneys, these extrapulmonary infections do not gener-

Table 6. Comparison of tuberculosis infection with active disease

	Latent infection	Active disease
Tubercle bacilli in the body	Yes	Yes
Tuberculin skin test	Usually positive	Usually positive
Chest radiograph	Usually normal	Usually abnormal
Sputum smears and/or cultures	Negative (usually not indicated)	Usually positive
Symptoms	None	Cough, fever, weight loss, fatigue
Infected	Yes	Yes
Infectious	No	Often, before treatment
A "case" of tuberculosis	No	Yes

ally pose a communicable disease risk. Persons co-infected with HIV and tuberculosis have a greater percentage of extrapulmonary disease (Centers for Disease Control, 1990a).

The American Thoracic Society (the medical arm of the American Lung Association) has developed a system for the classification of the various stages of tuberculosis infection (Table 7). This classic reference has been in use since 1975. Nurses should be familiar with these classifications and the implications of each.

Management of the Individual with Active Tuberculosis Symptoms of active tuberculosis may include cough, fatigue, weight loss, fever, and night sweats. Diagnosis is based on a combination of history and symptoms, reaction to a tuberculin skin test, chest radiograph findings, and laboratory studies. Definitive diagnosis depends on a sputum specimen that is culture positive for *Mycobacterium tuberculosis* (Centers for Disease Control & American Thoracic Society, 1991). Because of the nature of the organism, treatment for active disease is always prolonged (6 months or more) and involves more than one drug. With the development of multidrug-resistant organisms in the past few years, it is important that sensitivities also be obtained so appropriate drug therapy can be prescribed (Centers for Disease Control, 1992a).

The individual with active tuberculosis is infectious as long as viable bacilli can be found in the sputum. Isolation precautions and restriction from participation in program activities should be observed until the individual is no longer communicable.

The role of the nurse may include the following activities:

*   Recognize symptoms of active tuberculosis and arrange for further evaluation.
*   Educate individuals regarding the disease process and recommended treatment.
*   Monitor for side effects to medications and for compliance with medication regimen.
*   Report the case to the local health department.
*   Identify contacts to the active case of tuberculosis and arrange for contact testing and follow-up.
*   Be familiar with the recommendations for control of tuberculosis as they apply to a particular home or work setting.

Contact Testing and Screening for High-Risk Groups Preventive therapy is recommended for persons who have been infected with tuberculosis but do not have active disease in order to reduce their risk of developing tuberculosis in the future. Screening with an intradermal tuberculin skin test (the

Table 7.   Tuberculosis classification characteristics

Class 0	No tuberculosis exposure, not infected (no history of exposure, negative reaction to the tuberculin skin test)
Class 1	Tuberculosis exposure, no evidence of infection (history of exposure, reaction to tuberculin skin test not significant)
Class 2	Tuberculosis infection, no disease (positive reaction to tuberculin skin test, negative bacteriological studies [if done], no clinical and/or radiographic evidence of tuberculosis)
Class 3	Current disease (*M. tuberculosis* cultured [if done]; otherwise both a positive reaction to tuberculin skin test and clinical and/or radiographic evidence of current disease)
Class 4	No current disease (history of previous episode[s] of tuberculosis or abnormal stable radiographic findings in a person with a positive reaction to the tuberculin skin test, negative bacteriologic studies [if done], no clinical and/or radiographic evidence of current disease)
Class 5	Tuberculosis suspect (diagnosis pending)

Adapted from American Lung Association (1986).

Mantoux test) is the only reliable way to identify individuals in this group. Skin testing is recommended for all contacts of an active case, especially those identified as high risk. It is also recommended for certain high-risk populations as identified by the Centers for Disease Control (1990a). A positive skin test should be followed by a chest radiograph to rule out active disease. If there is no evidence of active disease and no other contraindications, 6–12 months of preventive therapy is recommended. It is important to screen not only program participants, but also caregivers in order to identify those at risk and initiate appropriate therapy. In addition, accurate record keeping of skin test results, recommendations, and completion of any recommended therapy is also part of the nurse's responsibility.

Final Comments Tuberculosis is a serious disease with grave consequences if not controlled. By applying the general principles of infection control, the nurse can establish workplace policies and procedures that ensure the success of tuberculosis prevention and control efforts.

Human Immunodeficiency Virus/Acquired Immunodeficiency Syndrome

A cluster of symptoms associated with severe impairment of the immune system of previously healthy young men was first documented in 1981. These symptoms were subsequently referred to as *acquired immunodeficiency syndrome*. From early on, scientists postulated that the world was dealing with a new infectious disease with a long incubation period. In 1983, a retrovirus named *human immunodeficiency virus* was linked with the development of AIDS (Henry, 1992a). Since that time, HIV/AIDS has become a major health care issue affecting all segments of society.

The Demographics of AIDS As of December 1992, more than 250,000 cases of AIDS had been reported to the Centers for Disease Control. Of those, more than 170,000 had died (Centers for Disease Control and Prevention, 1993). A shift in the demographics of those affected has been noted. Initially, AIDS was associated with homosexual activity and intravenous drug use. Currently, an increase in the percentage of heterosexual transmission and in the percentage of women with AIDS is reported (Centers for Disease Control, 1992c). AIDS is now the third leading cause of death for all U.S. women ages 15–44 (Henry, 1992b). This increase in females with AIDS is associated with an increase in pediatric AIDS cases as a result of perinatal transmission. In addition, as of 1988 AIDS was the sixth leading cause of death among 15- to 24-year-olds in the United States (Futterman & Hein, 1992). The magnitude of the problem cannot be overstated.

It is difficult to determine the full extent of HIV infection in persons with developmental disabilities because this characteristic is not linked with reportable data about those infected with HIV/AIDS. However, according to a study conducted by Kastner, Nathanson, and Marchetti (1992), "the number of adults with developmental disabilities and subsequent HIV infection has risen significantly. ... While the absolute number of infected individuals is relatively small, the rate of increase suggests that people with developmental disabilities have a substantial risk of becoming infected with HIV" (p. 130).

Transmission of HIV and Clinical Features and Progression of AIDS Since the first case of AIDS was diagnosed, much has been documented about HIV, including the means of transmission, the probable course of the infection itself, and appropriate interventions for preventing and controlling its spread.

Although HIV can be isolated in saliva, tears, and other body fluids, transmission of the virus to another person appears to occur only through sexual contact, parenteral blood contact, or perinatal transmission from the infected mother to her fetus or infant (Simonds & Rogers, 1992).

HIV infects white blood cells, the central nervous system, and other body tissues. Initially, the HIV-infected person may have no symptoms and be unaware that he or she is infected. Over the course of time (usually several years), the infection results in a reduction of the number of CD4+ T-lymphocyte cells (CD4 count), which leaves the immune system impaired and the individual unprotected against even minor infections. The infected individual is diagnosed as having AIDS once he or she has acquired one of the AIDS indicator conditions designated by the Centers for Disease Control, or has a CD4 count below 200/mm. Table 8 lists the AIDS indicator conditions as designated by the Centers for Disease Control in the 1993 revised classification system for HIV-infected adolescents and adults (Centers for Disease Control, 1992b).

Infection with HIV is detected through blood tests that identify antibodies to the virus. The tests most commonly used for screening are the enzyme immunoassay (EIA) and the enzyme-linked immunosorbent assay (ELISA). Positive results on either of these screenings should be confirmed with the Western blot assay. It usually takes 6 weeks to 6 months after exposure for the individual to develop detectable antibodies. False-negative results in adults after 6 months are rare.

For infants born to HIV-positive mothers, the testing presents some difficulties. An infant may initially test positive because of the presence of maternal antibodies. It is estimated that up to two thirds of the infants testing positive at birth are not infected with HIV (Sicklick

Table 8.   1993 AIDS defining conditions for adolescents and adults

- Candidiasis of bronchi, trachea, or lungs
- Candidiasis, esophageal
- Cervical cancer, invasive
- Coccidioidomycosis, disseminated or extrapulmonary
- Cryptococcosis, extrapulmonary
- Cryptosporidiosis, chronic intestinal (>1 month's duration)
- Cytomegalovirus disease (other than liver, spleen, or nodes)
- Cytomegalovirus retinitis (with loss of vision)
- Encephalopathy, HIV-related
- Herpes simplex: chronic ulcer(s) (>1 month's duration); or bronchitis, pneumonitis, or esophagitis
- Histoplasmosis, disseminated or extrapulmonary
- Isosporiasis, chronic intestinal (>1 month's duration)
- Kaposi sarcoma
- Lymphoma, Burkitt (or equivalent term)
- Lymphoma, immunoblastic (or equivalent term)
- Lymphoma, primary, of brain
- *Mycobacterium avium* complex or *M. kansasii,* disseminated or extrapulmonary
- *Mycobacterium tuberculosis,* any site (pulmonary or extrapulmonary)
- *Mycobacterium,* other species or unidentified species, disseminated or extrapulmonary
- *Pneumocystis carcinii* pneumonia
- Pneumonia, recurrent
- Progressive multifocal leukoencephalopathy
- Salmonella septicemia, recurrent
- Toxoplasmosis of brain
- Wasting syndrome due to HIV

Adapted from Centers for Disease Control (1992b).

& Rubinstein, 1992). Other screening tests, such as the polymerase chain reaction (PCR), which can detect HIV antibodies produced by the infant, are being developed. Until more reliable tests are available, serial testing over a period of 1 year to 18 months may be required before the true status of the child born to an HIV-infected mother is known. The system for classifying pediatric HIV infection (children under 13 years of age) acknowledges this difficulty by designating the child as having indeterminate infection, asymptomatic infection, or symptomatic infection (Centers for Disease Control, 1987a). Table 9 lists these classifications along with a brief description of each.

The increase in infants born with HIV infection is a growing area of concern for those working with persons with developmental disabilities. Although individual response varies, HIV infection in infants often is associated with encephalopathy, microencephaly, and brain atrophy, opportunistic infections of the central nervous system, and other neuropathology (Kozlowski, 1992). It can be anticipated that there will be an increase in infants dually diagnosed with HIV infection and developmental delays. The need for expansion of early detection and intervention services to meet the health care and developmental needs of these children will become increasingly evident during the next decade.

Responsibilities of the Nurse At the present time there is no vaccine to prevent infection with HIV, nor is there a cure for HIV infection or AIDS. There are, however, medications and approaches to treatment that have prolonged the asymptomatic period between initial infection with HIV and the development of AIDS. The trend in both children and adults is to see HIV infection less as an acute disease process resulting in rapid death, and more as a chronic condition that requires close supervision and careful management to delay or prevent complications (Henry, 1992b). The nurse's responsibilities when working with persons with developmental disabilities who are also infected with HIV should focus on three major areas: education, health care management, and coordination and referral.

Education Education remains the most effective means available to prevent the further spread of HIV infection. Educational programs concerning the basics of HIV/AIDS infection should be an ongoing part of every community-based program relating to persons with developmental disabilities. Educational programs should be developed for both program participants and caregivers and individualized for the needs of each.

Understanding of the nature of HIV infection, and how to minimize one's risk of exposure to the virus, is a central ten-

Table 9. Classification of HIV infection in children under 13 years of age

Class P-0	Indeterminate infection	Includes perinatally exposed infants up to 15 months of age who test positive for antibody to HIV, but have no other indication of HIV infection
Class P-1	Asymptomatic infection	Includes those children over 15 months of age who test positive for HIV antibody, but have no symptoms of infection; includes those under 15 months if they test positive for HIV antibody and have evidence of cellular and humoral immune deficiency
Class P-2	Symptomatic infection	Includes those children who test positive for HIV antibody and have signs and symptoms of infection; there are several subclasses based on the types of signs and symptoms present

et of such programs. Programs about sexuality and safer sex practices that address the needs of the person with developmental disabilities are imperative. Understanding the basics will help reduce unnecessary fear and develop constructive approaches in relating to program participants who are either HIV positive or at risk for HIV infection. Morse and Roth (chap. 12, this volume) address approaches for dealing with sexuality issues with this population. The consistent implementation of universal precaution procedures by caregivers as described later in this chapter is essential.

Health Care Management It is generally accepted that the person with HIV/AIDS does not pose a threat to other program participants under ordinary circumstances, and there is no need to restrict activities. However, the person with HIV infection will have special medical needs as his or her condition progresses. It is important that individuals have consistent and regular medical care from a primary care provider. The nurse is often in a key position to coordinate this care. Responsibilities of the nurse may include the following:

• Education of individuals and caregivers regarding the disease process and recommended treatment, including modifications in routine health practices such as vaccinations
• Assessment of developmental and adaptive functioning as this relates to the disease process
• Awareness of current health status of individuals with HIV/AIDS and any special needs this may generate
• Creation of a safe environment that reduces the risk of exposure to infectious diseases for the immunocompromised individual
• Recognition of symptoms of progression of HIV infection in both children and adults

• Monitoring for side effects and response to medications
• Regular communication with the primary medical provider concerning the individual's progress
• Counseling about risk reduction to avoid additional exposure and transmission to others

Coordination and Referral The nurse, as coordinator of the health care services, needs to be aware of appropriate community resources and assist individuals and their caregivers in utilizing these as indicated. The following is a listing of the types of referral services that should be considered in meeting the needs of a person diagnosed as having AIDS:

• Nutritional counseling
• Legal advice
• Financial resources
• Psychological counseling
• Respite care
• Home care or hospice care
• Spiritual counseling/support

The challenge for the future will be to utilize resources in a coordinated way to maximize cost effectiveness and accessibility for all.

Final Comments No segment of our society has escaped the impact of the HIV/AIDS epidemic of this past decade. It is anticipated that during the next decade this epidemic will affect more individuals with developmental disabilities. As the numbers of HIV-infected children increase, more resources to manage their special needs will be necessary. It is anticipated that there will be a growing problem with increasing infection rate among sexually active adolescents and adults within this population. If the needs of persons with developmental disabilities in the future are to be met, nurses must be cognizant of their roles in ensuring that a coordinated approach is implemented that addresses each person's individualized health needs.

SPECIAL CONSIDERATIONS FOR PERSONS WITH DEVELOPMENTAL DISABILITIES

Five areas that affect persons with developmental disabilities and place them at increased risk for infection and/or transmission of diseases have been identified: environmental/living settings, cognitive limitations, physical skill limitations, special health risks, and problems in obtaining health services.

Environmental/Living Settings

Group living, whether within the context of a family, group home, or institution, generates a potential for exposure to infectious diseases. During the course of the day, each individual comes in contact with many other people. Schools, workshops, and recreational facilities are settings that inadvertently may promote the transmission of infection. Factors including poor sanitation and sharing of personal care articles such as hair brushes, towels, and razors frequently occur in these settings.

Cognitive Limitations

Individuals with cognitive limitations have varying degrees of ability to participate in health practice routines that lower the risk of infection. One area to consider is the individual's limitations in following good personal hygiene practices. Infants explore their environment by placing objects and hands in their mouths. Drooling and the consequent spread of body secretions are expected behaviors during infancy. Diapering or assistance with toileting is required. In some individuals with developmental delays these behaviors may persist for many years or over a lifetime, placing them at continuing risk for infection. Because so many illnesses are spread by direct contact or by the fecal–oral route, all care providers must be diligent in practicing good hygiene measures. For individuals with milder cognitive limitations, consistent teaching with opportunities to demonstrate learning of basic hygiene measures are important.

An individual's impaired decision-making ability may affect disease transmission. Persons with developmental disabilities may be accustomed to having parents, staff, or job supervisors make decisions for them. Some individuals may benefit from assertiveness training that is appropriate to their development level. If they are not taught to be assertive, these individuals are vulnerable to being persuaded or manipulated in social settings. This can lead them to engage in sexual behaviors that place them at high risk for sexually transmitted diseases (Crocker et al., 1992).

Physical Skill Limitations

Persons with chronic health problems and physical impairments may have difficulty maintaining good health. Difficulty with performing tasks associated with personal hygiene may increase the person's susceptibility to infections. Individuals with decreased mobility skills often have moisture collect in skinfolds. This warm, moist environment harbors microbial organisms, leading to an array of infections such as candidiasis and tinea pedis.

Special Health Risks

Certain types of developmental disabilities may predispose an individual to infection. For example, children with Down syndrome are reported to have a higher incidence of respiratory infections. Individuals with spina bifida are prone to frequent urinary tract infections. Individuals with impaired immune systems have increased susceptibility to any infectious agent (Batshaw & Perret, 1992).

Problems in
Obtaining Health Services

Families and caregivers of individuals
with developmental disabilities often experience many obstacles in seeking and
obtaining high-quality health care services. Many physicians and nurses have
had little contact with this population
and are not cognizant of approaches to
use in assessing these individuals and
communicating with them. Most individuals with developmental disabilities
use health care that is reimbursable under the Medicaid program. Health care
workers who are Medicaid providers receive much less reimbursement for their
services than they could obtain through
private insurance sources. Therefore,
many persons with developmental disabilities have difficulty receiving coordinated
primary health care services with an
emphasis on prevention. Consequently,
health care efforts frequently are directed at curing a disease rather than
preventing it.

STRATEGIES FOR
INFECTION CONTROL

Nurses working with individuals with
developmental disabilities practice in a
variety of settings ranging from large institutions to classrooms and workshops
to residential facilities. Regardless of
the setting, there is a need to implement
basic strategies to reduce or eliminate
the incidence of infectious diseases.

The purpose of any infection control
program is to prevent the spread of infection. Understanding the cycle of disease transmission and the principles of
prevention enables the nurse to develop
approaches that are individualized for a
particular setting and the persons encountered there. Interventions based on
these principles seek to keep the infectious agent away from the susceptible
host or to minimize its impact on the

host through attention to one or more of
the following elements of disease transmission:

- Modifying the environment
- Interrupting direct transmission
- Increasing the host's resistance

By identifying factors to be addressed in
these three areas, the nurse can develop
a written infection control plan (Table
10). The infection control plan must be
communicated to caregivers and program participants, monitored periodically to evaluate effectiveness, and
changed to meet needs as they arise.

Modifying the Environment

The environment (i.e., the workplace,
classroom, or living area) frequently determines the degree to which infectious
agents can grow and multiply. Environmental factors also contribute to the in-
direct transmission of the infectious
agent to susceptible hosts. The first
grouping in Table 10 identifies some of
the factors that nurses should consider
in assessing the environment as a potential source of the spread of infectious diseases.

Overcrowding long has been known to
contribute to the transmission of certain
diseases. Infectious agents that are
transmitted through airborne droplets
(e.g., measles, chickenpox) find environments where there is overcrowding and
inadequate exchange of room air very favorable for transmission. Consideration
should be given to how many persons
work, study, or live in a particular area.
Room air should not be recirculated in a
closed system. Ideally there should be
several air exchanges per hour (Centers
for Disease Control, 1990a). In some programs and services, there are legal mandates that govern how many square feet
of space must be allocated for each program participant.

Table 10.   Considerations for developing an infection control plan

Modifying the Environment
- Provide adequate physical space for the number of program participants.
- Provide adequate bathroom facilities with appropriate adaptive equipment.
- Have sinks accessible, conveniently located, and in good working order.
- Provide soap and disposable towels, electric hand dryers or adequate clean towels.
- Maintain adequate air exchange and circulation.
- Control room temperature; avoid extremes of hot or cold.
- Provide food preparation areas that are properly equipped (i.e., running water, refrigerator, cleaning supplies accessible).
- Maintain separate storage of trash; use covered trash containers.
- Clean all work/living areas periodically according to established procedures.
- Clean up spills promptly and properly dispose of contaminated waste.

Interrupting Direct Transmission
- Practice good hand washing techniques at all times (all program participants and caregivers).
- Utilize universal precautions.
- Use gloves and other personal protective equipment appropriately.
- Screen participants for signs and symptoms of infectious diseases; treat promptly.

Increasing the Host's Resistance
- Assess immunization status of all new employees and program participants.
- Review and update immunization status periodically in order to remain current.
- Incorporate health promotion practices into the daily routine.
- Encourage periodic physical exams for all employees and participants.

Other environmental factors to be considered are the cleaning schedule for each work area and the types of products used to provide disinfection. A routine schedule for cleaning should be established and carried out by a designated person. Places for food preparation, bathroom facilities, and any other special areas identified must be cleaned and disinfected on a daily basis. Infectious a-gents such as *Salmonella* and hepatitis A virus are carried in the digestive tract. Their transmission often is aided when there is insufficient attention to the cleanliness of the immediate environment (Benenson, 1990). A regular cleaning schedule for other areas, such as classrooms, workshops, and recreational settings, should be established. The frequency and type of utilization of each area must be considered. Cleaning products that will kill or inactivate both bacteria and viruses should be used. The Environmental Protection Agency (EPA) publishes a list of approved disinfectants that is updated periodically. It can be obtained by contacting the local health department.

Particular attention should be given to food preparation sites. Food must be prepared on properly disinfected surfaces, using clean utensils. It must be stored at the correct temperature; otherwise, it can become a reservoir for infectious organisms. Persons with developmental disabilities who cannot practice good, appropriate hygiene measures should not assist in the preparation or serving of food. The local health department can provide guidelines and information on regulations concerning the preparation, storage, and serving of foods.

Interrupting the Direct Transmission

In establishing infections control practices in any setting, attention must be directed to the personal hygiene practices of caregivers and program participants. In controlling the spread of all infections, careful, frequent hand washing has been found to be the single most important factor in reducing transmission (Butz, Laughon, Gullette, & Larson, 1990).

Hand washing is usually a simple procedure for most individuals, but persons with severe impairments (cognitive and/ or physical) may find the task to be a challenge. Persons with developmental disabilities need ongoing learning opportunities, including frequent, consistent demonstrations of correct techniques and monitoring of performance during hand washing. These strategies ensure effective hand washing practices to prevent the spread of disease. Fingernails frequently harbor many different microorganisms and often are overlooked as potential sources of infection. Keeping nails trimmed and clean is important. Nail brushes can be useful in removing dirt and infectious agents from under the nails.

If staff fail to comply with regular hand washing procedures, they expose themselves and program participants to a variety of organisms. Butz et al. (1990) suggested four factors that may contribute to staff members' laxity in hand washing: 1) inconvenience of hand washing facilities, 2) perceived lack of need (familiarity of setting and persons being served), 3) poor skin conditions resulting from repeated hand washing, and 4) insufficient time available between tasks. The nurse should observe staff and determine if any of these factors are contributing to a lack of compliance with regular hand washing. The nurse then can identify the most appropriate actions to take in order to encourage good handwashing practices.

Butz et al. (1990) determined that noncompliance with adequate hand washing by staff in nonacute health care settings usually can be attributed to the inaccessible or inconvenient location of soap and water. If this is a problem at the program site, consideration should be given to the use of alcohol-impregnated wipes or other alcohol-based products available as gels or foam. These have been shown to be effective in reducing surface bacterial counts.

Table 11 describes the proper hand washing technique for decreasing the transmission of infectious organisms. Reminders about hand washing can be posted at appropriate hand washing areas throughout the work place, school, or living environment. Everyone must be aware of his or her potential role as a carrier of an infectious organism.

Under certain circumstances, the use of protective equipment will help interrupt the transmission of infectious organisms to a susceptible host. In situations in which care providers assist program participants with their personal hygiene needs, specimen collection, or wound care, there is a risk of exposure to infectious organisms in body fluids. The risk is increased if the care provider's own skin is not intact. The use of gloves will greatly reduce the care provider's risk of exposure. Care providers should be reminded that using gloves does not replace the need for good hand washing techniques. Gloves should be changed between procedures so they do not become sources of disease transmission.

In response to the need to contain infections associated with blood-borne pathogens such as HBV and HIV, the

Table 11.   Steps for proper hand washing technique

The most effective method to prevent and control the spread of disease is proper handwashing.
1. Use continuously running water.
2. Wet hands and apply soap.
3. Scrub vigorously all surfaces of the hands, including back of hands and between fingers, for at least 15 seconds.
4. Rinse thoroughly.
5. Dry well with a paper towel.
6. Use the paper towel to turn off faucet.
7. Discard paper towel in the trash can.

Centers for Disease Control issued universal precautions guidelines (Centers for Disease Control, 1987b, 1988). The basic principle underlying these guidelines is that all blood and body fluids contaminated with blood, as well as certain other potentially infectious materials, should be considered infectious without regard to their source. Table 12 outlines basic points to consider when implementing universal precautions in any program setting. Universal precautions should be explained to all care providers and program participants on initial entry into the program. A mechanism to review and reinforce understanding of these guidelines should be established and implemented in every program. All facilities must comply with the OSHA regulation on blood-borne pathogens and must have a system to ensure that universal precautions are known and observed.

Nurses must be able to assess program participants for early signs and symptoms of an infectious illness. Family members and other caregivers should be taught basic assessment techniques. With early recognition of the presence of an infection, steps can be taken to limit the exposure of others. This is especially important in a group setting. The appendix at the end of the chapter provides a quick reference guide for the nurse working with persons with developmental disabilities. The nurse must be cognizant of the basic features of various communicable diseases in order to provide relevant health teaching, coordinate needed medical referrals, and provide epidemiological follow-up as indicated.

Increasing the Host's Resistance

In developing an infection control program, the nurse also must take into consideration ways to increase the resis-

Table 12.   Principal aspects of universal precautions

What Are Universal Precautions?
These are steps designed to protect oneself if the possibility of contact with *anyone's* blood or body fluids exists. Universal precautions are intended to supplement rather than replace recommendations for routine infection control, such as hand washing and using gloves to prevent microbial contamination of hands.
How Are Universal Precautions Put into Practice?
1. Handwashing remains the most effective infection control procedure. Immediately and thoroughly wash hands and other skin contaminated with blood or other body fluids.
2. Prevent injuries when using needles, scalpels, and other sharp instruments by implementation of the following:
    a. Do not recap needles by hand.
    b. Do not bend, break, or manipulate used needles by hand.
    c. Place all used, disposable syringes and needles and other sharp items in a puncture-resistant container for disposal
    d. Locate the puncture-resistant container as close to the use area as practical.
3. Protective barriers can prevent or reduce incidence of exposure to blood and other body fluids. The type of protective barrier should be appropriate for the procedure performed and the type of exposure anticipated.
    a. Use gloves when contact with blood or other body fluids is anticipated, including the following:
        - Assisting program participants with bathing.
        - Giving mouth care (e.g., toothbrushing).
        - Handling laundry soiled with blood or body fluids.
        - Obtaining specimen (e.g., urine, stool, blood).
        - Changing a bandage or dressing a wound.
        - Providing skin care (e.g., shaving, application of topical ointments to skin lesions).
        - Treating cuts, bites, nosebleeds, burns, or bee stings.
        - Cleaning emesis.
    b. Change gloves and wash hands between client contacts.
    c. Do not wash or disinfect gloves for reuse.
    d. Replace torn or punctured gloves immediately.
    e. Cover cuts, rashes, or other breaks in the skin with bandages and gloves.
    f. Use general-purpose utility gloves for cleaning instruments or areas involving blood/body fluid contact.

tance of individuals who are at risk of exposure to infectious agents. Vaccination is one of the most effective means to accomplish this because vaccines offer immunity to specific diseases. Although the need for vaccination in early childhood is generally accepted, often older children and adults with developmental disabilities do not have current immunizations. This may be due to a variety of reasons, but the most common are:

- Delay of regular immunizations as a result of frequent illnesses or chronic health problems
- Tendency to be seen by medical specialists without access to a primary health care provider who will focus on preventive aspects of health care
- Frequent residential changes without someone coordinating health care and ensuring transferral of health history

In many programs that offer services to persons with developmental disabilities, documentation of current immunization status is required prior to enrollment. The nurse at the program site is responsible for obtaining this information. The nurse can use this opportunity to teach program participants and their family members about the importance of vaccinations and accurate documentation of immunization status. According to Orenstein, Atkinson, Mason, and Bernier (1990), many children fail to complete their primary series of immunizations because of barriers created by the health care delivery system. (See Steadham, chap. 7, this volume, for a guide to valid and invalid contraindications to immunizations.)

Often the need for adult vaccinations is overlooked. A number of vaccine-preventable diseases, such as hepatitis B, influenza, and pneumonia, affect adults greatly. Vaccines for these diseases are discussed in detail by Steadham and by O'Brien (chaps. 7 and 8, this

volume). It is important that both program participants and caregivers have current immunizations.

The nurse can be instrumental in promoting healthy lifestyles that are known to increase host resistance to disease. Adequate nutrition, proper rest, daily exercise, and stress reduction techniques will enable the person with developmental disabilities to resist certain infectious organisms (Valanis, 1986). (See Steadham, chap. 7, and O'Brien, chap. 8, this volume, for additional discussions of health promotion throughout the life span.)

DEVELOPMENT OF POLICY AND PROCEDURES FOR INFECTION CONTROL—THE NURSE'S ROLE

Regardless of the setting, every agency or institution that offers services to individuals with developmental disabilities must have a written infection control plan. Frequently, portions of these plans are mandated by federal or state regulations that specify the conditions under which services can be rendered. Often it is the nurse who is involved in the development and implementation of policies and procedures that address infection control issues. Although these policies and procedures are individualized according to the needs of each setting, there are certain basic areas that every plan should address. The following list of questions should be answered in the development of a written policy and procedures for infection control.

What is to be done?
- Are there federal, state, or local regulations that must be addressed?
- Does the OSHA blood-borne pathogen regulation apply to your setting?
- Are there preadmission or preemployment physical exams required? Immunizations? Initial screening exams such as tuberculin skin test or chest

radiograph? How often should these be repeated?

- Are there space requirements? Food preparation areas that need special attention?
- Are there special concerns to be addressed with program participants or care givers?
- What is the responsibility for reporting communicable diseases to local health authorities?

Who is responsible for what aspects?

- What are the administration's responsibilities and duties in seeing that policy is implemented?
- What are the nursing responsibilities?
- What are the responsibilities of the caregivers—paid staff? Volunteers?
- What are the responsibilities of the program participants and family members?

When is the plan to be implemented?

- Does a specific date have to be established?
- Is there need for periodic review?
- Is there a mechanism for revising and updating the policy and/or procedures?
- How will all parties be informed as to their responsibilities?

How will the policy be enforced?

- Do portions of the plan depend on voluntary compliance?
- Are there any reward mechanisms set up to encourage compliance? Are there any consequences if any of the parties involved do not fulfill their responsibilities?
- Are there penalties if all or part of the infection control policy is not carried out as stated?

How will you tell if the plan is working?

- What are the means for ongoing monitoring?

- Is there a specific plan for evaluation? Does a written report need to be completed? Recommendations made?

In setting up the plan, the nurse must know the pertinent federal, state, and local laws and regulations. There are a variety of regulations that exist and define the basic parameters of the infection control policy. Organizations must meet the basic requirements mandated by law, but also may elect to go beyond the basics to address other issues.

SUMMARY

All individuals have the right to good health and an environment that protects them from diseases and illnesses. Significant progress has been made since the 1940s in medication and vaccine development. At the same time, new infectious and/or drug resistant diseases, such as the hepatitis B, tuberculosis, and human immunodeficiency virus, have emerged with unrelenting persistence. The basic principles of infection control must be understood and adhered to if continued progress is to be made.

In addition to a solid knowledge base regarding epidemiological factors, resourcefulness and vigilance are crucial elements in this endeavor. Nurses who work with persons of all ages with developmental disabilities in a variety of settings have opportunities to identify factors and educate others about preventing and controlling the spread of infection. The nurse's responsibilities include the development and implementation of effective policies and procedures for promoting infection control and a healthy environment.

REFERENCES

American Lung Association. (1986). *Tuberculosis: What the physician should know.* New York: Author.

Batshaw, M.L., & Perret, Y.M. (1992). *Children with disabilities: A medical primer* (3rd ed.). Baltimore: Paul H. Brookes Publishing Co.

Benenson, A.S. (Ed.). (1990). *Control of communicable disease in man* (15th ed.). Washington, DC: American Public Health Association.

Blumberg, B.S. (1989). Feasibility of controlling or eradicating the hepatitis B virus. *American Journal of Medicine, 87*(3A), 2S–10S.

Butz, A.M., Laughon, B.E., Gullette, D.L., & Larson, E.L. (1990). Alcohol-impregnated wipes as an alternative in hand hygiene. *American Journal of Infection Control, 18,* 70–76.

Centers for Disease Control. (1987a). Classification system for human immunodeficiency virus (HIV) infection in children under 18 years of age. *Morbidity and Mortality Weekly Report, 36*(15).

Centers for Disease Control. (1987b). Recommended for prevention of HIV transmission in health care settings. *Morbidity and Mortality Weekly Report, 36*(2-S).

Centers for Disease Control. (1988). Update: Universal precautions for prevention of transmission of human immunodeficiency virus, hepatitis B virus, and other blood borne pathogens in health care settings. *Morbidity and Mortality Weekly Report, 37*(24).

Centers for Disease Control. (1989). A strategic plan for the elimination of tuberculosis in the United States. *Morbidity and Mortality Weekly Report, 38*(S-3).

Centers for Disease Control. (1990a). Guidelines for preventing the transmission of tuberculosis in health-care settings, with special focus on HIV-related issues. *Morbidity and Mortality Weekly Report, 39*(RR-17).

Centers for Disease Control. (1990b). Protecting against viral hepatitis: Recommendations of the immunization practices advisory committee (ACIP). *Morbidity and Mortality Weekly Report, 39*(RR-2), 1–26.

Centers for Disease Control. (1990c). Screening for tuberculosis and tuberculosis infection in high risk populations, and the use of preventive therapy for tuberculosis infection in the United States: Recommendation of the Advisory Committee for Elimination of Tuberculosis. *Morbidity and Mortality Weekly Report, 39* (RR-8).

Centers for Disease Control. (1991). Recommendations for preventing transmission of human immunodeficiency virus and hepatitis B virus to patients during exposure-prone invasive procedures. *Morbidity and Mortality Weekly Report, 40*(RR-8), 1–9.

Centers for Disease Control. (1992a). National action plan to combat multidrug-resistant tuberculosis. Meeting the challenge of multidrug-resistant tuberculosis: Summary of a conference. Management of persons exposed to multidrug-resistant tuberculosis. *Morbidity and Mortality Weekly Report, 41*(RR-1).

Centers for Disease Control. (1992b). 1993 Revised classification system for HIV infection and conditions included in the 1993 AIDS Surveillance Case Definition. *Mortality and Morbidity Weekly Report, 41*(RR-17), 1–19.

Centers for Disease Control. (1992c). The second 100,000 cases of acquired immunodeficiency syndrome: United States. *Morbidity and Mortality Weekly Report, 41*(2).

Centers for Disease Control and Prevention. (1993). *HIV/AIDS surveillance report,* 1–23.

Centers for Disease Control & American Thoracic Society. (1991). *Core curriculum on tuberculosis* (2nd ed.). New York: Author.

Ching, T.Y., & Seto, W.H. (1989). Hospital use of chlorine disinfectants in a hepatitis B endemic area: A prevalence survey in twenty hospitals. *Journal of Hospital Infection, 14,* 39–47.

Committee on Infectious Diseases, American Academy of Pediatrics. (1991). *Report of the Committee on Infectious Diseases* (22nd ed.). Elk Grove Village, IL: American Academy of Pediatrics.

Crocker, A.C., Cohen, H.J., & Kastner, T.A. (Eds.). (1992). *HIV infection and developmental disabilities: a resource for service providers.* Baltimore: Paul H. Brookes Publishing Co.

Futterman, D., & Hein, K. (1992). Medical care for HIV infected adolescents. *AIDS Clinical Care, 1*(12).

Henry, K. (1992a). Essential HIV/AIDS facts. What you need to know in 1992. *Postgraduate Medicine, 91,* 84–95.

Henry, K. (1992b). HIV and AIDS challenges and rewards for primary care physicians. *Postgraduate Medicine, 91,* 83.

Kane, M.A., Alter, M.J., Hadler, S.C., & Margolis, H.S. (1989). Hepatitis B infection in the United States. *The American Journal of Medicine, 87*(3A), 11S–13S.

Kastner, T.A., Nathanson, R.S., & Marchetti, A.G. (1992). Epidemiology of HIV infection in adults with developmental disabilities. In A.C. Crocker, H.J. Cohen, & T.A. Kastner (Eds.), *HIV infection and developmental disabilities: A resource for service providers* (pp. 127–132). Baltimore: Paul H. Brookes Publishing Co.

Kozlowski, P.B. (1992). Neuropathology of HIV infection in children. In A.C. Crocker, H.J. Cohen, and T.A. Kastner (Eds.), *HIV infection and developmental disabilities: A resource for service providers* (pp. 25–31). Baltimore: Paul H. Brookes Publishing Co.

Orenstein, W.A., Atkinson, W., Mason, D., & Bernier, R.H. (1990). Barriers to vaccinating preschool children. *Journal of Health Care for the Poor and Underserved, 1,* 315–330.

Sicklick, M.J., & Rubinstein, A. (1992). Types of HIV infection and the course of the disease. In A.C. Crocker, H.J. Cohen, & T.A. Kastner (Eds.), *HIV infection and developmental disabilities: A resource for service providers* (pp. 15–23). Baltimore: Paul H. Brookes Publishing Co.

Simonds, R.J., & Rogers, M.F. (1992). Epidemiology of HIV infection in children and other populations. In A.C. Crocker, H.J. Cohen, & T.A. Kastner (Eds.), *HIV infection and developmental disabilities: A resource for service providers* (pp. 3–13). Baltimore: Paul H. Brookes Publishing Co.

U.S. Bureau of the Census. (1975). *Historical statistics of the United States, colonial times to 1970* (bicentennial ed., Part I). Washington, DC: Author.

U.S. Department of Labor, Occupational Health and Safety Administration. (1991, December 6).

Occupational exposure to bloodborne pathogens: Final rule. *Federal Register, 56*(235), 64175–64182.

U.S. Public Health Service. (1990a). Protection against viral hepatitis (Part I). *Epidemiology Bulletin, 90*(4), 1–7.

U.S. Public Health Service. (1990b). Protection against viral hepatitis (Part II). *Epidemiology Bulletin, 90*(5), 1–11.

Valanis, B. (1986). *Epidemiology in nursing and health care.* Norwalk, CT: Appleton-Century-Crofts.

Appendix. Communicable Disease Chart for Personnel Working with Persons with Developmental Disabilities

Disease	Causative agent(s)	Symptoms	Incubation period	Transmission	Persons at risk	Diagnostic tests
Athlete's foot (tinea pedis)	*Trichophyton rubrum, T. mentagrophytes var. interdigitale, Epidermophyton floccosum*	Scaling or cracking of the skin, especially between the toes, or blisters containing a thin watery fluid	Unknown	Direct or indirect contact with skin lesions of infected persons or contaminated floors, shower stalls, or other articles used by infected persons	A common disease; occurs in adults more than children; males more than females; infections are more severe in hot weather	Microscopic examination of potassium hydroxide–treated scrapings from lesions between toes
Candidiasis (thrush, moniliasis)	*Candida albicans, C. tropicalis*	Oral— creamy white patches of exudate Vulval— irritation and vaginal discharge	Variable; 2–5 days for thrush in infants	By contact with secretions or excretions of mouth, skin, vagina, feces from infected individuals; during vaginal deliveries; by endogenous spread	Those with general debilitation, diabetes mellitus, antibiotic and corticosteroid therapy, chemotherapy, immune deficiencies	Presence of pseudohyphae and/or yeast cells in infected tissue or body fluids
Chickenpox[a] (varicella)	Herpesvirus group	Sudden onset of slight fever,	2–3 weeks (com-	From person to person by direct	Neonates whose mothers	Usually not done; antibody

Developed by Shirley P. Roth, MSN, RN, and Adrena J. Mahu, MSN, RN. From Roth, S. P., & Clausen, P. W. (1994). The role of the nurse in infection control. In S. P. Roth & J.S. Morse (Eds.), *A life-span approach to nursing care for individuals with developmental disabilities* (pp. 305–349), Copyright © 1994 by Paul H. Brookes Publishing Co.

Sources: Beneson (1990); Committee on Infectious Diseases, American Academy of Pediatrics (1991).

[a]Generally considered to be a reportable disease. Check reporting requirements in locality of practice setting.

(continued)

(*continued*)

Treatment	Preventive measures	Immunization	Control measures	Period of communicability	Recurrence	Exclusion from program
Topical fungicides such as miconazole, clotrimazole, ketoconazole, ciclopirox or tolnaftate; expose feet to air by wearing sandals; use dusting powders	Maintain good personal hygiene; special care in drying areas between toes after bathing; use powder containing an effective fungicide on the feet and particularly between the toes	None	Thoroughly clean and wash floor of showers and bathtubs with a fungicidal agent; educate concerning mode of spread	As long as lesions are present and viable spores persist on contaminated materials	Frequent	None
Ameliorating underlying causes (i.e., indwelling catheters); topical nystatin or an imidazole, oral clotrimazole (for infant thrush)	Treat vaginal candidiasis during pregnancy to prevent neonatal thrush; detect early, treat locally to prevent systemic spread; disinfection of secretions and contaminated articles	None	Hematogenous dissemination may produce lesions in other organs, such as kidney, spleen, lung, liver, endocardium, eye, and brain	Presumably while lesions are present	May occur	None
Acyclovir (IV or oral) for immuno-	Protect from exposure; varicella-	Being developed; not yet avail-	See preventive measures	As long as 5 but usually 1–2 days before	Infection apparently remains	At least 5 days after the

(continued)

Disease	Causative agent(s)	Symptoms	Incubation period	Transmission	Persons at risk	Diagnostic tests
Chickenpox *(continued)*		mild constitutional symptoms, maculopapular skin erruption	monly 13–17 days)	contact, droplet, or airborne spread of secretions; highly contagious	are not immune; persons with leukemia and/or immunodeficiency	assays may be useful in complicated cases
Chlamydia[a]	*Chlamydia trachomatis, C. pneumoniae*	*Trachomatis*—in neonates: congestion, edema, and discharge; vaginitis or cervicitis, infection can be acute or become chronic (PID) and lead to infertility; in males epididymitis *Pneumoniae*—severe pharyngitis, hoarseness, fever, productive cough, and cervical adenopathy	Variable but usually 7–14 days	*Trachomatis*—sexually transmitted; from genital tract of the mother to the newborn *Pneumoniae*—not defined; possible direct contact with secretions via fomites and airborne spread	*Trachomatis*—in persons with multiple sex partners, infants of mothers with chlamydia *Pneumoniae*—has been found in persons from 8 to 90 years of age	Serological testing to determine complement fixation antibody titer—isolate organism in tissue culture cells
Conjunctivitis (acute bacterial conjunctivitis, pink eye)	*Haemophilus influenzae*, bio-group *aegyptius*, and *streptococcus pneumoniae* are most common	Lacrimation, irritation and hyperemia of the palpebrae and bulb or conjunctivae of one or both eyes, edema of lids, photophobia, and mucopuru-	Usually 24–72 hr	By contact with discharges from the conjunctivae or upper respiratory tracts of infected persons, from contaminated fingers, using	Children under 5 years and older persons with debilitating conditions are most likely to be affected	Microscopic examination of stained smear or bacteriological culture of discharge.

(continued)

[a]Generally considered to be a reportable disease. Check reporting requirements in locality of practice setting.

(continued)

Treatment	Preventive measures	Immunization	Control measures	Period of communicability	Recurrence	Exclusion from program
compromised persons or those at increased risk; salicylates should not be given because of increased risk of subsequent Reye syndrome	zoster immune globulin modifies or prevents disease if given within 96 hr after exposure	able in United States		onset of rash to 5 days after appearance of first vesicles; may be prolonged with altered immunity	latent and may recur years later as herpes zoster in older adults	eruption first appears or until vesicles become dry
Treat neonates with oral erythromycin or sulfonamide; others—tetracycline, doxycycline, or erythromycin	Screen neonates of mothers treated for trachomatis; treat sexual partners who are symptomatic; educate about disease and to avoid contact with infected persons	None	Education, management of sexual partners, early identification of pregnant mothers	*Trachomatis*—unknown; relapses common *Pneumoniae*—not defined but outbreaks have lasted up to 8 months	*Trachomatis*—recurrence common *Pneumoniae*—immunity following infection incomplete	None
Topical antibotics such as tetracycline, erythromycin, chloramphenicol, and gentamicin; a sulfonamide such as sodium sulfaceta-	Good personal hygiene, hygienic care and treatment of affected eyes; investigations of contacts and source of infection; disinfection of secre-	None	See preventive measures	Variable, depending on organism; usually 1–5 days	May recur	Until antibiotic treatment completed (usually 3–5 days)

(continued)

(*continued*)

Disease	Causative agent(s)	Symptoms	Incubation period	Transmission	Persons at risk	Diagnostic tests
Conjunctivitis (*continued*)		lent discharge; in severe cases, ecchymoses of the bulb or conjunctiva and marginal infiltration of the cornea are observed		shared eye makeup, poorly sterilized instruments		
Cytomegalovirus (CMV)	Human (beta) herpesvirus 5	During perinatal period severe generalized infection, especially involving the CNS and liver; lethargy, convulsions, jaundice, petechiae, intracerebral calcifications, pulmonary infiltrates occur in varying degrees	Information is inexact; 3–8 weeks following blood transfusion, 3–12 weeks after birth	Intimate exposure by mucosal contact with infectious tissues, secretions, and excretions	Women of childbearing age working in delivery and pediatric units; preschool workers	Increased serum antibody titers; virus found in urine, saliva, cervical secretions, semen, or breast milk
Gonorrhea[a]	*Neisseria gonorrhoeae* (the gonococcus)	Newborn—ophthalmia Prepubertal children—vaginitis; Females—very mild urethritis or cervicitis may lead to PID Males—purulent discharge from urethra with dysuria 2–7 days after exposure; rectal infec-	Usually 2–7 days, sometimes longer	Contact with exudates from mucous membranes of infected persons, usually as a result of sexual contact; for infants and children, via vaginal canal or result of sexual abuse	Infants born to mothers with gonococcal infection; children and adolescents sexually exposed to persons with gonococcal infection; persons with multiple sex partners	Gram-stained smears of exudate from the eyes, endocervix; vagina, male urethra, skin lesions, synovial fluid, or cerebrospinal fluid

(*continued*)

[a]Generally considered to be a reportable disease. Check reporting requirements in locality of practice setting.

(*continued*)

Treatment	Preventive measures	Immunization	Control measures	Period of communicability	Recurrence	Exclusion from program
mide sometimes is used depending on the causal agent	tions and soiled articles					
Gancyclovir has been approved for CMV retinitis in immunocompromised persons	Observe universal precautions	None	See preventive measures	Virus is excreted in urine and saliva and may persist or be episodic for several years; excretion recurs with immunodeficiency and immunosuppression	N/A	None
Ceftriaxone, cefotaxime, doxycycline, or tetracycline (not under 9 years); evaluate for concurrent syphilis and chlamydia; follow-up cultures 4–7 days after meds; in infants use penicillin, also irrigate eyes with saline stat	Health promotion measures and sex education; discourage sexual promiscuity; teach personal prophylaxis; provide facilities for early diagnosis; use prophylactic agents in the eyes of the newborn	None	Give all neonates silver nitrate solution to eyes; infants with infected mothers receive ceftriaxone; educate, evaluate for other STDs if infected; endocervical culture for preg-	While discharge persists if untreated	For 24 hr following initiation of specific treatment	None

(*continued*)

(continued)

Disease	Causative agent(s)	Symptoms	Incubation period	Transmission	Persons at risk	Diagnostic tests
Gonnorhea (continued)		tions common in homosexual males				
Hepatitis A[a]	Hepatitis A virus (HAV)	Fever, with jaundice, anorexia, nausea, and malaise; infants and preschoolers may be asymptomatic or have mild symptoms with no jaundice	15–50 days (average 28–30 days)	Person to person by fecal–oral route	Diapered children in day care; persons having sexual contact with infected person; IV drug users; travelers to countries where disease is endemic	Serological tests for anti-HAV and IgM-specific anti-HAV antibodies
Herpes simplex type I	Virus from Herpesviridae, subfamily alphaherpesviridae	Conjunctivitis, keratitis, skin lesions on face and skin above the waist	2–12 days	Contact with saliva of carrier	Health care workers; infants born to infected mothers via the birth canal	Tissue culture, fluorescent antibody staining, or ELISA detection of HSV antigens
Herpes simplex type II	Virus from Herpesviridae, subfamily alphaherpesviridae	Vesicular lesions on the male or female genitals and perineal sites; also may be in the mouth	2–12 days	Sexual contact	Multiplicity of sex partners; newborns with infected mothers	Tissue culture, fluorescent antibody staining, or ELISA detection of HSV antigens
Impetigo	Staphylococcus aureus	Skin lesions initially vesicular, rap-	Variable and indefinite;	Contact with person with purulent le-	Newborns; chronically ill persons	Culture of lesion and/or nasal se-

(continued)

[a]Generally considered to be a reportable disease. Check reporting requirements in locality of practice setting.

(*continued*)

Treatment	Preventive measures	Immunization	Control measures	Period of communicability	Recurrence	Exclusion from program
and hourly until discharge is eliminated then less frequently			nant women; case reporting & follow-up			
Supportive; isolation for 1 week after onset of jaundice of hospitalized patients who are not toilet trained, have diarrhea or stool incontinence	Education for good sanitation and personal hygiene; proper water treatment, distribution systems, and sewage disposal; wash and/or cook raw foods; prophylactic doses of IG for travelers to countries where exposure is expected	Passive immunization with IG as soon as possible after exposure, but within 2 weeks	Isolation for 1 week after onset of jaundice; sanitary disposal of the body's waste products; immunize contacts; case reporting and follow-up	Latter half of the incubation period, continuing a few days after onset of jaundice	Homologous immunity after attack probably lasts for life	For 1 week after onset of jaundice; enteric precautions for 2 weeks
Acyclovir and vidarabine	Health education and good personal hygiene	None	Keep persons with lesions away from newborns, children with eczema/burns, and immunosuppressed patients	Up to 7 weeks after recovery from stomatitis	Frequent	None, but all personnel need to practice universal precautions
Acyclovir and vidarabine	Health education and good personal hygiene; use of latex condoms; C section when pregnant woman is infected	None	See preventive measures	Lesions infective for 7–12 days, with recurrent disease for 4–7 days	Frequent	None
Penicillin for 10 days; if resistant,	Strict adherence to personal	None	Development of drug-	Until after antibiotic treatment for 24 hr	May recur	Until treatment

(*continued*)

(*continued*)

Disease	Causative agent(s)	Symptoms	Incubation period	Transmission	Persons at risk	Diagnostic tests
Impetigo (*continued*)		idly turning seropurulent, with an erythematous base	commonly 4–10 days	sion, usually occurring via hands and nasal discharges	receiving systemaic steroid, antimetabolite therapy, or prolonged continuous IV therapy with indwelling catheters	cretions
Lyme disease[a]	*Borrelia burgdorferi*	Erythema migrans, a distinctive skin lesion that appears as a red macule or papule, accompanied by malaise, fever, headache, stiff neck, myalgia, lymphadenopathy, & neurological and cardiac involvement; may occur over extended period of time	Erythema migrans, a distinctive skin lesion, from 3–32 days; in early stages may be asymptomatic	Tick-borne: Transmission does not occur until tick has fed for several hours	All people who are out doors in tick-infested areas	Clinical findings and serological tests, biopsies of skin lesions
Measles[a] (rubeola, red measles	Measles virus, a member of the genus *Orbillivirus* in the Paramyxovirus family	Prodromal fever, conjunctivitis, cough, and Koplik spots on the buccal mucosa; red blotchy rash beginning on face and becoming generalized; leukopenia	Variable; 7–18 days from exposure to onset of fever	Airborne by droplet spread by direct contact with secretions of nose, throat; less commonly, by articles freshly soiled with secretions; highly communicable	All people who have not had the disease or have been inappropriately immunized, including very young and malnourished children, are at greatest risk	Blood test to confirm presence of IgM antibodies may be done
Mononucleosis	Epstein–Barr virus (EBV)	Fever, exudative pharyngitis,	4–6 weeks	Person-to-person spread via	Young children, particularly	Finding of a lymphocytosis ex-

(*continued*)

[a]Generally considered to be a reportable disease. Check reporting requirements in locality of practice setting.

(continued)

Treatment	Preventive measures	Immunization	Control measures	Period of communicability	Recurrence	Exclusion from program
methicillin or vancomycin	hygiene measures, especially hand washing; frequently change indwelling catheters and sites of IV infusions		resistant strain may require IV therapy			with antibiotics for at least 24 hr
Antibiotics such as tetracycline or doxycycline; children under 8 years can be treated with amoxicillin or phenoxymethyl penicillin (if allergic to this, can use erythromycin), ceftriaxone also used with neurological involvement at any age	Education about mode of transmission by ticks; avoidance of tick-infested areas, use of repellents, removal of ticks without crushing	None	See preventive measures	No evidence of person-to-person transmission; congenital transmission very rare	May occur	None
None	Vaccinations according to schedule	Two-dose measles live vaccine scheduled at 15 months and 4–6 years of age; both doses generally should be given as a combined MMR	See preventive measures	Before the beginning of prodromal period to 4 days after rash appearance; vaccine virus is not communicable	For 4 days after appearance of rash	
Rest and symptomatic treatment; steroids for	Good hand washing and personal hy-	None	See preventive measures	Indeterminate; may be prolonged	Unusual	Until medical clearance is

(continued)

(continued)

Disease	Causative agent(s)	Symptoms	Incubation period	Transmission	Persons at risk	Diagnostic tests
Mononucleosis (continued)		lymph-adenopathy (posterior cervical); jaundice in 4% of young adults, although 95% will have abnormal liver function tests; spleno-megaly in 50%; symptoms persist from 1 to several weeks		saliva; may be spread by infected saliva on hands, toys, equipment, or by kissing; also spread via blood transfusions	among eco-nomically depressed groups; group settings of adolescents, such as educational settings	ceeding 50% (including 10% or more abnormal forms); variability in tests and timing of each; consult resource for further guidance
Mumps[a] (infectious parotitis)	Paramyx-ovirus	Fever, swelling and tenderness of salivary glands, usually the parotid; orchitis may occur in postpubertal males or oophoritis in females	12–25 days (most commonly 18 days)	Droplet spread and direct contact with the saliva of the infected person	All people; however, greater risk has shifted to older children/adolescents and young adults	Serological tests; skin tests are unreliable
Pediculosis	Pediculus capitis (head louse), P. humanus (body louse); phthirus pubis (crab louse)	Severe itching and excoriation of scalp or body	Eggs of lice hatch in 1 week; sexual maturity is reached approximately 8–10 days after hatching	Direct and indirect contact (clothing) with infested person	All people	Visualization of nits and lice through inspection of hair shaft
Pinworm disease (entero-biasis)	Enterobius vermicu-laris	Anal pruritis, possible vaginitis,	2–6 weeks; reinfec-	Direct fecal–oral; indirect via	Suscep-tibility is universal;	Application of transparent adhe-

(continued)

[a]Generally considered to be a reportable disease. Check reporting requirements in locality of practice setting.

(*continued*)

Treatment	Preventive measures	Immunization	Control measures	Period of communicability	Recurrence	Exclusion from program
problematic cases	giene measures					obtained based on case-by-case findings
None	Vaccine, single or combined with rubella and measles vaccine (MMR)	Available as single vaccine or combined with rubella and measles vaccine; should be administered after 1 year of age; if combined, after 15 months of age	See preventive measures	6–7 days before overt parotitis, up to 9 days after; maximum infectiousness occurs about 48 hr before onset of illness	Immunity is generally lifelong	Until 9 days after onset of parotitis
For head and pubic lice, 1% permethren creme rinse (NIX); in case of body lice, laundering clothing and bedding in hot water and dry cleaning is recommended	Avoid physical contact with infested persons and their belongings, especially clothing; periodic inspection in primary schoolchildren for head lice, also institutions, nursing homes, and summer camps	Not applicable	See preventive measures	As long as eggs or lice are alive	As many times as people are exposed to infested subjects or articles of clothing	Until 24 hr after application of effective insecticide/treatment
Pyrantel pamoate, mebenda-	Good personal hygiene, daily	None	Change bed linen and un-	As long as gravid females are discharg-	Very common	Until treatment is

(*continued*)

(*continued*)

Disease	Causative agent(s)	Symptoms	Incubation period	Transmission	Persons at risk	Diagnostic tests
Pinworm disease (*continued*)		salpingitis, and pelvic peritonitis if aberrant migration occurs	tions may occur months after initial infection	contaminated items; dust-borne in heavily contaminated households	frequency and intensity relative to differences in exposure	sive tape to perianal skin to pick up any eggs; tape examined under microscope; best collected on waking in morning before washing
Ringworm of the scalp	Fungi of the genera *Microsporum* & *Trichophyton*	Erythema and scaling of the scalp with short broken hairs and localized alopecia; possible fever	10–14 days	Direct skin to skin; indirect from contaminated items such as backs of seats, clothing, hats, hairbrushes	Children below puberty; also found in adults	Fungal culture or demonstration of fungus by potassium hydroxide wet mount preparations
Ringworm of the body	Fungi of the genera *Microsporum* & *Trichophyton*	Circular, slightly erythematous, well-demarcated, scaly, vesicular or postular lesions; pruritis	4–10 days	Direct or indirect contact with skin and scalp lesions or from contaminated items	All ages, especially during periods of high humidity	Microscopic examination of the scrapings in a potassium hydroxide mount; tissue culture
Rubella[a] (German measles)	Rubella virus (family Toga-	Diffuse punctate, maculopapular	Usually 16–18 days with a	Contact with nasopharyngeal secretion of	In unvaccinated population, primarily a	Blood titer to determine antibody response

(*continued*)

[a]Generally considered to be a reportable disease. Check reporting requirements in locality of practice setting.

(continued)

Treatment	Preventive measures	Immunization	Control measures	Period of communicability	Recurrence	Exclusion from program
zole, alben-dazole, or pyrvinium pamoate; eggs are killed in laundry with tempera-tures of 55°C (131°F)	showers, frequent change of under-clothing and sheets, reduce overcrowd-ing, main-tain clean toilet areas, clean and vacuum house after treatment has begun		derwear of infected person daily, use closed sleeping garments, clean & vacuum sleeping and living areas daily for several days after treatment; examine all mem-bers of af-fected family or residential setting	ing eggs on perianal skin and eggs re-main infective; about 2 weeks		com-pleted
Oral grise-ofulvin with possible concurrent topical ther-apy with selenium sulfide shampoos	Education of the public; in epidem-ics, survey heads of young chil-dren by ul-traviolet light	None	Avoid direct contact with known or suspected sources, including dogs, cats, oth-er animals	As long as ac-tive lesions are present	Can occur	Until treat-ment is com-pleted
Miconazole, clotrima-zole, halo-progin, econazole, tolnaftate, naftifine, or ciclopirox 2 times daily, or keto-conazole, oxicon-azole, or sulcon-azole once daily	Good per-sonal hy-giene; use of fungici-dal agent in showers and dress-ing rooms of gyms	None	Avoid direct contact with known or suspected sources; frequent laundering of clothes	As long as ac-tive lesions are present	Can occur	Exclude from swim-ming pools, gymna-siums, and ac-tivities likely to lead to expo-sure of others until treat-ment is com-pleted
None	Education regarding immuniza-tion of all	Available sin-gle dose of live, attenu-ated rubella	See pre-ventive measures	About 1 week before and at least 4 days after onset of	None	For at least 4 days af-ter on-

(continued)

(continued)

Disease	Causative agent(s)	Symptoms	Incubation period	Transmission	Persons at risk	Diagnostic tests
Rubella (continued)	viridae; genus Rubivirus)	rash; in children few symptoms, in adults 1–5 days of low-grade fever, headache, and malaise; post-auricular and posterior cervical lymphadenopathy precedes the rash by 5–10 days; leukopenia is common; thrombocytopenia may occur	range of 14–23 days	infected persons; infection is spread by droplet or direct contact with persons	childhood disease; however, also frequently occurs in adolescents and adults	
Salmonellosis[a] (salmonella)	Serotypes of Salmonella	Fever, headache, malaise, anorexia, lethargy, abdominal pain and tenderness, constipation followed by diarrhea	6–72 hr (usually 12–36 hr)	Ingestion of contaminated foods, including raw or uncooked eggs, raw milk and milk products, poultry and poultry products	Persons with AIDS, malnourishment, GI problems; septicemia in those with sickle cell disease	Cultures of stool, rectal swabs, blood, urine, bone marrow aspirates, and foci of infection
Scabies (sarcoptic itch, acariasis)	Sarcoptes scabiei (a mite)	Papules, vesicles, or tiny linear	2–6 weeks before	Direct skin-to-skin contact	All people; individuals with immu-	Lesion scraping or biopsy

(continued)

[a]Generally considered to be a reportable disease. Check reporting requirements in locality of practice setting.

(continued)

Treatment	Preventive measures	Immunization	Control measures	Period of communicability	Recurrence	Exclusion from program
	children 15 months of age or older; susceptible population, especially adolescents, adult females of childbearing age, and postpartum women; young adults who have congregate living arrangements; IG given after exposure may modify or suppress symptoms	virus vaccine; elicits antibody response in approximately 98%–99% of susceptible persons		rash; infants with congenital rubella may shed virus for months after birth		set of rash; highly communicable
Antimicrobial therapy in persons with increased risk of invasive disease and other complications; ampicillin, amoxicillin, trimethoprim–sulfamethoxazole are drugs of choice	Thoroughly cook all foodstuffs derived from animal sources, expecially poultry, pork, egg products, and meat dishes; refrigerate prepared foods; educate food handlers; control infection in animals; inspect food processing plants; instruct carriers on good hand washing technique	None	Investigation of contacts; do not treat uncomplicated enterocolitis because this may prolong carrier state and lead to resistant strains	Throughout course of infection, may be several days to weeks; administration of antibiotics can prolong communicability	Possible	For food handler or client care provider, two consecutive negative stool cultures not less than 24 hr apart may be advised prior to returning to work
1% gamma-benzene hexa-	Education on mode of transmis-	Not applicable	Lesions secondarily infec-	Until mites and eggs are destroyed by	Infrequent	Until 24 hr after the start

(continued)

(continued)

Disease	Causative agent(s)	Symptoms	Incubation period	Transmission	Persons at risk	Diagnostic tests
Scabies (continued)		burrows on skin (they contain the mites and their eggs); intense itching, especially at night	onset of itching; 1–4 days after reexposure		nodeficiency are most susceptible to hyperinfestation	
Shigellosis[a] (shigella)	Genus *Shigella*	Loose or watery stools with minimal infection; more severe cases: fever, systemic toxicity, headache, and profuse watery diarrhea; abdominal cramps, tenderness, tenesmus, and mucoid stools as disease progresses	12–96 hr (usually 1–3 days)	Direct or indirect fecal–oral transmission from a patient or carrier	Children, elderly, debilitated individuals, and persons suffering from malnutrition	Culture of feces or rectal swab specimens; blood culture in severely ill patients
Shingles (herpes zoster)	Reactivation infection from the herpes virus that causes	Vesicles with erythematous base may appear in crops in irregular fashion	2–3 weeks (commonly 13–17 days)	Contact with vesicle fluid (lower transmission rate than chickenpox)	10% of children treated for malignant neoplasm; persons with HIV in-	Antibody assays are available but not routinely done

(continued)

[a]Generally considered to be a reportable disease. Check reporting requirements in locality of practice setting.

(continued)

Treatment	Preventive measures	Immunization	Control measures	Period of communicability	Recurrence	Exclusion from program
chloride (Kwell, Eurax, or Tetmosol); itching may persist for 1–2 weeks and should not be regarded as a sign of drug failure; overtreatment is common and may be toxic to the skin; treatment may be repeated after an interval of 7–10 days if eggs survived first treatment	sion; early diagnosis and treatment		ted from scratching; if scabies is complicated by beta-hemolytic streptococcal infection, a risk of acute glomerulonephritis is present	treatment, usually after one or two treatments, a week apart		of treatment
Trimethoprim–sulfamethoxaxole, ampicillin-resistant antimicrobial, antidiarrheal drugs	Health education and good personal hygiene; sanitary disposal of feces; water treatment systems; control fly breeding; refrigeration of foods; exclude carriers from handling food, and persons from patient contact	None	Isolation during acute illness; terminal cleaning; management of contacts; good personal hygiene	During acute infection and until infective agent is no longer present in feces, usually within 4 weeks after onset	Can recur if exposed again	Until diarrhea ceases and two successive negative stool cultures are obtained 48 hr after cessation of antibiotics
Acyclovir (IV or oral) for immuno-compromisd persons or those at in-	Varicella-zoster immune globulin effective in modifying or prevent-	None currently available	See preventive measures	Up to 7 days after appearance of vesiculopostular lesions	May occur	Up to 7 days after lesions first appear

(continued)

(continued)

Disease	Causative agent(s)	Symptoms	Incubation period	Transmission	Persons at risk	Diagnostic tests
Shingles (continued)	chicken-pox	along nerve pathways; severe pain and paresthesia are common			fection; occurs mainly in older adults	
Streptococcus A group (beta-hemolytic)	Streptococcus pyogenes	Acute sore throat, fever; may lead to scarlet fever	1–3 days	Direct or intimate contact with carriers; may be caused by ingestion of contaminated foods	Persons in school, day care centers, and day programs	Culture of secretions/exudate
Streptococcus B group (newborn disease)	Streptococcus agalactiae	Early onset—respiratory distress, apnea, shock, pneumonia, meningitis Late onset—meningitis, osteomyelitis, and septic arthritis	Early onset—less than 3 days Late onset—7 days to 3 months	Person-to-person contact, usually via the genital tract during birth	Premature babies of mothers with streptococcus genital tract infection	Blood or body fluid cultures
Syphilis[a]	Treponema pallidum	Primary stage—painless indurated ulcers of skin, mucous membranes, most commonly on the genitalia Secondary stage—rash on palms and soles with fever, malaise, sore throat, headache, arthralgia Latent stage—recurrence	10 days to 3 months (usually 3 weeks)	Sexual contact; blood transfusions; placental transfer	Persons with multiple sexual partners; fetus of infected mother; persons who have been sexually abused	Darkfield examinations of specimens, serological testing: non-treponemal antigen (e.g., RPR), VDRL treponemal antigen (e.g., FA)

(continued)

[a]Generally considered to be a reportable disease. Check reporting requirements in locality of practice setting.

(continued)

Treatment	Preventive measures	Immunization	Control measures	Period of communicability	Recurrence	Exclusion from program
creased risk	ing disease if given within 96 hr after exposure					
Penicillin V, benzathine penicillin G, erythromycin, cephalosporin	Education on modes of transmission, proper preparation of foods; exclude carriers from food handling	None	Isolation and full medication therapy to prevent rheumatic heart disease	Untreated uncomplicated 10–12 days; untreated complicated, weeks or months; treated, 24–48 hr	Frequent	Until 24–48 hr after antibiotic treatment
Penicillin and ampicillin	Parenteral administration of ampicillin to high-risk colonized, pregnant women; health education for caregivers	None	Treatment of high-risk mothers; intrapartum treatment of mother with previously infected infants; universal precautions in nurseries	Unknown	Frequent	Until treated
Aqueous crystalline penicillin G; benzathine penicillin G; if allergic to penicillin, tetracycline or erythromycin	General health promotion measures, sex education; syphilis serology in all STD cases; discourage sexual promiscuity; teach personal prophylaxis; provide easy access to facilities for early diagnosis and treatment	None	Isolation for primary, secondary, and congenital if hospitalized; refrain from sexual intercourse until lesions clear and meds completed; management of contacts	Variable and indefinite during primary, secondary, and first 4 years of latency; adequate penicillin treatment usually ends infectivity within 24–48 hr	Infection may lead to gradual development of immunity, unless treated in the primary and secondary stages	None

(continued)

(*continued*)

Disease	Causative agent(s)	Symptoms	Incubation period	Transmission	Persons at risk	Diagnostic tests
Syphilis (*continued*)		of secondary symptoms Tertiary stage— aortitis, changes in skin, bones, viscera (occurs 15 years after primary stage)				
Trichomoniasis	*Trichomonas vaginalis*	Frequently asymptomatic; foamy, yellowish vaginal discharge and mild vulvovaginal itening; dysuria and lower abdominal pain; in males, possible urethritis or prostatitis	4–20 days	Contact with vaginal and urethral discharges through either sexual intercourse or contaminated articles; more common in females	Females with multiple sexual partners	Examination of wet mount preparation of vaginal discharge

(*continued*)

Treatment	Preventive measures	Immunization	Control measures	Period of communicability	Recurrence	Exclusion from program
Metro-nidazole (Flagyl) for both males and fe-males; con-traindicated during first trimester of pregnancy	Education of public of symptoms and mode of transmis-sion; en-courage treatment	None	Avoid sexu-al rela-tions during in-fection and treat-ment; concurrent treatment of sexual partners is neces-sary	Several years in untreated carriers	Frequent	None

14

The Impact of Technology

Joyce S. Morse and Sally L. Colatarci

OBJECTIVES

On completion of this chapter, the reader will be able to:

- Identify the types of medical assistive technology available to individuais with developmental disabilities and discuss the impact of this technology on the life of the individual and his or her family.
- Identify the types of nonmedical adaptive technology available to individuals with developmental disabilities and discuss the impact of this technology on the life of the individual and his or her family.
- Describe the implications for participation in programs when technology is utilized by an individual with developmental disabilities.
- Describe the role of the nurse working with individuals with developmental disabilities who are dependent on adaptive technology.

OVERVIEW

The Technology-Related Assistance for Individuals with Disabilities Act of 1988 (PL 100-407) defined *assistive technology* in a broad sense, encompassing anything that can be used to enhance the lives of persons with disabilities. Assistive technology is "any item, piece of equipment, or product system, whether acquired commercially off the shelf, modified, or customized, that is used to increase, maintain, or improve functional capabilities of individuals with disabilities" (29 U.S.C. 2202, §3 [1]).

During the prenatal and neonatal period, medical technology enables physicians to diagnose and treat potentially life-threatening conditions. Assistive technology, both medical and nonmedi-

351

cal, then is used to improve and enhance the quality of life for individuals with developmental disabilities throughout the life span. The nurse, as a member of the interdisciplinary treatment team, must be knowledgeable about the types of technology available, its use, and how technology affects the life of an individual with developmental disabilities and his or her family. This chapter discusses both medical and nonmedical technology. Medical technology is referred to as *assistive,* as in PL 101-407, whereas nonmedical technology is referred to as *adaptive.*

MEDICAL ASSISTIVE TECHNOLOGY

The Congressional Office of Technology Assessment has defined *medical technology* as "the set of techniques, drugs, equipment, and procedures used by health care professionals in delivering medical care to individuals and the system within which such care is delivered" (Banta, 1990, p. 7). Health care professionals have integrated an increased use of technology for diagnosis, treatment, and monitoring into practice settings. At the same time, consumers have become more knowledgeable about health and health care technology. They expect an increase in the use of technology in the form of laboratory, radiological, diagnostic, and therapeutic services in the treatment process (Stanhope & Lancaster, 1992). As a result of the increased availability and utilization of technology, a generation of children and adults are surviving and living with conditions that require technological intervention and support.

Technological advances have increased the survival rate of extremely low birth weight and premature infants. Recent improvements in medical and surgical care have resulted in improved survival rates and outcomes for individuals with developmental disabilities. A dramatic

example of this trend is the child with spina bifida. In 1955, 90% of the infants born with spina bifida died in infancy; today 90%–95% survive infancy and have a normal life expectancy if they receive appropriate and timely medical intervention (Whaley & Wong, 1991). The frequency with which children require medical technology assistance is estimated to be about 1 in 1,000 (Haynie, Porter, & Palfrey, 1989). By definition, a child who is dependent on technology is one between the ages of birth and 21 years with a chronic disability that requires the routine use of a medical device to compensate for the loss of a life-sustaining body function; daily ongoing care and/or monitoring by trained personnel is required (Report to Congress, 1988).

Individuals who are dependent on technology rely on assistive devices to replace or compensate for vital body functions or to avert immediate threats to life. The primary categories of technology assistance are described in Table 1. The individuals in these categories usually require continual nursing care to address their ongoing, complex health care needs. This section describes aspects of nursing care for individuals with developmental disabilities in relation to the following types of medical assistive technology:

Respiratory technology: supplemental oxygen, mechanical ventilation, tra-

Table 1. Categories of technology assistance

Type	Description
I	Requires mechanical ventilation at least part of each day
II	Requires prolonged intravenous nutrition or drug therapy
III	Requires support for tracheostomy tube care, suctioning, oxygen supplementation, or tube feeding
IV	Requires cardiorespiratory monitoring, kidney dialysis, or ostomy care

Source: Office of Technology Assessment, Congress of the United States. (1987).

cheostomy, continuous positive airway pressure, humidification, aerosol therapy, chest physiotherapy, suctioning

Nutrition assistive devices: tube feeding (nasogastric, gastrostomy, jejunostomy) devices; ostomy devices to remove body wastes

Intravenous therapy devices: parenteral nutrition, medication infusion administration

Surveillance devices: pulse oximeters; cardiac and/or respiratory monitors, including apnea monitors

Kidney dialysis: peritoneal and hemodialysis

Respiratory Technology

About one half of all children with developmental disabilities who are dependent on medical technology require some form of respiratory assistance. This is used when there is a failure of the respiratory system to maintain normal gas exchange in the lungs. Respiratory system dysfunction in individuals with developmental disabilities may be caused by extreme prematurity or low birth weight, neuromuscular diseases (e.g., Duchenne muscular dystrophy), disorders of the central nervous system or spinal cord (e.g., myelodysplasia or spinal cord injury), and skeletal deformity (e.g., severe scoliosis secondary to cerebral palsy). Any dysfunction of the components of the respiratory system or its neurological/hormonal controls can result in the need for respiratory technology assistance.

The indication for the use of respiratory technology assistance is the presence of hypoxemia, as evidenced by reduced pulmonary artery oxygen levels and cyanosis. Supportive respiratory care includes a variety of therapies that involve changing the composition, volume, or pressure of inspired gases. This can include:

Oxygen therapy: increasing the oxygen concentration of inspired gas

Humidification: increasing the water vapor content of inspired gas

Aerosol therapy: adding airborne particles with beneficial properties

Mechanical ventilation: employing a variety of techniques to control or assist ventilation

Continuous positive airway pressure (CPAP): providing distending pressure to the airway to improve oxygenation and gas exchange

Chest physiotherapy, suctioning of respiratory secretions, and maintaining a tracheal airway (tracheostomy) are also techniques used to promote optimal respiratory function. One or several of these techniques may be used with a given individual.

Aita Kim Sung is a 6-year-old girl who resides at home with her parents and an older brother. Kim has a medical diagnosis of bronchopulmonary dysplasia (BPD) secondary to cerebral anoxia and cerebral palsy. She attends her local public school. The school nurse gives Kim supportive respiratory care twice during her normal school day. Kim receives a nebulizer treatment with Intal (cromolyn sodium) and normal saline. This is followed by postural drainage and manual percussion (chest physiotherapy) for 10 minutes to loosen secretions. The nurse performs oral/pharyngeal suctioning on Kim as needed. The nurse determines the need for supplemental oxygen therapy by assessing Kim's respiratory status before and after care. The nurse utilizes a pulse oximeter to monitor Kim's arterial oxygen saturation while
(continued)

respiratory care is being performed. Kim also has a portable oxygen retrieval machine that she uses if oxygen is needed before, during, or after the respiratory care.

Kim often is distracted during her respiratory care. Sometimes she fights the use of the mask to administer aerosol medication. The nurse, with the help of a music therapist, plays tape recordings of the country and western music that Kim likes in an effort to gain her cooperation. The music also helps Kim to slow her breathing and increase the volume of her respirations. This permits a greater percentage of oxygen and medication to be delivered during the course of the treatment.

The school nurse has educated the staff and the students who interact with Kim about her oxygen therapy and the precautions that must be taken when she is using oxygen. (For example, Kim cannot attend cooking class when oxygen is being used if an open flame will be in use.) The nurse also has instructed the school staff in the signs and symptoms of respiratory distress in an individual who depends on oxygen, and has provided them with guidelines for intervention in case Kim has a respiratory emergency.

Oxygen Therapy Oxygen may be administered by mask, hood, nasal cannula, face tent, tent, or ventilator. The method of delivery used is determined by the concentration needed and the individual's ability to cooperate. The goal of oxygen therapy is to maintain arterial blood oxygen saturation levels of 95% or more.

The nurse should be aware of and monitor for the potential deleterious effects of prolonged oxygen therapy. These include gradual impairment of alveolar ventilation as a result of damage to the capillaries of the lungs. In turn, this causes diffuse microhemorrhagic changes, decreased mucus flow, inactivation of surfactant, and altered ciliary function. Children with BPD often are affected by this problem, which is known as "lung burn" (Batshaw & Perret, 1992).

Atelectasis may occur in individuals with low tidal volume and inability to mobilize mucus or other secretions.[1] Oxygen-induced carbon dioxide narcosis is a complication that may be seen in individuals with developmental disabil-ities who have chronic pulmonary disease, or during the administration of sedative drugs.

Individuals who use oxygen therapy during school or day programs must bring an oxygen source and a delivery system with them. The rate of oxygen administration may need to be increased during periods of increased activity (Ahmann & Lipsi, 1991).

Consideration must be given to safety in the environment of the individual who uses continuous oxygen administration. The length of tubing attached to the oxygen mask, catheter, or cannula must be considered. Tubing between 6 and 30 feet in length permits greater mobility in the individual who is oxygen dependent. However, the length of the tubing may affect the total amount of oxygen being delivered, and therefore it should be evaluated periodically (Ahmann & Lipsi, 1991).

Oxygen itself is not combustible; however, it causes sparks or flames to burn at a higher temperature and a more rapid rate. Therefore, it is important for the

---

[1]The signs and symptoms of specific pulmonary dysfunction will vary with the cause and extent of the problem. The nurse might observe dyspnea with rapid shallow respirations, tachycardia, or cyanosis. Specific diagnosis can be determined based on physical examination including auscultation and percussion. Radiologic findings will confirm the medical diagnosis.

nurse to evaluate and/or instruct others to monitor the physical environment when oxygen is in use. Electrical appliances and devices, cigarettes and other smoking products, products that contain alcohol, petroleum jelly or petroleum-based products, and aerosol sprays should be kept away from oxygen (Whaley & Wong, 1991).

Nurses are able to bring valuable information about oxygen therapy to the treating team. All team members who interact with an individual who is oxygen-dependent should be familiar with the signs and symptoms of respiratory distress and know when to seek medical/nursing assistance for that individual (see Table 2).

Humidification Any individual who is receiving oxygen therapy will require humidification as well. Because oxygen is dry, the water vapor content must be increased during the delivery process to avoid dehydration of the mucous membranes. If an individual with a tracheostomy requires supplemental oxygen, it also is always delivered with a humidification system in order to prevent drying of the mucosa. Direct humidification can be supplied via a tracheostomy mask. This can be done during rest periods and/or at night so the person is unencumbered during day programs or classes. Room humidifiers can be used as long as the respiratory secretions are thin enough to be coughed or suctioned out. For individuals who are prone to mucus plugs, increasing the humidification will help to liquefy secretions and facilitate suctioning.

Aerosol Therapy Aerosol therapy, or the deposition of medication directly into the airway, is used to avoid the systemic side effects of some drugs. Bronchodilators, steroids, and some antibiotics can be inhaled so the medication is directed into the bronchi. Small, compact air compressors may be purchased or rented for use at home or during the day program. Some individuals with developmental disabilities may be frightened by the noise of the compressor or may resist the use of a nebulizer mask. The use of distraction, desensitization, or relaxation techniques (e.g., music therapy) may be helpful in obtaining cooperation (Colatarci & McConnell, 1991).

The primary nursing responsibility associated with the use of aerosol therapy is to assess the effectiveness of the treatment and the individual's response to the procedure (Whaley & Wong, 1991). Breath sounds should be auscultated before and after treatment, and a record should be maintained for comparison purposes. At home, the family should be encouraged to incorporate the aerosol treatments into the course of the daily caregiving routine. When appropriate, the individual should be given as much responsibility as possible for managing his or her treatment.

Mechanical Ventilation Mechanical ventilation is used to replace the function of the diaphragm and thoracic chest wall muscles in persons who require prolonged assistance with respiratory function. The lungs are inflated by application of either positive or negative pressure through a ventilator system

---

Table 2. Signs and symptoms of respiratory distress in an individual who is oxygen dependent

- Chest retractions (subclavicular, intercostal, substernal and suprasternal, and sternal)
- Nasal flaring
- Circumoral pallor
- Marked increase in respiratory rate
- Difficulty returning to resting respiratory rate after activity
- Increased duskiness or mottling of the skin
- Clammy skin or appearance
- Flailing of limbs (in infants or young children)
- Changes in muscle tone
- Tremors
- Hiccoughs
- Defecation
- Excessive crying
- Persistent gaze aversion

From Matheny School and Hospital. (1993). *Matheny School and Hospital nursing department policy and procedure manual.* Peapack, NJ: Author; reprinted by permission.

that often is connected to a tracheostomy. Individuals vary in their need for mechanical ventilation. Some require assistance for some part of the day or at night, whereas others may need assistance 24 hours a day.

Mechanical ventilators are classified according to the factors that regulate cycling: pressure, volume, and time. *Pressure-cycled ventilators* terminate the respiratory cycle when a preset inspiratory pressure is reached. *Volume-cycled ventilators* terminate respiration when a predetermined tidal volume is delivered. *Time-cycled ventilators* terminate inspiration when a predetermined time is reached. The type of ventilator selected for use is determined by the individual's size, the etiology of the respiratory condition, and the need for portability.

The nurse can assume an active role in teaching family and/or program staff how to optimize the effectiveness of ventilation by suctioning, positioning, and providing support to the individual receiving mechanical ventilation. For example, the nurse should advise caregivers and staff to monitor the integrity of the ventilator system to ensure that all connections are intact when the person is being transferred or positioned. Frequently, the ventilator tubing becomes disconnected at the tracheostomy site. The low-pressure alarm on the ventilator will sound if this happens. The tubing must be reconnected as quickly as possible. The risk of disconnection can be reduced by securing the connection with ties and observing it often during interactions (Ahmann & Lipsi, 1991).

Sometimes kinks in the tubing may cause the high-pressure alarm on the ventilator to sound. The high-pressure alarm also will sound if there is coughing, bronchospasm, or accumulated mucus in the tracheostomy tube. Kinked tubing or the presence of humidification for inspired air can result in the accumulation of water in the ventilator tubing. Accumulated water must be drained periodically; the tubing then is resecured. It is very important to prevent the accidental spillage of water into the trachea.

The use of mechanical ventilation to facilitate respiratory function during infancy and childhood affects growth and development in many ways. Some children are vulnerable to growth retardation resulting from compromised nutritional status because of increased risk for esophageal reflux and consequent vomiting associated with the use of mechanical ventilation. Other children may experience behavioral disturbances associated with prolonged hospitalizations and/or repeated illnesses and medical interventions related to the respiratory condition necessitating ventilation (Levy & Pilmer, 1992). In addition, many individuals who utilize mechanical ventilation spend prolonged periods of time in supine or side-lying positions. This provides few opportunities for playing, interacting with the environment, and building muscle strength, which can facilitate the handling of respiratory secretions. Alternate positioning in a semi-Fowler or prone position is generally possible. Either of these positions will enhance the individual's ability to function at his or her full potential.

The most notable impact on growth and development is that in expressive language; use of mechanical ventilation precludes speech. Outbursts of problem behavior and frustrations related to inability to communicate can be diminished by early intervention by the interdisciplinary team; because of this a speech-language pathologist should be included as part of the team. Age-appropriate language interventions might include sign language, a manual communication board, an electronic augmentative communication device, or the use of the Pasasy-Muir tracheostomy speaking valve (see "Tracheostomy," p. 358).

Therese is a quiet and shy 3-year-old with cerebral palsy and spastic quadriplegia. She attends a center-based early intervention program. She has a tracheostomy that is connected to a ventilator for respiratory support. The nurse and her teacher devised a program of positioning in which Therese is placed in a prone position over a bolster pillow. This position enables Therese to use her hands to play and to hit switches that activate specially designed toys. Therese gradually has increased her tolerance for this position, by 2-minute intervals each day, until she is able to tolerate it for the desired goal of 20 minutes. She also has been introduced to symbolic language. In this position, she is able to access a picture symbol system devised by the speech-language pathologist.

The nurse can assist caregivers and program staff to retain the focus on the assets as well as the needs of the person who is dependent on a ventilator. Whenever possible, the team is encouraged to anticipate the eventual weaning of the individual from ventilator dependence. Weaning may be done by decreasing the number of mechanical breaths per minute being delivered or gradually, over time, by decreasing the amount of time spent on the ventilator. Usually nighttime support is the last to be withdrawn. The amount of time it takes to wean a person from mechanical ventilation varies widely and the program is always highly individualized. Caregivers and staff must be sensitive to the activity tolerance of the person being weaned, and program schedules should be adjusted as necessary.

Continuous Positive Airway Pressure CPAP is created by the use of a device that imposes resistance to exhalation (Levy & Pilmer, 1992). It provides constant distending pressure to the airway in an individual who is able to breathe spontaneously, thus improving oxygenation, and lowers the carbon dioxide level by opening the alveoli so they can effectively allow gas exchange. CPAP is useful for individuals who have recurrent collapse of the lungs and/or moderate disturbances of pulmonary function. It is also useful in persons with central hypoventilation syndrome (sleep apnea).

CPAP can be delivered via nasal prongs or a tight-fitting mask. For an individual who uses a mechanical ventilator, CPAP can be delivered via an endotracheal airway or tracheostomy tube. It

Ralph, a 22-year-old with hazel eyes and light brown curly hair, has a medical diagnosis of spina bifida. When his school program ended, at age 21, Ralph was unable to find a job. He has spent the past 12 months watching TV and snacking. In the past year, Ralph has gained 20 pounds as a result of immobility and his sedentary life-style. One night, Ralph's mother noticed that his breathing was irregular while he slept. A thorough medical evaluation, including sleep studies, revealed obstructive apnea secondary to obesity. In an effort to promote weight reduction, Ralph has begun a strict 1,000 calorie diet. He now has an upper extremity and cardiovascular exercise program. Ralph is using nasal CPAP during sleep in order to provide consistent distending pressure to his airway and reduce the risk of sleep apnea.

is then known as positive end-expiratory pressure (PEEP). PEEP provides increased end-expiratory pressure that prevents alveolar collapse during controlled ventilation.

Chest Physiotherapy Chest physiotherapy refers to the use of postural drainage alone or in combination with any of the following techniques: manual percussion, vibration, and/or squeezing of the chest; cough; forceful expiration; and breathing exercises. Postural drainage is indicated whenever excess fluid or mucus in the bronchi is not being removed by normal ciliary activity and cough. Chest physiotherapy can be taught to parents and program staff and incorporated into an individual's daily routine. Chest physiotherapy is contraindicated for persons with increased intracranial pressure, osteogenesis imperfecta, minimal cardiac reserves, or end-stage renal disease.

Suctioning In suctioning, a catheter is used to remove secretions from the mouth, nose, or trachea in order to maintain a patent airway. It is usual to hyperventilate an individual with a tracheostomy with 100% oxygen just prior to and immediately following suctioning. This strategy prevents hypoxia. Suctioning should not require more than 3–4 seconds, and the person should be allowed to rest for at least 30–60 seconds between aspirations in order to allow the oxygen tension to return to normal (Whaley & Wong, 1991). Oximetry can be utilized to monitor suctioning and prevent hypoxia. Small, lightweight portable suction machines now are commonly available. A portable suction trap (e.g., the DeLee suction trap) may be utilized when a mechanical suction machine is not available. The need for suctioning may increase during activity. According to the Matheny School and Hospital Nursing Department, the indications for suctioning include:

- Copious secretions in the oropharynx, nasopharynx, or tracheostomy tube
- More tenacious secretions
- Audible bubbling, wheezing, or dry raspy sounds heard during respiration
- Signs of respiratory distress (see Table 2)

Tracheostomy A tracheostomy is a surgically created opening into the trachea. It usually is situated between the second and fourth tracheal ring. It is performed to bypass upper airway obstruction in certain conditions (e.g., infants with BPD who have tracheal airway narrowing secondary to numerous intubations for resuscitation), or to provide access to the airway for long-term ventilatory support.

The focus of nursing interventions for the individual with a tracheostomy is maintaining a patent airway, facilitating the removal of pulmonary secretions, and preventing complications. The most serious complications of a tracheostomy are tube occlusion and accidental decannulation. The risk of occlusion is greater in infants and children than in adults because of the smaller diameter of the trachea in these individuals. Maintaining the patency of the tracheostomy tube is accomplished by frequent suctioning and routine tube changes in order to prevent the formation of crusts that could occlude the tube (Whaley & Wong, 1991).

The nurse can reassure the family and other members of the interdisciplinary team that the tracheostomy itself does not interfere with most therapy treatment interventions (Ahmann & Lipsi, 1991). However, it is important to avoid extreme flexion in positioning as well as activities that potentially could occlude the tracheostomy tube itself. During all activities, it is important to protect the tracheostomy opening from particles of dust and other substances.

The treating team should be made a-ware of any medications being taken and their impact on the tracheostomy. Some medications, such as anticholinergic drugs, can affect the person's ability to swallow by decreasing the amount of saliva available to make a swallow. This makes the person more prone to the formation of mucus plugs, which can occlude the tracheostomy tube. Muscle-relaxant drugs may block the skeletal nerve–muscle connection, and thereby interfere with the voluntary part of the swallow. Seizure control medications may affect oral or motor function by affecting the trigeminal nerve. Any medication that affects general alertness may interfere with a person's ability to manage his or her secretions orally (Ahmann & Lipsi, 1991).

It is also important for the nurse to stress the positive effect of active or passive movement on the person who has a tracheostomy. Active movement helps secretions drain naturally. When the person is horizontal, the flow of secretions from the lower lungs is facilitated. An upright posture allows the upper lungs to drain. The individual with a tracheostomy may need assistance in order to clear mucous secretions and prevent obstruction of the tracheostomy opening. When secretions are coughed out of the tracheostomy opening or bub-

Table 3. Tracheostomy emergency supply kit contents

- Extra tracheostomy tubes (one that is the correct size and one that is a size smaller; in an emergency, a smaller size is sometimes more easily inserted because of tracheal swelling or narrowing of the stoma)
- Scissors
- Saline
- Ambu bag
- DeLee suction trap
- Sterile gauze pads
- Tracheostomy tube ties
- Stethoscope
- Written identifying information (including a list of allergies and current medications)
- Emergency instructions

From Matheny School and Hospital. (1993). *Matheny School and Hospital nursing department policy and procedure manual*. Peapack, NJ: Author; reprinted by permission.

ble from it, they may be removed by wiping with a clean gauze pad. A suction machine is used to assist an individual to clear excess mucous secretions from the mouth, nose, or tracheostomy.

In addition to being able to perform suctioning, families and program staff should be taught how to perform routine tracheostomy care and tracheostomy tube changes. Someone who is trained in basic life support and cardiopulmonary resuscitation should be available, and an emergency supply kit should accompany the person with a tracheostomy at all times. Table 3 describes the contents of a tracheostomy emergency kit.

José is a 12-year-old boy with dark brown curly hair and a wide, engaging grin. He has a medical diagnosis of Lesch-Nyhan syndrome. A tracheostomy was performed 6 months ago as a result of postsurgical complications. The community health nurse has taught José's mother and father how to suction and perform routine and emergency tracheostomy care. José sleeps with oxygen administered via tracheostomy mask with supplemental humidity to prevent drying of the mucosa.

José lives in a residential hospital setting. He receives a full range of medical/nursing, education, and therapy services. José fatigues easily, and his program plan incorporates frequent rest periods during the day. José takes Valium (diazepam) for the relief of painful dystonia. This medication decreases his ability to

(continued)

swallow and increases drowsiness. The nurse, in consultation with his family and the rest of the interdisciplinary team, develops a schedule for José that includes an alternative positioning plan to promote the effective draining of secretions and promote rest.

The nurse teaches all of José's teachers and therapists the indications for suctioning and routine and emergency tracheostomy care. A tracheostomy emergency kit is placed in his wheelchair bag, along with a portable suction machine. José's schedule identifies the specific individual who knows basic cardiac life support and the specific time(s) when that person is available.

In education and workshop settings, the specific responsibilities of caregivers, program staff, and any personnel involved in transporting and caring for the person with a tracheostomy should be delineated in a formal agreement (Kelly, 1993).

In individuals who utilize a tracheostomy, speech usually is precluded because inhaled air directed through the tracheostomy tube into the lungs is expelled in the same way, by passing the vocal cords. The Passy-Muir trachea valve can be utilized to redirect air into the normal passages of the larynx and the oral and nasal chambers. This permits the production of audible speech. The device fits most child-size and adult-size tracheostomy tubes. The only contraindication to its use is blockage of the air passages to the nose and mouth (e.g., the presence of scar tissue). The Passy-Muir valve allows individuals who have a tracheostomy as a result of problems with sleep apnea, bilateral vocal cord paralysis, tracheomalacia, neuromuscular disease, chronic obstructive pulmonary disease, head trauma, and quadriplegia to experience speech (Bunch, 1988).

Nutrition Assistive Devices
Neurological disorders such as cerebral palsy may lead to inadequate nutritional intake over time as a result of impaired swallowing (dysphagia). When dysphagia is present, swallowed contents do not traverse the normal route of the swallow (deglutition) in a timely fashion. Several events may occur: drooling, nasal regurgitation, esophageal regurgitation, and aspiration. Silent aspiration of salivary secretions and thin liquids can go undiagnosed for many years, and can result in chronic pulmonary change such as bronchiectasis or chronic reactive airway disease. In addition, retention of the swallowed contents as a residual in the oropharynx can manifest as any of the previously mentioned problems (Eddey, Newsome, Stringer, & Call, 1992).

Apprehension about mealtimes, fatigue, and recurrent episodes of aspiration may cause an individual to cease enjoying the eating process. The individual may begin to refuse food, and thus perpetuate a cycle of poor nutritional status and increased health risks. A videofluoroscopic swallowing study can be utilized effectively to determine if there is delayed initiation of the swallow, aspiration of thin liquids, or increasing risk of aspiration as the individual fatigues during the feeding process (Eddey et al., 1992). In cases of severe dysphagia, and/or in the presence of gastroesophageal reflux (GER), enteral tube feedings may be utilized to ensure adequate caloric intake and prevent aspiration.

Individuals with developmental disabilities also may have compromised bowel and/or bladder function as a result of congenital malformations such as Hirschsprung disease (congenital megacolon), bladder exstrophy, or a neural tube defect such as spina bifida, which often is accompanied by a meningocele or myelomeningocele. Spina bifida with myelomeningocele occurs approximately once in every 1,000 life births (Khoury, Erickson, & James, 1982). The degree of neurological dysfunction and its impact on the individual is directly related to the anatomic level of the defect, which determines which nerves are involved. Defective innervation to the bladder will affect sphincter and detrusor tone. This can cause constant dribbling of urine or result in overflow incontinence during childhood. There also may be poor anal sphincter tone and poor anal skin reflex. This results in lack of bowel control and rectal prolapse. Individuals who have a defect below the third sacral vertebra will have bladder and anal sphincter paralysis secondary to saddle anesthesia even though there is no actual motor impairment (Batshaw & Perret, 1992). Many individuals who have such problems with removal of body waste will require an ostomy, which surgically creates an opening in order to permit the elimination of urine and/or feces from the body.

Enteral Tube Feeding The initial decision to insert an enteral tube is not easy. A team effort is required to determine whether an individual who is having medical or nutritional problems because of dysphagia or GER would benefit from the placement of an enteral tube. An optimal team would consist of the individual and his or her family, a primary health care provider (i.e., physician or nurse–practitioner), a registered dietitian, a speech-language pathologist, and a nurse. The gastroenterologist, pulmonologist, radiologist, and surgeon all contribute to the assessment and treatment process.

Types of Enteral Tubes Tube feedings are used when it has been determined that an individual has normal function of the gastrointestinal tract but is unable to meet his or her metabolic and nutritional needs by oral feedings. The presence of gastroesophageal reflux and/or chronic aspiration reinforces the need for an alternative feeding method. Enteral tubes include nasogastric, gastrostomy, and jejunostomy tubes. A nasogastric tube (i.e., nose to stomach) is most commonly used for temporary problems. When a nasogastric tube is utilized, it should be paired with positive oral sensory experiences. An activity such as placing scented lip balm on the individual's lips continues to foster mealtime as a social and sensory event (Fraser, Hensinger, & Phelps, 1990). Long-term tube feeding techniques are most often used for individuals with multiple physical disabilities. A gastrostomy involves a permanent opening between the outside surface of the abdominal wall and the stomach. A jejunostomy involves a permanent opening between the small intestine and the outside surface of the abdominal wall. The decision to utilize a particular enteral site must take into account an individual's posture, muscle tone, age, feeding requirements and seating/positioning options. Gastrostomy tubes are the most common for long-term use. For some individuals, a gastrostomy feeding button may be utilized in lieu of a tube. The advantages and limitations of the gastrostomy feeding button are listed in Table 4.

Enteral Feeding Products There are a large number of commercially available products for enteral feeding. These can be divided into five categories: lactose-free, milk-based, elemental, modular, and specialty formulas. In addition, blender-processed food may be used. The lactose-free formulas are the most common, and include brand names such as Osmolite and Ensure. Although all formulas are produced to meet basic nutritional requirements, the choice of a particular formula may be determined by

Table 4. Advantages and limitations of the gastrostomy feeding button

Advantages	Limitations
Appearance is pleasing	Gastrostomy site must be well established
Care is simplified	
Permits greater mobility and comfort	Limited number of sizes
Decreased risk of migration and/or obstruction	Valve becomes clogged easily
Leakage and/or reflux is minimal	Requires more specialized connector tubing
Durable	More expensive than conventional gastrostomy tube
Fully immersible in water	
Clamp is unnecessary	Individual must remain fairly still during feedings, because tubing easily disconnects during activity
Radiopaque	
	If button size is too small, pressure necrosis can occur

Adapted from Huth and O'Brien (1991).

the presence of known allergies, cost, availability, and appeal to the family. The final decision is usually made by the primary care physician with input from a registered dietician.

Several factors must be considered in formula selection for enteral tube feeding:

• Nutritional status of the individual
• Nutritional requirements of the individual for maintenance of ideal body weight
• Complete medical history, including the presence of any known allergens
• Complete physical assessment, including blood studies for serum total protein and albumin:globulin ratio
• Underlying medical pathophysiology, especially diabetes mellitus or renal or hepatic failure

It must be noted that the concept of "ideal body weight" lacks standards in persons with paraplegia or constant choreoathetoid movements, and cannot be considered reliable in these individuals. Also, neurological disorders usually are accompanied by extremity wasting, independent of nutritional status; thus muscle circumference and skinfold thickness measurements do not have as much value in assessing nutritional status (Rombeau & Caldwell, 1984).

Enteral Feeding Methods In collaboration with the family, the health care provider, and a dietitian, formula and delivery methods are selected. Delivery methods include bolus feedings, intermittent gravity drip feedings, continuous infusion, and cyclic continuous infusion. Each method has advantages and disadvantages. Bolus feeding describes the introduction of a given amount of formula over a short period of time (i.e., 10–15 minutes). The frequency of bolus feedings is determined by the individual's nutritional and fluid requirements. The bolus of fluid is pushed into the stomach by attaching a bulb-syringe to the feeding tube. Frequent small bolus feedings can be used as opportunities to promote socialization in infants or other individuals who cannot tolerate large volumes of formula in a single dose. Large bolus feedings can be tolerated by some persons; however, when the stomach is very full, distention, reflux, and aspiration can be problems.

The most commonly used feeding method is the intermittent gravity bag. The feeding tube is held 1–2 feet above the tube insertion site, and the feeding solution is delivered into the stomach over a 30- to 45-minute period with the assistance of gravity. This is done several times a day, usually on a schedule that approximates regular mealtimes. It is an inexpensive method, and it reduces the risk of aspiration that is associated with larger bolus feedings. It is also tolerated better than bolus feedings by most individuals. Mobility is not impaired, as it may be with some of the continuous infusion feeding systems that require a pump system (Young & White, 1992).

If a decision is made to utilize an infusion pump to deliver enteral feedings, the individual, his or her family, and the nurse should evaluate the various options and then select the pump that best fits the individual's lifestyle. In addition to these considerations, families should be informed that some pumps work on gravity and must be positioned so that the container with the feeding product is above the level of the person's torso. Other pumps work by utilizing a bellows mechanism to regulate the flow of formula. As technology has improved, many pump-operated devices now come with battery packs that allow mobility during feeding. For individuals who utilize a wheelchair, modifications to the wheelchair permit the pump to travel and be utilized inconspicuously throughout the person's daily routines.

The social implications of enteral feeding also should be considered. In many cultures, mealtime is a social event. It provides an opportunity for interaction with family or significant others. Persons requiring enteral feedings may be intentionally or unintentionally isolated at mealtimes. In the home, the individual may be fed separately from the family because of the work involved in preparation of the feeding, or because the feeding schedule does not coincide with family mealtimes. The nurse should encourage the family to promote social interaction by including the individual who is receiving tube feedings at mealtimes. In the individual who has some swallowing ability, encouraging oral intake at mealtimes may enhance social interaction and a sense of belonging. These principles apply in any setting and at any stage in the life cycle.

Rose is an 18-year-old woman who is bright, inquisitive, and sociable and has a wonderful sense of humor. Rose has a primary medical diagnosis of cerebral palsy with a secondary diagnosis of reactive airway disease. Throughout her life, Rose had experienced frequent hospitalizations as a result of the reactive airway disease. During childhood, Rose was diagnosed with attention deficit disorder. She was very distractible at all times, including mealtimes. She always experienced coughing and choking spells during meals. Her family thought that it was because she was so distractible and because of the spasticity associated with the cerebral palsy. Rose remained small of stature, and very slender. At age 16, she weighed only 65 pounds.

At that time, the nurse at her day program recommended evaluation of Rose's pulmonary status. The pulmonologist then referred her to a gastroenterologist. Radiological studies were performed and it was determined that Rose was experiencing dysphagia and GER. The nurse, physician, and a dietitian then met with Rose and her parents. The findings of the evaluations, as well as the benefits and risks associated with continued oral feedings versus the use of a gastrostomy tube, were discussed. Rose wanted to know if she could still eat. Her family was concerned because they felt that a gastrostomy represented an increased level of medical intervention.

In order to address these concerns, a sophisticated oral motor evaluation was performed by a speech–language pathologist. On the basis of that evaluation, a videofluoroscopy was performed. This study proved conclusively that Rose had silent aspiration. Meanwhile, Rose began to eat less at each meal and to lose

(*continued*)

weight. This convinced Rose's parents that a gastrostomy was necessary. Rose was assured that she could remain at the family dinner table but would be eating in a different way. A gastrostomy tube was inserted percutaneously under local anesthesia at a same-day surgical center. Rose began her gastrostomy feedings gradually, and tolerated them well.

Now, at age 18, the quality of Rose's life has improved. Because of improved nutrition, she is no longer so distractible and she has experienced growth in height and weight. Her secondary sexual characteristics have appeared and she feels prettier. Her parents feel more comfortable about feeding because they realize that Rose is not dependent on oral intake to maintain adequate nutritional status. Rose is able to enjoy the socialization of mealtimes without fear of choking.

Aspiration is a major complication of tube feedings, especially in individuals who have a diminished level of consciousness (as seen in postictal lethargy), have absent or weak cough reflex, are noncommunicative, or are in a predominantly recumbent position (Young & White, 1992). The person receiving the feeding should have his or her head elevated, at least 30 degrees, for a period of time that may vary from 30 minutes before to 30 minutes after feeding, to reduce the risk of aspiration. This is especially important in individuals who have not had a Nissan fundoplication done to prevent GER and/or aspiration. Also, it is important to remember to check for gastric residual contents prior to each feeding, and delay feeding if there is more than 50–100 ml of residual content (Matheny, 1993). Other potential complications of enteral tube feeding include tube obstruction or dislodgment, electrolyte imbalance, and diarrhea.

Ostomy Devices to Remove Body Wastes As a result of various health problems, some individuals with developmental disabilities may require a bladder or bowel stoma to permit elimination of urine or stool. The type of surgery and the location of the resultant stoma are based on etiological considerations, the person's age, and whether the stoma is intended to be temporary or permanent. In addition, it is important to consider whether the individual has the cognitive and motor skills necessary to manage the ostomy on his or her own.

Periodically, the ostomy equipment should be evaluated for appropriateness. During childhood, growth may affect the size and location of the stoma. In the adult, stoma revision may be necessary periodically in order to maintain optimal placement. This is especially true for persons with progressive scoliosis who may have had a stoma placed on the lower part of the abdomen. As the person ages and scoliosis progresses or obesity develops, it may be difficult to find an appliance that the person can use independently because the stoma site will no longer be visible to him or her. If a body jacket is used to minimize the progression of scoliosis, it will be necessary to cut out a portion of the body jacket in order for the ostomy appliance to be visible and accessible for care. Another difficulty with lower abdominal stoma sites is that the collecting device tends to pull away from the body as it fills with urine or stool.

The availability of a wide variety of ostomy care appliances for persons of all ages permits every individual with a stoma to participate fully in all aspects of life. The nurse can act as a resource to the treating team by providing information and advocating for inclusion in all activities. The presence of a stoma should not keep a person from participating in exercise or sports such as swimming (Matheny, 1993).

Management of Urinary Function When neurological impairment results in impaired urinary storage, altered bladder tone (increased or decreased), and inadequate or increased resistance in the bladder neck and urethra, the individual is at risk for pyuria and renal complications. Individuals with increased bladder tone have a spastic bladder with uninhibited bladder contractions, which can cause high intravesical pressure. This predisposes the bladder to vesicoureteral reflux and incomplete emptying. The reflux can lead to hydronephrosis, and the presence of the residual urine predisposes the individual to urinary tract infection. Persons with decreased bladder tone have a flaccid bladder, which also results in incomplete emptying and the presence of residual urine (Mitchell & Rink, 1987).

In the individual who has bladder neuropathy, bladder capacity is impaired and he or she is unable to determine when the bladder is full. There is also no awareness of urine passing through the urethra, and the individual is unable to stop the urinary flow (Lozes, 1988). In such cases, it is important to establish a regimen of complete bladder emptying. Clean intermittent catheterization is a technique that can be taught to parents and caregivers and to individuals as young as 4 years of age. In combination with medications such as Ditropan, Pro-Banthīne, and Sudafed, clean intermittent catheterization can make it possible for an individual to achieve dryness (Solomon, personal communication, 1991).

A number of surgical procedures are used to manage urinary incontinence. These include the implantation of an artificial bladder sphincter, bladder augmentation, creating a continent ileal reservoir (Kropp procedure), or creating a urinary diversion such as a ureterostomy, cystostomy, or ureteroileostomy. When an ostomy is performed, an enterostomal nurse–therapist can assist the individual and/or the family to select a cost-effective urine collecting system for daytime and, if necessary, another system for nighttime use. Protocols for maintaining skin integrity around the stoma site and procedures for eliminating odors associated with poorly cared for or ill-fitting devices must be established and monitored. Older children, adolescents, and all adults should be involved, to the extent of their capabilities, with the self-care of bladder continence management (Matheny, 1993).

Astrid is a shy and quiet 23-year-old woman who enjoys singing in the choir and listening to music. Astrid has spina bifida, arrested hydrocephalus, severe scoliosis, and a ureteroileostomy. At birth, Astrid had many medical problems, including kidney failure. At 18 months of age, her urinary diversion was performed.

At age 8, Astrid was placed in residential care. For several years after her admission, Astrid was cared for by nursing staff, who performed all care related to her urostomy appliance. Astrid was not expected to learn to care for her urostomy. Her family maintained very limited contact with her. When she did go home, her family complained about the difficulty of managing her urostomy appliance.

The nurses began a program of teaching Astrid to provide and advocate for her own care. The nurses believed that, with instruction and assistance, Astrid could become independent in some of her care activities. An enterostomal nurse–

(continued)

therapist was consulted to assess Astrid's ostomy site and her equipment needs. A new type of self-adhesive appliance was prescribed.

Astrid's nurse began teaching her the skills necessary to manage her own ostomy care. When an appliance change was needed, Astrid was asked to assemble all of the necessary equipment. It took about 2 months until Astrid was comfortable with this activity. Then she was asked to direct her nurse in changing her appliance. It took about 3 months for her to reach a level of comfort with this responsibility.

Finally, the nurse suggested that Astrid begin the procedure by herself. Astrid occluded her stoma and the nurse had to help her to start all over again. After numerous failures, the nurse consulted with an occupational therapist. Together, the nurse and the therapist developed strategies that allowed Astrid to accomplish this task successfully and independently. (She was taught to put her finger through the hole in the appliance and feel her ostomy for proper placement.) Repetition and praise were utilized to promote successful task completion.

The process of teaching Astrid to care for her own urostomy appliance ultimately took about 2 years. However, Astrid's quality of life improved as a result of this teaching program. She experienced more age-appropriate independence, was able to participate in activities where no nursing services were available (e.g., Special Olympics), and, at age 21, was able to secure supported employment in a workshop.

The nurse should teach the person with developmental disabilities who has an ostomy, and his or her caregivers, about the importance of adequate fluid intake, the need for regular emptying of the collecting device, and the actions to take if skin integrity is compromised. If urine is allowed to come in contact with the skin surrounding the stoma site, irritation can occur. If the urine pH is too alkaline, the resultant irritation may have the appearance of barnacles. A solution comprised of equal parts of water and white vinegar can be applied in the form of compresses three to four times daily until improvement is noted (Matheny, 1993). If the urine pH is too acidic, a raw open area around the stoma will be seen. Zinc oxide paste, alone or with karaya paste, can be used with the appliance to encourage healing.

In order to prevent renal failure, a regular schedule of urological care and monitoring should be established. There should be periodic monitoring of kidney function through blood and urine studies (i.e., serum creatinine, serum calcium, blood urea nitrogen levels, and creatinine clearance). Imaging studies such as intravenous pyelograms, renal ultrasound, and renal scans should be used to detect the early presence of renal calculi. If renal calculi are present, lithotripsy, which is a nonsurgical procedure, can be utilized to fragment the calculi (Matheny, 1993).

Management of Bowel Function   The bowel problems seen in individuals with developmental disabilities are the result of ineffective ability to relax or contract the internal anal sphincter in conjunction with decreased or absent sensation around the anal opening. The presenting problems are alternating constipation and diarrhea. The lack of sensation causes fecal soiling.

Twenty years ago, colostomies were performed routinely on individuals with spina bifida and myelomeningocele. Therefore, today it is not unusual to see adults with spina bifida who have a colostomy. Presently, most individuals with spina bifida are placed on a bowel regimen early in childhood. A routine of timed toilet training combined with careful attention to dietary and fluid intake and judicious use of rectal suppositories (e.g., Dulcolax) permits most individuals to attain bowel continence (Batshaw & Perret, 1992). Although colostomy is no longer performed as a routine procedure, necrotizing enterocolitis, imperforate anus, Hirschsprung disease, and inflammatory bowel disease can affect persons with developmental disabilities and result in the need for a colostomy or ileostomy.

zinc oxide ointment or karaya paste will protect the skin adequately. As soon as the stoma is healed and the baby's size permits use of a collecting device, an appliance should be introduced. Toddlers and preschoolers can assist with daily care by handing the items used in care to the caregiver. School-age children, adolescents, and adults should be taught to manage their own ostomy care to the extent possible (Whaley & Wong, 1991).

Program staff, as well as parents, need information about strategies to maintain skin integrity, early signs of skin

---

Schabaz is a 42-year-old man who enjoys his job in a local supermarket. Schabaz has a medical diagnosis of spina bifida and mental retardation. He has a long history of perianal skin breakdown secondary to inability to contract the internal anal sphincter. He also has an absence of sensation around the anal opening. These problems were causing frequent absences from his job. He had to remain home and carry out elaborate skin-healing protocols with the assistance of his family. Unpredictable, frequent soiling also was occurring. This was embarrassing to Schabaz.

The community health nurse frequently visited Schabaz at home and had identified his family's difficulty in dealing with his skin and bowel issues. The nurse referred Schabaz to a gastroenterologist. After extensive evaluation, it was determined that Schabaz had inflammatory bowel disease, and a colostomy was performed. Postoperatively, an enerostomal nurse–therapist taught Schabaz how to irrigate and care for his colostomy.

When Schabaz returned home, the community health nurse visited to ensure that he was able to manage his own care at home. In order for Schabaz to perform the colostomy irrigation, he needed to hang the irrigation bag. The nurse and the family devised a plan to accommodate Schabaz in his wheelchair. A coathook at wheelchair-accessible height was hung on the bathroom wall adjacent to the commode. Schabaz was then able to carry out his own care. The quality of life for Schabaz was improved postsurgically. He no longer experienced skin breakdown, and was able to establish a normal bowel management routine that did not interfere with his job.

An enterostomal nurse–therapist can assist the individual and his or her family to understand the surgery and plan for daily care. For infants, a gauze dressing is left over the stoma and the skin is cleansed well after each bowel movement. A protective barrier such as

breakdown, and signs of stomal complications, such as ribbon-like stools, excessive diarrhea, bleeding, prolapse, or failure to pass flatus or stool. Staff and parents must be advised to contact the nurse or physician if any of these problems arise (Matheny, 1993).

368 Morse and Colatarci

Intravenous Therapy Devices

Prolonged intravenous (IV) therapy is used when there is a need to provide medication such as antibiotics or chemotherapy over a prolonged period of time and there is no other acceptable mode of administration. Venous access can be provided via a heparin lock device or a venous access device (VAD). Nursing responsibilities in the care of an individual with developmental disabilities who is receiving IV therapy are consistent with those for individuals who are receiving IV hyperalimentation.

Intravenous hyperalimentation, also known as *total parenteral nutrition* (TPN), is used to provide for the total nutritional needs of individuals with developmental disabilities whose lives are at risk because feeding via the gastrointestinal tract is impossible, inadequate, or hazardous (Whaley & Wong, 1991). In infants, necrotizing enterocolitis may result in a shortened gut that will not handle an adequate amount of nutrients to support life. Older children and adults might require TPN because of chronic malabsorption, inflammatory bowel disease (e.g., Crohn disease), chronic intestinal obstruction, extensive burns, acquired immunodeficiency syndrome, or the presence of abdominal tumors being treated by radiation or chemotherapy (Atkins & Oakley, 1986). TPN can be delivered via a peripheral venous site; however, for long-term use the preferred route is via a VAD. Table 5 describes and compares various long-term VADs.

The nurse is responsible for teaching the individual and/or the caregiver how to manage ongoing IV therapy. The nurse must ensure that sterile technique is utilized to control local infection and protect against sepsis. Parents, caregivers, and anyone who works with an individual who has a VAD should be aware that infection, leaking, or a clotted catheter represent complications that should be brought to the attention of the nurse immediately (Whaley & Wong, 1991).

There must be monitoring of the infusion rate, and ongoing monitoring to assess the individual's response to this therapy. Nurses should monitor vital signs, intake and output, and fluid and electrolyte balance frequently during the introductory phases of TPN. In persons with decreased renal function or metabolic defects, an imbalance of sodium and potassium can occur. There also may be other metabolic responses to the TPN solution that may require modifications of the TPN formula. Occasionally, hyperglycemia can occur during the first few days on TPN. The nurse can teach the caregiver to monitor blood glucose levels using a testing kit developed for home use. Sometimes insulin is given to assist the individual's body to adjust to hyperglycemia. When TPN is being discontinued, it is important to taper the rate of infusion slowly and taper the use of insulin. This protects the individual from hypoglycemia, which can cause osmotic diuresis and the risk of hypertonic dehydration (Whaley & Wong, 1991).

Parents and program staff must provide stimulation that minimizes developmental delays in infants and children who are treated with TPN for prolonged periods of time. A written information sheet about the purpose of TPN and the VAD's management should be provided to teachers and therapists. All caregivers should be provided with opportunities to handle and manage the VAD so that they become comfortable working with the individual and the device.

The VAD is not a deterrent to inclusion in most activities, including bathing. If the exit site is well healed and the cuff adheres to the tissue, swimming may be permitted. A transparent dressing (e.g., Op-Site) can be used to protect the catheter and the exit site. Generally, participation in contact sports is prohibited in order to protect the catheter.

Table 5. Comparison of long-term venous access devices

Device	Description	Advantages	Disadvantages
Hickman/Broviac catheter (includes several other trade names)	Silicone, radio-paque, flexible catheter with open ends One or two Dacron cuffs on cathe-ter(s) enhance tissue ingrowth	Reduced risk of bacterial mi-gration after tissue adheres to Dacron cuff Easy to use for self-administered infusions	Requires daily heparin flushes Must be clamped or have clamp nearby at all times Must keep exit site dry Heavy activity restricted until tissue adheres to cuff Risk of infection still present Protrudes outside body; sus-ceptible to damage from sharp instruments and may be pulled out; may affect body image More difficult to repair Patient/family must learn catheter care
Groshong catheter	Clear, flexible, sil-icone, radiopaque catheter with closed tip and two-way valve at proximal end Dacron cuff on catheter en-hances tissue in-growth	Reduced time and cost for maintenance care; no heparin flushes needed Reduced catheter damage—no clamping needed be-cause of three-way valve Increased patient safety be-cause of minimum potential for blood backflow or air embolism Reduced risk of bacterial mi-gration after tissue adheres to Dacron cuff Easily repaired Easy to use for self-administered infusions	Requires weekly irrigation with normal saline Must keep exit site dry Heavy activity restricted until tissue adheres to cuff Risk of infection still present Protrudes outside body; sus-ceptible to damage from sharp instruments and may be pulled out; can affect body image Patient/family must learn catheter care
Implanted ports (Port-a-cath, Infus-A-Port, MediPort)	Totally implantable metal or plastic device that con-sists of self-sealing injection port with precon-nected or attach-able silicon catheter that is placed in large blood vessel	Reduced risk of infection Placed completely under the skin; therefore cannot be pulled out or damaged No home maintenance care and reduced cost for family Heparinized monthly and af-ter each infusion to main-tain patency No limitations on regular physical activity, including swimming No dressing needed No or only slight change in body appearance (slight bulge on chest)	Must pierce skin for access; pain with insertion of nee-dle; can use local anesthet-ic before accessing port Special needle (Huber) with angled tip must be used to inject into port Skin preparation needed be-fore injection Hard to manipulate for self-administered infusions Catheter may dislodge from port, especially if child "plays" with port site ("twid-dler syndrome") Vigorous contact sports (football, soccer, hockey) generally not allowed

From Whaley, L.F., & Wong, D.F. (Eds.). (1991). *Nursing care of infants and young children* (3rd ed., p. 1271). St. Louis: C.V. Mosby; reprinted by permission.

Home care is a viable option for the long-term use of TPN in individuals with developmental disabilities. A community-based home health care agency can as-sess the home environment and family support systems. The community nurse can coordinate arrangements for the de-livery and storage of the hyperalimenta-tion solutions. A physician should be designated to handle emergency medical needs. Funding for such TPN programs is yet to be determined (Wilhelm, 1985).

Surveillance Devices

Surveillance devices are used to provide early warning of complications in individuals with developmental disabilities who have problems associated with cardiorespiratory functioning and blood gas exchange. Infants with BPD can be discharged from the acute care hospital when they are gaining weight, oxygen need is low (less than 1 liter/min), and they can sustain a blood oxygen saturation of 85% or greater for 20–30 minutes in room air (Batshaw & Perret, 1992).

Cardiorespiratory Monitoring The typical cardiac monitor consists of a pulse rate indicator that signals each ventricular contraction with a flashing light and an electrocardiograph (ECG) tracing. The indicator is integrated with an alarm system so that, when the heart rate falls below or rises above preset limits, an audio and visual alarm will be activated. Factors other than changes in the cardiac status also can activate the alarm. For example, movement or problems with the electrodes (e.g., loose electrodes, poor contact with the skin, poor placement, inadequate grounding, soiled electrodes) can trigger the alarm.

Respiratory activity also should be monitored, because the heart rate does not always drop with apnea, although bradycardia frequently follows an apneic episode.

An apnea monitor consists of an impedance monitor that measures the electrical resistance across the chest as it changes with respiration. The alarm usually is set at a 15- to 20-second delay. Apnea and cardiac monitoring can be combined in one unit. In long-term use, the placement of electrodes to avoid skin irritation can be problematic (Perry & Hayes, 1988).

The nurse should instruct parents and caregivers to assess the individual immediately for signs of respiratory distress, color, state of alertness, and cardiac abnormalities on the monitor when an alarm sounds. A respiratory arrest almost always precedes cardiac arrest in children; therefore, all caregivers for individuals on cardiorespiratory monitoring should be competent in the performance of cardiopulmonary resuscitation (Levy & Pilmer, 1992).

Nurses also can assist families who must deal with the day-to-day care issues of an individual who requires constant monitoring. Sometimes simple chores such as laundry and vacuuming may become overwhelming to the caregiver who is afraid that an alarm will not be heard over the noise of the appliance. The nurse can help the parent develop a realistic schedule for household activities and incorporate help from other family members or neighbors to watch the individual using a monitor. Handling, positioning, and age-appropriate developmental stimulation will foster normal development of the infant or young child on a cardiorespiratory monitor.

Oximetry Pulse oximetry measures the amount of light absorbed by oxyhemoglobin through a sensor with a bright light placed on a finger, toe, or earlobe. This information is used to calculate the saturated arterial oxygen level. Pulse oximetry can be intermittent or continuous, and it maintains an accurate measurement regardless of the individual's age or skin characteristics, or the presence of pulmonary disease. However, oximetry is ineffective in discerning hyperoxia (Whaley & Wong, 1991). If an individual is ill and his or her oxygen requirements are increased, activity may need to be curtailed and the oxygen concentration increased (Levy & Pilmer, 1992). Random oximetry readings can be utilized to evaluate the overall effectiveness of some of the oxygen therapies (e.g., CPAP) that were discussed earlier in this chapter.

The alarm on the oximeter will sound when there is a change in the individual's condition, the probe has become disconnected, or the oxygen delivery system has failed. The nurse can assist parents and caregivers by working with them to develop strategies that minimize episodes of probe disconnection and false alarms. Movement can trigger a false alarm with some instruments. Other devices synchronize the arterial saturation reading with the heartbeat, thereby reducing the interference caused by motion.

Renal Dialysis

Technological advances in the care of individuals with developmental disabilities who have acute or chronic renal failure have provided a means for maintaining kidney function in acute disease as well as prolonging life for those individuals with end-stage renal disease. The following methods of dialysis are available for the clinical management of renal failure:

Hemodialysis: Blood is circulated outside the body through artificial cellophane membranes that permit a similar passage of water and solutes.
Peritoneal dialysis: The abdominal cavity is used as a semipermeable membrane through which water and solutes of small molecular size move by osmosis and diffusion.
Hemofiltration: Blood filtrate is circulated outside the body by hydrostatic pressure exerted across a semipermeable membrane, and simultaneously replaced by electrolyte solution.

The choice of which type of dialysis to utilize depends on the nature and cause of the renal failure as well as the personal preferences of the individual and his or her family or caregivers. Peritoneal dialysis and hemodialysis can be performed at home. When dialysis treatments are performed at home, the time spent in transportation is eliminated. In addition, the environment is more stable and less threatening.

Peritoneal dialysis is the preferred method for intervention in acute conditions. It is quick, relatively easy to learn to perform, and requires a minimum of equipment. The two types of peritoneal dialysis used at home are continuous ambulatory peritoneal dialysis (CAPD) and continuous cycling peritoneal dialysis (CCPD). Both methods utilize commercially available sterile dialysate solution that is instilled into the peritoneal cavity via a surgically implanted indwelling catheter.

CAPD generally is performed three times during the day and once at night. It permits most individuals to maintain their usual daily routine. CCPD utilizes an automatic dialysis machine. The dialysis exchange is performed only at night. The use of a nighttime-only dialysis schedule permits the individual with developmental disabilities to maintain full participation in his or her day program or work schedule.

A primary requirement for home *hemodialysis* is the placement of a cannula that permits access to the blood supply. The nurse can provide training and support for the individual, family, and/or caregivers. The parent or caregiver must be taught how to operate the equipment, connect the unit to the vascular access, and evaluate the status of the individual who is receiving treatment. The nurse must teach how to palpate the internal shunt for patency and how to auscultate it for a bruit sound.

The initiation of a hemodialysis regimen can be frightening, traumatic, and anxiety provoking. It involves surgery to implant the vascular access site. The initial encounter with the hemodialysis machine also may be frightening. Each individual needs teaching at his or her own level of cognitive ability. Individuals with developmental disabilities will need support and reassurance from the nurse as well as the family.

Infants and young children are dependent on caregivers for their dialysis management. School nurses can assist the school-age child. Adolescents and adults should be encouraged to carry out the procedure to the fullest extent of their capabilities. This provides the individual with some control and fosters independence (Sander, Murray, & Robertson, 1989). Renal dysfunction also brings with it the need for dietary restrictions or controls, frequent laboratory studies, limitations to physical activity, and a sense of being different. The nurse must be sensitive to and support age-appropriate health teaching activities (Walker, 1991).

NONMEDICAL ADAPTIVE TECHNOLOGY

When nonmedical adaptive technology is utilized by individuals with developmental disabilities, it is typically with two major purposes in mind: 1) to correct or remedy a specific impairment, and 2) to assist the individual to learn specific material and/or specific tasks (Garner & Campbell, 1987). There is a wide variety of such adaptive technology available for individuals with developmental disabilities. Some devices, such as eyeglasses or hearing aids, compensate for sensory deficits. Others, such as ankle–foot orthoses and body jackets, provide physical support in order to maximize independent motor function and/or minimize deformity.

It has been suggested that the term *nonmedical adaptive technology* is also applicable to a range of highly specialized mechanical, electronic, and computerized tools that commonly are used in both rehabilitation and special education settings. These technologies are designed to perform specific orthotic or prosthetic functions, although they are not orthotics or prostheses in the tradi-

tional sense. Such a definition would include positioning and mobility devices, augmentative adaptive eating utensils, and specialized switch access devices (Brady, 1988). Such adaptive devices may enable the person with developmental disabilities to overcome environmental obstacles that could impede the acquisition of developmental skills and interfere with learning (Behrman & Lamm, 1983). "Adapted switches are those which are used to bypass normal on-off switches . . . They can be made to accommodate any body part movement that an individual is capable of controlling" (Fraser et al., 1990, p. 216). Toys such as remote-controlled cars, games such as Nintendo, or environmental controls such as light switches are all examples of the uses of adaptive switches.

All of the above examples of adaptive technology can be utilized to improve the lives and functional capabilities of individuals with developmental disabilities. However, those devices that optimize skill development in either communication or mobility or both areas can significantly improve the quality of life for a person with developmental disabilities. Opportunities for learning are fostered when the person with developmental disabilities has increased opportunities to interact with others as well as the environment. As a member of the interdisciplinary team, the nurse participates in the assessment and program development and implementation process. The community health nurse, in particular, may be the professional who assists a family to integrate new program components into the home. Parette (1991) cautioned that the introduction of technology into the family support system may have pronounced, but poorly researched and documented, effects on family members and the quality of parent–child interactions. In collaboration with other members of the interdisciplinary team, the nurse ensures that adaptive technology is made available and smoothly incorporated into the environment and life-style of a person with developmental disabilities.

Each team member has discipline-specific expertise that focuses on a particular aspect of function. For example, the occupational therapist can assess an individual's capacity to perform activities of daily living (ADLs) and make recommendations for equipment and strategies to enhance independence. Thus, when collaborating with the individual with developmental disabilities, his or her family, and an occupational therapist about an effective ADL routine, the nurse can ensure that health maintenance activities such as medication self-administration, as well as the more traditional activities such as bathing, dressing, and grooming, are considered.

Information Technology

Information technology is a subset of adaptive technology that can be utilized by interdisciplinary team members to: 1) assess and evaluate the cognitive, linguistic, and motor strengths and weaknesses of an individual with developmental disabilities; and 2) gain the best possible effects from rehabilitation measures by using specialized software and databases to further therapy and training.

According to Soede (1989), a person with developmental disabilities can use information technology to:

1. Augment and assist a direct person-to-person communication when there is an impaired communication ability.
2. Control transportation/wheelchairs.
3. Control information to and from remote databanks (i.e., shopping, banking).
4. Perform tasks at school or the office.
5. Control and supervise warning and alarm systems.
6. Control prostheses and/or orthoses.
7. Control muscles by electrostimulation.
8. Provide access to leisure/recreational opportunities (i.e., computer art, music composition and playback, video games).
9. Control environmental manipulators (i.e., page turners for individuals who lack hand skills).

Information technology often is incorporated with other types of adaptive technology to maximize the quality of life of a person with developmental disabilities.

Lee is a 50-year-old man who sets high standards for himself in all areas of job performance. He has a medical diagnosis of spastic/athetoid cerebral palsy. Lee works for a law firm doing data entry; he can type 30 words per minute using one finger. He has an IBM computer at home, and he accesses a computer network using electronic mail (e-mail). This enables him to work at home and also have a wide circle of "computer friends."

Because Lee spends so much time at the computer, he occasionally experiences painful muscle spasms due to the need to maintain a sitting position against gravity for computer use. Lee attended a seating clinic at his local disabilities center. He was examined by a physical therapist, an occupational therapist, and a physiatrist. Together with Lee, they decided to try a "tilt-in-space" seating system. This would allow Lee to alter his position for comfort to enable the relaxation of muscle spasms. After 3 weeks in the new chair, Lee reports that he is more comfortable.

Communication

The ability to communicate enables people to interact with others and the world around them—receiving, processing, and sending information to exchange thoughts, feelings, desires, and ideas, and to monitor changes in the environment. Communication takes place constantly and is involved in every activity. We communicate in many different ways—through touch, sight, hearing, smell, speech, writing, gesturing, and reading. It is impossible for any individual *not* to communicate, because any behavior transmits information. Speaking and listening are the most common ways in which human beings communicate.

Individuals with developmental disabilities experience communication disabilities when their ability to receive, send, or process information is reduced. For individuals with developmental disabilities and communication disabilities, Kangas and Lloyd (1988) state "there are compelling reasons to begin communication interventions at a young age in order to prevent the development of maladaptive communication patterns" (p. 219). Table 6 describes priority goals and strategies for promoting communication abilities. These are general recommendations for interventions that the nurse can utilize as adjunctive measures to more sophisticated technology.

The term *augmentative/alternative communication* refers to any mode of expressive communication other than speech. This includes systems such as sign language, symbol or picture boards, electronic devices, and synthesized speech. *Communication modes* refers to the general categories of behavior that are used to communicate. These modes can be vocal, gestural, written, or pictorial. *Communication systems* refers to specific sets of responses used to communicate within a particular mode. American Sign Language is an example

of a communication system within the gestural mode. Blissymbolics is an example of a communication system within the pictorial mode (Orelove & Sobsey, 1991). Although the same system can be used for either augmentative or alternative communication, there is a difference between the two.

Augmentative systems are used by people who already have some speech but either are unintelligible or have limited abilities to use their speech (e.g., individuals with cerebral palsy). For these individuals, other modes of communication are used to support, or supplement, what the person is able to say verbally. **Alternative communication** is the term used when a person has no vocal abilities. These individuals must rely on another method to make all of their ideas, wants, or needs known.

Sometimes parents or program staff will express concern that the individual with developmental disabilities will stop trying to talk if he or she is given another way to communicate. The use of augmentative communication, although not strictly necessary in some cases, may promote overall communication and facilitate social interaction for those with severe oral language deficits. However, they should not be viewed as substitutes for either oral or sign language.

For most individuals who use augmentative systems, the most efficient and reliable means with which to communicate becomes a combination of speech and the augmentative system; therefore, they continue to use speech also. As the individual, his or her family, and the team consider the usefulness of an augmentative system, the nurse can act as an advocate to ensure that health issues and concerns are considered in selecting and programming a system. Table 7 lists considerations in selecting an augmentative/ alternative communication aid.

Communication disorders affect more than 3 million Americans of all ages. Some individuals are unable to use

Table 6. Priority communication goals and strategies for individuals with developmental disabilities

Goals	Strategies
Socialization	
• Facilitate family bonding process • Ensure families have time and energy to interact with person with disabilities effectively • Establish an exchange (turn-taking, stop and wait) • Expand social communication beyond family to peers, familiar/unfamiliar listeners	• Look at positioning, movement, and mobility to support interaction • Teach caregivers to treat everything the individual does as meaningful language and respond accordingly • Help identify ways a person with developmental disabilities can indicate messages; don't pick reflexive movements or movements that increase muscle tone
Comprehension	
• Provide receptive language training using traditional approaches and aided language stimulation • Lay groundwork for skills-related communication (e.g., cause/effect) • Facilitate the individual's perception, comprehension, and use of symbols and train caregivers to reinforce and treat all behaviors as language • Expand range of communication capabilites—*do not rely* on a single modality • Provide opportunities for the person to shift modes (greeting, protesting, demanding)	• Engineer the environment so the individual is immersed in language; attach communication symbols to all objects and places • Make and use communication boards for different components of the person's day (i.e., recreation, ADL, etc.) • Replicate daily situations and role play communication activities (e.g., ordering from a menu, directing personal care)
Expression	
• Facilitate speech • Provide ways to respond and follow simple instructions • Provide mechanisms for mobility, manipulation, and expression • Indicate • Make choices • Initiate • Express wants and needs • Control behavior of other people	• Plan everyday events so that there is something to talk about • Use photo albums to create "memory books" that can be used to establish topics, and encourage information exchange between home and the school/program setting • Provide many ways to make choices • Use communication strategies that are as interactive and developmentally appropriate as possible • Don't use static boards; if possible, teach person to draw symbols • Use routinized choral speaking and songs as part of activities • Use generic rather than specific vocabulary (some, this, here, there, mine) • Use music imagination, fantasy, and imagery • Work technology into the daily routine (e.g., tape recorder, battery-operated toys or devices, dedicated communication devices such as Min-Speak or Touch-Talker)
Interaction with environment	
• Provide individual with sense of control and power • Provide ways to interact with toys and equipment • Set up environment so that there is a need to communicate	• Provide opportunities to move about that stimulate interest and curiosity • Increase use of tools • Pursue ways of providing independent mobility • Provide opportunities for contact with peers without disabilities • Develop individual's responsibility for success/failure of communication • Integrate augmentative communication techniques into home, classroom, and program settings • Provide opportunities for experiences that are similar to those of peer group without disabilities • Create opportunities for communication rather than eliciting responses • Use different modes concurrently • Encourage person to perceive self as a competent communicator • Don't "overtechnologize" the individual

Adapted from *Augmentative Communication News* (1990).

Table 7. Considerations in the selection of an augmentative/alternative communication device

Preference of the user
What type of device does the person want?
What type of special features are desired (e.g., small, portable, speech output, printer)?

Physical capabilities
Assessment for optimal use of body movement, assurance of proper positioning for the prevention of deformities, assessment of vision and hearing capabilities; all of these will determine the size, configuration, distance of the aid from the user, information to be communicated, usefulness of auditory feedback.

Communication needs
Cognitive capabilities and communication environment must be determined.
Aid must provide an acceptable level of content.
Environment may be home, school, workshop, etc.

Developmental considerations
Age, responsiveness to therapeutic interventions, potential for vocabulary and academic gains, nature of the individual's disability (static vs. progressive disability; e.g., cerebral palsy [static] vs., Duchenne muscular dystrophy [progressive])

Control interface
Interface selection depends on the person's available motion/activity (e.g., head pointer, mouthstick, joystick, pneumatic [puff/sip], air cushions, rocking lever, arm slot control).
The aid responds to the interface via the operating techniques of row–column scanning, directed scanning, and direct selection.
The location of the control interface and the aid must be selected carefully in order to elicit reliable responses and to accommodate the conditions of the environment in which the system will be used (e.g., wheelchair, bed, school desk).

Output
The output of the system may be in the form of pictures, symbols, letters, or words, and may be via manual indication (e.g., pointing for immediate, basic needs), lighted display or voice (for social, more personal communication), or printed output (very useful for academic/vocational needs).

Flexible control
Various components among aids enable the diversity of human needs to be met via different aids. Changing needs within the individual may be accommodated with a microprocessor-based unit.
General features should include portability, battery power (rechargeable), interchangeable control interfaces to permit environmental controls, computer access and/or mobility units to operate together, adjustable installation, durability, modular construction (so additional components can be added if the physical/mental capability of the user changes); also, the user should be able to program the aid as his or her needs and capabilities change.

speech or language at all. Many use adaptive devices (e.g., manual or electronic communication boards, speech output devices) to enhance their speaking and communication functioning. Some individuals with developmental disabilities have multiple impairments (i.e., vision, mobility, and speech) that can affect their ability to communicate. Other individuals have hearing disorders that result in communication difficulties; these persons also can benefit from various adaptive devices. Nurses who work with individuals with developmental disabilities may encounter persons with a variety of communication disorders.

Speech Disorders. Speech disorders may include articulation disorders, stuttering, resonance abnormalities, and voice disorders. *Dysarthria* is a motor speech disorder commonly associated with cerebral palsy. It is characterized by abnormal articulation caused by impaired oral motor muscle control. It is difficult to understand the speech of persons with dysarthria. In *verbal dyspraxia,* the individual has normal oral motor muscle control, but he or she has severely impaired articulation (Batshaw & Perret, 1992). Individuals with dysarthria and dyspraxia are good candidates for the use of augmentative/alternative communication systems.

Language Disorders Language development begins at birth. In young children, language development is the best predictor of future intellectual functioning (Blackstone & Painter, 1985). Individuals with developmental disabilities may experience delays in the development of expressive and/or receptive language. For example, some individuals have word-finding problems or difficulty in using mature sentence structure (lexical–syntactic disorders). Others may have poor ability to participate in conversation (semantic–pragmatic disorders). Some people (i.e., persons with autism)

Penny is an attractive 30-year-old woman who has an engaging smile and an infectious laugh. Her primary medical diagnosis is spastic cerebral palsy. Penny's speech is severely dysarthric; however, until 1 year ago, she believed that everyone was able to understand her.

At that time she moved into a group home and began a new day program. The staff and clients in her new home could not understand her. This led to some confusing situations. The nurse at the new day program spoke to Penny about the benefits of a consultation with a speech-language pathologist (SLP), and Penny agreed to a speech assessment. The SLP made several recommendations, and Penny was asked to establish her own priorities. She chose to utilize a user-friendly laptop computer with voice-synthesis output because this device required only a short period of instruction. Penny was then able to make her needs known.

Next, Penny and the SLP made up a small book with phrases and sentences in it to be utilized if the computer was not available. Penny determined when each method of communication would be appropriate. She was encouraged to use oral speech as often as possible, but she now had alternative communication systems to be used as necessary. Penny was able to communicate her health concerns to her physician without someone to "translate" for her.

may have limited speech or be mute. Others may be verbose or echolalic, or may have only a limited understanding of what is said to them (Batshaw & Perret, 1992). Early intervention, including therapy and education, can be helpful. Interactive computers also are utilized to promote language development.

Nurses must be aware of the person's language capabilities in order to perform valid nursing assessments and develop appropriate communication strategies to permit effective health teaching. Throughout the life cycle, the nurse encourages, facilitates, and advocates for the individual with developmental disabilities to assume an active role in the management of his or her health care issues. This cannot occur unless the individual has the ability to identify and communicate health needs.

Hearing Disorders Hearing disorders affect between 21 and 28 million Americans of all ages (about 10% of the U.S. population).

Approximately 10% of preschool children fail hearing tests. In the United States, about 22,000 children, or 1%, are born with or acquire permanent hearing loss each year (Northern & Downs, 1991). Approximately one third of these children will have one or more additional disabilities, including disorders of vision, learning disabilities, and mental retardation (Karchmer, 1985).

Hearing loss in children may be the result of genetic disorders, structural defects, prematurity and complications during the neonatal period, trauma, intrauterine infections, chronic recurrent middle ear infections or mastoiditis during infancy and childhood, and antibiotic toxicity (Batshaw & Perret, 1992). Hearing disorders also are very common among older individuals, affecting up to 60% of those people over 65 years of age. Hearing losses in this population range from mild impairment (difficulty hearing soft sounds) to profound deafness (difficulty or inability to hear even loud sounds).

Early detection of hearing loss is important. Prompt intervention at a young age can maximize the development of communication skills, minimize or prevent developmental delays, and allow learning.

Prior to any form of audiological testing, the nurse should assess the individual's ear canals, because the presence of excessive or impacted cerumen will interfere with the testing process and/or the test results. A regimen of regular ear hygiene that includes the use of Debrox on a weekly basis should be considered for individuals who demonstrate cerumen buildup that has the potential to interfere with hearing (Matheny, 1993).

For any type of audiometric testing that requires a participant's cooperation (e.g., pure-tone audiometry), an individual with developmental disabilities may need more than one opportunity to experience the testing situation. Role-playing and allowing the person to handle the equipment used in testing may decrease fear and anxiety and improve performance. Brainstem auditory evoked response can be performed on individuals with developmental disabilities, infants under sedation, or older individuals who are unable to participate in pure-tone audiometric testing techniques to evaluate hearing loss. Otoacoustic emission testing is a newer form of audiology evaluation technology. It measures movement of the hairs lining the inner ear. It does not require active cooperation from the individual being tested. Unlike brainstem auditory evoked potential, the use of sedation is not necessary. The results of otoacoustic emission testing are not specific for hearing acuity. They can be used to determine the presence of physiological malfunction of the inner ear (G. Sundar, personal communication, 1993). Impedance audiometry is a technique that is used to assess pressure levels behind the eardrum. It will detect the presence of middle ear fluid, which collects during episodes of otitis media.

There are a number of adaptive devices to improve the communicative ability of a person with a hearing disorder in specific listening situations, particularly when environmental noise and distraction may interfere with the message. For example, the majority of individuals with hearing impairment are "hard of hearing" and rely in varying degrees on adaptive devices for communication. Many use amplification (i.e., hearing aids) to enhance their communication and listening functioning (Stanhope & Lancaster, 1992). Adaptive hearing devices are defined by their specification or function (Pehringer, 1989) and include:

- Adaptive listening devices (e.g., a personal amplifier used independently or in conjunction with a personal hearing aid to improve discrimination).
- Adaptive alerting devices (e.g., loud bells, buzzers, or ringers to alert the listener to sounds around him or her).
- Adaptive signaling devices (e.g., flashing lights or vibrating devices to signal an event or emergency).
- Telecommunications devices (e.g., telephone amplifiers, fax machines).
- Informing devices (e.g., telecommunications devices for the deaf, computers, closed-captioned television).

Many individuals use a combination of adaptive hearing devices and augmentative/alternative communication systems to achieve the best possible communication skills.

Mobility

Mobility is an integral component of daily activities. Several types of positioning and movement activity are essential to all types of independent functioning. These include selecting a position that matches the practical and movement demands of the task, assuming that position and balancing the body in it, and coordinating the movements required to participate in the task (Fraser et al., 1990). These positioning and movement activities often present challenges to the individual with devel-

Mario is a 46-year-old man who lives with his sister and her family. He has a medical diagnosis of spastic/athetoid cerebral palsy and is deaf. Mario's athetoid head movements make it very difficult for his hearing aids to remain in place. Therefore he was fitted with circular hearing aid devices (called "huggies") that fit around the ear. Mario then was able to hear sounds, although he was not able to hear speech. In order to understand communication from others (receptive language), Mario learned American Sign Language. In order to communicate his wants and needs (expressive language), he learned to use a voice-synthesizing computer. This arrangement was efficient and effective, and permitted Mario to interact with the world around him.

opmental disabilities and his or her caregivers. Persons who have developmental disabilities accompanied by any type of neuromotor involvement often have abnormal movement and posture patterns that limit skill development and impair mobility.

As a member of the interdisciplinary team, the nurse works with the individual and his or her family to develop and implement programs that enhance skill development and foster maximum mobility. For example, a prone stander may be used by an individual with cerebral palsy in order to promote skeletal alignment, permit weight bearing on the lower extremities, and allow the individual to participate in household tasks such as dish washing.

Physical exercise, such as passive or active range of motion, can be utilized at any age, with either static or progressive developmental disabilities, to strengthen muscles and bones, enhance motor skills, and prevent contractures (Orelove & Sobsey, 1992). The nurse can encourage the family to carry out exercise programs set to music as a fun activity. All activities and exercise aid in achieving mobility to some degree.

Surgical interventions (i.e., adductor tenotomy, Achilles tendon release, Girdlestone procedure) to facilitate balance and improve sitting ability and ambulation potential may be necessary in some children and young adults with cerebral palsy. Surgical interventions such as the Lucque procedure to stabilize scoliosis may be necessary to maintain an adequate sitting posture and avoid respiratory compromise.

Many people equate the term *mobility* with *ambulation*. An ongoing concern of the family of an individual with developmental disabilities who has severely impaired mobility is whether or not the individual will ever be able to walk. The nurse can assist the family to understand that mobility can take various forms. For some individuals, transferring from one surface to another is a form of mobility, however limited. For others, a wheelchair may represent optimal mobility and function.

Mobility in Ambulatory Individuals For those individuals with varying ability to ambulate, many types of adaptive devices are available. Gait analysis and gait training, as well as adaptive ambulation aids such as canes, crutches, and walkers, are helpful for some individuals with mild motor/balance/coordination problems. The use of splints, orthoses, prostheses, and bracing devices can be effective for others. In some cases, an ambulatory individual may benefit from occasional use of assistive devices commonly employed by those persons who are not ambulatory.

Mobility in Nonambulatory Individuals There are a number of manual and powered mobility devices available

Rhonda is a 16-year-old girl who is part of a group of friends who like to go every-
where together. Her father calls them "the giggle girls." Rhonda has a low-level
myelomeningocele repair secondary to spina bifida. She ambulates with crutches,
but she tires easily. At Rhonda's high school, the school nurse advised her to speak
to the school occupational therapist (OT) about this problem.

At an OT assessment, it was decided that Rhonda's need for mobility could be
met by the occasional use of a scooter. This three-wheeled vehicle folds down and
fits into the trunk of a car. Rhonda now uses the scooter in situations in which
fatigue or distances were causing a problem (e.g., on a trip to the shopping mall).
This system also works very well at school. The use of an alternative means of
mobility has greatly improved the quality of Rhonda's life, and the lives of "the giggle
girls," for whom she now enjoys the ability to carry packages.

for the individual who is unable to ambulate effectively, the most common of
which are wheelchairs. As mobility devices, wheelchairs allow an individual
with developmental disabilities who is
unable to ambulate to have the freedom
to learn, move, work, and live (Nelson,
Leonard, Fisher, Esquenazi, & Hicks,
1989, p. 202). Nurses who work with any
individual who utilizes a wheelchair for
mobility should be familiar with the
most common types of wheelchairs and
their control devices. The *manual wheelchair* category may be subdivided into
standard, lightweight (also called sports),
special purpose (e.g., hand lever drive
and hemidrive), travelchairs, and stroll-
ers. All of these are controlled by hand.
Powered wheelchair systems include
standard electric wheelchairs, power
packs that attach to manual wheelchairs, electric three- and four-wheeled
carts, and powered riding toys (Nelson et
al., p. 202).

Powered mobility controls are of two
main types: standard commercially available ones or modifications or special adaptations of these. Standard controls include propulsional control and microswitch control. The former provides the
smoothest ride and is best used by persons with fair to good upper extremity
control. Microswitch control can be
turned on or off like a lightswitch and

tends to be most appropriate for persons
with minimal upper extremity control.
Common modifications of these controls
include joystick extensions, T-bars, and
special knobs. Special adaptations include a variety of switches, such as leaf,
touch plate, lever, pneumatic, and toggle
switches. Switch and proportional control may be accessed by any reproducible
movement of the body, such as a hand
joystick, chin or foot controller, head
switch, or pneumatic switch (Nelson et
al., 1989, p. 202).

Individuals with impaired mobility
secondary to neuromuscular abnormality or deformity may not be able to be
comfortable or be positioned adequately
in a standard wheelchair. For these individuals, specialized seating is available.
According to Nelson et al. (1989), the
goals of specialized seating and mobility
devices are to maximize function, increase comfort, provide pressure distri-
bution, enhance upright posture, nor-
malize tone, decrease the influence of
primitive reflexes, decrease the tendency to skeletal deformity, and improve the
quality of life.

Nurses must become knowledgeable
about the wide variety of mobility and
seating systems that are available. The
type of positioning and seating system
utilized influences the respiration, visual field, oral motor function, skin condi-

tion, alertness, use of available muscle strength, sitting comfort, and ability to perform functional activities of an individual with developmental disabilities (Kreutz, 1993). A thorough nursing assessment can provide important information to be utilized in the selection and/or fabrication of an individualized seating system. The nurse also must be aware of the resource centers that provide and service individualized systems. The nurse may refer the person with developmental disabilities to such a center, act as a liaison with the family, assist with obtaining prescriptions and funding, and maintain ongoing records relating to the seating and mobility device.

Positioning Considerations An interdisciplinary team approach to obtain optimal wheelchair positioning for a person with developmental disabilities involves a review of the diagnosis and prognosis and assessment of developmental level, skin condition, sensation, muscle strength and tone, reflexes, joint range of motion, and body dimensions, as well as special considerations such as respiratory status, unique feeding considerations, and the setting in which the wheelchair will be used. Early intervention with appropriate seating can decrease the risk of decubitus ulcers, postural deformities, joint contractures, atelectasis, aspiration, and hypotension. An effective seating system can improve mobility to allow the young child to interact with the environment. This enhances learning in the various developmental domains. An effective seating system for adults will affect sitting balance, mobility, transfers, daily activities, comfort, and appearance in a positive manner (Kreutz, 1993). RESNA (Rehabilitation Engineers of North America) is a national organization dedicated to developing state-of-the-art assistive technology. RESNA publications and conferences provide excellent orientation and education information that

nurses can incorporate into their practice settings.

The nurse who works with an individual with developmental disabilities who uses a wheelchair also should teach the individual and his or her family about the importance of using alternative positioning on a regular basis to relieve pressure and change posture. Pressure relief can be obtained by tilting the wheelchair in space, using the arms to lift the body and do pressure release exercises, or taking time out of the wheelchair. Any of these actions will be of benefit to the individual who is prone to skin breakdown secondary to immobility. Alternative positioning also changes body posture. This improves sitting tolerance and minimizes the impact of gravity on the development of kyphosis and scoliosis (Waugh & Bullard, 1992). The individual, his or her family, and the interdisciplinary team must develop, implement, and monitor an alternative positioning program. A good pressure relief program enables the individual to remain free of skin breakdown.

SUMMARY

The increasing use of technology in all areas of life is reflected in the range of medical and nonmedical adaptive technologies available to the person with developmental disabilities across the life span. Such devices include rapidly evolving medical adaptive technologies and supports such as light weight portable oxygen-retrieval devices that enhance mobility for individuals with compromised respiratory capacity. Adaptations of existing technology are now being designed to allow individuals with developmental disabilities more options in communication, mobility, leisure/recreational activities, computer access, environmental controls, and work skill tools (Arkwright, 1990). This chapter has identified some forms of medical and nonmedical technology available to individuals with developmental disabilities. We have attempted to identify the impact of technology usage on the individual and his or her family. The nurse, as a member of the interdisciplinary treating team, participates in the assessment of technology needs and brings the benefit of a health and wellness focus to the use of any technological devices. Nurses also educate individuals with developmental disabilities, their families, and program staff about the health implications of technology utilization. In educational and vocational settings the nurse works with the individual with developmental disabilities and his or her family, as well as the program staff, to successfully integrate technology that maintains or promotes healthiness into the person's daily routine. By obtaining feedback from the individual and/or his or her family about the impact of technology on the person's quality of life, the nurse acts as an advocate for the technologies that promote wellness, comfort, and optimal adaptive functioning for each individual with a developmental disability.

REFERENCES

Ahmann, E., & Lipsi, K.A. (1991). Early intervention for technology-dependent infants and young children. *Infants/Young Children, 3*(4), 67–77.

American Academy of Pediatrics (AAP), Committee on Children with Disabilities, Committee on School Health. (1990). Children with health impairments in schools. *Pediatrics, 86*(4), 636–637.

Arkwright, J.C. (1990). Adaptive devices for function. In B.A. Fraser, R.N. Hensinger, & J.N. Phelps, *Physical management of multiple handicaps: A professional's guide* (2nd ed.) (pp. 215–223). Baltimore: Paul H. Brookes Publishing Co.

Atkins, J.M., & Oakley, C.W. (1986). A nurse's guide to TPN. *RN, 49*(6), 20–24.

Augmentative Communication News. (1990). Vol. 3, no. 1. (Available from Gary K. Poock, Publisher, 1 Surf Way, #215, Monterey, CA 93940)

Banta, H.D. (1990). Technology assessment in health care. In A. Kovner (Ed.), *Health care delivery in the United States.* New York: Springer.

Batshaw, M.L., & Perret, Y.M. (1992). *Children with disabilities: A medical primer* (3rd ed.) Baltimore: Paul H. Brookes Publishing Co.

Behrman, M.M., & Lamm, L. (1983). Technology and handicapped babies: The future is now. *Communication Outlook, 5,* 4–6.

Behrman, R.E., & Vaughan, V.C. (1991). *Nelson textbook of pediatrics* (14th ed.). Philadelphia: W.B. Saunders.

Blackstone, S.W., & Painter, M.J. (1985). Speech problems in multihandicapped children. In J.K. Darby (Ed.), *Speech and language evaluation in neurology: Childhood disorders* (pp. 219–242). New York: Grune & Stratton.

Brady, M.E. (1988, March). *Implementing a service delivery program: Experiences in Pennsylvania.* Paper presented to the Annual Convention of the Council for Exceptional Children, Washington, DC.

Bunch, D. (1988). The respiratory patient as inventor. *American Association of Respiratory Care Times, 12*(8), 16–18.

Colatarci, S., & McConnell, J. (1991, June). *The use of music therapy in giving medical treatments to individuals with developmental disabilities.* Paper presented at the annual meeting of The American Association on Mental Retardation. Atlanta, GA.

Eddey, G., Newsome, L., Stringer, M., & Call, G. (1992, October). *Improving the quality of life for a person with dysphagia in a residential setting.* Paper presented at the annual meeting of the American Association on Mental Retardation, Annapolis, MD.

Fraser, B.A., Hensinger, R.N., & Phelps, J.A. (1990). *Physical management of multiple handicaps: A professional's guide* (2nd ed.). Baltimore: Paul H. Brookes Publishing Co.

Garner, J.B., & Campbell, P.H. (1987). Technology for persons with severe disabilities: Practical and ethical considerations. *Journal of Special Education, 21,* 122–132.

Haynie, M., Porter, S., & Palfrey, J.S. (1989). *Children assisted by medical technology in educational settings: Guidelines for care.* Boston: The Children's Hospital.

Huth, M.M., & O'Brien, M.E. (1991). The gastrostomy feeding button. *Pediatric Nursing, 13*(4), 243–245.

Kangas, K.A., & Lloyd, B. (1988). Early cognitive skills as prerequisites to augmentative and alternative communication use: What are we waiting for? In *Augmentative and Alternative Communication* (pp. 219–236). Baltimore: Williams & Wilkins.

Karchmer, M.A. (1985). A demographic perspective. In E. Cherow, N.D. Matkin, & R.J. Trybus (Eds.), *Hearing-impaired children and youth with developmental disabilities* (pp. 36–58). Washington, DC: Gallaudet University Press.

Kelly, M. (1993). Safe transport of technology dependent children. *Maternal Child Nursing, 18,* 29–31.

Khoury, M.J., Erickson, J.D., & James, L.M. (1982).

Etiologic heterogeneity of neural tube defects: clues from epidemiology, *American Journal of Epidemiology, 115,* 538–548.

Kreutz, D. (1993). Seating and positioning for the newly injured. *Rehabilitation Management, Dec./Jan.,* 67–83.

Levy, S.E., & Pilmer, S.L. (1992). The technology-assisted child. In M.L. Batshaw & Y.M. Perret, *Children with disabilities: A medical primer* (3rd ed.) (pp. 137–157). Baltimore: Paul H. Brookes Publishing Co.

Lozes, M.H. (1988). Bladder and bowel management for children with myelomeningocele. *Infant and Young Child, 1*(1), 52–62.

Matheny School and Hospital. (1993). *Matheny School and Hospital nursing department policy and procedure manual.* Peapack, NJ: Author.

Mitchell, M.E., & Rink, R.C. (1987). Pediatric urinary diversion and undiversion. *Pediatric Clinics of North America, 34,* 1319–1332.

Nelson, V.F., Leonard, J.A., Fisher, S.V., Esquenazi, A., & Hicks, J. (1989). Prosthetics, orthotics, and assistive devices. 2: Specialized seating and assistive devices. *Archives of Physical Medicine and Rehabilitation, 70,* 202–205.

Northern, J.L., & Downs, M.P. (1991). *Hearing in children* (4th ed.). Baltimore: Williams & Wilkins.

Office of Technology Assessment, Congress of the United States. (1987). *Technology-dependent children: Hospital v. home care—a technical memorandum* (OTA-TM-H-38). Washington, DC: U.S. Government Printing Office.

Orelove, F.P., & Sobsey, D. (1992). *Educating children with multiple disabilities: A transdisciplinary approach* (2nd ed.). Baltimore: Paul H. Brookes Publishing Co.

Parette, H.P. (1991). Use of technological assistance and families of young children with disabilities. *Psychological Supports, 68,* 773–774.

Pehringer, J.L. (1989). Assistive devices: Technology to improve communication. *Otolaryngologic Clinics of North America, 22*(1), 143–173.

Perry, M.A., & Hayes, N.M. (1988). Bronchopulmonary dysplasia: Discharge planning and complex home care, *Neonatal Network, 7*(3), 13–17.

Report to Congress and the Secretary by the Task Force on Technology-Dependent Children. (1988). *Fostering home and community-based care for technology-dependent children* (Vol. 2) (HCFA Pub. No. 88-0217. Washington, DC: U.S. Department of Health and Human Services.

Rombeau, J.L., & Caldwell, M.D. (1984). *Clinical nutrition. Volume one: Enteral and tube feeding.* Philadelphia: W.B. Saunders.

Sander, V., Murray, C., & Robertson, P. (1989). School and the in-center pediatric hemodialysis patient, *American Nephrology Nurses Associaton Journal, 16,* 72–79.

Soede, M. (1989). The use of information technology in rehabilitation: An overview of possibilities and new directions in applications. *Journal of Medical Engineering and Technology, 13*(1–2), 5–9.

Stanhope, M., & Lancaster, J. (1992). *Community health nursing: Process and practice for promoting health.* St. Louis: C.V. Mosby.

Walker, P. (1991). Where there is a way, there is not always a will: Technology, public policy, and the school integration of children who are technology-assisted. *Children's Health, 20*(2), 68–73.

Waugh, K., & Bullard, M. (1992). *Towards sitting the unsittable: Alternative therapeutic positioning equipment for the severely posturally challenged.* Paper presented at the 15th annual meeting of the Rehabilitation Engineers of North America, Washington, DC.

Whaley, L.F., & Wong, D.F. (1991). *Nursing care of infants and young children* (4th ed.). St. Louis: C.V. Mosby.

Wilhelm, L. (1985). Helping your patient "settle in" with TPN. *Nursing 85, 15*(4), 60–64.

Young, C.K., & White, S. (1992). Preparing patients for tube feedings at home. *American Journal of Nursing, April,* 46–53.

15

The Role of the Nurse as a Case Manager/Qualified Mental Retardation Professional

Deborah A. Natvig

OBJECTIVES

On completion of this chapter, the reader should be able to:

- Discuss the concept of case management as it is applied in the field of developmental disabilities.
- Describe how the knowledge and skills of professional nurses prepare them to be effective case managers.
- Describe the role of the case manager or qualified mental retardation professional in fulfilling the case management functions and responsibilities in residential and nonresidential settings.

OVERVIEW

Case management is a practice model that is ideal for assisting persons with developmental disabilities in meeting their health and daily living needs. It integrates planning, implementation, and evaluation of services that often are provided by more than one professional discipline or agency. A primary objective of case management is to enhance the continuity of care by eliminating overlap and preventing gaps in services provided. Two types of case management have been developed. In *clinical case management,* the case manager is involved in providing direct care to the individual and his or her family, as well as coordinating services provided by others. In the *brokerage case management* system, the case manager focuses on the coordination of services provided by others and does not have direct care responsibilities. Within the field of mental retardation, the case management role often is assumed by a professional designated as the qualified mental retardation professional (QMRP).

The case manager or QMRP works with other members of an interdisciplinary team in assisting individuals with developmental disabilities and their families to make decisions about how to meet the individual's needs most effectively. The interdisciplinary team develops a plan of care for the individual based on the assessments of the individual's strengths and needs (Gardner & Chapman, 1990). The case manager or QMRP is the member of the team responsible for integrating, coordinating, and monitoring each individual's plan of care (Natvig, 1991). The plan of care often is referred to as the individualized program plan (IPP), individualized habilitation plan (IHP), or individualized education program (IEP). For purposes of this chapter, the term IPP is used when referring to the plan developed by the interdisciplinary team.

This chapter discusses how the knowledge and skills of professional registered nurses prepare them to be effective case managers of QMRPs. It describes how integration and coordination of the interdisciplinary team can be accomplished through case management and illustrates the effective use of case management to meet the needs of individuals with developmental disabilities in both residential and nonresidential settings.

PROFESSIONAL NURSES AS CASE MANAGERS/QMRPS

If individuals with developmental disabilities are to benefit from the programs designed to assist them in achieving their true potential, it is necessary for them to be in the best health possible. It is important for the individual coordinating the IPP to understand what is needed for a person with developmental disabilities to attain a high level of health. When special health needs of the individual have underlying implications for other aspects of his or her activities, both the individual and the team may benefit if the case manager/QMRP is a professional registered nurse.

The nurse serves as a resource to other team members regarding health-related issues, just as the psychologist serves as a resource for psychological and behavioral issues. If the case manager/QMRP understands how health impacts and influences each individual's response to program opportunities and activities, a better IPP may result. For example, the individual's tolerance level for physical activity may be a significant issue in determining the most effective program of active treatment. The nurse case manager/QMRP would be able to guide the team in the selection of activities and programs that would meet the needs of the individual without compromising his or her physical capabilities. In addition, the nurse case manager/QMRP would be able to assess how well the individual was physically tolerating the program.

Although the term *case management* is relatively new, the concept is very similar to community health nursing, which is a recognized speciality in nursing practice. In community health nursing, the nurse works collaboratively with other members of the health care team to meet the needs of individuals. The community health nurse coordinates each individual's health care plan and works with the individual and other health care providers to enhance the continuity of care. Direct services may be provided by the community health nurse, or he or she may be instrumental in teaching a caregiver or family member how to provide the services needed. The nurse serves as an advocate by assisting the individual and his or her family to obtain services they may have difficulty procuring on their own. In addition, community health nurses educate other providers about the special needs of the individuals with whom they are working. This ongoing advocacy helps make human service systems more aware of and responsive to the special needs of certain groups of individuals in the community (Mudd & Cookfair, 1991).

Case Management Skills

In general, to monitor and coordinate an individual's IPP effectively, the case manager must be knowledgeable about human behavior and the process of growth and development. Awareness of social, behavioral, and health-related intervention techniques also strengthens one's ability to monitor and evaluate services. The case manager must have sufficient knowledge and experience to determine the appropriateness and quality of services provided to individuals with developmental disabilities. Because the case manager is responsible for procuring services once needs have been identified, he or she also must have knowledge of community resources and funding mechanisms available. Case managers often assume the role of chair of the interdisciplinary team, a role that requires skills in group process as well as knowledge of group dynamics. (See Russell & Free, chap. 3, this volume, for a discussion of the composition of an interdisciplinary team.) Skills that will facilitate effective written and verbal communication among team members, other service providers, and the individual and his or her family also are essential to effective case management.

Through his or her educational preparation, the professional registered nurse acquires knowledge and skills that are an integral part of the case management role. Nurses are among the few professionals who receive specific education in assessment, care planning, service delivery, discharge planning, evaluation, quality assurance, and leadership. Nurses have knowledge of acceptable documentation practices that enable them to develop and maintain monitoring and record-keeping systems, which can be used to track programs and progress involving individuals with complex health and medical needs.

Another benefit of having a nurse as a case manager/QMRP is that nurses have the ability to communicate with other health care providers. In addition, because they are familiar with terminology used by health care providers, nurses should be able to translate information from other health care providers into clear and understandable language for other members of the interdisciplinary team.

There are several ways in which the educational background, experience, and expertise of a professional registered nurse would be particularly beneficial in fulfilling the role and responsibilities of the case manager/QMRP. Some programs for which it is particularly beneficial to have a nurse as a case manager/QMRP include early intervention programs, programs for individuals who have complex medical needs and persons who have multiple disabilities, and programs designed to meet the needs of the aging individual.

Education and Experience Requirements

Recommendations and standards vary regarding the education and experience needed in order for a nurse to qualify as a case manager or QMRP. The American Nurses' Association recommends that nurse case managers have a baccalaureate degree and 3 years of appropriate clinical experience (Bower, 1992). The National Institute on Community-Based Long-Term Care (1988) proposes a minimum requirement of a 4-year college degree and 2 years' experience in human services.

The concept of the QMRP originated from the regulations governing intermediate care facilities for persons with mental retardation (ICFs/MR), promulgated in 1977 by the Health Care Financing Administration (HCFA). The concept is closely aligned with the case management concept used in nonresidential settings. In some instances, the term *QMRP* is used in nonresidential settings even though the ICF/MR regulations do not apply there. In an ICF/MR, case management generally is provided by QMRPs. The HCFA (1988) provided qualification guidelines for QMRPs that must be met if the facility is receiving federal funding. To become a QMRP, the professional must have a bachelor's degree in a human services field or be licensed as a doctor of medicine, registered nurse, physical or occupational therapist, social worker, speech pathologist or audiologist, or dietitian. In addition, the professional must have at least 1 year of experience working directly with persons with mental retardation (HCFA, 1988). Because individuals with various educational backgrounds may be licensed as registered nurses, some programs consider only those nurses with a 4-year baccalaureate degree as meeting the qualifications of the QMRP. In some programs, a nurse without a baccalaureate degree can be employed as a QMRP but carry out only some of the case management functions as part of his or her job.

CASE MANAGEMENT AND THE INTERDISCIPLINARY TEAM

The involvement of an interdisciplinary team working together to meet an indi-vidual's needs is not a new concept in nursing. Henderson's (1966) conceptual model for nursing is based on the assumption that the nurse is an active member of an interdisciplinary health care team. This team, which includes the individual needing assistance and his or her family, develops a plan of care designed to meet the needs of the individual. The purpose of the care plan is to assist the individual to perform basic activities of daily living (ADLs), or to provide an environment in which he or she can perform ADLs unaided. Henderson (1966) suggested that each individual should be encouraged and allowed to live as normal a life as possible. This model of nursing is consistent with the principle of normalization (Wolfensberger, 1980), which serves as an underlying philosophy of service delivery for individuals with mental retardation.

Figure 1 illustrates how the members of the interdisciplinary team relate to one another. Each petal of the flower represents a member of the team. The largest part of each petal represents the role and function that is unique to each professional discipline or team member. In addition, there are many areas in which team members have similar education, training, or experience. The overlapping sections of the petals represent the roles and functions that may be carried out by team members from more than one area of expertise (Creekmur, DeFelice, Doub, Hodel, & Petty, 1989). The center of the flower depicts how the unique and overlapping roles of each team member come together into one client-centered plan designed to meet an individual's needs in a holistic manner.

The primary role of the nurse on the interdisciplinary team is to ensure that the 14 fundamental needs of the individual identified by Henderson (1966) are met. These 14 needs reflect physiological, psychological, social, cultural, behavioral, and environmental aspects of

Figure 1.   The overlapping relationships of team members of interdisciplinary health care teams. (Adapted from Adam [1983]).

health (Table 1). According to Henderson (1966), the goal of nursing is to encourage independence of the individual by increasing his or her level of understanding and knowledge of his or her own potential. In cases in which the individual will continue to be assisted by a family member or other care provider, the nurse strives to give these caregivers the knowledge and skills necessary to function as independently as possible in providing that care. Case management provides a means to achieve this goal while addressing the individual's fundamental needs.

In clinical case management situations, the nurse case manager/QMRP would be involved directly in providing the care needed in order for the individ-

Table 1.   Fundamental needs of all individuals that reflect the physiological, social, cultural, behavioral, and environmental aspects of health

1. Breathe normally.
2. Eat and drink adequately.
3. Eliminate body wastes.
4. Move and maintain desirable positions.
5. Sleep and rest.
6. Select suitable clothes; dress and undress.
7. Maintain body temperature within normal range by adjusting clothing and modifying the environment.
8. Keep body clean and well groomed and protect the integument.
9. Avoid dangers in the environment and avoid injuring others.
10. Communicate with others in expressing emotions, needs, fears, or opinions.
11. Worship according to one's faith.
12. Work in such a way that there is a sense of accomplishment.
13. Play or participate in various forms of recreation.
14. Learn, discover, or satisfy the curiosity that leads to normal development and health and the use of available health facilities.

ual to meet his or her fundamental needs. In a brokerage case management system, the nurse case manager/QMRP would contract with the nurse on the interdisciplinary team to provide the direct care services needed.

IMPLEMENTATION OF CASE MANAGEMENT

The purpose of case management is to make the service delivery system more effective and to ensure that individuals receive assistance that is responsive to their needs (National Institute on Community-Based Long-Term Care, 1988). The primary components of case management are: 1) assessment, 2) planning, 3) implementation (procurement, delivery, and coordination of services), 4) monitoring, and 5) evaluation and reassessment. Table 2 describes the purpose of these components, with a brief explanation of what is included in each. Although all of the components of case management are essential in providing quality programs, the focus here is on implementation.

Service delivery programs vary depending on the needs of the individuals being served and the aims and objectives of their IPPs. Although programs may vary, the components of case management are common to each, and the roles of the nurse case manager/QMRP are similar. A primary role of the nurse case manager/QMRP is the coordination of services provided by families, professionals, and agencies that are necessary to meet the individual's needs. Other roles of the nurse case manager/QMRP include advocacy, counseling, gatekeeping, and recordkeeping.

Service Coordination

Coordination of services provided by the interdisciplinary team is one of the primary responsibilities of the nurse case manager/QMRP. It is important that the techniques and procedures developed to help the individual and his or her family are used in a consistent manner. This consistency should be demonstrated from one provider to another, and from one time of day to the next. For example, if an individual is learning to feed himself or herself, the same procedures should be followed during all meals, both in the day program setting and in the home. Also, when possible, services should build on the individual's strengths and progress in a developmental sequence. Proper sequencing of assessments, services, and client training will maximize the time spent by the client, his or her caregivers, and special service providers. Finally, the case manager should ensure that all professionals and service providers are working toward the same goals and are aware of the approach being taken by the other providers. In this way, programs from one discipline can

Table 2.   Components of case management

Responsibilities	Purpose	Areas of consideration
Assess	Determine the functional level and/or impairments. Identify strengths and needs.	Physical, cognitive, social, developmental, and emotional aspects of the individual
Plan	Development of an IPP.	Specific goals and objectives to be achieved
Implement	Ensure linkage between strategies and outcomes.	Implementation of the IPP in an organized, cost-efficient manner
Monitor	Observe and review progress.	Observing the individual, documentation review, and working with caregivers
Evaluate	Determine the effectiveness/ appropriateness of services.	Measuring the progress in attaining the individual's goals, documentation of progress, and revision of IPP if needed

build on and support the programs from another discipline. This also will reduce the likelihood that the individual will be exposed to programs that do not complement, and may even conflict with, one another.

Scheduling One aspect of service coordination may include scheduling appointments for the individual with developmental disabilities. In order for assessments and services to be of maximum benefit to the individual, the individual's schedule and tolerance level should be taken into account. For some individuals, participating in more than one or two activities in one day may overtax their strength, energy, and ability to absorb what is being presented. For these individuals, the plan of care may be more effective if the services and activities are spread throughout the week rather than being provided all on one day.

In some cases, specialty services are not always readily available and the individual may have to travel in order to receive some services. The individual or his or her family also may have other commitments that prevent them from making several, more frequent appointments. For these individuals, it may be necessary to schedule as many services as possible in one day. When this occurs, every effort should be made to schedule the appointments so that those needing maximum response and cooperation from the individual are at a time when he or she is best able to participate.

Because some professional resources are scarce, difficult to obtain, and expensive, the proper utilization of the professional's time is also important. If assessments and services are completed in the proper sequences, the individual will benefit and the professional will be able to provide services in the most time-efficient manner possible. Lack of coordination may result in return visits, incomplete services, or ineffective services because the individual had not completed the requisites necessary in order for the next stage of service to be effective.

Assuring Relevance and Quality of Services A well-coordinated, high-quality plan will demonstrate consisten-

---

Yvonne, an alert and cheerful young girl with mental retardation, has just been diagnosed as having cerebral palsy. Her physician requests that Yvonne be evaluated by a physical therapist, occupational therapist, and speech-language pathologist. Because the therapists' offices are in close proximity to one another, the nurse case manager schedules all three appointments for one afternoon. At each of the appointments, the therapist does a thorough assessment and presents Yvonne's mother with a series of exercises or activities that are to be performed daily. Yvonne, who normally naps in the afternoon, becomes increasing irritable and uncooperative as the afternoon progresses. The speech-language assessment is scheduled as the last appointment of the day, and the therapist has an extremely difficult time because Yvonne is tired and therefore uncooperative. By the end of the day both Yvonne and her mother are tired and confused and able to absorb little of the information presented to them. In addition, because of her fatigue, the assessments completed by the therapists do not reflect Yvonne's true abilities or potential. If Yvonne's appointments had been scheduled for mornings and spread out over several days, the results may have been far more accurate and satisfying to Yvonne, her mother, and the therapists.

Rasul, a young man with mental retardation, does not seem to be responding as he should to verbal cues and instructions. The team thinks that Rasul may have a hearing impairment. Rasul's special education teacher makes arrangements for Rasul to have his hearing tested by an audiologist. When he arrives for his appointment, the audiologist finds an excessive buildup of earwax in Rasul's ear canals, which prevents proper testing. The appointment must be rescheduled to allow time for the earwax to be removed. If the nurse case manager had been able to examine and clean Rasul's ears prior to his appointment with the audiologist, the hearing tests could have been performed during the first appointment, saving time, money, and frustration. In addition, Rasul would have obtained the services he needed without unnecessary delay.

cy, proper sequencing of assessments and services, and high-quality services that are relevant to the individual. The need for coordination of services in acute care, community-based, and residential settings has become more evident as the demand for containing costs and providing more comprehensive services has increased. The case manager must be aware of professional and community resources that are available to the individual. In addition, he or she should be able to determine if the services provided are of high quality and appropriate for the individual. Table 3 presents a checklist of questions that may be considered when determining the quality of services being provided.

In many instances, a professional with broad general knowledge is considered the best person to be the case manager. Because the case manager is considered the generalist on the team, the level of quality may be difficult to determine, particularly if the service provided is highly specialized. For individuals with more intense or specific needs, the case manager may be more effective if he or she is knowledgeable about how to meet the specific needs of the individual. Expertise in the area of concern will help the case manager determine whether appropriate services are being provided, and if the individual is progressing in a satisfactory manner. In instances in which the primary needs of the individual are health related, the nurse may be the most appropriate professional to serve as the case manager.

Gatekeeping

Another role of the nurse case manager/ QMRP is to obtain services in the most cost-effective manner possible. This role is referred to as gatekeeping. As the gatekeeper, the nurse case manager/

Table 3. Case managers' checklist for assessing quality of services

	Yes	No
1. Are services provided on a timely basis in accordance with the written plan?		
2. Is the individual and his or her family satisfied with the approach taken and do they feel the services are relevant to the individual's needs?		
3. Is the progress or lack of progress made by the individual addressed by the service provider?		
4. If the individual is not making satisfactory progress, does the service provider initiate alternative methods and techniques?		
5. Is the feedback from other professionals on the team regarding the services provided to the individual positive?		
6. Is there consensus and general agreement among members of the interdisciplinary team about the overall progress of the individual and the need to maintain or modify services?		

QMRP should evaluate the cost of a service relative to its amount and quality. Theoretically, case management will reduce cost of care by linking the individual with appropriate providers and thereby eliminate wasted or unneeded services (Franklin, Solovitz, Mason, Clemons, & Miller, 1987).

The nurse should realize that the initiation of a case management program does not always result in the least expensive service delivery model. For example, in a study by Franklin et al. (1987), a program was implemented to determine whether case management would reduce hospital admissions, increase utilization of community-based resources, affect cost, and improve the quality of life of individuals with chronic mental health problems. Because of the comprehensive nature of case management, more services were provided after the case management model was implemented. The total cost of services therefore increased. Another study also found that the cost of services increased when case management programs were initiated (Kemper, 1990). In this study, however, it was determined that a high percentage of the costs were related to the initial enrollment functions of outreach, screening, assessment, and care planning. After the individual was part of the case management system, the cost of ongoing services was reduced by 75%.

Advocacy

Although the interdisciplinary team strives to provide integrated, comprehensive services, the case manager is the only member of the team who has been given the primary responsibility of being aware of the "whole" individual (Intagliata, 1982). Therefore it is the case manager who must act as an advocate to ensure that the focus of team efforts remains on the individual and his or her needs.

The nurse case manager/QMRP must remain in regular contact with the individual, carefully monitoring his or her status. This allows for communication of crucial information (Intagliata, 1982) and permits the case manager to remain sensitive to the changing needs of the individual. If appropriate services are not being provided, the case manager has the responsibility as the individual's advocate to determine if the current situation can be improved, and, if not, seek out another way to obtain the services.

Additionally, the nurse case manager/QMRP should identify and work to remove any barriers that are restricting the services needed. These barriers may include such things as limited availability of professional resources, service providers who are not willing to provide services to individuals with developmental disabilities in the same manner as individuals without developmental disabilities, and financial resources that limit the amount and quality of services that can be purchased. In addition to serving as an advocate for an individual or group of individuals, the nurse case manager/QMRP should also teach individuals and their families to become their own advocates (Morse, chap. 2, this volume).

Counseling

The case manager is often one of the first people contacted in a crisis situation. The nurse case manager/QMRP may need to give emotional support in addition to the other services he or she arranges. Counseling may be provided to the individual who has developmental disabilities or it can focus on giving support to the family or caregivers.

Recordkeeping

Recordkeeping requirements will vary from program to program, and the nurse case manager/QMRP must be knowledgeable about all aspects of the recordkeeping system. The essential components

Jeremy Evans is a sandy-haired 28-year-old young man who lives with his parents in a middle-class neighborhood. Although he has mental retardation, cerebral palsy, and diabetes, Jeremy continually strives to remain as independent as possible. He and his family have worked diligently in order for Jeremy to continue to live at home.

Jeremy's father built ramps, enlarged doorways, and remodeled bathrooms to make their entire house accessible to Jeremy and his large electric wheelchair. Mr. Evans purchased a van with a lift to make it easier for Jeremy to travel. Although Mr. Evans was concerned about Jeremy, his role had always been that of chauffeur, carpenter, and social companion. He had never become involved in Jeremy's physical care.

Jeremy's mother was the primary caregiver for Jeremy. She was skilled at special meal preparations, adjusting insulin needs, providing range-of-motion exercises, and working with Jeremy on his new electronic communication system and programs recommended by the speech therapist. Jeremy's care encompassed her life, and she felt his progress was her reward.

Mrs. Evans suddenly became ill and was rushed to the hospital. The initial report was that she would be in the hospital between 2 and 3 weeks and would need to restrict her activity for at least 6 months after she returned home. With Mrs. Evans hospitalized, Jeremy's health care needs became an immediate concern and problem for his father. Mr. Evans contacted Larraine Anderson, R.N., who was Jeremy's case manager, for assistance.

Ms. Anderson was able to arrange for immediate respite care for Jeremy in an approved foster home for individuals with complex medical needs. Because the foster care workers already had been trained in meeting basic health care needs, Ms. Anderson focused her attention on teaching them about Jeremy's diet, exercise program, electronic communication system, and speech programs. Ms. Anderson also arranged for a licensed nurse to administer Jeremy's insulin each day.

Before taking Jeremy to the foster home, Ms. Anderson carefully explained to Jeremy what had happened to his mother, the changes that were being made in his life, and what he might expect during the next few weeks. Ms. Anderson visited Jeremy frequently to monitor his progress and help him adjust to the changes that had occurred. She remained in close contact with Jeremy's father not only to keep abreast of Mrs. Evans' progress but also to reassure Mr. Evans that, although Jeremy missed daily contact with his parents, he was adjusting well. As Mrs. Evans regained her strength, Ms. Anderson met with Mr. and Mrs. Evans to discuss the options available to them regarding Jeremy's future.

Although long-term residential placement could have been pursued, the Evanses remained steadfast in their commitment that Jeremy should live with them in their home. Ms. Anderson worked out arrangements that would allow Jeremy to come home after Mrs. Evans had regained enough strength. A part-time housekeeper was hired and taught to prepare Jeremy's special diet and assist him in his activities of daily living. Arrangements were made with a day program to take over responsibility for much of Jeremy's exercise and speech and communication programs. Mr. Evans was taught the basics of Jeremy's care and was able to assist him when the housekeeper was not available. A nurse came in to give Jeremy his insulin the

(continued)

first week that Jeremy was home, and after that Mrs. Evans was able to take care of Jeremy's insulin needs.

Throughout the entire process, Ms. Anderson visited frequently to offer encouragement and support and to assess how well the Evanses were coping with the situation. The option of short-term respite services was kept open to the Evanses in the event the situation became too taxing for them. With the combination of in-home assistance and the support and guidance that Ms. Anderson was able to give them, Jeremy was able to remain at home with his parents.

that should be a part of all systems include a written IPP, progress reports, and evidence of periodic evaluation of the plan, including reassessment of the individual's needs. As discussed earlier, the IPP should be based on assessments completed by all members of the team. The specific services to be provided, when they will be provided, and by whom should be documented clearly in the IPP. The progress of the individual should be documented by those providing direct care or therapy, as well as by the nurse case manager/QMRP. Periodically, written evaluations of the IPP should be completed that address the continued relevance of the plan, the progress the individual is making in meeting the goals, and the need for modification. Any revisions of or additions to the IPP must be documented clearly.

USE OF CASE MANAGEMENT IN THE PROGRAM SETTING

It is essential that case management services be designed specifically to meet the needs of persons with developmental disabilities in a variety of settings. These include community-based residences where individuals live independently, semi-independently, or with family members. Other individuals may live in larger residential settings where case managers have integral roles. To discuss how case management is utilized in the field of

developmental disabilities, two types of programs are used as examples. First, case management in residential settings (ICFs/MR) is examined. Next, case management for services provided in non-residential, community-based programs are reviewed.

Residential Programs

An ICF/MR generally utilizes a more administrative approach to case management, referred to as the brokerage system. In this system, the QMRP, who is the case manager in the ICF/MR setting, provides case management services but no direct care or therapy (Lamb, 1980; Maurin, 1990). For example, if the QMRP in this system is a nurse and direct nursing care is needed, the QMRP would arrange for nursing services to be provided by a nurse on the interdisciplinary team rather than perform the services directly. In reviewing the various roles of the case manager that are assumed by the QMRP in an ICF/MR, coordination of services, advocacy, counseling, and recordkeeping are the most prominent. Because ICFs/MR have direct care staff on duty 24 hours a day, and either have professionals on their staff or have contractual agreements for professional services, the QMRP is less involved in gatekeeping than are case managers in other settings. In an ICF/MR, the gatekeeping functions generally are assumed by an administrator.

The interdisciplinary team identifies specific training programs to be implemented and makes referrals for additional services or evaluations that are to be obtained. The QMRP has the responsibility to see that programs identified in the IPP and other recommendations made by the team are implemented. Some programs may be implemented by the professional staff who made the original assessments. More frequently, however, the directions for program implementation will be developed and written by professional staff and implemented by direct care staff. Direct care staff must be trained so that programs can be carried out on a consistent basis. The QMRP may be involved directly in providing training to staff or ensuring that the staff training occurs.

To coordinate the delivery of active treatment across all program areas, the QMRP must visit residential areas and program sites. The QMRP observes the interaction between staff and the individual as well as the individual's response to his or her training programs. At each site, the QMRP serves as a resource to staff and assists them in learning new approaches and training techniques. Minor adjustments may be made in programs as a result of ongoing monitoring of the individual by the QMRP. The observations made by the QMRP also are shared with the other members of the interdisciplinary team so modifications in the IPP can be made if needed.

The QMRP also provides follow-up services for team recommendations and program referrals for services that must be obtained outside the ICF/MR. The QMRP may reconvene the team so that decisions can be made about new information that has been obtained from outside referrals.

Programs for the Aging Individual

It is estimated that currently there are over 315,000 individuals with develop-mental disabilities over the age of 65 in the United States and that, by the year 2020, the number will exceed 526,000 (Nutt & Malone, 1992). These individuals share the same concerns about aging as other members of the population. Their need for case management services may be increased because they generally will not have a spouse or children on whom they can depend for support or assistance (Cowan & Millsap, 1988).

Nurses traditionally have been involved in care of the aging population because of the developmental decline in functional ability and the concurrent increase in physical frailty common in this population. Exposure to community health nursing practice and long-term nursing care situations prepares nurses to manage the problems and challenges that must be met in providing comprehensive care for aging individuals. A nurse case manager/QMRP will be able to identify approaches to care that will contribute to the maintenance of the physical and cognitive capabilities of the individual.

It is anticipated that the average age of individuals living in ICFs/MR will be increasingly older during the next decades (Gardner & Chapman, 1990). As this population ages, program practices and services will need to be refined to reflect the special needs of aging individuals. The nurse case manager/QMRP will be able to guide the team in developing programs and activities that take into account the physiological changes that occur with aging. Attention to daily orientation may enhance the individual's ability to maintain his or her cognitive skills at their optimal level. For example, a morning awareness program may be implemented wherein the individuals are brought together in small groups or one-to-one with staff. Daily topics of interest are discussed, and basic information about the events that are to occur during the day are reviewed.

This program will give the elderly individuals time to relax and "get their bearings" before other scheduled activities for the day begin. It also gives staff an opportunity to assess each individual for subtle changes that may be occurring.

The nurse case manager/QMRP also will be able to guide the team in determining the amount and type of physical activity in which the individual should be encouraged to participate. Some individuals may need to have their activity paced throughout the day or week, whereas others may have to be encouraged to increase their physical activity in order to maintain their health.

Nonresidential Programs

In nonresidential community-based programs, an individual who has developmental disabilities lives independently, semi-independently, or with his or her family. This individual may enter the case management system through a variety of mechanisms, including referral from a physician, public health nurse, school, family, or friends. The continuum of services available in community-based programs may include prenatal and at-risk pregnancy services, early childhood services, services for the school-age youngster, young adult services, and services that meet the special needs of the aging population. To include all these services, active outreach programs must be available with information referral systems that are well known and easily used.

Home-Based Programs for Persons with Complex Medical Needs

Programs for individuals with complex medical and health-related needs often are provided in residential programs designed for individuals with mental retardation. There are many individuals, however, who are able to remain in their family home or foster home with the assistance of case management services. For those individuals, the case manager helps determine the direct care and professional services that must be provided in the home environment.

A nurse is particularly effective in the case management role for these individuals because their complex medical needs often call for a variety of specialized health services. The nurse's education and background enables him or her to communicate effectively with the health care specialists on the team. The nurse case manger is able to interpret findings and incorporate the services needed into a workable plan for the family, school, or day program setting. In the school or program setting, the nurse case manager also may serve as a member of the interdisciplinary team to ensure that continuity of health care services is provided in the school or program environment.

The nurse, as a health care generalist, serves as a resource to the family. Because many of these individual have special equipment needs, the nurse case manager may assist the family in selecting and purchasing equipment. Accompanying the individual to doctor's appointments or providing follow-up services after appointments also may be a significant role for the nurse case manager caring for individuals with complex medical needs.

One of the factors that may determine if an individual can remain in the family home or a community-based environment is whether or not adequate medical and health-related resources are available. As the case manager, the nurse can be instrumental in identifying and obtaining services from qualified service providers. For persons with complex medical needs, the gatekeeping role of the case manager is prominent.

Case managers need extensive knowledge of the services available in the community to be effective. In addition, because services from individual providers

Cynthia is a vibrant 10-year-old girl with mental retardation. Although nonverbal, Cynthia communicates her satisfaction and displeasure through facial expressions. Positive responses from Cynthia are characterized by her beautiful smile and dancing eyes. Cynthia has partial paralysis of her arms and legs, a gastrostomy feeding tube, and a tracheostomy. She lives at home with her parents and attends the local elementary school, where she also receives physical therapy and meets regularly with the speech therapist to improve her communication skills. The school nurse visits Cynthia daily to give her anticonvulsant medication.

Tanya Long, R.N., Cynthia's case manager, is actively involved in coordinating Cynthia's care. Because of the complexity of Cynthia's medical problems, Cynthia is seen by numerous medical specialists. Mrs. Long helps Cynthia's mother arrange for medical and other health-related evaluations and often accompanies Cynthia and her mother to appointments. Mrs. Long assists Cynthia and her parents by acting as a liaison between the medical specialists and Cynthia's interdisciplinary team at school. This team is comprised of a physical therapist, a speech therapist, the school nurse, Cynthia's teachers, and other classroom caregivers. Mrs. Long ensures that information is transmitted accurately, programs and procedures are carried out correctly, and follow-up consultation visits are made. Prior to medical appointments, Mrs. Long confers with members of Cynthia's team at school. Mrs. Long then is able to relay to medical specialists information that accurately reflects Cynthia's current status at school and to ensure that specific concerns of the team are shared with the physician. Following the medical appointments, Mrs.Long also meets with the team to share with them the results of the visit and help them incorporate necessary changes into Cynthia's care plan. If necessary, Mrs. Long also provides training to caregivers on new procedures that have been incorporated into Cynthia's care plan.

Because Cynthia's overall level of care is more complex than that of other children in school, Mrs. Long has helped identify special equipment needed for her care. The school purchased suctioning equipment needed for Cynthia based on the documentation provided by Mrs. Long that explained Cynthia's complex health care needs. Mrs. Long's ability to communicate with health care professionals and interpret the findings of specialists to Cynthia's family and interdisciplinary team at the school has enabled Cynthia to receive coordinated health care services. Mrs. Long's background in nursing has been instrumental in Cynthia receiving the care she needs while living at home and attending school.

often must be purchased, with the growing cost of health care, services and systems for reimbursement must be evaluated carefully. The case manager must be familiar with Medicaid, private insurance, and the state and local funding mechanisms that are used to fund services.

The case manager in the nonresidential community system may be an individual in a branch of the human services system that is part of the state government. In other instances, the state government has contracted these services out to private vendors or organizations. Occasionally, there may be more than one organization working with the individual that can provide case management services. In those instances, one organization should be designated as having responsibility for the case management services. If this does not occur, services may become fragmented and the original intent of the case management concept will be defeated.

Although there may be a variety of agencies providing services to the individual, one agency usually is designated as having primary responsibility. The case manager generally works for that agency. If the agency focuses on clinical case management, the case manager will have in-depth clinical knowledge and the skills to provide assessment and therapy or services directly to the individual. Additionally, the clinical case manager coordinates services provided by others. The brokerage system also may be employed, whereby the case manager provides no direct care services but provides the other case management functions of coordinator, advocate, counselor, recordkeeper, and gatekeeper.

It may be beneficial to have a nurse as the case manager for individuals participating in some types of nonresidential community programs. For example, case managers for individuals in early intervention programs need a strong background in health to meet the needs of the individual and his or her family. As a clinical case manager, the nurse is equipped to complete developmental assessments. The nurse provides direct nursing care to the child and family in areas of counseling, health care teaching, nutritional management, and growth and development. The nurse case manager identifies and coordinates the services that are provided by other members of the interdisciplinary team. When the nurse case manager functions as a broker in a nonresidential case management system, the direct nursing care responsibilities are delegated to another nurse and the gatekeeping role becomes more evident.

SUMMARY

Case management can improve the continuity and quality of services provided to individuals with developmental disabilities. Professional nurses have an excellent background to provide case management services, particularly to those individuals with significant health-related problems or needs. Individuals receiving case management services may be receiving services in a residential program or a nonresidential community-based program. In community-based programs, the individual may live independently, semi-independently, or in the family home. In any of these settings, case managers are often referred to as QMRPs.

Depending on the focus of the case management program, the nurse case manager may provide clinical case management services or brokerage case management services. A primary responsibility of the nurse case manager in either situation is coordinating the plan of care developed by the interdisciplinary team. In addition to coordinating the IPP, the nurse case manager often assumes the role of counselor, advocate, recordkeeper, and gatekeeper.

REFERENCES

Bower, K.A. (1992). *Case management by nurses.* Washington, DC: American Nurses Publications.

Cowan, M.K., & Millsap, M. (1988). The developmentally disabled population. In M. Stanhope & J. Lancaster (Eds.), *Community health nursing: Process and practice for promoting health* (pp. 519–538). St. Louis: C.V. Mosby.

Creekmur, T., DeFelice, J., Doub, M.S., Hodel, A., & Petty, C. (1989). Evelyn Adam: Conceptual model for nursing. In A. Marriner-Tomey (Ed.), *Nursing theorists and their work* (2nd ed., pp. 133–145). St. Louis: C.V. Mosby.

Franklin, J.L., Solovitz, B., Mason, M., Clemons, J.R., & Miller, G.E. (1987). An evaluation of case management. *American Journal of Public Health, 77,* 674–678.

Gardner, J.F., & Chapman, M.S. (1990). *Program issues in developmental disabilities: A guide to effective habilitation and active treatment* (2nd ed.). Baltimore: Paul H. Brookes Publishing Co.

Health Care Financing Administration. (1988, October). *State operations manual. Provider certification: Appendix J. Interpretive guidelines for ICFs/MR.* Washington, DC: Author.

Henderson, V. (1966). *The nature of nursing: A definition and its implications for practice, research, and education.* New York: Macmillan.

Intagliata, J. (1982). Improving the quality of community care for the chronically mentally disabled: The role of case management. *Schizophrenia Bulletin, 8,* 655–674.

Kemper, P. (1990). Case management agency systems of administering long-term care: Evidence from the Channeling Demonstration. *The Gerontologist, 30,* 817–824.

Lamb, H.R. (1980). Therapist case-managers: More than brokers of services. *Hospital and Community Psychiatry, 3,* 762–764.

Maurin, J.T. (1990). Case management: Caring for psychiatric patients. *Journal of Psychosocial Nursing, 28*(7), 6–12.

Mudd, T.M., & Cookfair, J.M. (1991). Developmentally disabled persons in the community. In J.M. Cookfair (Ed.), *Nursing process and practice in the community* (pp. 485–510). St. Louis: C.V. Mosby.

National Institute on Community-Based Long-Term Care. (1988). *Care management standards: Standards for practice.* Washington, DC: National Council on Aging.

Natvig, D.A. (1991). The role of the interdisciplinary team in the use of psychotropic drugs. *Journal of Psychosocial Nursing and Mental Health Services, 29*(10), 3–8.

Nutt, L.M., & Malone, M. (1992). Gerontology. In P.J. McGaughlin & P. Wehman (Eds.), *Developmental disabilities: A handbook for best practices* (pp. 277–297). Boston: Andover Medical Publishers.

Wolfensberger, W. (1980). A brief overview of the principles of normalization. In R.J. Flynn & K.E. Nitsch (Eds.), *Normalization, social integration, and community services* (pp. 7–30). Baltimore: University Park Press.

Appendix
Resources Across the Life Span

Linda J. Ross

This appendix is intended as a resource guide for parents and professionals. Nurses can use these listings as a referral source for individuals with developmental disabilities and their families, and can access the professional organizations listed for information useful in their personal practice. The first two sections are a compilation of organizations that provide a wide range of services to individuals with developmental disabilities and their families. The first section provides listings of national organizations that can supply general information and services; organizations that may be more useful at the state and local level are listed in the second section. Another source for assistance is the state or province library association. Checking with local groups is helpful for listings of books, videos, and other materials.

This is a representative rather than inclusive listing of resources. New resources for special interest groups are emerging constantly, so that one telephone call to an organization can lead to referrals to other resources. An attempt has been made to make this listing as current as possible, with the realization that there is constant change.

The third section lists various organizations that provide information and services to professionals working with persons with developmental disabilities and their families. These resources can be of valuable assistance to those nurses who are not specialists in developmental disabilities but need additional information to provide enhanced services to some individuals in their practice settings.

SELECTED NATIONAL ORGANIZATIONS

Accessibility
The Association for Persons with Severe Handicaps (TASH)
7010 Roosevelt Way, NE
Seattle, WA 98115
(206)523-8446
TDD: (206)524-6198

Barrier-Free Design Centre
2075 Bayview Avenue
Toronto, ON M4N 3M5
CANADA
(416)480-6000
FAX: (416)480-6009

National Association of Protection and Advocacy Systems (NAPAS)
900 Second Street, NE
Suite 211
Washington, DC 20002
(202)408-9514
TTD: (202)546-8206
FAX: (202)408-9520

Protection and Advocacy, Inc.
230 North Maryland Avenue
Suite 107
Glendale, CA 91206
(818)546-1631

The Research and Training Center for Accessible Housing
North Carolina State University
School of Design
Box 8613
Raleigh, NC 27695-8613
(919)515-3082

U.S. Architectural and Transportation Barriers Compliance Board
1331 F Street, NW
Suite 1000
Washington, DC 20004
(202)272-5434
FAX: (202)272-5447

Adaptive Equipment and Technology

Alliance for Technology Access Parent-Run Resource Centers
1307 Solano Avenue
Albany, CA 94706-1888
(415)528-0747
or
Massachusetts Avenue
Lexington, MA 02173
(617)863-9966

Bulter
P. O. Box T
Hewitt, NJ 07421
(800)736-2216
(201)853-6585

Center for Applied Special Technology (CAST)
39 Cross Street
Peabody, MA 01960
(508)531-8555

PAM Assistance Centre
601 West Maple Street
Lansing, MI 48906
(517)371-5897
(800)274-7426

Rehabilitation Engineering Society of North America (RESNA)
1101 Connecticut Avenue, NW
Suite 700
Washington, DC 20036
(202)857-1199
FAX: (202)223-4579

Toys for Special Children
385 Warburton Avenue
Hastings-on-Hudson, NY 10706
(914)478-0960

Adoption

Adopt a Special Kid
3530 Grand Avenue
Oakland, CA 94619
(510)451-1748

Adoptive Families of America
3333 Highway 100N
Minneapolis, MN 55422
(612)535-4829

Children's Adoption Support Services
1039 Evarts Street, NE
Washington, DC 20017
(202)362-3264

National Adoption Center
1500 Walnut Street
Suite 701,
Philadelphia, PA 19102
(215)735-9988
(800)TO-ADOPT
FAX: (215)735-9410

National Adoption Information
11426 Rockville Pike
Suite 410
Rockville, MD 20852
(301)231-6512

AIDS

National AIDS Hotline
(800)342-AIDS
(800)342-2437
(800)344-SIDA
(800)344-7232 (Spanish access)
deaf access (800)AIDS-TTY (800)243-7889

National AIDS Information Clearinghouse
P. O. Box 6003
Rockville, MD 20850
(800)458-5231
TTY/TTD: (800)243-7012

Project STAR
1800 Columbus Avenue
Roxbury, MA 02119
(617)442-7442

Aging

Alzheimer's Alternative Resources Center
230 5th Avenue
Suite 607
New York, NY 10001
(212)980-4280

Alzheimer's Disease and Related Disorders Association (ADRDA)
70 East Lake Street
6th Floor
Chicago, IL 60601
(800)621-0379

Alzheimer's Disease Education and Referral Center
P. O. Box 8250
Silver Spring, MD 20907-8250
(800)438-4380
FAX: (301)587-4352

Alzheimer's Resource Center of New York
280 Broadway
Room 213
New York, NY 10007
(212)442-3086
FAX: (212)442-3162

American Association of Retired Persons (AARP)
601 E Street, NW
Washington, DC 20049
(202)434-2277

National Association of Area Agencies on Aging (NAAAA)
1112 16th Street, NW
Suite 100
Washington, DC 20036
(202)296-8130
FAX: (202)296-8134

Alcohol and Drug Abuse

The Clearinghouse for Drug Exposed Children
400 Parnassus Avenue
Room A203
San Francisco, CA 94143-0314
(415)476-9691

Fetal Alcohol Syndrome Network
7802 SE Taylor
Portland, OR 97215
(503)246-2635

National Association for Perinatal Addiction Research and Education (NAPARE)
11 East Hubbard Street
Suite 200
Chicago, IL 60611
(312)329-2512
FAX: (312)329-9131

Resource Center on Substance Abuse— Prevention and Disability
1331 F Street, NW
Suite 800
Washington, DC 20004
(202)783-2900
TDD: (202)737-0645
FAX: (202)737-0725

Autism

Autism Society of America
7910 Woodmont Avenue
Suite 650
Bethesda, MD 20814
(301)657-0881
(800)3-AUTISM
FAX: (301)657-0869

Institute for Autism Research
4182 Adams Avenue
San Diego, CA 92116
(619)281-7165
FAX: (619)563-6840

National Autism Hotline/Autism Services Center
Prichard Building
605 9th Street
P. O. Box 507
Huntington, WV 25701-0507
(304)525-8014

Career Counseling

ERIC Clearinghouse on Handicapped and Gifted Children
1920 Association Drive
Reston, VA 22091-1589
(703)264-9474

Higher Education and Adult Training for People with Handicaps (HEATH Resource Center)
1 Dupont Circle
Washington, DC 20036-1193
(800)54-HEATH; (202)939-9320

Job Accommodation Network (JAN)
West Virginia University
P. O. Box 6080
Morgantown, WV 26506-6080
(800)526-7234
(800)526-2262 In Canada: voice/TTD
(800)DIAL-JAN

National Clearinghouse on Postsecondary Education for Individuals with Disabilities— HEATH Resource Center
1 Dupont Circle
Washington, DC 20036-1193
(800)54-HEATH
(202)939-9320

Partnership for Training and Employment Careers
1620 I Street, NW
Washington, DC 20006
(202)887-6120

President's Committee on Employment of People with Disabilities
111 20th Street, NW
Suite 636
Washington, DC 20036
(202)653-5029

Technical Assistance for Special Populations Program (TASPP)
National Center for Research in Vocational Education (NCRVE)
University of Illinois Site 45 Education Building
1310 South Sixth Street
Champaign, IL 61820
(217)333-0807
FAX (217)244-5632

Cerebral Palsy

American Academy for Cerebral Palsy and Developmental Medicine
1910 Byrd Avenue
Suite 100
P.O. Box 11086
Richmond, VA 23230-1086
(804)282-0036
FAX: (804)282-0090

United Cerebral Palsy Association
1522 K Street, NW
No. 1112
Washington DC 20005
(800)872-5827
(202)842-1266
FAX: (202)842-3519

Chronic Illness

Families of Children Under Stress (FOCUS)
P. O. Box 1058
Conyers, GA 30207
(404)483-9845

Parents of Chronically Ill Children
1527 Maryland Street
Springfield, IL 62702
(217)522-6810

Computers

CompuAbility Corporation
40000 Grand River
Suite 109
Novi, MI 48375
(313)477-6720

Computer Access Center
2425 16th Street
Room 23
Santa Monica, CA 90405
(310)450-8827

Disabled Children's Computer Group (DCCG)
2547 8th Street
No. 12A
Berkeley, CA 94710
(510)841-3224
FAX: (510)841-7956

Trace Research and Development Center
1500 Highland Avenue
S-151
Madison, WI 53705-2280
(606)262-6966
TDD (608)263-5408

Dental Care

National Foundation of Dentistry for the Handicapped
1800 Glenarm Place
Suite 500
Denver, CO 80202
(303)298-9650
FAX (303)298-9649

Down Syndrome

Association for Children with Down Syndrome
2616 Martin Avenue
Bellmore, NY 11710
(516)221-4700

Canadian Down Syndrome Society
12837 76th Avenue
Suite 206
Surrey, BC V3W 2V3, CANADA
(604)599-6009; FAX: (604)599-6165

Caring Inc.
P. O. Box 400
Milton, WA 98354
(206)922-8607

National Down Syndrome Congress
1605 Chantilly Drive
Suite 250
Atlanta, GA 30324
(800)232-6372
(404)633-1556
FAX (404)833-2817

National Down Syndrome Society
666 Broadway
Suite 810
New York, NY 10012
(800)221-4602
(212)460-9330
FAX (212)979-2873

Education

Association on Higher Education and Disability (AHEAD)
P. O. Box 21192
Columbus, OH 43221
(614)488-4972

Council for Exceptional Children
1920 Association Drive
Reston, VA 22091
(703)620-3660

Head Start—Resource Access Projects (RAPS), Region II
New York University
Resource and Training Center
School of Continuing Education
48 Cooper Square
Room 103
New York, NY 10003
(212)998-1205

IN*SOURCE Indiana Resource Center for Families with Special Needs
833 Northside
Boulevard, Building No. 1–Rear
South Bend, IN 46617
(219)234-7101
Indiana toll free: (800)332-4433

National Committee for Citizens in Education
900 Second Street, NE
Suite 8
Washington, DC 20002
(202)544-9495
(800)NETWORK

National Information Center for Educational Media (NICEM)
P. O. Box 40130
Albuquerque, NM 87196
(505)265-3591
(800)468-3453

Epilepsy

America's Pharmacy Services for People with Epilepsy
6109 Willowmere Drive
Des Moines, IA 50321
(800)247-1003
FAX (515)237-2329

Epilepsy Foundation of America
4351 Garden City Drive
Suite 406
Landover, MD 20785
(301)459-3700
information and referral: (800)332-1000

General

ACCENT on Information
P. O. Box 700
Bloomington, IL 61702
(309)378-2961

**American Association for the Advancement of Science
Project on Science, Technology, and Disability**
133 H Street, NW
Washington, DC 20005
(202)326-6672

American Association of University Affiliated Programs for Persons with Developmental Disabilities
8630 Fenton Street
Suite 410
Silver Spring, MD 20910
(301)588-8252
FAX (301)588-2842

American Council on Rural Special Education (ACRES)
National Rural Development Institute
Miller Hall 359
Western Washington University
Ballingham, WA 98225
(206)676-3576

American Preferred Prescription Pharmacy
1750 New Highway
Farmingdale, NY 11735
Long Island: (800)227-1195
NY: (800)445-4519

American Society of Allied Health Professions (ASAHP)
1101 Connecticut Avenue, NW
Suite 700
Washington, DC 20036-4387
(202)857-1150

Association for the Care of Children's Health (ACCH)
710 Woodmont Avenue
Suite 300
Bethesda, MD 20814
(301)654-6549; FAX: (301)986-4553

Avenues
P. O. Box 5192, Sonora, CA 95370
(209)928-3688

Canadian Association for Community Living
Kinsmen Building
York University
6700 Keele Street
North York, ON
M3J 1P3 CANADA
(416)661-9611
FAX: (416)661-5701

Center on Human Policy
Syracuse University
200 Huntington Hall
Syracuse, NY 13244-2340
(315)443-3851

Children's Defense Fund
25 E Street, NW
Washington, DC 20001
(202)628-8787
FAX (202)622-3520

Christian Council on Persons with Disabilities
1324 Yosemite Boulevard
Modesto, CA 95354
(209)524-7993

Clearinghouse on Disability Information
Office of Special Education and Rehabilitative Services
U.S. Department of Education
Room 3132
Switzer Building
Washington, DC 20202-2524
(202)732-1241
(202)732-1245
(202)732-1723

Coalition on Sexuality and Disability, Inc.
122 East 23rd Street
New York, NY 10010
(212)242-3900

Council for Exceptional Children
1920 Association Drive
Reston, VA 22091-1589
(703)620-3660
FAX: (703)264-9494

Council on Family Health
225 Park Avenue South
17th Floor
New York, NY 10003
(212)598-3617

Early Recognition Intervention Network (ERIN)
376 Bridge Street
Dedham, MA 02026
(617)329-5529

Federation of the Handicapped, Inc.
211 West 14th Street
New York, NY 10011
(212)206-4200

Keshet—Jewish Parents of Children with Special Needs
3525 West Peterson
Suite T-17
Chicago, IL 60659
(312)588-0551

March of Dimes Birth Defects Foundation
1275 Mamaroneck Avenue
White Plains, NY 10605
(914)428-7100
FAX (914)428-8203

MedicAlert
P. O. Box 1009
Turlock, CA 95381-1009
(800)ID-ALERT

Mobility International
P. O. Box 10767
Eugene, OR 97440
(503)343-1284
FAX (503)343-6812

National Association for the Dually Diagnosed
110 Prince Street
Kingston, NY 12301
(914)331-4336
(800)331-5362

National Association of Developmental Disabilities Councils
1234 Massachusetts Avenue, NW
Suite 103
Washington, DC 20005
(202)347-1234

National Association of Protection and Advocacy Systems
900 Second Street, NE
Suite 211
Washington, DC 20002
(202)408-9514
FAX: (202)408-9520

National Catholic Office for Persons with Disabilities
P. O. Box 29113
Washington, DC 20017
(202)529-2933
(202)529-4678

National Center for Clinical Infant Programs
P. O. Box 7270
McLean, VA 22106-7270
(703)356-8300

National Center for Education in Maternal and Child Health
38th and R Streets, NW
Washington, DC 20057
(202)625-8400

National Center for Youth with Disabilities
University of Minnesota
420 Delaware Street SE
Box 721
Minneapolis, MN 55455-0392
(612)626-2825
(800)333-6293
FAX (612)626-2134

National Council on Independent Living
Troy Atrium
4th Street and Broadway
Troy, NY 12180
(518)274-1979

National Easter Seals Society
70 East Lake Street
Chicago, IL 60601
(312)726-6200
(800)221-6827
TDD (312)726-4258

**National Information Center for
Children and Youth with Disabilities
(NICHCY)**
P. O. Box 1492
Washington, DC 20013
(703)893-6061
(800)999-5599
FAX (703)893-1741
TDD (703)893-8614

**National Information Clearinghouse
for Infants with Disabilities and Life-
Threatening Conditions, Center for
Developmental Disabilities**
School of Medicine, Department of
  Pediatrics
University of South Carolina
Columbia, SC 29208
Voice TT: (800)922-9234, ext. 201

**National Information System for
Health-Related Services**
(800)922-9234

National Organization on Disability
910 16th Street, NW
Suite 600
Washington, DC 20006
(202)293-5960
(800)248-ABLE

**National Parent Network on
Disabilities (NPND)**
1600 Prince Street
Suite 115
Alexandria, VA 22314
(703)684-NPND
TDD/voice (703)684-6763

**Sick Kids (Need) Involved People, Inc.
(SKIP)**
990 Second Avenue
New York, NY 10022
(212)421-9160

Society for Developmental Pediatrics
P. O. Box 23836
Baltimore, MD 21203
(410)550-9446
(410)550-9420

**Specialized Training of Military
Persons (STOMP)**
c/o Washington PAVE
12208 Pacific Highway SW
Tacoma, WA 98499
(206)588-1741

Genetics

Alliance of Genetic Support Groups
38th and R Street, NW
Washington, DC 20057
(202)625-7853
(800)336-GENE

Hereditary Disease Foundation
1427 7th Street
Suite 2
Santa Monica, CA 90401
(310)458-4183
FAX (310)458-3937

**International Center for the Disabled
(ICD)**
340 East 24th Street
New York, NY 10010
(212)679-0100
TDD (212)889-0372

**National Foundation for Jewish
Genetic Diseases**
250 Park Avenue
Suite 1000
New York, NY 10017
(212)371-1030

National Society of Genetic Counselors
233 Canterbury Drive
Wallingford, PA 19086
(215)872-7608

Hearing Impairments

**Alexander Graham Bell Association for
the Deaf**
3417 Volta Place NW
Washington, D.C. 20007-2778
(voice/TTY (202)337-5220)

**American Deafness and Rehabilitation
Association**
P. O. Box 251554
Little Rock, AR 72225
(501)663-7074

**American Society for Deaf Children
(ASDC)**
814 Thayer Avenue
Silver Spring, MD 20910
(800)942-ASDC

Auditory–Verbal International, Inc.
6 South Third Street
Suite 305
Easton, PA 18042
(215)253-6616
(215)253-4434
FAX (215)253-6709

Better Hearing Institute
P. O. Box 1840
Washington, DC 20013
(800)EAR-WELL
FAX (703)750-9302

Canadian Hearing Society
271 Spandina Road
Toronto, ON M5R 2V3
CANADA
(416)964-9595
TDD (416)964-0023
FAX (416)964-2066

Captioned Films and Videos for the Deaf/Modern Talking Picture Services
5000 Park Street N
St. Petersburg, FL 33709
(800)237-6213
(813)541-7571

The Deafness Research Foundation
9 East 38th Street
New York, NY 10016
(212)684-6556

Deafpride
1350 Potomac Avenue, SE
Washington, DC 20003
(202)675-6700

Deaf-REACH
3521 12th Street, NE
Washington, DC 20017
(202)832-6681
FAX (202)832-8454

Hearing Aid Helpline
20361 Middlebelt Road
Livonia, MI 48152
U.S. & Canada: (800)521-5247

John Tracy Clinic
806 West Adams Boulevard
Los Angeles, CA 90007
(800)522-4582
(213)748-5481
(213)747-2924
FAX (213)749-1651

Listen, Inc.
P. O. Box 27213
Tempe, AZ 85285
(602)921-3886

National Association for the Deaf (NAD)
814 Thayer Avenue
Silver Spring, MD 20910-4500
(301)587-1788
TDD (301)587-1789
FAX (301)587-1791

National Captioning Institute (NCI), Inc.
5203 Leesburg Pike
15th Floor
Falls Church, VA 22041
(800)533-9673
TDD (800)321-8337
(703)998-2400

National Cued Speech Association
P. O. Box 31345
Raleigh, NC 27622
(919)828-1218
FAX (919)828-1862

National Information Center on Deafness
Gallaudet University
800 Florida Avenue, NE
Washington, DC 20002
(202)651-5051
TDD (202)651-5052
FAX (202)651-5054

National Technical Institute for the Deaf
Rochester Institute of Technology
Lyndon Baines Johnson Building
52 Lomb Memorial Drive
Rochester, NY 14623-5604
(716)475-6400
FAX (716)475-6500

Self Help for Hard of Hearing People, Inc. (SHHH)
7800 Wisconsin Avenue
Bethesda, MD 20814
(301)657-2248
TDD (301)657-2249
FAX (301)913-9413

Signing Exact English (SEE) Center for the Advancement of Deaf Children
P. O. Box 1181
Los Alamitos, CA 90720
(213)430-1467

VOICE for Hearing-Impaired Children
124 Eglinton Avenue W
Suite 420
Toronto, ON M4R 2G8, CANADA
(416)487-7719
FAX (416)487-7423

Hotlines
DIRECT LINK for the disABLED, Inc.
P. O. Box 1036
Solvang, CA 93464
voice/TDD (805)688-1603

**National Digestive Diseases
Information Clearinghouse**
9000 Rockville Pike
Box NDDIC
Bethesda, MD 20892
(301)654-3810
FAX (301)496-2830

**National Jewish Center for
Immunology and Respiratory
Medicine**
1400 Jackson Street
Denver, CO 80206-2762
(800)222-LUNG

National Spinal Cord Injury Hotline
Montebello Hospital
2201 Argonne Drive
Baltimore, MD 21218
(800)526-3456

Social Security Administration Hotline
(800)227-1213
TDD (800)325-0778

**U.S. Architectural Transportation
Barriers Compliance Board**
(for information related to the Americans
with Disabilities Act)
(800)USA-ABLE

Learning Disabilities

**Center on PostSecondary Education
for Students with Learning
Disabilities**
The University of Connecticut
School of Education, 249
Glenbrook Road
Box V-64
Storrs, CT 06269-2064
(203)486-0163

**CH.A.D.D. National (Attention Deficit
Disorders)**
499 NW 70th Avenue
Suite 308
Plantation, FL 33317
(305)587-3700

Council for Learning Disabilities
P. O. Box 40303
Overland Park, KS 66204
(913)492-8755

Dyslexia Research Institute
4745 Centerville Road
Tallahassee, FL 32308
(904)893-2216

**Learning Disabilities Association of
America**
4156 Library Road
Pittsburgh, PA 15234
(412)341-1515

Learning Disabilities Network
25 Accord Park Drive
Rockland, MA 02370
(617)982-8100

**National Attention Deficit Disorder
Association (NADDA)**
Local support groups
19262 Jamboree Road
Irvine, CA 92715
Membership in NADDA:
P. O. Box 488
West Newbury, MA 01985
(800)487-2282

**National Center for Learning
Disabilities (NCLD)**
99 Park Avenue
New York, NY 10016
(212)687-7211

**National Network of Learning Disabled
Adults (NNLDA)**
800 North 82nd Street
Scottsdale, AZ 85257
(602)941-5112

The Orton Dyslexia Society
724 York Road
Baltimore, MD 21204
(410)296-0232

Legal

ACLU Children's Rights Project
132 West 43rd Street
New York, NY 10036
(212)944-9800

**American Bar Association Center on
Children and the Law**
1800 M Street, NW
Suite 200, South
Washington, DC 20036
(202)331-2250; FAX (202)331-2225

The Bazelon Center
1101 15th Street NW
Suite 1212
Washington, DC 20005
(202)467-5730
FAX (202)223-0409

Children's Defense Fund
25 E Street, NW
Washington, DC 20001
(202)628-8787
FAX (202)622-3520

Disability Rights Education and Defense Fund (DREDF)
2212 6th Street
Berkeley, CA 94710
(510)644-2555

Estate Planning for the Disabled (EPD)
955 West Center Avenue
Suite No. 12
Manteca, CA 95336
(209)239-7558
(800)448-1071

Mental Health Law Project
2021 L Street, NW
Suite 800
Washington, DC 20036
(202)467-5730

National Center for Law and the Deaf
Gallaudet University
800 Florida Avenue, NE
Washington, DC 20002
(202)651-5373

National Center for Law and the Handicapped
P. O. Box 477
University of Notre Dame
Notre Dame, IN 46556
(219)283-4536

N. Neal Pike Institute on Law and Disability
Boston University
School of Law
765 Commonwealth Avenue
Boston, MA 02215
(617)353-2904
FAX (617)353-2906

Mental Health

Academy of Clinical Mental Health Counselors
5999 Stevenson Avenue
Alexandria, VA 22304
(703)823-9800, ext. 384
FAX (703)823-0252

Federation of Families for Children's Mental Health
1021 Prince Street
Alexandria, VA 22314
(703)684-7710
(703)684-7722
FAX (703)684-5968

Mental Health Policy Resource Center
1730 Rhode Island Avenue, NW
Suite 308
Washington, DC 20036
(202)775-8826

National Mental Health Association
1021 Prince Street
Alexandria, VA 22314
(703)684-6642
(703)684-7722
FAX (703)684-5968

Mental Retardation

American Association on Mental Retardation
1719 Kalorama Road NW
Washington, DC 20009-2683
(202)387-1968

The Arc (formerly Association for Retarded Citizens of the United States)
500 East Border Street
3rd Floor
Arlington, TX 76010
(817)640-0204

Canadian Association for Community Living
Kinsman Building
York University
6700 Keele Street
North York, Ontario
M3J 1P3 CANADA
(416)661-9611
FAX (416)661-5701

The Joseph P. Kennedy, Jr. Foundation
1350 New York Avenue, NW
Suite 500
Washington, DC 20005-4709
(202)393-1250

National Association of State Mental Retardation Program Directors
113 Oronoco Street
Alexandria, VA 22314
(703)683-4202

President's Committee on Mental Retardation (PCMR)
330 Independence Avenue
Cohen Building
Room 5325
Washington, DC 20201
(202)609-0634

Mental Retardation/Mental Illness

National Organization of the Dually Diagnosed (NADD)
110 Prince Street
Kingston, NY 12401
(914)331-4336
(800)331-5362

Music Therapy

American Association for Music Therapy
P. O. Box 80012
Valley Forge, PA 19484
(215)265-4006

National Association for Music Therapy, Inc.
8455 Colesville Road
Suite 930
Silver Spring, MD 20910
(301)589-3300
(301)589-5175

Occupational Therapy

American Occupational Therapy Association, Inc.
1383 Piccard Drive
Rockville, MD 20850
(301)948-9626

Physical Therapy

American Physical Therapy Association
1111 North Fairfax Street
Alexandria, VA 22314
(800)999-2782, ext. 3210

Rare Disorders

Lethbridge Society for Rare Disorders
No. 100B
515-7 Street S
Lethbridge, Alberta T1J 2G8
CANADA
(403)329-0665

National Organization for Rare Disorders, Inc. (NORD)
100 Route 37
P. O. Box 8923
New Fairfield, CT 06812
(203)746-6518
(800)999-NORD

National Resource Library
University of Minnesota–NCYD
P. O. Box 721
420 Delaware Street, SE
Minneapolis, MN 55455
(800)333-6293
(612)626-2825

Recreation, Sports, and Leisure

Access: The Foundation for Accessibility by the Disabled
P. O. Box 356
Malverne, NY 11565
(516)887-5684

American Athletic Association of the Deaf
Shirley Hortie Platt
Executive Secretary
1052 Darling Street
Ogden, UT 84403
(202)224-8637

American Camping Association
Bradford Woods
Martinsville, IN 46151
(317)342-8456

American Therapeutic Recreation Association (ATRA)
P. O. Box 15215
Hattiesburg, MS 39404-5215
(800)553-0304
FAX (601)264-3337

Boy Scouts of America, Scouting for the Handicapped Division
1325 Walnut Hill Lane
Irving, TX 75062
(214)659-2127

Girl Scouts of the U.S.A.
420 Fifth Avenue
New York, NY 10018-2702
(212)852-8000

National Handicapped Sports
National Headquarters
1145 19th Street
Suite 717
Washington, DC 20036
(301)217-0960
FAX (301)217-0968
TDD (301)217-0963

National Recreation and Parks Association
2775 South Quincy Street
Arlington, VA 22206
(703)820-4940

National Therapeutic Recreation Certification
P. O. Box 479
Thiells, NY 10983-0479
(914)947-4346

National Therapeutic Recreation Society
2775 South Quincy Street
Arlington, VA 22206
(800)626-6772

National Wheelchair Athletic Association
3595 East Fountain Boulevard
Suite L1
Colorado Springs, CO 80910
(719)574-1150

Special Olympics International
1350 New York Avenue, NW
Suite 500
Washington, DC 20005-4709
(202)628-3630

Special Recreation, Inc.
362 Koser Avenue
Iowa City, IA 52246-3038
(319)337-7578
(319)353-6808

Travel Information Center
Moss Rehabilitation Hospital
15th Street and Tabor Road
Philadelphia, PA 19141
(215)329-5715

Very Special Arts
1331 F. Street, NW
Suite 800
Washington, DC 20004
(202)628-2800
TDD (202)737-0645
FAX (202)737-0725

Wilderness Inquiry
1313 Fifth Street, SE
P. O. Box 84
Minneapolis, MN 55414-1546
Twin Cities
(612)379-3858
(800)728-0719

Rehabilitation

**Canadian Rehabilitation Council for
  the Disabled**
45 Sheppard Avenue E
Suite 801
Willowdale, Ontario M2N 5W9
CANADA
(416)250-7490
FAX (416)229-1371

**Kinsman Rehabilitation Foundation of
  British Columbia**
2256 West 12th Avenue
Vancouver, British Columbia V6K 2N5
CANADA
(604)736-8841
TDD (604)738-0603

National Rehabilitation Clearinghouse
816 West 6th Street
Oklahoma State University
Stillwater, OK 74078
(405)624-7650
FAX (405)624-0695

**National Rehabilitation Information
  Center (NARIC)**
8455 Colesville Road
Suite 935
Silver Spring, MD 20910
(301)588-9284
voice/TDD (800)346-2742
FAX (301)587-1967

**Rehabilitation Engineering Society of
  North America (RESNA)**
1101 Connecticut Avenue, NW
Suite 700
Washington, DC 20036
(202)857-1199

World Rehabilitation Fund
386 Park Avenue S
Suite 500
New York, NY 10016-4901
(212)725-7875

Self-Help

American Self-Help Clearinghouse
St. Clares-Riverside Medical Center
Denville, NJ 07834
(201)625-7101
TDD (201)625-9053

National Self-Help Clearinghouse
Graduate School/University Center
City University of New York
25 West 43rd Street
Room 620
New York, NY 10036
(212)642-2944

Sexuality

**Coalition on Sexuality and Disability,
  Inc.**
122 East 23rd Street
New York, NY
(212)242-3900

**Sex Information and Education
  Council of U.S. (SIECUS)**
130 West 42nd Street
Suite 2500
New York, NY 10036
(212)819-9770
FAX (212)819-9776

Siblings

Siblings for Significant Change
United Charities Building
105 East 22nd Street
Room 710
New York, NY 10010
(212)420-0776

Siblings Information Network
A. J. Pappanikou Center on Special
    Education and Rehabilitation: A
    University Affiliated Program
1776 Ellington Road
South Winsor, CT 06074
(203)648-1205
FAX (203)644-2031

Specific Disabilities and Conditions[1]

Arnold-Chiari Family Network
c/o Keven and Maureen Walsh
67 Spring Street
Weymoth, MA 02188
(617)337-2368

**Arthritis, American Juvenile Arthritis
    Organization**
1314 Sprint Street NW
Atlanta, GA 30309
(404)872-7100
FAX (404)872-0457

**Cornelia de Lange Syndrome
    Foundation, Inc.**
60 Dyer Avenue
Collinsville, CT 06022
(203)693-0159

**International Rett Syndrome
    Association, Inc.**
8511 Rose Marie Drive
Ft. Washington, MD 20744
(301)248-7031

**Joubert Syndrome—Parents-in-Touch
    Network**
c/o Mary Von Damme
12348 Summer Meadow Road
Rock, MI 49880
(906)359-4707

National Fragile X Foundation
1441 York Street
Suite 215
Denver, CO 80206
(800)688-8765
(303)333-6155

**The National Neurofibromatosis
    Foundation, Inc.**
141 5th Avenue
7th Floor
Room 75
New York, NY 10010
(212)460-8980

**National Tuberous Sclerosis
    Association**
8000 Corporate Drive
Suite 120
Landover, MD 20785
(800)225-NTSA
(301)459-9888

Prader-Willi Syndrome Association
6940 Excelsior Boulevard
Edina, MN 55436
(612)926-1947

Spina Bifida Association of America
4590 McArthur Boulevard
Suite 250
Washington, DC 20007
(202)944-3285

Spina Bifida Association of Canada
220-388 Donald Street
Winnipeg, Manitoba R3B 2J4
CANADA
(204)957-1794

**Support Organization for Trisomy 18,
    13, and Related Disorders**
c/o Barb Van Herreweghe
2982 South Union Street
Rochester, NY 14624
(716)594-4621

Tourette Syndrome Association
42-40 Bell Boulevard
Bayside, NY 11361
(718)224-2999
FAX (718)279-9596

**The 5p− Society (Cri du Chat
    Syndrome)**
11609 Oakmont
Overland Park, KS 66210
(913)469-8900

Speech-Language Pathology

**American Speech-Language-Hearing
    Association**
10801 Rockville Pike
Rockville, MD 20852
(301)897-5700
TDD (301)897-0157

Better Hearing Institute
P. O. Box 1840
Washington, DC 20013
(800)EAR-WELL
FAX (703)750-9302

---

[1]The organizations listed here provide information and support to both parents and professionals.

Canadian Hearing Society
271 Spadina Road
Toronto, Ontario M5R 2V3
CANADA
(416)964-9595
TDD (416)964-0023
FAX (416)964-2066

Travel
Mobility International
P. O. Box 10767
Eugene, OR 97440
(503)343-1284
FAX (503)343-6812

Travelin' Talk
P. O. Box 3534
Clarksville, TN 37043-3534
(615)552-6670

Vision Impairment

American Council of the Blind
1155 15th Street, NW
Suite 720
Washington, DC 20005
(800)424-8666
(202)467-5081

American Foundation for the Blind, Inc.
15 West 16th Street
New York, NY 10011
(212)620-2020

American Printing House for the Blind
P. O. Box 6085
Louisville, KY 40206
(800)223-1839
(502)895-2405
FAX (502)895-1509

Association for Education and Rehabilitation of the Blind and Visually Impaired
206 North Washington Street
Alexandria, VA 22314
(703)548-1884

Blind Children's Center
4120 Marathon Street
Los Angeles, CA 90029
(800)222-3566

Blind Children's Fund
230 Central Street
Auburndale, MA 02166
(617)332-4014

Canadian National Institute for the Blind
1929 Bayview Avenue
Toronto, Ontario M4G 3E8
CANADA
(416)480-7415
(416)480-7414
FAX (416)480-7699

Institute for Families of Blind Children
P. O. Box 54700
Mail Stop No. 111
Los Angeles, CA 90054
(213)669-4649

Job Opportunities for the Blind (JOB)
National Center of the Blind
1800 Johnson Street
Baltimore, MD 21230
(410)659-9314
(800)638-7518

National Association for Visually Handicapped
22 West 21 Street
6th Floor
New York, NY 10010
(212)889-3141
FAX (202)727-2931

National Federation of the Blind
1800 Johnson Street
Baltimore, MD 21230
(410)659-9314
FAX (410)685-5653

National Retinoblastoma Parent Group
603 Fourth Range Road
Pembroke, NH 03275
(603)224-4085

National Society to Prevent Blindness
500 East Remington Road
Schaumburg, IL 50173
(800)331-2020
(708)843-2020
FAX (708)843-8458

Recording for the Blind
20 Roszel Road
Princeton, NJ 08540
(609)452-0606

Retinitis Pigmentosa International Society for Degenerative Eye Diseases
P. O. Box 900
Woodland Hills, CA 91365
(800)344-4877
(818)992-0500

RP Foundation Fighting Blindness
1401 Mt. Royal Avenue
4th Floor
Baltimore, MD 21217
(800)683-5555
(410)225-9400
TTD (410)225-9409
FAX (410)225-3936

Stargardt Disease Self-Help Network
P. O. Box 136
West Chicago, IL 60186
(708)206-5017

Vision Foundation
818 Mt. Auburn Street
Watertown, MA 02172
(800)852-3029
(617)926-4232

STATE-SPECIFIC RESOURCES[2]

The resources listed in this section are designed to enable families to work more effectively with professionals to meet the needs of the family member with developmental disabilities. The protection and advocacy center for each state is listed first, followed by various state organizations that can provide information, support, and parent training.

Alabama

Alabama Developmental Disabilities Advocacy Program
The University of Alabama
P. O. Drawer 870395
Tuscaloosa, AL 35487-0395
(205)348-4928

Special Education Action Committe, Inc. (SEAC)
P. O. Box 161274
Mobile, AL 36616-2274
(205)478-1208
(800)222-7322
FAX (205)473-7877

Alaska

Advocacy Services of Alaska
615 East 82nd Avenue
Suite 101
Anchorage, AK 99518
(907)344-2002

Alaska PARENTS Resource Center
(Parents as Resources Engaged in Networking & Training Statewide)
540 International Airport Road
Suite 250
Anchorage, AK 99518
(907)563-2246
(800)478-7678
FAX (907)790-2248

American Samoa

Client Assistance and P and A Program
P. O. Box 3937
Pago Pago, AS 96799
(684)633-2441

Arizona

Arizona Center for Law in the Public Interest
363 North First Avenue
Suite 100
Phoenix, AZ 85003
(602)252-4904

Pilot Parent Partnerships
2150 East Highland Avenue
Suite 105
Phoenix, AZ 85016
(602)468-3001
(800)237-3007

Arkansas

Advocacy Services, Inc.
1120 Marshall Street
Suite 311
Little Rock, AR 72202
(501)371-2171

---

[2]Adapted from *Exceptional Parent,* 23(7), D-20–D-23.

Arkansas Disability Coalition
10002 West Markham, Suite B7
Little Rock, AR 72205
Voice/TDD (501)221-1330
(501)221-9067

FOCUS, Inc.
2917 King Street, Suite C
Jonesboro, AR 72401
(501)935-2750
Voice/TDD (501)221-1330
FAX (501)931-1111

California

Protection and Advocacy, Inc.
100 Howe Street
Suite 185N
Sacramento, CA 95825
(916)488-9950
(800)952-5746

Parents Helping Parents
1801 Vincente Street
San Francisco, CA 94116
(415)564-0722
FAX (415)681-1065

Northern Coalition for Parent Training and Information (NCC)
Parents Helping Parents
535 Race Street
Suite 140
San Jose, CA 95126
(40-8)288-5010
FAX (408)288-7493

DREDF
2212 6th Street
Berkeley, CA 94710
(510)644-2555
FAX (510)841-8645

Matrix, A Parent Network and Resource Center
P. O. Box 6541
San Rafael, CA 94903
(415)499-3877
FAX [call first] (415)499-3864

Exceptional Parents Unlimited
4120 North 1st Street
Fresno, CA 93726
(209)229-2000
FAX (209)229-2956

Team of Advocates for Special Kids, Inc. (TASK)
100 W. Cerritos Avenue
Anaheim, CA 92805-6546
(714)533-TASK
FAX (714)533-2533

Colorado

The Legal Center
455 Sherman Street
Suite 130
Denver, CO 80203
(303)722-0300

PEAK Parent Center, Inc.
6055 Lehman Drive
Suite 101
Colorado Springs, CO 80918
(719)531-9400
TDD (719)531-9403
(800)284-0251
FAX (719)531-9452

Connecticut

Office of Protection and Advocacy for Handicapped Developmentally Disabled Persons
60 Weston Street
Hartford, CT 06120-1551
(203)297-4300
(203)566-2102
(800)842-7303

CT Parent Advocacy Center, Inc. (CPAC)
5 Church Lane, Suite No. 4
P. O. Box 579
East Lyme, CT 06333
(203)739-3089
(800)445-2722
FAX (203)739-7460

Delaware

Disabilities Law Program
144 East Market Street
Georgetown, DE 19947
(302)856-0038

Parent Information Center of Delaware, Inc.
700 Barksdale Road, Suite 6
Newark, DE 19711
(302)366-0152
TDD (302)366-0178
FAX (302)366-0276

District of Columbia

COPE
P. O. Box 90498
Washington, DC 20090-0498
(202)526-6814
FAX (202)832-2180

I.P.A.C.H.I.
300 I Street NE, Suite 202
Washington, DC 20002
(202)547-8081

Florida

Advocacy for Persons with Disabilities
2671 Executive Center
Circle W, Suite 100
Tallahassee, FL 32301-5024
(904)488-9071
Statewide toll free: (800)342-0823
(800)346-4127

Family Network on Disability
5510 Gray Street
Suite 220
Tampa, FL 33609
Voice/TDD (313)289-1122
FAX (813)286-8614

Georgia

Georgia Advocacy Office, Inc.
1708 Peachtree Street NW
Suite 505
Atlanta, GA 30309
(404)885-1234
(800)537-2329

Parents Educating Parents (PEP)
  Georgia ARC
1851 Ram Runway, Suite 104
College Park, GA 30337
(404)761-3150
Voice/TDD (404)761-2745
(800)966-3150
FAX (404)767-2258

Guam

The Advocacy Office
P. O. Box 8830
Tamuning, Guam 96911
(671)646-9026

Hawaii

Protection and Advocacy Agency of
  Hawaii
1580 Makaloa Street
Suite 1060
Honolulu, HI 96814
(808)949-2922

AWARE/Learning Disabilities
  Association of Hawaii (LDAH)
200 North Vineyard Boulevard
Suite 103
Honolulu, HI 96817
Voice/TDD (808)536-2280
FAX (808)543-2222

Idaho

Co-Ad, Inc.
1409 West Washington
Boise, ID 83702
(208)336-5353

Idaho Parents Unlimited, Inc.
Parent Education Resource Center
4696 Overland Road, Suite 478
Boise, ID 83705
Voice/TDD (208)342-5884
(800)242-IPUL
FAX (208)342-1408

Illinois

P & A, Inc.
11 East Adams
Suite 1200
Chicago, IL 60604
(312)341-0022

Designs for Change
220 South State Street
Suite 1900
Chicago, IL 60604
(312)922-0317
(800)952-4199
FAX (312)922-6993

Family Resource Center on Disabilities
  (FRCD)
20 East Jackson Boulevard
Room 900
Chicago, IL 60604
(312)939-3513
TDD/TTY (312)939-3519
(800)952-4199
FAX (312)939-7297

Indiana

Indiana Advocacy Services
850 North Meridian Street
Suite 2-C
Indianapolis, IN 46204
(317)232-1150
(800)622-4845

Indiana Resource Center For Families
  with Special Needs (IN*SOURCE)
833 East Northside Boulevard
Building 1–Rear
South Bend, IN 46617
(219)234-7101
(800)332-4433
FAX (219)287-9651

Iowa

Iowa P and A Service, Inc.
3015 Merle Hay Road
Suite 6
Des Moines, IA 50310
(515)278-2502

Iowa Pilot Parents (IEPC)
33 North 12th Street
P. O. Box 1151
Fort Dodge, IA 50501
(515)576-5870
(800)952-4777 (parents only)
FAX (515)576-8209

Kansas

Families Together, Inc.
1023 S.W. Gage Boulevard
Topeka, KS 66604
(913)273-6343
(800)264-6343
FAX (913)273-1385

**Kansas Advocacy and Protection
  Services**
513 Leavenworth
Suite 2
Manhattan, KS 66502
(913)776-1541
(800)432-8276

Kentucky

**Kentucky Special Parent Involvement
  Network (KY-SPIN)**
2210 Goldsmith Lane
Suite 118
Louisville, KY 40218
(502)456-0923
(502)456-0893
(800)525-7746

**Office of Public Advocacy, Division for
  Protection and Advocacy**
Perimeter Park West
1264 Louisville Road
Frankfort, KY 40601
(502)564-2967
(800)372-2988

Louisiana

**Advocacy Center for the Elderly and
  Disabled**
210 O'Keefe
Suite 700
New Orleans, LA 70112
(504)522-2337
(800)662-7705

**Program of Families Helping Families
  of Greater New Orleans**
4323 Division Street
Suite 110
Metairie, LA 70002-3179
(504)883-9111
(800)766-7736
FAX (504)888-0246

Maine

Maine Advocacy Services
One Grandview Place
Suite 1
P. O. Box 445
Winthrop, ME 04364
(207)377-6202
(800)452-1948
(207)289-2394 (Augusta area)

**Special-Needs Parent Information
  Network (SPIN)**
P. O. Box 2067
Augusta, ME 04338
(207)582-2504
(800)325-SPIN
FAX (207)582-5022

Maryland

Maryland Disability Law Center
2510 St. Paul Street
Baltimore, MD 21218
(410)333-7600

Parents Place of MD, Inc.
7257 Parkway Drive, Suite 210
Hanover, MD 21076
Voice/TDD (410)712-0900
FAX (410)712-0902

Massachusetts

Disability Law Center, Inc.
11 Beacon Street
Suite 925
Boston, MA 02108
(617)723-8455

**Federation for Children with Special
  Needs, Inc.**
95 Berkeley Street, Suite 104
Boston, MA 02116
(617)482-2915
(800)331-0688
FAX (617)695-2939

Michigan

Citizens Alliance to Uphold Special Education (CAUSE)
313 South Washington Square
Suite 040
Lansing, MI 48933
Voice/TDD (517)485-4084
(800)221-9105
FAX (517)485-4145

Michigan Protection and Advocacy Service
109 West Michigan, Suite 900
Lansing, MI 48933
(517)487-1755

Parents are Experts: Parents Training Parents Project
23077 Greenfield Road
Suite 205
Southfield, MI 48075-3744
Voice/TDD (313)557-5070
FAX (313)557-4456

Minnesota

Minnesota Disability Law Center
222 Grain Exchange Building
323 Fourth Avenue, S.
Minneapolis, MN 55415
(612)332-7301

PACER Center, Inc.
4826 Chicago Avenue South
Minneapolis, MN 55417
(612)827-2966
(800)53-PACER (parents only)
FAX (612)827-3065

Mississippi

Association of Developmental Organizations of Mississippi (ADOM)
332 New Market Drive
Jackson, MS 39209
(601)922-3210
(800)898-1026
FAX (601)922-6854

Mississippi Protection and Advocacy System for Developmental Disabilities, Inc.
4793-B McWillie Drive
Jackson, MS 39206
(601)981-8207

Missouri

Missouri Protection and Advocacy Services, Inc.
925 South Country Club Drive
Unit B-1
Jefferson City, MO 65109
(314)893-3333

Missouri Parents Act (MPACT)
1722W South Glenstone
Suite 125
Springfield, MO 65804
Voice/TDD (417)882-7434
(800)743-7634
FAX (417)882-8413

MPACT—Kansas City Office
1115 East 65th Street
Kansas City, MO 64131
(816)333-6833
TDD (816)333-5685
FAX (816)333-2267

MPACT—St. Louis Office
8631 Delmar, Suite 300
St. Louis, MO 63124
Voice/TDD (314)997-7622
(800)995-3160
FAX (314)997-5518

Montana

Montana Advocacy Program, Inc.
1410 8th Avenue
Helena, MT 59601
(406)444-3889

Parents Let's Unite for Kids (PLUK)
EMC/Special Education Building
1500 North 30th Street
Billings, MT 59101-0298
(406)657-2055
(800)222-7585
FAX (406)657-2061

Nebraska

Nebraska Advocacy Services
522 Lincoln Center Building
215 Centennial Mall South
Lincoln, NE 68508

Nebraska Parents' Center
3610 Dodge Street
Omaha, NE 68131
Voice/TDD (402)346-0525
(800)284-8520
FAX (402)346-5253

Nevada

Nevada Parent Connection
3380 South Arville Boulevard
Las Vegas, NV 89102
(702)252-0259, ext. 112
FAX (702)252-8780

Office of Protection and Advocacy
205 Capuroo Way
Suite B
Sparks, NV 89431
(702)789-0233
(800)992-5715
FTS 4705911

New Hampshire
Disabilities Rights Center, Inc.
P. O. Box 19
Concord, NH 03302-0019
(603)228-0432

Parent Information Center
151A Manchester Street
P. O. Box 1422
Concord, NH 03302-14226
(603)224-6299
Voice/TDD (603)224-7005
(800)232-0986
FAX (603)224-4365

New Jersey
**Office of Advocacy for the
Developmentally Disabled**
Hughes Justice Complex
CN 850
Trenton, NJ 08625
(609)292-9742
(800)792-8600

**Statewide Parent Advocacy Network,
Inc. (SPAN)**
516 North Avenue East
Westfield, NJ 07090
(908)654-7726
(800)654-SPAN
FAX (908)654-7880

New Mexico
**EPICS Project
S.W. Communication Resources, Inc.**
P. O. Box 788
2000 Camino del Pueblo
Bernalillo, NM 87004
Voice/TDD (505)867-3396
(800)767-7320
FAX (505)867-3398

Parents Reaching Out
1127 University Boulevard NE
Albuquerque, NM 87102
Voice/TDD (505)842-9045
(800)524-5176
FAX (505)842-1451

Protection and Advocacy System, Inc.
1720 Louisiana Boulevard, NE
Suite 204
Albuquerque, NM 87110
(505)256-3100
(800)432-4682

New York
**Advocates for Children of New York,
Inc.**
24-16 Bridge Plaza South
Long Island City, NY 11101
(718)729-8866
FAX (718)729-8931

**New York State Commission on Quality
of Care for the Mentally Disabled**
99 Washington Avenue
Albany, NY 12210
(518)473-4057

Parent Network Center (PNC)
1443 Main Street
Buffalo, NY 14209
(716)885-1004
(800)724-7408
FAX (716)885-9597

**Resources for Children with Special
Needs**
200 Park Avenue South
Suite 816
New York, NY 10003
(212)677-4650
FAX (212)254-4070

North Carolina
**Exceptional Children's Assistance
Center (ECAC)**
P. O. Box 16
Davidson, NC 28655
(704)892-1321
(800)962-6817
FAX (704)892-5028 (call first)

**Governor's Advocacy Council for
Persons with Disabilities**
1318 Dale Street
Suite 100
Raleigh, NC 27605
(919)733-9250

Parents Project
300 Enola Road
Morganton, NC 28655
(704)433-2662
FAX (704)438-6457

North Dakota
Pathfinder Family Center
1600 Second Avenue SW
Minot, ND 58701
(701)852-9426
TDD: (701)852-9436
(800)245-5840
FAX: (701)838-9324

Protection and Advocacy Project
400 East Broadway
Suite 515
Bismarck, ND 58501
(701)224-2972
(800)472-2670

North Mariana Islands
Catholic Social Services
Box 745
Saipan, CM 96950
(670)234-6981

Ohio

Child Advocacy Center
1821 Summit Road
Suite 303
Cincinnati, OH 45237
(513)821-2400
FAX (513)821-2442

Ohio Coalition for the Education of Handicapped Children (OCEHC)
1299 Campbell Road
Suite B
Marion, OH 43302
Voice/TDD (614)382-5452
(800)374-2806
FAX (614)382-2399
Worthington Office: (614)431-1307

Ohio Legal Rights Service
8 East Long Street
6th Floor
Columbus, OH 43215
(614)466-7264
(800)282-9181

Oklahoma

Parents Reaching Out in Oklahoma Project (PRO-OK)
1917 South Harvard Avenue
Oklahoma City, OK 73128
Voice/TDD (405)681-9710
(800)PL9-4142
FAX (405)685-4006

Protection and Advocacy Agency for DD
9726 East 42nd Street
Osage Building
Room 133
Tulsa, OK 74145

Oregon

Oregon Advocacy Center
310 Southwest 4th Avenue
625 Board of Trade Building
Portland, OR 97204-2309

Oregon COPE Project, Inc.
999 Locust Street, NE
Box B
Salem, OR 97303
Voice/TDD/FAX (503)373-7477

Pennsylvania

Mentor Parent Program
Route 257
Salina Road
P. O. Box 718
Seneca, PA 16346
(814)676-8615
(800)447-1431
FAX (814)676-8615

Parent Education Network
333 East 7th Avenue
York, PA 17404
Voice/TDD (717)845-9722
(800)522-5817
FAX (717)848-3654
Spanish (800)441-5052

Parents Union for Public Schools
311 South Juniper Street
Suite 602
Philadelphia, PA 19107
(215)546-1166
FAX (215)731-1688

Pennsylvania Protection and Advocacy, Inc.
116 Pine Street
Harrisburg, PA 17101
(717)236-8110
(800)692-7443

Puerto Rico

Asociación de Padres Por Bienestar de Ninos Impedidos de PR, Inc.
P. O. Box 21301
Rio Piedras, PR 00928-1301
(809)763-4665
(809)765-0345

Protection and Advocacy
Governor's Office
P. O. Box 5163
Hato Rey, PR 00918-5163
(809)766-2388
(809)766-2333

Rhode Island

Rhode Island Protection and Advocacy System (RIPAS), Inc.
55 Bradford Street
2nd Floor
Providence, RI 02903
(401)831-3150

**Rhode Island Parent Information
   Network (RIPIN)**
Independence Square
500 Prospect Street
Pawtucket, RI 02860
(401)727-4144
FAX (401)725-9960

South Carolina

PRO-PARENTS
2712 Middleburg Drive
Suite 102
Columbia, SC 29204
Voice/TDD (803)779-3859
(800)759-4776
FAX (803)252-4513

**South Carolina P and A System for the
   Handicapped, Inc.**
3710 Landmark Drive
Suite 204
Columbia, SC 29204
(803)282-0639
(800)922-5225

South Dakota

South Dakota Advocacy Project, Inc.
221 South Central Avenue
Pierre, SD 57501
(605)224-8294
(800)742-8108

South Dakota Parent Connection
P. O. Box 84813
Sioux Falls, SD 57118-4813
Voice/TDD (605)335-8504
(800)640-4553
FAX (605)335-8504

Tennessee

E.A.C.H., Inc.
P. O. Box 121257
Nashville, TN 37212
(615)298-1080
(800)342-1660

**Support & Training for Exceptional
   Parents (STEP)**
1805 Hayes Street, Suite 100
Nashville, TN 37203
(615)639-0125
(800)280-STEP
TDD (800)848-0298
FAX (615)327-0827

Texas

Advocacy, Inc.
7800 Shoal Creek Boulevard
Suite 171-E
Austin, TX 78757
(512)454-4816
Voice/TTY (800)252-9108

**Partners Resource Network, Inc.
PATH**
227 North 18th, No. 2
Beaumont, TX 77707-2203
(409)838-2366
(800)866-4726
FAX (409)866-2351

Project PODER
2300 West Commerce
Suite 205
San Antonio, TX 78207
(210)732-8247
(800)682-9747
FAX (210)732-8249

Special Kids, Inc. (SKIP)
P. O. Box 61628
Houston, TX 77208-1628
(713)643-9576
FAX (713)643-6291

Utah

Legal Center for the Handicapped
455 East 400 South
Suite 201
Salt Lake City, UT 84111
(801)363-1347

Utah Parent Center
2290 East 4500 South
Suite 110
Salt Lake City, UT 84117
(801)272-1051
(800)468-1160
FAX (801)272-3479

Vermont

Vermont DD Law Project
12 North Street
Burlington, VT 05401
(802)863-2881

**Vermont Parent Information Center
   (VPIC)**
The Chase Mill
1 Mill Street
Burlington, VT 05401
Voice/TDD (802)655-4016
(800)639-7170
FAX (802)655-5976

Virgin Islands
Committee on Advocacy for the Developmentally Disabled, Inc.
31A New Street
Apartment No. 2
St. Croix, VI 00840
(809)772-1200

Virginia

Department of Rights for the Disabled
James Monroe Building
101 North 14th Street
17th Floor
Richmond, VA 23219
(804)225-2042
(800)552-3962

Parent Educational Advocacy Training Center (PEATC)
228 South Pitt Street
Suite 300
Alexandria, VA 22314
(703)836-2953
TDD (703)836-3026
(800)869-6782 (VA, WV, MD)
FAX (703)836-5869

Washington

PAVE/STOMP
Specialized Training of Military Parents
12208 Pacific Highway, SW
Tacoma, WA 98499
Voice/TDD (206)588-1741
FAX (206)984-7520

A Touchstones Program
6721 51st Avenue South
Seattle, WA 98118
(206)721-0867
FAX (206)721-2422

Washington P and A System
1401 East Jefferson
No. 506
Seattle, WA 98122
(206)324-1521

Washington PAVE
6316 South 12th Street
Tacoma, WA 98465
Voice/TDD (206)565-2266
(800)5-PARENT
FAX (206)566-8052

West Virginia
West Virginia Advocates
1524 Kanawha Boulevard
East, Charleston, WV 25311
(304)346-0847
(800)950-5250

West Virginia PTI
104 East Main Street
Suite 3-B
Clarksburg, WV 26301
Voice/TDD (304)624-1436
FAX (304)622-5861

Wisconsin

Parent Education Project of WI, Inc. (PEP-WI)
2001 West Vliet Street
Milwaukee, WI 53205
(414)937-8380
(800)231-8382
FAX (414)933-6077

Wisconsin Coalition for Advocacy, Inc.
16 North Carroll Street
Suite 400
Madison, WI 53703
(608)267-0214

Wyoming
Wyoming Protection and Advocacy System, Inc.
2424 Pioneer Avenue
No. 101
Cheyenne, WY 82001
(307)638-7668
(800)624-7648

Wyoming PIC
5 North Lobban
Buffalo, WY 82834
Voice/TDD (307)684-2277
(800)660-WPIC
FAX (307)684-5314

Index

Page numbers followed by t *and* f *denote tables and figures, respectively.*

case studies, 123–127
developmental, 21–22
elements of, 120, 120*t*
forms for, 134*f*–139*f*, 140*f*–145*f*
process of, 120–121, 123–127
of school-age children, 71
Nursing care
approaches for adolescents, 72
approaches for preschool children, 69
approaches for school-age children, 71
changes in, 4–8, 5*t*
early, 2–3
guidelines for, 6
definitions related to, 98*t*
historical perspectives, 1–9
legislative reforms, 6–7
professional reforms, 6–7
Nursing care plans, case study, 114, 115*t*,
115, 116*t*
Nursing diagnoses, 7, 119, 128–131
case studies, 123–133
collaborative, 131–132
definition of, 106
developing, 128–130
for drug therapy in relation to self-care
deficits, 196, 196*t*
prioritizing factors, 130, 130*t*
reference materials, 130–131, 131*t*
Nursing education, in developmental disabilities, 10–13
Nursing position statement, 10
Nursing process
definition of, 106
Self-Care Deficit Theory and, 112–116
Nursing services
evaluation of, 100
standards for, 99, 100*t*
Nutrition, 183–185
assistive devices, 353, 360–367
considerations for adolescents, 165
Nutrition/metabolic pattern, 122

Obesity, 183–184
Occupational hazards, 188–190
Occupational therapy resources, 411
Older adults
habilitation for, 74–75
health maintenance approaches for,
74–75
program models for, 75
routine health examinations for, 177–178
see also Adults
Oral motor difficulties, medication administration with, 197–202
techniques for, 198, 199*f*–202*f*
Oral motor specialist
definition of, 194
signs of need for assessment by, 197*t*,
197–198

Oral polio vaccine, contraindications, 159*t*
Orem, Dorothea, Self-Care Deficit Nursing
Theory, 105–117
Osteoporosis, and epilepsy, 245
Ostomy devices, 364–367
Our Home, 93
Oximetry, 370–371
Oxygen therapy, 353, 354–355
signs and symptoms of respiratory dis-
tress with, 355, 355*t*

Pain, Wong–Baker rating scale, 197, 197*f*
Pamelor, 210*t*
Paraldehyde, 226*t*
Parents
adolescent, 79
with mental retardation, 81–82
single, 81
Pediculosis, 338*t*–339*t*
PEEP, *see* Positive end-expiratory pressure
Pentobarbital coma, 226*t*
Peritoneal dialysis, 371
Person-centered approach, 35
Personal rights education, 291
Personal skills safety training, 291
Personality development theories, 21, 22*t*
Personnel, medication administration,
214–215
Persons with developmental disabilities, *see*
Individuals with developmental dis-
abilities
Pertussis vaccine, *see* Diphtheria–
tetanus–pertussis vaccine
Pharmacological therapy, *see* Medications
Phenergan, 210*t*
Phenobarbital, 210*t*, 226*t*, 231–232
drug interactions, 232*t*
laboratory monitoring protocols for, 235,
236*t*
pharmacokinetics, 233*t*
Phenylketonuria (PKU), 83
Phenytoin (Dilantin), 210*t*, 226*t*, 234
drug interactions, 232*t*
laboratory monitoring protocols for, 235,
236*t*
pharmacokinetics, 233*t*
Philadelphia General Hospital ("Blockley
Hospital"), 1–2
Physical examinations, periodic, 176–178
Physical hazards, job-related, 188
Physical skill limitations, and infection control, 319
Physical therapy
chest, 358
resources, 411
Pink eye, *see* Conjunctivitis
Pinworm disease, 338*t*–341*t*
PL 94-142, *see* Education for All Hand-
icapped Children Act of 1975